THE BEST PLAYS OF 1923-24

THE
BEST PLAYS OF 1923-24

AND THE

YEAR BOOK OF THE DRAMA
IN AMERICA

Edited by

BURNS MANTLE

DODD, MEAD AND COMPANY
NEW YORK : : 1969

CONTENTS

INTRODUCTION

BOTH professional playgoers and their friends, those old-time followers of the theater who delight to write the editor, are agreed that the New York theater season of 1923–24 was more productive of good drama than any previous season within their memories.

Selecting ten plays from the hundred and fifty that came within the scope of this work was, therefore, a more difficult task than usual. To have chosen fifteen, or even twenty, would have been comparatively simple. But we have held to our original determination to take but ten.

Addressing those newer readers of " The Best Plays " who are joining our family circle for the first time we repeat that it is the object of this annual yearbook of the drama both to record the activities of the theater and to reflect the taste of the American theater-going public, as represented by the so-called commercial theater, and to make note of the trend of dramatic authorship in America as it is determined by that reflection of taste.

Therefore, to repeat what we have said in previous volumes, the ten plays included herein are not presented as merely the arbitrary selection of one individual, but as a carefully considered compromise that shall do justice to his personal choice and the choice of that greater public that by its support of the theater makes possible the development of the American drama.

In furtherance of this determination we have included " The Swan," a comedy of the better class written by Ferenc Molnar of Hungary, but adapted for the American theater by Melville Baker, a young man employed by

INTRODUCTION

honest conclusion so far as it is concerned with the particular children of these particular parents.

Mr. Dodd's " The Changelings," on the other hand, is adult in both theme and treatment, in addition to being a well written play, and conveys an observing message that we feel may profitably be pondered in many American communities.

There were few farces produced last season. Guy Bolton's "Chicken Feed," which has been renamed "Wages for Wives," is an American comedy with a farcical touch. So is Owen Davis's "The Nervous Wreck," the plot of which was taken from a short story written by E. J. Rath. "The Nervous Wreck" was the more successful. But of the two we have selected "Chicken Feed" because we feel that it is more truly characteristic and decidedly more purposeful than "The Nervous Wreck." The division of the net family income, even when treated farcically, is a debatable American family problem, and for all the fun he has extracted from it, Mr. Bolton leaves a thought in the minds of his audiences that we feel it will do them good to heed.

We selected Gilbert Emery's "Tarnish" for much the same reason. Its purpose is worthy and sanely reasoned. There were other dramas which we thought somewhat less technically artificial, and others that created more stir. But none of the others so clearly nor so definitely stated its theme nor held to it to so satisfying a conclusion.

Of the other plays that we could have justified using, though not without regret for having had to exclude those they would have replaced, we wish to name Bernard Shaw's " Saint Joan," Leon Gordon's " White Cargo," J. P. McEvoy's " The Potters," Rachel Crothers's " Expressing Willie " and Martin Flavin's " Children of the Moon." Each has a definite claim. But there is room for only ten — so why go into detail?

Again the editor wishes to extend grateful thanks to

INTRODUCTION

Charles Frohman, Inc., as playreader, after other dram-
atizations had failed to satisfy the producers of the
play. "The Swan" may be reasonably classified as the
high comedy success of the year.

We have included "Outward Bound," the work of a
young English dramatist, Vane Sutton-Vane, as the most
original of the dramas of the year and one that shares
with "Beggar On Horseback" the honor of being the
season's dramatic novelty.

George Kelly's "The Show-Off," which was easily the
outstanding light comedy success of the year, is its own
justification. And Hatcher Hughes's "Hell-Bent fer
Heaven," in addition to being a particularly fine example
of the native folk drama, was also selected by the Pulitzer
Prize Committee as the best American drama of the year.

"Beggar On Horseback," a satire so keen and so whole-
some that it made an immediate appeal to the American
playgoing public somewhat satiated with the buncombe
of less radical and less courageous writers, is also its
best excuse for inclusion. Messrs. George Kaufman and
Marc Connelly, its authors, built it upon the foundation
of a foreign dramatist's idea, but so complete and so
entirely characteristic is their work that it deserves to
stand as practically a native composition.

Lula Vollmer's "Sun-Up" was the first of the Southern
folk dramas. Handicapped in many ways, it still was
able to complete a two-seasons' run on its merit as drama
and as entertainment.

Lewis Beach's "The Goose Hangs High," and Lee Wilson Dodd's "The Changelings" represent to me the best
of the dramas dealing with American home life and the
common problems with which they deal. Mr. Beach's
play is a sincere study of the so-called younger-generation
menace. If any care to argue that it does not, with its
typically American happy conclusion, truthfully represent the reactions of that generation, we will answer that
we are pleased to agree with the author that it is an

INTRODUCTION

those who have written to express their appreciation and those who have bought the previous volumes of this series. Their endorsement and their encouragement have made the compilation a pleasure. He trusts they will not consider the fifth volume unworthy of a place on their bookshelves alongside the other four.

Forest Hills, L. I.
June, 1924.

THE BEST PLAYS OF 1923-24

THE BEST PLAYS OF 1923-24

THE SEASON IN NEW YORK

THE good record of the theater season of 1922-23 in New York was kept up and, we believe, improved upon in the season of 1923-24. The general quality of drama was higher than it ever has been before. There were fewer trivial plays and fewer of those musical entertainments of which kindly disposed reviewers are wont to write that the librettos were terrible but the music good. Of the hundred and ninety-six productions, of which this volume of the yearbook is a record, less than forty were musical. Last year there were nearer sixty. And of cheap farces there were practically none at all.

It was not a season of sensational successes, however. No one play, starting early, romped away with a record similar to that achieved some years back by "Lightnin'," and more recently by "Rain." With the exception of "The Swan," the most successful play came after the holidays. "The Miracle" was not produced until January, "Outward Bound" was also a January production, and both "The Show-Off," the light comedy success of the year, and "Beggar on Horseback," the outstanding dramatic novelty, were February contributions.

The native drama prospered exceedingly and achieved, we believe, a record to which future historians of our theater will point with pride as a turning point in its upward progress. It was distinguished by a noteworthy group of Southern folk plays, including the Pulitzer prize play, Hatcher Hughes's "Hell-Bent fer Heaven," Lula Vollmer's "The Shame Woman," Nan Bagby Stephens's "Roseanne," and Percy Mackaye's "This Fine-Pretty World." It included the successful revival of Cora

1

Mowatt's " Fashion," the first comedy of American au-
thorship and manners of which there is record, and it
boasted a fine list of domestic comedies and dramas
headed by George Kelly's "The Show-Off," J. P. McEvoy's
" The Potters," Lewis Beach's " The Goose Hangs High,"
Rachel Crothers's " Expressing Willie," George Cohan's
" Song and Dance Man," and Lynn Starling's " Meet the
Wife."

It will be remembered as the season in which the
Actors' Equity successfully defended its fight for an
Equity contract and sanely accepted a compromise on
its demand for an Equity shop, by the terms of which
no actor was to be permitted to play without joining the
actors' association and contributing his bit to its support.
By the terms of a ten-year agreement, signed by a majority
of producing managers, 80 per cent of the actors employed are to be Equity members while 20 per cent are
permitted to retain their independence upon payment of
a sum equivalent to the Equity dues.

It will be remembered, too, as the season in which
Eleanor Duse paid her last visit to America. Mme. Duse
was enthusiastically greeted by huge audiences in all
the major theatrical centers. Her death in Pittsburgh
near the conclusion of her tour was deeply and sincerely
regretted.

The Russian players of the Moscow Art Theater, following their sensational triumphs of the season before,
returned to give an additional hundred performances.
They were successful, but the society stampede which was
a feature of their first visit was over. Their second, and
more legitimate appeal, was made to their own country-
men.

The summer shows were of a familiar pattern. George
White started his " Scandals " June 18 and they continued prosperously for twenty weeks thereafter. A day
later, "Helen of Troy, N. Y.," a musical play that gained
some distinction because the dramatic authors, Kaufman

and Connelly, agreed to revamp its somewhat lame book, and because a gifted young dancer, Queenie Smith, romped away with one of those overnight ovations that nearly made a star of her in " Sitting Pretty," the spring following, began a run that continued through the fall.

In July Earl Carroll entered the lists with a revue. The first of his " Vanities" was written, composed and staged by Mr. Carroll, and its cast was headed by Peggy Hopkins Joyce, who had devoted her recent years to matrimony and not to the stage. The feminine interest in Miss Joyce and the masculine interest in Joe Cook, a vaudeville comedian making his first appearance in what is known as " the legitimate," served to inspire a lively interest in the Carroll production, which ran on for 204 performances. " In Love With Love," a light but pleasant comedy farce, beat the August barriers a week and lasted well into the fall.

The rush began, as usual, the second week in August. There were twenty new plays introduced that hot month, most of them disappointing. Booth Tarkington's " Twee-dles " was one of these, Mary Roberts Rinehart's " The Breaking Point " another and the late Aaron Hoffman's " Good Old Days " (originally called " Light Wines and Beer "), a third. " Children of the Moon," a thoughtful drama by a Chicagoan, Martin Flavin, stirred the interest of so many of the intellectuals as were left in town to appreciate it, and continued for a creditable run at the Comedy. " Little Jessie James," a musical comedy, and " Artists and Models," a revue revamped by the Shuberts from an amateur show staged by the Illustrators' society, ran the season out.

September, usually one of the busiest months with the producers, offered only seventeen new plays this year, and few hits among them. Lee Wilson Dodd's " The Change-lings," at the Henry Miller, was the first of the serious domestic dramas to attract general attention, and Mrs. Fiske, appearing in St. John Ervine's graceful comedy,

"Mary, Mary, Quite Contrary," enjoyed a half success at the Belasco. Two Chicago hits, "Peter Weston" and Jules Eckert Goodman's "Chains," both suffered reverses in New York, though "Chains" held on for better than a hundred performances. The first of the light comedies to score was Guy Bolton's "Chicken Feed." There were only three music plays — "Poppy," which introduced Madge Kennedy, the dramatic comedienne, as a singing star for the first time; the new Music Box Revue, which ran through the season, as usual, and the Sam Bernard-William Collier "Nifties," which died quickly and in considerable pain.

October made up for the short September list by adding twenty-six to the current entertainments. And there were many hits among them. Gilbert Emery's "Tarnish" was one, Owen Davis's "Nervous Wreck" another, Lulu Vollmer's "The Shame Woman" a third, Franz Molnar's "The Swan" a fourth.

Eleanor Duse's gala reception at the Metropolitan was a stirring event of the month, and Mr. Ziegfeld's annual "Follies," a lighter musical piece, "Battling Buttler," and a colorful romp called "Runnin' Wild," supplied tuneful entertainment.

The Eleanor Duse reception was tremendously inspiring. Probably five thousand persons rose to cheer the little gray lady who had chosen the colorless Ibsen heroine in "The Lady from the Sea" for her debut. Afterward Mme. Duse played eight additional matinee performances at the Century Theater, each of them crowded with wildly enthusiastic patrons.

"The Swan" was the most immediate of the comedy successes, and easily ran the season through, as did "The Nervous Wreck," the first of the farces to score. William Hodge brought the newest of his Christian Science dramas, "For All of Us," to town the 15th, found his devoted public early and continued his healing services for 216 performances thereafter. Richard Bennett got

133 performances with an English melodrama, "The Dancers."

There were also several picturesque failures. Julia Marlowe and E. H. Sothern suffered one of these with their revival of "Cymbeline," which the Shakespearean dears read to death on the 2d, and retired to the storehouse lofts fifteen performances later. The Theater Guild, too, suffered its first failure with John Galsworthy's "Windows," from which much had been expected. Arthur Hopkins, bringing Pauline Lord home from her London success with "Anna Christie," presented her as the slightly demented heroine of "Launzi," which lasted but a fortnight and never enjoyed a normal respiration during that time. The players from the Grand Guignol, Paris, began a ten-week season at the Frolic and were glad to quit in seven. Sir Martin Harvey had a hard time at the Century with a repertoire which he opened with "Œdipus Rex" and closed with "Hamlet." He had little to show for his season but a neat little package of press clippings.

November was also an interesting month. The twenty-five plays produced included Walter Hampden's happy revival of "Cyrano de Bergerac," the production of two historical plays, the English John Drinkwater's American drama, "Robert E. Lee" and the American Walter Prichard Eaton and David Carb's English chronicle play, "Queen Victoria." The Moscow Art players returned for a revival of their repertoire. "Laugh, Clown, Laugh," was produced by Mr. Belasco for Lionel Barrymore and John Barrymore's revival of "Hamlet," with which he drew $30,000 in one week to the Manhattan opera house, probably set the shade of William Shakespeare cheering in heaven. A bright satire making fun of celebrity worshiping wives, called "Meet the Wife," was also successful.

This was the month Father Fred Stone introduced Daughter Dorothy in "Stepping Stones," and enjoyed the double thrill of having his play called the best of the Stone list and his daughter the greatest of dancing comediennes in musical comedy. The Stones (Mother Aline Crater Stone was also in the cast) carried "Stepping Stones" through the winter, and were only stopped then by the Equity strike order of June 1.

Otis Skinner started with "Sancho Panza," knowing that whatever his reception in New York the road would prove loyal. There was a virile drama called "White Cargo," by Leon Gordon, produced obscurely in Greenwich Village that later ran the season through up town. A mystery melodrama, "In the Next Room," which boasted Eleanor Robson Belmont as part author (Harriet Ford being the other part), scored a success in spite of its social register handicap, and the Theater Guild suffered its second failure with Lenormand's "The Failures."

Jane Cowl, eager to begin the building of a repertoire upon the fine foundation she had established with her success as Juliet, came early in December with a revival of Maeterlinck's "Pelleas and Melisande." But a part of her public did not understand Maeterlinck, another part did not like what they did understand and a considerable part remained away from the theater entirely. So the poetic tragedy was withdrawn after thirteen showings, and "Romeo and Juliet" was revived.

December was further distinguished by the success of J. P. McEvoy's "The Potters," a life-like study of American family life in Chicago, and the production by the Theater Guild of George Bernard Shaw's "Saint Joan," an unlifelike but interesting discussion of the miracle days in France when the Maid of Doremy led her mystified followers to victory.

There was also a fine little folk drama called "Roseanne," a study by Nan Bagby Stephens of negro life in Georgia, in which all the characters were negroes, and to close the month George Cohan brought his veracious " Song and Dance Man " to the Hudson and Eddie Cantor came with " Kid Boots " to the Carroll on New Year's eve.

" The Miracle " was produced in the transformed Century theater, now become a massive Gothic cathedral, in January. For some weeks thereafter there was not much else talked about in theater circles. The production of this German pantomime unquestionably set a new mark for similar achievements. It cost something like a half million dollars, and returned a profit of less than half that amount. But its backers appeared satisfied, and are expecting to recover some, at least, of their losses from a limited showing of " The Miracle " in the larger eastern and middle western cities the coming fall.

The most unusual drama of the year was also a January entrant, this being Sutton Vane's " Outward Bound," more about which appears in other chapters of this volume. A third highlight of the month was the importation by the Selwyns of " Charlot's Revue " from London, which registered an immediate success with both the Broadway crowd and their social betters. " The Goose Hangs High " came in January, too, introducing the Dramatists Theater, Inc., as producers. Five playwrights (Owen Davis, Edward Childs Carpenter, Arthur Richman, James Forbes and Cosmo Hamilton) banded together ostensibly to present their own plays, offered this drama by Lewis Beach, an outsider so far as their organization is concerned, as a sample of what they hoped to do. Its immediate success was heartening both to playwrights and playgoers.

Probably the most characteristic Broadway success of the season was that of George Kelly's " The Show-Off," which came in February. Not only was the response of the boulevardiers and their ladies immediate but the town followed after them with such enthusiasm there was not an empty seat in the Playhouse at any performance given the following five months.

This hit had no more than been recorded when the Kaufman-Connelly " Beggar on Horseback " was revealed at the Broadhurst and scored immediately with the public that is ever on the look-out for the more adult offerings of the theater.

It was in February that the still ambitious Jane Cowl suffered her second disheartening experience with her production of " Antony and Cleopatra." The reviewers had many words of hope and praise to cast at the actress's feet, and a few words of advice that she should have a particular care in the selection of her support. An Antony, whose youth was unsatisfactorily disguised by his whiskers, was charged with having sadly unbalanced her production.

This month there were a few afternoon performances of " Hannele " and the Equity players revealed an interesting study of native character in " The New Englander."

Not much happened in March to cause unusual excitement. The Theater Guild, having sent " Saint Joan " uptown, presented the Hungarian " Fata Morgana " in the Garrick, and registered its first popular success of the season with the story of an attractive seductress and an idealistic adolescent.

Eugene O'Neill, the most promising and least dependable contributor to the native commercial theater the last few seasons, helped with the production of a new play of his called "Welded." It proved a drama impressively human in conception and treatment, but monotonous in the playing, and lasted but three weeks. J. K. Hacket, having returned from Paris with a decoration and the assurance of the French critics that he is the greatest of American Macbeths, revived the tragedy under the guidance of the Equity players, giving thirty-three performances. Maurice de Faraudy, for forty-four years a member of the Comedie Francaise, paid us his first visit. He had two good weeks with a repertoire of his better known character

creations. "The Outsider," a London success, with Lionel
Atwill and Katherine Cornell playing the leading roles,
started in March and grew slowly into one of the popular
successes of the late season. It was forced to retire by
the Equity fuss while its receipts were still big.

April brought fifteen additions to the list, but nothing
in the way of quality to brag about, excepting the Equity
Players production of "Expressing Willie," by Rachel
Crothers — the actors' first popular hit in two years. Mrs.
Fiske, having finished with "Mary, Mary, Quite Con-
trary," on tour, came back with a younger generation
comedy, "Helena's Boys," which served her joyfully for
a spring season of five weeks. There was an all-star re-
vival of "Leah Kleschna," and a striking staging of "The
Ancient Mariner" by a newly formed triumvirate of
Provincetown Players — Eugene O'Neill, Kenneth Mac-
Gowan and Robert Edmund Jones.

There was also uncovered a vivid drama called
"Cobra." It was written by Martin Brown and played
so well by Judith Anderson, Ralph Morgan and Louis
Calhern that it ran through the summer.

By May there were many promises of crowds that were
coming to the Democratic convention in late June. Production was therefore kept up to an unusual state of
activity. Usually this closing month of the legitimate
season offers no more than a half dozen plays. This year
there were sixteen of them. But not more than four or
five any self-respecting delegate would give a fifty-cent
piece to see. One of these was a joyous burlesque,
"I'll Say She Is," in which the Four Marx brothers from
vaudeville figured amusingly. Another was, "Plain
Jane," a musical comedy with an excellent imitation prize
fight in it. A third covered the début of the French
soubrette, Mistinguett, in still another music play called
"Innocent Eyes," and a fourth was a "Keep Kool"
revue properly spiced with vaudeville and tunefully
supplied with a score. Down in Grand Street, a district

which none but the Al Smith delegates ever heard of,
the Neighborhood Playhouse staged the brightest of the
local revues. Society from the west side took it up, made
a fad of it, and helped to keep it running through June
and into July. " The Grand Street Follies," they called it.

On May 31 the agreement signed by the Producing
Managers' Association and the Actors' Equity Association
at the termination of the first actors' strike five years before, expired. A Shubert group of independents, including the Selwyns and A. H. Woods, had already signed
a new agreement and this permitted their attractions to
continue. An Erlanger group of " regular " or " die-
hard " members, however, including Sam H. Harris,
Charles B. Dillingham, Arthur Hopkins, John Golden,
Gilbert Miller, Henry W. Savage and others, were still
demanding better terms of the actors, and as a result
seven of their attractions: " Stepping Stones," " The
Swan," " Seventh Heaven," " The Nervous Wreck,"
" Rain," " The Outsider " and " Lollipop," were closed.
Late summer compromises brought practically all the
producing managers into working agreement with the
actors' organization.

The first half of June, still with the convention in sight,
brought four additional plays, including a revival of the
twenty-year old " The Fatal Wedding." The hope of the
producers was that the crudities of the old thing would
highly amuse the sophisticated playgoers of today. They
did, for twenty minutes. But two hours of it was an hour
and a half too much. A week of " She Stoops to Conquer," with a Players' club cast that included Elsie
Ferguson, Pauline Lord, Helen Hayes, Margola Gillmore, Henry E. Dixey, Francis Wilson, Dudley Digges,
Ernest Glendinning, Basil Sydney, Maclyn Arbuckle, Paul
McAllister, A. G. Andrews and many others of equal
prominence, brought the season to a close. There were, as
noted, counting from one June 15 to another, 196 new
plays and important revivals. Enough to satisfy almost
anyone.

THE SEASON IN CHICAGO

By Frederick Donaghey

Drama-Critic of The Chicago Tribune

THIS is written as of June 28, which is as good a date as any other to mark the end of a season which, like most stage seasons in Chicago, was without a beginning. The theaters are opened and closed, sometimes with and sometimes without discernible reason. Hits are whisked away on a day's notice because, as the managers whimsically explain, New York is calling; and failures are held here weeks and weeks after the public has given its answer. . . . As an art, the Drama remains the least logical of the trades: not only is it, as Bagehot would have called it, the "commerce of the imponderable," but it is also the commerce of the incredible, the inexplicable, and the inexcusable. . . .

Now, let's see as to the season which may be said to have had an emergence from the preceding season along in August of 1923, and which I have sumptuarily ended June 28, 1924. There have been acted here ever so many plays, of this kind and that kind, which New York has not seen. Some of them New York will never see. Others, better dead, will be pulmotored into a night or two of Broadway life because their sponsors have been told by the authors that the plays were over (meaning above) Chicago's 2,890,784 heads. Here they are:

"A Bit of Dust," by Willis P. Goodhue: pretty bad, and not helped any by Taylor Holmes's trying to play an Irish priest of the Boucicault epoch.

"A Rainy Day," by Fred Ballard: based on an idea,

11

and badly worked out. Might repay skilful tinkering.

"Peacocks," by Owen Davis: the winner of the 1923 Pulitzer Prize (with "Icebound") trying to be Clyde Fitch, and making an awful mess of it.

"King for a Day," by Cæsar Dunn: three acts of what the two-a-day performers regard as snappy chatter when it is put into a twenty-minutes sketch. Gregory Kelly was in it. . . . To be revived for New York as "Engaged to be Married."

"The Horse-Thief," by Louis B. Ely and Sam Forrest: dull chatter in the Kaintuck *patois* about a bad father and the daughter he has never seen until Act I, with plenty of stuff lifted out of "Lightnin'." The performance made endurable by Miss Ann Harding, new here, with much of her charm offset by the "character-acting" of George Marion. . . . Promised for New York.

"Silence," by Max Marcin: another about a bad father and the daughter he has never seen until Act II (Act I being cut-back stuff, which explains the delay in bring- ing 'em together). A play with an idea calling for a Cohan to work it out. . . . New York's to get it with H. B. Warner.

"The Best People," by David Gray and Avery Hop- wood, based on the former's published story called "The Self-Determination of the Lennoxes." This was one of the first two or three successes of the Chicago season, run- ning through more than twenty weeks. And a success of the type academically known as fluke. A failure left a three-weeks hole in the bookings of a theater. The play, knocking about on the byways, was rushed in, brushed up, and crushed through an opening on three days' notice, and within a week was a sell-out. It is second-generation stuff, like "The Goose Hangs High," "We Moderns," "Helena's Boys," et cætera, with a fine satirical theme. This bothered nobody hereabout, how- ever; for Mr. Hopwood, the well-known gag-master, wise- lined it with odds-and-ends left over from "The Gold-

Diggers," and the actors, a fair corps of somebodies, kicked the laughs across from the outer edge of the footlight trough. . . . Due in New York soon.

"The Highwayman," by Biro, who wrote "The Moonflower," adapted by Miss Gladys Unger: Hungarian social satire that was topical previously to 1914, and without edge as a result of the war. Miss Unger didn't help it much. Joseph Schildkraut, who seemed to be a good actor in "Liliom," was a comic blunder in the part of a romantic blackleg.

"Kelly's Vacation," by Vincent Lawrence: a comedy about golf with a first act that had the golfers in the audience on their feet and cheering, and other acts that made me wonder if, after all, we ought not to have a censor of plays. Robert Ames did well by an impossible rôle; and Miss Mary Newcomb made us like her. . . . A. H. Woods, who doesn't play golf, says he will give the piece to New York as "Kelly."

"Honeymoon House," by Emil Nyitray and Herbert Hall Winslow: a comedy of minor domestic troubles said to have been a wow in the Magyar original; and I should be sad if I thought the United States collected import duty on it. It was as juvenile as something "advanced" by Tchekhoff or Eugene O'Neill; and it had Jack Norworth, once of Miss Nora Bayes's act, in the principal part.

"Patches," by Joseph E. Graham: melodrama about a murder and a girl waif who saves an innocent man. Pretty bad, even when it lifted stuff by the handful from "Peg o' My Heart."

"Grounds for Divorce," by Ernest Vajda, author of "Fata Morgana," in an adaptation by Guy Bolton: a gay piece of Paris locale about a sedulous divorce lawyer and his pretty wife, who throws an inkwell at him. The good plotting survives Mr. Bolton's hand-me-down text; and the piece is a neat medium for Miss Ina Claire, who again is a good woman pretending to be a bad woman in order to convince the man she loves that she is a good

woman.   You know how it is when Ina has a rôle: just
like "Polly with a Past," and "The Gold-Diggers," and
"Bluebeard's Eighth Wife," and "The Awful Truth."
And both Bruce McRae and H. Reeves Smith are there to
help her along.   (She's better than she used to be, but
still slovenly in speech.) . . . New York will get it in
due time.

"The Breed of the Treshams," by John Rutherford,
who is the old-time collaboration of Beulah Marie Dix
and Evelyn Greenleaf Sutherland: a bit of cheap shop-
ware about Cavaliers and Roundheads, and Oliver Cromwell, who isn't in it, and a reckless hero called the Rat,
who is in it, worse luck!   For the part was acted, as one
says when euphemistic, by Martin Harvey, who has used
the play for years and years and years on the other side,
where they think he's pretty good.   One of the world's
ten worst plays.

"The Great Lady Dedlock," a disarray of scenes from
"Bleak House" by Paul Kester: just another attempt to
crowd too much Dickens into a play.   Miss Margaret
Anglin, who's forever fooling with such things, put a
lot of money into it, and, following the Janauschek tradition, undertook to perform as both Lady Dedlock and
Hortense, the maid.   The hit of the venture was made by
the reviewers trying to kid Miss Anglin's French dialect
as Hortense.

"Simon Called Peter," made from Robert Keable's
nasty best-seller by Jules Eckert Goodman and Edward
Knoblock: the two dramatists have done so well that four,
six, or eight others couldn't have made a worse play out
of the book.   Cold dirt about sex, with offstage airplane
effects.

"Easy Street," by Ralph Kettering: no use in telling
about this one; for you wouldn't believe it.   I've seen
it; and I don't believe it!   Miss Mary Newcomb is in it,
and is good.

"The Werewolf," by Rudolph Lothar, adapted by Miss

Gladys Unger: most audacious of the light comedies yet brought hither from Germany or any other place, and a good play, as to workmanship. Miss Unger has done her part of it without disaster either way; and that's a lot. The trouble with it as an entertainment is that it has been staged in the key of something by Somerset Maugham about a week-end party in the English shires, and is acted pretty much that way, whereas it calls for Latin color, pace, and feeling. I note an exception in favor of Miss Laura Hope Crews, who is immense in the most exacting part she has ever had. (To keep the record straight, permit me to explain that this play is in the volume called *Erotic Comedies* by Angelo Cana, as translated from the Spanish into German by Fraulein Helen Richter, and that there isn't any such person as Cana or Miss Richter, that the play was not written in Spanish, and that saying so was a device of Lothar's to fool his colleagues of the Berlin press.) . . . New York is sure to get " The Werewolf," — and, I pray, with a cast more nearly suitable to the requirements.

A work twice tried without success in New York is new here in " The Deluge," by Henning Becker; and this is far-and-away the best play made known in Chicago in 1923-24. And it is badly acted, on the whole, with Miss Emelie Polini (she should always be remembered and thanked for her acting in " Hindle Wakes," back in 1912-13) seeking to make a sweet-souled ingénue of the tough little street-walker: this, however, by direction, as it is the notion of the producer, Guy Bates Post, that he should let a little sunshine in at the end, and, so, the girl is " redeemed." Even this bit of actory insolence does not notably weaken the gorgeous satire of this true comedy. But one of the New York actors is in the cast — Robert E. O'Connor, as the saloon-keeper; and the others are so bad that they make him seem better than he is.

There have been some revivals local to Chicago, and

not likely to be proffered in New York. One was of " A
Woman of No Importance," the worst of Oscar Wilde's
plays, atrociously acted by Miss Anglin's company, although she was bully as the bleary mother. . . . Another
was of the late Edward Locke's " The Climax," something of a sensation in New York when new, about sixteen
years ago, and a pitiful thing in its restoration by Guy
Bates Post. . . . A third was of " Mr. Wu," a piece by
two English actors which ran for ever so long in London
before the war, and was given in New York about ten
years ago by Walker Whiteside, who made the revival.
It was new to us this last season, and bad: about the
weakest of all the make-overs of Sardou's " La Tosca."
. . . And a fourth restoration was of Miss Rachel
Crothers's early comedy, " The Three of Us ": one of those
things about the clear, open spaces where men are
actors, and the women, also, pay their dues to Equity.
The excuse for the revival (another of Mr. Post's ex-
humations) is to highlight Miss Maude Hanaford, whom
he regards as ready for the big type and the electric sign.
She is, perhaps — but not in " The Three of Us."

Of plays with music as yet unknown in New York,
there have been four. Easily the best of them is (it
is still here) " No! No, Nanette!" — a making-over of
the farce called " His Lady-Friends," acted some years
ago in Chicago by Jack Norworth, in New York by the
late Clifton Crawford, and in London by the late Charles
Hawtrey. The farce always fairly cried for some tunes;
and now has them — plenty of them, and all good —
by Vincent Youmans, who wrote some of the good
music of " Wildflower." With the first cast, the fun in
the farce died on the vine; but Miss Blanche Ring,
Miss Louise Groody, Miss Mary Lawlor, Miss Eleanor
Dawn, Charles Winninger, and Bernard Granville have
been brought in, and the piece is a hit. The first cast,
too, was made up of somebodies in musical comedy; but
they were all wrong for this job.

A freak of the season has been "Topsy and Eva," running since the end of December. It purports to be a musical comedy version of "Uncle Tom's Cabin"; and it is a terrible thing, with lucid intervals for the Duncan Sisters, one of whom blacks up and does comic falls as Topsy, while the other "plays straight" as Eva.

"The Town Clown," based on Aaron Hoffman's farce called "Nothing But Lies," was taken off for repairs after a fortnight. Repaired, it will be given in New York as "Good-for-Nothing Jones," with Eddie Buzzell, who was in it here. . . . The revision of the piece was the last work done by Hoffman before his death, in May.

The fourth of the musicals, "In Bamville," was a Negro show by Sissle and Blake, who helped to manufacture "Shuffle Along!" They called Julian Mitchell in to stage the new one, and he did it, with fond remembrance of most of the things he used to do for Weber and Fields. The trouble with the show here was that it was shy on laughter.

Another 1923-24 group in Chicago may be classified as plays shown here before they were given in New York. In that list belong "Spring Cleaning," a hit here; "The Lady," a failure; "The Deep-Tangled Wildwood," a pity (for it dripped rich ideas of travesty); "Laugh, Clown! — Laugh!" popular here; "We Moderns," a stupid and vulgar piece whose run of nine weeks in Chicago was in reality a forced crawl; and "Henky" (which became "The Melody-Man" for Broadway), a failure. . . .

Musical pieces now known in New York after a hearing here have been: "The Rise of Rosie O'Reilly," which prospered in spite of the wit which Cohan put into his travesty on the Cinderella thing; "Mr. Battling Buttler," known here as "The Dancing Honeymoon"; "Moonlight," which was quickly taken beyond the city's precincts; and "Innocent Eyes," wherein Mistinguett had all too little to do to make clear the fine talent whereof she is in outright possession.

Of plays and the like brought hither after New York
runs, the proportion has been about as in earlier seasons.
Worst of the Broadway hits was " The Fool"; and it was
reasonably popular here with non-playgoers and the
come-ons. . . . Others were " Kiki," " Merton of the
Movies," " The Changelings," " Zander the Great,"
" Mary, Mary, Quite Contrary," " Sancho Panza," " Magnolia," " The Whole Town's Talking," " The Laughing
Lady," " The Business-Widow," " Give and Take," " Leah
Kleschna," " Whispering Wires," " On the Stairs,"
" The Lullaby," " Home Fires," " The Nervous Wreck,"
" You and I," " Children of the Moon," " Sun-Up," and
so on — each with its appropriate star or stars, *de jure*
and *de facto,* and some doing well, and some fair, and
some nothing, regardless of their deserts. . . .
We've had " The Old Soak," with Tom Wise, who
hasn't played in it in New York. . . . We've had Martin
Harvey in " Œdipus Rex," and emerged from the spell of
the great play to brood with wonder at the nerve of this
actor in undertaking the title-rôle. . . . We've had David
Warfield in " The Merchant of Venice," and refrained
from loud laughter; and Mr. and Mrs. Sothern and Mr.
Mantell in Shakespeare, and refrained from attending.
. . . As a community, we were successful in ignoring
performances of " The Devil's Disciple," " He Who
Gets Slapped," and " Peer Gynt " by a company saying
it belonged to the Theater Guild, although it didn't, and
although " Peer Gynt " was worth seeing in spite of
Basil Sydney's being in the title-part. . . . And Chicago
did pretty well in keeping away from the Moscow Art
Players and from the Chauve-Souris, although the former
were fine and the latter was bully fun. (And here, perhaps, is just the place to inform the strabismic world
that Leonidoff's in " The Brothers Karamazoff " was the
best individual achievement in the season's acting, most
of which was bad in the sense of not good, and some of
which was bad in the sense of felonious.)

We've had all the so-called revues: the most recent Passing Show, the fourth Greenwich Village Follies, the sixteenth Ziegfeld Follies (1922 issue), the second Music-Box, the 1923 Scandals, and the first Vanities; and the best of them has been " Artists and Models," here for the summer, and the only one of the string with a fresh idea in it, even if its population be lacking in performers of celebrity and high wage.

We've ignored " The Clinging Vine," hooted " Sally, Irene, and Mary," and been restrained in the case of " Up She Goes!" We've been kind to " The Gingham Girl," sorry in the matter of " Caroline," respectful to " The Lady in Ermine," charitable to " Little Jessie James," and are at present hospitable to " Wildflower."

And the record were incomplete if it failed to state that we have " Abie's Irish Rose," with what the management frankly boasts is " the original Erie cast." Instead of thinking less of Erie, we ponder on what a tough thing it would be if good actors were put into the play. . . . I vaguely recall having forgotten to mention that the season's plays from New York have included one called " We've Got to Have Money!" and one called "Guess Again!" — the latter having been done in New York as " The New Poor." They were terrible!

. . . And that's 1923-24 in Chicago. As was said in the beginning, this is written as of June 28; and the season of 1924-25 in Chicago will, therefore, start June 29 with the first performance here of " The Amber Fluid," by Arthur Lamb, and of " A Trial Honeymoon," by Harold Orlob. It seems that the latter has been done in New York, where it was called something else: " Ginger," perhaps. . . . And that doesn't matter.

THE LITTLE THEATERS

By Walter Hartwig

Director of the Little Theater Tournaments of 1923 and 1924

A DEVELOPMENT in the American theater that is forcing itself into some serious consideration is the so-called " Little Theater." This is not, as is popularly believed, the outgrowth of the old time " amateur show " which was purely dilettante and was not expected to be taken seriously either by the actors or the audience. Amateur theatricals are practised purely for the fun that is to be gotten out of giving a play and are usually hitched up to some other activity, such as a charity entertainment, a private club affair, or in schools and colleges where the technique of the theater is not a part of the curriculum.

This, however, is not the " little theater " that is getting the attention of some five hundred well organized groups throughout the country who are exciting a new interest in dramatics and another five hundred well-intentioned but poorly organized groups of people who are attempting something along this line, but who, through lack of good guidance and direction, achieve only an amateur theatrical result, however much they set out with an ambition for " little theater." The disconcerting feature is that the public has not keyed itself to distinguish between what is " amateur theatricals " and, therefore, not to be taken seriously, and what is " little theater " and to be considered quite differently. In theatrical parlance we have always had two classifications for the performers: professionals and amateurs. According to this classifica-

20

tion, anyone who had played an engagement and been paid for the effort, was considered a professional and this likewise established his status of ability and talent. Against this we had the amateur who worked for nothing and was, therefore, not to be considered seriously as having any real aptitude for dramatic interpretation.

With the advent of the little theater a new classification is being recognized. In amateur theatricals we have the untalented and the talented (by accident) but untrained — coaching is quite another thing than technical training. In the little theater we have only the talented person in training under good technical direction. The professional theater is supposed to have only talented and technically skillful players. About seventy-five per cent of those who profess the theater as an occupation have obvious talent and apparent technique. These the public is always willing to pay, and liberally, for their contribution to the theater.

The first Little Theater Tournament was held the week of May 7, 1923, at the Nora Bayes Theater in New York City. The idea of the tournament was to bring together in friendly rivalry the most important of the groups who were following the little theater idea in avocational dramatics. Its object was to give these groups, who came mostly from the metropolitan district, an opportunity to work with the advantage of a well equipped stage and an efficient stage crew, neither of which most little theaters can boast of. No thought was had of any comparison with the regular legitimate theater. The tournament was conducted entirely by, for, and in the interests of, little theater groups and more especially the groups entered in the contest. It received at once the endorsement of the New York Drama League which gave it valuable support. Mr. David Belasco, who had previously gone on record as having little respect for amateur theatricals, readily saw a new purpose underlying the tournament idea and by lending his interest to the undertaking gave it moral support without which the managers of the tournament could probably not have seen the first tournament to a successful conclusion.   Also Mr. Belasco offered a handsome trophy to the tournament to be awarded to the group making the best presentation.   This trophy is held by the winning group until the next tournament when it is again competed for.   Additional prizes of $100 each are awarded to the groups making the three best productions, for the tournament is essentially a presentation contest, the awards being made on the following basis: 50% for presentation, meaning, interpretation, or " how well the idea of the play is gotten over "; 25% for acting; 15% for setting and 10% for the selection of a play.

During the first tournament four one-act plays were produced each evening by four different groups for five evenings until twenty presentations had been made.   Five judges passed on these productions and selected three out of the twenty as being plays especially well interpreted.

Thirty-two responses were received from the first notice sent out to the groups in the metropolitan district. And twenty of the thirty-two were entered in the first tournament.

It was expected that the event would arouse considerable interest among the competing groups, but the unexpected happened when the press recognized it as a noteworthy adventure.   When it eventually proved that it actually paid for itself — the tournament represented an expenditure of $5,000 — it was regarded as a successful achievement quite apart from the accomplishment of its original purpose, which was not contingent upon whether it came out well financially.

The prizes in the first tournament were won by the East-West Players of Manhattan, who presented George Calderon's " The Little Stone House "; the Fireside Players of White Plains, N. Y., in " The Crow's Nest " by William Manley; and the Gardens Players of Forest Hills, L. I., in " The Clock " by Robert Courtney.   The East-West

Players were awarded the Belasco trophy to hold for one
year or until the 1924 tournament.

With the announcement of the plans for the Second
Annual Little Theater Tournament the undertaking took
on a national aspect. The idea of such a development
had been dreamed of, but hardly for the second tournament. Among forty-two applications for entry in the
1924 contest one came from Dallas, Texas — 1,800 miles
from New York. An elimination scheme satisfactory to
every one was established, based on qualifications, and
when the second tournament opened on May 5, 1924, at
the Belasco Theater, the following entries were lined up:

The Montclair Repertoire Players of Montclair, N. J.
The Manor Club Players of Pelham Manor, N. Y.
The Bensonhurst Theater Guild of Brooklyn, N. Y.
The Lighthouse Players of Manhattan, N. Y.
The Brooklyn Players of Brooklyn, N. Y.
The Alliance Players of Jersey City, N. J.
The Fairfield Players of Greenwich, Conn.
The Stockbridge Stocks of Manhattan, N. Y.
The Adelphi Dramatic Association of Brooklyn, N. Y.
The Little Theater of Dallas, Texas.
The Kittredge Players of Manhattan, N. Y.
The Playshop of Pelham Manor, N. Y.
The Gardens Players of Forest Hills, Long Island, N. Y.
The Community Players of Mount Vernon, N. Y.
The Huguenot Players of New Rochelle, N. Y.
The MacDowell Club Repertory Theater of Manhattan, N. Y.
The Fireside Players of White Plains, N. Y.

The three prizes in the 1924 tournament were won by:
the Little Theater of Dallas, Texas, in a new play by a
Texan, J. W. Rogers, Jr., called "Judge Lynch"; the
Alliance Players of Jersey City, in Martin Flavin's
satirical comedy "Caleb Stone's Death Watch"; and
the Gardens Players of Forest Hills, Long Island, in
"Crabbed Youth and Age," a character comedy by
Lennox Robinson. A presentation of Thomas Wood
Stevens's miracle play "The Nursery Maid of Heaven,"
as offered by the Community Players of Mount Vernon,
N. Y., was given honorable mention. The Belasco
Trophy went to Texas, won by the Little Theater of
Dallas.

The interest in the second tournament was locally more acute than that shown in the first tournament and it was also far more extended. Newspaper clippings about the tournament were received from all parts of the country. An invitation was received from the Drama League of America to bring the prize plays of the contest for a showing at the annual convention of the League held in Pasadena the week of May 26 and a plan was worked out to accept this invitation. In order to finance such an undertaking the scheme was to play a series of one-night stands on the way to Pasadena and back, but here the limitations of the little theater groups were probed. The three prize plays were offered as an attraction to some twenty of the most important little theater groups along the way to California at $600 for one performance each, but this was evidently beyond their resources. Offers of acceptance came only from the Drama League itself at Chicago and from the center at Pasadena and the plan was finally abandoned for this year's convention.

The annual convention of the Drama League of America at Pasadena gave considerable recognition to the little theater movement, devoting the entire first day of its five-day convention to conferences on the little, art and community theaters. Speeches were made by Capt. Paul Perigord, President of the Pasadena Community Playhouse Association which is generally regarded as the most important and best organized of the little theaters in the country; by Mrs. Clara Bryant Heywood, Drama Chairman for the Los Angeles District of the California Federation of Women's Clubs; by Oliver Hinsdell, Director of the Little Theater of Dallas, Texas; by Irving Pichel and Sam Hume, who impressed upon his audience the significant fact that too much importance cannot be given to the dramatic activities in all secondary and high schools of the land — not because of the potential actors they might develop but that through them a new crop of discriminating playgoers would be brought for the future. A tempest in a teapot was stirred up by Edith Ellis, a playwright, who denounced all little theaters and charged them with the present plight of the professional theater. She said that Broadway was broken-hearted because upstarts from the provinces were crowding off the professionals. This rather spectacular expression of apprehension, even if not too well founded in fact, was a great compliment to the little theater which has hitherto never asked for, nor received, any recognition from its parent, the legitimate theater. If this is the age of youth it may very well be that as little "Willie" is growing up and beginning to "find out things" it may be that "Mother" will have to watch her step a little more. This will do "Mother" no harm and "Willie" is probably only being smart — much more genuinely concerned with his toys than the conduct of his elders.

" THE SHOW-OFF "

A Comedy Drama in Three Acts

By George Kelly

THE author of " The Show-Off " was not unknown to
Broadway when, in February, this newest play of his
achieved the quickest and most definitely popular success
of the season of which this book is a record. The year
before he had offered " The Torchbearers," a smartly
written comedy with the Little Theater movement as a
target, and before that he was well known as the contributor of some of the best of the comedy and dramatic
sketches that entertain the followers of vaudeville. But
he was still, in a sense, on probation. His " Torchbearers " had tickled the few, but the many found it a
trifle subtle and " highbrowish."

" The Show-Off " was greatly to the crowd's liking and
from the first performance, February 5, 1924, to well into
the summer there was not, according to the accepted
record, a vacant seat at any performance given in the
Playhouse.

Heywood Broun, who contributes a preface to the published play, frankly declares " The Show-Off " to be
" the best comedy which has yet been written by an American." Mr. Broun is not one to weigh phrases when he
is pleased, and " The Show-Off " may not quite reach
that high level, but it certainly is to be numbered with
the plays that must be considered in any search for the
best. It is, to me, more a comedy farce than a legitimate comedy, for all it holds closely to its author's
classification as " a transcript of life." Its farcical ex-

travagances are apparent, though they are neither cheap nor impossibly motivated.

It is an early evening in May. The Fisher family, living in North Philadelphia, is scattered. Clara Hyland, a married daughter, finds the living room deserted when she drops in. But she soon brings her mother from upstairs, and Mother locates Joe, Clara's brother, fussing with a radio in the basement.

Amy, the unmarried sister, expecting company, is upstairs primping and Father Fisher is out seeking entertainment and an evening paper at Gillespie's. This leaves the situation clear for such neighborhood and family gossip as Clara and her mother consider important.

So far as the family is concerned, this gossip is principally concerned with Amy and her newest beau. Amy, a somewhat flighty, extravagant girl, has become greatly interested in a gabby young man who has recently taken to calling regularly both Wednesday and Sunday evenings. This, to the more observing of the Fishers, is indicative of a serious intention. Inasmuch as he is not the type of young man calculated, from family observations, to make Amy happy, even if he can support her in the manner in which she has been supporting herself, the family is considerably perturbed. Particularly Mrs. Fisher.

MRS. FISHER — . . . It looks like a steady thing. And you never in your life heard anybody talk so much, Clara — I don't know how she stands him. Your Pop can hardly stay in the room where he is. I believe in my heart that's the reason he went over to Gillespie's tonight — so he wouldn't be listenin' to him.

CLARA — Doesn't she take him into the parlor?

MRS. FISHER — She does, yes; but she might just as well leave him out here; for he's not in there five minutes till he's out here again — talkin' about Socialism. That's all you hear — Socialism — and capital and labor. You'd think he knew somethin' about it. And the Pennsylvania Railroad. He's always talkin' about that, too. That's where he works, you know. I don't know what he does down there. He sez himself he's head of the freight department; but as I sez to our Joe, I sez, " I don't know how *he* can be head of anything, from the talk of him." Joe sez he thinks he's a nut. And your Pop told him right to his face here last Sunday night — that he didn't know the meanin' of the word Socialism. (*She checks herself and gets up.*) I'd better not be talkin' so loud — he's apt to walk in on us. (*She goes to the hall door and glances out.*) He's a great joker, you know. That's what he did last Sunday night. I never got such a fright in my life. . . . But, you know, what'd kill you, Clara, you can't say a word about him in front of her. Oh, not a word. No matter what he sez, she thinks it's lovely. When Joe told her here the other night he thought he was a nut, she just laughed, and said that Joe was jealous of him — because he could express himself and he couldn't. You never heard such talk. And, you know, Clara, I think he wears a wig. (*Clara laughs.*) I do, honestly. And our Joe sez he thinks he does too. But when I asked her about it here one mornin', I thought she'd take the head right off me. You never seen anybody get themselves into such a temper. She sez, "It's a lie," she sez, "he don't wear a wig." She sez, "People always say somethin' like that about a fellow that makes a good appearance." But *I* think he does, just the same; and the first chance I get I'm goin' to take a good look. (*She moves around to her chair again.*) He often sits right here, you know, under this light, while he's talkin'; and I'm goin' to look close the very first chance I get. I can tell a wig as good as anybody. She won't make a liar out of me.

Clara has also heard something of this affair of Amy's, and Frank Hyland, Clara's husband, has met the man. His name, it appears, is Piper — Aubrey Piper — and they say around the places where he goes that he is not only a nut, as Joe Fisher suspects, but absolutely crazy as well. The way he talks so grand all the time, and swells around with a white carnation in his button-hole is enough to prove it. "I believe in my heart," Mrs. Fisher believes, "that's what's turned her head. . . . You often see things like that, you know. The worst fool of a man can put a carnation in his coat or his hat over one eye, and half a dozen sensible women'll be dyin' about him."

Amy is quite the independent sort. Coming down-stairs, completing the pinning up of her newest frock, bustling about to be sure the parlor is ready for her company, she pays little attention to the implied criticism of her mother and sister, giving them quite as good as they send, as the saying is, whenever she is drawn into the discussion. To Amy her own affairs are strictly her own affairs, and you have the feeling that she wishes to Gawd all the Fishers would mind their own business.

And yet Mrs. Fisher and Clara feel that something will have to be done to warn Amy about this Piper fellow. He is only a freight clerk in the railway offices, according to Hyland, and he can't possibly get more than $150 a month. If Amy were to marry him it would simply mean that she would be back on the family in no time. Even if she was able to stand Aubrey's talk two of them couldn't live on that salary — not the way Amy shops. And then Aubrey comes. They recognize his ring, and, not to be caught, the Hylands sneak out the back way. From the hallway the echoing boom of the Piper voice, and the merry but hollow tones of the Piper laugh float into the living room.

AUBREY — (*out at the front door*). Right on the job!

AMY — Hello!

AUBREY — The pride of old West Philly! (*He laughs, a bit boisterously.*)

AMY — I'll take your hat, Aubrey.

AUBREY — Anything to please the ladies. The boy rode off with many thanks, and many a backward bow. (*He laughs again, rather wildly. Mrs. Fisher tiptoes into the room from the right and stands, listening keenly.*) Do you know, I think I'll have to get hold of an airship somewhere, Amy, to come out here to see you.

AMY — It is quite a trip for you, isn't it?

AUBREY — Just one shining hour and a half, if you say it quick, by the little old Brill special. And how is the Mother? . . .

The mother, at the moment, is busy getting herself into a position of advantage near the folding doors leading into the parlor, where she can listen to Amy and her young man. She is there when Mr. Fisher returns from Gillespie's with the evening paper and in good humor. He enjoys making sport of a prying wife listening at a keyhole, however justifiable her curiosity.

Fisher confesses that he has as little use for " Windy " as any of them, but he has not started to worry about him yet. Neither has Joe, who comes up from below stairs with his latest radio improvement. But they are given cause for a little irritation, at least, when Aubrey, hearing their voices, comes blithely in from the parlor to join the family group.

AUBREY — (*coming out of the parlor*). Stay right where you are, folks, right where you are. (*He moves to the mirror over the mantelpiece.*) Just a little social attention — going right out again on the next train. (*He surveys himself critically in the mirror, touching his tie and toupé gingerly. Mrs. Fisher gives him a smouldering look, and Joe looks at his father. Aubrey turns from the mirror, and indicates his reflection with a wide gesture.*) There you are, Mother! Any woman's fancy, what do you say? Even to the little old carnation. (*He gives the table a double tap with his knuckles, then laughs, and moves up towards the kitchen door, and calls to Amy.*) Come on, Amy, step on the United Gas out there; customer in here waiting for the old aqua pura. Man's got to have something to drink — how about it, Pop? (*He gives Mr. Fisher a slap on the shoulder.*) You'll stay with me on that, won't you? (*Old man Fisher is very much annoyed.*) Yes, sir. I want to tell those of you who have ventured out this evening, that this is a very pretty little picture of domestic felicity. (*He laughs a little and looks from one to the other, patronizingly; but nobody pays the slightest attention to him.*) Father reading; Mother knitting. (*Mrs. Fisher withers him with a quick look.*) But then, Mama is always knitting. And little old Tommy Edison over here, working eighteen hours a day to make the rich man richer and the poor man poorer. (*He gives Joe a tap on the back, then moves back again towards Mr. Fisher.*) What about it, Popcorn? (*Slaps him on the back.*) Shake it up! Right or raving?

MR. FISHER — (*starting to his feet violently*). God damn it, let me alone! And keep your hands to yourself. I never saw such a damn pest in my life! (*He goes up the stairs bristling with rage, and muttering to himself. Aubrey is vastly amused.*)

AUBREY — Sign on the dotted line! And little old Popsy-Wopsy getting sore and going to leave us flat. (*He laughs again considerably; then turns to Mrs. Fisher.*) Nevertheless, and notwithstanding, Mrs. Fisher, I'd like to mention that the kid from West Philadelphia is giving the growing boy the said and done. (*He indicates Joe with a waving gesture. Turns to Amy.*) And there she is herself, and not a moving picture. (*Amy extends the glass of water, laughing, and with a touch of self-consciousness.*) Blushing as she gave it, looking down — at her feet so bare, and her tattered gown. (*Amy giggles, and her Mother looks sharply at Amy's shoes.*) How's that, Mother Fisher? Can't beat that little old Willie Shakespeare, can you? No, sir, I'd like to tell the brothers that that little old Shakespeare party shook a wicked spear. (*He laughs at his own comedy, and Amy is immeasurably delighted.*) Well, here's laughter, ladies! and (*turning to Joe*), Mr. Marconi — my best regards to you. (*He drinks.*)

A moment later he is off on a wild harangue against the capitalists who refuse to recognize the genius of young chaps like Joe — and himself. " Yes, sir, Mr. Joseph," he spouts, " I want to tell you you're wasting time; for when you're all through they'll offer you twenty cents for it and sell it for twenty millions. . . . Take it or leave it — sign on the dotted line."

Isn't that exactly what they did to Aubrey? It is. Didn't he have a formula to prevent the rusting of iron and steel ". . . a simple combination of chemical elements to be added to the metal in its molten state, instead of applied externally as they have been doing!" He did.

And why have they kept Aubrey out of his rightful triumphs as an inventor? Because, he assures Mrs. Fisher, because he works for a living. " That's the said and done on the whole business. Keep them poor and get them married; and then, as my darling old mother used to say, ' You've got them on their beams and hinges.' "

He is still talking as Amy shoos him toward the parlor.

AUBREY — Yes, sir, Amy, I want to tell you it's the poor man that gets it every time. I put a question up to Secretary Mellon — in a letter six weeks ago — that absolutely stumped him, because I haven't had a line from him since. (*Amy is smiling into his eyes. He passes in front of her and goes into the parlor. The curtain commences to descend slowly.*) I simply asked him to what extent his proposed program of Income Tax Revision would affect the Great American Railroad Employee.

The curtain is down for a moment to denote the three hours that have passed. At its rise Mrs. Fisher is asleep over her knitting, Joe is still busy with his radio set. From the parlor float the strains of Amy's accompaniment to Aubrey's singing of " Rocked in the Cradle of the Deep." It is enough to awaken anybody, even Mrs. Fisher. And she, in turn, is terribly worried for fear it also will awaken Father — which it does. From the head of the stairs he protests roughly, but no more profanely than the circumstances would seem to warrant. Mrs. Fisher is thereupon emboldened to approach the parlor with the idea of suggesting, timidly, that perhaps midnight is not just the time for loud singing, seeing the neighbors are what they are. But before she has a chance to protest Aubrey and Amy appear. Aubrey is just about to take his reluctant leave. " In fact," says he, " the recent outburst was in the nature of a farewell concert. . . . The little old song at twilight, you know, Mother Fisher, to soothe the savage breast."

Now Aubrey has finally said his farewells to the giggling Amy in the hallway, and Joe has explained to his mother that all that fancy talk of Aubrey's about the anti-rust invention was funny — seeing it was he (Joe) who had given him the idea weeks before and he had forgotten where it came from.

Amy is back and struggling to control her rage. What right had they to treat Aubrey the way they had? Walking out on him while he was talking? What right have they to be interfering in her affairs, anyway? Or questioning her choice of friends?

MRS. FISHER — (*trying to quiet Amy*). Oh, don't fly into a temper, if anybody speaks to you!

AMY — (*stamping her foot*). Well then, don't speak to me about things that put me in a temper!

MRS. FISHER — You're not frightenin' anybody around here.

AMY — No, and nobody around here is frightening me, either — our Clara took who she wanted. And I guess you took who you wanted. And if I want Aubrey Piper I'll take *him!*

MRS. FISHER — (*taking Amy's tone*). Well, take him then! — and the sooner the better; for it's a pity to spoil two houses with you. (*She leans forward a little.*) Only remember this, Amy — if you do take him, be sure that you keep him — and that — he — keeps — you. (*Amy looks at her keenly.*) And don't be comin' around here cryin' for your Pop to keep you.

AMY — (*with amused derision*). Don't make me laugh.

MRS. FISHER — You can laugh all you like; there's a lot of that kind of laughin' goin' on these days. But they change their tune as soon as the rent begins to come due; and it's the mothers and fathers that has to listen to the changed tune. But nothin'll do but they'll get married.

AMY — You got married, didn't you?

MRS. FISHER — Yes, I did.

AMY — Well ——

MRS. FISHER — To a man that was able to keep me.

AMY — And how do you know that Aubrey Piper wouldn't be able to keep his wife?

MRS. FISHER — Because I know what he earns; (*she strikes the table with her fist*) and it isn't enough. This fellow's got you so crazy about him that I believe you'd take him if you knew he had a wife and family somewhere, and not two cents in his pocket.

AMY — Well, I guess we'd get along some way even if I did.

MRS. FISHER — All right.

AMY — Everybody else does.

MRS. FISHER — (*in a rage*). That's the kind of talk that leaves them livin' in garrets! And back at their jobs ten days after the weddin'.

AMY — Oh, you talk as though everybody that was married was starving to death.

MRS. FISHER — There are ways of starvin' to death, Amy, besides not gettin' enough to eat. (*With a change to great shrewdness of tone and manner.*) And the funny part of it is, Amy — like a lot of others, you're very shrewd about money while you're at home, as far as what you give your mother and father is concerned; but the minute some clown, with a flower in his coat and patent-leather shoes, winks at you, you seem to forget there's such a thing in the world as a ton of coal. And then it's just as Clara sez, it's your people that has to come to the rescue.

AMY — (*furiously*). I wish I'd been here while she was talking! I bet I'd a told her a thing or two!

MRS. FISHER — Oh, you needn't try to turn it onto Clara; she wasn't talkin' at all.

AMY — She must have been talking!

MRS. FISHER — She simply asked me where you were — and I told her you were gettin' dressed — that this fellow was comin' here tonight; so then she told me that Frank Hyland knew him, and where he worked, and what he got and all about him. (*There is a slight pause.*)

AMY — (*half-crying*). I'd just take him for spite now.

MRS. FISHER — (*deliberately*). Well, let me tell you, Amy — the day a girl that's used to spendin' money the way you do, takes a thirty-five-dollar-a-week man, the only one she's spitin' is herself. There'll be no more permanent waves after that — you can make up your mind to that. Nor fifty-five dollar beaded dresses, neither.

AMY — (*in a crying temper*). Well, I'd never bother anybody around here if I needed anything, I'll tell you that.

MRS. FISHER — Maybe you won't.

AMY — I won't — you needn't worry.

MRS. FISHER — (*with a bitter levelness*). Time'll tell that, Lady Jane; I've heard the likes of you before. (*She goes to the hall door.*) Put out that light and go to bed, it's twelve o'clock.

"Mrs. Fisher goes up the stairs. Amy stands for a second, fuming; then she swings suddenly to the middle of the room and stops, with her hands on her hips, irresolute. Then she comes forward and stands above the table, thinking. As she clasps her hands together she becomes conscious of the ring in her hand. She tiptoes to the hall-door, stands listening for a second, then looks up. She hurries back to the table, looks at the ring, slides it onto the third finger of her left hand and holds it so that the diamond will catch the light from the chandelier. But the reflection is evidently unsatisfactory; so, with a furtive glance toward the hall-door, she shifts her position to a point nearer the table-lamp and holds her hand so that the ring will reflect the light. The curtain commences to descend slowly; and she stands, holding her hand at arm's length, lost in the melting wonder of her engagement ring."

ACT II

The scene is the same, the time six months later. Joe has finished at least one radio set and Mrs. Fisher is listening in on what we judge is a pleasant program. And then Aubrey comes.

Aubrey, a bit more dapper, if anything, than before, sports a new light overcoat and the traditional carnation. He is looking for Amy. There is an automobile show on and he thinks perhaps she might enjoy it. And that she may attend it in comfort he has borrowed a car to take them there.

The fact that Aubrey and Amy have been married for five months has not in the least changed Mrs. Fisher's opinion of the young man. Her distrust of him, in fact, has been considerably intensified. Even now, to hear him talk so grandly of going to automobile shows — and possibly buying a car — when she knows that he has considerable trouble paying the rent of the few rooms

he and Amy call home irritates her excessively. Her
caustic criticisms, however, leave Aubrey untouched. He
admits that he will soon have to move and that he is on
the lookout for a house. But he wants to buy, rather than
rent. And if he has to rent he wants something attractive, something with a little ground, where he can
" do a bit of tennis in the evening," if he feels like it.
He has been thinking seriously of going out along the
Boulevard.

AUBREY — Lot of people out that way, Mother.
MRS. FISHER — Well, if there is they're payin' more than you're able to pay.
AUBREY — Man's got to live somewhere, Mother.
MRS. FISHER — Well, if he's wise, he'll live where he's able to pay for it;
unless he wants to be breakin' up half a dozen times a year — like a lot of them
are doin'. Makin' a big show. Buyin' ten thousand dollar houses, and puttin'
fifty dollars down on them. (*He turns to her.*) Besides, you haven't got any
furniture for a house, even if you got one — unless you want to be sittin' on the
floor.
AUBREY — The matter of furniture nowadays, Little Mother, is a very inconsequential item, from what I can gather.
MRS. FISHER — You ought to price it sometime when you're in the city, and
see how inconsequent it is.
AUBREY — (*settling himself for a golf shot, using his cane for a club*).
I've investigated the matter very thoroughly, Mrs. Fisher, and I find that there
are at least fifteen first-class establishments right here in this city that will furnish a man's house from garret to garage, and give him the rest of his life to
pay for it. (*He hits the imaginary golf ball.*)
MRS. FISHER — They'd need to give some of them the rest of their lives, at
the rate they're goin' now.
AUBREY — Give the growing boy a chance, Mrs. Fisher, give the growing boy
a chance. You know what Mr. L. D. Brophy of the American Can Company
said in the September number of the *American Magazine*, don't you?
MRS. FISHER — No, I don't.
AUBREY — Well, I'll tell you. (*Mrs. Fisher shifts her knitting, giving
him a wearied glance.*) He said, " I would say to that innumerable host of
young men, standing on the threshold of life, uncertain, and, mayhap dismayed — as they contemplate the stress of modern industrial competition —
' Rome was not built in a day.' " Those were his very words. I wouldn't kid
you, and I think the old boy's got it right, if you ask me.

He is on his way back to his own home to find Amy
when she walks calmly in from the parlor. She has
heard him talking and knows his plans. But she did not
want to go to the Automobile Show and has waited until
he left. Amy is pretty well tired out. She has been
hunting flats all day — and found nothing she can afford.
Marriage has proved a little disillusioning to Amy,
but her faith in Aubrey is still firm, and she loves him
a lot. Nor can her mother discourage her or change

her opinion of her husband. Aubrey has to dress well to preserve his standing at the office. And if it costs more money than they can save out of his $32.50 a week, that is their affair. They have borrowed, yes. But they have always paid back what they have borrowed. At least she has. And she knows Aubrey has, too.

She is more excitedly moved to defend herself and Aubrey when Clara propels herself into the discussion. Clara has come over to see what's happening, having found a phone call at home saying her brother Joe was eager to see her. But she is quite ready for an old-time fight with her sister while she is waiting. And she has something to say about Aubrey, too. What he spends and how he spends it may be no business of hers, as Amy intimates, but it happens that he has been borrowing most of what he spends from Frank Hyland, and that does concern her. Twice Frank has helped Aubrey pay his rent, she charges, and if Amy doesn't believe it she can come over to Clara's house and read some of Aubrey's written appeals.

AMY — What do you do, open them?

CLARA — I do now, yes — since I found out who they're from.

MRS. FISHER — (keenly). Do you mean to tell me, Clara, that he's writin' to Frank Hyland for money?

AMY — No, he doesn't do anything of the kind, Mom, that's another of her lies!

MRS. FISHER — I'm not talkin' to you, Amy.

AMY — She just makes those things up.

CLARA — I make them up!

AMY — (crying). Yes!

CLARA — And I've got at least twelve letters right in my bureau drawer this minute that he's written within the last two months.

MRS. FISHER — What does he write letters for?

CLARA — For money — so he can pay seven dollars for a seat out at the football game — as he did Thanksgiving afternoon. Frank saw him there.

MRS. FISHER — Why don't he just ast Frank Hyland for the money when he sees him, instead of writin' to him?

CLARA — I suppose he thinks a written request is more appropriate, coming from one of the heads of the Pennsylvania Railroad.

MRS. FISHER — How much does he ast for, when he asts him?

CLARA — There was one a couple of weeks ago, for three hundred.

MRS. FISHER — (aghast). Three hundred dollars?

CLARA — That's what the letter said.

MRS. FISHER — What would he have wanted three hundred dollars for, Amy?

AMY — Oh, ask her, Mom; she's good at making things up.

MRS. FISHER — Oh, you wouldn't believe it, even if it was true, if it was against him.

AMY — Well, I wouldn't believe her, anyway. (*Amy goes out and slams the parlor door.*)

MRS. FISHER — (*raising her voice*). You wouldn't believe your own mother, never mind your sister. (*She turns to Clara.*) She flew at me like a wildcat, when I told her he wore a wig. I guess she knows it herself by this time.

CLARA — She's for him, Mom; and the sooner you get that into your head the better.

MRS. FISHER — I know very well she is, you needn't tell me. And she'd turn on everyone belongin' to her for him. The idea of askin' anybody for three hundred dollars. I suppose he wanted to buy an automobile or something. That's where he is tonight, out at the Automobile Show — and not two cents in his pocket — like a lot of others that'll be out there, I guess. And I'll bet he'll be doin' more talkin' out there than them that'll buy a dozen cars.

CLARA — I think that's what he did want the money for.

MRS. FISHER — It wouldn't surprise me — the damned fool. It'd be fitter for him to be thinkin' about gettin' a house to live in.

CLARA — He doesn't think he needs to think about that; he thinks he's coming in here.

MRS. FISHER — Comin' in here to live, do you mean?

CLARA — That's what he told Frank, the day before yesterday.

MRS. FISHER — Well, he's very much mistaken if he does, I can tell you that. I'd like to be listenin' to that fellow seven days in the week! I'd rather go over and live with your Aunt Ellie in Newark.

CLARA — Well, that's about what you'll have to do, Mom, if you ever let them in on you.

MRS. FISHER — I won't let them in on me, don't fret. Your father 'ud have something to say about that.

CLARA — Pop may not always be here, Mom.

MRS. FISHER — Well, I'll be here, if he isn't; and the furniture is mine. And there's very little danger of my walkin' off and leavin' it to any son-in-law. (*The front door closes.*) I guess this is your Pop, now, and I haven't even got the kettle on.

It isn't Pop who has opened the door. It's Joe, and he brings bad news. Pop has had a stroke at his work and has been taken to the Samaritan Hospital. The doctors think it would be well for the family to come to him at once.

It isn't easy to tell Mrs. Fisher. They stutter a good deal about it, as families will, until she guesses for herself that something is wrong with their father. And then they tell her, minimizing the seriousness of the situation as much as possible. But she knows. Two of Pop's brothers died from strokes. The same thing is likely to happen to him.

The preparations for the hurried trip to the hospital are nervously gone through with. Even in the shadow of a possible tragedy Mom must look neatly dressed to anyone she may meet at the hospital. She doesn't intend to go there " lookin' like a dago woman."

They are just about to start when Aubrey arrives. Suddenly Mrs. Fisher looks up and sees him framed in the hall door. He is pale and a little battered. There is a bandage around his head, through which a suggestion of red shows. And he is, for Aubrey, noticeably subdued. And yet, if he could, he would have it appear that nothing unusual has happened.

AUBREY — (*coming forward, removing his hat*). It's beginning to rain.

MRS. FISHER — Never mind the rain, the rain didn't do that to you. I guess you ran into somebody, didn't you?

AUBREY — (*with a shade of nonchalance*). Don't get excited, Mother — just a little misunderstanding on the part of the traffic officer.

MRS. FISHER — You don't mean to tell me that you ran into a traffic officer!

AUBREY — Control, now, Little Mother. I assure you there is no occasion for undue solicitation. (*He turns and sees Clara.*) Good evening, Mrs. Hyland.

CLARA — Hello! What happened to your head?

MRS. FISHER — You look like a bandit.

AUBREY — The veriest trifle, Mrs. Hyland — just a little spray from the windshield.

MRS. FISHER — Where's the car you borrowed? Smashed, I guess, ain't it?

AUBREY — The car I borrowed, Mother Fisher, is now in the hands of the bandits of the law, the judicial gentlemen, who have entered into a conspiracy with the regulators of traffic — to collect fines from motorists — by ordering them to go one way — and then swearing that they told them to go another.

MRS. FISHER — Never mind your fancy talk, we've heard too much of that already! I want to know who you killed — or what you did run into; for I know you ran into somethin'. And where's the automobile that someone was fool enough to lend you?

AUBREY — The automobile, Little Mother, is perfectly safe — parked and pasturing — in the courtyard of the Twenty-second and Hunting Park Avenue Police Station.

MRS. FISHER — Did you get arrested, too?

AUBREY — I accompanied the officer as far as the station house, yes; and I told them a few things while I was there, too, about the condition of traffic in this city.

MRS. FISHER — I guess they told you a few things, too, didn't they?

AUBREY — Beg pardon?

MRS. FISHER — (*starting abruptly for the hall door*). Never mind; you're welcome.

The accident in which Aubrey has figured, though a mere incident to him, assumes increasingly serious proportions as he reluctantly reveals the details. He had, he insists, not struck anything much. Only a traffic cop. And the cop should have been struck — seeing he was jay walking and paying not the least attention to where he was going. He was, in fact, trying to beat Aubrey to the crossing, after having given him the right of way. There probably wasn't anything at all the matter with

the poor straw ride, although he was faking a broken
arm when they took him to the hospital.

Aubrey's appearance excites Amy, when she comes in,
but he quickly reassures her that nothing at all has
happened. Just a little shake-up — that's all. And everything's all right. Nothing will happen until ten o'clock
Monday, when he thinks he will probably have to call
for the car. Until then he is out on bail.

AMY — (*very quietly*). How much bail did they put you under, Aubrey?
AUBREY — One thousand berries, Amy.
AMY — A thousand dollars!
AUBREY — That's regulation. (*Amy gives her mother a troubled look.*) A
little chicken feed for the stool pigeons.
MRS. FISHER — Did he say they put him under a thousand dollars' bail?
AUBREY — That's what I said, Mrs. Fisher, one thousand trifles — I wouldn't
kid you.
MRS. FISHER — You wouldn't kid anybody that'd listen to you for five
minutes. And who did you get to go a thousand dollars' bail for you?
AUBREY — Don't be alarmed, Little Mother — I saw that the affair was kept
strictly within the family.
MRS. FISHER — What do you mean?
AUBREY — Your other son-in-law — was kind enough to come forward.
MRS. FISHER — Clara's husband!
AUBREY — That's the gentleman, Mrs. Fisher — Mr. Francis X. Hyland.
MRS. FISHER — (*helplessly*). My God! (*To Clara.*) Do you hear that, Clara?
CLARA — What?
MRS. FISHER — He got Frank Hyland to go his bail for a thousand dollars.
CLARA — (*looking bitterly at Aubrey*). What did you do, write him another
letter?
AUBREY — That was not necessary, Mrs. Hyland, not giving you a short
answer. Your husband was fortunate enough to see the whole affair from the
trolley car. He was just returning from his business, and happened to be on
the trolley car that ran into me.
MRS. FISHER — How many more things ran into you — besides traffic cops
and trolley cars! I suppose a couple of the buildin's ran into you too, didn't
they?
AUBREY — You'll find out all about that Monday morning, Mrs. Fisher.
MRS. FISHER — Well, see that nothin' else runs into you between now and
Monday.

They get away to the hospital finally, leaving Amy
and Aubrey alone. Again he gently assures her that she
has nothing to fear as a result of his accident. He will
be perfectly able to manage all that and it is altogether
likely that they will be apologizing to him before he is
through with them. True, they may try to take away
his license — even though he doesn't happen to have one.
But what's that? And courts have been known to fine

people for driving without a license, unless those accused were smart enough to beat them to it.

A workman from Fisher's shop arrives with further details of the stroke. He is bringing back Pop's lunch box and his overcoat and hat. And he describes how the unfortunate workman was found, not fifteen minutes after another friend was talking to him, lying prostrate in front of a boiler. He never came to after that.

Even while he is telling the story Amy is called to the telephone, and when she comes back it is with the news that her father is dead. She clings a little helplessly to Aubrey in her misery and he, awkwardly, blunderingly, but with as much gentleness as he can command, tries to comfort her.

AUBREY — Don't let it get you, Honey — you have nothing to regret; and nothing to fear. The Kid from West Philly'll never go back on you — you know that, don't you, Baby? (*She continues to cry.*) You know that, don't you, Amy? (*She doesn't answer him.*) Amy.

AMY — What?

AUBREY — You know I'm with you, don't you?

AMY — Yes. (*He kisses her hair affectionately.*)

AUBREY — Don't cry, Honey; the old man's better off than we are. He knows all about it now. (*He kisses her again.*)

AMY — What do you think we ought to do, Aubrey?

AUBREY — They's nothing at all that you can do that I can see, Sweetheart; except to sit tight till the folks get back. They'll be down there themselves in a few minutes, and they'll know all about it.

AMY — They said that Pop died at a quarter of six.

AUBREY — Was that the Hospital on the telephone?

AMY — Yes.

AUBREY — Something we ought to have in here, Amy; a telephone — not be letting the whole neighborhood in on our business. (*Amy is crying softly.*) Now, pull yourself together, Sweetheart. (*He goes to her and puts his arm around her shoulders.*)

AMY — This is where Pop always used to sit in the evening. It'll seem funny not to see him here any more. (*She breaks down again.*)

AUBREY — (*after a slight pause*). The old gent had to go sometime. Your mother'll have you and me to comfort her now.

AMY — I don't know how Mom'll keep this house going now, just on Joe's pay.

AUBREY — Why don't you say something to your mother about letting us come in here? She'll need a man in the house. And my salary'ud cover the rent.

AMY — Mom doesn't have to pay rent, Aubrey — she owns this house. Pop left it to her. He made his will out the week after we were married. (*Aubrey looks at her keenly.*) Clara got him to do it.

AUBREY — Who's the executor, do you know?

AMY — Clara is. (*Aubrey nods comprehendingly.*)

AUBREY — (*looking away off*). Too bad your father didn't make me the executor of that will — I could have saved him a lot of money.

AMY — I suppose he thought on account of Clara being the oldest.

AUBREY — I wonder why your father never liked me.
AMY — Pop never said he didn't like you, Aubrey.
AUBREY — I always tried to be clubby with him. I used to slap him on the back whenever I spoke to him.
AMY — Pop was always very quiet.
AUBREY — And the Kid from West Philly had too much to say. Well — forgive and forget. It's all over now. And the old man can be as quiet as he likes. (*Amy cries again.*)
AMY — (*pulling herself together*). You haven't had anything to eat tonight yet, have you, Aubrey?
AUBREY — (*coming out of his abstraction*). Don't worry about me, Sweetheart.
AMY — I'll get you something.
AUBREY — It'll be all the same at the finish — whether I've had my dinner or not. (*He gazes starward.*) "Sic transit gloria mundi." And we never get used to it. The paths of glory lead but to the grave. And yet we go on — building up big fortunes — only to leave them to the generations yet unborn. Well — so it goes. And so it will always go, I suppose. "Sic transit gloria mundi."
AMY — What does that mean, Aubrey, "Sic transit gloria mundi"?
AUBREY — (*casually*). It's an old saying from the French — meaning, "We're here today, and gone tomorrow."
AMY — (*wretchedly*). I'm worried about tomorrow, Aubrey.
AUBREY — What are you worried about, Sweetheart?
AMY — I mean Monday.
AUBREY — Now — "Sufficient unto the day is the evil thereof," — you know that, don't you, Baby?
AMY — But, you didn't have a license, Aubrey. And if that traffic officer should be seriously injured ——
AUBREY — Don't you worry about that, Sweetheart — we're here today; and if he's seriously injured — we'll know all about it Monday. "Sic transit gloria mundi."

The curtain falls

ACT III

It is a week later. The agent for the insurance company has called with a check for $1,000, payable to Mrs. Fisher. It is money, he explains, that his company likes to pay — and doesn't like to pay. But at least it is money that doesn't make things any less pleasant.

He inquires also about Mr. Piper. He has brought with him a memorandum for Aubrey detailing the cost and upkeep of a life and accident insurance policy for fifty thousand dollars, in which Mr. Piper has taken great interest. But Mrs. Fisher does not encourage his leaving it.

"He was showin' off, Mr. Rogers — what he's always doin'," she explains. "Why, that fellow don't make enough salary in six months — to pay one year's premium on a policy like this. So, if I was you, I'd just put this paper right back in my pocket, for you're only wastin' it to be givin' it to him."

The agent is reluctant to give up the Piper prospect, even in the face of so unpromising a report. But he is forced to bide his time. Aubrey is not at home, and his coming is uncertain. At the moment he is in court, being tried for driving without a license a car he didn't own, and running into a traffic officer. He may not be back for six months, it is Mrs. Fisher's belief, unless the magistrate discharges him to get rid of him, after listening to his talk.

Clara, come to stay with her mother while the others are in court, is inclined to defend Aubrey this morning. She at least can understand how Amy feels about him, which is more than her mother can do.

CLARA — (*looking straight ahead, wistfully*). She's in love with him, Mom — she doesn't see him through the same eyes as other people do.

MRS. FISHER — You're always talkin' about love; you give me a pain.

CLARA — Well, don't you think she is?

MRS. FISHER — How do I know whether she is or not? I don't know anything about when people are in love; except that they act silly — most everybody that I ever knew that was. I'm sure she acted silly enough when she took him.

CLARA — She might have taken worse, Mom. He does his best. He works every day, and he gives her his money; and nobody ever heard of him looking at another woman.

MRS. FISHER — But he's such a rattle-brain, Clara.

CLARA — Oh, there are lots of things that are harder to put up with in a man than that, Mom. I know he's terribly silly, and has too much to say, and all that, but — I don't know, I feel kind of sorry for him sometimes. He'd so love to be important; and, of course, he never will be.

MRS. FISHER — Well, I swear I don't know how Amy stands the everlastin' talk of him. He's been here now only a week, and I'm tellin' you, Clara, I'm nearly light-headed. I'll be glad when they go.

CLARA — I'd rather have a man that talked too much than one of those silent ones. Honestly, Mom, I think sometimes if Frank Hyland doesn't say something I'll go out of my mind.

MRS. FISHER — What do you want him to say?

CLARA — Anything; just so I'd know he had a voice.

MRS. FISHER — He's too sensible a man, Clara, to be talkin' when he has nothin' to say.

CLARA — I don't think it's so sensible, Mom, never to have anything to say.

MRS. FISHER — Well, lots of men are that way in the house.

CLARA — But there are usually children there — it isn't so bad.

MRS. FISHER — Well, if Amy ever has any children, and they have as much to say as their father, I don't know what'll become of her.

CLARA — She'll get along some way; people always do.

MRS. FISHER — Leanin' on somebody else — that's how they get along.

CLARA — There are always the Leaners and the Bearers, Mom. But, if she's in love with the man she's married to — and he's in love with her — and there are children ——

MRS. FISHER — I never saw a married woman so full of love.

CLARA — I suppose that's because I never had any of it, Mom. (*Her mother looks at her.*)

MRS. FISHER — Don't your man love you? (*Clara looks straight out, shaking her head slowly.*)

CLARA — He loved someone else before he met me.

MRS. FISHER — How do you know?

CLARA — The way he talks sometimes.

MRS. FISHER — Why didn't he marry her?

CLARA — I think he lost her. I remember he said to me one time — " Always be kind, Clara, to anybody that loves you; for," he said, " a person always loses what he doesn't appreciate. And," he said, " it's a terrible thing to lose love." He said, " You never realize what it was worth until you've lost it." I think that's the reason he gives Piper a hand once in a while — because he sees Amy's in love with him, and he wants to make it easy for her ; because I have an idea he made it pretty hard for the woman that loved him.

MRS. FISHER — Well, a body can't have everything in this world, Clara.

The others are back from court, now — Amy looking a little worn and ragged from the strain; Frank Hyland, calmly quiescent and possibly a little disgusted with all the fuss. Aubrey has stopped at the cigar store.

The judge fined Aubrey a thousand dollars, Amy admits to Clara, without her mother's hearing her. And Frank Hyland paid the money to save his brother-in-law spending six months in jail. Amy expects to pay Frank back — as soon as she can go back to work.

But they have little success fooling Mrs. Fisher. She'll know the truth some way, she assures them, when they try to dissemble. It'll be in the papers, most likely.

CLARA — I wouldn't say anything to Amy about it, even if it is; she has enough to bother her now.

MRS. FISHER — Well, she brought it on herself if she has — nobody could tell her anything.

CLARA — Well, there's nothing can be done by fighting with her, Mom.

MRS. FISHER — (*with conviction*). There's nothing can be done by anything, Clara, when once the main thing is done. And that's the marriage. That's where all the trouble starts — gettin' married.

CLARA — If there were no marriages, Mom, there'd be no world.

MRS. FISHER — Oh, everybody sez that! — if there were no marriages there'd be no world.

CLARA — Well, would there?

MRS. FISHER — Well, what if there wouldn't? Do you think it'd be any worse than it is now? I think there'll be no world pretty soon, anyway, the way things are goin'. A lot of whiffets gettin' married, and not two cents to their names, and then throwin' themselves on their people to keep them. They're so full of love before they're married. You're about the only one I've heard talkin' about love after they were married. It's a wonder to me you have a roof over you; for they never have, with that kind of talk. Like the two in the parlor there — that has to kiss each other, every time they meet on the floor.

CLARA — (*quietly*). Amy's going to have a child, Mom.

Mrs. Fisher — How do you know?

Clara — She told me so.

Mrs. Fisher — (*softening a bit*). Why didn't she tell me?

Clara — I suppose she thought it'd start a fight.

Mrs. Fisher — (*indignant again*). I don't know why it'd start a fight; I never fight with anybody, except him; and I wouldn't fight with him only for his impudence.

Clara — Has Amy said anything to you about coming in here to live?

Mrs. Fisher — She said something to me the night your father was laid out, but I wasn't payin' much attention to her.

Clara — I think you ought to let her come in here, Mom. She'd be company for you, now that Pop is gone. And you don't know what day Joe might take a notion to get married.

Mrs. Fisher — What's changed your ideas so much about lettin' her come in here? You were very much against it when she was married.

Clara — I'd be against it now if things around here were the way they were then. You didn't even own this house, Mom, when Amy was married. It was Pop's; and I knew if anything ever happened to him, and there was no will, you might not find it so easy to order anybody out of it.

Mrs. Fisher — It isn't that I'd mind lettin' Amy come in here, Clara, but I wouldn't like to please him; for I know the first thing I'd know, he'd very likely be tellin' somebody that he'd let me come in. Oh, I wouldn't put it past him; he's told bigger lies than that. And if I ever found out that he said that, he'd go out of here inside of five minutes, bag and baggage.

It is arranged that the Pipers shall move over to the Fisher house, but not until Clara has undertaken to make Aubrey see the light. It happens that she, and not Mrs. Fisher, is the executor of Pop's estate, she tells him, and it is only on her conditions that Aubrey need expect to be permitted to live there.

" What do you want me to do?" he asks meekly.

" I want you to stop telling lies," she warns him; " for that's about all everything you do amounts to. Trying to make people believe that you're something you're not — when if you'd just stop your talking and your showing off you might be the thing that you're trying to make them believe you are. . . . Your wife's going to have a child one of these days, Aubrey, and you want to pull yourself together and try to be sensible, like the man of a family should be. You're smart enough; — there's no reason why a fellow like you should be living in two rooms over a barber shop. I should think you'd have more respect for your wife."

" A man doesn't stand much chance of getting ahead, Clara, when the boss has got a grudge against him," protests Aubrey.

"Well, stop your silly talk and get rid of that carnation, and the boss might get rid of his grudge."

The family has just settled down. Amy and Aubrey have gone to look at the side room Mom is to let them have; Clara is next door telephoning her maid that she won't be home for dinner and Mom has taken up her knitting for as peaceful a moment as she can expect, with Aubrey's gay laughter booming down the hall to her — when in rushes Joe with a piece of news that *is* news.

Right there in the evening's paper is something Mom should enjoy reading: "Philadelphia Youth Makes Important Chemical Discovery. Mr. Joseph Fisher of North Philadelphia Perfects Rust-Preventive Solution."

And Joe is the fortunate youth. His patented formula has been bought, the contracts are signed and a check for $100,000 first payment is even then resting in his attorney's safe.

Mom is duly impressed, though she might be more excited if she could remember exactly how many noughts there are in a hundred thousand. She realizes, however, that it is enough to permit Joe to stop working if he wants to. He has no intention of doing that. He thinks he may go over to Trenton, where he can have access to some completely equipped laboratories, now that she isn't going to be alone without him. He is rather pleased that the Pipers are coming in. As a matter of fact he feels a little as though he owes Aubrey something.

JOE — You know, Mom, I kinda feel that there's somethin' comin' to that nut out of this thing.

MRS. FISHER — How do you mean?

JOE — He gave me the idea one night.

MRS. FISHER — (*seizing him suddenly by both arms*). Well, for God's sake, don't tell him that, Joe! — or, as sure as you live, he'll be tellin' everybody that he done the whole thing.

JOE — You remember the night he was sayin' here about bein' at work on a solution for the prevention of rust in iron and steel?

MRS. FISHER — Yes.

JOE — Well, you know, I'd been tellin' him somethin' about it a week or so before ——

MRS. FISHER — Yes, you told me.

JOE — While he was waitin' here for Amy one night.

Mrs. Fisher — Yes.

Joe — Well, he forgot that night he was tellin' me about it that it was me that had been tellin' him about it; and he got it mixed.

Mrs. Fisher — That's the way he does with everything.

Joe — And it was the way he got it mixed, Mom, that gave me the idea. He said that it was a combination of chemical elements to be added to the metal in its molten state, instead of applied externally, as they had been doin'. And I landed on it — the way Howe did when he dreamed of puttin' the eye in the point of the needle instead of the other end. That was exactly what I'd been doin'— applying the solution externally — in a mixture of paint. But the next day, I tried adding parts of it to the molten state of the metal, and it did the trick. Of course, he didn't know what he was sayin' when he said it ——

Mrs. Fisher — He never does.

Joe — And he didn't know anything about the solution-formula. But it was the way he got what I'd been tellin' him twisted, Mom — that put the thing over.

Mrs. Fisher — Well, that's no credit to him, Joe.

Joe — I know.

Mrs. Fisher — He was only blowin' when he said it.

Joe — Sure.

Mrs. Fisher — He don't know what a formula means. And I'd have told him where he heard it, too, if I'd been you.

Joe — (thoughtfully.) I'd like to give him a little present of some kind.

Mrs. Fisher — What would you give him a present for?

Joe — For makin' a mistake.

Mrs. Fisher — That's all everybody's doin' around here — givin' that fellow presents for makin' mistakes. That's what Frank Hyland said here today, when I ast him why he paid his fine. He said, " Oh, you've got to give a little present here and there once in a while." There's no use tryin' to be sensible any more.

Joe — I'd like to give him somethin'.

Mrs. Fisher — I'll tell you what you can do, Joe, if you're so anxious to give him somethin'. Find out what fine Frank Hyland paid for him this afternoon, and tell him you're goin' to give him that. But don't tell him what you're givin' it to him for, Joe, or we won't be able to live in the house with him. And don't give him money, Joe; for he'd only be goin' from one room to another here in an automobile. And don't give it to her neither, Joe; for she'll only hand it right over to him. Give it to me. (Joe looks at her.) And I'll give it to them when I think they need it.

Clara, back from her telephoning, is properly impressed with her brother's luck, and Aubrey, again easing himself into the family circle with his customary confidence, has words of congratulation and advice as well to offer.

Aubrey — (to Mrs. Fisher). If he's a wise bird, he'll let me handle that money for him. I could give him a couple of very fly tips on that.

Mrs. Fisher — He don't want your tips; nor your taps neither. We know about one tip you gave a man, and his arm has been in a sling ever since.

Aubrey — That's all right, Mrs. Fisher; but if he's a wise bimbo, he'll take the drooping left (he lowers the lid of his left eye, very mysteriously), and I'll double that money for him within the next two weeks; and give him an extra pair of trousers.

Mrs. Fisher — I guess he'd need an extra pair of trousers if he was sittin' around waitin' for you to double his money for him.

Aubrey — Well, I'm telling you, Mother, he's an awful straw ride if he doesn't get in on some of that copper-clipping that those people are writing me about.

MRS. FISHER — What is it, a copper mine this time?
AUBREY — 'Tain't a mine at all — it's a mint.
MRS. FISHER — What are they writin' to you about it for?
AUBREY — They're writing to everybody.
MRS. FISHER — They must be.
AUBREY — Prospective investors — They hear a man's got a few dollars lay-ing around idle, and they get in touch with him.
MRS. FISHER — Well, nobody's heard that you have any dollars layin' around idle, have they?
AUBREY — (with a touch of consequence). Oh, I don't know — they may have.
MRS. FISHER — Listen, boy, if you've got any dollars layin' around idle, it'd be fitter for you to pay Frank Hyland the money he paid to keep you out of jail, than to be lookin' around for an investment for it — in some old copper mine, out in God-knows-where — that you don't know no more about than them that's writin' to you about it.

But Aubrey almost has his moment of triumph. He has stood by as complacently as possible while Mrs. Fisher discovers from the evening paper that he was fined the thousand dollars and that Frank Hyland paid it for him. With more satisfaction than humiliation, he hears her tell Clara to take the life insurance money and pay Hyland back. " I don't want Frank Hyland goin' around payin' out thousand dollar bills on account of this clown. . . . It's bad enough for me to have to do it," she says. And he has accepted a second lambasting inspired by his admitted temerity in looking up the terms on the fifty-thousand-dollar insurance policy.

AUBREY — A man 'ud certainly have a swell chance trying to make anything of himself around this hut.
MRS. FISHER — Listen, boy, any time you don't like this hut, you go right back to Lehigh Avenue to your own two rooms over a dago barber shop. And I'll be glad to see your heels.
CLARA — Stop talking, Mom.
MRS. FISHER — Nobody around here's tryin' to stop you from makin' some-thin' of yourself.
AUBREY — No, and nobody's trying to help me, either; only trying to make me look like a pin head — every chance they get.
MRS. FISHER — Nobody'll have to try very hard to make you look like a pin head; your own silly talk'll do that for you, any time at all.
AUBREY — I suppose it's silly talk to try to make a good impression.
MRS. FISHER — Yes; it's silly to try to make an impression of any kind; for the only one that'll be made'll be the right one — and that'll make itself.
AUBREY — Well, if you were out in the world as much as I am, you'd very soon see how much easier it is for a fellow to get along if people think he's got something.
MRS. FISHER — Well, anybody that 'ud listen to you very long 'ud know you couldn't have very much.
AUBREY — Is that so.
MRS. FISHER — You heard me. (Clara rises and moves toward her mother.)
AUBREY — People that are smart enough to be able to make it easier for you —
CLARA — Aubrey — that'll do.

Then he hears Joe repeat to Clara the details of his getting the check from the people who bought his invention and his putting it temporarily in his lawyer's safe. Immediately Aubrey is himself again. There is a new light of hope in his eyes as he carelessly flicks the ashes from his cigar and engages Joe in conversation.

" Joe," he says, grandly; " Joe — what do you think we ought to do with that money?"

Joe tries to hide his laughter. So do they all, except Amy. But the query has served to remind Joe that he was really considerably surprised when they made him so large a cash payment.

Joe — You know, it was a funny thing, Mom — when I first talked to the Meyers & Stevens people I was only to get fifty thousand dollars advance; and when I went up there today they had the contracts all made out for a hundred thousand.

Aubrey — And they're getting away with murder at that.

Mrs. Fisher — Oh, keep still, you! You don't know anything about this at all.

Aubrey — I made them think I knew something about it.

Mrs. Fisher — You made who think?

Aubrey — The Meyers & Stevens people.

Joe — What are you talkin' about, Aubrey, do you know?

Aubrey — Certainly, I know what I'm talking about. I went to see those people last Saturday afternoon, after you told me they'd talked with you.

Joe — And what'd you do up there?

Aubrey — Why, I told them that they'd have to double the advance, if they wanted to do business with us.

Mrs. Fisher — And what business was it of yours?

Aubrey — Well, I'm Joe's guardian, ain't I?

Mrs. Fisher — Who told you you were?

Aubrey — Well, he's got to have somebody tend to his business, doesn't he? He's only a lad.

Mrs. Fisher — Well, he doesn't need you to tend to his business for him. He tended to his business long before he ever saw you.

Aubrey — He never landed a hundred thousand dollars, though, till he saw me, did he?

Joe — Well, what did you say to them, Aubrey?

Aubrey — Why — I simply told them that your father was dead, and that I was acting in the capacity of business adviser to you; and that, if this discovery of yours was as important as you had led me to believe it was, they were simply taking advantage of your youth by offering you fifty thousand dollars for it. And that I refused to allow you to negotiate further — unless they doubled the advance, market it at their expense, and one-half the net — sign on the dotted line.

Joe — Well, did they know who you were?

Aubrey — I told them — that I was head of the house here; and that I was also connected with the Pennsylvania Railroad.

Mrs. Fisher — It's too bad they didn't know what you do down there; and call your bluff.

Aubrey — I beat them to it; I called theirs first.

Joe — Well, I certainly have to give you credit, Aubrey; that's the way the contract reads.

Aubrey — I told it to them; and I told it to your lawyer, too.

JOE — I'll have to give you a little present of some kind out of this, Aubrey.
AUBREY — You'll not give me any present, Joe. Give it to your mother.
She'll need it more than I will. Amy — have you got the financial page there?
AMY — Is this it, Aubrey?
AUBREY — Thank you. (*Amy looks at him wonderingly.*)
AMY — Aubrey, you're wonderful!
AUBREY — A little bit of bluff goes a long way sometimes, Amy.
AMY — Isn't he wonderful, Mom?
MRS. FISHER — (*after a long sigh*). God help me, from now on.

" The curtain descends slowly, with Amy standing lost in admiration of the wonder of Aubrey. When the curtain rises again Aubrey is reading, Mrs. Fisher is knitting, Clara is sitting reading the ' Delineator,' over on the arm of the arm-chair at the right, Joe is putting on his overcoat and hat at the mantelpiece mirror, and Amy is sitting just looking at Aubrey."

THE END

"HELL-BENT FER HEAVEN"

A Play in Three Acts

By Hatcher Hughes

THE Pulitzer Prize for 1923 was awarded this play of the Blue Ridge mountain folk written by Professor Hatcher Hughes of Columbia College. Not, however, without a contest. The special jury of three selected by the Pulitzer Prize committee to offer suggestions as to the best American play of the year gave one first and two second votes to George Kelly's " The Show-Off," and only one first vote to " Hell-bent." The prize committee, however, after due deliberation, reversed this recommendation. Whereupon Owen Johnson, the novelist, serving on the jury with Prof. Clayton Hamilton of Columbia and Prof. William Lyon Phelps of Yale, made public the jury's expressed preference for " The Show-Off " and resigned his membership. Professor Phelps publicly endorsed the statement of Mr. Johnson, but did not resign. And nothing was heard from Professor Hamilton, save that he was the member who voted for the Hughes drama as first choice and " The Show-Off " second. Professor Phelps's first choice was for " The Changelings " and his second for " The Show-Off."

" Hell-bent fer Heaven " was written and accepted by the Klaws for production a year before it finally reached the stage. It was not, therefore, inspired by the success of Lula Vollmer's " Sun-up " and " The Shame Woman," the other mountain-folk plays that preceded it, though that impression was general, following its production.

It was ready for presentation, after a week of trial performances on the road, in December, 1923, but there was no theater available for it in New York. The Klaw Theater, for which it was intended, was housing at the time a comedy called " Meet the Wife," which had scored a promising hit. So, rather than disband the " Hell-bent " company, Alonzo Klaw, who produced the play, decided to start it at a series of special matinées. The first of these was given January 4, 1924.

The public's response was so immediate and seemingly so genuine that the play was continued at special matinées for four weeks, when it was moved to the Frazee Theater for a regular engagement. Here it continued for 112 additional performances. Patronage was always good, but never such as to tax the capacity of the theater. That portion of the public that is easily offended by anything less than a kind of awesome reverence for a religious subject, however hypocritical such a reverence may obviously be, took exception to Prof. Hughes's exposé of a somewhat fanatical convert to " camp-meeting religion " and stayed away.

The scene of " Hell-bent " is " A room in Matt Hunt's home in the Carolina mountains. The walls and ceilings are of rough boards, smoked and stained with age. There being no floor above, the gable roof is visible, with its rough hewn timbers. The furniture is old and hand-made, of natural wood stained and polished by wear and time. The place is neat and homelike." . . . . " It is late afternoon of a midsummer day and through the windows and the open door can be seen the sunlit hills across the valley, bathed in a bluish vapor. Sunlight floods the porch and streams in through the window."

Old David Hunt and Meg, his daughter-in-law, are home. David " is a rugged, well preserved man of 80. His snow-white hair and long beard contrast vividly with the ruddy glow of his face. A rich personality, humorous, virile and mellow." Meg Hunt is " a wiry, active woman of forty-odd."

They are waiting for Matt Hunt, who is driving his son, Sid, just back from a year overseas with the A. E. F., up from the railroad station.

They are wondering, too, what the war has done to Sid. It may have changed him a lot. Made him more religious, his mother thinks, or less so, as David suspects. It evidently has not changed his instinctive habits much, for now, when he comes, it is through the kitchen, where he has helped himself to a large slice of pie. " I jist natchelly come 'round to the place where the cookin's done," he explains.

Sid is a handsome, vigorous young fellow, a little flustered by the excitement of his homecoming, a little embarrassed by their references to the pieces in the paper about his being a sort of hero, and glad of a chance to relieve the strain by fussing with his grandpap as to the relative merits of their two wars. Grandpap, having fit with Stonewall Jackson and Robert E. Lee, doesn't think much of Pershin' and Foch.

Living with the Hunts is Rufe Pryor, a shifty, sallow-faced boy " of medium height; young but of uncertain age." He has been doing Sid's work in the general store run by Matt Hunt and, because he is weaker and more helpless than her other men-folk, who are always " pickin' " on him, Mrs. Hunt has felt obliged to mother and protect him a good deal. Rufe comes downstairs from his room now, almost slyly edging his way into the group, and plainly resentful of Sid's popularity.

Rufe is a good deal of a whiner. He would have been in the army, too, he says, if it hadn't been for his health, which somebody told him would never stand it. And he just knows he's not wanted even there, at the Hunts', nor deservin' of all Mrs. Hunt's kindness. Everybody's down on him, Rufe's convinced. But, thank heaven, he's stout of heart and able to stand their taunts. Especially is he fortified against the railing of David and Matt, who find it hard to stomach him and his constant " bellyachin'."

Even now, when Matt sends him for Sid's pack, left at the barn, Rufe accepts the task as a hardship and something he wasn't hired to do. Being humble, however, he allows he will go. " I'll be a nigger fer Sid — or anythin' you say " he agrees, with mock humility. Which doesn't serve to calm Matt Hunt's temper. But Sid saves the situation. He doesn't take Rufe's part, but he allows he understands his mother's protection of the boy. " I've seed folks like him," he explains. " Kinder tetchy. But I reckon he don't mean no harm."

MEG — Course he don't! An' he wouldn't be tetchy neither if your paw an' grandpap wusn't allus a-pickin' on 'im jist 'caze he ain't so big an' strong as they aire.

DAVID — You don't ketch Matt and me a-pickin' on chil'en jist 'caze they ain't so big and strong as we aire. I'v noticed 'at if folks gits picked on it's ginerally 'caze they desarve it.

MEG — Oh, you could get along with Rufe if you tried.

MATT — Yeh, I expect we could if we laid awake o' nights figgerin' how to keep from hurtin' his feelin's — like you do — an' if I didn't expect him to do no work. 'Tain't only he's tetchy — though God knows I'm sick o' hearin' him bellyache — but he's lazy or born tired — why when it comes to work he ain't worth his salt! (During this speech Meg anxiously notes the effect of it upon Sid.)

DAVID — 'Specially sence he got that camp-meetin' breed o' religion. I never seed a man so Hell-bent fer Heaven as he is! (Rufe enters carrying Sid's pack.)

RUFE — (putting the pack down). Thar 'tis.

SID — Much obliged, Rufe.

RUFE — No 'casion, Sid. I'm glad to do anything I kin fer Matt.

MATT — Well, I got jist one thing more fer you to do. I want you to pack up your duds and make tracks away from here. (Rufe and Meg are stunned. He looks to Meg to help him.)

MEG — Matt! You ain't a-goin' ter turn 'im off at this time o' year?

MATT — O' course! I didn't adopt him fer life. I agreed to keep him till Sid come back!

MEG — But he cain't git another clerkin' job an' it's too late to start a crop now.

MATT — He'd orter thought o' that before. He knowed a month ago 'at Sid was a-comin' home.

MEG — Yeh, but when you didn't say nothin' more 'bout his leavin' he natchelly thought 'at . . .

MATT — Now, Meg, I ain't a-goin' to argue about it — he cain't stay here. (Meg is silenced. She looks helplessly at Rufe. Having leaned upon her as long as she fought for him, he now strikes out for himself.)

RUFE — He's right, Meg. I might ha' knowed this would happen. But, Matt, I'm a-goin' to tell you sompen for your own good. The Scripture says as how anybody as wants to can be saved. But you've never took advantage o' the offer. I cain't understand that in a close trader like you, Matt. If the offer o' free salvation 'us a hoss swap or a case o' free goods fer the store you'd never let it git by. Understand I'm a-sayin' this in a true Christian sperit. The Scripture says to love our enemies an' do good to them that despitefully uses us.

MATT — Dadburn you, I don't want you a-lovin' me ner doin' good to me nuther!

RUFE — I know you don't, Matt. But I jist cain't help it. An' you cain't neither; that's one thing you ain't the boss of.

MATT — (*rising and exploding*). Go on up an' pack your duds!

RUFE — All right, Matt, you're the boss o' that. You kin hector me an' bully me about the things o' this world, but you cain't keep me from lovin' your immortal soul! (*He starts upstairs.*) An' you cain't take away my reward, which is in Heaven! An' you cain't escape yourn, which ain't! (*As he goes through the door.*) Unless you have a change o' heart!

MEG — It's the truth that hurts, Matt! your reward ain't in Heaven!

MATT — I hope it ain't if that's whar he's a-goin'!

DAVID — I cain't make him out. If he 'us jist a plain hypocrite I could understand him. But he 'pears to honestly believe that everybody's got to be like him before they're saved.

MEG — Mebbe they *has* got to be different from you an' Matt.

At Sid's suggestion a compromise is effected. Rufe is to stay on for another month while Sid is getting settled in the home ways again and attending to his private business. Part of this latter, we gather, is concerned with Jude Lowry. The Lowries have lived neighbors to the Hunts for a good many years, and Jude, if not the handsomest mountain girl in the district, could never reasonably be left out of any such beauty competition. She and Sid have been as good as engaged a number of times. Were as good as engaged when the war came, in fact, for all they had quarreled.

The first of the Lowries to be a party to Sid's homecoming, however, is not Jude, but her brother Andy. Andy is carrying the mail, and swings off his cart at the sight of his old friend in the Hunt doorway. He is a healthy, happy young fellow, but easily excited. Just now his face is slightly flushed with the whiskey he has drunk, but not noticeably so.

Andy is another of the mountain boys who wanted to go to war, but was kept at home because his Mam and Pap had wheedled him into claiming exemption so he could help cut timber for the government. And now he's "totin' the mail." This has all made Andy a little bitter. "I want a job that gives me more elbow room," he protests to Sid. "Every time I look at that piddlin' mail sack an' think o' what you've been through, I git so goddern mad at myself an' everybody else, 'at I feel like startin' a war o' my own right here in the mountains!"

He swings the mail sack playfully at Sid's head and they scuffle good-naturedly. They have long been friends, but there is a suggestion that they have long been rivals, too. This thought is strengthened a moment later when Andy asks Rufe to fetch him a box of revolver cartridges from the store.

The subject of guns and ammunition starts the boys inspecting a " Dutch peacepipe " Sid has brought home from France — a souvenir from a Dutchman who hadn't any more use for it after he had shot at Sid and missed. It's an automatic, which doesn't mean much to mountain men. Grandpap Hunt insists he wouldn't " be ketched dead in the woods " with one of 'em. " It's an insult to shootin' men," says he, pushing it from him. " It's built on the notion that you're a-goin' to miss all your fust shots."

But Sid thinks it will shoot pretty well, and Andy is keen for a shooting match to test it. They start for the yard, but meet surprising opposition. Meg is the first to oppose the match, much to her son's amazement.

SID — (looking at her puzzled, then placing his hands on her shoulders). Why, Mam! What sort of a graveyard rabbit has crossed your path? Me an' Andy used to have shootin' matches out thar an' you never made no fuss about it!

MEG — I don't keer! I've seen enough shootin' an' fightin' in my time! An' I've hyeard enough talk about war!

SID — 'Tain't a-goin' to do no harm fer us to shoot at a spot on a tree.

MEG — 'Tain't a-goin' to do no good! (With a sudden flare of passion.) An' I wisht you'd throw that pistol in the river! The man it belonged to had a mammy too! Think how she feels — wherever she is!

ANDY — If he'd been to as many shootin' matches as Sid mebby you'd be the one 'at's a-feelin' that way!

RUFE — It wasn't the shootin' matches 'at saved Sid. It 'us the will o' God!

SID — Mebby so, Rufe, but I've noticed other things bein' equal, God generally sides 'ith the feller that shoots the straightest.

MEG — Oh! Cain't you talk o' nothin' but shootin' an' killin'? I wish I could go some place whar I'd never hear guns mentioned agin as long as I live!

RUFE — You kin! We can all go thar if we live right! An' that 'minds me, boys; if I 'us livin' I wouldn't have no more shootin' matches. It 'us at a shootin' match that the feud fust started 'twixt your two gran'-daddies. (In an instant the faces of the men become tense with amazement. Rufe is conscious of this, but continues with a show of innocence.) An' they 'us both fetched home on stretchers, 'long 'ith lots more o' your kin on both sides, afore it 'us patched up. I know 'tain't none o' my business ——

MATT — (his right fist trembling dangerously). Then why the Hell don't you keep your mouth shet?

Rufe — I 'us only warnin' 'em fer their own good! They're frien'ly now an' I want 'em to stay that way!

Matt — You've got a dam' poor way o' showin' it! You know that's sompen we don't talk about here! If I didn't know you 'us a born fool I'd ——

Meg — He meant everything fer the best, Matt!

Matt — That's what you allus say.

Rufe — All right, if you don't want me to do you a good turn, I won't! Hereafter they can shoot er do what they please. I won't open my mouth!

Sid — You needn't pester your mind about me an' Andy, Rufe. We've knowed all about the war 'twixt our fam'lies sence we 'us knee-high to a duck. An' it's never made our trigger-fingers itch none, has it, Andy?

Andy — Not a durned bit! We natchelly hain't talked about it, but I reckon we could if we had to.

Sid — I don't reckon nothin' about it, I know it! Me an' you could talk about anything 'thout fightin' — 'cept religion!

Andy — (laughing). I'd even take a crack at that with you, fer I expect we've got about the same sort!

Sid — Well, my mouth ain't no prayer book, an' I don't try to make it sound like one.

Andy — (uproariously). Me, nuther!

Grandpap David doesn't see anything smart in their " a-runnin' " down religion." " I've lived in this ole world longer'n both of you put together, an' they ain't nothin' to be ashamed of in bein' a Christian," says he.

He knows, too, does Grandpap. He has had experience. Once, when he was " jist such a jackass " as Sid or Andy he undertook to put in his place a militant Baptist who had come to the mountains to preach the gospel. David attended the first meeting, and when the preacher pointed him out as one of the worst sinners of the community, David called him out of the pulpit. And he came. And David smote him on the right cheek. And the minister turned t'other cheek. And David smote him again. And minutes afterward, when David recovered consciousness, he found two men a-rubbin' of him and the minister goin' right ahead explainin' Scripture as though nothin' had happened. " He said the Savior never told us what to do after we'd turned t'other cheek once," David concludes; " fer he took it fer granted any dern fool'd know."

Sid and Andy enjoy the story. But Rufe is convinced such a preacher couldn't have been a Christian at all, and Meg is so stirred by the argument that follows that she decides she had about as soon listen to them talk

war as religion. " It allus was a peacefuller subjec', "
admits David. To stop the argument he goes with Meg
to rob a bee-gum to sweeten Sid's supper.

Andy is for Sid's having a drink. He has a bottle of
" blockade " in the mail pouch he would like to have him
sample. But Sid declines. Rufe, of course, has " gone
prohibition," but he has a proposition to make. If Andy
is going to drink it would be a lot better if he was to
drink good stuff. Which Rufe knows where to get, seeing
he has been hiding some 20-year-old he found in a cache
one day when he was dynamitin' fish, afore he joined the
church.

RUFE — . . . An' it's the best stuff you ever stuck your tongue into! So
thick an' sirupy it clings to the sides o' the bottle jist like 'lasses!
ANDY — (interrupting him). Stop! Is they any left?
RUFE — Some. Why?
ANDY — Why! Ha, ha! Did you hear that, Sid? He wants to know why?
(To Rufe.) 'Course you don't want to sell any of it?
RUFE — Well, my advice to everybody is to let licker alone. But if folks
is bound they're a-goin' to drink the stuff. I s'pose tain't no more'n right to
help 'em git sompen good.
ANDY — Spoke like a true Christian!
RUFE — That's what I try to be, Andy. An' ef that licker o' mine'll help
you out I don't want to make nothin' on it. The only thing is — I bought Bill
Hedgepeth's share an' if I'm a-goin to be out of a job soon I would kinder
like to git back jist what I paid fer it.
ANDY — Well, you won't have no trouble a-squarin' yourself if it tastes anythin' like you say.
RUFE — You don't have to take my word for it. I got a sample bottle in my
trunk. (Coaxingly to Andy, as he goes to the stairs.) Come on up an' try it!
ANDY — Well, I've had about all I can tote — but I reckon one more drink
like that won't load me down. (As he turns to follow Rufe he looks off in the
direction of the store.) Oh, hell! Thar's Sis — out at the store!
SID — What's the trouble?
ANDY — Trouble? Jude's got religion sence you left — like Rufe — an' she
has a jeeminy fit every time she smells licker on me! But drive on, Rufe!
Damn it all, I'm free, white an' twenty-one!

It is Rufe's idea that Sid should drink with them, and
he suspects the reason he won't is that he is trying to
make Jude Lowry think he's " a-sproutin' wings." Sid's
coming back a sort of hero seems likely to interfere
somewhat with Jude's interest in the meek and penitent
Rufe, and the latter resents it.

When, a moment later, Jude bounds into the room in
search of Meg Hunt, Sid is playfully hiding behind the
door. When she goes into the kitchen he comes out and

plants himself in the middle of the floor, standing straight
and stiff in the position of a soldier at attention. When
she comes again into the room and sees him and is properly and rather happily surprised he continues to stand
rigidly and stare at her. When she tries to talk with him
he makes signs, indicating that he has lost the power of
speech. She is shocked at the mere thought of such
a possibility. Suppose he should have been shell-shocked
or "tetched in the head"! With a great surge of sympathy she goes close to him and shakes him by the arms.
"Why don't you say sompen? You know me, don't
you?"

He does, and the next minute she finds herself held
tight in his arms and vigorously kissed. At which action
she pretends to be righteously indignant.

JUDE — . . . Sid, if you don't tell me why you're actin' this way I'm a-goin'
to scream!
  SID — I ain't actin'. This is natchel!
  JUDE — Natchel!
  SID — Yeh, don't you mind the last time you seen me you told me never to
speak to you agin as long as I lived?
  JUDE — (freeing herself and backing away). Oh! So that's it!
  SID — (laughing). Yeh! you know I allus did try to please you!
  JUDE — If you didn't aim to speak to me what'd you go an' kiss me fer?
  SID — You didn't say nothin' about not kissin' you!
  JUDE — I never kick afore I'm spurred! You knowed all the time I didn't
mean it when I told you never to speak to me no more! An' anyhow, you could
ha' writ!
  SID — (gradually working over to her). I thought o' writin'. But I ain't
much of a hand at settin' things down on paper. I 'lowed I could argy with you
better when I got you where I could sorter surround you!
  JUDE — (stepping away). That's another thing! You'd ought to kep' your
hands offen me! (With a suggestion of coquetry.) I still ain't a-goin' to marry
you!
  SID — Oh! (Teasing her.) Well, nobody axed you!
  JUDE — (her eyes blazing). You needn't throw that up to me!
  SID — (going to her). Oh, come on Jude, le's be sensible! (He tries to
take her hands.) I'll quarrel with you an' court you all you want me to after
we're married!
  JUDE — You act like you thought you had a morgidge on me!

Andy, lunging through the door at the head of the
stairs, puts an end to their talk. Andy is not drunk,
but he "is in the state of exhilaration that precedes complete intoxication," and inclined to be ugly. Evidently
Rufe has been filling him full of ugly thoughts as well
as "blockade" liquor.

Jude indicates her humiliation and disappointment. She had hoped Andy would keep his promise to leave the stuff alone. Sid is worried, though he tries to make light of the situation. He agrees to fetch the cartridges for Andy from the store, though he thinks they had probably better call the shooting match off, considering how Mrs. Hunt feels about it.

" She's afeard we'll start another war," sneers Andy. " All right. It's off. But bring me a box o' caterdges just the same as if it wusn't."

With Sid and Jude gone to the store Rufe continues his insinuations to Andy. He knows, he says, Sid and Jude are talking about gettin' married, which is a lot different way of " swoppin' blood " than the way the Hunts and Lowries used to do it in the old feud days. But perhaps Andy's a little afraid o' Sid Hunt, like a certain man said.

" Any man 'at says I'm afraid o' Sid Hunt's a damn liar!" shouts Andy.

RUFE — I ain't a-sayin' who it wus. But as your friend, Andy, I'm a-goin' to warn you o' one thing: don't you start nothin' 'ith Sid that you ain't prepared to end! Rickollect the last time the Hunts an' Lowries fit they 'us three more Lowries killed 'n they wus Hunts!

ANDY — (with the superhuman calm of the drunken man). Did Sid brag about that?

RUFE — I ain't a-sayin' what Sid done! I'm a-talkin' to you now as a friend fer your own good!

ANDY — Three more Lowries 'n Hunts! (Weeping with rage.) The dirty skunk! Where is he? Where is he? (He starts out through the door. Rufe, terrified, grabs his arm.)

RUFE — Ca'm yourself, Andy! He'll be back here any minute! (Rufe tries to get to the kitchen door but Andy heads him off.)

ANDY — Rufe, are you fer me or agin me?

RUFE — I'll stick by a friend, Andy, tell Jedgment Day!

ANDY — Then gimme your hand! Fer jist as shore as sunrise I'm a-goin' to equalize things!

RUFE — I'm sorry to hear you talk this way, Andy!

ANDY — (pulls out his pistol). You b'lieve in Provydence, don't you?

RUFE — (staring at the pistol). Yeh — I — I — believe in Provydence.

ANDY — Look! (He opens the pistol.) It's a-goin' to take six Hunts to make things equal, an' I got jist six caterdges in my pistol! That's Provydence!

RUFE — (with a strange mingling of fear and fascination). My advice to you, Andy, is to drop this! The Hunts are dangerous folks! Sid in pertickler, now 'at he's been through the war! You'd a heap better pocket your pride an' live in peace with him if you can, fer if he gits started he won't stop at nothin'! I know him!

ANDY — Ah! But you don't know me, Rufe! You think I'm skeered! Well, jist wait! This is a free country, an' everybody in it ought to be equal! Three more Lowries 'n Hunts — that ain't equal! (*He drops down in the chair and weeps with rage.*)

The curtain falls

ACT II

The scene is unchanged. The time a few minutes later. Andy has placed a chair opposite the door and sits, with his pistol in his hand, waiting the return of Sid.

Rufe, standing at the window, is acting as lookout. Now he sees Sid and Jude returning from the store and turns to beg Andy not to kill Sid now. But Andy, " with the unnatural calm of the drunken man," allows that every man has to die when his time comes.

For a moment after entering neither Sid nor Jude notice anything unusual in the attitude of Andy. Jude calls to him that she is ready to go home and passes on through the room to say good-bye to Mrs. Hunt. Sid circulates naturally about the room and finally comes to Andy to deliver the cartridges he has brought for him. Even when Andy insists on paying for them then and there Sid accepts his attitude more as a joke than anything else.

" I don't want no Hunt — in hell ner out — to say 'at I killed him on credit," mutters Andy. And that starts Sid thinking that perhaps he is in earnest. He turns inquiringly to Rufe.

SID — (*very uneasy, but concealing it*). What's the trouble with him, Rufe? He seems to have sompen on his mind.

RUFE — I don't know! He's been a-talkin' plumb wild! I tried to ca'm him, but I couldn't!

ANDY — You keep out o' this, Rufe! (*To Sid with the same deadly calm.*) Sid Hunt, this is a free country, ain't it?

SID — That's what they call it, Andy.

ANDY — If it's a free country, then everybody in it ought to be equal!

SID — Well, ain't they, Andy? Some's had more to drink 'n others, but that's nothin' to quarrel about.

ANDY — I admit it, but that ain't the p'int. When the Hunts and Lowries fought the last time, the Hunts killed three more Lowries 'n the Lowries killed Hunts. Do you call that equal?

SID — That's all over now, Andy.

ANDY — But it ain't equal — is it?

SID — Why, Andy, that happened so long ago — afore you an' me 'us born!

ANDY — That ain't the p'int! It ain't equal!

SID — All right then, it ain't. But what do you want me to do to equalize things?

ANDY — I don't want you to do anythin' but holler! I'll do the equalizin'! An' they's only one way! The Hunts killed three more Lowries 'n the Lowries killed Hunts. (*Pulls gun.*) I'm a-goin to kill three more Hunts 'n the Hunts killed Lowries!

SID — Three more. That sounds reasonable enough. Now lemme see, how many Hunts'll that make in all?

ANDY — Only six! An' I got jist six caterdges in my pistol. That's provy-dential!

SID — It does look like it. The only question is which six Hunts it's a-goin' to be. (*Coaxingly.*) Now I'll tell you, Andy, I've got lots o' no 'count kin —— (*Steps toward him.*)

ANDY — (*points gun at Sid and keeps it that way*). No, you cain't pull that on me! I got no 'count kin too! They ain't wuth killin'!

SID — I expect you're right about that, Andy.

ANDY — I know damn well I'm right!

SID — Now look here, Andy, I want this thing done like it ought to be. (*Persuasively.*) Now I'll tell you what I'll do: you go home an' study 'bout this overnight an' come back tomorrow morning. If you still want to kill six of us then, I'll let you take your pick. (*He starts to the door but Andy heads him off.*)

ANDY — Ha, ha! You think I'm a damn fool, don't you? Well, I am; but I ain't that sort!

SID — All right, Andy, jist as you say! If you'd ruther begin on what you got here now I'll send fer 'em. Only they ain't enough to make out your six.

But Andy is not to be fooled that way either. He orders both Sid and Rufe to stand where they are on penalty of having their heads blown off. Then he orders Rufe to fetch his banjo and play " Turkey in the Straw."

" When the Hunts an' Lowries fought afore the Hunts made my gran'daddy dance when they shot him," he sneers as he cocks his pistol. " This is the time to dance."

And Sid dances. With such grace as he can muster he executes the steps that Andy calls off. Occasionally he " sashays " a little too close to the door or the window and is promptly called back by his drunken master.

For two or three tense moments the dance continues. Then Jude appears suddenly in the kitchen door. Startled for a second, she realizes the next instant what is happening and jumps between her brother's gun and her dancing sweetheart. Sid, taking advantage of Andy's momentary confusion, grabs his arm, thrusts it up with a quick twist and disarms him.

A moment later Grandpap David and Meg Hunt have joined them. Hearing what has happened convinces

David that Rufe's the real one to blame, for having started
all that feud talk when Andy was drinkin', but Sid insists Rufe did what he could to quiet Andy. A moment
later Sid leads Andy out of the house. He will put him
on his horse, he says, and start him home, seeing he has
sobered up somewhat.

Jude tries to get from Rufe some explanation of what
has occurred, and why. But he claims to be as mystified
as she. He has an idea that Sid wasn't altogether innocent. Sid can be mighty overbearin' when he wants
to, as he insists she will find out if she marries him.
Jude doesn't know that she is — or isn't — going to marry
Sid. Nor does she see where it is any of Rufe's business what she does. In which conclusion Rufe insists she
is entirely wrong. He loves her, too, he says, with such
a love as only the Creator can understand, and when
it comes to deciding which of them will get her he is
inclined to think that God will side with him, for reasons
he would like to explain.

JUDE — I got too much else to think about with killin' in the air!
RUFE — But I want to explain afore it's too late. I want you to know that
my love fer you wus ordained from above. (She turns to him.) The first time
I ever thought o' marryin' you, Jude, 'us when I seen you in church the day I
got religion!
JUDE — (turning from him). Mebby you wouldn't ha' thought of it then if
you'd been a-studyin' 'bout your religion like you'd ought ha' been!
RUFE — I wus, Jude! That's jist the p'int! The whole thing 'us spiritual!
(Jude turns to him and is somewhat moved by the religious trend of his appeal,
in spite of an instinctive distrust of the man.) I mind it jist as well as if it
'us yistidy! Preachin' 'us over an' they 'us a-singin', an' when they come to the
verse:

> " I sighed for rest an' happiness
> I yearned fer them, not Thee;
> But while I passed my Savior by
> His love laid hold o' me "

I looked across the aisle an' seen you a-settin' thar a-singin'! An' sompen hot
swep' over me jist like fire! At first I thought it 'us Satan a-temptin' me, an' I
tried to look t'other way! I don't never look at the women's side in the meetin'-
house! Anybody 'at knows me 'll tell you that! But I couldn't look no other
way then! Some Power greater an' stronger'n me seemed to have holt o' my neck
a-twistin' it around toward you! I 'us absolutely helpless, jist as helpless as a
child! But I didn't know what it wus till they got to the last verse. You know
how it goes:

> " Thy pleasures lost I sadly mourned,
> But never wept for Thee,
> Till grace my sightless eyes received,
> Thy love-li-ness to see."

It 'us then that the scales dropped from my eyes! An' I seen the Truth! An'
when I did everything in the whole world 'us changed fer me! (Going toward

her, his arms outstretched.) I 'us so happy I felt jist like I 'us a-floatin' away on a ocean o' joy!

JUDE — (*throwing off the spell that has crept over her in spite of herself*). Well, if you felt like that you'd better let well enough alone. I couldn't make you no happier by marryin' you.

But Rufe continues of a contrary opinion and becomes more wildly eloquent in his pleading than he was before. He is a pure and lonely soul, is Rufe, and his only sustaining hope is that Jude will some day be his wife. When Sid appears and interrupts the flow of his passion at its peak he turns ugly — or would turn ugly if his religion did not restrain him. As it is he merely suggests that he is mighty thankful that he (Rufe) is able to bare all his thoughts about women to Jude, which is more, he is sure, than Sid can do. Especially his thoughts about those French women he met on the other side.

But Sid is not disturbed. "I don't know whether you're a trouble breeder or whether you're jist tetched in the head with religion," he says to Rufe. "But whichever it is I want you to git this much straight: Me an' Jude's a-goin' to be married, an' everything I want her to know about them French gals I'll tell her myself."

Nor does Jude's denial that she has ever agreed to this arrangement worry him. With Rufe out of the room Sid repeats his conviction that Jude will marry him. She again denies it. She might have — once, she admits. But now — with this new trouble between him and Andy looming up — she isn't sure it would be right.

SID — Now see here, Jude! (*He seizes her wrists in a strong grip.*) If this trouble with Andy is a-standin' between us we might as well settle it right now.

JUDE — (*with a flare of passion*). You got no right to make me take sides agin my own flesh an' blood!

SID — I ain't a-goin' to try to make you. That's sompen you'll have to decide fer yourself. The Bible says a man an' woman ought to leave their daddy an' mammy an' all the rest o' their kin an' stick together in spite o' the devil — at least that's the sense of it. I don't purtend to pattern after Scripture like Rufe, but that part allus hit me as bein' jist about right. An' if you don't feel the same way I want to know it.

JUDE — (*looking at him dumbly*). But I — er — er — but I ——

SID — They ain't no room for "buts" here, Jude. If you've got any doubts about whose side you'd be on in a fight between me an' your folks, you'd better give yourself the benefit of 'em.

JUDE — I couldn't never go back on my own kin!

SID — Then that's settled. (*He releases her and turns away.*) We don't belong together.

JUDE — You don't actially think our folks are a-goin' to start fightin' agin, do you, Sid?

SID — Not if I can keep 'em from it. (*He turns to her again.*) But that ain't the p'int; if they do start I don't want no weak sister fer a wife. If a woman ain't fur a man she's purty apt to be agin him. They don't come a-settin' on the fence.

JUDE — You mean — you mean I — I got to ——

SID — I mean — you've got to stand by me if you marry me.

JUDE — But it ain't right! You know it ain't right to go agin my own blood!

SID — Well, nobody ain't a-makin you marry me.

JUDE — (*flaring up hysterically*). What do you keep on *a-sayin'* that fer when it ain't *so!* (*Then breaking into sobs as she goes to his arms.*) You know I cain't do nothin' else!

SID — I sorter hoped you couldn't, Jude. But I wanted you to find out fer yourself.

JUDE — (*still sobbing*). I'm a-goin' to do what's right, but it's terrible hard — Andy's my own brother! 'Tain't in human nacher to ——

SID — Don't you worry about that, Jude! They ain't a-goin' to be no trouble. I jist wanted to find out whar you stood in case they wus. But you jist leave all that to me. Nothin' ain't a-goin' ter happen to Andy ner nobody else.

The Hunt men are excited. David and Matt have heard of the quarrel with Andy and they are of the opinion that the sooner they have a talk with Andy's paw the better chance they will have of stopping the story before it spreads far and grows big.

Sid is satisfied everything is all right. He and Andy are perfectly capable of patching things up if they're let alone. Which shortly appears to be the case. Andy, sobered somewhat, is brought in by Jude as they are about to start home. She has told him about Sid's asking her to marry him, and he has come to make his apologies. He allows he has made a fool of himself, and the fact that the liquor helped is no excuse.

The restoring of peace is further assisted by Sid's giving Andy back his pistol, and agreeing to ride a piece up the road with him and Jude on their way home. Sid has gone to saddle his horse, and the others are bustling about getting things closed up against the oncoming rain, when Rufe finds the morose and remorseful Andy alone.

He, too, is glad that everything has been smoothed over and that there isn't going to be any more trouble, Rufe assures Andy. But just the same, if he were in

Andy's place he would not take any chances. Nor would he let the fact that Sid has made Jude promise to marry him fool him any. There have been things hinted between the Hunts, Rufe intimates, that sound mighty like they were a-holdin' an inquest over Andy.

RUFE — I'm a-takin' a big chance to tell you! But you've allus been my friend, Andy! An' I'd walk through hell on a greased pine pole fer my friends! They're all I got left in the world!

ANDY — (impatiently). Well, come on! What are they up to?

RUFE — Jist now — afore you come in — (He looks around.)

ANDY — Yeh?

RUFE — Sid an' his daddy, an' the old rooster 'us a-holdin' a inquest over you!

ANDY — A inquest!

RUFE — That's what I'd call it!

ANDY — What 'us the verdick — death from natchel causes?

RUFE — They didn't edzackly say that.

ANDY — But you know what they meant?

RUFE — We never know nothin' in this world. But my advice to you is not to let Sid ketch you by yourself in a lonesome spot in the woods 'less you want to wear a wooden overcoat. (Leaving Andy to let this sink in, he wanders up to the door.)

ANDY — If that's his game why didn't he let daylight through me when he had a good excuse? (Lays his hand on his pistol.) And what'd he gimme back my pistol fer?

RUFE — You don't know Sid like I do. He's deeper'n he looks. If he'd ha' killed you while ago when he had a chance Jude 'd never ha' married him. But he's made hisself solid 'ith her now by lettin' you off. He can afford to wait to put you to sleep tell they ain't nobody a-lookin', though that ain't pesterin' his mind much fer he knows the law cain't tetch him.

ANDY — Why cain't it?

RUFE — 'Caze you threatened his life in the presence o' witnesses.

ANDY — Has he got all that figgered out aforehand?

RUFE — That an' more.

ANDY — Well, I've done all I could! I admitted to 'em 'at I 'us wrong to breach that ole fight agin!

RUFE — I know you did, Andy. An' 'tain't a-goin' to do you no good to eat more dirt fer 'em 'less you're prepared to eat six feet of it. Fer I hyeard Sid tell his daddy that you wusn't the sort o' man as could be bound by his word to keep the peace.

ANDY — That's sompen I cain't understand, Rufe. If I had it in my heart to kill a man I couldn't act toward him like I 'us his friend.

RUFE — Me nuther. I b'lieve in speakin' my mind, an' lettin' whatever comes up come out. But you have to fight fire with fire; you cain't afford to take no chances when your life's at stake.

ANDY — What 'ld you do if you 'us in my place, huh?

RUFE — I ain't a-sayin' what I would do, but I know one thing I wouldn't; I wouldn't wait fer him to git the drop on me! I'd be the early bird!

ANDY — No! I won't shoot fust 'less he starts it! But I'm a-goin' to keep my eyes on him, an' the fust suspicious move he makes — (he pats the handle of his pistol) — one or t'other of us'll be buzzards' meat!

RUFE — That's all right — (insinuatingly) — if he don't take a crack at you from the bushes!

The storm becomes more threatening. Sid suggests that both Andy and Jude stay over awhile. Nobody will expect them home in a storm. But Andy is bound to go, storm or no storm. And Sid refuses to let him go alone. Besides he has his own reasons for wanting to have a talk with Jude's father before anything can happen to his engagement. But Jude decides to stay.

The boys are off and riding hard to beat the storm. Meg Hunt is worried and Jude is anxious. But Rufe is comforting. " If any harm's goin' to come to 'em worryin' won't stop it," he preaches.

A moment or two later, above the occasional thunderclaps of the approaching storm, a revolver shot is distinctly heard. Then another. Meg and David start with fear. Jude all but collapses on the bed. Rufe's eyes brighten. Before anyone can make a move toward an investigation there is a further racket in the yard. Meg, rushing to the door, starts violently at what she sees. Sid's horse has returned with an empty saddle! The very shock of this conclusive evidence of tragedy serves to calm her.

MEG — They ain't no use in foolin' ourselves! It's happened! He's dead! Andy's killed him!

DAVID — Now stop your ravin', Meg! They's a thousand ways that horse might ha' got loose! It might ha' throwed him! (*Matt enters at the door, grim and determined.*)

MATT — (*as he takes a gun from the rack and some cartridges from the top drawer*). No it didn't! It's not a buckin' horse! You know that as well as I do! I've never seed it skeer at nothin' sence I got it! (*He starts out.*)

DAVID — Wait! I'm a-goin with you an' see what's happened! (*He crosses to the gun rack, takes down his gun and puts in a percussion cap.*)

MEG — Matt! Don't take the guns! If Sid's dead fightin' won't bring him back!

MATT — (*loading his gun*). I never said it would. But if he's dead my business is 'ith the man that killed him!

RUFE — Vengeance is mine, saith the Lord! I will repay!

DAVID — He has to have an instrument to work through! (*He follows Matt out.*)

MEG — (*staring in front of her, blankly*). God! If He's almighty like they say, I cain't see why He don't stop things like this!

RUFE — I wouldn't say things like that, Meg! All His jedgments are jest an' righteous altogether!

JUDE — But it don't seem right fer Sid to go through the war an' then be struck down by Andy the minute he gits home.

RUFE — That ain't fer us to say. (*Piously.*) He knows what Sid done while he 'us away in the war! We don't!

JUDE — Andy ain't a God-fearin' man neither!

RUFE — I know he ain't! An' vengeance is on his track too! It's writ that the heathen shall rage an' the wicked shall destroy one another! That seems to be a part of God's plan! Let Him be right if you have to make out everybody else wrong's what I say, an' they's good Scripture fer it.

JUDE — They's Scripture fer everything! Job's wife told him to cuss
God an' die. (*There is a loud clap of thunder. Rufe shrinks away. Meg rises
and glances out through the window.*)
  RUFE — If you're a-goin' to talk blasphemy, 'ith a thunder-cloud a-comin'
up, I'll have to leave you!
  JUDE — (*to Meg*). Are you a-goin' out?
  MEG — Yes! I cain't set here!
  JUDE — Neither can I. I'll go with you and see if they've found him. If
Sid's dead I'll kill the man 'at killed him — even if it's my own brother! I'll
kill him with my own hands!

Rufe doesn't like this idea. He could not think of
marrying a girl who killed her own brother, and he feels
that he should advise God to prevent it. The room has
darkened as the storm continues. Only the fitful flames
in the fireplace and an occasional flash of lightning
sharpen the scene. Rufe is still muttering his prayer,
"Lord, don't let her commit a sin she could never git
fergiveness for," when he looks up to see Sid calmly
entering the room from the kitchen. He recoils in terror.
as though he had seen a ghost, and for a moment is completely unnerved.

Gradually he recovers himself enough to learn what
has happened. Riding through the woods Sid had dis-
mounted to tighten a saddle girth. Andy had seen him
reach in his back pocket for a knife and had promptly
shot at him. There is a bullet hole through his hat at-
testing the accuracy of the aim and the seriousness of
Andy's intentions. Realizing these Sid has turned his
horse loose and cut for the bushes.

Sid is more puzzled than ever about Andy. He can't
understand why he should do the things he has done
since he got that liquor from Rufe. He has a feeling
that Rufe can enlighten him as to this, and the boy's
actions at the moment confirm him in the belief. He
questions Rufe pointedly and Rufe grows more and more
confused and more shrill in his denials of any knowledge
of a reason for Andy's state of mind. His determination
to hold Sid there becomes increasingly suspicious.

Gradually, despite Rufe's protests and his lies, Sid uncovers most of the truth. He knows that his people be-

lieve him dead, and that his father and grandfather have taken their guns and are on the way to the home of the Lowries.

Determined to save Andy and to prevent further trouble he seeks a way of stopping the Hunts. At every turn he is blocked by the now thoroughly frightened Rufe.

RUFE — (*rushes to door*). Hold on, Sid, you cain't do nothin' 'bout it now. They must a-left afore you come in and they'd natchelly go the short way and be half way over the mountain by this time! It's too late to stop 'em now.

SID — By God, you don't want me to stop 'em! I believe you knowed all along where they wus, only you 'us afraid o' what Andy could tell!

RUFE — That's right! Blame it on me! I don't wish him no harm! I don't wish nobody no harm!

SID — (*moves about nervously, then suddenly turning to Rufe as an idea occurs to him*). Does that telephone wire along the river run from the dam to the settlement over thar?

RUFE — Why — er — are you a-thinkin' o' 'phonin' from the dam to head off Matt an' your grand-daddy?

SID — That's my business.

RUFE — It's too late, Sid! You'd have to go afoot all the way!

SID — As I remember it the phone is in that toolhouse on a ledge right down under the dam. Is that right?

RUFE — You'd never git to that house now! You'd have to walk out to it on boards across that sluice of water! (*This gives Sid the necessary information and he starts quickly to the door, but Rufe arrives there at the same time and holds the door closed.*) Sid, it's dangerous when the river ain't up. You might jist as well commit suicide as try it now! (*Sid starts out but Rufe pulls his hand away from the door handle.*) I wouldn't do it to save my own brother let alone a man 'at had tried to kill me. An' all you'll git out o' Andy is a passel o' lies about me. Natchelly he'll say I agged him on — that I told him ——

SID — (*seizing him by the throat*). By God, I believe that's jist what you did do!

RUFE — (*screams hysterically*). No I didn't, Sid! I swear I didn't! All I said wus 'at you 'us a dangerous man an' not to cross you — that if you started ——

SID — (*tightening his grip*). So! I'm right! You *wus* at the bottom of it. Did you do it a-purpose?

RUFE — God forgive you, Sid, fer such a thought!

SID — An' God damn you!

Sid hurls Rufe to the floor and rushes out of the door, leaving it open. A blinding flash of lightning envelops him. Rufe lies on his elbow, cowering in fear, till the thunder crashes and reverberates. Then suddenly, as if struck by an idea, he rises to his knees and clasps his hands in prayer.

RUFE — Did you hear what he said, God? I can put up 'ith his insults to me, but when it comes to blasphemin' Thy holy name it does look like it's time to call a halt! But you know what you're a-doin' Lord, an' I don't! I'm only a ignorant sinner! You know more in a minute 'n I could ever know in a million years! It bothers me though, Lord that you left the wicked prosper more'n the righteous! They git the best o' everythin' in this world now! It wusn't so in Bible times, Lord! Then you cut the wicked down afore the congregation o' Israel! An' the dread o' you an' the fear o' you wus on

all people! But now your name is a by-word among sinners! You hyeard
that yourse!f jist now! I ain't presumin' to give you advice, Lord! You
know your own business! But if you'd make an edzample o' this blasphemer
— if you'd strike him down in the abomination of his wickedness by a bolt
o' lightnin', it 'ld serve as a warnin' to all like him! An' they'd be sich
another revival o' ole time religion in these mountains as you've never seed
sence the earthquake!

(*He pauses again as if struck by a new thought. His knees gradually give
way beneath him and he sinks to the floor.*)

In your holy word Lord, I know you command your servants to slay all
blasphemers! Mebby you think that's enough! An' mebby it ought to be!
But I'd druther you'd do it yourself, Lord! You can do it better'n me!
An' it 'ld have more effect! But I want you to understand, I ain't no coward!
If it don't suit you to do it yourself — I'll do it fer you — I don't keer if
they hang me! You died for me once, an' I'm a-willin' to die for you if
you want me to! You can do with me what you please, Lord! If it's your will
that this blasphemer shall die, I've got a whole box o' dynamite out thar
in the store, an' a time fuse long enough so's I can get back here afore it
explodes! I can blow up the dam while he's under thar a-telephonin' an' the
waters o' your wrath'll sweep over him like they did over Pharaoh an' his hosts
in olden times!

(*There is a blinding flash of lightning, followed instantaneously by a terrific
crash of thunder. Rufe rises to a standing position, his knees trembling with
fear. As the noise of the thunder dies away his fear is transformed into
joy. He stands firmly on his feet and looks toward Heaven, his voice ringing
out triumphantly.*)

" I hear you, Lord! An' like Joshua of old I go to do your will!"

He rushes from the house as the curtain falls.

ACT III

The scene is the same. Night has come. The storm
is passing. There are still occasional flashes of lightning
and a distant rumble of thunder. Above these the steady
roar of a swollen stream is noticeable.

The Hunt living room is empty and lighted only by the
flickering fire. Matt Hunt and Grandpap David bring in
Andy. He is shuffling along ahead of them, practically
at the tip ends of their guns, and he seems defiantly eager
to bait them into shooting him and getting it over with.

Matt is ready enough to oblige Andy, but David will
not listen to it. True, they have not been able to find
Sid, and there is nothing to indicate that he has been
home. But there is also the chance that he has escaped.
Or is still lying wounded in the woods.

Suddenly a shadow flits past the windows of the porch
and emerges as Rufe, stopped in the doorway by the dis-

covery of Grandpap guarding Andy. Rufe is plainly excited, but controls himself.

He has only been out of the house a minute, he tells them — just down to the spring and back. And he hasn't seen Sid at all. Not since they left. Meg and Jude have gone up the road thinking they might meet Sid, or find him, if he is hurt. Certainly, Rufe insists, Sid couldn't have come back to the house without his seeing him.

Again Matt Hunt is for evening the Hunt-Lowry score by doing for Andy, but David is still able to restrain him. From up the river there comes the sound of a muffled explosion. Sounds like blasting to everybody but Rufe. He thinks it must have been some sort of thunder. "Mebby it 'us the stopper blowed out o' hell," suggests Andy. "You'll be in p'sition to tell more about that a little later when you git thar!" Matt grimly assures him.

Jude and Meg are back from their search, having found no trace of Sid. They are sick with grief and anxiety and Jude is ready to help force the truth from her grinning brother's lips, even to the point of threatening him with Matt's gun. But Andy is not frightened.

ANDY — All right, Sis, blaze away! (*She releases the gun.*) But I'd ruther you'd let Matt do it. He's a better shot 'n you are. As for Sid, at the rate he 'us a-goin' the last time I seen him he'd ought to be in China if he hain't run hisself to death!

MATT — That's a lie on the face of it!

ANDY — Well then, I killed him an' buried him in the mud. How's that fer the truth? (*Meg and Jude turn away shuddering.*)

MATT — You'd be closer to it in my opinion if you said you killed him and throwed him over the cliff into the river.

ANDY — That would ha' been less trouble 'n buryin' him if I'd ha' hit him!

MATT — You missed him a-purpose I reckon!

ANDY — No, Matt! Don't git no wrong notions about me! I missed him becaze I couldn't hit him.

MATT — It's jist as well you ain't axin' fer no mercy, for all you're a-goin' to git is jestice an' plenty of it!

ANDY — You don't have to tell me that. I know you're a-goin' to send me to hell the short way. But I don't want you to make no mistake about one thing; when I go I'll go a-standin' up on my hind legs; I won't go a-crawlin' ner a-whinin' fer mercy. (*He sees Jude and is moved by her grief.*) To the best o' my knowledge an' belief I didn't kill Sid. That's the truth! (*Then to Matt, belligerently, to correct any impression of weakness.*) But I tried my damnedest to kill him! An' that's the truth, too!

They tie Andy's arms for fear he might put up a fight
against Grandpap while Matt goes on another search
for Sid, and have settled down for a long wait when the
roar of rushing water is heard. The river has never
sounded the same way before, and it often has run high
enough to reach the cellar of the Hunt house. Still,
Rufe is the only one who is much excited by the new
flood. He is breathless as he comes in from the porch,
" rolling his eyes in a fine frenzy." " It's come! It's
come!" he shouts.

DAVID — What's come?
RUFE — The Day O' His Wrath — when the saints an' the sinners shall
be parted right an' left! Brother, will you be able to stan' on that day?
That's the question every man here's got to answer — an' every woman too!
DAVID — You speak as one havin' authority, Rufe. Have you been to
heaven to git the latest news?
RUFE — No, I hain't been to heaven yit, but I've been about my Master's
business!
DAVID — Well, I hope fer His sake that you 'tended to it better'n you do
to ourn.
RUFE — I know I done what He told me! That's all I know an' all I
want to know on this earth!
MEG — I reckon that's enough fer any of us. But I would like to know
what's happened to Sid. I don't feel that I can ever close my eyes in sleep
or death tell I find out!
RUFE — It's too late! You cain't git to that patch o' woods now! The
river's come up all around it! Look!

David and the women go to the porch to see the flood.
The waters are continuing to rise and the cellar is threatened. Indoors Andy seeks to bargain with Rufe to release him. They are, after all, fellow conspirators. Why
shouldn't Rufe help him get away?

But Rufe can't see it. He is willing to pray for Andy,
but he sees no sense in cutting his thongs when he
is almost certain to be immediately recaptured. And
there couldn't be any doubt in the minds of the Hunt
men who had released him. This, Rufe argues, would
make it bad for him.

This line of reasoning sets Andy cursing, sometimes
under his breath and sometimes not. Cursing and threatening Rufe with exposure as well. Which starts that
young man a-trembling with fear, though he tries to

hide his fear by assuming a pious manner. Gradually, in an effort to frighten Andy so he will not tell on him, Rufe works himself into a religious passion that impresses Jude and Meg. It leaves David cold and Andy frankly cynical.

"Arter all, Meg," says David, when his daughter-in-law protests he has no right to permit Andy to blaspheme the way he is doing in making sport of Rufe; "arter all, the Lord's will's too big a thing fer any one man to git a strangle hold on it. Rufe's dead certain that God allus sees eye to eye 'ith him on every question. But fer all we know God hisself may c'nsider *that* more blasphemous 'n what Andy's doin'—— What makes you think what he's got is real religion?"

MEG — By their fruits ye shall know 'em! When I mourned fer Sid you an' Matt didn't bring me no comfort! All you thought of 'us vengeance! But I feel comforted some now, an' Rufe done it! (*She takes Rufe's hand.*)

DAVID — Shucks! If comfort in time o' trouble 'us religion most folks could git more religion outen a bottle o' licker'n they could out o' the Bible!

RUFE — (*angrily*). Are you accusin' me o' bein' loaded?

DAVID — Right up to the gills. You're drunk on sompen, Rufe. I dunno whether it's licker er religion.

ANDY — What difference does it make? One's jist as dangerous as t'other when it gits into a cracked head.

JUDE — The time'll come, Andy, when you'll wish you'd prayed stid o' scoffin'!

MEG — Father forgive them! They know not what they do!

RUFE — (*standing between Meg and Jude*). Let 'em revile me! I don't keer! Let 'em persecute me, lie about me, crucify me. I don't keer what they do (*to Andy*), fer verily I say unto you it'll be better fer Sodom an' Gomorrah on the Day o' Jedgment than fer you! An' that day ain't as fur off as it has been! If I 'us a mind to I could tell you things that 'ld curdle your blood and dry up the marrer in your bones!

MEG — (*credulously*). Have you seen a vision, Rufe?

RUFE — (*mystically, his eyes still on Andy*). What I've seen, I've seen! He that hath ears to hyear, let him hyear! An' lo, there wus a great earthquake; an' the sun become black as sackcloth o' hair, an' the moon become as blood; an' the stars o' heaven fell into the earth, even as a fig tree castest her untimely figs, when she is shaken of a mighty wind! An' the heavens departed as a scroll when it is rolled together; an' every mountain an' island were moved out o' their places! An' the kings o' the earth, an' the great men, an' the rich men, an' the chief captains an' mighty men hid themselves in the dens an' in the rocks o' the mountains; an' said to the mountains an' rocks, fall on us an' hide us from the face o' Him ——

(*He has gradually worked himself up to an emotional singsong like that of the old-fashioned mountain preacher. During this time Meg and Jude have been swaying rhythmically and crying " Hallelujah!", " Amen!", " Blessed be His name!" with increasing fervor.*)

that sitteth on the throne — ah! an' from the wrath o' the Lamb — ah! For the great day of His wrath has come — ah!

ANDY — Whoa, ole hoss, er you'll bust your bellyband! When I tell **my** religious experience I won't have to stop to suck wind. I'll spit it out quick!

(*Seeing Andy unmoved by his supreme effort and still determined to tell on him, Rufe is wild with fear.*)

RUFE — (*trying to frighten Andy*). If you'd seen what I've seen an' hyeard what I've hyeard your tongue 'ld cleave to the roof o' your mouth!

ANDY — No, Rufe, you cain't come that on me! Oath or no oath, my tongue won't cleave wuth a damn! (*Rufe glances fearfully at the others.*) It's loose at both ends and it's a-gettin' looser every minute. An' if you don't quit spoutin' Scripture it's a-goin' to spill all I know afore God can skin a gnat.

RUFE — (*to Meg and Jude*). Don't listen to him! His mouth is foul with blasphemy! (*He begins to sing, leading the women into the song. They join in and sing in religious ecstasy.*)

> I am bound fer the promised land!
> I am bound fer the promised land!
> Oh, who will come an' go with me?
> I am bound fer the promised land!

ANDY — All that ain't a-goin' to save you, Rufe. If you don't go to **hell** it's only because they ain't no place thar hot enough fer you!

RUFE — (*changing his tactics*). Meg, are you goin' to let him set thar **an'** revile and blaspheme like that?

MEG — No, I ain't! I've stood all I kin! If David won't do nuthin' 'bout it I will!

DAVID — What do you want me to do about it?

MEG — Git him out o' my sight — I don't keer whar! In the kitchen, **up-** stairs in the closet, some'eres.

At Rufe's suggestion they put Andy in the cellar. The water's comin' up a little, but not enough to be dangerous, Rufe insists, though there's a smile of triumph on his face as he says it. And now he turns his attentions to comforting Jude. She shouldn't grieve for Andy, he assures her. "Everybody cain't be saved. Some're born for glory and some fer shame." And it seems likely Andy's born for shame, and Sid wasn't born for glory, neither.

"You ought to build your hopes on a firmer foundation," he tells her, sitting down beside her on the edge of the bed. "There's still treasure in heaven if you'll seek it in the right way."

JUDE — (*choked with grief*). That's what I'm a-tryin' to do, Rufe! But all my faith — everything — seems gone now!

RUFE — (*gradually moving closer*). That's a good sign! The darkest hour o' the spirit is allus jist afore dawn! Think, Jude, what a friend we have in Him! "Oh, what peace we often forfeit; oh, what needless pain we bear — all because we do not carry everything to Him in prayer!"

JUDE — (*trying to get back into the religious ecstasy*). I want to carry it to Him, but I cain't! Seems like I'm froze up inside!

RUFE — I know what's the matter with you, Jude! You ain't a-trustin' Him! (*Stroking her gently on the shoulder.*) All you got to do is trust Him —

JUDE — (*softly*). I see! Hallelujah!

RUFE — He'll save you! (*Stealing his arm further around her.*) You're on the right track. Go right on trustin Him! He'll comfort you!

JUDE — (*louder*). Halleluyah! Bless His name!

RUFE — (*his arm around her*). That's it! You're a-gittin' right now! Jist imagine you're a-leanin' on the everlastin' arms! (*She inclines her head slightly toward his shoulder in a state of half-conscious religious ecstasy. He kisses her. She half awakes from her stupor and gets up.*)

RUFE — (*nervously*). Don't look at me like that, Jude. It's perfectly all right! The Scripture says fer the brethren an' sisteren to greet one another with a holy kiss! An' that's all it wus, Jude! A holy kiss! Go right on trustin' — sweetly trustin'!

JUDE — (*as the religious ecstasy again creeps over her*). Halleluyah!

RUFE — Always trustin'! (*He is moving toward her almost imperceptibly.*)

JUDE — (*a little more audibly*). Halleluyah!

Meg's voice breaks the spell. She has come, at David's orders, to untie Andy so he can be free to keep himself above the water that may seep into the cellar. Rufe offers to undertake to do this, while the women are looking after the young turkeys caught in the rising waters. And he is much disappointed when he discovers that the water's going down and Andy is more determined than ever to tell the Hunts of Rufe's part in the shooting of Sid.

"All I wanted, Andy," he calls down the cellar stairs, "was to tell you 'at if you'll gimme your solemn word not to tell a livin' soul, I might mebbe could help you now!"

"Not by a damn sight," shouts back Andy. "I'm goin' to hell astraddle o' your neck!"

Rufe thinks perhaps he has trusted too implicitly in the Lord's handling of the situation. He rushes to the gun rack and takes down a gun and makes sure that it is loaded. He turns toward the cellar, then stops, suddenly, as though he had forgotten something. Laying the gun down, he drops to his knees and begins to pray.

"Oh, Lord, Thy will be done, not mine," he intones. "I won't kill him lessen you want me to. But you had the chance and now the river's goin' down! So mebby you meant for me to do this, too. I'll do anything you say, Lord. If it's your will. . . ."

While he prays, Sid appears in the door at back. "He is hatless, his clothes torn and his face smeared with mud." He starts toward Rufe and then changes his mind.

He stands back watching him, and as Rufe stretches his arms heavenward, awaiting the Lord's answer, Sid speaks in a deep voice:

" Mene, mene, tekel, upharsin!"

" Is that you, Lord?" queries Rufe, not daring to look around.

" I'm the ghost o' Sid Hunt," answers Sid.

And Rufe believes him. He has come back, Sid says, with the orders from above to ha'nt Rufe for having killed Sid Hunt. And when Rufe insists that it was the Lord who attended to that matter Sid insists that they shall proceed at once to the judgment seat and make good that charge. Let Rufe be a witness.

" But," protests the boy, " you can't accuse *Him* o' murder. He's *Almighty!*"

" He's almighty tired o' bein' a scapegoat fer folks that do all the meanness they can think of an' callin' it religion," Sid answers.

Gradually Sid worms what amounts to a confession from Rufe, and learns of Andy's being tied up in the cellar. He goes to get the rest of the story from Andy, and Rufe throws himself again upon the mercy of the God to whom he prays.

A minute later Andy and Sid are up from the cellar and Meg and Jude are affectionately reclaiming their lost man. In the cellar Andy and Sid have " swapped experiences," and have managed to piece together the story of Rufe's activities, including the blowing up of the dam.

The women find it hard to believe so earnest a Christian as Rufe could ever conceive such dastardly conspiracies, and for a moment Rufe sees a hope of retreat under this cover of their sympathy.

MEG — Don't pay no 'tention to them Pharisees, Rufe!

JUDE — Go right on an' tell what happened!

RUFE — It 'us while you 'us all out a-lookin' fer Sid. He come in an' accused *me* o' aggin' Andy on to shoot him. He cussed me an' reviled me an' took God's name in vain.

MEG — Sid!

RUFE — Then he went out to the dam to telephone an' head off Matt. I knowed the blame 'us all a-goin' to fall on me — an' I knelt thar to pray — (*pointing*) right thar in that very spot. An' all of a sudden God appeared to me in thunder an' lightnin' an' spoke in a still small voice, but loud a-plenty for me to hear.

MEG — Halleluyah!

JUDE — What'd he say?

RUFE — " Gird up your loins," He says, " an' take the box o' dynamite you got thar in the store an' go forth an' blow up the dam while he's under thar a-telephonin'!" (*The men exchange glances.*)

MEG — (*recoiling with horror*). Oh!

JUDE — Then you done it to kill Sid!

RUFE — I know it seems quair now, but He works in a mysterious way! (*Meg rushes at Rufe with a cry of rage.*)

DAVID — Ca'm yourself, Meg!

MEG — Take him out o' here an' kill him!

RUFE — I didn't do it, Meg! I 'us only His instrument!

MATT — (*reaching for the gun on the rack*). Yeh, an' so 'm I!

ANDY — (*crossing a step and rolling up his sleeves*). No, Matt! This is my job! Sid's done promised me I could do it! An' I don't want no weapons. (*Holding up his two hands*) Jist these two instruments!

He makes a dash for Rufe, who runs into the cellar and pulls the door shut after him. From there they hear him shout his last prayer for help. " O, Lord, if you're ever goin' to help me, help me now!" And he sings frantically and out of tune,

> " I am bound for the promised land!
> I am bound for the promised land!
> Oh, who will come and go with me?
> I am bound for the promised land!"

" The son of a biscuit eater! He's actially tryin' to play the same trick on God that he played on me!" shouts Andy, begging a chance to pull the door off its hinges and be at the hypocrite.

David holds him back long enough to suggest that he take the key to the other cellar door and go around that way. Then he makes a long and fruitless search for the key. Finally it dawns on the men that David is trying purposely to detain them, and both Matt and Sid are for joining Andy and getting Rufe before he gets away. But the old man will not let them go.

DAVID — (*emphatically, grabbing Andy by the arm and stopping him, and holding Matt at bay*). Now boys, hold off a minute an' listen to me! You say the Lord didn't punish Rufe. But He might yit if you give Him a chance. (*The others show signs of impatience, but David holds them.*) An' arter what's happened here tonight we orter be willin to foller the Lord uphill back'ards 'ith our eyes shut.

SID — What!

ANDY — Arter what's happened tonight!

DAVID — Edzactly. Seems to me He's been workin' fer us from beginnin' to end. Jist run it over in your minds an' see. (*To Matt.*) You wanted Rufe to make tracks away from here an' he'll do it if you let him.

ANDY — Aw!

DAVID — (*turning to him*). Andy wanted a war of his own an' he got it. An' they ain't none of us been scratched. Take it right straight through, an' the Lord's been on our side every pop — even to blowin' up that dadburn dam that never'd orter been put in! (*All but Andy now admit, although grudgingly, that there is something in David's argument.*)

MATT — That's so! (*Meg nods her assent.*)

SID — I hadn't thought o' that!

JUDE — Me nuther!

DAVID — I tell you, religion's a great thing when the Lord's on your side!

Another minute they hear the slamming of the outside cellar door and know that, thanks to David's ruse, Rufe has escaped. They are after him, with their guns ready — or would be if David did not again bar the door. He had unlocked the cellar door, he admits — but he had done it some time before, when he told Meg to see that Andy's hands were untied. And they know that Grandpap David has been working quietly for all their best interests the last several hours.

"You durned ole Christian! You'll save me from hell yit!" snorts Andy, giving up the pursuit of Rufe.

"Anyhow," sighs Grandpap, "I've saved a lot of folks from a run-in with the sheriff!"

The men are samplin' a bottle of "coneyack" Sid brought home from the war, as the curtain falls.

THE END

" THE SWAN "

A Romantic Comedy in Three Acts

By Ferencz Molnar

(Translated by M. P. Baker)

THE production of " The Swan " at the Cort Theater
on October 22, 1923, seemed to find New York playgoers
hungry for romance. They had had samples of almost
every kind and character of play the first ten weeks of
the season and had paid comparatively little attention
to any of them. Up to this time there had been fifty odd
plays produced and there was not a real hit among them.

" The Swan," however, was an immediate success, and
continued to build on this early popularity until it was
closed by the Equity trouble on May 31.

Gilbert Miller, the producer, bought the rights to the
Hungarian original some time back. Two English translations were made, one by Granville Barker and another
by Benjamin Glazer. Neither quite fulfilled the hopes of
Mr. Miller, however, and he suggested to young Melville
Baker, a Frohman playreader and a year out of Harvard,
that he try his hand at translation. The result was a
happy accident. The blend of Baker enthusiasm and
Molnar romance, pointed with many clever shafts of
satire, produced a delightful entertainment.

The story is one of the always dearly beloved mythical
kingdom series. It starts on a summer morning in a
pavilion in the garden of the Princess Beatrice's castle.
" It is a square room which has been fitted up to be used
as a schoolroom," reports the author, and its principal

77

articles of furniture are a long study table with a chair at either end for the use of the young sons of the household. George and Arsene, and one in the center at back for their tutor, Professor Agi. There are maps of Central Europe on the rear wall, and scattered about the usual paraphernalia associated with study rooms.

The boys have been at their studies for some time, and the day's exercises are being concluded by the young professor reading aloud to them selections from the history of Napoleon. A timely selection, inasmuch as there has been a recent disagreement in the family as to Napoleon's proper status as a hero and a genius. It is the opinion of the Princess Beatrice that the great Frenchman was a Corsican upstart, and that if it had not been for him her own noble family never would have suffered the loss of its crown. She is a little angry at Agi for not having taught the boys to hate Napoleon.

Professor Agi, seeking to keep the minds of his charges unprejudiced, is still free to admit that his own opinion of Napoleon is much opposed to that of their mother. He sees him as one of the world's greatest geniuses — " one who succeeded because he knew how to seize and make the most of the opportunities which the revolution cast at his feet."

It further transpires that the current sensitiveness of Princess Beatrice on the subject of thrones is heightened by the presence as a guest in her house of Prince Albert, a royal neighbor and heir to a throne. The boys discuss the situation with Agi.

ARSENE — Mother is rather touchy about thrones now that Prince Albert is here.

GEORGE — Prince Albert is a real heir-apparent — and when Mother sees one of those, she can't eat.

ARSENE — Poor Mother. Just because her great-grandmother had a throne of her own, Mother can't bear to think that *she* can never have one.

GEORGE — Never?

AGI — It's hardly likely — thrones are rather difficult to obtain these days.

ARSENE — But suppose the Prince marries Alexandra?

GEORGE — He won't.

ARSENE — How do you know he won't? If he does, we'll all be at the court because Alexandra will be queen. And if I know Mother, the Prince will not be the one who does the ruling.

GEORGE — *If* he marries her.

ARSENE — He will.

GEORGE — Why should he?

ARSENE — Because Mother wants him to — all of us want him to. **Aunt** Symphorosa — Alexandra — I — and you — and the Professor.

GEORGE — I'm not sure I want him to, are you, Professor?

AGI — (*embarrassed*). Well, her Highness would grace the most exalted position.

GEORGE — Yes, I know — but you don't want her to marry him, do you?

AGI — Why do you say that?

GEORGE — Well, the way you said — " Her Highness would grace the most exalted position."

AGI — It— comes as rather a surprise to me. I can hardly grasp the idea all at once. Since — it has been my good fortune to be with your family, her Highness, your sister, has been very gracious to me — to all of us. And then besides I have been allowed to instruct her in fencing. When I try to realize, so suddenly, that my pupil is to become a bride — and a queen — well, I find it rather difficult.

GEORGE — I shall be sorry to leave this place. Everyone has been so nice to us. But you'll be coming with us, won't you?

AGI — If I am asked to.

ARSENE — It won't be so bad and maybe politics will keep Mother so busy, we'll be left to ourselves.

Princess Beatrice and Alexandra come from the garden to warn Professor Agi and the boys that Prince Albert has announced an intention of visiting them in their schoolroom. He is interested in their studies and he would also like to see them fence. The Princess is a matronly woman, though still the better side of middle age, and plainly a dominating spirit in her own household. Alexandra, the daughter, is a slim, beautiful girl in her early twenties, serene and wistful, a passive and rather interested figure in the royal game, who has so far accepted without protest the positions into which the older and presumably wiser players of her family have moved her.

She listens a little amusedly as her mother scolds the boys for their past and their threatened slips of conduct, displaying a maidenly irritation when young George blurts out his conviction that his mother has come to tell them that Alexandra is to be a queen!

Now, with Beatrice and the boys gone to meet Father Hyacinth (still the boys' favorite uncle, even though he has deserted the court for the monastery), Alexandra takes a hand in arranging the day's program with the tutor.

The fencing will take place in the gymnasium, she says, immediately following a tour of inspection of her own rose garden. She will act as Prince Albert's guide to the rose garden, but she will take no part in the fencing. Which disappoints Professor Agi greatly.

AGI — I regret that your Highness is not to have an opportunity to display her skill with the foils.

ALEXANDRA — That was not intended when the program was arranged. If I change my clothes I shall have no time to show him the garden. So it has been arranged that only the boys fence.

AGI — May I, in all deference, inquire whether someone else might not as well accompany his Highness through the garden?

ALEXANDRA — Why do you ask that?

AGI — In that case your Highness would have time to change her costume.

ALEXANDRA — Why are you so anxious that I should fence?

AGI — I merely thought — it seemed to me that since your Highness fences with such rare skill and grace and —

ALEXANDRA — And?

AGI — And someone else *could* just as well show off — could as well escort his Highness through the garden.

ALEXANDRA — Yes, no doubt.

AGI — Forgive me, Princess. It was the pride of the teacher that made me speak. (*George, in door, turns to hear.*)

ALEXANDRA — Your pride was not considered in arranging the program. In any case, please allow me to take care of it.

AGI — As it pleases your Highness.

Father Hyacinth, a gentle man but keenly alert, laughingly accepts the rapturous and somewhat rough greetings of his nephews as he enters the schoolroom and makes himself known to Professor Agi. And it is soon plainly evident that the professor and the priest have much in common — including a veneration of Napoleon — and their agreement that the best of all educations is one which seasons book learning with sports. This bond of sympathy does not altogether please Princess Beatrice, but there seems little she can do about it.

Aunt Symphorosa, who would doubtless have carried the title of lady-in-waiting to the queen had Beatrice been a queen, but who now merely serves without title, announces from time to time the whereabouts and probable movements of his Highness the Prince. At the moment he is sleeping, lying comfortably and wisely on his right (or liver) side, as reported by his aide. For four days Beatrice has practically had hourly reports of her

royal guest, and yet, with all her most skillful management, she has not been able to bring about the situation
nearest to her heart.   Prince Albert has been graciously
appreciative of everything done for him — but not once
has he exhibited anything more than the most casual interest in Alexandra.   And this lack of interest spells
tragedy for Alexandra's distraught mother.   Especially
as Albert is leaving next day.   Father Hyacinth's attempt
to cheer her avails but little.

BEATRICE — Oh, Karl, I have no illusions. I know they are considering
us — Alexandra, that is — only because two or three reigning families whom
they don't wish to offend have made simultaneous advances to them. The Czar
wants him for Olga, Constantine's daughter. And Edward for Helen of England.
HYACINTH — Albert can't keep his heart to himself forever.
BEATRICE — Of course not. Rome is out of the question and he must marry
someone.
HYACINTH — Perhaps he will go to Montenegro.
BEATRICE — I have thought of that. He is such a dutiful son — his mother
dominates him absolutely. It was because of her that he set out to dispose
of his heart. First there was Charlotte at Dresden — but she was hardly satisfactory — a pronounced tendency towards plumpness. From there he and his
heart went to Lisbon. The Infanta Silvina Gonzaga he found to be the most
exemplary young lady, but a perfect fright. And now he is with us. And if we
let him get away, he will go straight to Montenegro.

Symphorosa is back to report that his Highness has
stretched, yawned, turned over and drunk his barley
water.   Otherwise the situation remains unchanged.

BEATRICE — Karl, you know that this marriage was the dearest wish of my
husband. Indeed his great friendship for Albert's father sprang from that.
HYACINTH — No, that sprang from his heart.
BEATRICE — Perhaps. But he nourished it with the thought of the marriage. And now that they are both dead, the fulfillment of the dream rests
with me. Oh, Karl, if I could be assured that my daughter was to have
a throne, I would willingly die this minute.
HYACINTH — There's not much of Christian humility in that wish, Beatrice.
BEATRICE — Forgive me, Karl, but after three days of this I am no longer
myself. I know that he came because of Alexandra. But now that he is here,
it is as if she didn't exist. And no word from his mother. If his intentions
were serious she would be here now. (Weeps.)
HYACINTH — Come, now, Beatrice.
BEATRICE — I told you I wasn't myself. And to think we have only one day
more. This afternoon and this evening — if nothing happens by that time —
why, then it will be the end of everything.
HYACINTH — No signs at all?
BEATRICE — Nothing at all — and you may be sure I have had my eyes open.
HYACINTH — Perhaps Alexandra —
BEATRICE — She is beautiful and clever — and such dignity and reserve.
Her father, you know, always called her his swan. " My proud white swan,"
he used to say. And she does impress you that way. Always proudly silent —
with head high. Indeed, she is quite beyond criticism. And Albert doesn't
even notice her. It's enough to drive one to distraction.

HYACINTH — Beatrice, you are losing control of yourself.
BEATRICE — I know, but I can't help it. This is my last, my very last chance.
And I will not lose it. I may have to perform a miracle, but I will succeed if it
is the last thing I do.

Now Symphorosa has something real to report. The
Prince is arising. Count Lutzen has coughed at his door
and his Highness is stirring. Colonel Wunderlich would
have coughed, but the colonel's cough is so rasping it
invariably irritates Albert, so Lutzen is really the official
cougher of the Prince's suite. The Prince also has taken
a cup of tea, and is dressing, and the probabilities are
reasonably strong that he soon will be ready to continue
with the day's program. Beatrice is quite flustered as
she goes to meet him, Father Hyacinth following a moment later.

And now Prince Albert, attended by Wunderlich and
Lutzen, and incidentally by Symphorosa, Alexandra,
Beatrice and Father Hyacinth, enters the pavilion. He
is tall, about 35, gracious and handsome. He wears
a general's uniform. As Albert enters he is explaining
to Hyacinth the success of the cough as a gentle reminder
that it is time to arise. Now he has finished and, graciously deploring the stiffness and formality of their
several attitudes, insists that they all be seated.

BEATRICE — (*sweetly*). Did you sleep well?
ALBERT — Astonishingly well. I really don't know why it is that I do sleep
so well here. Whether it is the mild climate, or the spring mattress, or simply
the pervading atmosphere of calm and repose. I wake from my sleep as refreshed
as if I had taken a bath in warm milk. . . . Oh, I wish I could tell you how
happy I have been here. Indeed, I shall never forget these past few days. Aunt
Beatrice so thoughtfully attentive, and — the old castle encircled by these gently
rolling hills. Mother, you know, has always looked upon this as the ideal
retreat — and so shall I hereafter. But more than anything else, I shall remember
the charm and — spiritual harmony of your family life. Oh, I can only say that
I am in love with you all.
BEATRICE — We are more than delighted that you are so enjoying your visit
with us.
ALBERT — When I am alone in the evening, I think of my father and your
husband — Uncle Henry — and how they loved to walk together in the park.
BEATRICE — And talk of their children.
ALBERT — Yes, they were exemplary fathers — their only thought was for the
welfare of their children.
BEATRICE — It was what they lived for. Always the children and their future
— what would become of them. How some day they would have families of
their own.
ALBERT — (*To Hyacinth.*) Evenings when I stand looking out of my window,

I can still see the two old men walking together along the white gravel path beyond the lawn. And the fragrance of the roses pouring in upon me —
BEATRICE — Alexandra's roses.
ALBERT — (to Alexandra). Your roses?
ALEXANDRA — Yes, mine.
ALBERT — Did you plant them?
ALEXANDRA — Not exactly — but I take care of them.
ALBERT — Do you find that amusing?
ALEXANDRA — Yes.
ALBERT — Do the thorns prick your fingers?
ALEXANDRA — Yes, quite often.
ALBERT — You should wear gloves then.
ALEXANDRA — I do.
ALBERT — And still you prick your fingers?
ALEXANDRA — Yes, through the gloves.
ALBERT — You should wear thicker gloves.
ALEXANDRA — Thank you — I shall try that.
ALBERT — C'est ça. Such is life. One must always be prepared.
BEATRICE — How truly you speak!
ALBERT — It's nothing — simply — that is — one can't help learning a little — from experience — but I learned that at home from Mother, about the gloves, I mean. Well — (he stands up) — suppose we take a look at the children. Is this where you study?

Before the fencing Beatrice does what she can to start Albert toward the rose garden with Alexandra as guide. But his Highness is still either consciously or unconsciously stubbornly opposed to the excursion. He had much rather see the new dairy. The cows, Wunderlich tells him, are milked by vacuum — think of that! And what chance has a pretty rose garden, even with a pretty girl as guide, against so strong a counter attraction?

Beatrice is distressed by this turn of affairs, for which she blames not only Albert's abnormal frigidity, but the subtle influences of his staff as well. But she is not yet defeated. There is a way. She still has one trick left in her hand and now, in her desperation, she is determined to play it.

SYMPHOROSA — You alarm me, Beatrice.
BEATRICE — You may as well be alarmed. For what I am about to do is so unspeakable that I could never forgive anyone else who ——
HYACINTH — Beatrice ——
BEATRICE — God will forgive a mother what she does for the sake of her child. (Tears in her eyes — to Hyacinth.) And you will forgive me.
HYACINTH — Consider yourself absolved.
SYMPHOROSA — When I hear you talking in this way all I can say is — "Don't do it."
BEATRICE — Please have the kindness to be quiet. And pay attention. The whole trouble is that Alexandra has not succeeded in arousing Albert's interest — I mean she has not appealed to his feelings as a man.
SYMPHOROSA — Oh, dear, oh, dear.

BEATRICE — What is the matter with that? He must have some feelings —
He is a man, isn't he?

SYMPHOROSA — I know, but —

BEATRICE — Furthermore, there are very definite limits as to what Alexandra
can do in that direction. She can hardly make eyes at him or —

SYMPHOROSA — It gives me some comfort to hear you say that.

BEATRICE — Alexandra — simply cannot throw herself at him.

HYACINTH — Well, what then?

BEATRICE — There is only one thing which can arouse a man's interest in a
woman; the interest of another man in the same woman.

SYMPHOROSA — This is the unspeakable part.

HYACINTH — Not yet — we are still talking in generalities. Go on, Beatrice.

BEATRICE — Well, in short, Albert must be made to respond to the woman
in Alexandra — the rest will follow of itself. Alexandra is clever and — open
to reason — and Albert told us he found the tutor charming —

HYACINTH — This is the interesting part.

BEATRICE — I know what you will say — but you can't stop me now.

HYACINTH — Yes, but what about the tutor?

BEATRICE — We — are going to invite him to the reception tonight. And
Alexandra will — will notice him. Oh, I should never have dreamed of it
if Albert himself had not suggested the idea. You remember how he praised
the professor? That was what gave me the inspiration. To think that I should
be forced to employ such an outgrown stratagem. The tutor and the princess!
So hackneyed — and still so effective. Because you see, a rival of his own
rank wouldn't bother him in the least. But when his rival is a petty tutor, then
he will realize the danger.

SYMPHOROSA — This is more than I can bear.

BEATRICE — You must bear it. Alexandra will look at the tutor — and
Alexandra will dance with the tutor. And God will forgive me and God will
forgive Alexandra — and I shall never forgive the tutor.

HYACINTH — And why not?

BEATRICE — Because I shall be indebted to him.

Father Hyacinth is not at all surprised at the audacity
of his sister's plan. It represents no more than "the
customary tactics of the harassed mother." But he is
a little worried about the effect on the tutor — this game
they are planning to play with him. Beatrice, however,
fails either to understand or to appreciate his concern
for the young man. If he has any fear that the tutor will
be permitted to put a false interpretation upon Alexandra's conduct toward him, let him have no fear. "I
shall take care of *that* danger!" confidently announces
Beatrice.

HYACINTH — Yes, I suppose you will. But — the tutor is young and, being
young, not incapable of fashioning dreams. Perhaps my eyes have lost their
old skill in reading the face of a young man, but there was something in the
way that boy looked at your daughter that I could not mistake. There was
reverence in his look but it was reverence not without desire. He was like a
cat watching a beautiful bird — the cat has a certain respectful admiration for
the bird, but it would also like to eat it.

BEATRICE — Are you trying to tell me that he is in love with her?

HYACINTH — No, but at least Alexandra has aroused *his* interest.

BEATRICE — But what of it?

HYACINTH — What of it? Nothing, except that a brave lad like that was not meant to be used as a tool and then thrown away.

BEATRICE — In other words, it is the tutor you care about?

HYACINTH — No, not the tutor — the man.

BEATRICE — What is the difference? What it amounts to is — that the happiness of your niece and the fate of our house interests you less than the feelings of this tutor!

HYACINTH — My dear Beatrice, you have seen me in this frock so long that you no longer notice it. You know what interests me — the only thing that has any meaning for me; and that is the dignity of the human heart, and the divine life, which flows from it. What are your little schemes — or Albert's throne — or Alexandra's crown to me? What are they, that you should sacrifice for them the peace of a man's soul? Now, when I kept my racing stables, I used to enter two of my horses in the same race, so that one of them would set the pace for the other — and then I would let the second horse come up and win. But those were horses — not men. A woman who would so use a man — who would so lightly break his pride — such a woman, my dearest sister, has every reason to explain that she does so for her daughter's sake. Now do you understand, my dear? (*Change of tone.*) Well, I believe I'll have a look at this vacuum machine myself.

Beatrice is still obdurate. Her mind is made up and she knows what she is doing. Curtly she dismisses Symphorosa and sends for Alexandra, to whom she, a little hesitantly, outlines the plan. Alexandra listens respectfully and without comment. There may be a barely perceptible blush upon her cheek, but she is a dutiful daughter and not without her own royal ambitions. If stratagem must be employed to bring Albert to a consciousness of her nearness to him, she is willing to lend herself to it. But — she, too, is a little worried about the possible reactions of the professor.

ALEXANDRA — Don't misunderstand my hesitation — but — I need just a minute to — adjust myself to the idea. Why, the tutor is the son of a common farmer. And when I think that his arm will rest on mine —

BEATRICE — You will have gloves, my child.

ALEXANDRA — It is not so much the touching him that I mind — it is the thought of it.

BEATRICE — Do you ask your flowers or your pets who their ancestors were? Or does it trouble you to smile at a dog or a pretty squirrel?

ALEXANDRA — Of course if you look at it in that way.

BEATRICE — The only possible way to look at it.

ALEXANDRA — Still there *is* a difference, isn't there — It —

BEATRICE — Don't be ashamed to tell me what you are thinking.

ALEXANDRA — Well, he is a man, isn't he?

BEATRICE — Of course — but —

ALEXANDRA — And he must think about— such things; that's the difference between him and the pretty squirrel.

BEATRICE — His thoughts are his own concern.

ALEXANDRA — But he might misunderstand.

BEATRICE — There will be nothing in your conduct toward him that *could* be misunderstood. I am confident of that.

ALEXANDRA — And you can be. Yet this change in my manner toward him — it can't help but have some effect on him.

BEATRICE — That again is his concern.

ALEXANDRA — Nevertheless I feel I ought to be prepared — to know what to do if — I'm merely supposing — one has to think of these things — but suppose he should — feel himself — well, attracted to me?

BEATRICE — Is there anything to make you think he feels this way already?

ALEXANDRA — I said I was only supposing.

BEATRICE — But you haven't noticed anything?

ALEXANDRA — There are certain things one *never* notices.

BEATRICE — Then you have.

ALEXANDRA — He does sometimes appear rather embarrassed when he speaks to me.

BEATRICE — Oh that is nothing — nothing for you to trouble about. All that you have to think of is your own goal — toward that you must resolutely advance, looking neither to the left nor the right but always forward.

ALEXANDRA — (*obediently*). Yes, Mother.

The boys are dressed for the fencing and with them Professor Agi is awaiting further instructions in the gymnasium. Prince Albert is still inspecting the cows. Now, apparently, is the time for Alexandra to make the first move with and toward the tutor. Beatrice sends for him and leaves Alexandra to take care of the meeting. "And now, my dearest child — courage! Courage!" she sighs, as she kisses her, and leaves her.

Professor Agi is in fencing costume when he comes, and carries a foil. Alexandra may never before have realized how romantic a figure Agi commands. And even now she is eager to dismiss the thought quickly from her mind. She questions the tutor as to his plans for the evening. He had intended, he explains, taking the boys to watch the stars from the observatory. But now he cannot do that, she ventures, a little embarrassedly.

ALEXANDRA — We — We are giving a reception this evening in honor of the Prince's departure. He is leaving in the morning.

AGI — That is a pity.

ALEXANDRA — Only the most important people have been invited — so there will not be many of us. I — have expressed the wish that you should be among the guests.

AGI — I!

ALEXANDRA — And so you can hardly be stargazing this evening.

AGI — I feel deeply honored, Princess, particularly to have received the invitation from your own lips.

ALEXANDRA — It will be a somewhat formal affair. I hope you won't find it stupid.

AGI — I could hardly find it stupid when your Highness is to be present.

ALEXANDRA — If you find the company of so many notables tiresome — please come and talk with me.

AGI — If your Highness will allow me to —

ALEXANDRA — I want to hear you talk of something beside fencing. For you know that is all you have ever spoken to me about.

AGI — I had no choice, Princess.

ALEXANDRA — You shall tell me of the stars — about that blue star and the golden star.

AGI — It will give me the greatest pleasure, Princess.

ALEXANDRA — Strange — that I should feel — a little afraid of you, now.

AGI — Afraid?

ALEXANDRA — There's something formidable about you as you stand there, sword in hand.

AGI — It is not the first time that your Highness has seen me with my sword.

ALEXANDRA — But in the fencing hall I have a sword too. Now I feel quite defenseless.

AGI — Do I appear as fierce as that?

ALEXANDRA — Not fierce but —

AGI — But?

ALEXANDRA — Rather aggressive.

AGI — (surprised). Aggressive? But Princess, it is I who feel defenseless.

ALEXANDRA — Then you will come?

AGI — Yes, Princess.

ALEXANDRA — You would not rather watch the blue star?

AGI — No, Princess.

ALEXANDRA — At nine, then.

AGI — You are most kind, Princess.

ALEXANDRA — No, Professor, no, not at all.

Alexandra nods briefly, then goes into the garden. Agi stands looking after her for a moment.

The curtain falls

ACT II

The banquet hall of the castle is set for the late evening supper. "It is a large, sumptuous, square room, richly decorated, lighted by a massive chandelier and brackets." Near the center of the room there is " a long table, elaborately spread with lace cloth and china and gold service for seven persons, and dressed with smilax and flowers. There are five chairs back of and one at each end of this table, richly upholstered in blue with coat-of-arms showing on their backs, and in front of the table are two stools matching the chairs." From a distant ballroom dance music is frequently heard, as doors are opened and closed. The hall is unoccupied until Symphorosa hurries in, followed a second later by Beatrice.

The ball has been going on for some time and it is easily to be gathered from the flustered attitude of the ladies that something momentous is happening. Alexandra, it appears, has been having altogether too much success with the professor. For the last few minutes she has been sitting quite contentedly under the mirror with him, and certainly everybody will be noticing it if she does not move soon. Symphorosa is quite upset about it.

Beatrice is also worried, but not unduly. She can trust Alexandra, and she has been greatly thrilled by Prince Albert's confession — once repeated — that he never before had realized how pretty Alexandra really is. This, argues the anxious mother, indicates that he will not go home in the morning, and the day following, his mother, Maria Dominica, will be there. And Maria Dominica, Beatrice feels certain, will not only approve of Alexandra, but will see that her backward son does, too. She turns now to a final consultation as to the arrangements for serving the supper with Cæsar, her major-domo. The menu, Cæsar reports, has been made up from the Prince's favorite dishes, as suggested by his staff. It is a cold menu — so cold Beatrice thinks perhaps she had better have some hot tea poured into her cold consommé. Hot enough, that is, to warm her, but not hot enough to steam and expose the substitution. A difficult commission, but one Cæsar will see is carried out.

Now Alexandra and Professor Agi come from the ball-room. Alexandra felt, she says, that she should inspect the table. And she did not mean that Agi should follow her. But — now that he suggests his regret that he did not understand and his willingness to go — she thinks, perhaps, he had better stay. She does not want to be rude to him. Or to hurt him. But she is a little inexperienced in such affairs. She does not know exactly what she does want. He has been telling her of his stars. Not of the mystery and beauty of them. But of their remoteness. And she is not interested in remote things tonight.

Agi — I would have spoken of the thoughts with which the stars inspire me ——

Alexandra — That might have been more interesting.

Agi — Among those far-off stars lie my thoughts of the Unknown — of birth and death — of life and — (softly) — love.

Alexandra — (coldly). Can you conceive of such remote things?

Agi — When I look up to you, Princess ——

Alexandra — (still colder). And the Unknown?

Agi — When I look into my own heart.

Alexandra — And do you believe in these miracles?

Agi — I must believe in them, Princess — what else could give me courage to endure my life?

Alexandra — Is your life then so unendurable?

Agi — It would be if ——

Alexandra — If ——?

Agi — If I did not have two lives. There is the life you know — but I have another life, quite apart from that — a burning, inextinguishable life.

Alexandra — Why have I never suspected that?

Agi — Because your Highness evidently believes in miracles, too. At least, you have been able to believe that the cold, impassive expression of my face was real — even when struck.

Alexandra — You are struck — in the face?

Agi — Every day.

Alexandra — By whom? (Agi does not answer.) Who strikes you in the face? Who? Do you mean I do? (Agi nods.) Without knowing it?

Agi — That is why it hurts so much.

Alexandra — This is stranger than your stars. You mean I hurt you?

Agi — Your Highness witnesses a miracle every day. You see a young man whose face, whose voice, whose outward bearing all remain composed and expressionless while in his heart there is a raging fire. And yet it never occurs to you to ask for the explanation of this miracle.

Alexandra — The explanation?

Agi — Yes. Why do you think I bear all that I do? Why do I teach so humbly, and silently submit to everything? Why do I allow my pride to be trampled upon? Why am I here where I am? Why do I live as I have to live here?

Prince Albert interrupts them. He is apparently on a casual tour of inspection with two ladies clinging to his arms. But he is not too occupied to notice the princess and the tutor. He stops a moment to speak with them, and then passes on. Not altogether pleased, it may be, but giving no outward indication of such a feeling.

Agi is not so successful in hiding his feelings. The appearance of Albert, his complaisance, his slightly patronizing attitude, saddens if it does not anger the tutor and Alexandra senses the change in him. Which forces from his unhappy lips finally the confession that he is jealous.

AGI — I should have left it unsaid — but this evening ——
ALEXANDRA — Yes, I know — this evening.
AGI — For months you have been cold and reserved towards me. Your politeness was as false as your indifference was real. And now tonight — this evening — you suddenly begin to look at me as if I were a man — and you even speak with a little kindness.
ALEXANDRA — I said nothing that ——
AGI — Perhaps — but everything you have said and done and looked — has left me shaken and bewildered — and no longer able to subdue my feelings. When you were so far removed from me, so hopelessly unattainable, then your remoteness gave you the beauty of the stars. And now that beauty is lost — because of this evening.
ALEXANDRA — I don't know what to say — only I wish I could give it back to you.
AGI — That is beyond your power, little Princess.
ALEXANDRA — Why do you call me that? I don't like it.
AGI — You will not hear it again. I shall leave, if you ask. Indeed, even if you ask me to stay, I shall go. Oh, I can't speak to you as I used to — you have sent my thoughts twirling, Princess. But tomorrow, tomorrow ——
ALEXANDRA — No, now. I must make you understand now. Oh, I am so ashamed. I want you always to respect me — and I want to be at peace with myself — once more. I think we can rely on you as a good friend. My family — that is, my mother — has but one aim in life — to see me a Queen, so that I may restore our family to its lost throne. Oh, Professor, cherish always this moment. Respect me for every word that I am trying to say — for I feel as if each one was drawn bleeding from my heart. The Prince paid no attention to me, and so my mother thought that if there were another man — Albert's interest might be aroused. Oh, believe me, I can feel for you in your suffering, but — I must unburden my heart. I never harmed anyone before — you are the only man I ever hurt — and I wouldn't have hurt you. Indeed, I always treated you coldly just because I felt — well, because you seemed embarrassed when you spoke to me, but I'm weak and mother knows so well how to handle me. Never since I was a little child have I said "No" to her. It was she who suggested that I invite you here this evening. Had I dreamed, Professor, had I foreseen what no one could have foreseen — or if I had known how the eyes of a man can smoulder when his heart is on fire — or that any man would dare look at me as you do. (Pause.) Now I have told you everything, Professor, and there is a peace in my heart again. Can't you respect me a little even for what I have done? I can thank my dear mother — because without her, I might never have known what it was to suffer for another's pain.
AGI — (bows his head). Alexandra.
ALEXANDRA — Have you nothing to say?
AGI — You did only what you were told.
ALEXANDRA — I don't want to seem less guilty than I am. It was hateful of me to make it appear all my mother's fault. I, too, am to blame. (Pause.) I want to be a queen.

It is not easy for Agi to take this blow gracefully. He would, if she would let him, quietly retire with his misery. But Alexandra cannot have him go thinking the worst of her. She has told him what she has because of her respect for him, and she is ever so eager that he shall understand.

"I worship you, Princess," he exclaims; "and now I can worship hopelessly again. But have no anxiety on my account, I shall be properly submissive and I am

quite at the disposal of your distinguished family. I
bleed a little — perhaps it is a mortal wound — nevertheless I can enjoy the interesting rôle you have given
me. It amuses me and appeals to my sense of the dramatic. What better way of serving a beautiful princess — with a smile on your lips and a dagger in your
heart!"

The assembling guests find them smiling bravely and
pretending a deep interest in the story of the stars the
professor has been telling. Prince Albert again has his
suspicions of the situation and there is a growing curtness
in his attitude toward Agi. Why, he would like to know,
has he not been told of all this interest in stars, and the
observatory? Because, as Alexandra explains to him,
"Your Highness goes to bed too early. The stars have
no regard for etiquette." A good epigram, Albert admits. But it is plain to be seen that he does not find it
altogether satisfying as an explanation.

The guests take their places at the table, and as Albert,
with more alacrity than usual, offers his arm to Alexandra, Professor Agi stands stiffly and consciously to one
side. Symphorosa and Beatrice are again noticeably
eager to cover the situation. Agi should be sent away,
Symphorosa insists in a whispered voice. And Beatrice
agrees. But how? They try to do something by suggestion and by hinting, but Agi, a little flushed and defiant now, pretends not to understand them.

Tired? Not he! Not well? He never felt better in
his life. Have his supper sent to his room? No, indeed! He had much rather eat it there, with them.
And when they try to shoo him to that end of the table
farthest from Alexandra he promptly takes the chair next
her with a polite but final "Thank you! This will do
very well!"

There are many awkward pauses during the serving of
that supper, and once or twice a threatened conversational catastrophe. Alexandra, between his Highness

and the tutor, finds it no easy task to direct and control the conversation. Prince Albert seems determined to lead Agi on, and the professor, flushed and resentful, is easily led. Once, when he has finished a long and personal account of his life, his work and his hopes, he reaches for his glass of Tokay. " I drink to the very beautiful daughter of the house!" he cries and drains the glass at a gulp.

The company is a little startled by this. Even Father Hyacinth politely protests that so heavy a wine is never drunk either so soon or so fast. But Agi didn't know, not being used to it, and he did not care, being miserably unhappy. This, he admits, is the first glass of wine he ever took. But anything might happen on a night like this!

And anything does, for now Alexandra has also drained her glass of Tokay at a single draught! Beatrice is quite dismayed, but there is not much that can be done. And Albert, seeking to make light of the matter, accepts it quite calmly as Alexandra's generous impulse to shield the embarrassed professor.

With the wine to add zest to his spirits Agi is soon taking the center of the conversational stage again. And now he is in what promises to be rather an unpleasant argument with Albert.

AGI — . . . I am an astronomer, your Highness. And astronomy teaches you not to despise even the tiniest specks, for these minute specks in the sky are each worlds in themselves.

ALBERT — All of them?

AGI — All of them.

ALBERT — And these little specks, are they aware of that?

AGI — Yes. I know that is something that you rulers of the earth can hardly appreciate. You speak of ten million inhabitants, an army of two millions, quite as if these millions were not all sovereign worlds — worlds that one may not destroy.

ALBERT — But, Professor, no one here wants to destroy any of your worlds.

AGI — Women sometimes do it with a smile. (*To Alexandra.*) Your gracious Highness is looking at me very intently.

ALEXANDRA — I like what you say.

AGI — (*to Beatrice*). And your Highness is looking at me very nervously and anxiously. Perhaps you do *not* like what I say.

BEATRICE — I am not quite accustomed to hearing you speak in this way, Professor.

AGI — I am in exceptionally good spirits this evening, your Highness.

BEATRICE — Perhaps a little more so than one would wish.

ALEXANDRA — Mother, this is a ball and we have been drinking wine.

BEATRICE — Nevertheless, you astonish me, Professor.

SYMPHOROSA — (*suddenly*). And this salmon, Albert, you must notice this salmon — it is quite the pride of the chef.

ALBERT — He talks very prettily, you know. That's why Zara is so pleased with him. What's wrong with the salmon? You said something about the salmon.

WUNDERLICH — Her Highness remarked it was quite the pride of the chef.

ALBERT — Yes, yes, that's splendid. What of it?

SYMPHOROSA — I just said it, that's all.

ALBERT — I see. H-m-m-m. Little specks in the sky — Astronomy — worlds one may not destroy —pretty phrases —

AGI — Not phrases, your Highness.

ALBERT — Yes, phrases — pretty phrases to impress the ladies with. Every star a sovereign world!

AGI — Not every one, your Highness.

ALBERT — No?

AGI — No! There is that great white moon up there. It seems very bright and shines with a rather imposing splendor — and yet it has no light of its own, it only reflects the sun's rays. But take Vega, now — the one you ridiculed so a little while ago — well, that remote, barely discernible little star, for all its modesty, shines a thousand times more brightly than the sun.

ALBERT — How considerate of it to be so modest!

AGI — It isn't modest — simply a great way off.

ALBERT — All the more reason for it to twinkle modestly.

AGI — It twinkles modestly only for you, your Highness. But for me who can appreciate it, it shows its true strength. And I take pride in proclaiming that it shines more brightly than the sun — and that it shines with its own God-given radiance, your Highness. Its own!

ALBERT — No doubt, Professor, but of course you know these are things I can't understand.

AGI — No, your Highness.

BEATRICE — (*to Symphorosa*). Oh, I can't bear this any longer.

ALBERT — Splendid! At last someone who dares to tell me there is something I don't understand.

AGI — Yes, your Highness, this is something you know nothing about.

ALBERT — For twenty years I have longed to be addressed in that tone. Let me tell you, that as an astronomer, and as a man, you have delighted me — and your manner is charming.

AGI — Whether or not I have delighted you, doesn't interest me.

ALBERT — And so frank. Charming! Charming!

Beatrice can stand no more. Something, she realizes must be done, and so she elects to faint. Soon the supper table is deserted and Symphorosa and the attendants are helping Beatrice to her room. Albert insists upon following, to see that she is properly disposed.

And now the two enraptured folks are alone with Father Hyacinth, and eager to explain to him their respective views of the unhappy scene.

ALEXANDRA — It is my fault. I am responsible for everything. That's why I stayed, so that I ——

HYACINTH — Gently, gently, my dear. Let us talk quietly. That's what I stayed for. As long as I am here, you needn't worry. (*To Agi.*) But you are trembling.

AGI — I am not trembling.

ALEXANDRA — Hyacinth. (*Leaning on Hyacinth's shoulder.*)

HYACINTH — Rest there, my dearest. I understand it all — I know so well how it happened.

AGI — I couldn't stand it any longer, Father, I couldn't. God knows I meant to bear it in silence until tomorrow — but I am a man — and in love, Father — and I didn't know what I was saying. I don't even know now what I did, except that it was something unpardonable. But when I saw that I was being used as a mop to clean the floor for someone else to walk over, then something inside me gave way, my blood began to boil, and when he ridiculed me in that cold, sarcastic way of his, my anger couldn't be held back — even now it is raging within me.

HYACINTH — Tell me, my boy, are you angry at me, too?

AGI — At you?

HYACINTH — Then don't shout at me. I can hear what you say and understand it, too.

AGI — I have reached the end — but I will not give my life away so cheaply again. Not even for this beautiful princess. Yesterday, this afternoon, I would have laid down my life for her handkerchief — but now that I have been wounded, my life seems dearer to me.

HYACINTH — What you have done ——

AGI — Is done. And I'll face the consequences.

HYACINTH — I was sure you would say that.

AGI — I know — it was *lèse majesté* and worse. But I am ready to answer for it to anyone — the family — the prince, the colonel, with swords, cannons — whatever —— But what I did I had to do, and now I must do more.

For Alexandra's part, she, too, has something to say, though what it is is not altogether clear in her mind. The wine — the first glass she has ever drunk — has made her feel very warm and comfortable. She thinks, with her head tipped against Hyacinth's breast, that perhaps it would be nice to die that way. But first she must be sure of Professor Agi's forgiveness. She is very sorry for the unhappy tutor.

ALEXANDRA — I never was so sorry for anyone in my life.

HYACINTH — And when he looks at you, you are still sorrier for him.

ALEXANDRA — When he looks at me, my face burns — as when the oven door is open.

HYACINTH — The oven door — and —

ALEXANDRA — And then his eyes look into my heart, and it's as if someone had touched a piano key — lightly — with one finger.

HYACINTH — A piano key, I know — and then——

ALEXANDRA — When he speaks to me — when he speaks to me, his voice rings through my conscience — like a bell — and that hurts. Oh, I am so sorry for him.

HYACINTH— So! I wonder if this isn't a case of something else besides pity or remorse?

ALEXANDRA — What could it be?

HYACINTH — A case of — let me see — (*bends physician-wise over her breast*) something wrong here — no, not there — it's on the left side — I wonder could it be —— Now take a deep breath — sigh — and say "Professor."

ALEXANDRA — (*sighing*). Professor.

HYACINTH — (*dryly, straightening and looking at her*). Heart trouble!

But it isn't easy for a proud young lover to forgive —
until he realizes that Alexandra is quite sincere. And
then Hyacinth seeks diplomatically and kindly to explain to them that what they have done is very foolish —
and very beautiful. He tries ever so hard to be severe
with them — but what is he to do, sitting between them,
as they gaze first at each other and then so earnestly,
so helplessly, at him?

"I look at you," he stumbles along; "and then — I
just look at you — that's it — I look at you and my
heart aches for you. You two dear children, so young
and so innocent — and I, how can I judge you? I try
to, but it's no use. How can I judge you as you sit there
in this hour of glorious beauty — the boy so brave and
foolish, the girl so guiltless and foolish — two brave
children in such a plight — and so happy — happier than
they can ever be again — for your happiness will vanish
with the night's breeze. You hardly knew it when you
had it. Now the daylight is almost here — the daylight
that must separate you. What a sad awakening for you,
you poor children! I had such an awakening once in
the days when I still wore my uniform and a sword —
but that was long ago — so very long ago."

From the table he fetches a glass of wine and with it
drinks to them: "To your happiness!" he cries. Then
the majordomo comes to summon him to his sister's room.
Alexandra would go, too, if her mother wished it. But
it seems the only request Beatrice has made in respect
to her daughter's actions is that she keep out of her sight!

Now the princess and the tutor are alone again — and
each of them flustered a little by the nearness and the
dearness of the other. Alexandra would know, in a
breath, all there is to know of Agi — his name, which he
tells her is Nicholas, and his age, which is 24, and where
he was born —

Suddenly she is aware of the majordomo pretending
to be busy at the back of the room, and dismisses him

with some curtness. It is not a time even for princesses to be chaperoned. She would have the servant tell the orchestra to play something — something that is not usually permitted.

AGI — They have all gone; the guests, too. We are alone together, dear Princess. Perhaps only a few minutes, and then the end of this — the only thing of beauty in all my life. Are you afraid of me?

ALEXANDRA — I don't know. But if it is fear, then let me always be afraid.

AGI — The last hour, perhaps the last minute I can be with you. Do you love me?

ALEXANDRA — (like a child). If this is love, then it is very much like the time when I was a little girl and the Emperor —— (Agi looks at her astonished.) I had seen many portraits of the Emperor — with a crown of gold on his head — in all his pomp and glory — and then when he came to visit us, dressed like any other man, I didn't know him.

AGI — Yes dear, clever princess. (Goes toward her.)

ALEXANDRA — Don't come any nearer, Nicholas. This is the first time I have ever seen a man in love — and he happens to be in love with me.

AGI — Are you so very much afraid of me? (He takes her hand.)

ALEXANDRA — Frightfully — at the thought of your being — so close to me — how cold your hand is.

AGI — And yours is warm. What do you feel that makes it tremble so in mine?

ALEXANDRA — Something that burns and ——

AGI — And ——?

ALEXANDRA — And my rank. Why can't I forget that? How odd that I should speak of it! Do you know what I would like to do? I would iike to give you something to eat — I would like to do something to make you happy. Supposing I tell you that I adore Napoleon?

AGI — Adore him? Adore is too much.

ALEXANDRA — What shall I do with him then? Tell me and I will do it always. Now you are laughing at me.

AGI — I laugh very sadly, Princess.

ALEXANDRA — Why is it — I feel as if I wanted to do something I shouldn't — something wicked. Suppose I tell you all our secrets — did you know that we once had an actress in our family? But that's nothing — it must be worse than that.

AGI — It will be dawn soon — the time goes very quickly.

ALEXANDRA — (nervous). Now he is hurrying me. Oh, what is there I can do for you? Tell me, would you like to call me Zara?

AGI — Your Highness ——

ALEXANDRA — No? Did you know that the blood of the Bourbons runs in my veins?

AGI — I knew it, Princess.

ALEXANDRA — And yet —— (She looks at the table.) Will you have something to eat?

AGI — No.

ALEXANDRA — Why not?

AGI — I am not hungry — I am thirsty.

ALEXANDRA — Do you want some wine?

AGI — No, it is you — your mouth — your eyes — your throat that I am thirsty for.

ALEXANDRA — Must you look at me like that — when I only want to be kind to you?

AGI — It is not kindness I want — no, not that — to look into your eyes — deep into your eyes, and then to see them close as ——

ALEXANDRA — What do you mean?

AGI — And then to go on and on — never to stop — on the way which you have shown me.

ALEXANDRA — Which I have shown you?

Agi — Yes — without knowing it. In my cowardice, this evening, I did not dare to think I could be the rival of a king, but I know now that I am, and I know, too, that I am the victor. Before I had no voice but now I can sing aloud for I am young, Princess — and a man. A man triumphant over all. And now —

Alexandra — And now?

Agi — And now for the morning. Now we shall see who is King — he or I?

Alexandra — (drawing a little away). Oh, please, please, have mercy on me.

Agi — When I said nothing, that was the time for you to be afraid.

Alexandra — Do you want to be revenged on me?

Agi — I am in love, Princess, and this is my one hour of life.

Alexandra — Poor boy!

Agi — I will not have you pity me. They will be here soon — a minute more and then I am the disgraced servant. Will it end so? Shall I see you once more in all your proud disdain and ever after regret that I didn't carry you away — carry you away through the rose trellis out into the summer night beyond — and there — (Attempts to embrace her.)

Alexandra — (resisting). Nicholas!

The major-domo is back with two announcements. First, Prince Albert is about to retire and will pass almost immediately through that room, and, second, he (Albert) has just received a telegram announcing that his mother, the Princess Maria Dominica, will be there the next day.

When Albert comes, formally attended by his staff, he pauses to say good-night to Alexandra. He is in jovial mood. There is a suggestion that he is a bit excited but holding his emotions well in hand. For the moment he ignores the presence of Professor Agi. But when he does notice him it is with a none too carefully guarded tone of contempt in his voice.

Albert — (as if he has just seen Agi). Ah, the professor! Good-night Professor. I like what you said — and the way you said it. A little defiant, but very original. When her Highness was taken ill, I was just about to make my modest comment — I had no idea you were such a rebel.

Alexandra — Albert, you are mistaken.

Albert — No, I find these astronomical outbreaks very interesting — something new and unconventional. What I like to think of as temperament. (To Hyacinth.) He sat down so unobtrusively with us and then the first thing we knew he had lifted us to the skies and there he stayed — after letting me drop back to earth. (To Agi.) There was inspiration in your words — it was very pretty — upwards, ever upwards ——

Alexandra — Your ridicule is unjust, Albert — he is not like us.

Albert — So I observed.

Alexandra — (more and more excited). He is a scientist, a free spirit — he is not bound by our conventions.

Albert — You defend his bad manners now with as much grace as you tolerated them a while ago. You are a brave-hearted girl, a little martyr. I have just learned from your mother that you have been the uncomplaining object of certain unwelcome attentions — and that ——

Alexandra — (very excitedly). Mother is mistaken, Albert, and your insinuations are unjust. You do not understand him.

Albert — (ironically). It's not easy then to understand him?

ALEXANDRA — But you don't understand him now. (*Albert laughs.*) Don't laugh at him, Albert. He is a scholar and a poet — an astronomer.
ALBERT — (*calmly*). An ill-bred little stargazer.
AGI — (*taking a step forward*). Your Highness!
ALEXANDRA — You are going too far, Albert. You mustn't say such a thing.
ALBERT — Ah, but I do.
ALEXANDRA — I will not allow it — when it was for my sake that ——
AGI — Your Highness, I — I ——
ALBERT — (*coldly and calmly*). You are a presumptuous intruder.
AGI — (*with a step forward*). You ——
ALEXANDRA — (*at the height of her excitement*). Don't answer him, Nicholas. (*She looks at him.*) I forbid you to. (*With her voice breaking.*) Nicholas!

For a second or two Alexandra hesitates. Then she deliberately throws her arms about Agi's neck and kisses him passionately. Shocked into absolute stillness those who have been entering the room in the wake of Albert silently withdraw. Father Hyacinth alone stands his ground.

Albert, completely taken aback, slowly gathers his wits and bows formally. "I beg your pardon!" he half mumbles. "That is another matter — quite another matter. In that case I most humbly beg your forgiveness, Professor."

He bows stiffly to them, repeats his good-nights and is gone. Symphorosa, noticing that Alexandra seems in danger of collapsing, leads her gently out of the room. Agi, with head bowed and cheeks flushed, stands alone. Seeing him, Father Hyacinth advances upon him almost threateningly, stops in front of him — and kisses him on both cheeks. Agi stares wonderingly after him, as he hurries out of the room.

The curtain falls

ACT III

It is early morning of the following day. In the rooms being prepared for the Princess Dominica there is a general recapitulation of the situation as it stands.

Alexandra, having arisen early, is out riding — alone.
Prince Albert has not yet been coughed into consciousness by the mellow-throated Lutzen. Symphorosa is
bustling about nervously, seeing that everything is in
readiness for the expected guests. And Beatrice, after a
sleepless night, during a part of which Alexandra sat
at her bedside and told her everything that had happened,
is hoping for the best but fearing the worst that can happen. Father Hyacinth has not yet appeared and Professor Agi is reported packing.

The Princess Dominica, having arisen at two in the
morning, arrives early by motor. She is large and dom-
inant and immediately prepared to take command of any
situation that may present itself. She is not one to beat
about the bush. "Now," says she, once the rather elaborate greetings are over, "now to business. Do I have
to tell you what I am here for?"

BEATRICE — Oh, Dominica!

DOMINICA — I have come to you almost as joyfully as a bride. To tell the
truth, much more joyfully than when I really was a bride. Poor Victor — well
— never mind. Beatrice, my son wishes to marry your daughter!

BEATRICE — Dominica!

DOMINICA — Beatrice! Why do you weep? Is it as bad as that?

BEATRICE — I am so overwhelmed.

DOMINICA — Then collect yourself. You must sooner or later make up your
mind to it. His Majesty is more than pleased to approve the marriage. And
I had a long wire from Albert yesterday, explaining that he did not dare to
show how delighted he was with Alexandra until I came. You know he never
commits himself without first consulting me.

BEATRICE — He is such a perfect son.

DOMINICA — Happy the people with such a king! Albert wrote that he was
beginning to find his enforced silence very irksome and he begged me to come
at once so that he could tell you how delighted he was and how happy he
could be with her.

BEATRICE — Oh, Dominica!

DOMINICA — I am not surprised. Your daughter is truly beyond criticism —
beautiful, intelligent and dignified. That's what I like about her — her dignity
— her magnificent reserve.

BEATRICE — How sweet of you to say that!

DOMINICA — I mean it. I do not at all approve of the modern tendency
toward freedom of manner, so noticeable in the younger generation. Fortunately there is not even a suggestion of it in Alexandra — one could not ask
for more perfect stateliness and *aloofness*. In fact, she is, if anything, a little
too aloof — a little unnecessarily cold with her inferiors.

BEATRICE — Cold? You could hardly say that.

DOMINICA — But I told you that that was what I particularly admired in her.

BEATRICE — She has changed lately. She treats her inferiors almost warmly
now.

This reported change in Alexandra, however, does not impress Dominica as anything to worry about. She regrets a little that the incompetency of her diplomats practically forces Albert to marry for love, but she is really fond of Alexandra and always has been. During all the time they were shopping in Europe for a fitting consort for their heir apparent, she still thought often of Alexandra. And — now that everything has been arranged she is much relieved.

Father Hyacinth, however, coming upon these maternal felicitations, proceeds to stir a bit of excitement by insisting on telling Dominica everything that has happened. Nor will he let Beatrice resume her fainting spells and escape. His attitude is both forceful and determined, and he tells the story, beginning at the beginning, so to speak, by assuring Albert's mother that during her son's visit he had behaved like a fish.

After which he relates the young man's coldness, his positive lack of interest in Alexandra and finally the necessity, as Beatrice felt it, of bringing the good-looking young tutor into the scene to develop a needed action. He tells her of the scene at the supper, and of the discovery that Agi was secretly in love with Alexandra.

HYACINTH — Imagine the cruel suffering of this good young man, so pitifully in love, when he discovered his part in this innocent game was only to serve as a means to an end.

DOMINICA — Albert is to blame — why couldn't he speak out? There was no need for him to be so over cautious.

HYACINTH — He did it for your sake. I don't think you know what a dutiful son you have.

DOMINICA — Of course, it is gratifying. Well, and then — ?

HYACINTH — And so the boy sat down to supper with us — the martyr — there is no other word to describe him — this self-sacrificing martyr — and the agony he endured brought tears to my eyes.

DOMINICA — I don't blame you.

HYACINTH — And Alexandra — with her kind heart — couldn't bear to see him suffer either. She would have liked to have sent him away. But the professor — merely out of loyalty to the family and to Alexandra — and to your son, too, for that matter, was determined to play the game out, in spite of his breaking heart.

DOMINICA — The poor boy.

HYACINTH — Until Albert, who of course knew nothing of what was going on — *insulted* him.

DOMINICA — The professor?

HYACINTH — Yes, the professor.

DOMINICA — That poor boy?
HYACINTH — That poor boy — imagine it!
DOMINICA — How did Albert insult him?
HYACINTH — He called him an intruder.
DOMINICA — How awful — why didn't you stop him?
HYACINTH — How could I?
DOMINICA — And the poor boy?
HYACINTH — What could he do? He bowed his head — I thought my heart would break.
DOMINICA — The brave fellow — and Alexandra?
HYACINTH — I knew you would be sorry for him.
DOMINICA — And Alexandra?
HYACINTH — You are not only the cleverest, but also the best-hearted woman in Central Europe. If you could have seen him as he stood there, with his hopeless, desperate love — with his romantic dream so cruelly shattered — with his heart torn and bleeding — while Albert, in all his perfect elegance, insulted him. And the boy stood there with his head bowed, humiliated, disgraced, all because of his loyalty to the family. I appeal to you as a woman — wasn't that brave of him?
DOMINICA — Very brave.
HYACINTH — Does such a man deserve to be sent away?
DOMINICA — No.
HYACINTH — Does he deserve to be insulted, to be disgraced, to be punished?
DOMINICA — God forbid.
HYACINTH — I ask you once more — does such a man deserve to be sent away, to be treated with contempt, to be insulted? Doesn't he rather deserve to be — to be — how shall I say it — to be — I don't know myself — but doesn't he deserve to be — ?
DOMINICA — To be kissed.
HYACINTH — Exactly what happened to him.

Dominica is not altogether certain she can as freely excuse this impulsive action on Alexandra's part as she thought she could before she knew about it, but Hyacinth, by talking fast and with great emotional enthusiasm, soon convinces her that to have kissed the tutor under the circumstances was really the only thing a princess could have done. " If you must know — I kissed him myself," he concludes. " Of course you did," agrees Dominica; " there was nothing else for you to do. When his wife recovered from her confinement Louis XVI kissed the nurse. The most natural thing in the world."

And so the recital of Beatrice's " great calamity " is successfully negotiated. Dominica understands perfectly. But she does think something should be done by way of seeing that the young professor leaves well provided for. " Men in his position usually turn up again — as writers of memoirs, publicists for the opposition or American lecturers," she warns.

When Alexandra comes back from her ride she finds Professor Agi waiting to see the Princess Dominica. He is wearing the clothes he expects to travel in. She is surprised to hear that he is going. What is to become of the boys?

The Professor is sorry to leave — the boys. But he must go. Yes, he knows the Princess Dominica has arrived, and he knows the object of her visit is to see Alexandra and Prince Albert engaged. But there is nothing that he can do that he is not doing.

ALEXANDRA — Have you forgotten what happened — last night?
AGI — I have forgotten.
ALEXANDRA — Even when I —
AGI — Even that. I must forget — and your Highness must deny it — and he — he must not have seen it.
ALEXANDRA — I will not deny it, and he did see it. (*Turns her back to him.*) It seems to me you took a very precious gift from me — more precious than you deserve — perhaps a kingdom.
AGI — That is not so much — There was one offered once in exchange for a horse.
ALEXANDRA — Do you want to insult me? You are behaving like a sulky child.
AGI — No, your Highness. My action, my speech, my departure today — they are simply my answer to your Highness's kiss.
ALEXANDRA — I didn't ask you to use that word.
AGI — What harm to name it? When the receiving was so much more painful.
ALEXANDRA — More painful than the giving?
AGI — Much more — Because I felt all the pity in it and the contempt. It was a little too condescending. It meant that I was not a man, but a child or a dog that you could pat on the head.
ALEXANDRA — Was that how you took it?
AGI — If I could have taken it in any other way.
ALEXANDRA — Then — ?
AGI — I would have returned it.
ALEXANDRA — Then, in other words, it was a very stupid thing that I did.
AGI — It was a little too much, your Highness, too sudden.
ALEXANDRA — Too sudden?
AGI — We had not gone that far. But you did kiss me — and so I went out into the cool morning air, after the kiss — I went out through the park, where the wind could clear my head. I walked about there — not near the roses, but under the oaks where the air is fresh and not heavy with fragrance. There my heart became quiet, and I could think once more — then I felt very much like a beggar who has had a thousand-crown note cast into his hat and is half inclined to run after his benefactor for fear it was a mistake, that it was too much.
ALEXANDRA — (*proud, nervous*). I am glad that now you see things so clearly.
AGI — It is the morning light, your Highness. The sun is shining.
ALEXANDRA — And not the stars.
AGI — No, no, not the stars.
ALEXANDRA — I am very glad. It is well as it is.
AGI — It could not be better.

Father Hyacinth again serves as the understanding peacemaker between them. He knows why Agi feels as he does. And he tries to make the tutor's seeming change in attitude plain to Alexandra. But he is not entirely successful. Her pride is still hurt.

ALEXANDRA — (*her head on his shoulder*). I am very sad, Hyacinth, but when you talk to me — don't you suppose you could stay on a little longer and talk to me some more? It comforts me so.

HYACINTH — I'll stay, my dear, for three days — four days, if you want.

AGI — Will you permit me to leave?

ALEXANDRA — I marvel at your calmness, your self-control. But I know it's not real the way you are acting today. You would like to act quite differently.

AGI — Perhaps, your Highness.

ALEXANDRA — You would like to speak in another way.

AGI — No, your Highness.

ALEXANDRA—Where was this self-control last night? I would like to know that.

HYACINTH — I'll stay a week.

ALEXANDRA — (*more and more nervous*). If you can be so calm now, why did you act as you did last night? What was it you wanted then? I'm sure I don't know.

AGI — Nor do I. That was the most beautiful thing about last night — I didn't know what I wanted.

ALEXANDRA — You didn't know?

AGI — No.

ALEXANDRA — You didn't know!

HYACINTH — I'll stay two weeks.

ALEXANDRA — (*with growing excitement*). He didn't know what he wanted! And yet he went right on. He played upon my kind-heartedness, my inexperience — so that he carried me along through it all — and I was ready to go — with him — even in his defiance — to the end of the world — and he — (*Albert enters. Alexandra sees him, but pays no attention to him.*) He didn't know what he wanted. (*Speaks to Albert.*) He only wanted to destroy things — to give way to the excitement of the moment. You called him a rebel — you should have called him a rebellious child.

ALBERT — (*lightly and ironically*). You judge him unjustly — he is a free spirit — he is not like us.

ALEXANDRA — All he wanted was to defy us — to make a scene — he had no decency.

ALBERT — You forget, he is an astronomer.

ALEXANDRA — And now I say his behavior was presumptuous.

AGI — Your Highness.

ALBERT — Not a word, Nicholas, I forbid you.

And before he knows it Prince Albert himself has added one more kiss to the startled and flushed cheek of the tutor. Agi leaves them now, unhappy, but a little proud, it may be, of his martyrdom, and the boys run after him to give him bouquets they have picked for him.

And now Alexandra, Prince Albert and Father Hyacinth are alone. Albert is the least flustered of the three and frankly seeks peace. He begs that Alexandra will

not be angry with him. He holds nothing against her, and he understands everything — even her kissing the professor.

ALBERT — Alexandra! Last night you righted a wrong that my weakness made me commit. I would like to ask you to stay by my side always so that when I make a mistake again you will be there to — to act as bravely as you did last night. Will you? (*He takes her hand.*)

ALEXANDRA — (*after a pause*). Albert, I must be trustful with you. If I say that at this moment I feel nothing more for you than respect — and friendship —

ALBERT — Then I will say that that is quite enough for me.

ALEXANDRA — (*sadly*). This is hardly a love match.

ALBERT — No, no — decidedly not.

ALEXANDRA — No.

HYACINTH — No.

ALBERT — I would like to say this ——

ALEXANDRA — Yes.

ALBERT — We have something even finer — the love which comes after marriage. That deep and abiding happiness which — which —

HYACINTH — Comes later and lasts longer.

ALBERT — Extraordinary how you can express exactly what's in one's mind. I was about to say that Katharine of Wurtemburg was one of the happiest of wives — and her marriage was entirely the result of Napoleon's — (*Pause. Dominica enters.*) Well — so it goes.

Now Dominica has come back and heard the news. And she is pleased with everything — including the general habit of kissing the professor that appears to have attacked the household. And she is particularly pleased that Alexandra has agreed to become her daughter.

ALEXANDRA — My dearest Aunt, if you deem me worthy —

DOMINICA — Worthy in every way, my dear daughter. (*Kisses her.*) But with this one word of advice — remember that your dear father used to call you his Swan. Never forget that — and think always of what it means to be a Swan. You may glide proudly, superbly over the smooth surface of the lake — but you must never approach the shore. For when the swan tries to walk, when it waddles up the bank, then it painfully resembles another bird —

ALEXANDRA — A goose?

DOMINICA — Exactly, my dear. The nature books teach us that the Swan is no more than a very haughty duck. So it must stay out on the lake — be a bird, but never fly; know one song but never sing it — until the end. So for you, my dear daughter, the unruffled waters of the lake — there you must remain — with head high, oblivious of the crowds along the shore — and the song, never. (*Pause.*)

Caesar enters to announce the serving of breakfast. Hyacinth proffers Dominica his arm. Next go Beatrice and Symphorosa, alone. Then Albert and Alexandra, arm in arm.

The curtain falls

THE END

" OUTWARD BOUND "

A Drama in Three Acts

By Sutton Vane

SUTTON VANE'S drama concerned with the flight of the human soul after death, called " Outward Bound," proved the most provocative play of the year. It came to Broadway with the endorsement of a London run, which meant that its chances of success here were strengthened, though not secured.

The first night New York audience was typical of such gatherings — which is to say it was made up of playgoers 100 per cent experienced and 80 per cent hardened to the influences of a première. Apparently it was too moved for utterance. The play's reception was noticeably undemonstrative.

The professional reviews ranged from accounts that were wildly enthusiastic to others significantly noncommittal. For weeks afterward the correspondence of interested lay critics followed a similar trend in argument. " Outward Bound," in other words, proved, in New York at least, one of those plays about which there are few carefully qualified opinions. People either like it immensely — are quite fascinated by it, in fact — or loathe it with like passion. Fortunately the play found a public that did like it early in its engagement, and continued at the Ritz Theater, under the direction of William Harris, Jr., from January 7, 1924, to well into the spring of 1924, playing to audiences that kept the theater filled.

In " Outward Bound " the curtain " rises on a room

105

which suggests rather than represents the lounge smoke room of a small ocean liner." There is a drinking bar at the stage right and writing tables at the left. The room is carpeted in " a warm, neutral tone," and around the edge at back is a red-cushioned wallseat under a row of portholes. Through the door letting onto the deck at back center " the color of the sky arrests the attention at once. It is a curious color — vague and almost non-descript. The sun is shining, and it is a clear still morning. Behind the bar stands Scrubby, busy polish-ing the glasses — preparatory to the boat sailing. He is dressed in the usual uniform of a ship's steward. His manner is always calm and reposeful, and his voice gentle and kindly. He is an elderly man, typically English."

One by one the passengers enter the lounge and make themselves known — either to Scrubby, the steward, or to each other. There are Ann and Henry, a young couple apparently laboring under a peculiar strain and each greatly dependent upon the moral support of the other.

There is Tom Prior, " a slight young man, highly strung. He is not specifically drunk at the moment, but rather more displays the mellow and bland cock-sureness of a youth who for some time has kept himself going with constant stimulants. He is wearing a lounge suit, and is very cheerful and smiling."

Prior is amiably inquisitive, and pleasantly communi-cative. He is much in need of " pulling together," and he is convinced that a drink or two of Scotch will help. He at least is eager to try that remedy.

Soon he is joined by Mrs. Cliveden-Banks. " She is a withered old harridan of fifty odd — probably once beautiful," records the author. " Smartly frocked in traveling costume, she carries an armful of magazines."

Her greeting of young Prior is jovial and friendly. " I saw your name on the passenger list, so I asked for the bar at once, and here you are," she chirrups.

Mrs. Cliveden-Banks is taking the trip to join her husband, but she fears it is going to be a very dull trip. " There is nobody on board — at least nobody who *is* anybody — though of course the poor creatures can't help that." There is, however, one passenger who threatens to be a somebody very much to Mrs. Cliveden-Banks' disliking. He is a young clergyman, and clergymen at sea, she declares, are dreadfully unlucky. She, for one, purposes to cut the fellow dead and seeks Tom's support in doing likewise. A moment later the Rev. William Duke, " a sincere, earnest, young clergyman," enters the lounge and gives them their chance. Mrs. Cliveden-Banks can barely see him at all, even when he addresses a direct question to her, and Tom, alcoholically accommodating by this time, somewhat cumbersomely follows her lead, greatly to Duke's surprise and confusion.

The organized snobbery of the upper class representatives receives a setback with the entrance of Mrs. Midget, who now appears in the doorway. Mrs. Midget " is a poor charwoman in black little bonnet, black shawl and dress — her best. Very humble, simple and obviously out of place in these strange surroundings. But sweet and motherly."

MRS. MIDGET — (*to Mrs. C-Banks*). You'll excuse me speaking up as it were, but I must say something to someone. And as you're the only other lady I've seen about, bar myself, I must ask you to give me a ——

MRS. C-BANKS — Mr. Prior, am I to be attacked from all sides?

MRS. MIDGET — (*starts suddenly on hearing the name*). Mr. Prior?

TOM — Any objections?

MRS. MIDGET — No, very pleased to meet you. You see, mum, I 'ad to follow yer because yer see, mum, I've been struck all of a 'eap.

MRS. C-BANKS —- You've been what?

MRS. MIDGET — Struck all of a 'eap.

MRS. C-BANKS — Mr. Prior, rescue me. And you had better do something for this woman, too. It appears she has been struck all of a heap ——

TOM — Well — what's the trouble?

MRS. MIDGET — Well, sir, thanking you, it's like this, as it were ——

MRS. C-BANKS — " As it were." How quaint! " As it was " is correct, of course — we all know that from our Prayer Book. Go on.

MRS. MIDGET — Well, sir, it were like this, *as it was;* only last Saturday, Mrs. Roberts and I were talking about the sheets being damp, and I says ——

MRS. C-BANKS — Ah! Sheets — damp. The good woman is, of course, a stewardess.

— Are you?

Mrs. Midget — Am I what?

Tom — A stewardess on this boat?

Mrs. Midget — No, I'm a passenger.

Mrs. C-Banks — She's a passenger! Oh, I see it, she's a passenger! I see it all! The whole thing has come to me in a flash! She's a passenger. Don't worry yourself any more, Mr. Prior, I have solved the good woman's trouble. She's a passenger and she's lost her way; haven't you, good woman?

Mrs. Midget — Exactly, mum.

Mrs. C-Banks — Mr. Prior, tell that steward fellow to tell somebody to take the good woman back to her proper place immediately. She's been wandering. She's on the wrong deck, she's in the wrong class. Good-bye, good woman, good-bye. So glad to have been so helpful.

Mrs. Midget — Thank you, mum.

Tom — (going to her). Oh, steward, just get someone to show this woman steerage — er — third class deck — or something, will you?

Scrubby — (turns to Tom). The third class, sir?

Tom — Yes, please.

Scrubby — I think you've made some mistake, sir. There is only one class on the boat.

Mrs. C-Banks — (faintly). What was that?

Tom — Only one class?

Scrubby — Yes, sir. It's the same on all this line.

Mrs. C-Banks — What was that?

Tom — Oh, sorry — I didn't know. (Returning.) Er — Mrs. Cliveden-Banks ——

Mrs. C-Banks — Mr. Prior, did I, or did I not hear that fellow say there is only one class on this boat?

Tom — He said so, certainly.

Mrs. C-Banks — Mr. Prior, the thing's impossible.

Tom — Well, he ought to know.

Mrs. C-Banks — How dare she — how dare my secretary book me a passage on a vessel with only one class? How am I to know who are the ladies and gentlemen, and who are not?

Tom — Now, now, don't get excited.

Mrs. C-Banks — Excited! Mr. Prior, a terrible thought has struck me. That woman there —

Tom — Well, what about her?

Mrs. C-Banks — She probably eats.

Tom — Extremely likely, I should say.

Mrs. C-Banks — Well, then — if she eats — and if there's only one class — she will eat in the same place as we shall. It can't be done. I shall disembark immediately.

Tom — Now look here, Mrs. Banks — Mrs. Cliveden-Banks — she's probably only a lady's maid or something.

Mrs. C-Banks — Who would have a maid like that — outside a theatrical boarding house?

Tom — The idea of your landing is absurd. Don't get nervy about nothing. We can easily avoid her. If you're really upset ——

Mrs. C-Banks — And I am, I am!

Tom — Then I'll question her.

Mrs. C-Banks — Yes. Do, do, quickly. It would be quite impossible for me to lunch at the same table with a woman who has been struck all of a heap.

Mrs. Cliveden-Banks is finally dissuaded from disembarking, and Tom seeks to clear away the Mrs. Midget irritation by helping the puzzled charwoman back to her cabin. He finds the task a little difficult, seeing that Mrs. Midget is not quite certain how she came aboard or why. Nor does she know exactly where she is bound for. She is quite willing, however, to follow any of the company's suggestions and is soon on her way to her own, or at least another, section of the ship under Scrubby's guidance.

Out from under Mrs. Cliveden-Banks's dominating influence Tom is frankly ashamed of his part in snubbing the Rev. Duke and frankly confesses as much. He is, he admits to the padre, just naturally a weak character, but the padre insists the admission itself is proof of strength rather than weakness of character.

The Prior apology accepted, these two are soon friendly voyagers, planning this and that activity to relieve the tedium of the trip. But the padre does most of the planning. Tom agrees only to help organize the entertainments, and he will do most of that from the lounge.

The next passenger to appear is Mr. Lingley. " He is a hard and unpleasant business man, aged 55 or 60. He is loud and officious, and is obviously self-made. He has on a traveling cap and a heavy overcoat, and he is carrying an attaché case, containing business papers. He is evidently in a great hurry."

Lingley is considerably excited at having nearly missed the boat. He had flown from his office to make it, and he has brought loads of work with him. He can't stop work, even though he has often been advised to do so. Not only is he a member of parliament but he has numerous other interests. " I'm on the London County Council as well," he explains to Duke and Prior. " Incidentally I own twenty-one music-halls, a chain of cinemas, two gold mines and a Methodist chapel. Naturally they want looking after."

Tom recognizes the great man now. Once he had worked for him — for two days. He was discharged for drinking and Lingley would not give him a second chance. Exasperated by the memory of that humiliating experience, he takes delight now in telling Lingley what

he thinks of him. He is, among other things, " a pompous old idiot," and also a " blue-nosed baboon." Likewise he is a " pink-eyed rabbit, a rotter and a grasper —"
The shock is too much for Lingley. A moment later, working himself into a state of wrath, he suffers a minor stroke and is in a state of collapse from which a drink of spirits, kindly furnished by the cause of the trouble, only partially revives him. He thinks that if he can get on deck he will be all right. His physicians have warned him that he must never get excited and that he must have more air and sunshine, and worry less, if he is to keep going.
Lingley makes his way uncertainly to the deck, and Duke is about to follow to see that he is all right, when Tom stops him.

Tom — In strict confidence — now we're friends again — has it struck you by any chance that there's anything queer about this boat? Strictly between ourselves.
Duke — No, it hasn't.
Tom — It has me.
Duke — How do you mean?
Tom — I think there's something jolly queer about her. By Jove, if I were right it *would* be a joke!
Duke — I don't follow you.
Tom — It's difficult to explain. But Mr. Lingley — and — and — oh, I'm not quite sure myself. It may be only my ——
Duke — Imagination?
Tom — Exactly. Only somehow I don't think it is.
Duke — Go on. I must hurry.
Tom — Yes. Well (*turns to Duke*), there was a sort of charwoman here just now — you didn't see her — a very decent sort of a soul, of course, but — well — hardly the kind of person you'd expect to find here. And she couldn't remember where she was going. Excepting she was going to meet someone. Now this Lingley fellow's just told us the same thing in different words. He couldn't remember where he was going either, at least not clearly. And I've noticed lots of other little things. For instance, it's absurd sailing with our passenger list — there are so few of us. I tell you it's queer — and ——
Duke — Really, I can't follow you.
Tom — Then there's old Mrs. Banks drivelling on about joining her husband — Good Lor'! It's just struck me.
Duke — What has?
Tom — Colonel Cliveden-Banks kicked the bucket over a month ago. Surely she can't have forgotten *that*. Or — or would *that* be her father?
Duke — Mr. Prior, if you take my advice, you'll follow Mr. Lingley's example and get some fresh air on deck.
Tom — Yes, I think I will. All the same it *is* queer. (*Rises.*) Certain you're not angry with me?
Duke — Oh yes, certain. Shipmates, eh? (*Shakes hands.*)
Tom — Oh yes, shipmates. But I bet you cut me the moment we land.
Duke — Rot!
(*He follows Lingley on to the deck. Henry has entered and is lighting his pipe from a match which he has taken from the table.*)

TOM — Excuse me, sir, after you. (*Coming up to him he takes his match and lights his cigarette from it.*) Thanks. I say, do you mind if I ask you a question?
HENRY — Of course not.
TOM — It's rather a queer question.
HENRY — Go on.
TOM — Do — you — know — where — you — are — going — to?
HENRY — Are you a Salvation Army man or what?
TOM — No, I'm quite serious.
HENRY — Of course I know where I'm going to.
TOM — On this boat?
HENRY — Certainly.
TOM — Thank goodness! I'm going to get some fresh air!

Ann and Henry are still worried. Something has happened to them from the consequences of which they fear they must suffer, but what it is they can but vaguely remember. Henry is anxious, too, about Jock, his pet dog. How will Jock get along, left as they had left him? And if anything should happen — is there, does Ann think, a heaven for dogs?

She thinks there must be. A heaven without cats — " just lots of bones and meat and water. And hot fires to lie in front of in the winter. . . . And some arrangement so that the good dogs can't remember the kind masters." All their memories are muddled, but gradually the muddle is getting a little clearer.

HENRY — I can't quite remember, Ann, not clearly, not yet — it's coming back gradually of course, but — but ——
ANN — Yes, dear?
HENRY — Ann, haven't you and I sinned in some way?
ANN — We've been true to each other. How can we have sinned?
HENRY — If we had, Ann, could they separate us?
ANN — Hold my hand tightly.
HENRY — I'm trying so hard to remember.
ANN — What, dear?
HENRY — What it is we've done that isn't right.
ANN — We've done nothing that isn't right.
HENRY — No. Not in our light, of course. But have we from other — from the world's ——
ANN — We've never cared for the world. We're not going to care for it now.
HENRY — If we were wrong and if it were something very, very wrong, they couldn't separate us, could they?
ANN — That sort of thing's all over now, Henry. You've forgotten our secret.
HENRY — No, I haven't. It's all perfect, of course — excepting this one thing. (*Tom enters from the deck and unobserved by them stands quietly at the back leaning against the doorway.*) Don't laugh — don't laugh at me, Ann, I'm only trying to remember, and asking for your help. But it seems to me this thing — this crime, if it is one — that we've committed, is something big, and yet that it's — now don't laugh — that it's only something to do with gas.
ANN — (*sits beside him*). Gas?

HENRY — Yes.
ANN — You silly.
HENRY — It seems to me that before we left the flat ——
ANN — Our sad little flat!
HENRY — I forgot — to turn off — the gas.
ANN — You terrible silly! Of course you did. We — agreed — that. That's what we agreed.
HENRY — There's nothing very wrong in not turning off gas!
ANN — Don't worry, dear. Take my hand.
HENRY — Nothing so bad that they could separate us for it. You can't blame people for not turning off gas! And yet, I'd have sworn — Ann, you're quite certain that there isn't something else we've done? Something big?
ANN — There's nothing else, dear, I'm certain. You've nothing to be ashamed of.
HENRY — I love you so.
ANN — Thank you, Henry. Don't worry, dear.
HENRY — I wish I could remember *how* we got here. We wanted to so long. Anyway, now we have.
ANN — Let's go out on to the deck.
HENRY — Yes, let's — bless you. (*Both turn and see Tom.*) Hello, sir.
TOM — (*quietly*). Hello!
HENRY — We didn't notice you ——
TOM — It's all right. I just came back to ——
HENRY — May I introduce my wife? Ann, this is the gentleman who asked me if I knew where I was going.
ANN — How do you do?
TOM — How do you do?

Tom is a changed man. His tone is quiet and sad, and he stands perfectly rigid. The awful truth which has dawned upon him has completely sobered him. There is a pause. Then Ann goes out onto the deck, and Henry follows her.

HENRY — (*as he exits*). We'll see you later. We've sailed, you know. (*Scrubby appears behind the bar.*)
TOM — Yes, I am right. (*Comes to bar.*) Scrubby!
SCRUBBY — Yes, sir?
TOM — I am right, aren't I, Scrubby?
SCRUBBY — Right, sir, in the head, do you mean?
TOM — You know what I mean.
SCRUBBY — Right about what, sir?
TOM — You — I — all of us on this boat.
SCRUBBY — What about all of us on this boat, sir?
TOM — (*trembling with apprehension*). We are — now answer me truthfully — we are all *dead*, aren't we?
SCRUBBY — (*after a pause. Very quietly with firm conviction*). Yes, sir, we are all dead. Quite dead. They don't find out so soon as you have as a rule.
TOM — (*pause*). Queer!
SCRUBBY — Not when you get used to it, sir.
TOM — How long have you been — you been — oh, you know?
SCRUBBY — Me, sir? Oh, I was lost young.
TOM — You were what?
SCRUBBY — Lost young, sir.
TOM — I don't understand.

SCRUBBY — No, sir, you wouldn't, not yet. But you'll get to know lots of things as the voyage goes on.
    TOM — Tell me — tell me one thing — *now*.
    SCRUBBY — Anything I can, sir.
    TOM— (*terrified*). Where — where are we sailing for?
    SCRUBBY — Heaven, sir. (*Pause*.) And hell, too. (*Pause*.) It's the same place, you see.

The curtain falls, with Tom, in a state of dreadful apprehension, gazing blankly at Scrubby.

ACT II

It is evening of the same day.   The scene is the same, but " the curtains are drawn over the portholes and the electric lights are on.   The center door is open from time to time and it is pitch black outside."
    Mrs. Cliveden-Banks, who, naturally, dressed for dinner, is in the lounge.   So, too, is Mr. Lingley of Lingley, Ltd.   It is practically their first meeting.   They were introduced at dinner, but their names were somewhat confused.   " Being introduced during the soup has its disadvantages," as Mr. Lingley explains.   " The lady sitting next to us made it a little difficult to hear concisely." The " lady " was Mrs. Midget.
    The Rev. William Duke joins the party.   At least the Rev. Duke is willing to join if Mrs. Cliveden-Banks can be prevailed upon not to continue making everybody uncomfortable by trying to ignore him.   Mrs. Cliveden-Banks thinks, after some deliberation, that she can afford to make some concessions.   She is a generous woman and willing to sacrifice herself for the sake of the others. " But, remember, Mr. Duke," she warns, " if you *do* drown us all, I'll never speak to you again."
    The arrival of Mrs. Midget a moment later presents a further complication.   Mrs. Cliveden-Banks is not yet

prepared to lower her standards completely. To meet
the little charwoman as a social equal, as it were, is
asking too much. So she decides to make sport of her.
She does not get far, however, and the others find Mrs.
Midget's autobiographical reminiscences quite interesting.

MRS. MIDGET — . . . Do you know, all of yer, believe me or believe me
not, I once had a house of my very own.
MRS. C-BANKS — How magnificent!
MRS. MIDGET — Yes, wasn't it? Though of course it wasn't *all* my own. No.
Semi-detached, and lodgers, yer know. Payin' guests and very well it *did* pay for
donkey's years. Well enough for me to make my son a gentleman anyway, and
send him to college to prove it.
MRS. C-BANKS — Quite romantic. Perhaps I have met your dear boy? Where
is he now? Cambridge or Cologne?
MRS. MIDGET — Well, 'avin' become a gentleman 'e naturally lost all 'is
money. And 'is money was my money. And I ain't seen him since. 'E hasn't
seen me, not to know me, since 'e was a little boy. I got my brother-in-law,
'e's rich, to take him over and manage things for me. You see I didn't want to
disgrace 'im. 'E's been a good boy.
LINGLEY — Sounds it.
MRS. MIDGET — (*resentfully*). 'E *was*, I tell yer. But you know what it
is yerself, sir.
LINGLEY — I do not — I have never lost a penny in my life.
MRS. MIDGET — Ah! then you can't be a gentleman.
LINGLEY — What?
MRS. MIDGET — Now the gentlemen my — my boy mixed with *were* gents.
Always broke, bless 'em, and then 'avin' "another one" just to make 'em
forget about it. And my boy the life and soul of the 'ole crowd. At least
so the letter told me from the brother-in-law. And you can't 'ave your cake
and eat it, as the sayin' goes, nor your gin and drink it *as* you well know, sir.
LINGLEY — Confound it, madam, I do *not* know.
DUKE — Sorrow's sent to us to try us, Mrs. Midget.
MRS. MIDGET — Cors' it's sent to try us. What else could it be sent for?
And it does try us very much.
DUKE — Yes — but sometimes, as in your case ——
MRS. C-BANKS — Mr. Duke means you would never have the steady poise,
you would not be the woman of the world you so obviously are unless —
MRS. MIDGET — You're trying to pull my leg, aren't you?
DUKE — I'm afraid Mrs. Cliveden-Banks *was* trying to. I certainly didn't
mean that.
MRS. MIDGET — Thank you, sir. (*To Mrs. C-Banks.*) Mum, I may not know
the manners of Society, and if them is such as yours I do *not* want to. With
which terse remark I shuts up, being sorry for anything I've said.

The conversation turns to Tom Prior, who has not appeared at dinner. Probably, suggests Lingley, he has
been "sleeping it off," considering the condition he was
in. Before they get far with their comments Prior
appears. "He is very pale, tense, and very quiet."
And he has come to tell them that they are trapped — all
of them. Trapped!

They are inclined to laugh at him. Do laugh, in fact. But their merriment is hardly contagious. Lingley is blusterous, Duke plainly worried. Mrs. Midget thinks someone should put that poor young man to bed. But Tom is determined they shall know the truth and realize its fateful significance. "You shall have the word of the — the man who calls himself a steward, and the words of two of our fellow passengers," he all but shouts at them.

LINGLEY — But what about, sir? What are you driving at?

TOM — I began to suspect this morning before lunch. Nobody seemed to know where they were going to. I'd forgotten myself, though I didn't admit it. I didn't want to. I didn't dare to. I daren't now. When I was quite convinced, I got drunk. That was only natural. All my life I've started to face facts by getting drunk. Well — when — when — I woke up again — about an hour ago, you were all in the saloon. I was frightened, terribly frightened. At last I got out of my cabin and went over the ship. I made myself. Yes, over her, all over her. Into the officers' quarters and everything. No one said a word to me for a very simple reason. There's no one on board to say anything. No captain, no crew, no nothing.

MRS. C-BANKS — If there's no crew on board this ship, Mr. Prior, may I ask who waited on me at dinner?

TOM — There's no one at all on board this ship, excepting we five — and those two — and the steward. He waited on you at dinner. He's in charge of the ship. I made myself find out. Do you know where that steward is now? He's in the rigging — sitting cross-legged — high up in the rigging. I've just seen him.

MRS. MIDGET — It's takin' 'im in a funny way, ain't it?

DUKE — (advancing on Tom). Really, Prior, I think that —

TOM — I don't know what I'm talking about? Very well, then, answer me this. Who have you, any of you, seen on board this ship since she sailed? Excepting ourselves? Mrs. Midget, perhaps you can help. When I sent you to your stewardess this morning, did you see her?

MRS. MIDGET — See who? I saw no one except the fellow I went with. And first rate he looked after me. Got me a cup of tea and —

TOM — I tell you I — (Turns to Duke.) Padre — Padre, think carefully, who exactly have you spoken to?

DUKE — I — really, I — I have seen men about of course.

TOM — Have you? Have you indeed? What sort of men, sailors?

DUKE — Yes, I think so.

TOM — In the same way that you thought I was sober.

MRS. C-BANKS — You don't expect us to talk to sailors, do you, Mr. Prior, able-bodied though they may be?

TOM — Have any of you met anybody else then? A purser, an officer of any sort, even a stoker?

LINGLEY — That reminds me. In your gigantic tour of this vessel did you by any chance strike the engine room?

TOM — No, I couldn't find it.

LINGLEY — A pity! I'd hoped you were going to say the ship was worked by elastic — ha, ha, ha.

(Mrs. Cliveden-Banks laughs also.)

TOM — Joke if you want to. If that is a joke. Well Padre, speak up.

DUKE — Well, I — must have met someone of course.

Tom — You *should* have met someone, you mean. But you've not. Padre, where are *you* landing?
Duke — Landing? I'm going to — of course I'm going to — mind your own business.
Tom — *Where are you landing?*
Duke — I'm taking a little holiday, that's all. I'm going first to — to —
Tom — You see you can't remember. I'm right! I knew I was. Why, look at the quiet way we sailed. Was anybody here to see any of us off? No, you know they weren't. Because you can't see people off — not right off — to where we're going.

But he cannot convince them. Even Henry and Ann, entering the room a moment later, still clinging consciously and a little desperately to each other, refuse to back him up. And when he speaks of the gas he had overheard them talking about Ann becomes visibly panicky.

It is then time, concludes Lingley, to put a stop to Tom's "madness." They must get him either to a doctor or lock him up. And yet when Tom dares them — any of them — to go on deck and see for themselves if there are lights there they hesitate. Lingley refuses. He would "never dream of interfering with the ship's discipline." And though the Rev. Duke had rather not go, he agrees to make the inspection on condition that Prior will go quietly to his room if he finds everything all right.

It is a tense moment they spend in waiting for Duke's return, though they severally try to make light of it. There is the muffled roll of Drake's drums, though none but Tom hears it. Mrs. Cliveden-Banks can't see the least use of worrying about things there in the dark when they might all be concentrating on making it nice and comfortable inside.

"Mrs. Cliveden-Banks, you're an ostrich!" Prior answers. "I'm sorry, but you are. You're in danger, great danger of something out there — something, I don't know what it is — but it may affect your very soul — yet all you can think about is light and warmth and cards in here. So the only word for you *is* ostrich."

Now the Rev. William Duke is back. " He is pale and
agitated, terrified — but tries to conceal it."

They appeal to him anxiously for a report. Everything, he assures them, is all right. And they sigh with
relief — all but Tom. He is immediately beside himself with anger, throwing himself violently at the Reverend Duke and calling him " Liar!"

As Duke struggles to free himself Lingley takes a hand
and between them they succeed in forcing Prior into a
chair, where he collapses and sobs hysterically. Both
Mrs. Cliveden-Banks and Mrs. Midget decide to withdraw, and Henry and Ann follow them, leaving the
lounge to the unhappy Tom, Duke and Lingley.

LINGLEY — (to Duke). And now, sir.
DUKE — (coming to Prior). Prior, I apologize.
LINGLEY — What do you mean?
DUKE — That Mr. Prior was perfectly right.
LINGLEY — What?
DUKE — There is no — there's no starboard — no —
LINGLEY — There's not!
DUKE — No. There's no light on the boat at all. She's black as pitch.
LINGLEY — Impossible.
DUKE — Look for yourself.

Lingley, alarmed now, crosses to the center door,
opens it and glances out into the dark, then shuts it.
Then he hesitates and turns. " But — the bridge?"

DUKE — As far as I could see there's nothing — nothing anywhere.
LINGLEY — Nothing — nobody?
DUKE — I'm not even certain that we're moving.
LINGLEY — Good heavens, man, why didn't you tell us this at once?
DUKE — I didn't want to alarm the ladies.
LINGLEY — Women drown as easily as men.
DUKE — Is this a question of drowning? Something must be done — we must
all do something immediately.
TOM — Exactly, but what?
LINGLEY — (thoroughly rattled). To begin with — well — somebody ought to
ring a bell.
TOM — And get someone else to explain.
LINGLEY — Duke — do you — do you believe in all this?
DUKE — I don't understand it.
LINGLEY — (to Henry). And you, sir?
HENRY — I don't understand it either.
TOM — That's not true! And you know it's not true!
DUKE — Prior! Now look here, when did you first feel certain, in your mind,
about all this?
TOM — (pointing at Henry). After I'd heard something he said. I spoke

to the steward, I asked him if — he told me the truth, I'm sure — it seems we're sailing for (*pause*) — both Hell and Heaven.
DUKE — Very interesting from a professional point of view, of course.
TOM — If there's anything else you want to know, better ask him, the steward.

It is precious little satisfaction that Mr. Lingley gets from the steward when he brusquely demands an explanation. Scrubby is quite accustomed to seeing gentlemen lose their temper in similar cimcumstances. And he is not at all upset by Lingley's threats to report him to the London office.

TOM — What you told me this morning was true, wasn't it?
SCRUBBY — That we're dead, sir? Yes, quite dead if that's what you mean.
LINGLEY — You speak for yourself.
DUKE — It is queer.
SCRUBBY — Why, sir? We didn't think it was queer when we were born.
LINGLEY — Now listen. I don't want any mysteries.
SCRUBBY — There are none, sir.
LINGLEY — And I mean to get in touch with someone at once — ah! I have it, the wireless!
SCRUBBY — She doesn't carry any, sir.
LINGLEY — That's illegal anyway. Duke! Duke!
DUKE — I'm afraid I can't suggest anything.
LINGLEY — But — but — ! (*Suddenly overcome with fear.*) I must get out of this — I must get out of it.
SCRUBBY — That, sir, is imposible until after the examination.
LINGLEY — What examination?
SCRUBBY — You'll find out later, sir.
LINGLEY — The ladies ought to be warned immediately.
SCRUBBY — I should leave them to find out for themselves, sir, if I were you. I have known some of them not to like the idea to begin with and get hysterical. It is kinder to let them find out for themselves.
DUKE — They will find out?
SCRUBBY — Undoubtedly, sir.
LINGLEY — (*suddenly seeing Henry*). Damn it — don't stand there saying nothing — get upset!
HENRY — I am, of course.
LINGLEY — You're a bright lot, all of you, aren't you? So helpful — but — but — what are we to do? What are we to do? (*To Duke.*) You're always talking about doing things? What are we to do?
DUKE — I really — don't know. Of course, if we were all quite certain — a prayer —
LINGLEY — Is praying going to bring the captain or the crew to life?
TOM — Or any of us for that matter.
SCRUBBY — There's no danger, gentlemen, if that's what you're frightened of.
LINGLEY — Isn't there?
SCRUBBY — No, sir.
LINGLEY — I'm not frightened.
DUKE — I am. How many times have *you* made this passage, steward?
SCRUBBY — About five thousand times, sir.
LINGLEY — Five —
SCRUBBY — Yes. I was lost young.
DUKE — And it's always like this?
SCRUBBY — Not always, sir. No. As I was telling this gentleman (*referring to Prior*), the passengers don't find out so quickly as a rule. I suppose it's because of the half-way's we've got on board this trip.

Duke — Half-ways?

Scrubby — Yes, sir, it sometimes does work like that.

Lingley — There is no point in standing here talking to a lunatic. The question is, " What is — ?"

Scrubby —— to be done? That's what they all ask, sir. There's nothing to be done. Just go on as if nothing had happened.

Tom — How simple.

Lingley is still unconvinced and stormy. But suddenly he finds some relief in deciding that he is merely asleep and dreaming. And he is doubly pleased to find that he can walk. In some dreams it is not so easy.

The Reverend Duke is still puzzled, but calm. And Tom, from a matter of habit, helps himself to another drink.

Tom — (toying idly with glass). I'm awfully sorry. I'm afraid I'm a fearful rotter, I'm so used to it. Any crises you know — I say — I say — (Pause.) Charles Reade — or some other rotten novelist once said, " Never too late to mend," didn't he? Do you think there's any truth in novels? And then there was that other chap — the Great One, you know, in the Bible, he said — he — There you are, you see; that's the sort of fellow I am! I've forgotten what he said.

Duke — Does it really much matter what either of them said? Isn't it more to the point what you have got to say?

Tom — No sermons! But, if you please, I would like to talk to you seriously if you'd listen to me, out there in the dark.

Duke — (rises). Shall we go out there — in the dark — and talk to each other, shipmate?

Tom — (humorously). This is a great chance for you, isn't it?

Duke — We must both, my dear Prior, keep our sense of humor.

As they pass out to the deck they meet Henry coming in. He is alone, but Ann is close by on the deck. He calls her when the others have gone. She is still wistfully anxious.

Ann — What is it?

Henry — Come here.

Ann — I'm with you.

Henry — Ann — listen — they know we're dead — they're — they're finding out our secret.

Ann — (frightened). I know! I know they are! (They look at each other.)

Henry — What will they do to us, dear?

Ann — (getting closer to him). They won't separate us — will they?

The curtain falls

ACT III

It is afternoon and some days later. The scene is the same, save for such rearrangement of the furniture as Mr. Lingley thought necessary for a meeting of the passengers, which he has arranged.

It is Mr. Lingley's belief that he and his fellow travelers should settle a few matters definitely before they arrive wherever it is they are going. First, is it the sense of a majority of those making the journey that they are, as alleged, all dead? Or is it not? And, if they are dead, what, in the opinion of the company, will be the most effective way, in all their interests, to meet and talk with the Examiner who is later to board the ship?

The attitude of the company is widely varied. Prior, nearer to hysteria and more oppressed by doubts than most of them, is inclined to be flippant and cynical and thoroughly disgusted with Lingley for suggesting that they should all sit down and seek to determine whether or not they have immortal souls! And, if they have, what sort of bargain they can make as to their reception by the Examiner.

Duke, suddenly freed of the responsibility of his job, is inclined to be a bit flighty; to say and do the things a decent churchly inhibition had prevented his saying and doing on earth. He recalls, and takes boyish delight in recalling, a limerick he overheard one of his choir boys reciting on one occasion, the one beginning " There was a young girl of Hong-kong." He even becomes quite free with Mrs. Cliveden-Banks, addressing her as " Banky " in the cause of their better acquaintance.

Mrs. Cliveden-Banks, a little shaken as to her complete confidence in the immediate future, is still certain that nothing really disturbing can ever happen to a Cliveden-Banks, and Mrs. Midget is amiably indifferent to what happens. Nothing much is known as to the feelings of

the mysterious young lovers, Henry and Ann, who drift
in and out of the cabin from time to time, still fearful
of being separated but never taking much part in what
is going on.

Mr. Lingley, in consequence of this diversity of moods,
has some little difficulty in bringing his meeting to order.
Nor can he do much with it after it has been brought
to order. He does, however, finally bring them all to
the point of agreeing that, if such action seem wise later,
he shall represent them all before the Examiner, and
shall, in preparation for that meeting, sort of tabulate
them, as it were.

LINGLEY — Excellent. Then I can put all the cases before this — this examiner briefly and to the point.

MRS. C-BANKS — It should save us a great amount of trouble.

LINGLEY — So, if you will all just give me a few details about yourselves —
and any special little reference you might like me to bring forward. Mrs.
Cliveden-Banks, let me start with you. What shall I say about *you* to this
— er — examiner?

MRS. C-BANKS — I should just say I am — or *was* — Mrs. Cliveden-Banks —
and leave it at that.

LINGLEY — Um! Oh, very well; you, Mrs. Midget?

MRS. MIDGET — Oh, I dunno.

LINGLEY — Oh, dear, dear, dear! Is that really all?

MRS. MIDGET — Yes, please sir.

LINGLEY — All right — not at all satisfactory, but I suppose all right — in
my hands. I can answer for myself of course. You, Mr. Prior?

TOM — Oh, say, I'm an old drunk. Or rather a young one.

LINGLEY — That won't help you very much.

TOM — How do *you* know?

LINGLEY — But you must have had some redeeming qualities that will help
you? For instance, were you good to your mother or — did you go to Oxford?

TOM — Put down the truth — he will know it anyway.

LINGLEY — Really, you're none of you being very helpful. (*Writes.*) A
drunk — er — a Mrs. Cliveden-Banks — er — and an I dunno.

MRS. C-BANKS — I should prefer to precede the drunk.

LINGLEY — Very well. (*To Henry.*) Now, sir, how can you assist me?

HENRY — I can't.

LINGLEY — But — you then, madam?

ANN — He speaks for both of us.

HENRY — We have nothing to say.

LINGLEY — It is really most discourteous of you! Mr. Duke, I can rely on
you at any rate.

DUKE — You can rely on me for *one* piece of information.

LINGLEY — Thank you very much.

DUKE — I now entirely agree with Mr. Prior for calling you a pompous
old idiot!

TOM — Cheers.

LINGLEY — What? — just because I'm trying to do my duty!

DUKE — Your duty! Your rubbish! You're doing what you are because
you're in a blue funk! And I don't blame you. I'm in a blue funk, too! But
not so much as to make an utter ass of myself by trying to get out of this

with balance sheets and board meetings! You want to try and impress this examiner with your cleverness, your business importance, your supposed interest in your fellow creatures. You're hoping to save your own skin that way. And I think it's pretty rotten!

LINGLEY — Indeed. Destructive criticism is very simple. Then perhaps *you* can advise me.

DUKE — I can advise nothing.

LINGLEY — Um! That's *very* useful.

MRS. MIDGET — Oh, sir, not just *one* word of 'elp?

DUKE — That is different. If I can *help* I will. But you mustn't take anything I say in the nature of advice. The blind leading the blind, you know. I can only tell you what I am going to do myself, and I may be wrong.

TOM — *What* are you going to do, Duke?

DUKE — I have been trying to look into myself silently, trying to examine my past thoughtfully and humbly — to seek out all the faults and not try to excuse them. But to know all that I am responsible for; and when I see my life, lying before me like a blurred map, I am going to pray to be able to make one more prayer. But for myself; I am not fit to pray for others. If any of you care to do likewise please do so if it will comfort you. Look back.

MRS. C-BANKS — I *could* look back, of course, but I don't intend to. Remember Mrs. Lot.

MRS. MIDGET — Thank you, sir.

DUKE — No, no, now that's just what I didn't *want* you to do. You see, Mrs. Midget — try to understand — we're just shipmates, you and I — trying to help one another. I'm not a captain any longer. I cannot pray for others. Perhaps the realisation of that is the beginning of my punishment. I've *lost* my job.

LINGLEY — I don't suppose it was worth much anyway.

DUKE — It was the most glorious job in the world. I suppose a man never really knows he's incompetent until he's sacked, and I can't, I can't understand and I *ought* to. It's my *job* to; and it's beastly hard not to be able to. It's heartbreaking — it's — (*To Prior.*) Give me a cigarette.

A moment later the sound of the ship's siren is heard, and a little later they know the boat has made port. The knowledge that the journey is over quite upsets them. Young Prior goes all to pieces, wildly protesting his fear of meeting the final test. Suddenly he feels in need of prayer — the prayer of a man, whether he be a clergyman or not. And Mrs. Midget agrees with him. "There's no 'arm in 'abits, if they're good 'abits," says she; "and prayer *is* a good 'abit."

So the Reverend Duke offers up the simple prayer of his childhood — the first one he ever learnt, he tells them, and probably the finest: " Gentle Jesus, meek and mild, look upon a little child — children — pardon our simplicity, suffer us to come to Thee. God bless father and mother, Harriet (she was my nurse), all kind friends, make me a good boy. Amen. Say it to yourselves if you want to; and remember Harriet — she was a worthy soul."

Then Scrubby comes to announce that the boat is in and the Examiner's cutter alongside. A moment later they hear his voice from the deck, gaily hallooing for Duke. And then he appears, filling the cabin door with his bulk and beaming good naturedly upon the company. He is the Rev. Frank Thomson, " an elderly and massive clergyman, rotund, rubicund and jovial. He is dressed in white drill and a topee. But he wears a clergyman's collar and black bib." Suddenly the surprised Duke recognizes him.

THOMSON — (*beamingly*). Ah, there you are! Duke, my old boy, how are you?

DUKE — Good — ! My — ! Well — ! Well, I'm dashed if it isn't old " grease spot." (*Crossing and shaking hands.*)

THOMSON — It is, sir, and greasier than ever. Phew! This climate! Well, I am glad to see you after all this time. How are you, Duke? Have a good passage? You're looking fit. (*Taking off topee and wiping forehead.*)

DUKE — I'm not *feeling* it.

THOMSON — I only heard this morning your boat was due in this afternoon. I'd seen your name on the passenger list of course — so I hurried down especially to meet you, I'd been up country.

DUKE — Thank you.

THOMSON — Well, how goes everything? I'm bursting for news! How's Ferguson — still in the same old place?

DUKE — No, they've made him a bishop now.

THOMSON — Good Lor', they *would*. Well, I hope he likes it. And what's become of Maltby; and that little fellow with the red hair and spectacles? I never could remember his name. (*Lights a cigarette.*) And do you still go for your blow-out at Simpson's every pay day, you young rascal? Tell me, what's the meat like there now?

DUKE — (*greatly agitated and in no mood for Thomson's frivolity*). Thomson, I'm delighted to see you again, of course, and I'm dying to tell you everything afterwards — *if I can* — but can't you realise — at this moment — how terribly worried I am?

THOMSON — Worried — worried about what?

DUKE — This — this person.

THOMSON — What person?

DUKE — This person — or whoever it is — who's just coming to examine us.

THOMSON — The examiner! Oh, I shouldn't worry about him!

DUKE — What — do — you — mean?

THOMSON — *I'm* the examiner!

(*General movement.*)

DUKE — You — you are!

THOMSON — Well, I'm one of 'em anyway. We've got dozens on the job. And they *will* shove all the duds on to it. My dear boy, our profession is not what it used to be. Terribly overcrowded, too, believe me.

DUKE —You're — my — examiner?

THOMSON — Yes — you're under *my* orders now. And I tell you, my boy, you'll have to mind your p's and q's; and *how* you'll have to slog at it! But I've fixed your " digs " up for you all right; they're not up to much, but clean, in the same house as myself; the old woman's quite a decent sort. And it's near your work, right in the center of the parish, so you couldn't do better, really.

Duke — Work?

Thomson — I find it quite handy myself.

Duke — " Parish — slog at it." Thomson, Thomson, you don't mean I haven't lost my job after all? Don't torture me, tell me quickly.

Thomson — Of course you haven't lost it. You haven't started it yet. You're just beginning it.

Duke — Not lost my job? Still got my job. Oh, thank you! Oh, thank God! I will work harder now every moment, I swear I will, Mr. Thomson. Harder than ever! Oh, do you all hear? My job I was so keen on — it's not been taken from me after all. My — oh! (*sits at table, and quietly cries*) job.

Thomson — (*patting him on shoulder*). There, there, boy, there, there! Whatever made you think it would be taken from you? There, there, it's quite all right.

With Duke recovered the Reverend Thomson suggests that he may as well begin his apprenticeship by assisting in the examination of his fellow passengers, an action that indicates to both Mr. Lingley and Mrs. Cliveden-Banks that favoritism is likely to play a large part in the inquiry. But neither their remarks nor their attitude has any effect on the Examiner. Lingley is dismissed as a nuisance the minute he seeks to assert himself. In fact they are all sent to the deck to await their calls, while the Examiner goes over the list with Duke.

According to his notations all those on the ship are expected ashore excepting Henry and Ann, and of them there is no record. This is rather puzzling to Duke, but of seemingly no great importance to the Examiner, who proceeds at once to the examination of Lingley.

" I am Lingley, of Lingley, Limited!" announces that worthy, as he faces the Reverend Thomson.

" Never mind the Limited. You are just Lingley now," replies Thomson.

And thereafter the experience of the big business man is not pleasant. The record in the book is decidedly against him. What he boasts of as enterprise the Examiner sets down as plain dishonesty, and when he characterizes that statement as a lie he is sent peremptorily from the room.

Lingley — I — I'm afraid you don't understand business.

Thomson — Not the way *you* conduct it. Why, you've been a rascal from the very start. You commenced your career by breaking a playmate's head against a granite curb because he had a painted tin horse. You wanted to get it.

LINGLEY — Well, I got it.

THOMSON — Oh, I grant you that! That's how you've made that glorious straight path you boast about. By knocking down anyone who came across it or tried to turn you off it. The foundation of Lingley, Limited, was laid when you stole the plans of a turbine engine — and let the inventor die in poverty.

LINGLEY — I've not been wicked. People respect me.

THOMSON — Do they? To your face, perhaps. Some men get found out during their lives, Lingley. You are only found out now. Come; off you get.

Again Duke suggests that Henry and Ann be called. They seem such a worthy young pair of lovers. But the Examiner repeats his regret that he can find no record of them in his books. He asks Scrubby about them, and discovers from the steward that Henry and Ann are " halfways," which appears to account for everything. But what a " half-way " is he does not then explain. He must get on with the others.

Mrs. Cliveden-Banks is called. Her experience is no happier than was that of Mr. Lingley. She begins by patronizing Duke, seeking in that way his good offices as a friend at court. And she tries desperately to make up to the Reverend Thomson. But he knows her — and knows her husband, too, Colonel Cliveden-Banks. The colonel is known as " Bunny " to his friends and is even then a popular golfer on shore. " Bunny," the Examiner reports, is eagerly awaiting the coming of his wife — though why eagerly he (Thomson) is at a loss to understand.

The news is not pleasant to Mrs. Cliveden-Banks. Having escaped from " Bunny " in life, she considers it a scurvy trick that she should have to take up with him again in death. And the Examiner's announcement that not only will she meet " Bunny," but that she will live with him and be a wife to him until she learns to be a *good* wife fills her with dismay. She refuses, absolutely. She could not, she admits, face her husband again. She could not stand the look in his eyes.

THOMSON — . . . You never could look him in the eyes. You're a thoroughly bad lot. You trapped him; you were grasping, you made him marry you. You — you — you —

MRS. C-BANKS — Don't let me down before *him*. (*Indicating Duke.*)

THOMSON — I wouldn't if you'd been a *good* harlot; but you weren't, you were a bad one.

MRS. C-BANKS — Rather a vulgar way of putting it!

DUKE — Dear, dear, only a poor unfortunate after all.

THOMSON — No, Duke, *not* a poor unfortunate. This old woman was once a beautiful young girl, outwardly, but she was never an unfortunate, never. She's been just a schemer. And somehow she's always managed to fall on her feet. There were two other men before she met Cliveden-Banks, richer men too than he was then. But she saw something *steady* in Bunny, so she made him marry her. He found out all about it later — and he's never told her. Too unselfish — too " big " — too loyal. So she goes back to him. I hope he *beats* her — but I know he won't. Anyway, she'll get her punishment. The eyes that made her run away. Only remember, Mrs. Cliveden-Banks, it won't be Bunny who'll know now, it will be you and I and everybody *except* Bunny. He'll have forgotten.

Tom Prior comes next. He has not yet recovered from his panic and his nerves are all to pieces. But he wants to know the worst. And he wants to die — really die and forget. But that, Thomson tells him, is impossible. He must go on, like the others. And in time he will forget ——

TOM — As if I could! As if I would anyway. You damned torturer. I see what you want me to do. You want me to chuck drink, develop a nice clear brain and remember all the other horrors! No, I won't do it. It's all I've got, it's my only comfort and if I'm to go on I won't give it up. See? But I'm not going to go on. Kill me! There, it's not asking much. And look at all the trouble it will spare you. I'm not worth saving. I'm not really.

THOMSON — You've suffered.

TOM — Ha! (*As if to say, " Haven't I?"*)

THOMSON — Can't I do *anything?*

TOM — No, you can't.

MRS. MIDGET — (*quietly*). Perhaps *I* could, sir.

THOMSON — (*sharply*). What do you want?

MRS. MIDGET — My name's Midget, sir. Excuse me bargin' in as it were, but —

THOMSON — I'm very pleased to meet you — yes, yes, I know all about you. But you've no business here yet.

MRS. MIDGET — Oh, but I *have*. You see, yer Reverence, when I first got on to this big boat nobody would speak to me. I was lost as it were — was — and then young Mr. Prior was very kind to me. 'E spoke to me and broke the icicles, as is said, and if he is in trouble I really don't feel I could put my 'ead on my pillow to-night — if I 'ave one — after what 'e done for me.

She understands young men of the Prior type, does Mrs. Midget, and she thinks maybe, if he will let her, she can help him a bit. What he really needs is a good, honest, respectable housekeeper to take care of him.

" Then all your things would be properly looked after," she promises. " With everything mended and darned ready for yer to put on. Someone to see yer didn't sit up too late, too often. No fussing mind, and call you in the morning with a nice 'ot cup of tea. What time do you get up?"

TOM — Oh, don't!

MRS. MIDGET — Oh, you can 'ave your drinks, as long as you don't let them interfere with your meals or take away your appetite. I'm a good cook I am, and if you left anything untouched it would upset me awful.

THOMSON — Mrs. Midget, you're suggesting.

MRS. MIDGET — I was thinking of it, yes.

THOMSON — Very fine, very fine of you. There's a little cottage waiting for you, with a garden by the sea.

MRS. MIDGET — There we *are* then! The very spot. (*Sudden change to the practical.*) 'As it got a good sink?

THOMSON — You don't quite follow. True, Mr. Prior is free to do as he chooses but he has not yet arrived on the same plane as you have. He would not be allowed to live there to begin with anyway.

MRS. MIDGET — Then why can't I go where he's going? That's simple enough.

THOMSON — It would mean going back to the slums.

MRS. MIDGET — And what's the matter with the slums? They're all right.

TOM — I won't listen to the idea.

MRS. MIDGET — (*pleading*). You can always give me a week's notice.

TOM — I'm not worth bothering about.

MRS. MIDGET — I'm willing to 'ave a shot.

TOM — I can't understand this extraordinary interest anyway.

MRS. MIDGET — One good turn deserves another. Sir, wouldn't the people who spoilt you be glad if they knew you was in capable 'ands?

TOM — They would be, I suppose.

MRS. MIDGET — *And* doing well? (*With growing fervour.*)

TOM — Er — yes —of course.

MRS. MIDGET — That might ease those 'orrid thoughts of yours a bit too, mightn't it?

TOM — It might.

MRS. MIDGET — Well then, ain't it worth it, sir?

TOM — Please don't keep calling me " sir." I'm not a gentleman really.

MRS. MIDGET — Aren't you, sir?

TOM — No, I'm not. If I were, I shouldn't be hesitating as I am. Mr. Examiner, help me. *You* must be experienced in making decisions.

THOMSON — No, boy, I can't help you in this. It's your own choice.

It is not an easy decision for Prior to make. He can't promise to be good. And he is thoroughly convinced that he isn't worth anybody's bothering about. But — he'll try!

Prior has gone back to the deck. Mrs. Midget is following happily after him. The Examiner smiles benignly upon her. " Good-bye Mrs. *Prior*," he calls. " You're a good mother!"

She turns ferociously to check him. " Blast you," she screams, " how did you find out?" But in a minute she is pleading pitifully that no one shall ever be told. And

when they promise her they will not tell she is joyously
happy again.

"Oh, sirs, ain't it wonderful?" she beams. "He
doesn't know me, and I've got him to look after at last
— without any fear of me disgracing him. It's 'Eaven,
that's what it is, it's 'Eaven!'"

The examinations are over and the Examiner is about
to leave. But as he turns toward the deck door Henry
and Ann suddenly reappear, bewildered and frightened,
still clinging to each other. Again Duke tries to put in
a good word for them, but Thomson cannot help. "He
gazes at them thoughtfully, then shakes his head as if
regretfully, and most tenderly. 'Not yet, my children,'"
he says as he passes out the door.

"Henry and Ann stand hopeless and bewildered, they
look from one to the other curiously; then, she, terror-
stricken in awful apprehension of the uncertainty of their
plight, at their being ignored, at the mystery of it all,
suddenly clutches Henry's arm and holds to him tightly."

There is a moment's darkness to indicate the passage
of hours. It is night again. "The moonlight pours
in through the portholes and through the center door
which is wide open — Scrubby is tidying up—Once more
the mysterious drum is heard, and Ann appears from
the deck."

The boat has sailed, and Ann and Henry have been
left behind. Why, they can't understand. They are unhappy and still fearful of that dreaded separation.
Henry, too, has imagined that he has heard his pet dog,
Jock — the one they had left staring in at the window
of their flat. Jock had barked — and there was a tinkling
sound, like the crash of glass. Henry's nerves are all
on edge because of the cries that rush in suddenly upon
him.

HENRY — And since we left that harbour I feel we are bound for some
dimly remembered place — Ann, I feel — a breeze like a breath of new — of
different air.

ANN — They didn't question us. Perhaps it's freedom.

HENRY — Ann, Ann, wife, wife. Don't let's get away from each other. We don't know where we are, we don't know what's becoming of us, or where we're going.

ANN — I don't really care what's becoming of me as long as I am with my husband. What else matters? But if *you* went away from me —

HENRY — It seems you're rather leaning on me now!

ANN — Shares, Henry.

HENRY — Shares, Ann.

ANN — You see, I love you. I love you so much. I love the way you walk, the way you hold your head. I love *you*. I love your mouth. (*Ann sits down. Henry kneels with arm around her.*)

HENRY — My wonderful Ann. They won't separate us now, will they, Ann? Nothing can take one from the other now?

ANN — Nothing — nothing.

HENRY — Keep close though, keep close — Are *you* cold?

ANN — (*takes hold of him*). No. I've got you, darling, I've got you.

HENRY — Never let go.

ANN — Why aren't we closer? I thought we would be when we were dead.

HENRY — I thought there would be no need for speech. That *we*, the *real* you and I would drift away together. Where is the utter completeness? Oh, Ann — Ann —

ANN — Supposing, after all, we were wrong.

HENRY — Wrong? — how wrong? What was that?

It is only Scrubby, come back to continue his tidying up. And now from him they learn why it is they have been left behind, and why they must always be left behind, and spend eternity making trips from shore to shore — as he has done. They are half-ways, like himself. " We're the people who ought to have had more courage," he explains; " more courage to face life."

ANN — Do you remember how you became a half-way?

SCRUBBY — Oh, no. I've been allowed to forget. I hope you'll be allowed to forget. It would be too cruel if they didn't let you forget in time that you killed yourselves.

ANN — Scrubby! (*A pause.*)

HENRY — (*cries out*). My God! that's it! Now I remember! Suicide!

SCRUBBY — Keep closer to him, madam.

HENRY — The people who ought to have had more courage! I see. *That's* what we've done that wasn't right.

ANN — Henry! (*Goes to him.*)

HENRY — The little bits are fitting together.

ANN — Dear, don't worry.

HENRY — Ann, I wanted to forget. Oh, don't say the damned torture's going to start all over again. We'd reached the end of our tether as it was. Ann —

ANN — I'm with you still. (*She stands behind his chair and puts her arms around him.*)

HENRY — But you can't face it, Ann, you can't stand it any more. I won't let you suffer — not another second. We'll kill ourselves, dear, and forget in each other's arms. Then we'll be so happy, sweet, so happy for ever. Oh, but it's over. We *have* killed ourselves. And we're *not* happy.

They had taken their own lives, they explain to Scrubby, because they realized the hopelessness of their great love and had given themselves to each other without the sacrament of marriage. And then, because they had been brave, they had been beaten down gradually by the malicious gossip of their friends until, finally, they had decided to wipe out the "one minute spiritual barrier between them," which, they believed, was death. And now they find themselves just the same as though they had never died.

Again Henry is assailed by memories of the dog, Jock. And there is a great longing in his heart to go back to life — just for a little while — to try again, to try to right the wrong he feels he has done Ann. There must be some way, he thinks. He will go on deck by himself, and perhaps it will be made clear to him.

"Don't let him go too far, madam. Call him, now," warns Scrubby.

From the deck Henry answers her halloo, but rather faintly. And when she calls again a moment later there is no answer. Wildly she runs to the deck, calling, calling — but there is no answer. Nor is there comfort in Scrubby's words when she appeals to him.

SCRUBBY — He has gone.
ANN — (screams). Henry! ! (To Scrubby.) You haven't looked.
SCRUBBY — Useless.
ANN — What do you mean? (Quiet now.)
SCRUBBY — I know what's happened to him.
ANN — What?
SCRUBBY — He lives again!
ANN — Lives! Henry gone back?
SCRUBBY — The dog, ma'am, outside the window. Perhaps broke through.
ANN — Henry is gone back, alone.
SCRUBBY — The dog, ma'am, outside the window! to resist the fumes, maybe.
ANN — Gone back. I'll follow him.
SCRUBBY — You can't.
ANN — Henry wouldn't leave me alone.
SCRUBBY — He couldn't help himself, madam.
ANN — But we've been dead a week —
SCRUBBY — A week! A century! A moment! There's no time here. He's gone back, madam.
ANN — Then I'll go too.
SCRUBBY — You can't.
ANN — I will. I must!
SCRUBBY — It's impossible.

Ann — *I will follow.* Henry! Henry! Henry, dear, where are you? It's Ann, dear. Where are you, baby? Just tell me where you are? *Where are you?* I'll come, darling. Just tell me. Henry! Henry!

Scrubby — He won't answer. (*Standing in shadows.*)

Ann — Henry! Henry, are you in the flat? I believe you are, Henry; you mustn't be there by yourself — you won't know how to manage anything.

Scrubby — It's useless.

Ann — I will follow him! I *will!* I will! Henry, listen, Henry. Our love, our great love. (*The drum is heard again.*) It's speaking, Henry, the little wedding ring, that wasn't a wedding ring at all — put it on my finger again. It's on the mantel-piece. Henry, don't leave me alone for ever. It's Ann, your Ann, who wants you. Henry! Henry dear! (*The drum stops.*)

Scrubby — Quiet! Quiet! I heard something out there — on the deck. (*Another pause, then Henry appears in the centre doorway.*)

Ann — (*without seeing him, still facing front*). Hello, Henry!

Henry — (*coming toward her*). Hello, Ann. Quick, dear, be very quick! There's only a second or two. I've come to fetch you home, dear! Ready, sweetheart? (*Holding out his hand.*)

Ann — Ready, Henry, ready! (*Turning and taking his hand.*)

Henry — We've such a lot to do, my love. And such a little time to do it in. Quick. Quick.

They go out together. The drum starts again very softly. Scrubby watches them go.

THE END

"THE GOOSE HANGS HIGH"

A Comedy in Three Acts

By Lewis Beach

OF the plays written with the younger generation and its alleged irresponsibility as a theme, none that New York saw last season scored as definitely pleasant an impression as Lewis Beach's "The Goose Hangs High."

Produced at the Bijou Theater January 29, 1924, it found a public immediately. A few of the reviewers acknowledged a half-suppressed fear that the story had too happy an ending to be wholly artistic, but they all admitted that as a transcript of life it was mostly true and observantly written.

Additional interest attached to this play's production by reason of its backing. The producers, the Dramatists' Theater, Inc., had been organized some months before by five active and successful playwrights — Edward Childs Carpenter, Owen Davis, James Forbes, Cosmo Hamilton, and Arthur Richman.

Their experiences in the theater had convinced them it was possible for authors to finance, direct and manage their own productions and they were eager to try. For one reason or another — perhaps they did it deliberately to prove the sincerity prompting their experiment — they selected a drama by an author outside their group as their first play. Mr. Carpenter handled most of the business connected with the enterprise and Mr. Forbes did a particularly good job as director of the rehearsals, while the other three probably were quite free with suggestions for improvements.

132

It is two days before Christmas when "The Goose
Hangs High" begins.   The scene is the living room of
the Bernard Ingals's home " in a small city in the middle
West."   It is a " charming, restful, Colonial living room,
obviously long lived in by people of breeding and taste
. . . . It is 5 o'clock in the afternoon.   The lamps are
lighted."

The Ingals, Bernard and Eunice, are still a happily
married pair, even though they have reached middle
age — happy in their mutual love and twice as happy
in their love of their children.   " They have charm and
distinction," reports the author, " and they will always
be respected.   One feels — on seeing them — that he
would like to know them personally.   Eunice is tall and
slender; a beautiful woman in her late forties.   Bernard
is fifty-one, thin, and fairly tall.   He has never lost his
youthful enthusiasm and his manner is often very boyish."

There is some natural family excitement incident to
the holiday preparations.   Two of the children, Bradley and Lois, the twins, are coming home from college.   But Hugh, the oldest, out of college six years and
working in New York, has written that he cannot make
it.   Which, seeing it is the first Christmas he has missed,
is rather distressing news to his fond mother.   However — She is one to make the best of it — even if her
husband does catch the glimmer of a furtive tear or two
on her cheek.   There must be some good reason for
Hugh's not coming — seeing they both had written him
offering to pay his fare.

Noel Derby drops in.   Noel is an old friend of the
family, and the nearest thing to a man chum Bernard
still clings to.   Their mutual interest in floriculture appears to be the thing they hold most in common.
They both love to work around growing plants and it
long has been Noel's ambition to induce Bernard to give
up the thing he is doing and join him in a greenhouse
business.   Right now he can buy a place at a great

bargain, and he has come again to see if there isn't a chance —

But there isn't. Bernard had rather own a greenhouse and grow plants and flowers than anything else he can think of — but when a man has two children in college, at the present cost of things — adventuring in business is one of the things he can't do.

A second caller is Leo Day. "Day is a handsome man in his early thirties, but he is quite without poise or breeding. He wears a fine raccoon coat, cutaway, spats, a derby tilted a trifle too much on one side, and he carries a stick. He has an unlighted cigar in his mouth. He does not take off his hat until he sees Eunice."

Day is one of the newly elected members of the City Council. This, his first call, is partly social, partly business, and entirely personal. The Ingals, to him, represent a stratum in local society to which he is hopeful of climbing. Eunice Ingals is Roger Bradley's daughter — and the thought of being an invited guest at the table of a Bradley intrigues the recently elevated politician. He is quite frank, even a little fresh, in saying so.

A moment later, with Noel Derby gone, Day has a chance to state the real object of his visit. He is, he reminds Bernard, entirely self-made. He was reared in the orphan asylum on the hill and often, as a kid, when he looked down upon the city he would tell the Mother Superior that some day he would be somebody in that city.

In pursuing that ambition consistently he has had himself elected councilman — not because he wanted the salary; any one of his thirty gasoline stations pays him more than he gets for lawmaking — but to help him get in with the right people. He has made his way through the business world, he has acquired money and he has achieved political distinction. Now he wants to get in with the right people socially. He wants the right kind of a wife. And he would like to have Bernard advise him.

DAY — . . . Is anything wrong with me?

BERNARD — Why, no!

DAY — Then what's the trouble?

BERNARD — I don't think there is any.

DAY — Then why aren't people taking me up? They certainly know about me. I've been in office a month but —

BERNARD — I don't believe local politics are much of a stepping stone to social advancement. But, Day, there's nothing in that.

DAY — I want it. I'm going to fight for it. And I want your help.

BERNARD — Oh, but I — I'm not in the social crowd.

DAY — You could be if you wanted to — and your children are. Well, what about it? Will you help me?

BERNARD — If I can do anything.

DAY — You can and you're going to.

BERNARD — What do you mean?

DAY — I've been snubbed — I'm not going to be again. I can do a lot for you at City Hall, Ingals, if you return the compliment. If you don't — (*Shrugs his shoulders.*)

BERNARD — (*surprised*). What?

DAY — I'm up for membership at the Country Club. You can help me.

BERNARD — I'm not a member.

DAY — But friends of yours are.

BERNARD — What do you mean, Day?

DAY — There's no use beating about the bush: I've got to have your help and I'm going to have it.

BERNARD — (*angered*). You mean part of my job as City Assessor is to help you socially?

DAY — Yes.

BERNARD — Good God! We've had unpleasantness at the City Hall — things have been particularly trying with some of the new councilmen, but — Day, I can't.

DAY — Why not? You mean you won't take me up?

BERNARD — No. But think, man, it's not square.

DAY — You want to keep your position?

BERNARD — Yes, of course. Why, I — (*stops.*)

DAY — Councilmen always have friends they want jobs for. And the friends can be damned insistent. But I'm for you if ——

BERNARD — (*breaking in*). You mean the council wants to get rid of me?

DAY — I don't say there's a plan actually on foot, but it's well for you to have me pulling for you. And I can make it worth your while, if —

BERNARD — No!

DAY — A check — or slip you some cash —

BERNARD — No!

DAY — Well, that's up to you. (*Laughs.*) I shan't insist on that. But I want you to speak to your friends at the Country Club — they vote next week. And what's the matter with inviting me here to dinner some night soon?

BERNARD — Day!

DAY — Why not? Would you be ashamed?

BERNARD — Oh, don't you understand? It isn't that. It's like taking a bribe.

DAY — Bah! To invite me to dinner, to tell your friends it'd be a good thing to have me in the Club? Why it won't hurt your conscience a damn bit. (*Pause.*) Well? It's just a part of your job, Ingals. And you want to keep your job.

BERNARD — (*does not look at Day*). I'll do what I can.

As Bernard closes the door on Day, refusing his tender of cigars and his kind offer to take him any place he wants to go in his waiting Mercer, " he stands still for a

moment, thinking. He is angry, but he is caught; he
can't do anything else." A moment later he has, a little
shamefacedly, asked Eunice if she thinks they might invite Day to dinner some day the following week, and
she, surprised, has replied cheerily: "Of course, dear,
if you'd like to."

Living with the Ingals is Eunice's mother, Mrs. Bradley. "Granny" is the family name for her. She is
just back from a walk, during which she picked up a
family friend, Julia Murdoch. "Julia is a rather large,
dark complexioned woman of middle age. She is dressed
as though she's just left a Fifth Avenue shop. Granny is
in her early seventies; she's rather small, physically, but
is an aristocrat through and through."

The talk is desultory, until it is turned into such chan-
nels of implied criticism as Granny sometimes likes to
employ. She has a favorite family complex — that the
Ingals children are a pampered set and that their parents
have quite deliberately made fools of themselves sacrificing everything for the children's happiness. In this
argument Julia Murdoch sides with Granny. She doesn't
approve of Eunice wearing her old clothes so Lois can
have a new frock. She doesn't, as a matter of fact, think
very much of the kind of education the children are getting. Which is the reason she and her husband had not
urged their son, Ronald, to go to college.

"At the time Cal and I didn't feel we could afford to
send him. I don't think so much of this college business
anyhow. It just gets it into their heads they're ladies
and gentlemen."

"Is that a bad thing?" Eunice asks.

"Oh, you know what I mean," Julia explains. "They
seem to think their parents are made of money and all
they have to do is have a good time. And where are
they when they graduate? They don't learn anything
about making money but every way to spend it. And as
for religion, college makes them all atheists."

Julia has also heard, she mentions incidentally, that Hugh Ingals and Dagmar Carroll are engaged. Which is news to the Ingals and a bit of a shock to Eunice, even though she doesn't believe it. And she asks Granny not to say anything about even the rumor to Bernard.

Bernard is back from the store, loaded with " cash and carry supplies " and bringing a missing present bought for Bradley — a rare volume that he needs in his work. Bradley hopes to be a painter and designer of stage scenery when he gets out of college. The book cost $30, but — as the parents repeat — he wants it.

" 'Wanting' and 'getting' mean the same thing in this house," Granny explains to Julia. " Oh, their goose hangs high!"

Eunice catches Bernard trying to unload his pockets without exposing a telegram among his papers. She is immediately anxious. Perhaps the children can't come! Perhaps one of them is ill! He is forced to show the wire to her to quell her fears. It is from Lois, and reads:

" Terribly sorry but I can't leave until you wire me fifty dollars with loads of love Lois."

BERNARD — You see.

GRANNY — (*disgusted*). Oh!

EUNICE — Oh, she won't get home tomorrow.

BERNARD — Yes, she will! The wire came three days ago.

EUNICE — Poor Lois, she always runs short at the last moment.

BERNARD — (*laughing*). Can't you see her, forgetting all about having to buy a railroad ticket? Next time I think I'll buy the ticket myself.

EUNICE — Do you suppose Bradley has enough money?

BERNARD — (*laughs*). Oh, we'd have heard from him if he hadn't.

GRANNY — Oh, you two make me tired! Julia, can't you bring them to their senses?

BERNARD — Well, Eunice, listen to that!

GRANNY — You let the children think you're made of money. They get anything they want.

BERNARD — Oh, no, they don't.

GRANNY — There's Eunice in a dress that's been made over and made over. You've even given up your greenhouse because it costs a few dollars to heat. And Eunice has gone without a maid all fall so you could send more money to them. And do you think they appreciate it?

EUNICE — Oh, Mother, they do!

GRANNY — If Lois didn't realize she had to save enough money to get home with, she should have been made to stay in school for the holidays. Oh, you can't blame them for trampling on you when you lie right down at their feet.

EUNICE — Mother, this isn't very pleasant for Julia.

JULIA — Oh, it's none of my business, I know. But I think your mother's
right. We've taught Ronald to do things for himself. He knows the value of
a nickel. How can any one appreciate *filet mignon* if he doesn't know what
round steak's like?

A moment later the excitement begins. First, and
without previous warning, Hugh Ingals, the unexpected,
appears suddenly in the doorway, with a cheery "Good
afternoon, Mr. and Mrs. Ingals." A second later his
mother has him in her arms and his delighted Dad is
pumphandling his arm with enthusiasm.

Hugh had no intention of coming, but he changed his
mind at the last minute — changed it because he could
not bear to think of the twins and his fond parents weeping over his empty chair at the Christmas feast. The
suspicious Julia, however, is inclined to think that Dagmar Carroll's coming home had something to do with it.
Hugh evades that issue. . . .

There is another commotion at the door, preceded by
the hearty yowling of " Hail, hail, the gang's all here!"
and followed by a march of the celebrants.

The twins are home. " Before anyone can move, the
street door is opened and Lois and Bradley tear into the
living room. Lois comes first; she has a hat box, an
ukulele, and three flower boxes. Bradley holds three
suitcases on his extended arms, a bag hangs from his
elbow, and golf clubs are strapped across his back. Immediately they take possession of the house and seem
to charge the atmosphere with electricity. They are in
their early twenties. At times they seem younger —
thoughtless, vapid creatures. Then they surprise by
abruptly revealing keen, informed minds. They're a fine-
looking, healthy pair who live every moment of the day.
There's great commotion throughout the following scene,
which is played with great speed. Every one seems to
be talking at once."

For the next five minutes something strongly resembling pandemonium reigns. Everybody has to greet
everybody else, and everybody does so heartily and

explosively. Even Granny is drawn into the whirling
enthusiasm of the homecoming, though you feel that a
moment later the strain on her nerves is going to tell —
which it does the moment Bradley drags Dazzler the
dog into the party. Still, there might easily be another
reason — " the three children make more fuss over the
dog than they have over their family," reports the author.
" The din is terrible."

Finally, as the scene quiets, the twins are induced to
tell how they got there, and why they did not write.
Bradley, it appears, aided and abetted by five other vaca-
tioners, had pooled his funds with theirs and bought a
considerably used Ford for $150. And six of them had
reached their homes in that, though not without a
struggle.

"Jack and Barron escaped with eight-fifty apiece —
they were dumped at Albany," Brad reports. " Ted,
fifteen; he lives in Syracuse; Jerry and Alan crawled
out at Toledo — they antied twenty-five dollars each.
Frank vamoosed at Detroit — his share was thirty-one;
and I picked Sis up at Fordville and made her pay five
dollars of my thirty-seven."

The children now, as apparently is their custom, take
charge of the house. Bradley, having sent on two
favorite Holbein prints ahead of him, unpacks them and
hangs them in place of the much-prized family portraits
of himself and Lois his mother has insisted on having
in the living room. Lois accepts and approves the new
dinner gown her mother has made her and immediately
begins picturing its first appearance. Their planning
and their thought is for and of themselves. Granny is
quite disgusted. She begs Julia to take her home
to dinner. " Not tonight — their first night!" pleads
Eunice. " Oh, I'll see enough of them before they get
away," significantly answers Granny.

Now the twins have bolted upstairs to freshen up.
Word has come that there is dancing at the Chapmans'

and they are keen to go over. Hugh is alone with his parents. He takes advantage of the moment to clear his mind of a secret he had planned to keep.

HUGH — . . .You know, Dagmar and I are engaged. (*Slight pause.*) Hang it all, we weren't going to tell any one just now. But Mrs. Carroll had suspicions; she got all worked up last night and Dagmar had to tell her. She swore her to secrecy but Mrs. Carroll blabbed it the first thing.

BERNARD — But why did you want to keep it secret?

HUGH — Oh, I don't know; we just did. Course we intended to tell you and the Carrolls but the others weren't to know till we were married.

EUNICE — It's to be soon then?

HUGH — Next month, we hope.

EUNICE — Hugh!

HUGH — It's the hardest thing to find the kind of apartment we want. We've been looking for a month.

BERNARD — Hugh — how about finances?

HUGH — I've enough saved to buy the furniture for a little apartment. Dagmar's going on with her work.

BERNARD — What?

HUGH — She wouldn't give it up for any one. As long as she feels that way I don't want her to. Neither of us has to pay much of an income tax; but we love each other so why shouldn't we get married?

EUNICE — I never dreamed you were in love.

HUGH — You've known Dagmar. Didn't you see I was bound to fall in love with her? She's the finest girl in the world — she's wonderful!

BERNARD — (*jesting*). In a month — better get my evening clothes out of mothballs, Eunice.

HUGH — The wedding isn't going to be here.

BERNARD — Then we'll have to go to New York.

HUGH — Oh, of course, it'd be great to have you there. But I think you'd have more fun if you'd wait and come on a little later. You see, we're just going to drop in on a minister some Saturday afternoon and then run over to Atlantic City for the weekend. (*Pause.*)

EUNICE — It's such a surprise — I can't understand why you've never said anything to me.

HUGH — You never asked. (*Laughs.*) You must have realized I'd get married some day.

EUNICE — Of course. but —— (*breaks off; goes to him.*) I hope you'll be very happy, Hugh. (*She kisses him.*)

HUGH — Thanks, Mother.

BERNARD — (*goes to Hugh*). I guess Hugh knows what we hope. (*Gives him his hand. Pause.*)

HUGH — But I don't see why there has to be such gloom about it.

EUNICE — (*quickly; almost beseechingly*). Oh, there isn't, Hugh, there isn't! We're happy for you.

It is a sad sort of happiness, however. Nor is it brightened perceptibly by the developments of the next few minutes. Lois is down again, proud of her record dressing, and bringing with her the gift she has bought for her mother's Christmas present. She just couldn't wait till Christmas. It happens to be a handsome ostrich feather fan that just matches Lois's costume.

"Dad, did you ever hear about the woman who gave her husband lace curtains for Christmas?" laughs Hugh.

But Lois dodges the impeachment. She really wanted her mother to have something nice. And so did Dad. And it was awfully sweet of him to wire the money.

Now Hugh, urged by Lois, has decided to run over to the Chapmans with the twins. Of course his father and mother won't care! Why should they? There will be lots of time to visit, and this will give him a chance to see all the old crowd! He is up the stairs in two bounds to get ready.

With the boys upstairs donning their makeup, Lois chats affably if a little critically with her father and mother.

LOIS — . . . You've a new council, haven't you?
BERNARD — Yes. And they're raising Cain.
LOIS — How so?
BERNARD — Upsetting everything. They act as though this was the first council the city ever had.
LOIS — Who are they?
BERNARD — Frank Monroe, John Teed, Elliott Kimberly ——
LOIS — (breaking in, interested). Not that terrible Kimberly who used to run a livery?
BERNARD — The same.
LOIS — But he's a crook! Good Lord, a hundred thousand people here and a man like Kimberly can get elected. Aren't people like you ever going to wake up?
BERNARD — (smiling). What do you mean?
LOIS — It makes me so damn mad!
EUNICE — Lois!
LOIS — (with increasing excitement). Mother, you ought to swear about it too! Decent people absolutely dodge their responsibility. (Bradley enters.) Look what you did about prohibition — let a lot of half-baked W. J. Bryans and W.C.T.U.'s turn us into law-breakers. The same busy-bodies that ——
BRADLEY — (cutting in). Who wound her up?
LOIS — It makes me furious! But if you go on sleeping the first thing you know there'll be a revolution. Then you'll wake up.
BRADLEY — Oh, get off the soap box, Sis!
LOIS — Yes, that's the whole thing — laissez faire.
EUNICE — Oh, Lois, come here.
LOIS — What is it? (Goes to Eunice.) Too much powder?
EUNICE — Just let me put my arms around you. I want to be sure ——
LOIS — What is the matter, old sweetheart?
BRADLEY — Speaking of the affairs of government. (Holding up a bottle of gin which he has taken from the suitcase.) There, Dad, with my compliments.
BERNARD — By George, where'd you get it?
BRADLEY — From one of the rising millionaires.
EUNICE — Bradley, you might have been arrested.
BRADLEY — I'd like to see any one go through my bag without a search warrant.

EUNICE — But in Cambridge ——
BRADLEY — When he delivered it the bootlegger had a policeman on the front seat of his car.
BERNARD — You're sure it's O.K.?
BRADLEY — One of the fellows analyzed it. If Prohibition continues, chemistry will be a required course in every high school. (*Hugh enters. Lois puts on her coat. Eunice helps her.*)
HUGH — All ready. (*Sees the gin.*) Ho! Fire-water!
BRADLEY — (*picking up his coat and hat*). I'll show you how to make the peppiest cocktail, Dad.
HUGH — I bet I can beat you. (*Goes to hall and gets coat and hat.*)
BRADLEY — Let me have the key to the car, will you, Dad?
BERNARD — (*gives him the key*). If you'd come home when you said you were coming it would have been washed.
BRADLEY — I'd hoped you might surprise us with a new one. If you don't get rid of the old bus soon you'll never be able to.
LOIS — Come along. Oh, Mother, do you mind putting my flowers in water? Ready, Hugh? (*Hugh and Lois go into the hall.*)
BRADLEY — (*following them*). We'll be back soon. Hugh, have you tried loganberry and gin?
HUGH — Grenadine and lemon juice are better.

They leave the house, laughing. The street door bangs. After a pause Eunice sits. Bernard goes to one of the windows and looks out. Rhoda comes from the dining room.

RHODA — Dinner is served.
EUNICE — All right, Rhoda. But there'll only be two after all.
RHODA — Have they gone again?
BERNARD — Yes.
RHODA — They didn't even say hello to me.
EUNICE — They didn't think, Rhoda. They didn't mean anything by it.
BERNARD — (*to Eunice*). You're not upset because they went off the first minute?
EUNICE — I'm glad they could go and have a good time.
BERNARD — So'm I, so'm I.
EUNICE — They're all right. They're all right.
BERNARD — They're great.
EUNICE — (*rises and goes to Bernard*). Come, dear, dinner'll get cold. (*Bernard puts his arm in Eunice's. They go toward the dining room.*)
BERNARD — George, I wish I'd had the car washed today. It looks pretty punk.

The curtain falls

ACT II

It is four days after Christmas, and the holiday decora-tions are still up. It is early evening and the Ingals family is at dinner. At least as many of the Ingals family as are at home.

Hugh is not with them. He has been at the Carrolls and now he and Dagmar Carroll sneak into the Ingals living room hoping to retrieve Hugh's pipe without arousing the family. "Dagmar is a tall, slight, dark-haired girl of Hugh's age. She has a great deal of distinction."

Hugh and Dagmar are very much in love and therefore extremely sensitive to each other's criticism. They are having some little trouble at the moment over the furnishing of the apartment they hope to have in New York. Hugh is strong for comfort, even though it means a conventional arrangement of the furniture. Dagmar is for comfort, too, but she feels strongly against robbing her home of all individuality.

Each of them, it develops, has made a rough sketch showing how their living room should be furnished, and now, with some little trepidation, they respectively submit them.

HUGH — You've put the smoking stand by the Windsor chair.

DAGMAR — You didn't back the sofa with a table.

HUGH — You can reach the magazines when you're stretched out on the sofa!

DAGMAR — There's a box for flowers at the windows! But where's that floor lamp of yours?

HUGH — You haven't left a space for that writing table you like. You must have it, Dagmar.

DAGMAR — No.

HUGH — I insist.

DAGMAR — My old desk will do.

HUGH — But I want you to have a new one.

DAGMAR — We'll save the money for something else.

HUGH — But you wanted it.

DAGMAR — We can't have everything. And, Hugh, we must have a portable table we can pull up to the fire for Sunday night supper. We've always planned that.

HUGH — (*hurries to her, drops on his knees, puts his arms round her*). Just you and I — no guests ever for Sunday supper? (*Dagmar shakes her head. They kiss.*) I'm sorry I was a brute.

DAGMAR — I wasn't laughing at you.

HUGH — It's because you're so wonderful that I'm always afraid I'm not half good enough.

DAGMAR — (*touching his hair*). Oh, my dear!

HUGH — Brad does know more about such things than I.

DAGMAR — I don't care how the apartment's furnished if you're there with me.

HUGH — My sweet! Oh, Dagmar, in a month — together in a month.

DAGMAR — It's the loveliest dream one could dream coming true.

HUGH — It is coming true. And nothing can spoil it.

DAGMAR — Nothing!

Bradley, coming from the dining room, surprises them in their embrace, but he doesn't mind. He is, he assures them, used to suffering.

Now Hugh and Dagmar have hurried on. Dinner is waiting for them at the Carrolls' and there really isn't time to wait and explain to Eunice.

In truth, Eunice has been pretty generously overlooked this day. Hugh was to call for her — and forgot. So she walked home in the rain and is chilled and unhappy as a result of that economy. Then Lois, who was expected to be home to dinner to meet Leo Day, the alderman, had been delayed down town and when she did come late — in a taxi she had to charge — she had just rushed upstairs to change for an evening party without letting anyone know.

Mr. Day, as it has turned out, did not come to dinner after all, thanks to young Bradley. There was something wrong with the gas at lunch, and when it had not been fixed by 5 o'clock and Day had called to find out at what hour he was expected for dinner, Bradley, meeting him in the hall, frankly assured him he did not see how there could be any dinner in that house that evening. Which sent the alderman away a trifle peeved.

Lois and her escort are off for a dance. Granny, more than ever disgusted with the children's lack of consideration for their father and mother, has gone next door to visit old Mrs. Holden, and Bradley is waiting for a chum to pick him up and wheel him over to the party, even though, as he tells his mother, he is not particularly keen to go.

BRADLEY — . . . Hang, I'm not keen for this dance tonight. Not much fun in being a stag.

EUNICE — Why didn't you invite some girl?

BRADLEY — Didn't get around to it in time. It's hardly fair to invite them in September for parties in December. And you have to if you want a girl. (*Stretches out on the sofa.*) Besides, how do I know I'll want to take her when the time comes? This whole woman business is pretty much of a nuisance, Mother.

EUNICE — Have you become a misogynist too?

BRADLEY — Hardly! I thrill at them too much. That's the nuisance. Ever read any D. H. Lawrence, Dad?

BERNARD — No.

BRADLEY — He sizes women up as deadly. They destroy — or want to. He thinks they should only be a functional thing with men. Course that'd do away with the family — but that wouldn't be so bad.

BERNARD — (surprised). What? You're against the family as an institution?

BRADLEY — Naturally! Everyone'd be a whole lot better off if the children were brought up by the State. You'd probably be taxed so much a head for us — but you shouldn't even have that responsibility. It's coming. Things are all wrong as they are now.

BERNARD — But, Brad, don't you feel — why, your mother ——

BRADLEY — (breaking in). Oh, I know what you're going to say, but that's sentimentalism. I'm all for the complete freedom of the individual, and sloppiness and family life raise Cain with it. I say, hand me that ash tray, will you? I'll spill the ash if I get up. (Bernard hands him a tray.) Thanks. Yes, sir, the sooner the family disappears as an institution the sooner the complete freedom of the individual will come. Sentimentality will disappear then. And sentimentality is enervating.

BERNARD — (really disturbed). But see here, Brad ——

BRADLEY — (breaking in). Just a minute, Dad. Take yourself — you really are a good sort.

BERNARD — Oh, come on!

BRADLEY — Oh, I'm not going to ask for money. Remember I sold that Ford. When you got through high school you were all for being a horticulturist, weren't you?

BERNARD — I'd thought of it.

BRADLEY — Well, why didn't you go through?

BERNARD — Well, I — Father really needed me in the store.

BRADLEY — You see — sentimentalism — you sacrificed yourself.

BERNARD — He wasn't well — he'd always been kind to me.

BRADLEY — Why shouldn't he have been? He was your father. But when the store was sold, why didn't you go in the nursery business then?

BERNARD — Oh — I don't know ——

BRADLEY — Because of Mother and us?

BERNARD — There were reasons.

BRADLEY — Were you afraid? (Bernard does not answer.) I'd like to see anyone persuade me to give up my life. Nothing can stop me. And our crowd's taken a solemn oath never to sacrifice art to money, no matter what the circumstances may be. This summer in Maine under Stiles will help me worlds. And when I've had a year or two in Europe I'll really be ready to get started.

BERNARD — You want to go to Europe after graduation?

BRADLEY — Ted and I've got it all fixed for summer after next. (Rises; throws cigarette into the fire.) Life's a damn fine thing if you know how to use it. (Pause. Stretches.) Mother, have I any clean white kid gloves?

EUNICE — I put a pair in the top drawer of your chiffonier this morning.

BRADLEY — Fine! (He turns and goes upstairs.)

It is plain that, seemingly for the first time since the children have come home for their holidays, Bradley's youthful and rather hard philosophy has hurt Eunice. She says nothing, but Bernard senses her disappointment, and tries to cheer her.

BERNARD — My dear — he doesn't know — he doesn't mean ——

EUNICE — I wonder.

BERNARD — (surprised). What?

Eunice — Am I getting old, supersensitive —? They seem to have become so callous, flippant ——

Bernard — They've really hurt you?

Eunice — We seem to mean —— (*Breaking off.*) But it's not we I'm thinking of. Oh, Bernard, we're responsible for what they are. Have we done the right thing?

Bernard — We did what we thought was right.

Eunice — We wanted to give them as fine a start as we could — to educate them — to let them know what is good and true. That's what we wanted to do. But have we bungled? (*Bernard turns away.*) Answer me, Bernard.

Bernard — I don't know, I don't know.

Eunice — If our giving has injured them ——

Before she can finish the doorbell rings loudly. Evidently Alderman Kimberly has arrived. And Bernard wants to see him alone.

Kimberly is a " large, big-bellied, coarse-grained man of 50. He's had a drink or two. He does not take off his hat during the scene." Also, it may be mentioned, Kimberly is furious. " Who in the devil do you think you are, Ingals?" he bawls; " God almighty?"

It appears that Kimberly, when he came into office as one of the new councilmen, had been instrumental in having Bernard's stenographer, a capable young woman who had worked in the office ten years, fired and a friend of his appointed in her place. Bernard, having done his best to put up with the incompetence of the newcomer, had finally been forced to tell her that she was unequal to the work. She had run to her friend the alderman with the story and he was now prepared to demand an accounting of Ingals.

Kimberly — . . . Well, Miss Plummer is a particular friend of mine. I'm your boss. I put her in your office and I want her to stay there. I expect you to apologize.

Bernard — (*furious*). What? (*Then taking himself under control.*) You're making it very difficult for me. I've been assessor for eighteen years. There's never been any complaint of the way I've done the work. But I don't seem to be able to satisfy you. Is it a feeling you have against me personally? It's getting almost unbearable.

Kimberly — Then why don't you quit?

Bernard — Why ——

Kimberly — You've had the job for eighteen years. Don't you think it about time some one else — or do you think you're indispensable? You're not!

Bernard — You mean — you want me to get out?

Kimberly — Did you scurry around and help elect me? Fat chance! But I'm in office. And I want people who worked for me, my friends, around me. And I'm not the only councilman who feels that way — and about you, too.

BERNARD — I didn't realize it was a game you were playing to get me out.

KIMBERLY — Either you do what I want you to do or I swing things against you. It's coming, Ingals! And don't forget Miss Plummer stays at her desk.

BERNARD — But, good God, Kimberly, I can't let incorrect statements leave the office, I can't see to every detail myself ——

KIMBERLY — (breaking in). It's your woman or mine.

BERNARD — What?

KIMBERLY — And naturally it's mine.

BERNARD — (beside himself with anger). Get out of here! Get out at once!

And Kimberly goes. Still smarting under the sting of his anger Bernard turns to his desk, adjusts his fountain pen and writes rapidly. He finishes quickly, having a letter signed, sealed and ready to deliver to Bradley when the latter starts for the party. He hesitates just a second before letting the letter go — but Brad has taken it out of his hand and is on his way before he knows it.

With Bradley and the letter gone Bernard is stricken with doubt as to the wisdom of his move. He runs to the door and tries to call his son back, but without success — He goes immediately to the telephone, calls a number and begs the person at the other end to please have Bradley Ingals call his home the minute he arrives. He calls another number and asks that Mr. Kimberly be given word to call Mr. Ingals as soon as he returns.

Eunice, finding him in an excited state, is worried. She tries to divert his mind by talking of Bradley and his ambitions as a scenic artist. It is no use. A fear has laid hold of Bernard that he cannot shake off. Another moment he is at the phone again, trying to head young Bradley off. Presently he is getting into his coat with the idea of stopping the letter at the postoffice. Finally he is forced to confess to Eunice what he has done and the importance of his getting the letter back.

BERNARD — Oh, I've been a fool — an impetuous, mad fool. Eunice, I've resigned.

EUNICE — What?

BERNARD — Given up my position — as though I were wealthy, independent.

EUNICE — I don't understand.

BERNARD — (quickly and excitedly). Kimberly was here — he provoked me

— drove me — I lost my temper — I guess that's what he's been trying to do — I didn't see.

EUNICE — Driving you?

BERNARD — For weeks — ever since the new council came into office — it's been hell there at the City Hall. Day's been threatening. Tonight Kimberly practically said I had to be his slave to hang on — he said — he made me wild — I ordered him out of the house — and then I actually wrote out my resignation and gave it to Brad to mail.

EUNICE — Bernard!

BERNARD — Kick me, call me fool, idiot —

EUNICE — No!

BERNARD — I deserve everything.

EUNICE — I'm glad you did what you did.

BERNARD — (amazed). Eunice!

EUNICE — Why didn't you resign when they first began — ? (Telephone rings.) Let me go.

BERNARD — I'll —

EUNICE — (goes quickly to telephone). It's Brad — I'll talk to him. (At telephone.) Hello — yes, Brad — that letter your father gave you to mail — well, put it in the box now.

BERNARD — Eunice, don't you see? I've got to have a job.

EUNICE — Are you afraid you can't get one elsewhere?

BERNARD — Can a man my age just walk into a good salaried position? Haven't I already tried to find one?

EUNICE — I'd rather starve than have you lick boots.

BERNARD — Yes, I know you'd go through with me. But what about them — our children? (Eunice starts.) If I've no job they can't go back to college, and — You see now? (Pause.)

EUNICE — (fearfully). Oh, Bernard, what have we done?

BERNARD — " We?" You've nothing to blame yourself for. I'm the one who has failed them.

EUNICE — (taking hi hand). Oh, I love them so, and I'm afraid.

BERNARD — What will they do? What will they say?

EUNICE — (terrified). Suppose they — No, no! I can't. Bernard, we must do something.

BERNARD — I'll fix it some way. I'll go to the City Hall early in the morning. I'll get that letter. I'll make Kimberly and Day ——

EUNICE — No.

BERNARD — I can even play their game if necessary.

EUNICE — You can't go back there.

BERNARD — Of course I can. It's not so bad.

EUNICE — To let you dishonor yourself to give them money — no. That would be like having you steal for them. It would be criminal of you and me. They can't have it if that's the price.

Granny is back from Mrs. Holden's. Perhaps, thinks Eunice, Granny would help. Guardedly she suggests as much. Bernard, she explains, has lost his position, and there is a question as to whether the twins can finish their college work. The expense the previous year was something like $3,000. It might, of course, be cut a little, but it would probably take something like that sum. And if Granny could advance it, why ——

But Granny is not of a mind to lend them a cent.

"Not even sure where your own bread's coming from, but you'll borrow to keep them in luxury!" She sneers a little as she makes the charge. She is perfectly willing to help Bernard and Eunice, but not the children. Already they have been made vain and empty headed by too much coddling.

GRANNY — For years you've denied yourself for them. With the money Bernard's father left him, he could have gone into business for himself. No, it had to be saved for them. It saw Hugh through college. But what's he done in the six years since he graduated? Has he paid you back?
BERNARD — We never wanted or expected him to.
GRANNY — And for the last two and a half years everything you could get your hands on has gone to the twins. You've simply poured affection on them — you wanted to keep them laughing. From the time they were infants — you dropped everything to answer their demands.
EUNICE — To find out why they asked for it — sympathy ——
BERNARD — Eunice, what's the use?
GRANNY — Well, you ought to see what your sympathy has done for them. I don't blame the children — it's not their fault — but yours. You've only yourselves to blame.
EUNICE — Don't think of them. Think of me. I'm asking you ——
GRANNY — That's what I am doing. (Rises.) And I say no. Oh, I pity you, you fools. But you must face it. You've had it coming to you.
EUNICE — What do you mean?
GRANNY — What do you think they're going to do now?

Granny flounces up the stairs and leaves them discouraged and puzzled. This much they know they must face: with Bernard's position gone, willing as they are to make every sacrifice, college for the children will be impossible for the present. And the children must be told. That's the hard part —" Don't tell them tonight. Let them be happy while they can be," pleads their father. " How long the night will be," sighs their unhappy mother. " But I don't want it to pass. Oh, I can't sit still and think! Let's do something — let's walk — fast — till we're tired —— "
Granny hears them leaving the house — hears Eunice tell Bernard to leave the door unlocked for fear one of the children has forgotten the key. She hurries down as the door slams — evidently of a mind to call them back. They have doubtless started in search of funds, she thinks. But they are out of reach of her voice. For a moment she is soberly thoughtful, but there is firmness of purpose

in her decision when she makes it. She is at the phone calling the Carrolls and asking for Hugh as the curtain falls.

A half hour later Bernard and Eunice are still walking. Lois, Hugh and Bradley have been rounded up and told the truth by their grandmother. "Your father has lost his position! He's bankrupt! You can't go back to college! That's what's happened!"

With which succinct statement of facts she leaves them to their own reactions.

"There is complete silence. They do not move a muscle of their bodies. Finally Hugh speaks."

HUGH — (*quietly*). Poor Dad.

LOIS — Oh, where are they?

BRADLEY — It's beastly for him and Mother.

LOIS — (*with a movement of her hands*). Like that — everything. (*Loudly.*) No, no! I don't believe it.

BRADLEY — Kimberly was here —

HUGH — (*almost with a cry; as though she were slipping away from him*). Dagmar!

LOIS — (*turning toward Hugh; surprised*). What? (*Then realizing what's in Hugh's mind.*) No, Hugh, no! Everything can't stop so suddenly.

BRADLEY — (*very quietly*). "You can't go back to college." (*The matter is settled as far as he's concerned.*)

LOIS — What does it mean? Why? Everything was all right. Bankrupt. There's always been money. Where's it come from if — ?

HUGH — Dad's lost his position. (*Loudly.*) Oh, don't you see? Everything has gone to us.

BRADLEY — (*amazed*). What?

HUGH — Oh, God, what fools we've been! Oh, they had no right! It was wrong! I've never questioned.

LOIS — I couldn't have taken if I'd known. I'm not so low.

BRADLEY — It makes us seem like bloodsuckers. (*Pause. Lois bursts out laughing.*) Don't! Sis!

LOIS — It *is* funny. Don't you see? The bottom's fallen out of everything. Where are we at? What's going to happen now?

BRADLEY — I tell you it's wrong, wrong! They shouldn't have had this responsibility. Giving us till —

HUGH — (*breaking in*). "Responsibility?" It was love made them give.

LOIS — There's a girl at college. She never gets a letter from home but they tell her what they're sacrificing to keep her there. She's sick — a melancholic — her mind's warped —

BRADLEY — Dad wanted to be a horticulturist — he's sacrificed — No! You don't give up what you care for most! You can't! (*Suddenly realizing.*) Oh, my God, for us, for us. *We* are what they care for most. Oh, what are we? Oh, to put such a burden on a person — to force him to live up to your ideals. It's too much! It isn't fair!

HUGH — (*quietly*). Life and love. Brad — you can't get away from it.

LOIS — But other parents — that girl at college — is that love?

HUGH — I don't know, I don't know.

LOIS — (*trying to think it out*). Selfish love, unselfish —

BRADLEY — (*suddenly; pulling the letter from his pocket*). Wait! I took this letter from Dad to mail. I forgot. Then they called me. Mother told me to put it in a box at once. But I could hear Dad shouting " No! No!" I didn't know what to do.

HUGH — Who's it for?

BRADLEY — (*reading the address*). " The Council of the City of

LOIS — (*cutting in*). Open it.

HUGH — (*hesitates; then*). Yes. (*The children's distaste for this sort of thing is evident. But they feel the circumstance justifies, rather than forces them, to open the letter.*)

BRADLEY — (*unseals letter and reads*). " . . . Please accept my resignation as City Assessor to take effect immediately. I cannot go on longer . . ."

LOIS — What? He resigned?

BRADLEY — " I cannot go on longer — " (*breaking off.*) Mother told me to mail it. Dad — (*Hugh takes the letter from Bradley; reads it.*) They told me at the hall my father was trying to reach me. But Mother —

HUGH — I'd scarcely recognize his writing — why, he's even left an " s " out of assessor, a word he's written for years.

BRADLEY — Kimberly was here while I was upstairs — then Dad wrote the letter — Kimberly must have given him hell. By God! (*Hurries to his coat; picks it up.*)

LOIS — Where are you going?

BRADLEY — (*putting on his coat*). Never mind!

On his way out Brad takes the letter with him. He'll not forget to mail it this time, although Hugh warns both the twins that they must weigh well what it means to them. If it is not sent they probably can go back to college.

" Be honest with yourselves," he warns the young individualists. " Oh, *please,* no false sentiments. *Don't do anything you don't want to do.*"

But their minds are made up. The letter is readdressed to the council and Brad takes it.

Lois and Hugh try to put as cheerful a face on the matter as possible. In their hearts there is a secret exultation that they want to meet this particular crisis decently. It is a wrench for Hugh to think of his and Dagmar's plans being smashed, but he refuses to compromise. He writes a check for the savings that were to provide for the wedding and the apartment that he may have it ready. And Lois — finding that she isn't so very different from other daughters — realizing what it would have meant to her if the news that had brought her home had meant she would never have been able to talk to her Dad again — is glad of her chance to do even a little to help.

When Bernard and Eunice return — they have only been walking a half hour, though it seems hours to them — they are pretty wretched. They find Hugh building a fire, and trying bravely to appear as though nothing had happened.

When Lois comes, she, too, would convey the impression that quitting a dance thus early is a most natural proceeding for her. She was disgusted with her escort, she explains. The idiot! He had proposed on the way *to* the party! Could anything be more stupid?

Besides, she wanted to come home to talk to them. She suddenly has come to a great decision. She is not going back to school. She has had enough of it. Too much, in fact. Anyway ——

Before they can quite grasp the meaning back of this announcement, in bursts Bradley. He is pretty well dishevelled and he fears he may be followed by a policeman. He has just taken a punch or two at Alderman Kimberly. He never had liked Kimberly — not since he kicked his dog something like fifteen years back. Which so pleases Lois that she takes his breath by throwing her arms around him. And his mother, as she begins to grasp the situation, encircles him in another embrace and cries a little on his shoulder. "Even Mother falls for the vim and vigor stuff!" Brad chuckles.

And the joke of it, as it happens, is that it wasn't Kimberly at all who had kicked Brad's dog — but Sam Streeter.

There is still a faint hope in Bernard's mind that the resignation has not been sent. But Brad's announcement that not only had he mailed the letter but registered it, does for that. "Just wanted to prove that for once I had remembered to do something," says he, cheerfully.

BERNARD — That settles it. (*Seems to crumple up.*)
LOIS — (*going to him*). Don't, Dad, don't.
BERNARD — (*rising immediately*). You must know. I've done a very foolish, dastardly thing.
EUNICE — Bernard, please!
BERNARD — I've failed you. I've gone back on —

EUNICE — (*breaking in*). It's not true. Don't you believe him.

HUGH — (*quietly*). Dad, we know, all of us. Granny told us.

BERNARD — What?

BRADLEY — The council ousted you. That's all.

BERNARD — That isn't true. I —

HUGH — (*quickly*). Everyone knows what they are. Of course they couldn't appreciate you.

BERNARD — Hugh, please!

HUGH — You'll get into another berth — and a better one right away. But until you do, well you and Mother may feel just a little more comfortable if — (*Pulls the check from his pocket and tries to put it into Bernard's hand without the others seeing.*) I don't need it just now. (*Laughs; whispers.*) Bank on me.

(*Bernard does not realize that it is a check. He unfolds it.*)

BERNARD — Oh, no!

EUNICE — You sha'n't, Hugh.

HUGH — (*simply*). I've never been able to do anything that's made me so happy.

BERNARD — Oh, God! Eunice —

HUGH — Oh, I wish I could tell you — there's so much — I don't know how to say it.

EUNICE — Hugh, if you kiss me, that will say — (*Hugh takes her tightly in his arms and kisses her.*)

BRADLEY — You do know where we stand?

EUNICE — Yes. And I'm ashamed.

BRADLEY — Whatever do you mean?

(*Eunice looks at the children. She seems to be begging for forgiveness. Then she speaks.*)

EUNICE — Oh, I can't tell them, Bernard! But children, don't be afraid to show what you feel — ever.

LOIS — I don't understand.

EUNICE — Love's too beautiful to be hidden. (*Pause.*)

BRADLEY — Good Lord, but I'm hungry.

LOIS — So'm I. Why, I haven't eaten anything since tea.

EUNICE — I'll get a lunch.

HUGH — Come on, you twins. Let's raid the ice-box.

BRADLEY — Right! Sandwiches — dozens of them.

LOIS — We'll call when it's ready. (*Lois and Hugh go into the dining room.*)

BRADLEY — (*following them*). And Dad, if a policeman should come, remember he has to show the warrant before he gets in. (*Goes out. There is a slight pause. Then Bernard jumps to his feet.*)

BERNARD — (*with great determination*). God, I'm not beaten! Eunice, what must you think of me?

EUNICE — Dear, I understand.

BERNARD — I must carry on.

EUNICE — We can and we will.

BERNARD — Oh, Eunice, come, I'll get them to take me back.

EUNICE — (*with a restraining gesture*). Please.

BERNARD — If I can do for the children I sha'n't mind about Kimberly.

(*Bernard crumples the check and throws it into the fireplace.*)

EUNICE — (*turns, faces Bernard, and takes his hands in hers*). No, dear. But we'll find some way.

BERNARD — Maybe they think they're going to run this roost now. God bless them! But they're not!

The curtain falls

ACT III

It is morning of the following day. The Ingals family, having straggled in to breakfast, is straggling out again. Bernard is hurrying off to town when Hugh stops him. There is still the matter of the proffered check between them. Bernard had tossed it into the fireplace, but missed the fire. Hugh found it and is again insistent that his father take it. " I've always — dreamed that some day I could do — something fine for you and Mother," he half stammers, a little ashamedly. " But I just forgot how much little things could mean."

But Bernard is still firm, though greatly appreciative, and the coming of Dagmar and Eunice from the dining room gives him a chance to escape without giving Hugh a definite answer.

It isn't easy for Hugh to tell Dagmar that their plans will have to be changed; that they can't rent and furnish the apartment; that they can't even be married for some time. But he manages it finally:

HUGH — Do you understand, dear, how I feel? I want to give to them. It isn't conscience. It's love. (*Slight pause.*) So I have the courage to ask you to wait.

DAGMAR — Of course, Hugh.

HUGH — But do you understand?

DAGMAR — Yes, dear. It's beautiful.

HUGH — Oh, please!

DAGMAR — It is beautiful because it's love. Oh, don't ask me to explain why I know. Some children do things for their parents because of convention, public opinion, because they've been told it's the thing to do. If you did it just because you thought it your duty — as one's ashamed to pass a beggar — I believe I could hate you. But it's not sentimentality. It's real and true.

(*Hugh takes her hungrily in his arms. Dagmar puts her arms around his neck.*)

HUGH — My darling, I adore you. I want you, Dagmar. Don't think that I ——

DAGMAR — (*breaking in*). It will be hard, dear, to wait. Sometimes I shall probably beg you to forget them. I will cry for you. Don't listen to me then. If you do, some day I'll not love you as I do now.

HUGH — Dagmar!

DAGMAR — But, Hugh, when the day comes — Oh, dear, if we can inspire such love in our children — then our love will take on greatness.

HUGH — But, dear, don't all children feel — why you — ? (*Dagmar leaves him; shakes her head.*)

DAGMAR — No.

HUGH — But — ?

DAGMAR — Don't ask me. So many parents believe that simply because they bring children into the world they take out a patent on their love — it

Now the force of the blow falls on Granny. She hears Eunice 'phoning the want ad department of the town's newspaper to advertise two furnished rooms for rent after January 1. The twins will have gone back to school then and their rooms will be available.

The thought is shocking to Granny! A Bradley renting rooms! Lodgers in the home of one of the first families! She won't have it. The house is hers, really, even if Bernard does rent it from her. Then, Eunice tells her, it will be necessary for them to get another house. She is even cheerful at the thought. Nothing much matters now. The children — her children — have met the test and stood firm.

"It isn't the little things that reveal character," she says, a little proudly. "They'd seemed hard, indifferent. That's the outer spirit of the time. But if deep inside there's truth, who are we to criticize? Maybe they're finer. I believe they are. They're more honest and unafraid — If they had turned on us I could not have blamed them. I would have known I was the one who had failed. That's why I was afraid."

Bradley and Lois dash in from the street. They have been at their job early, and it is apparent from their manner that there have been developments — developments in which Granny is destined to figure. They are quite frank in hinting that they would like their mother to leave them with Granny — alone.

That being arranged they all but startle the old lady out of her wits by seating her mysteriously upon the sofa between them and asking her soberly if she has ever thought about dying? Not right away, of course, but some time? She admits that the idea may have occurred to her.

BRADLEY — Granny, how much do you know of what's happened?
GRANNY — I know that your father's lost his job. That he's got no money.

And that he's pretty much of a fool — and your mother too, though she is **my** daughter.

BRADLEY — And what do you think's going to become of him?

GRANNY — I can't see anything but the poorhouse or insane asylum.

LOIS — The asylum would be awful enough. But the poorhouse! The husband of a Bradley — maybe a Bradley herself. Oh, Granny, you couldn't endure that.

GRANNY — Rather the poorhouse — there's more than one fine family ended there — than tradespeople, shop girls, clerks living here.

BRADLEY — What do you think of street cleaners?

GRANNY — Street cleaners?

BRADLEY — Icemen, milkmen?

GRANNY — I don't!

LOIS — Well, Dad will have to do something. He's too able-bodied to get into the poorhouse.

GRANNY — What are you driving at?

BRADLEY — (*seriously*). Granny, he's fifty years old.

GRANNY — Fifty-one.

BRADLEY — It's going to be pretty difficult for a man of his age to step into a good position.

GRANNY — I dare say.

BRADLEY — A respectable one, I mean. Fine concerns want young chaps — like me, for instance.

GRANNY — Do they?

BRADLEY — Yes. Of course, the other fields are open to him — soda fountains, haberdashery stores, street-car conducting —

GRANNY — (*already feeling herself insulted*). What?

BRADLEY — He hasn't your pride, Granny. He'll feel he must do something.

LOIS — Oh, Bud, wouldn't it be awful to see him carrying a sign through the streets — a sandwich man, everybody staring, saying " Eunice Bradley's husband," " Mrs. Roger Bradley's son-in-law."

GRANNY — (*unable to sit still*). Stop it! Stop it!

BRADLEY — That Swede who runs the gasoline station on the corner — he's always been friendly — Sis, maybe he'd let Dad squirt gas into people's cars.

GRANNY — Oh, how can you?

LOIS — It's terrible, Granny. But we've got to face it.

GRANNY — Never!

LOIS — Then what can you suggest? We've racked our brains.

GRANNY — Can't you think of something that *is* all right?

BRADLEY — He might start a second-hand clothes store. (*Acting it out.*) You know the way they come sidling up to you intimately on the street and sort of whisper — " Any old clothes to-day, Madam?"

GRANNY — I'd make Eunice divorce him.

LOIS — But she'd still be Mrs. Bernard Ingals.

GRANNY — Oh, can't you think of anything respectable for him?

LOIS — What can you suggest?

GRANNY — Think! Use your heads! What were you sent to college for?

BRADLEY — Let's see — the most respectable thing in the world — a church. Sis, he might get a job as janitor.

GRANNY — No, no!

LOIS — He'd have to mow the grass, shovel the snow —

GRANNY — I've got some money.

Thus is the old lady's mind prepared for their great scheme. They have been talking with Noel Derby, and Noel has told them of the market gardener's place he can buy dirt cheap. If Dad, for instance, could go in with Noel, and they could buy the place and realize their dream of starting a nursery! Wouldn't that be great? Of course Dad wouldn't think of taking Granny's money — but if she were to buy the place with Noel, and then hire Dad to look after her interests? Wouldn't that be wonderful?

Before she quite has time to resent the conspiracy there is Noel Derby at the door beaming with joy at the thought of the plan! Another minute and the children have herded Granny and Noel upstairs to settle the details.

Which probably would have been simple if Bernard did not suddenly appear with a new complication. He also had fixed things. His resignation has been refused — and everything is as it was before anything happened.

BERNARD — Brad, you and Lois can go back just as you'd planned.

EUNICE — Dear, please explain.

BERNARD — (*taking off his coat; exuberantly*). I went into Day's office. He almost embraced me; his application for membership in the club was accepted. He thinks I'm responsible. He was furious — frightened — when he heard of the resignation. Wouldn't hear of my getting out. He called the councilmen together. Kimberly and Sands, of course, wanted to accept it. But Day, Teed, and Monroe refused. So I'm back. Oh, isn't it great! (*Eunice shudders. The others do not move; they are aghast.*) Oh, Brad, Kimberly has got a black eye. But he says he fell. (*Pause.*) Well, can't any of you say anything? You might at least congratulate me. Lois, what's your chum's address? We'll wire her not to cancel that room reservation. (*Starts toward telephone.*)

LOIS — Oh, damn!

BERNARD — Eunice, can't you speak?

EUNICE — I've nothing to say.

BERNARD — Is something the matter with all of you? Do you realize what I've said? I've got my job back! Hugh, I don't need your assistance. And Lois and Bradley go east on Monday.

But it is not as easily rearranged as that. Lois is not going back. She has accepted a position at Wingate's. Neither is Brad going back. He has found himself a job with the local stock company. Part of the time he expects to carry a spear and the other part he will spend painting scenery. Hugh and Dagmar have also made other arrangements. Having deposited their home fund to Dad's credit so the twins can go back to school, they are prepared to wait ——

But they are all reckoning without Dad himself. He listens patiently and appreciatively to their fine plans for him. But when they begin to raise their voices, Hugh

insisting the twins shall go back to school and the twins
insisting they will not, he takes a hand:

BERNARD — (*more loudly and furiously than they*). Silence! All of you!
(*The children are amazed at this strange tone from Bernard, and to see him
so angry.*) If you think you're going to run things here you're sadly mistaken.
A lot of nerve you had, doing what you've done without my permission. But
I still am boss.
HUGH — That's the stuff, Dad!
BERNARD — I mean you too. You're as bad as they are.
HUGH — But, Dad —
BERNARD — I don't want to hear another word from any of you.
EUNICE — Bernard!
DAGMAR — I think I'd better go.
BERNARD — No! You're in this too. Stay here. The twins go back to
college.
BRADLEY — Dad!
BERNARD — And Dagmar and Hugh are getting married. (*To Hugh.*) How
dare you deposit money to my account?
HUGH — (*weakly*). I thought we'd —
BERNARD — Well, we hadn't!
LOIS — I won't, Dad, I won't!
BERNARD — Did you hear me say to be quiet?
BRADLEY — But, Dad —
BERNARD — I meant it.
EUNICE — (*appalled*). Oh, what are we doing? We've never quarreled.
BERNARD — There's no quarreling. I've said my say and that's the end of
it. (*Turns.*) I'm going for a walk.
LOIS — (*desperately*). Mother, what can we do?
BERNARD — Don't try and get your mother mixed up in this. I'm going
to buy your Pullman reservations. (*Hugh runs upstairs.*) Bradley, telephone the
theater and resign at once.
BRADLEY — You've never talked to us this way before.
BERNARD — Not since the last time you tried to disobey me. I thrashed
you then. I can do it again.
EUNICE — Oh, let's calm down. Let's —
BERNARD — (*breaking in*). Eunice, I asked you to be quiet.
EUNICE — (*amazed*). Bernard!
LOIS — I never knew you were such a stubborn —
BERNARD — You go call up Mr. Wingate.
LOIS — I tell you I will not.
BERNARD — Lois, do as I say.

Noel Derby does not help much when he comes gaily
down stairs to congratulate Bernard on their new business.
He and Granny have settled all the details and Bernard
is to be hired — but for a salary that will not be big
enough to allow him to spend too much on the children.

Bernard does not like that suggestion. He is still able
to decide such matters for himself, and he does not like
their somewhat patronizing disposition of him.

BERNARD — (*to Granny*). There's a string to it? You mean I can't be my
own boss in my private affairs? Thank you, no!

Eunice — Mother doesn't mean that, Bernard. But if you go back to the City Hall I'll leave you.

Bernard, Granny and Noel — Eunice!

Hugh, Lois and Bradley — Mother!

Dagmar — Mrs. Ingals!

Eunice — I shall! I will not have that.

Bernard — Eunice, how can you — ?

Hugh — He can't go, Mother. We won't let him.

Bradley — I'll black Kimberly's other eye if necessary.

Bernard — It's a conspiracy.

Lois — (putting her arm in his). Oh, Dad, don't you understand? You and Mother have always stacked the pack to give us all the face cards and aces. But you have taught us the game. We know how to play.

Bradley — We can't cheat.

Bernard — But your work, children, we want you to go on with it.

Bradley — Whatever makes you think I shan't? Good Lord, you don't think I'd give it up?

Bernard — But if you turn to something else —

Bradley — But I'm not. Why, I need the practical experience round the theater.

Lois — I think I want to do advertising. But I shan't stick if I've a wrong hunch. Why, I may even end up a rum-runner. Or daub scenery — like Bud.

Bradley — You?

Eunice — Well, Bernard?

Bernard — What can I do?

Eunice — We can't dictate in this. We haven't the right. But, dear — (puts her hand on his arm). We'll be ready — to carry on.

Noel — Don't you understand, Bern? It was they who came to me this morning?

Bernard — The children?

Noel — Yes. Oh, these parents who rave because their children don't love them — why don't they look into their own hearts?

Hugh — Dagmar, what are we going to do?

Eunice — (going to them). If you could be married before you leave!

Bernard — (brightens). Of course, they can!

Eunice — If it's right with your mother and father?

Dagmar and Hugh look at each other. Then they embrace. Lois and Bradley hurry to them. Granny turns to them — even she is pleased at the idea of a wedding.

Lois — What will you wear?

Bradley — Can I be best-man?

Noel — It's " yes," Bern?

Eunice — (going to Bernard and Noel). It is " yes," Noel.

Bernard — But, Eunice, it's adventuring. You said yourself we must be ready.

Eunice — We will be! Don't you see?

Bernard — Eunice!

Eunice — We'll all be ready always.

THE END

BEGGAR ON HORSEBACK

A Fantastic Comedy in Two Parts

BY GEORGE S. KAUFMAN AND MARC CONNELLY

UNQUESTIONABLY if the manuscripts of all the foreign plays that are even now kicking around the offices of the New York producers were gathered up and laid end to end they would make an impressive magazine story.

"Beggar on Horseback," up to and including a part of last season, was one of these. It was known then, I believe, as "Hans Sonnenstoesser's Hohlenfahrt." The Theater Guild had it and passed it by. Several other managers were consulted and could see nothing promising in its possibilities.

Then it came to Winthrop Ames's attention and he saw a play in it. Suggesting to him a modern satire he naturally thought first of George Kaufman and Marc Connelly as the best of working collaborateurs to whom to turn it over. Their success with "Dulcy," "To the Ladies" and "Merton of the Movies" had brought them prominence as two who delight in calling attention to the native weakness for boastfulness in achievement. The pretense and affectation that are so common and so pitiful a part of the exhibition given by the new rich are a favorite target with them.

"Beggar on Horseback" represents, as Alexander Woollcott has written in the preface to the published version of the play, "the distaste that can be inspired by the viewpoint, the complacency and the very idio of Rotarian America. It is a small and facetious di

160

turbance in the rear of the Church of the Gospel of Success."

The original play was no more than a story to its adapters. Mr. Ames told them the general scheme of it and they fashioned their own American version. An important feature of the play, the pantomime called "A Kiss in Xanadu," was not included in the original version, and the authors give entire credit for its creation to Mr. Ames.

"The Beggar" was first played in New York the night of February 12, 1924, at the Broadhurst Theater, achieved an immediate popularity and easily ran out the season.

The scene is the apartment of a young composer, Neil McRae. The living room, in which the action begins, "is plainly an artist's room, and furnished with as many good-looking things as the occupant could afford — which are not many. The most luxurious piece of furniture in the room is a grand piano, which Neil has probably hung on to with no little difficulty. The door into the apartment is at the right — somewhere beyond it is the elevator, and one needs only a look at the room to know that it is an elevator that requires four minutes to ascend the three floors. The time is about four thirty of a spring afternoon."

A young man lets himself into the room, after getting no response to his knock. He is followed shortly by a young woman, a suspicious young woman, who might think he was a gentleman burglar if she believed the combination possible. He is, it transpires, Dr. Albert Rice, an old friend of McRae's. And she is Cynthia Mason, a comparatively new friend of the same young man.

The doctor is pausing briefly on a visit from Chicago. Miss Cynthia lives across the hall and sometimes she sort of looks after young McRae, who isn't exactly practical. For example, this very afternoon he has invited folks to tea and apparently done nothing more about it.

Rather important visitors, too. The Cadys of Livingston, which happens to be the home town of both Dr. Rice and Neil. Gladys Cady has been studying piano with Neil — is, in fact, his only pupil. Not that he wants to give music lessons, but — well, he has to do something. Writing symphonies doesn't pay particularly well at first.

Neil is home now, loaded down with an armful of books and a music portfolio — the books expensive editions he had no business buying, the music certain cheap orchestrations on which he has been working nights, much to Miss Mason's disgust and very little to his own profit. This overwork has brought him nearer a state of nerve collapse than he imagines.

Dr. Rice notes the symptoms. Neil needs rest, and that immediately. Also he needs a change of scene, and release from the grind of work that is painfully uncongenial, if he is going to realize at all on the talent that is his. The problem of the moment, however, is the tea. And Cynthia, as usual, agrees to see to that. The Cadys must be looked after.

ALBERT — How soon will they be here?

NEIL — Any minute, I guess. Why all the questions?

ALBERT — I just wondered. (*He takes a medical case from his pocket and shakes out a pill.*) I want you to take one of these before they come, and another one later on.

NEIL — Good heavens, there's nothing the matter with me.

ALBERT — I know there isn't.

NEIL — What'll they do — make me sleep?

ALBERT — They'll quiet you.

NEIL — But I don't dare go to sleep. In the first place the Cadys are coming, and — (*Cynthia re-enters. She is now hatless, and carries a folded tablecloth.*)

CYNTHIA — (*to Albert*). I hope you scolded him.

ALBERT — Not enough, I'm afraid. (*To Neil.*) Do you think you have a glass of water left?

NEIL — (*starting*). Oh, of course!

ALBERT — No, no, I can find it. (*He goes into the bedroom.*)

CYNTHIA — (*with a glance at the portfolio*). You didn't let them give you more to do?

NEIL — Why, hardly any. It's all right.

CYNTHIA — It isn't all right. Oh, I wouldn't mind if it were something decent! But it's perfectly sickening to think of your genius choked to death in this way!

NEIL — I'll work on the symphony soon, honestly.

CYNTHIA — And then make up for it by mere hack work. I wish someone would subsidize you.

NEIL. — That would be nice.

ALBERT — (*coming back with water*). Here you are!

NEIL — Oh, all right. But there's nothing the matter with me. (*He takes the pill.*)

ALBERT — How was it?

NEIL — I've tasted better. (*The orchestra across the street is heard in another outburst of jazz.*) Would you believe that people actually enjoy that? Wait! I've got one here that will be next month's national anthem. (*He searches for it in the portfolio.*) There aren't any words to it yet, but it's going to be called " Sweet Mama."

CYNTHIA — Don't, Neil. Play Dr. Rice the second movement of your symphony.

NEIL — Want to hear it?

ALBERT — You bet.

NEIL — She calls it the second movement because there isn't any first.

There is not much time for music. The Cadys are prompt. They file in in order — Mrs. Cady, Gladys, Mr. Cady and the son, Homer. " Together they make up an average Middle West family. They have no marked external characteristics except that Homer is wearing a violent yellow tie."

The greetings are general, noisy, and familiar. There is much talk of Livingston and the old Livingstonians, married, dead, moved and moving. Often all the Cadys talk at once. But it doesn't matter. Nothing that they say is at all important.

Gladys and her mother are particularly interested in Neil. And not in Cynthia, who drifts in as " temporary hostess " with the tea things, and probably appears a little too much at home to please the visitors. But she is soon gone again and the elder Cady takes up the family interest in Neil.

CADY — (*noisily*). Well — how are things generally, Neil? Making a lot of money out of your music?

NEIL — No — with music you don't make a great deal of money.

CADY — I don't know about that. It's just like any other business. Maybe you're not giving them what they want.

MRS. CADY — I guess Neil's doing his best, aren't you, Neil?

CADY — We've all got to please the public. Eh, Doctor?

ALBERT — Oh, yes.

CADY — I've got to in my business. Of course I don't claim to know anything about music, but I think I represent about the average view point. Now, what I like is a good lively tune — something with a little snap to it. As I understand it, though, you sort of go in for — highbrow music.

NEIL — It isn't exactly that.

CADY — Well, there's no money in it. You know what happened to your father.

Mrs. Cady — Had to scrape all his life. (*Turns to Albert.*) Neil's father. Had to scrape all his life.

Cady — A young fellow's got to look out for his future, I claim — got to save up a little money.

Neil — (*puzzled*). Yes, sir.

Mrs. Cady — (*helping along what is clearly a prearranged conversation*). In some business, Mr. Cady means.

Cady — Yes. Now you take — well, my business, for example. We've always got an opening for — a bright young fellow.

Neil — You mean — *me* — in your business?

Cady — Well, I just mentioned that for example.

Neil — I'm afraid I wouldn't be much good in business, Mr. Cady.

Mrs. Cady — Of course you'd be good.

Neil — I did work once in an office, and I guess I wasn't — very —

Cady — That's all right. You'd learn. The idea is you'd be making money. Some day you'd maybe have a nice interest in the firm. 'Tain't as though you couldn't write a little music now and then in your spare time, and we'd be sort of all together. (*The jazz orchestra is heard again — this time louder.*)

Mrs. Cady — Just like one big family.

Gladys — (*singing and swaying to the tune*). Oh, they're playing "The Frog's Party." (*To Neil.*) Come on and dance!

Neil — I'm sorry, but I don't dance.

Gladys — Oh, so you don't — but I'm going to make you learn. I know a wonderful teacher. (*Turns to Albert.*) Dance, Doctor?

Albert — A little. (*Gladys and Albert take a few turns about the room. Mrs. Cady hums the tune, not knowing the words.*)

Cady — Great song! A man I played golf with yesterday tells me that for the first six months of the fiscal year that song'll make a hundred thousand dollars. Write something like that and you're fixed. That's music.

Gladys continues the campaign, while the others gossip in chorus. She draws Neil to the piano. She wants to talk with him about ever so many things. Miss Mason, for one. He doesn't like Miss Mason better than he does her, does he? He shouldn't. And won't he give her his photograph? And does he think she looks better in pink or in blue? She's been shopping and has the hardest time making a choice. She sort of prefers pink herself, but if he likes blue ——

They are going. At least they are starting to go. Gladys must get to the dressmaker's. But she doesn't have to go home with the family for dinner. Not if Neil would rather she'd stay and go with him to a new restaurant she knows.

Neil thinks, perhaps, he had better work. But — well, anyway, Gladys decides to phone him from the dressmaker's.

Now they're gone — only Homer lingering long enough to beg a whispered opinion from Albert Rice as to

Neil's possibilities as a brother-in-law. " Gladys's nutty about him," Homer admits. " Thinks he's artistic. My God! And did you hear the old man? Just because his father was John McRae!"

Alone with Neil, Albert again takes up the question of his physical condition. He positively must go to bed. He must rest. And if he won't go to bed at 5.30 in the afternoon, he can at least lie down in his dressing gown. And he can't go on working on his orchestrations until he does. Also, there is another matter ——

ALBERT — I want to talk to you about something else.

NEIL — Good heavens!

ALBERT — All right, but — somebody **has to.** (*Neil looks up, sensing something important.*) What are you going to do about your work?

NEIL — Huh?

ALBERT — Your real work, I mean. How much have you done since I went away?

NEIL — Well, what you heard. And Miss Mason and I are working out a little pantomime together. It's going to be a lot of fun ——

ALBERT — How much of it is written?

NEIL — A lot. About half, I guess.

ALBERT — About half a movement of a symphony and about half a pantomime.

NEIL — I still have to eat.

ALBERT — But Neil, don't you see — you're wasting your genius!

NEIL — Genius, my hat!

ALBERT — You're wasting the best years you'll ever have doing odd jobs just to keep alive. You've got to be free to write.

NEIL — Well, maybe some day I'll write a popular song and make a million.

ALBERT — If you ever did you'd either burn it or sell it for ten dollars. You'll never make any money, Neil. You know that as well as I do.

NEIL — Then what's the answer? Are you going to subsidize me?

ALBERT — I wish to God I could! But there's no reason why you shouldn't subsidize yourself.

NEIL — What do you mean?

ALBERT — I mean the Cadys.

NEIL — What are you talking — Oh, don't be foolish!

ALBERT — Why is it foolish?

NEIL — Gladys would never — why, you're crazy!

ALBERT — Am I? Think back. How did she behave this afternoon? And Papa Cady? " Nice little share in the business?" And — well, I know what I'm talking about.

NEIL — You mean you're seriously advising me to ask Gladys Cady to marry me?

ALBERT — That's exactly what I'm doing. She's a nice girl, and pretty. You'd have comfort and money and time —

NEIL — (*interrupting, with growing excitement*). Well, what about me? Do you think money and music and time would make up for everything else? No, sir! I'd rather keep on living right here — just as I am now — all my life long.

ALBERT — Now, now! Don't get temperamental! If you'll just — (*Cynthia opens the door.*)

CYNTHIA — May a poor girl call for her dishes?

NEIL — I'm sorry — I should have brought them over.

CYNTHIA — (*detecting a note in his voice*). Neil, there's nothing the matter?
ALBERT — I've been trying to persuade him to rest. (*To Neil.*) Won't you go in and — get ready?
NEIL — I — can't now.
CYNTHIA — Neil, please. (*A pause.*)
NEIL — All right. But don't go away. I want to talk to you. (*He goes into the bedroom.*)

Cynthia and Albert are agreed on one thing — and that is Neil's need of practical help. And they are agreed, too, on the practicability of his marrying Gladys Cady. At least Albert is agreed. Cynthia would like to feel a little more sure that such a marriage would be the right thing for Neil, and the wisest. But if the doctor is sure ——

"We only hurt people by being sentimental about them," he assures her. "That's one of the first things a doctor learns."

And as they shake hands she agrees to help him put the marriage through — "for Neil's sake."

Neil is back in his dressing gown. He submits with as much grace as he can muster to the administering of the pill the doctor gives him and agrees to take another when he goes to bed. Albert hurries away to his appointment and Cynthia gathers up the last of her tea things preparatory to leaving.

NEIL — He's been talking to you about me, hasn't he?
CYNTHIA — Why — you and other things.
NEIL — What did he say?
CYNTHIA — Don't you wish you knew — curiosity!
NEIL — I do know. I know exactly. He said the same thing to me. He said I was a failure — practically. That I'd have to depend on other people all my life.
CYNTHIA — Neil, you're just exciting yourself. You're tired, and you know he wants you to —
NEIL — No, wait! We've got to talk about this, you and I. He said more than that. He said that I ought to ask Gladys Cady to marry me. (*A pause.*) Well! You don't seem — surprised.
CYNTHIA — No, I'm not.
NEIL — Don't you even think it's — funny, a little bit?
CYNTHIA — No.
NEIL — Cynthia! (*He looks at her for a moment and then with a cry.*) Oh, Cynthia — dear! (*He takes her hand.*)
CYNTHIA — Don't, Neil! — Please don't!
NEIL — But Cynthia, don't you know — without my telling you — that I love only you and no one else?
CYNTHIA — Oh, Neil, please! (*Then, with an attempt at lightness.*) This is so sudden!

Neil — (*hurt*). Oh, Cynthia, please don't!

Cynthia — Oh, please don't *you!*

Neil — You know I love you, Cynthia! Of course you know; you couldn't help knowing! I thought maybe you — don't you, at all, Cynthia?

Cynthia — (*regaining control of herself*). Neil, let me tell you something. I have seen that you were growing to care for me, and I've — I've tried to think what I ought to do about it.

Neil — Do about it! What can you do about it if —

Cynthia — You can do lots of things — if you're practical and sensible.

Neil — Oh, my dear!

Cynthia — I said to myself, I think he's beginning to care about me more than he ought to, considering how we're both situated, and that nothing could come of it. And if I stay here I mightn't be sensible either. So, I'm going away.

Neil — What!

Cynthia — I'm going to move uptown and live with Helen Noland. I'm going tomorrow.

Neil — Cynthia — do you mean that you don't care about me at all?

Cynthia — Oh, yes, I do, Neil. I care about you very much. I think you're a great artist.

Neil — Artist! (*He turns away from her.*)

Cynthia — And I think it would be the greatest possible misfortune for your music for you to go on this way, living from hand to mouth. So — when Dr. Rice suggested that you marry Miss Cady, it seemed to me a very sensible thing to do.

Neil — (*faces her again*). Cynthia — do you know what you're talking about?

Cynthia — Perfectly.

Neil — You can't mean that music or no music I ought to marry Gladys.

Cynthia — I think you ought to do just that for the sake of your music.

Neil — (*hurt*). Oh! You're like Albert! You think my music is the only thing about me that's worth while!

Cynthia — Oh, Neil!

Neil — (*continuing*). It never was me that you cared about — only the music.

Cynthia — I want you to be happy, Neil.

Neil — (*mirthlessly*). I certainly got it all wrong, didn't I? (*A pause.*) Well, goodbye, Cynthia.

Cynthia — Oh, Neil! Don't say goodbye like that.

Neil — What other way is there? You're all being so sensible and practical. I might as well be practical and sensible too.

Cynthia starts to answer him, but her voice fails her. She is choked with tears as she hurries from the room, and he goes mumbling on in his mounting anger. " My music!" And again, a little less viciously, " My music!"

The phone rings. It is Gladys. She has finished at the dressmaker's. She selected the pink frock. And will he meet her? He can't do that, he tells her, because of the doctor's orders. He has to sleep for about an hour. Then — if she will come up there — there's something — he would like to ask her.

There is grim determination in his voice, but the effects of the sleeping medicine are becoming noticeable and the telephone receiver nearly falls from his hand.

"We thought — that is I thought — how would you like to marry a great composer?" he mumbles, sleepily.

And over the phone Gladys's exultant "Oh, darling! Do you mean it?" comes rumbling back to him.

Mean it? Sure he means it. But it is not easy for him at her dictation to call her "Sweetheart." Perhaps he can do better when she comes to him — in about an hour.

He tries to put the dangling receiver back on the hook, but he is too sleepy and it hangs dangling from its cord as he flops back into his chair. "And that's that!" he mumbles.

Across the street the cabaret orchestra begins again to play "The Frog's Party," and as Neil's imagination causes it to swell louder and louder, he staggers toward the window. "Now go ahead and play!" he sneers, defiantly. He staggers across the room and falls limply into an easy chair. "Play the wedding march, damn you! Play the wedding march!"

"The tune resolves itself into a jazzy version of Lohengrin's Wedding March. At the same time Neil finally collapses into the chair, and the lights of the room begin to go down. As it grows dark the music swells. Then, after a moment, it begins to grow light again — but it is no longer Neil's room. It is a railway station, with the arch of Track 37 prominently visible, and other arches flanking it at the side. A muddled train schedule is printed on the station walls, with strange towns that never existed. Neil's piano, however, has remained where it was, and so has his easy chair. Then, down the aisles of the lighted theater, there comes suddenly a double wedding procession. One section is headed by Mr. Cady and Gladys — Mr. Cady in golf knickers and socks, knitted vest, and frock coat, with a silk hat prominently on his arm. Gladys is the gorgeously attired bride, bearing proudly a bouquet that consists entirely of banknotes. Behind them stream four ushers

— spats, frock coats, and high hats, to say nothing of huge bridal veils, draped over their heads. If you could peer beneath their veils, however, you would find that all four of them look just alike. The procession that comes down the other aisle is headed by Mrs. Cady and Homer. Mrs. Cady wears a grotesque exaggeration of the dress that Neil has seen her in, and Homer's yellow tie has assumed tremendous proportions. Behind Mrs. Cady and Homer are four bandsmen. Like the ushers, they all look alike, all wearing bridal veils, through which they play their instruments. At the foot of the stage the processions halt; the music stops. Albert appears from nowhere in particular; he has turned into a minister."

Gladys calls to Neil. Albert reminds him that he is forgetting his wedding day. Gradually he realizes their presence and rises to meet them. The two processions stream up the stairs leading from the aisles to the stage. The wedding party is formed, with everybody swaying in a sort of rhythmic chant, " Glad to meet you," " Glad to meet you," " This is Fatty." " This is Lou." " Glad to meet you," etc.

The ceremony becomes a curious mixture of the wedding service and train calls. "Take this man to be your husband?" queries Albert, and before Gladys can answer a trainman has swung across the stage calling the " Wolverine, for Monte Carlo!" " Yes, I do," declares Gladys. " All your worldly goods and chattels?—" And then a trainboy yelling, " Latest magazines and papers!"

But finally they are married and off for the train, Gladys gaily flinging her bouquet of banknotes back to the ushers, who start a wild scramble for it.

The lights die down, and when they are raised the scene has changed to one suggesting an enormous living room, with rows of white marble columns, and between them gorgeous crimson curtains. Only the piano and the easy chair of the original set remain.

Soon Gladys and Neil enter this palace. He is still
in his bathrobe, but she has changed to a pleated dress,
a highly exaggerated copy of the one she wore in the
first act. And this is their beautiful home! Now Neil is
going to have everything he has ever wanted. Papa has
said so.

"Butlers!" calls Gladys, and two liveried servants,
exactly alike, step out smartly from behind two pillars.
"Announce somebody!" orders Gladys.

"Mrs. Cady and her chair and knitting," sing the
butlers.

And Mother appears with a rocking chair strapped to
her. Soon she is knitting and rocking as fast as she
talks.

"Two little lovebirds," she simpers. "Gladys and
Neil! Gladys and Neil! Are they happy? Oh, my
dear, you never saw anyone so happy! I was saying to
Mr. Cady, ' Well, Mr. Cady, what do you think of your
little daughter now? How's this for a happy family?'
And Mr. Cady says to me, ' Well, I never would have
believed it.' And I says to Mr. Cady, and Mr. Cady
says to me, and I says to Mr. Cady, and Mr. Cady says to
me, and I says ——"

Again the butlers are summoned. There are four this
time. And they announce in unison, " Mr. Cady, her
father!"

Cady is dressed for the golf links, but he does not
intend his game shall interfere with his business. There
is a small telephone attached to his chest through which
he keeps up a continuous chatter.

"Yep! Yep! Hullo! Well, I'll tell you what to
do! Sell eighteen holes and buy all the water hazards.
Yep! Yep! Hullo! Well, I'll tell you what to do!
I expect caddies will go up any time now. How's the
eighth hole this morning? Uh-huh. Well, sell it in
three. Yes, sir. That's fine. Yep! Yep! Hullo!
Well, I'll tell you what to do! Buy ——"

There are six butlers to announce Homer. His yellow
tie is at least twice as large as before and his jaundiced
disposition has become something awful.

"Oh, there you are, you dirty dog," shouts Homer, at
sight of Neil. "I'm on to you! You married her just
because Dad's got a lot of money, and you think you're
going to have a cinch. But if you think you're going to
get all of Dad's money, you're mistaken, because I'm
going to get my share and don't you forget it."

But poor Homer is sick and must be forgiven. Everybody says so. And this is to be their happy home!

There is no time for Neil to work on his symphony.
He must go shopping with Gladys, getting a little of this
and a little of that. And he must be ready to go to
business with father and learn the ins and outs. "Lots
of people think the ins and outs don't amount to anything;
but you can't get anywhere in business without them."

There is a crowd in for tea. Neil can't see them, but
all the others can. And they carry on the typical tea
time conversations. With each newcomer the butlers
increase in number. There are eight, then ten, then
twelve. "A great many other members of the family,"
they chant, in unison. "And all pretty terrible, if you
ask me," mumbles the first, not quite under his breath.

The Cadys are all talking at once, as they circle
about, greeting imaginary guests. "Neil moves through
it all, walking through guests, passing his hands through
the butlers' trays — bewildered."

CADY — Oh, hello, Ralph! I want you to meet my new son-in-law. Neil,
this is Mr. Umn.
GLADYS — Oh, have you been out to California? Did it rain much?
CADY — Yes, he's going to be very valuable to me in business, too.
HOMER — I'll bet he's rotten.
CADY — But after all there's nothing like business. It'll all be his when I
retire — his and Homer's, his and Homer's. (He slaps Neil on back.)
(The following four speeches are spoken simultaneously.)
MRS. CADY — Well, Miss Mmmm, you know Mmm, don't you? He's a
cousin of John's who knew Francis very well. She's Ted's aunt. Yes. It's
such a long time since you've been to see us. Gladys is always saying:
" Mama, why is it Mrs. Mmm doesn't come and visit us, or why don't we go
out and see her?" and all like that. You know Mrs. Mmm, don't you? You've
become very plump, or you've become very thin. You don't mind my not getting

up, do you? Mr. Cady says I'm chair-bound. But that's his way of making a joke. He's always making a joke. You know Neil, of course. Would you like to have Neil play for us? Would you like to have Neil play for us? Neil, play for us.

HOMER — Look at him, the dirty dog! He married her for her money all right, but if he thinks he's going to get it he's got another think coming. Pop's going to put him in business! Huh! He thinks he's going to get the business, too. Well, I'll show him — the dirty dog! He isn't going to get the business away from me — not while I'm alive and kicking. All because he's a musician. Yes, he thinks he plays the piano. Well — let him play it and see if I care. I dare him to play it. Go on and play for us.

MR. CADY — Well, well, well! You know Judge Mmm, of course. Old man, I want you to meet the Judge. Yes, they've got a very beautiful home here. Would you like a cocktail, eh? Yes, sir! Well, Judge, how's everything been going? Say, you know Mr. Mmm, don't you? How are you? How have you been all these years? Have a cocktail — that's the boy. Yes, she's a big girl now. Grown up — married. That's her husband there. That's the one I bought for her. Very talented. I'll get him to play. Neil, we'd like to hear you play. Come on, Neil, play something on the piano.

GLADYS — Oh, how do you do, Aunt Gertrude? You know Willie, of course. Willie, you remember Aunt Gertrude. Aunt Gertrude, you remember Willie. Yes, this is our beautiful home. My husband's very talented. No, you didn't interrupt him a bit. He's awfully glad you came. He wasn't going to do anything this afternoon. Anyway, we always have tea. And if it isn't tea, it's something else. We're always having such a good time, Neil and I. Yes, that's my husband there. He plays the piano beautifully. Shall I get him to play? I think he would if I ask him. Oh, Neil, darling, play something. Please, Neil! Neil, for my sake, you'll play, won't you?

Neil starts to play, a little defiantly, not the sort of thing they expect, but something " soft and flowing and reminiscent of Cynthia." And as he plays the lights fade and Cynthia comes, like a beautiful wraith, through the window.

But Cynthia can't help him. She's sorry, because she wants him always to be happy. But it is too late, now. And as his music, in spite of himself, turns to jazz she drifts out of the window again and is gone.

Immediately Mr. Cady is there to take her place. He wears his hat and is starting for business. Neil must go with him —— Now they are at the office. The man who was the trainman is the elevator man. They are riding in an express elevator with four other business men, dressed exactly alike and all carrying newspapers. They are all Cady associates and must be introduced to the new son-in-law. " I bought him for my daughter," Cady explains to them.

Now Neil has been put off at his floor and is looking

for the Ins and Outs department.   Failing that he discovers a small office presided over by Miss Hey, a
stenographer, and thinks he will begin his business career
by getting himself a pencil.

NEIL — I beg your pardon?
MISS HEY — Well?
NEIL — I want a pencil.
MISS HEY — (*still typing*). What is it?
NEIL — I want a pencil.
MISS HEY — Who sent you?
NEIL — I don't know. But I have to have a pencil. I worked in a place
like this once before. I had a great deal of difficulty getting a pencil then,
I remember.
MISS HEY — It's just as hard to get one here.
NEIL — I thought it would be. I suppose there's a lot of red tape to go
through.
MISS HEY — Yes. Now I understand it, you want a pencil.
NEIL — That's right.
MISS HEY — Of course you've filled out a requisition.
NEIL — No, I haven't. A piece of paper, isn't it? (*She hands him a tre-
mendous sheet of paper.   It is about twenty by thirty inches.   He studies it.*)
What I want is a pencil. There's a place for that to be put in, I suppose?
MISS HEY — (*wearily*). Yes — where it says: " The undersigned wishes a
pencil to do some work with." How old are you?
NEIL — Thirty-two.
MISS HEY — (*taking the paper away*). That's the wrong form. (*She gives
him another — a blue one this time.*) Parents living?
NEIL — No.
MISS HEY — What did you do with your last pencil?
NEIL — I didn't have any.
MISS HEY — Did you have any before that?
NEIL — I don't think I ever had any. (*He indicates the form.*) Is that all
right?
MISS HEY — It isn't as regular as we like, but I guess it'll do.
NEIL — What do I do now? Go to someone else, don't I?
MISS HEY — Oh, yes. Sometimes you travel for days.
NEIL — Are we all crazy?
MISS HEY — Yes. (*She resumes typing.*) You might try Room E — right
down the corridor.
    (*The curtains close over her, and the curtains at the left simultaneously
open, revealing another office just like the first.   Another stenographer, Miss
You, is at work on a typewriter.   Neil approaches her, requisition in hand.*)
NEIL — Is this Room E?
MISS YOU — (*mechanically*). Did you have an appointment?
NEIL — No — you don't understand. I'm trying to get a pencil.
MISS YOU — Well, what do you want to see him about?
NEIL — (*handing over the requisition*). It's this. Somebody has to sign it.
MISS YOU — (*takes the requisition*). Oh! (*Looks at it.*) Mr. Bippy! The
man is here to see about getting a pencil or something.
NEIL — It *is* a pencil.
MISS YOU — Did you see Mr. Schlink?
NEIL — Yes.
MISS YOU — Mr. Woodge?
NEIL — Yes.
MISS YOU — Mr. Meglup?
NEIL — Yes.
MISS YOU — What did *they* say?
NEIL — Why, they seemed to think it would be all right.

Miss You — (*calls again*). Oh, Mr. Bippy! (*To Neil.*) Belong to the Employes' Mutual Mutual?
  Neil. — Oh, yes.
  Miss You — Cady Golf and Building Fund?
  Neil — Yes.
  Miss You — Well — all right. (*She stamps the requisition with an elaborate machine, which rings a bell as it works. She hands the paper back to Neil.*)
  Neil — Oh, thanks. Do I get a pencil now?
  Miss You — Oh, no! It has to be O.K.'d by the President. All requisitions have to be O.K.'d by the President.
  Neil — Is he around here some place?
  Miss You — Oh, no! He's in a big office. Just keep going until you find a great big office.
  Neil — Where?
  Miss You — Oh, somewhere in the new building. (*She calls.*) Mr. Bippy!

In the big office Neil finds Mr. Cady engrossed in the greater and lesser details of the widget industry of which he is the presiding genius. " The turnover in the widget industry last year was greater than ever," his secretary reads from the annual report. " If placed alongside the Woolworth Building it would stretch to the moon. The operating expenses alone would furnish every man, woman and child in the United States, China and similar places with enough to last for eighteen and one-half years, if laid end to end." And in the coming September the whole nation is to celebrate National Widget Week.

Now they go into conference with other big business men. They have some very nice conferences in the widget business and quite frequently. In conference Neil, speaking as one newly come to the widget business, addresses the directors, explaining how, by application and self training he has been able to forge ahead until it is easy for him to solve problems that have puzzled the best brains of the business world for years. So they give him a million dollars and sign him up for the next annual quarter.

When he finds himself outside the meeting with the checks in his hand he can only vaguely remember that he was to match them for Gladys. Anyway, he doesn't want them. He wants to write his symphony.

Gladys finds him there and whisks him away to a restaurant, where the head waiter turns out to be Alfred.

The orchestra plays " The Frog's Party " insistently and Gladys dances round and round with Alfred.

As they whirl away Gladys flings back at Neil her conviction that if he had not married her he would have starved to death, which sets him thinking about Cynthia and what their life might have been together. Soon he sees it, a sunlit cottage with flowers about and Cynthia sitting across the breakfast table from him.

NEIL — (*calling*). Cynthia!
CYNTHIA — I'm coming!
NEIL — Are you coming, or must I use force?
CYNTHIA — It's the toast machine. You sit down and begin.
NEIL — As though I ever begin without you! Besides, I have something beautiful for you. (*Cynthia enters, bringing a tray laden with breakfast.*) See what I've done!
CYNTHIA — What?
NEIL — Nothing at all! Merely created an utterly beautiful morning!
CYNTHIA — *You* did? I started it an hour ago.
NEIL — Perhaps; but see those little powder-puff clouds? *They* weren't there ten minutes ago.
CYNTHIA — They *are* nice, darling. I didn't think you were so clever.
NEIL — And wait till you see the sunset I'm planning.
CYNTHIA — You can't beat last night's. What a scarlet!
NEIL — It blushed because we flattered it so. (*A pause.*)
CYNTHIA — Darling.
NEIL — What?
CYNTHIA — A letter. (*They stare at the envelope corner.*)
NEIL — Didn't you dare open it?
CYNTHIA — No. But let's be brave. (*They hold hands and take a long breath.*) Now — one, two, three! (*They tear the letter open and read it in silence.*) Do you believe it? (*The voice is ecstatic.*)
NEIL — No! Do you?
CYNTHIA — Darling!
NEIL — Darling!
CYNTHIA — But it *must* be real — it's typewritten.
CYNTHIA AND NEIL — (*reading in unison*). " Your symphony will be played by our orchestra on December the tenth."
NEIL — Darling!
CYNTHIA — Darling! They'll applaud and applaud! You'll have to come out and bow!
NEIL — I won't!
CYNTHIA — You'll have to have a new dress suit!
NEIL — And you'll have to have a new evening dress — yellow chiffon, too. I can do their damned orchestrations now. I can do a hundred of them between now and October.
CYNTHIA — No, you won't!
NEIL — But, my youngest child, we must continue to eat.
CYNTHIA — But, my dear, we're extremely wealthy. Have you seen my new housekeeping book?

The book proves that they have actually saved a hundred and seventy-seven dollars and seventy-seven cents, and they are wonderfully proud and gorgeously

happy — until Gladys calls. Then the picture fades and
Cynthia with it. Gladys is through dancing with Alfred
and has taken on a few of the attendants while she urges
Neil to hurry and pay the check and " tip the waiters,
tip the waiters, tip the waiters."

He hands them bundles of bills, but he is pretty mad
when he runs into Alfred. It was Alfred who got him
into this thing and now he will have to get him out. A
simple proceeding, according to Alfred. Let him kill
Gladys and all the other offending Cadys. It's simple
and practical.

So Neil goes home with Gladys, giving thought on the
way to the pretty slaughter suggested by Albert. And
when he finds Homer at the radio, and Father playing
golf with an imaginary ball, and Mother knitting, rocking and singing hymns; and particularly when he is
introduced to a sextette of exquisite young gentlemen
dancing teachers engaged to teach him to dance, he puts
Albert's idea into execution.

With his own favorite paper knife, grown to the
proportions of a scimitar, he neatly and quickly stabs
each of them and they all die. Not without some protest,
but at least without offering any unnecessary interference.
In fact they are all very pleasant about it — all except
Homer. Homer is a bit nasty.

NEIL — (as he finishes off Mr. Cady). Thank God, they're out of the way!
Peace! I can work at last!

THE RADIO — Stock market reports! Stock market reports!

HOMER — (coming from behind the radio machine). Is that so? I guess you
forgot all about me, didn't you?

NEIL — Forget you? Indeed I didn't! Homer, my boy! (He stabs him.
Homer crumples up on the floor.) I guess that ends that! Free! Free.

HOMER — (sitting up). Free nothing! We'll sue you for this, you dirty dog!
(He falls dead again.)

NEIL — It won't do you any good! Not when they know why I did it! Not
when I show them what you killed! Not when I play them my music! (Half
a dozen newspaper reporters enter. They are dressed alike and look alike; each
has a pencil expectantly poised over a piece of paper.)

THE REPORTERS — (speaking one at a time, as they surround Neil). The
Times! The World! The Post! The Globe! The Sun! The News! The
Times! The World! The Post! The Globe! The Sun! The News!

NEIL — Gentlemen, this is purely a family affair. I don't think I should say
anything at this time, but do come to my trial.

THE REPORTERS — *(again speaking one at a time)*. A statement! A statement! A statement! A statement! A statement!
NEIL — Well, gentlemen, it's a long story.

"Instantly a dozen newsboys rush down the aisles of the theater, crying, 'Extra! Extra! All about the murders!' The din is terrific. Simultaneously the theater lights up; the audience turns for a second to look at the newsboys, and in that second the curtain falls. The newsboys pass out copies of the Morning-Evening, containing a full account of the quadruple murder."

[The "Morning-Evening — With Which Has Been Combined the Evening-Morning, Retaining the Best features of Each," — is a complete, though small, four-page daily newspaper which cleverly burlesques all the set and popular features of the New York press. These include the extravagant crime story; the dotted-line-indicates-route-taken-by-murderer illustration; the blah-blah editorials; the mushy love letters offered as evidence in the suit of Miss Florence Thgly, ex-"Foibles" girl, for $500,000 against Herman Winkle, elderly millionaire; the dramatic criticism of many words and little sense; the more atrocious of the comic strips, etc. It is distributed by regular newsboys and keeps many a normally restless patron in his seat throughout the intermission. Thus held, observation indicates, the patron either enjoys himself hugely or spends the time trying to explain the Morning-Evening to his lady friend or family.—EDITOR.]

PART II

The scene is a court room. There are long black curtains at back and silhouetted sharply against them are "three major objects in red — the same red that appeared fitfully in Neil's chintz curtains, and again as draperies for the pillars in the Cady home."

These three objects are a block of twelve jury seats,
resembling a section of a theater auditorium, in the
center, a judge's bench at the right and a witness box
and ticket taker's stand at the left. Neil's piano and
easy chair are still in their accustomed places. Leaning
against the judge's bench is a frame of pictures, similar
to those shown of actors in theater lobbies. The pictures represent Judge Cady at the various trials he has
conducted.

When court is opened with the stentorian " Oyez, oyez,
oyez!" of the ticket taker the jurors file in. There are
check boys and ushers to meet them and each surrenders
a ticket of admission, retaining the coupon. They are
all dressed alike and look alike. They are, in fact, the
dancing teachers of the previous act. They also talk alike.
" Hello, Ed!" " Hello, Ed!" " Well, you old son-of-a
gun!" " Well, you old son-of-a-gun!" " How's every
little thing?" " How's every little thing?" And so on.

They are greatly interested in this trial, and in the
Cady pictures.

FIRST JUROR — (at the frame of photographs). Say, who's this?
NEIL — That's the judge. It's the opening night of my trial, you know.
That's the way he appeared in several famous cases.
SECOND JUROR — (joining them and pointing to a picture). Oh, yes! That's
the way he looked in the Watkins trial. He was terrible good. Did you see it?
FIRST JUROR — No, I was out of town. (Points to another picture.) There he
is in the Ferguson case! Gosh, he was good in that!
NEIL — I heard he was.
SECOND JUROR — Was he funny?
FIRST JUROR — Funny? He had that court room roaring half the time.
SECOND JUROR — I don't know another judge in the country who can deliver
a charge to a jury like he can. Pathos, comedy, everything.
FIRST JUROR — They say this will be the best trial he's ever done. I hear
they were sold out last Monday.

The orchestra plays the overture for the trial as more
jurors file in and are shown to their seats. Albert Rice
appears. He carries a camera. He represents the picture
papers. They don't use any writing, he explains. At
least not much. "We always have a few simple words
saying what the picture is about," says he. " A good
many of our subscribers can read, and they tell the
others."

There is excitement in the jury box over the election of a foreman. Smith is a candidate. So is Jones. And seeing that both are old Eighth Ward boys, known to the electorate since childhood, and pledged to give the jury a business administration, choice is difficult. Until Neil suggests a solution.

NEIL — (*going into the witness box*). Ladies and gentlemen of the **Fifth** Jury District: I know it is late to be putting forward a new candidate for foreman of this grand jury, but this is my trial, and it is my music that you're to hear. Both of the candidates who are now up before you are good dancers, but it is only fair that there should be someone on the jury who knows good music.

JURORS — Hooray!

NEIL — Therefore, when the light of the Times Building swings on tonight,, I want it to be a steady red light, which will show that we have elected the **Hon.** Albert Rice, of Chicago, a man of the people, for the people, and by the people, and the stars and stripes forever in the good old U. S. A!

There is a red light, the orchestra plays " Stars and Stripes " and the jurors, leaving their seats, march around the jury box cheering and waving small American flags. Albert is elected. He also takes a picture of the scene for his paper, and immediately thereafter produces the paper with the picture printed in it. Also the judge's address. " But he hasn't delivered it yet," Neil protests. " Well, we have to get things quick. Our readers expect it," explains Albert.

Judge Cady, entering to the tune of the soldiers' chorus from " Faust," wears a huge red robe over his golf costume. He poses modestly until the applause dies down and late comers are seated.

CADY — I declare the court to be in session. (*There is a round of applause. Cady bows.*) The business of the day is the trial of Neil Wadsworth McRae for murder. (*There is more applause. Neil is finally compelled to bow. Cady again addresses Neil confidently.*) Am I right?

NEIL — Yes. And don't forget, I'm going to play my symphony. That was the reason I did it, you know.

CADY — Yes, I remember. (*He is quite conversational.*) Now, the first thing to be done, I should say, is to have the prosecuting attorney make a sort of general charge. (*To Neil.*) What do you think?

NEIL — I guess that's right. How about it, Albert?

ALBERT — (*looking up from his program*). Yes, that's right.

TICKET TAKER — (*announcing*). The prosecuting attorney! (*Homer enters to the tune of " Tammany." He wears a long black robe. He receives a hearty round of applause, with a few hisses.*)

NEIL — Oh, it's you!

HOMER — (*quietly*). I'll get you now, you dirty dog!

NEIL — I think not.
CADY — Come, come, we can't be all day at this. I've got to get back to the office. Now, just what were these murders all about?

Homer reads the charge, struggling against a babel raised by the ushers, check boys, candy peddlers, etc. Neil personally is forced to silence them in order that Homer may be heard. " Some of us would like to hear the show," he protests, irritably. Later, after the State rests, partly because of Homer's state of health, Neil insists on putting Mrs. Cady on the stand. Can she or can she not prove an alibi? She doesn't know. Neither does the judge. There are several kinds of alibis and before they can agree on one Gladys is back. She has just dropped in to get the jury boys for the dancing. And borrow ten thousand dollars from her father. She is going to another opening.

Neil protests. She can't do that! She can't take the jury away right in the midst of everything! He appeals to the judge. The judge thinks she can, if it's a habeas corpus, which it is beginning greatly to resemble.

NEIL — But it isn't fair! They've got to hear my music. I know what I'll do! (He faces Cady.) I'll take it to a higher court!
CADY — (just a bit hurt). Oh, don't you like this court?
NEIL — It isn't that. It's a good court, I guess, and the people are lovely, but —
CADY — About how high a one would you want?
NEIL — I'd want the highest I could get.
CADY — All right. (Judge Cady slowly goes up in the air as his stand grows two or three feet higher.) Is this high enough for you?
NEIL — I guess so. Is this the superior court?
CADY — Oh, yes. Much superior. And more up-to-date. We send out all our verdicts by radio.
NEIL — She can't take them away with her now, can she — in this court?
CADY — Oh, no! You see, in a higher court the lower court is reversed.
NEIL — Good!
GLADYS — Oh, the devil! Well, then, I'll take Albert. He's only the foreman.

Gladys has danced away with Albert before anyone can stop them and Judge Cady has signified his willingness to proceed with the case if the jury is ready to report. Again Neil protests. They have not heard the music yet. And it is his music that was the very cause of the murders.

He wants to prove to the jury that he was justified

in killing anyone who would interfere with its creation. But when he tries to play his C minor symphony the result is discordant and meaningless. Then he realizes that Gladys has torn up the manuscript and he cannot play it. Again in his distress he calls aloud for Cynthia, and she appears, mysteriously, to stand by the piano. " She is calm and sympathetic, as always."

NEIL — Cynthia, she tore up my symphony! I can't remember it, and they're waiting for me to play!
CYNTHIA — You still have the pantomime, haven't you?
NEIL — Yes.
CYNTHIA — Then play that for them instead. (*She finds the pantomime music.*) They'll think it's better, anyhow.
NEIL — But it isn't finished.
CYNTHIA — Well, now you can finish it.
NEIL — Can I?
CYNTHIA — Of course. It'll be all right, dear — you'll see.
NEIL — You — you think we ought to do it?
CYNTHIA — Of course.
NEIL — All right. (*He faces his inquisitors.*) Ladies and gentlemen, instead of the symphony, we're going to play a little pantomime called " A Kiss in Xanadu " — written by Cynthia Mason and Neil McRae. We'll need quite a lot of room, so, if you don't mind clearing the court — (*The Judge's dais and the witness box disappear. The jury box, too, moves into blackness.*) The scene is the royal palace in Xanadu. It's a night in June — one of those spring nights that you find only in Xanadu. Now, if you're all ready — music! (*The music of the pantomime begins.*) Cynthia, we ought to have a window to show what kind of night it is. (*In the distance a great open window appears. Beyond a moonlight balustrade are flowers and trees and stars.*)
CYNTHIA — It's coming!
NEIL — Thanks. (*To the jury.*) The scene is the bedchamber of the Prince and Princess. On the right is the bed of the princess and on the left is the bed of the Prince.

" Two fairy tale beds appear from the darkness. They are canopied in pink. Above them are flower-draped testers that rise to golden points. Neil and Cynthia seat themselves at the piano and the pantomime begins."
The pantomime of " A Kiss in Xanadu " is the story of a Princess who was very beautiful, but restless, because she was a married Princess and romance had fled from her life. And a Prince who " would like to be a Gay Dog Prince," again and know the thrills of his earlier love affairs before he was married.
So after they have been put in their respective beds by the Lord and Lady of the Bedchamber, they separately respond to the call of the night. The Prince.

turning the royal dressing gown wrong side out as a disguise, and using the lining of the crown for a cap, is soon sneaking carefully out the window into the moonlit garden.

And no sooner has he disappeared than the Princess, awakened by the moon, decides to go adventuring, too. The Prince is sleeping, she decides, the curtains of his canopy drawn. Up she springs, taking a spread from the bed as her shawl, wearing the lamp shade as a very becoming hat and using the Prince's candle shade for a mask.

The music goes softly on, but now the lights are out, and when they are on again the scene is the public park of Xanadu. There the Prince and Princess meet, and flirt and kiss —— And then, as the clock strikes five and the dawn is threatening, they run back to the Palace.

In the bedchamber the Princess arrives first and is snugly in bed when the Prince tiptoes to his couch — The clocks strike eight. Lord and Lady of the Bedchamber arrive. The pages bring in the royal breakfast. The Prince and Princess make more than the usual fuss about getting up.

At breakfast " the Princess starts to pour her husband's coffee. Oh, yes, she had forgotten! She rises and offers a cheek to be kissed. He mechanically obliges. They sit down again. But they cannot eat. The music of the night is still with them. They steal wistful looks at the window. The Princess looks at the rose he gave her. The Prince looks at the one she first refused. The flowers are stealthily put away. The Prince and the Princess unfold their napkins. It is the humdrum of life once more."

From out of the darkness there come the protests of the court, relayed by radio to all parts of the theater. " Rotten!" "No good!" " High-brow!" " Terrible!" When the scene lightens Judge Cady is sitting cross-legged on top of Neil's piano, smoking. He calls for the verdict of the jury, now invisible but still roughly articulate. The verdict is " guilty!"

CADY — See, Neil? I told you so.

NEIL — Well — well, what are you going to do with me?

CADY — This thing of using the imagination has got to stop. We're going to make you work in the right way. You see, your talents belong to us now, and we're going to use every bit of them. We're going to make you the most wonderful song writer that ever lived.

NEIL — But I can't write that kind of music! You know I can't!

CADY — You can do it by our system. You are sentenced to be at the Cady Consolidated Art Factory at eight o'clock tomorrow morning!

NEIL — Art factory?

CADY — At eight o'clock tomorrow morning!

The scene changes. There is a tier of four cells, and the sound of discordant music. It is the Cady Consolidated Art Factory, and a guide is showing a party of visitors through the plant. He stops in front of the cells, a gong rings, the factory activities cease and the cell inmates walk quickly to the bars of their cells and stand, at it were, at attention.

GUIDE — Now this, gentlemen, is the manufacturing department. In this studio — (he indicates the first) we have Walter Carp Smith, the world's greatest novelist —

NOVELIST — (more or less routine). How are you?

GUIDE — (passing the second cage). In this studio, Neil McRae, the world's greatest composer!

NEIL — (listlessly). How are you?

GUIDE — (at the third cage). In this one, Finlay Jamison, the world's greatest magazine artist!

ARTIST — How are you?

GUIDE — (at the fourth cage). And in this, James Lee Wrex, the world's greatest poet!

POET — How are you?

GUIDE — (indicating the unseen cages beyond). The studios beyond are devoted to science and religion. Mr. Cady was the first person in the world to put religion up in ten-cent packages, selling direct to the consumer.

FIRST VISITOR — You don't say so!

GUIDE — He also prides himself on having the largest output of literature and music in the world. He's going to open two more plants the first of the month. Now, would you like to see how these men work?

FIRST VISITOR — Yes, indeed! (Goes toward the first cage.) Did you say this was the novelist?

GUIDE — The world's greatest. Author of more than two thousand published works.

FIRST VISITOR — What an imagination!

GUIDE — Yes, sir, none at all. Now if you're ready, I'll show you how he works. Go!

NOVELIST — (begins at once to dictate from a book in his hand). " Something closely resembling a tear fell from the old patrician's cheek. ' Margaret,' he cried, ' the people of the West have learned to love you, too.' ' Jackie boy,' she whispered. ' They have made you governor after all.' Far off on the — the — " (he hesitates: the stenographer takes up the story.)

STENOGRAPHER — " — desert, the caravan faded away. Night took them in its arms and a great hush fell on the forest. The two lovers — "
GUIDE — Stop! (*He turns to the visitors.*) There you are!
FIRST VISITOR — Was *she* writing it?
GUIDE — Oh, no! Sometimes she gets a little ahead of him, that's all.
FIRST VISITOR — Isn't he wonderful!
GUIDE — Forty-five minutes after he finishes a novel we have it printed and assembled and on its way to the movie men.

At the moment the novelist is at work on his forthcoming opus, " Love Eternal." The book from which he is dictating is his previous success, " Eternal Love." They move on to the cell of the artist. He can do them either a magazine cover or an advertisement in practically no time at all. The canvas he hands them is quite blank, but they see on it a beautiful picture and are thrilled to learn that it sells for $3,500 and will appear in thousands of magazines. They move on to the next cell.

GUIDE — And here, gentlemen, is our poet. His " Jolly Jingles " are printed in three million newspapers a day.
FIRST VISITOR — (*pointing to men in back*). Who are those men?
GUIDE — Those are his models. He is the only poet in the world who works from living models. That's why all his poetry is so true, so human. He'll show you. Go!
POET — I will now write a friendship poem. (*Motions to his models.*) Friendliness No. 3, please. " Friendship." (*The models strike a pose, hands clasped.*)
    " Goodbye, old pal; hello, old pal; the greatest pal I ever knew.
    A dog's your finest friend, my lad, when all the world is blue."
SECOND VISITOR — Ain't it human?
GUIDE — And here, gentlemen, is Mr. Neil McRae, America's foremost composer.
FIRST VISITOR — Who's that in back?
GUIDE — That's his lyric writer. You will now see how they work. What kind of a song will it be, McRae?
NEIL — A pathetic. (*He sits at the piano.*)
GUIDE — A pathetic. Go! (*Neil plays.*)
SINGER — (*in a horrible voice*).
    " You've broken my heart like you broke my heart,
        So why should you break it again?"
        (*Neil comes to the bars again.*)
GUIDE — That will sell one and one-half million.
SECOND VISITOR — I suppose you write other kinds of songs, too?
NEIL — Oh, yes — mammies, sweeties and fruit songs. The ideas are brought from the inspiration department every hour on the hour. After I turn them into music they are taken to the purifying department, and then to the testing and finishing rooms. They are then packed for shipment.
FIRST VISITOR — A wonderful system!
THIRD VISITOR — I should say so!
SECOND VISITOR — Do you work all the time?
NEIL — No, the night shift comes on at eight.
FIRST VISITOR — How long have you been here?

NEIL — For years and years.
SECOND VISITOR — Say, will you write another song for us — just as a souvenir?
NEIL — (desperately). Oh, why don't you all go away?
GUIDE — What's that? What was that? You get busy there and write another song!
NEIL — No! I've been writing forever — I'm tired of it.
GUIDE — Do you want me to call Mr. Cady?
NEIL — I don't care! I don't care what you do!
GUIDE — I'll give you one more chance.
NEIL — No! I won't!
GUIDE — All right, then! Mr. Cady! Mr. Cady!

Cady is of no mind to stand rebellion in his factory. He appears in back of the cages with a long snake whip, and the inmates of the cells slink fearfully into corners. But he concerns himself only with Neil. If Neil thinks he is going to escape his sentence he is much mistaken. He will go on and on until he dies. " You take our money and you live our life. We own you, we own you," he chants. The others join in, weaving back and forth in unison. " You sold your soul and you can't get away. We own you, we own you."

But there is a promise in that chant for Neil. He can at least die. " You can't keep me from it. Open the door," he shouts, shaking the bars of his cell. " Open the door!" It opens quite easily — it was never locked.

" Cynthia, Cynthia, I'm free! I can die!" he shouts, gleefully.

Cynthia comes in answer to his call, as she always does, and helps him with his arrangements. She knows a very good executioner. And a very careful one.

Now Neil is preparing for his execution, a little apprehensive and not altogether satisfied with the make-shift block Cynthia has fashioned from the armchair. But still eager to get it over with. If Cynthia will only promise to stay with him — always.

Before they can bring off the execution, however, Albert must come again and give Neil a pill. That guarantees absolute painlessness. Finally, Neil takes off his collar, advises the executioner that he prefers " just a once-

through, please," and the knife starts to descend ——
" There is a hum of voices. Presently one can discern
several chanting, ' You take our money and you lead our
life.' . . . The lights slowly go up again. We are
back in Neil's apartment. He is asleep in his chair. It
is sunset. There is a knock, a real knock, on the door."

NEIL — (half asleep). Yes? (Cynthia enters.)
CYNTHIA — Is anything the matter, Neil? I thought I heard you talking.
NEIL — It didn't hurt. Was it a success?
CYNTHIA — Neil, are you all right?
NEIL — (takes her hand). I need you, Cynthia!
CYNTHIA — Oh, Neil, do you? Are you sure you do? I — I couldn't stay
away, Neil. I tried to, but I couldn't. Because I need you, too. I just couldn't
give you up to anyone else on earth.
NEIL — Cynthia, dear.
CYNTHIA — It wouldn't have worked, Neil — with those people. Don't you
know it wouldn't?
NEIL — I think I do.
CYNTHIA — I've been sitting out on a bench in the square, trying to think
out what it would mean — what it would do to you.
NEIL — I know. Widgets.
CYNTHIA — That would be worse for you than any amount of poverty.
NEIL — Poverty in our cottage.
CYNTHIA — Did you think of a cottage, too?
NEIL — Of course — I lived there.
CYNTHIA — We could manage. I know quite a lot about raising chickens.
NEIL — (reminiscently). A little red hen and a little dun cow.
CYNTHIA — Yes, we might have a cow. Have you been thinking about it,
too? (She rises.)
NEIL — Well — let's say dreaming. (He rises and goes to the desk.) It was
terrible, Cynthia — do you know, I dreamed I was married to her?
CYNTHIA — To Gladys?
NEIL — When I thought you didn't care, I was hurt and angry. And I
dreamed she telephoned — (sees the receiver off the hook.) My God! Did she
telephone? Oh, Cynthia, it's real! I did do it! I did!
CYNTHIA — Did what?
NEIL — I did ask her to marry me!
CYNTHIA — Neil! You didn't! And she — accepted you?
NEIL — Yes.
CYNTHIA — Oh, Neil.

Gladys arrives. She has come to acknowledge her
engagement to Neil. She is very happy, of course. But
— there is a big favor she would like to ask him. Coming back from the dressmaker's whom should she meet
but Walter Craig — one of her very oldest boy friends.
And Walter, being in town only for a week, would like
to have her play around with him. Which, of course,
she couldn't do if she were engaged to Neil. Then, after
Walter has gone, and she and Neil are really engaged,

of course she expects to settle down to going with him exclusively — to parties and every place.

Neil doesn't quite appreciate her idea of an engagement. To him it would seem rather a solemn occasion. "I think I'd want to be somewhere alone," he suggests, "just the two of us, where we could talk."

GLADYS — Talk about what?

NEIL — (*with a meaning look*). I don't know.

GLADYS — You don't mean you'd *always* be like that, do you? I mean, when you're married?

NEIL — I might.

GLADYS — Well, where would I come in? Do you mean you'd expect *me* to sit around *every* evening and — just talk? I did think you'd be willing to — play around the way other people do.

NEIL — I see.

GLADYS — But, of course, if you wouldn't — well — why — there doesn't seem to be much sense in our being engaged, does there?

NEIL — It's to be just as you say, Gladys.

GLADYS — Well, I don't think we're exactly suited to each other — if you think it over. Honestly, I don't. Do you?

NEIL — No, Gladys.

GLADYS — I noticed the difference the minute I saw Walter again! I can kind of let myself go with Walter. You're sure you don't think I'm a quitter?

NEIL — I think you're all right.

GLADYS — And we'll still be friends, won't we? I've always thought you were nice, Neil. (*She gives a sigh.*) It's a sort of relief, isn't it?

NEIL — Yes, it is — rather.

GLADYS — Well, goodbye. I've got to go because I left Walter downstairs. (*She departs.*)

NEIL — Oh! (*Laughs. Starts to call out.*) Cyn — (*Looks across the hall, crosses to the piano and begins to play the music of the pantomime. After a moment Cynthia comes slowly into the room.*)

CYNTHIA — (*hesitatingly*). Want me, Neil?

NEIL — Do I want you? (*He continues playing as he hears her approaching. The curtain descends slowly.*)

THE END

" THE CHANGELINGS "

A Comedy in Three Acts

By Lee Wilson Dodd

HENRY MILLER began his season September 17, producing " The Changelings," an observant comedy of life and modern manners among native-born citizens, written by Lee Wilson Dodd. His company was one he was proud to present as the Henry Miller Players in the Henry Miller Theater, and " The Changelings " quickly found a public that patronized it generously for the succeeding four months.

Mr. Dodd takes as his text for this play a quotation from Talleyrand: " *Plus ça change, plus la même chose.*" His purpose, we gather, is to offer a word of cheer and suggest a helpful self-analysis to those flustered family folk who have been startled out of their wonted calm by a younger generation grown suddenly restless and more or less irresponsible. A timely theme, sanely and effectively handled, but slightly handicapped commercially by the fact that the younger generation, as such, is not greatly interested in the plays its elders write about it. And the older generation is a little ashamed when it sees itself exposed.

The story is dramatically holding and arrestingly intimate. The opening scene is laid in the library-living room of the Wallace Aldcrofts; he is a well-to-do book publisher of fifty, and she, Karen, his dutiful wife, eight years his junior. The Aldcrofts are entertaining at dinner the Fenwick Fabers; Mr. Faber a novelist of forty-five and Dora, forty-four, his loyal wife and most consistent reader.

188

These four have been the closest friends for twenty years or more. And their little dinner parties have been regular incidents in the usual exchange of social courtesies. As they come from the dining room, the women arm in arm, Dora Faber, the author suggests, " looks her age, while Karen Aldcroft does not. Karen is the prettier and the more sophisticated woman of the two. Fenwick Faber is a tall, dark, romantic looking man; obviously an ' intellectual.' Wallace Aldcroft is shorter, heavier, more genial; no less certainly a man of brains, but less distinguished in appearance than his friend."

Not only has this Aldcroft-Faber friendship existed many years, but it recently has been more strongly cemented by the marriage of the Faber son to the Aldcroft daughter. " Wicky " Faber is a young professor at Yale, recently appointed, and he and " Kay " live in New Haven. The young people boast the usual lack of interest in letter writing, and little has been heard from them for the past few weeks. Only one letter has come from Kay, and that was rather disturbing.

From the family chatter over the coffee there spring two significant guidelines to character and existing conditions. First, that there is an admitted bond of sympathy and understanding between Karen Aldcroft and Fenwick Faber, and an equally strong attachment between Dora Faber and Wallace Aldcroft. The men, for example, have been casually discussing business.

FENWICK — . . . Oh, while I think of it — Silberstein's doing a book on The Family. He calls it " The Last Bulwark." The last bulwark of tyranny against freedom, he means. It's a rotten title; but I've glanced through his first chapters, and they're remarkably stimulating! I think you'll be wanting the first look at it.

WALLACE — H'm. I'm not so sure. I've an idea the family is the last bulwark against social degeneration.

FENWICK — Pooh! You've a funny old-fashioned streak in you, Wally, haven't you? (With a friendly grin.) But look out for Karen! Karen wouldn't stand for such a blatant piece of Victorianism as that!

WALLACE — No. No — I suppose not. I suppose she wouldn't. But Dora would.

FENWICK — Oh — Dora, yes. But Dora, bless her, isn't exactly a philosophical thinker, you know.

WALLACE — H'm — Neither am I, if it comes to that. H'm — Dora and I aren't nearly so complicated as you and Karen, Fen. I've often noticed it — haven't you?

FENWICK — Queer you should put it like that! I mean — just as if —

WALLACE — (*sharing his sudden embarrassment*). Yes — wasn't it!

The opportune arrival of the butler with the coffee relieves the somewhat unexpected tension. But it is tightened a moment later by the announcement that " Wicky " Faber has telephoned that he is in the city and on his way to the house.

The fact that young Faber must skip two lectures to make such a trip on Friday, combined with the somewhat alarming and mysterious tone of Kay's letter, serves to set the quartet wondering what is happening to their young people. Could anything serious have happened? Can Wicky and Kay have quarreled?

The arrival of Wicky soon sets their wondering at rest. He is plainly excited, though, being naturally a quiet young man, he is politely self-contained about it. "He is an agreeable, refined, but rather indefinite personality; and resembles his mother far more than his tall, dark, distinguished father. Physically he looks a little soft; and while he is a thoughtful, sensitive boy there is, somehow, no edge to him."

Wicky's mother goes to him at once, sensing his disturbed state. His father would brace him up with a drop of cognac. But Wicky is not looking for that sort of stimulant at the moment. He is looking for Kay!

DORA — (*gently*). You say Kay has left you, Wicky? Why? We never doubted you were happy together.

WICKY — *I* never doubted it, mother, till five or six months ago — Just after we'd come down from Maine at the beginning of term.

KAREN — (*sharply*). What made you begin to doubt it then?

WICKY — Kay didn't seem like herself — for a week or two. She ——

WALLACE — (*exploding*). My God, am I to stand here and listen to a long tale of this and that — (*He advances on Wicky*). Where's my little girl now — that's what interests me.

WICKY — I don't know, sir.

WALLACE — You don't know!

WICKY — Do you suppose I'd be sitting here like this if I did?

KAREN — (*suddenly*). Kay's my daughter — but you dodge and dodge and force me to ask the one question that matters! (*She stops before Wicky.*) Do you know the man she's bolted with, or don't you?

WICKY — (*shakes his head miserably*). I'm not sure.

KAREN — (*with contempt in her tone*). Oh! — do you even know there **is a** man?

WICKY — (*quietly, but with something dangerous in his voice*). Yes, Mother Kay — I do know that.

DORA — (*before she can check herself*). He knows *Kay*, you see!

(*There is an instant of awful hush, and in that little instant it becomes evident that between those four friends nothing will ever be quite the same again. Dora rises in confusion. There is a pause.*)

FENWICK — (*to his wife*). That was below the belt, Dora. (*Turns to Karen.*) But you can understand — She was thinking only of Wicky. Dora has a one-track mind at times — It wasn't as if —

KAREN — Yes, I know — it just slipped out. The truth does, occasionally, and it's very illuminating! Oh, Dora — little things you've said — little puzzling things that I've passed over as of no consequence — ah, it all comes to me **quite** clearly now. You never really liked Kay or trusted her.

WALLACE — Oh, Karen! You're going too far. Dora's loved Kay like her **own** child.

DORA — Yes. I *do* love her. But a brilliant, nervous, temperamental **being** like that! You know, Karen dear, I've always felt you overstimulated all **that** dangerous side of Kay's nature and —

FENWICK — (*breaking in*). Good heavens, Dora — can't we keep away from these irritating personalities? You ——

WALLACE — Yes, yes, if we four old friends can't handle this situation without — (*Breaks off with a groan.*) Besides, I don't and won't believe my little girl would do such a thing! There's some ridiculous mistake. We all know how prone Wicky is to make ridiculous mistakes. What's happened, anyway? You seem incapable of telling us — but I insist! I'm Kay's father, and —

FENWICK — (*with badly concealed irritation*). My dear old friend, we all know you are Kay's father! But haven't you forgotten who Wicky is?

WICKY — I think you've all forgotten that Kay and I are not children. (*To Wallace.*) You want facts, sir. Well, Kay always has admirers, you know that. This summer she had two who were very much devoted. I was absorbed by my work. I've been very anxious to get on in the world — more for Kay's sake than my own. Besides, I'm a plodder. But I love Kay — who could help it? And I absolutely trusted her. I thought the admirers merely amused her — as they did me. No doubt I was a fool. Well, it's rather evident now that I *was* a fool. (*Wallace starts to interrupt. Wicky prevents him.*) Wait, please! — When we got home again and the fall term started, I was busier than ever. But I soon realized that Kay was moping — and that she no longer cared for me in the old way. I was very hurt about it. Instead of talking it all **out** frankly with her, I drew my head into my shell — and sulked. We didn't discuss the matter — and we didn't quarrel. Then, after a few weeks, the whole thing seemed to blow over. Kay cheered up — became much more like her old self; and — naturally — I fell into the trap ——

KAREN — (*sharply*). Trap?

WICKY — I'm sorry, Mother Kay — but I don't know what else to call it — now.

KAREN — Never mind. Go on, please.

WICKY — There's not much more to tell. I had class work this morning from eight to ten. I was home by eleven. Kay was gone — and her personal **effects** with her; except her engagement and wedding rings and the few bits of **presents** I've been able to give her from time to time. These were left **on my desk**; but no word with them.

Both families are quickly aflame with the desire to provide their respective offspring with a reasonable alibi. Karen stands stanchly back of Kay. She has not done, nor would she think of doing, a cowardly thing. Being

brave, and learning that her marrying Wicky has been a
mistake, Kay has probably gone straight to the man she
really loves.

"Straight? Gone *straight?*" laughs Dora, a little
shrilly. "Well, I'd hardly put it that way, Karen, if I
were you!"

Which starts a discussion that serves more definitely
to reveal the natural sympathies of this quartet of old
friends. Fenwick Faber understands Karen Aldcroft
perfectly. It is natural that she should stand up for her
own child.

And Wallace Aldcroft finds it equally easy to get Dora
Faber's point of view. There is nothing brave in what
Kay has done — if she has done it — and he cannot
understand how Karen can defend even her own daughter
if she has left her husband for another man.

Wicky is both surprised and hurt at the revelation
of his respected elders's pettiness. "Do you realize that
you are all quarreling like children?" he demands.

KAREN — (*at last, hanging her head*). Like children — yes. Fen, Wicky's
right. We've never been anything but children. We've played with ideas —
played at living our lives — played at being grown up — And now Kay — my
baby — has dared to do something honest — something *real!* Oh — no wonder
we're panic-stricken — It's laughable!

WALLACE — (*stupefied*). Laughable? I can't make you out tonight.

KAREN — Of course not! I don't blame you. I can't make myself out.
You can't expect a female infant to mature in five minutes. You must give me
a little time! (*She is laughing.*)

WALLACE — (*to Fenwick*). Is she hysterical, or what? (*He appeals to Dora,
helplessly.*) Do you understand a word she's saying, Dora?

DORA — (*quietly*). Perhaps. But I can still hope I'm mistaken, Wally — for
all our sakes.

KAREN — (*laughing*). Toys — toys — toys! Wicky — you're up against reality
now and you understand me. If Kay doesn't love you — if she does love another
man — do you want her back? No matter how it hurts — do you want her back?
And could you possibly respect her if she came?

WALLACE — That's pretty wild talk —

KAREN — (*cutting him off*). No, Wally, it isn't. But for years we've been
discussing these things in a vacuum — all of us. We've made a sort of word-
game out of it! And now, it isn't a game any more — it's right here among
us. And you're afraid of it! But Kay wasn't afraid of it! That's why I'm
proud of her — and I'd be ashamed not to take her part — Yes, against all of
you, if it's necessary.

FENWICK — But it isn't necessary, Karen.

DORA — (*on an involuntary breath of dismay*). Oh — *Fen* —

FENWICK — Please, please, don't misunderstand me, Dora. All my natural
sympathy goes to Wicky. On the other hand — we're supposed to be more or
less enlightened men and women, aren't we? Well, if we are — we must know

do can't mend things by taking a conventional attitude. Is there one of us who believes morality means obeying certain fixed rules handed down from above? Of course not! All life is chance — a continuous experiment; and —

DORA — (*interrupting*). Yes, dear, that will make a very nice editorial — perfectly cool and reasonable — and beside the point. Wicky, dear, wouldn't you like to take your unintelligent mother home? She wants to say foolish things and cry a little. I wish you would.

WICKY — (*quietly, but boyishly; his voice breaking a little*). Oh, Mother — thank God for you! (*He embraces her.*)

DORA — And for you, dear. Come, get your overcoat. My wraps are in the hall, I think.

But it is not as easy for them to walk away from this mounting domestic unhappiness as Dora thought. Wallace, for one thing, demands that Wicky shall *do* something. If he knows who have been Kay's admirers he should name them. If he has any idea where she is or whom she is with the least he can do is to try to save her from the mad thing she has done. It is probably his neglect that has driven her to it. And if he will not do anything to right the situation her father will.

But Wicky has no intention either of searching Kay out or of trying to browbeat her into returning to her home if she should be found. He loves her too much to beg her to come back to him.

It is not easy for either Dora or Wallace to understand Wicky's attitude. If he loves Kay he should try to save her if only for her own good, his mother believes. And it is Wallace's opinion that he is entirely responsible for the whole affair. But here Dora springs again to the defense of her son.

DORA — (*quickly — a hand on Wicky's arm*). Oh, Wally, how *stupid* of you! Now you force me to say something I — didn't want to say. Karen, have you ever given Kay a chance? Have you ever taught her — *anything* that matters? You've filled her vain foolish little head with fancies and ideas she couldn't possibly digest.

KAREN — (*her eyes flashing*). Really, Dee — there's a limit ——

FENWICK — (*breaking in*). Yes, *really*, Dora! I can't see the least excuse for such an attack on — (*He checks himself*) on your best friends!

KAREN — (*to Fenwick*). On *me*, you mean.

WALLACE — (*unexpectedly*). Well, I can and do! I thoroughly agree with Dora — so there. I've never approved of all this stuff you've foisted on Kay — this feminism — new freedom — whatever you want to call it. Social anarchy, *I* call it!

KAREN — (*with passionate scorn*). Ha! There we have it, Fen — the whole story! Our broad-minded publisher — bringing out, advertising, living on the sale of modern books; but secretly cherishing all the medieval prejudices of his Puritan ancestors! Scuttling like a rat for a dark hole at the first —

DORA — (*breaking in, with genuine anguish*). Oh, Karen, how *can* you! To — Wally — ?

KAREN — Yes — to Wally — and to *you* too — if you're both such hypocrites!

WALLACE — (*dangerously*). Be careful, Karen.

KAREN — Oh — be careful — be cautious — respect the sacred conventions — of course, of course! But I tell you both, they haven't been just a social game with me, my ideas. From now on I mean to live by them as Kay has.

WALLACE — Kay — ideas! Kay doesn't live on ideas — and neither do you. You both live on excitement — live on your nerves!

FENWICK — (*trying to speak gravely above the tumult within him*). Come, come, Wally — that's a cheap sarcasm. Now, let me put it to you this way —

DORA — Oh, another editorial.

FENWICK — Yes, if you like, Dora. (*To Wallace once more.*) You and Dora have drifted with the times, but you've never really broken with the past. Kay has, it seems — as for Wicky —

WICKY — (*breaks in roughly*). As for me, Dad — I'm sick of all this. Can I have my old room tonight, Mother? I've got to catch an early train back in the morning.

WALLACE — Now look here, you're not going to leave this room till you tell me the names of those men —

WICKY — (*shaking his head slowly*). Sorry — I've no real reason to suspect either of them, you see — How do I know that it isn't some other man — some one I've never even so much as thought of? (*Passionately.*) And besides — I'm not blaming Kay. People are made as they're made — and things work out as they work out. That's all there is to it.

Wicky and his mother have gone. Karen, Fenwick and Wallace continue to grope for some line of immediate action. Wallace would go at once in search of Kay if he had the least idea where to find her, or if he knew the name of the man she is suspected of being with. Kay must have mentioned him in some of her letters.

Karen still stands her ground as her daughter's defender, whatever she has done. And inasmuch as Kay's letters were written to her she refuses to have them searched for evidence. In this stand Faber upholds her.

KAREN — (*to Wallace, with passion*). Haven't Fen and I made it clear to you — hasn't Wicky himself made it clear to you — that we won't have Kay treated like the erring daughter in a melodrama? — Humiliated and — and bullyragged!

WALLACE — See here, Karen, I think we'd better understand each other. Can you seriously expect me to sit down with folded hands when —

KAREN — (*interrupting*). I'll tell you what I have the right to expect, Wally — That you'll stop thinking of Kay as a child and think of her as a woman — responsible for her own conduct to herself and to nobody else in the whole world. Am I right, Fen?

FENWICK — Of course, you're right —

KAREN — Ah!

FENWICK — . . . but — all the same ——

WALLACE — Exactly. You see even Fen can't swallow that! Why, you don't know what you're talking about.

KAREN — The old manly assumption. I thought so. (*Wallace, with an impatient shrug, turns to enter the bedroom.*) Where are you going, Wally?

WALLACE — Why, to get the letters, of course.

KAREN — Oh no — no! They happen to be *my* letters — shut up in *my* desk. If you'd asked me for them, I might or might not have refused. Now I'd rather die than give you permission —

WALLACE — (*curtly*). I haven't asked your permission. As your husband and Kay's father, I consider that I have that right.

KAREN — Wally! If you open my desk and take Kay's letters from it —

WALLACE — Yes — ? I advise you to weigh your words carefully, for that's precisely what I'm going to do. (*A pause.*)

KAREN — (*speaks very quietly*). Then — I bow to the inevitable.

WALLACE — (*misunderstanding her, in a deep breath of relief*). Ah — ! I thought you'd come to your senses. You too, Fen. After all — there can't be two heads to a family —

KAREN — No, no, Wally, there can't be — (*Wallace nods and passes on into the bedroom.*) There can't even be one. (*She moves swiftly to Fenwick and drops her hand as she gets close to him. He takes it.*) Ah! (*She slips into Fenwick's arms.*)

FENWICK — (*terrified, in a broken whisper*). Karen — not here — not like this — we've lost our senses —

KAREN — (*clinging to him*). No, no, I want him to find me in your arms. I want him to.

FENWICK — Sh! Sh!

They are standing thus, Karen's cheek pressed against his, when " Kay Faber rushes in breathlessly. She stops dead in her tracks staring at Fenwick and her mother. Karen utters a startled exclamation, hiding her head. Fenwick tries to prevent Kay from recognizing her mother."

Kay stands in the doorway completely taken aback by what she has seen.

" Daddy Faber — what is it? I don't understand," she cries.

And then, suddenly hiding her face in her hands, she wails, " Oh, I don't want to understand. I don't want to understand," and rushes from the room. The slamming of the outer door arouses Karen. " Fen, stop her! Do you realize ——"

Fenwick realizes. At least he realizes what may happen if Kay were to go straight to Dora and demand an explanation from her of what she has seen, and his sense of self-protection moves him suddenly to run after Kay.

Wallace returns with Kay's letters just in time to hear the slamming door and is puzzled by Fenwick's hurry.

But he is more puzzled a moment later when the former returns and reports to Karen that he was unable to overtake Kay. It is the father's first knowledge that his daughter had been there and he can't understand why he was not called. Or why Karen did not tell him? Or what it was that frightened Kay away again!

Now he is more determined than ever that he must find her. From her letters he has narrowed her possible affairs down to two. It is either Bob Grayling or Clyde Halstead, the latter a novelist of none too savory a reputation.

WALLACE — . . . Fen, I want you to go straight to Bob Grayling's rooms, will you?

FENWICK — But I don't know him ——

WALLACE — You don't know him? Neither do I — so much the better. Here's the address. I'll take on Clyde Halstead myself, damn him! But we can't afford not to get in touch with them both, Fen. I needn't give you any instructions; you're Wicky's father and —

FENWICK — (impatiently). Yes, yes, yes! I happen to know that. But what I'd like to know is whether you're going to Halstead's to lose your head and make some kind of ridiculous scene —

WALLACE — (breaking in). I'll make a ridiculous scene, thank you, if necessary, and otherwise, not. I don't need your advice, Fen — when it comes to protecting my family. Well — well, are you coming?

FENWICK — (after a deeply troubled glance at Karen, who almost imperceptibly signals him to go at once). Yes, yes — of course. Shall we report back here as soon as possible — either in person or by telephone? (Passes on out.)

KAREN — Wally — just a moment, please.

WALLACE — Well — ?

KAREN — (quietly, tensely). I haven't changed my mind, Wally. If you find Kay, I'll be glad. If you can persuade her to come here to me of her own free will — and talk things over, I'll be gladder still. But if you do anything foolish, or — worse than foolish —

WALLACE — Do you expect me to stand here and argue? I'll do what's right — what's my duty.

KAREN — (with irony). And of course you know what that is!

WALLACE — Better than you do, I'm afraid, Karen.

KAREN — (quietly). Very well. I've nothing more to say to you.

WALLACE — Thank God for that. (Goes to door. Stops.) Oh! — Tell Fisher he's not to turn in till I get back. And — please don't worry. It isn't my idea of protecting you and Kay to get your names in the newspapers. (Gravely.) In short, my dear, I'm not quite such an ass as you and Fen seem to imagine — not quite.

Alone, Karen is trying desperately to clear her mind as to a proper course to pursue when Clyde Halstead is announced. The announcement, however, is merely a formality, as Halstead immediately follows the butler into the room. At 34 " Halstead is a success, financially and socially; a popular novelist with an attractive person, who is getting from life almost everything he has it in him to care for. He is well-groomed, dressed for the evening. Something is disturbing him — obviously; yet he is making a gallant effort to conceal the fact."

He has come in search of Kay, and he is entirely honest and self-poised about it. He doesn't mind " fencing " with Mrs. Aldcroft and he admires her apparent determination both to shield her daughter and to pretend that she knows nothing of his and Kay's intimate friendship. But he is convinced that Kay, having left him, has returned to her home, and the fact that he picked up a scented handkerchief in the hall which he recognized as Kay's convinces him that his surmise is correct.

KAREN — (*frowning thoughtfully*). Mr. Halstead, I ought to be very angry with you — but I'm not. Do you know, I like you much better than your books, Mr. Halstead.

HALSTEAD — (*with irony*). I've never doubted you were a woman of taste, Mrs. Aldcroft.

KAREN — (*with a smile*). There. Now we're quits. Kay *has* been here.

HALSTEAD — Ah!

KAREN — And gone again.

HALSTEAD — What! (*Bursting forth.*) Gone back to that stupid husband of hers! Good God, if she has! It's the most dastardly thing I ever heard of —

KAREN — (*breaks in quickly*). Haven't you rather singular ideas of right and wrong, Mr. Halstead?

HALSTEAD — No! I have the ideas of my time. The normal, conventional ideas of my time. So have *you*, I think! I don't believe *you'd* call it straight if a woman arranged to leave her husband — to go to a man able to appreciate her, and then, at the last moment — with her baggage at his rooms, steamer tickets bought, everything — simply funked it! My God — if that isn't moral cowardice — lack of sportsmanship — I'd like to know what is!

KAREN — Why you amazing person!

HALSTEAD — Where is Kay?

KAREN — I don't know.

HALSTEAD — She mustn't be allowed to make a terrible mistake — spoil her whole life like this! What did she come for? Why did you let her go?

KAREN — (*trying for dignity*). My daughter is a free agent, Mr. Halstead. When will men ever learn to mind their own business — and let women attend to theirs!

HALSTEAD — (*impatiently*). Yes — that's all very well, of course! But I'm not discussing all that! I don't give a damn — Beg pardon, Mrs. Aldcroft, but *really* — *!* How do you suppose this sort of thing is going to make *me* look? It's certain to get out. This sort of thing always does. And here am I with the steamer tickets and a taxi ordered for twelve-ten and all Kay's stuff piled up in my rooms and —

KAREN — Oh! — Then if Mr. Aldcroft should force his way into your rooms somehow, he'd be sure to discover —

HALSTEAD — What are you talking about?

KAREN — (*with dignity*). My husband left for your place just before you arrived.
HALSTEAD — (*angrily*). Ah! — that's it! Well, let me assure you that Mr. Aldcroft will *not* force his way into my rooms. Furthermore, under the circumstances, you had better advise your husband to keep very quiet about all this — very quiet indeed. Kay's treated me damnably — and I'm not a very forgiving person, you understand. I've a certain reputation, I think, and I'm in no mood to be badgered — or made ridiculous.
KAREN — (*a step toward him*). Why — you insufferable person! You're thinking only of yourself!
HALSTEAD — Naturally — Aren't *you* — ? Good night.

He turns to the door, but before he can pass through, the outer door slams and Wicky Faber enters. For a second the two men stare at each other, Halstead a little apprehensive, Wicky calmly contemptuous even if he is a bit excited. He would like to know from Karen what Halstead is doing there, but when Karen hesitates before answering him, Halstead coolly takes it upon himself to explain.

" I'll tell you in three words, Mr. Faber," says he. " Your wife grew tired of you — thought she could use me as a convenient way station — found she couldn't — and is probably at this moment on her way back to New Haven again. I advise you to join her — and comfort her. Good-night — Good-night to you both!"

Wicky makes no move to follow, and has no words to protest, which angers Karen. Is he so spineless? Doesn't he even want to chastise this would-be despoiler of his home? No wonder Kay left him! Women hate cowards!

" What they really hate, Mother Kay, is civilization," the young philosopher answers her. " But don't try to understand that remark. It's too deep for you."

KAREN — I never realized before what a contemptible weakling you are.
WICKY — (*breaks in quietly, but firmly*). I wouldn't say things like that if I were you, Mother Kay. You'll regret them later.
KAREN — Oh — I don't understand you at all!
WICKY — No. But it doesn't surprise me. Understanding things isn't your strongest point, Mother Kay. You're an utterly instinctive creature, you know. Most women are — Why, look at poor Mother. Father Kay called her up just now before leaving here to go to Halstead's rooms.
KAREN — He called Dora up, did he?
WICKY — Yes, and now Mother's rushed off to join him, afraid Father Kay will get hurt, I guess.
KAREN — (*with contempt*). Oh, if you think you can excuse yourself by —
WICKY — (*interrupting her as before*). But why should the one halfway

reasonable being in this ridiculous family try to excuse himself? (*Karen starts to speak.*) Now don't interrupt me — I'm going to say my say and have done with it. When I first came tonight and told you Kay had left me — what happened? You and Dad — instinctively — took Kay's part. Why? Because of your modern ideas? Nonsense! Because, for years probably, you've both been wanting to kick over the traces yourselves. As for Mother — and Father Kay — they instinctively leagued together too.
    KAREN — (*impulsively*). Yes. They *did* — didn't they?
    WICKY — Why — it's obvious — it's pathetic. So far as your instinctive emotions go, you're all married to the wrong persons — whether you're aware of it or not. Any good Freudian would tell you to change partners — and be happy. Well — but I'm not a good Freudian, you see. If you *did* change partners you wouldn't be happy. Life isn't built for personal happiness — you can't get it at any price. Unless you've found God — which you haven't — for a very good reason. And no more have I — !

Fenwick Faber is back. He had found Grayling engaged in a poker game, so that clue is dead. Now, with Karen's help, he understands why. But he can see no reason why he and she should go chasing after Wallace and Dora, as she suggests. Surely the gathering at Halstead's rooms promises to be quite complete without them. But he agrees to go just the same, when Karen becomes a little peremptory about it.

Wicky watches them through the door with a rueful shake of his head. " Poor Dad — poor — everybody ——" he sighs.

" He reaches absent-mindedly for a drink, goes to tabouret for a match for his pipe and his hand encounters Kay's handkerchief. He takes it up — the scent is wafted to him and changes instantly his whole lackadaisical manner. He reads the initials, then suddenly dashes off through Karen's bedroom."

" Kay!" he calls, wildly; " Kay!"

But there is no answer and he stands in the center of the room " with his old air of utterly weary discouragement; but there is a subtle difference in him — a profounder note of wretchedness. Kay's handkerchief is still crumpled in his hand. He returns to the same chair. Finally, with a sudden passionate movement, he buries his face in the handkerchief, murmuring brokenly, ' My darling — my *darling* ——' "

The curtain falls

ACT II

The scene changes to Clyde Halstead's bachelor quarters in Central Park South. "The large comfortable living room is the workshop of a popular, affluent novelist, but at the moment it is a trifle mussed up with a steamer trunk, a suit case and a hand bag."

Barney Degan, Halstead's man, "a quiet young Irish-American with a pronounced limp—his personal souvenir from the late war," is engaged in painting out the initials on the steamer trunk, when the ringing of the phone bell interrupts him.

There is a visitor below stairs. She is to be sent up, Degan instructs. But no one else is to be admitted. "We're not at home to a livin' other soul tonight, understand? No matter what they say," he instructs the guardian below.

The visitor is Kay Faber. "Ordinarily a vivid, colorful, restless being, she drifts into the room like a wraith. She is white, still, repressed." Nor is Degan entirely successful in trying to make her feel at ease.

DEGAN — Now don't you worry, Miss. He called me up, see — and I'm wise to everything. It'll all go through now as smooth as silk — now you make yourself at home — and I'll be finishing this job, if it's the same to you ——

KAY — (*smiles faintly*). Clyde told me heaps about you, Barney Degan — last summer, you know. He was always wishing you were with him — to take charge of our picnics, and all that.

DEGAN — (*at work on trunk*). Well, he *made* me take the vacation. *I* didn't want to. It only got me into trouble, and I didn't need any more of it, Miss, believe me.

KAY — Vacations *are* rather dangerous, aren't they?

DEGAN — Terrible! Specially with the girls like they are nowadays. Gee — what my old mother'd think, if she was livin' — !

KAY — (*unexpectedly; with passion*). I know. She'd be right, too, Barney Degan. There's no excuse for us — any of us — that I can see. Don't you just hate life? Doesn't it disgust you? Of course it does!

DEGAN — (*flabbergasted*). Well — now — Miss — when you take a guy's breath away like that——

KAY — Don't pay any attention to me. It doesn't matter. Go on with your work. (*Drifts from him toward the window, wraith-like once more.*) What did Clyde say when he phoned you?

DEGAN — He — (*hesitates, then gets to his feet*). Mr. Halstead wanted to know if you'd arrived yet.

KAY — Didn't that surprise you?

DEGAN — Well, I didn't let on, Miss. I could tell Mr. Halstead was kind of upset. So I says no, the lady ain't here yet; and he says all right, if she gets there before I do make her comfy, see — but I won't be long myself.

KAY — (tonelessly). I ran away from him, Barney. I couldn't eat the
dinner — he knew how to order — so I slipped off to the dressing room while
he was paying the bill — and then I ran — and ran — (Gets cigarette, lights it.)
and ran. I've been running away from things so long now — it's a habit I
suppose. I keep running away and running away — but now I'm not going
to try any more. You see, the trouble is — I can't run away from myself.
There's only one way of doing that — (Drops head on table.) Oh God, why
did you mention your mother, Barney Degan, why did you — why did you?
    DEGAN — What is it, Miss? What is it?
    KAY — Don't pay any attention to my nonsense. I — I'm just having a fit of
nerves ——

She cannot eat the food he suggests she needs, nor
is she interested in amusing herself at the piano in the
library. But she does get a little comfort from his
quaint philosophy of life. A guy can't let anything get
him, Barney has decided. Out of the war a lot of guys
brought nothing but an overwhelming sense of disgust
with the whole bag o' tricks. What was there to life,
anyway? What was the use o' livin'?

"But, pshaw, Miss — a guy can't go on like that —
not unless he's plumb dippy," he adds. "It ain't
natural. Something turns up sooner or later, see? A
girl — or a ball game or something — and kind of gets
you thinking of something else. That's the real dope,
Miss — thinking of something else — see? (With a
grin.) Why, it's like you right now! You was sort of
all in. But the minute you started thinking of me 'stead
of yerself — you begins feelin' better straight off. Ain't
that right, Miss? Sure it is! But all the same I'm
going to get you just a little drop of something, eh ——?"

Kay doesn't want anything in the way of artificial
stimulants. Neither, she repeats, is she in a mood for
music. She probably will be ready for ragtime soon,
however. She's not going to let life beat her — of that
much she's certain.

Again the phone bell interrupts and Kay picks it up
before Degan can reach the stand. It is, she thinks, sure
to be Clyde Halstead. But it is her father instead —
and he has recognized her voice before Degan can get the
phone away from her.

A few moments later, despite Degan's efforts to stop

him, Wallace Aldcroft walks into the room. His manner, however, is more anxious than belligerent. He has come to take his daughter away, or at least to listen to her explanation of why she is there, and he has no intention of leaving at anyone's request until this mission has been accomplished.

Kay, taking charge of the situation with exceptional calmness, succeeds in sending Degan from the room. Then she turns to her father.

KAY — If you'll sit down with me, Daddy — and — and try not to feel I'm a soul on the brink of destruction — I'll talk to you. But — straight talk, dearest — between a grown woman and a man she respects and loves! — Oh, don't you understand — if it can't be that way it simply can't be at all?

WALLACE — (gravely, after a pause). Very well, Kay, straight talk. As you say, you've sneaked away from your husband to give yourself to another man. That's a rotten thing to have done — and a cruel thing as you chose to manage it. Without frankness — with no word of explanation left — cruel. I don't recognize you in it, Kay — I can't believe it of you yet — even here — in these rooms, my daughter — (A spasm of pain crosses his face; his hands drop from her shoulder.) I simply can't endure the thought of it ——! (He turns from her.)

KAY — (after a long pause; tonelessly). Rotten — cruel — yes. You're right, Daddy. I won't try to defend myself. But I can't turn back.

WALLACE — (wheeling round to her eagerly). Nonsense! Of course you can! Why, good heavens, sweetheart, if you're sorry already for what you've done ——

KAY — (with passion). Have you never done anything you hated? — but you had to go through with it — just because you were made that way — or pushed that way?

WALLACE — (struck by the phrase, and searching Kay's face). Pushed that way? I don't quite — (Breaks off, then speaks more gently.) Exactly what did you mean by — "Pushed that way — ?"

KAY — (who is thinking of her mother). Oh — everything — nothing! Things in me that — but I can't explain to you, Daddy. I won't.

WALLACE — Not to me? Not to your father? Well, I can understand that, perhaps — But to your mother?

KAY — (with sudden, impulsive violence). No, no, no! I don't want to see her, Daddy — ever again!

WALLACE — You don't want to see your mother — again? (Kay shakes her head, and turns from him to hide her emotion.) Kay, there's something more in all this — there's something behind your words that I don't — get hold of ——

KAY — (turns to him). You never will, Daddy— not from me.

Again, when her mother's name is brought into the conversation, Kay refuses to explain her meaning, even though her father is determinedly persistent. "Good heavens, Father, isn't it all plain enough?" she cries. "I've left Wicky and come to Clyde Halstead. I'm not sorry — I'm not ashamed — and I shall stay with him."

WALLACE — I see. Because you love him so deeply that nothing else — not even your hating the whole thing — weighs in the balance — · Is that it? (*Kay doesn't answer.*) Is that the truth of it, my dear?

KAY — Yes, yes, of course — of course it is! — Daddy, won't you please go now? It's no use, you see — I can't change — I'm only doing what I must do — what it's my *right* to do as a free human being — and if Clyde comes while you're here you'll only quarrel, make a scene! It would be so — disgraceful, Daddy. But it wouldn't do any good — not a bit of good — to anybody!

The phone rings and Wallace, reaching it first, listens in. Halstead is talking to Degan on the extension phone in the other room. The conversation over, Wallace quietly hangs up the receiver and orders a taxi for Kay. He will wait and meet Halstead, but his daughter, he tells Degan, will return to her home.

Kay, however, has no intention of doing anything of the kind, and when Degan starts moving her steamer trunk toward the elevator, she demands an explanation. Her father furnishes it. " Halstead's at his club," he explains. " He never wants to see you again. Says when you left him at dinner that ended it so far as he's concerned. He won't return until you and your things are gone. The man is to let him know."

Kay is stunned but not overcome by this turn of affairs. She soon recovers from a momentary weakness, and there is a note of relief in her voice as she says: " It serves me right. I suppose I ought to die of shame — or something — but I'm not going to — you'll see, Daddy ——"

She is on her way to the taxi when Dora Faber bursts into the room. She has come to see that no harm comes to Wallace.

DORA — I couldn't help it, Wally. I was so afraid, afraid something might happen — (*Breaks off lamely, turns to Kay putting out hands.*) Oh, my dear — if we can all be — just as we used to — to be ——

KAY — As we used to be — oh! That's almost — funny — Mother Dora!

WALLACE — Wait, please, Dora — let me tell you what I know. When Kay left home this morning she meant to elope with Clyde Halstead. There's no doubt of that. Her trunk and bags were sent here. But it was arranged between them to meet first at dinner — at some public restaurant. I don't know why — but when Kay did meet Halstead she found she couldn't go through with it. (*To Kay.*) Am I right, sweetheart? (*Kay does not answer.*) Yes. At any rate, she slipped off from him somehow — vanished; and there is no doubt she meant never to see him again — (*checks an attempted interruption from Dora*) for she came straight home to her mother.

KAY — · Oh, Daddy — then Mother told you — confessed —— ?

DORA — Confessed? Karen did? What does she mean, Wally?

WALLACE — What do you mean, dear — confess what, Kay? You know, Dora, how upset and overwrought Karen has been all day over a letter she received from Kay this morning — well — it's not surprising that when Wicky burst in on her this evening with the news that Kay had disappeared, her nerves gave way and she went all to pieces, fainted. Luckily, Fen who happened to be there, was just in time to catch her and save her from a nasty fall, and sent Wicky immediately for me. Wicky had barely left the room, so Fen explained, when Kay suddenly appeared and almost as suddenly turned and fled. When I arrived Karen was just coming to. Now, dear, what is all this mystery about confessing —

KAY — Oh, Daddy — Thank God. What a fool — how could I have thought —

WALLACE — Thought what, Kay?

KAY — Why, when I saw mother in Daddy Faber's arms, oh ——

WALLACE — Kay — Kay ——

KAY — Oh, what a fool! (*Kisses him.*) Forgive me, Daddy — (*Reaches for her coat and hat.*)

WALLACE — Where are you going?

KAY — I'm going home to my mother.

DEGAN — The taxi is waiting. (*He is very sullen.*) Shall I take the bags down, sir?

WALLACE — Yes, take them — if you will, please. You'd better go with her, Dora. I must see Halstead before I leave.

DORA — And I must see *you* before I leave, Wally.

KAY — I'm going on alone, Mother Dora.

WALLACE — Now ——

KAY — Now don't make a useless fuss, Daddy, I'm not a school girl and I've got to be alone. (*To Dora.*) Is Wicky with you tonight?

DORA — Yes, dear. But I'll bring him to you after you've seen your mother — shall I?

KAY — Please. But don't deceive yourself, Mother Dora. I'm not going back to him ever. I left him because I had to. Only — Daddy's right. It was rotten to sneak away. I should have had the courage to tell him. And now, when it's so much harder — well — now I must tell him. Then — perhaps — some day — I can hold up my head again. Now don't argue with me, Daddy. I tell you I'm going.

Left by themselves, Dora and Wallace, a little reluctantly, face their own problem. There is a boundless sympathy and complete understanding between them, but each knows that, whatever may happen to the others, they, at least, must go on doing what to them is the right thing.

WALLACE — . . . But think of Kay, almost driven back into Halstead's arms by the shock of seeing her own mother ——! My God, Dora, what is there in the world but being fathers and mothers to keep people decent — make them do what's right — by all of us — instead of grabbing at everything they want the moment they want it!

DORA — (*quietly, sadly*). We would have been so happy together, Wally.

WALLACE — (*deeply moved*). Dora! (*He takes her hand.*) Are we all wrong about this thing? Are we just conventional fools, sacrificing ourselves to no purpose? Suppose Karen and Fen, in spite of everything, do run off together — ?

DORA — It won't make any difference to us, Wally. We'll stick it out on the old line, whatever happens. You see, my dear, we just happen — both of us — to be made that way ——

WALLACE — Yes — yes — that's it, I suppose. What is the newfangled lingo for being decent — ?

Dora — (*smiling up at him, withdraws hand gently*).   Inhibited, Wally.   We're
inhibited ——
    Wallace — Yes.
    Dora —Only— *we* mustn't try to be up-to-date, Wally.   It doesn't become
us.   Let's put it the simple, old-fashioned way, my dear.   Let's say we believe
in being good ——
    Wallace — Well, yes — confound it —   We *do* — there you are!
    Dora — Ah — !   (*With a sigh, as her hand slips slowly from his shoulder.*)
There you are! ——

They do not hear Halstead when he enters and a little
insolently apologizes for the interruption.

Aldcroft is in fighting mood immediately.   He is of a
mind to chastise the " contemptible hound " who has
stolen his daughter, but he is restrained by Dora.

Halstead is rather amused at the older man's over-
confidence in his physical powers — and though he smarts
under the epithet applied, he is willing to overlook it —
for business reasons.

    Halstead — Why not — ?   Since I mean you to publish my next novel — pay
me an advance of twenty thousand on it — and advertise it as you've never
advertised a novel before.   If I can't thrash you one way, I can another — and
I intend to do it.
    Wallace — Never! — Dora!   Is the man mad or does he think for a moment
that I — !
    Halstead — Do you want it known that your daughter threw herself at my
head — sent her trunk to my rooms — came here uninvited — and was ejected
by my valet, at my request?   — No; you don't.   Neither do I care to have it
known, as it happens.   Our interests are identical.   And nothing will do more to
prevent malicious gossip than your bringing out my next novel.   " Contemptible
hound " isn't a pretty phrase, Mr. Aldcroft.   I don't forget such things easily —
You see, Mrs. Faber, I am really being generosity itself.
    Wallace — Come, Dora.   I apologize for my part in this disgraceful scene.
    Halstead — (*insolently*).   You agree, then, of course — ?
    Wallace — Never.   (*Quietly.*)   And let me tell you, if you spread lies about
my daughter you will be held responsible.   I'm not in the habit of yielding to
— blackmail.
    Halstead — What did you say?   Blackmail.   By — !

    (*His right fist shoots out to Wallace's jaw; Wallace collapses heavily onto
the sofa.   Dora, with a cry, throws herself down on her knees beside Wallace and
takes his head on her shoulders, murmuring broken expressions of love and pity.*)

All of which is highly diverting to Halstead.   The
discovery of this new entanglement is positively touching.   " What a revelation! " he almost shouts in his joy.
" Dear me, dear me — the secret wickedness of this wicked
world! "

The next minute the door bell rings and the voices
of Fenwick Faber and Karen Aldcroft are heard in the

hall. Neither Dora nor the now recovered but still
wobbly Wallace feels up to facing the others just now.
They leave quickly by an inner hall, and the discovery
of their flight adds considerably to Halstead's continued
enjoyment of the situation. His manner irritates Karen
excessively. If she were a man she would thrash the
novelist for his insolence, and Faber's refusal to do so
at her suggestion reveals clearly to her from which of his
parents Wicky Faber inherits his cowardice.

Halstead continues his cheerful review of the situation, subtly insinuating his conviction that Mr. Aldcroft
and Dora Faber are quite satisfied with the new family
arrangements. At which Faber flares up threateningly,
though he permits Halstead to leave the room with an
ironical smile of triumph on his face. Which again
serves to arouse the more excitable Mrs. Aldcroft.

KAREN — . . . If you were a man you'd go in there and thrash him within an
inch of his life — try to, anyway!

FENWICK — Be quiet, I tell you. Hasn't there been scandal enough? For
Kay's sake at least.

KAREN — Oh, you hypocrite. Wally's the only real man among you! Oh! —
how I could ever have supposed that I loved you — !

FENWICK — (in an agony). Oh — come now — as for there being anything
serious in that little flare-up between *us* tonight, I'd be the last man to ——

KAREN — (breaking in with contempt). Yes. The *very* last. I can see that
— now. (With a bitter little smile.) And so — everything's serene again, isn't it?

FENWICK — (fervently). I hope so. I *hope* so.

KAREN — I thought you would. Kay's saved! *I'M* saved! *YOU'RE* saved!
He! — it's like the end of a comedy! Forgiveness all round — kiss your partners
— quick curtain. I'm going. (Starts for hall.)

FENWICK — (following her). Wait! I'm coming with you.

KAREN — (scornfully and with rising emotion). Oh, no. We've made our
renunciation, Fen — our noble renunciation. Don't spoil the picture! — And
besides — I'm sick of the sight of you! But no doubt you feel — exactly the
same way about me — (Starting off again.)

FENWICK — (flaring up). Well, yes — if you will have it! You've opened
my eyes tonight. You — you're a dangerous woman!

KAREN — (a step toward him). Yes, I am. Most women are, you'll find out.
Even *Dora* ——

FENWICK — How dare you — Dora's an angel!

KAREN — Exactly. So is Wally! That's why we mustn't throw them together
any longer — !

FENWICK — Karen! You don't mean to say you — really think Dora and
Wally — care for each other — ?

KAREN — (with an hysterical touch of laughter). Of course they do. Don't
we *all* care for each other? Aren't we the four oldest and best friends in the
world?

FENWICK — (crushed). Dora and Wally! — Good God — how can you joke
about it! — You're heartless!

KAREN — (*suddenly breaking into tears*). I'm not — I'm not! If you **only** knew how I hate myself — you — everybody! Everybody but — but **Wally and** Kay. (*Then she flings up her head again and dashes the tears from her eyes.*) Oh — you go back to your wife, Fen — I'm going home. (*She turns and hurries off through the hall.*)

FENWICK — (*stands for a moment perfectly silent staring off after Karen; then his hand goes to his head and he mutters*). Dora and Wally ——

(*The bedroom door opens. Halstead re-enters, still with his insolent smile.*)

HALSTEAD — Oh — Still here, Mr. Faber — ? Have you anything further **to** say to me — ? If not ——

FENWICK — (*in a sudden frenzy of rage*). Yes. I've a lot to say, **you** home-wrecker! You're a cad — a bully — a sneak — and a damn bad **novelist!** (*He dashes down his hat.*) Now come on — ! (*He starts to take off his coat, springs at Halstead and grapples with him.*)

The curtain falls

ACT III

Back in the Aldcroft living room Wicky is waiting. " He has been drinking his father-in-law's cognac, which has merely intensified his over-wrought nervousness." At the ringing of the phone bell, or the slamming of the front door, he starts excitedly.

He hears Kay's voice in the hall; hears her ask for her mother; hears the butler tell her that Karen is not at home. He waits a little expectantly for her to enter the room, but the slamming door tells of her continuing her search elsewhere, and he sinks, a little weakly, into the chair. A moment later he is called to the phone in the next room.

Wallace and Dora are back from Halstead's, Wallace with a scraped chin where Halstead's fist had landed. Dora is all sympathy for him, and tender in her ministrations. They know, these two, that although their experiences of the last few hours have brought them closer together than they ever have stood before, the new friendship must end there, and this fact makes even these flustered moments together precious.

Wicky startles them from a threatened embrace when he returns excitedly from the phone. The phone message had been from the elder Faber, and was a call for help. In Halstead's room, when Faber and the novelist had grappled, they fell heavily to the floor. Halstead's head struck something and Faber fears that he is dead.

"I'm afraid it's serious," Wicky reports. "He's all to pieces, Mother. He wants you with him before he notifies the police."

Immediately Mrs. Faber's anxiety is all for her own husband rather than her friend's, and she and Wicky rush hurriedly away to the Halstead apartment. . . .

Kay is back. She has been to the Fabers's; she has not found her mother there and she is worried. Her father tries to reassure her, but it is not easy, particularly as he has some difficulty explaining his own recent adventures — including the patch of court plaster Dora Faber has put on his chin. Kay is a little too keen to be taken in by his too elaborate explanations.

KAY — You know very well what I mean, don't you? You've lied to me twice tonight, you're lying to me now. Every squirm of your body tells me so. There's no use, Daddy, fate's against you. Oh, I might have known there at Clyde's while you were telling me — but it was just that I wanted so to believe you.

WALLACE — Because of your mother — Kay, you mustn't misjudge your mother — no, nor YOURSELF — nor Fen either. We were just four old friends, I tell you — until Wicky came. (*Helplessly.*) It isn't anybody's fault. Only — you mustn't blame your mother — and idealize ME.

KAY — Daddy, when I know how big you are now — how fine ——

WALLACE — (*with a groan*). Me — ! Good God, I'm nothing. Your father's a very ordinary man — VERY ORDINARY. You think that it's been any different with your mother and Fen, than with US — Dora and me?

KAY — (*incredulously*). Daddy! YOU — and Mother Dora? (*Searching his face.*) You care for each other — THAT way? Oh no — no.

WALLACE — I don't wonder you can't believe it. I can't. It isn't real. We were four old friends — we had been dining together tonight — four old friends — It's impossible to understand the human heart, Kay — It's as if there were hidden forces — great black reservoirs of hidden forces — There they lie in us, quiet, deep and — terrible — until some shock comes — and they well up and transform us — change everything.

KAY — Poor Daddy — Oh, what have I DONE to all of you? What have I done?

WALLACE — No, no — you mustn't blame yourself. No one seems to be to blame. Come, come, I'm talking nonsense, Kay. The thing to do is to get hold of oneself — and — find out what one ought to do. Well, the thing's out of our hands now — for better or worse. Karen's had her way again. She's gone through with it — left us.

KAY — Yes — and for your sake, Daddy — yours and Mother Dora's — I think I'm glad.

WALLACE — No, no, Kay — you're not. There's no gladness in all this — not for any of us. The whole thing is — dreadful.

KAY — Yes — dreadful — (*Passionately.*) But I'm hanged if I see why. I don't see why it isn't the best thing for all of you. I don't see why you should all sacrifice yourselves to — idiotic, old-fashioned, used-up ideas. After all, Mother and *I* — we're two of a kind, Daddy. Why should *I* have been shocked by seeing her — Perhaps she's right. Perhaps she's the only one of us who is right — who sees things straight and — isn't a coward — But oh, Daddy, it's killing me. I am a coward. I can't bear Mother to be like that. (*And suddenly she flings herself into her father's arms and clings to him, weeping.*) Daddy, daddy, promise me not to change. I'm selfish — I'm frightened — I want something to hang on to — something bigger than — Oh, Daddy, I can't help it! I don't want you to be happy. Not if it means losing you — as you are. I want to feel you back of me — standing fast.

WALLACE — (*deeply moved*). Standing fast — Ah, my dear little girl, **you** must help me then. We must help each other. Your father's a very ordinary man ——

In the doorway Karen suddenly appears. She stops short at the sight of them. She is not just sure what her reception is to be. But a second later she is fast in her daughter's arms.

KAREN — My darling — my precious! I've been so afraid for you — If anything had happened to you — because of *me* ——

KAY — But nothing has, Mother.

KAREN — Oh — I've been driving about the streets — giving first one address and then another — like a crazy thing. The taxi driver must have thought I was mad. Perhaps I was — Wally, you, you and Kay were the only people in the world I wanted to see — and I didn't dare come back here — to my own house — for fear I might see you.

KAY — Come, come, Mother. This isn't a bit like you.

WALLACE — Not a bit, Karen.

KAREN — Isn't it? No, I suppose not — (*With a wan smile.*) for I've nothing to say for myself — nothing. I'm ashamed to look either of you in the face ——

WALLACE — (*above Karen's chair*). Nonsense, my dear. We've been badly shaken tonight — you and Kay and I — in the same leaky boat; human nature. It's a dangerous craft for every mother's son and daughter of us — for you can't catch a man, or a woman either, who isn't three-quarters at least an instinctive fool. When the unexpected happens, we don't use our heads — we *lose* 'em. Kay lost hers, you lost yours — I lost mine. Well, but now, thank God, we've found them again — and we're going to pull together again. There's to be no shame between us — none. The dream is ended.

There is some doubt in Kay's mind. She is a little afraid that she and her mother are " two of a kind," and that neither is worthy of so sweeping and complete a forgiveness. But so it stands, by her father's decree. And now she has her own problem to solve with Wicky. . . .

Young Faber is back from Halstead's, and what he has seen there convinces him that life, their part in it at least, is a good deal of a farce. "You left Dad with Halstead," he explains to Karen. "Well, Dad tackled him. Halstead fell and struck his head on something. Dad thought he had killed him. Halstead was just coming round when Mother and I reached his rooms. Now Halstead's on his way to Sicily — Dad's all to pieces at home — and Mother's comforting him. (*With a harsh laugh.*) I told you it was a farce."

Kay and Wicky, left alone, are naturally given to considerable self-accusation. Kay frankly confesses what she conceives to have been her deliberate guilt. " I treated you horribly — by sneaking off without a word — horribly. It makes me ashamed. There! I — I'd tell you that — if it killed me — It *has* almost killed me — And you, Wicky — Oh, how tired you look! I've never seen you look so ——"

But Wicky will have none of her pity. He loves her — he is crazy with longing for her. And yet he is glad she has left him because he feels now that they do not belong together. " — I've seen through it all tonight, I tell you — life — you and me — the whole show. And there's nothing in it — nothing to believe in — nothing to trust — nothing — nothing — nothing!"

KAY — Nothing — yes — I know that feeling — It came to me tonight when I saw my mother — in Daddy Faber's arms. (*Breaks off — then goes toward Wicky.*) Oh, I *am* grateful — to Clyde. It's thanks to him that I'm growing up at last — coming of age. And it wasn't his fault — any of it — I only used him — to strike at *you.*

WICKY — (*looking up slowly*). Then — you didn't love him, Kay?

KAY — Not even enough to — keep me from hating you. Oh, I tried to think I loved him. Perhaps I even did — a little — once — I don't know. But I do know all this couldn't have happened if I were anything but a sensual, self-worshipping little beast. No, let me tell you — It didn't begin last summer — it was long before that — when you took me, after our honeymoon, to — to settle down, and your year's work began and caught you up in it, and — and everything flattened out suddenly ——

WICKY — (*puzzled*). Flattened out —?

KAY — Yes; it did — for *me.* Because I'm no good, I suppose. Oh — it's clear enough to me now. I hated — settling down — all the details of trying to make a home — I hated them. Well — I simply didn't want to be your all, don't you see? I'd never thought of marriage as — as anything but love affair — in good standing. Marriage was just a sort of convenience passion was all that was real to me. Yes — and I wanted it to be every-*you.* I wanted to make it that — and keep it that. And, of course — n't. But what else could you have expected of me? What else was for? I've never done a single thing in my life but have a good time and and clever and let others adore and flatter me —

CKY — Nonsense. Only stupid women are like that. You ·——

KAY — But I *was* stupid. And mother — for all the brilliant effect she makes — has been stupid in the same way, always. Her ideas, as she calls them — all her chatter about freedom, self-expression — all the stuff I've gabbled after her like a damned little parrot — oh, what are they? Just so many demands on Daddy, her friends — everybody — for their exclusive attention and admiration. — Oh, Wicky, what's the matter with us nowadays? Why can't we be simpler, somehow — decenter? Why do we grab — grab — grab? Why are we so afraid of being bored?

WICKY — I've told you that. It's because we've both no faith in life — life itself. It doesn't *mean* anything. Why should I have taken it for granted that making a home for me, looking after my comfort, was all you needed from life? You say marriage meant nothing to you. It meant nothing to me. I had you — and I had my work. You had only the intervals — after my work was done. That isn't marriage, Kay. I should have brought you into my life — into every part of it — or helped you to find a life of your own — You have brains Kay. And God knows light housekeeping isn't a career.

KAY — Unless — unless there are — children ——

WICKY —(*his face lighting suddenly*). Ah, but then, of course, it isn't light.

KAY — Wicky, why have you never talked like this to me. If you only had ——

WICKY — Is it too late? (*He puts out his hands to her.*) It's all meaningless now — without you.

KAY — And — *with* me?

WICKY — You see, I need you, Kay — need you — to help me *find* a meaning. KAY — Ah — (*She puts her hands in his.*) *That's* why I ran and ran and ran — till I ran home — (*She is in his arms, clinging close to him as the curtain falls.*)

Now, in the epilogue, the four old friends are again coming into the living room at the Aldcrofts's in much the same formation and mood that they entered a year before — at the play's opening.

Dora and Karen are again chatting together cheerily, the men affably joining in whenever the conversation turns to subjects on which they feel they are privileged to express an opinion or at which they can rail with impunity.

On one subject, however, they are all agreed: there is a real thrill in being a grandparent. Wallace Aldcroft even goes so far as to try to epigram the situation, as it were.

" It isn't being fathers and mothers that counts," says he, a bit fatuously, " it's being *Grand*."

And when no one throws anything at him he continues joyously: " I say it's a perfectly marvelous thing that we four old friends should be happy grandparents. Now don't be so damned superior. Stand up, every one of you! (*They all rise, laughingly.*)   Here's to Fenwick Faber, 3d.   Bless him!   (*They drink the toast.*)   **And** ' God bless us, every one.' "

They forgive him his Dickens and soon they **are** getting settled for their regular evening of bridge.   But before they start there are certain plans to arrange.   If Karen is going up to New Haven the next day, why can't she stop for Dora that they may ride up together?   She can — and will.

And if Grandather Wallace is motoring up Sunday morning, why can't they all motor up with him — and stop in Stamford to call on old Bill Smith ——

They are all talking at once, as old friends will, **but** quietly and naturally, as few do, as the curtain falls.

THE END

A Drama in Three Acts

By Lula Vollmer

IN May, 1923, just before the 1922–1923 volume of
"The Best Plays" was closed up and sent to the printer,
there was produced at the Provincetown Playhouse in
Macdougal Street, Greenwich Village, New York, a
comedy drama called "Sun-Up."

The author, Lula Vollmer, was at that time a box
office executive for the Theater Guild, but otherwise
unknown to the theater. She had arrived in New York
in 1918 from Atlanta. Born and reared in the lowlands
of North Carolina, spending many summers with her
father in the lumber camps of the mountains, she was
greatly interested in the reported attitude of the illiterate
mountain folk toward the World War and the American
draft that was at that time being organized. Seeing in
them a theme for a play she wrote "Sun-Up" in two
weeks — and waited five years for a production.

The play was an immediate but inconsequential hit.
It was the end of the season. The Provincetown Theater
is obscurely placed and generally accepted as a home of
experimental drama, and the author was unknown. But
it clung on, attracting small but paying crowds all during
the hot weather. When the new season was started in
September "Sun-Up" was still there.

Moved to another small theater, the Lenox Hill, also
obscurely located in Seventy-eighth Street, it continued
for another ten weeks. In view of this show of strength
Lee Shubert took an interest in the play and it was
moved to the Princess Theater which, though small, is

well located in the theater district. And at the Princess
" Sun-Up " ran the season out. We feel that on this
record alone the play is entitled to inclusion in any
year book of American drama.

In the mountains of west North Carolina, near Asheville, the Widow Cagle has lived for the better part of
sixty years. She is, as Miss Vollmer sees her, " a frail,
but wiry type of woman " and " a very positive character,
but the tenderness in her nature shows in spite of her
efforts to conceal it."

The time of the opening act is a noonday in June, 1917,
and the scene the living room of the Cagle cabin, a
sparsely and typically furnished room. " The furniture
consists of a bed in the corner between the doors. A
rough table, covered with oil cloth, is in the center of
the room. A bench is beside the table. There are three
small, straight-back chairs, an old cupboard, and an old
trunk. Cooking utensils are near the fireplace. A gun
hangs over the door."

There have been rumors of a war, but they have not
reached the Widow Cagle's ears. Or if they have she
has promptly dismissed them as being unimportant.
Somebody may " be a-feudin' " somewhar, and likely
as not it's the Yankees agin', but, as she sees it, " Thar
ain't no reason fer war, unless us poor folks fight the
rich uns for the way they air bleedin' us to death with
the prices for meat and bread. I tell ye, Pap Todd,
we uns ought to rise up and fight the rich leeches, but
we won't. Poor folks ain't got guts 'nough. That's
whut makes 'em poor."

At the moment, as she tells her neighbor, Todd
— Pap being " old and wiry with a personality of the
' hound dog ' type " — at the moment she is more concerned about an offer of $800 she has had for her place.
Some city feller is thinking of buying it, but she ain't
selling out just to " 'blege no rich man."

But, on the other hand, she is not altogether satisfied

with what her son Rufe gets from the place. He's a good
boy and a good farmer, " but if he'd raise more corn and
fear the law less, he'd be more of a man like his pap."
Moonshinin', she insists, ain't a bad business if a man's
got nerve enough to stand behind a gun and shoot.

There has been some talk, too, of Rufe marrying Emmy
Todd, and the Widow Cagle isn't opposing the match.
Whatever she may think of Pap Todd, she admits
" Emmy's maw wuz good stock."

Rufe Cagle is back from town. He finds Emmy alone
in the cabin. Sheriff Weeks has come to look over the
boundary lines of the Cagle property in case the Widow
Cagle should decide she is willing to sell, and they have
gone to examine them. Rufe is young and good-looking.
" A positive character also. Gentle and kind in manner,
of a build to suggest great physical strength." Rufe is
in love with Emmy, and, having grown up with her, has
never considered marrying anyone else. She is of a
mind to tease him this day, however, both because he
suddenly has become anxious for her answer, wanting
to marry her right away, and also because the Sheriff,
an older man but still in his thirties, has also been after
her. Nor does all Rufe's pleading induce her to come
to a decision. She will tell him, she says, when she meets
him at the pasture gate at sundown — and not before.

The Widow and Sheriff Weeks are back, but there has
been no decision about a sale. The fact that it's war
time and prices are likely to drop doesn't worry the
Widow Cagle in the least — until she hears that Rufe
may have to go. Leastways he will have to register his
name and address, so the government can send for him
if it needs him.

MRS. CAGLE — What does Rufe or Bud owe the Guv'ment? The Guv'ment
kept Bud's daddy in jail for twenty year because he tried to make an honest
living outen the corn he planted and raised. What did the Guv'ment do to
Rufe's pap? Shot him dead. Shot him in the back while he wuz a-protectin'
his own property. Fight? Well, I reckon if either one of them boys fight,
hit will be their own fight, and agin, not fer the Guv'ment.

RUFE — (coming forward). Mom, ye air right as far as ye go. What ye say is true, but Pap Todd, and my pap too, wuz a doin' what the Government told them not to do. They wuz breakin' the law.

MRS. CAGLE — Whut right has the Guv'ment to tell us mountain folks whut to do or whut not to do? Air we beholdin' to them? Air they doin' anything fer us but runnin' up the prices of bread and meat till hit's all we kin do to keep body and soul together?

RUFE — Well, Mom, that ain't the Government's fault.

TODD — They treated me purty well while I wuz in jail.

MRS. CAGLE — Who kin ye lay the fault to then?

RUFE — It is because we don't know much. We need l'arnin'. We air ignorant.

SHERIFF — That's what the mountain folks need — l'arning.

MRS. CAGLE — 'Pears like the little ye both got ain't doin' ye much good, 'cept to make plum fools outen both of ye.

RUFE — (laughing). Neither one of us is got 'nough to run us crazy, Mom.

TODD — Emmy's eddicated purty well. Cain't tell much 'bout Bud. He won't talk. He kin write some.

MRS. CAGLE — Well, if l'arnin' air whut we need air the Guv'ment givin' us schools?

SHERIFF — Yes'um, and I reckon we would have more schools if our folks would patronize them. Last school we had in the village, the teacher said she had to quit because the children wouldn't come. I guess them that did come didn't l'arn nothin'.

MRS. CAGLE — Well, I reckon it wuz because the most of 'em wuz a hungry. Ye kin fill a young un's brain all ye want to, but hit's a-goin' to run out if thar's a hole in his stomach.

SHERIFF — You cain't say it's up to the government to feed 'em all, can you, Mis' Cagle?

MRS. CAGLE — No, but it kin let 'em alone when they try to make money the only way they know how — blockadin'.

SHERIFF — That's why I say they need l'arnin'. Learn how to do somethin' else.

MRS. CAGLE — I ain't never bin agin l'arnin'. I didn't have none, and Rufe's pap couldn't read, but I allus wanted Rufe to l'arn as much as he could.

RUFE — Yes ye did, Mom. Ye done all ye could. I kin recollect once when school wuz a-goin' on five miles down the road, I wuz too little to walk it. (Turns to others.) In the mornings Mom used to tote me most of the way. Then when I started home a'ter it wuz over, Mom would leave her work in the cornfield, meet me, and tote me the rest of the way home.

MRS. CAGLE — But I wouldn't a had ye l'arn nothin' if I'd a knowed it wuz a-goin' to turn ye into a law lover, and make yer fergit the laws of yo' own folks.

RUFE — I ain't fergot, Mom. I never will. But that little bit o' l'arnin' taught me to respect somethin' a little higher then my own way of wantin' ter do things. I'm a-goin' ter l'arn more, some day.

MRS. CAGLE — I want ye to l'arn books then, not foolishness.

RUFE — Well, Mom, ain't whut I knowed made the best farmer on the mountains? Don't I make ye a good livin'?

MRS. CAGLE — I ain't complainin'. I don't keer how much l'arnin' ye git if ye don't turn skeered puppy, and lick the boots of them lawmongers like Jim Weeks.

SHERIFF — Now Mis' Cagle.

RUFE — I ain't, Mom, but ye would want me to do whut I thought wuz right, even if it wuz to go to war, wouldn't ye?

MRS. CAGLE — In this Guv'ment feud? — No — if yer want to fight, son, get Zeb Turner, the man that shot your pap.

A barnyard commotion takes the family outside again. Only the Sheriff and Emmy are left. He counts the

circumstance lucky, but Emmy is not so sure. She is
somewhat less certain when the Sheriff takes advantage
of the moment to propose. He is, he allows, a good man
and true, and as between him and Rufe ——

SHERIFF — Well, the difference between me and Rufe — Rufe's a good boy
— but the difference is this. Rufe ain't got nothin' but a farm. I got a little
farm, and an office besides. Rufe ain't never made nothin' of hisself, and
I'm kinder looked up to, and respected.

EMMY — Yes ——

SHERIFF — I calculate I could be worse lookin', couldn't I? (*Emmy looks
him over.*)

EMMY — Yes, a little.

SHERIFF — I've told you that I love yer, and I figure there's a little love
in your heart for somebody, ain't there?

EMMY — I reckon so.

SHERIFF — Well, is it fer me?

EMMY — I ain't sayin' jest yet.

SHERIFF — Well, seein' us together, I'm willing to take my chances with Rufe.
I'll let you choose between me and him. But I'll say this much in my favor.
As conditions air, Rufe has got to go to war. I ain't. You stand more chances
of being Widow Cagle than you do of being Widow Weeks.

The news that Rufe will have to go to war is rather
unsettling to Emmy. She might have suspected it, but
she was never sure until the Sheriff explains. Rufe is
young and the government can make him go. But the
Sheriff is — well, not so young, and an officer of the
law besides. He won't have to go unless he wants to.
These admissions help Emmy to her decision. When
the folks come back from the yard she immediately
singles Rufe out.

"Rufe," says she, still a little in teasing mood, " I can't
come to the pasture tonight."

RUFE — (*as his countenance falls*). How come ye cain't, Emmy?
(*The Sheriff grins.*)

EMMY — I want to give ye my answer now, Rufe.

SHERIFF — That's right, Emmy.

EMMY — Air ye willin', Rufe?

RUFE — As ye say, Emmy.

EMMY — Then, Rufe, I'll marry ye.

RUFE — (*clasping her in his arms*). I knew ye would, Emmy.

SHERIFF — Why Miss Emmy!

TODD — Air yer proposin' to Rufe, Emmy?

MRS. CAGLE — Set down, Pap Todd. (*To Rufe.*) Well, son, if ye air a-goin'
ter marry Emmy, I reckon ye'll git over the notion of registerin' to fight in
this here Guv'ment feud of Jim Weeks!

RUFE — No, Mom, cause I done registered this mornin'.

The curtain falls

ACT II

The scene is the same. Three months have elapsed
It is early September and Rufe Cagle and his mother are
sort of straightening things up about the Cagle place
preparatory to Rufe's joining his regiment.

He has, he tells her, arranged for Bud Todd to look
after the crops, and paid him with the money he was
saving for his schooling. The Widow Cagle is not in
favor of any such generosity and she did not want Rufe
to spend his savin's thataway. But Rufe explains that
he won't need the money in France because he will be
paid wages by the government.

Mrs. Cagle is inclined to doubt the statement, and she
is not at all sure where France is. Rufe doesn't know
either, but Pap Todd has told him it is about forty
miles the other side of Asheville. Which, the old lady
insists, is " going a mighty long way to fight."

This leave-taking is awkward for both of them. There
is much explaining to be done, but neither finds it easy
to do. It is the first time they have been separated since
Rufe's pap was killed.

MRS. CAGLE — Yo' pap wuz a fine man, Rufe.

RUFE — I know he wuz. That reminds me o' somethin' I wanted to say to
ye, Mom. Sometimes I've felt that you thought I wuzn't like my pap — that I
wuz one of them skeered kind because I wouldn't make moonshine.

MRS. CAGLE — No, I never thought ye was a-skeered, but I thought ye wuz
kind o' foolish not to make money the easy way. Heap easier ter make moonshine then hit is to make a crop.

RUFE — Well, Mom, it's like this. I ain't feered o' nothin'. Ye ought ter
know that, but I don't believe in moonshine. It's bad stuff. I don't drink it
myself, and I don't want to sell it to nobody. Look at old man Todd, he made
it, and he drank it too. Bud told me jest 'tother day that he knowed he would
have more sense if the ole man hadn't been such a drunkard. Jest look whut
corn juice has made outen that old man.

MRS. CAGLE — Well, if corn-juice hadn't done it, killin', or somethin' else
would have. He wuz jest naturally born without any backbone.

RUFE —No, I reckon he ain't got much. Ye ain't a-mindin' me marryin'
Emmy, air ye, Mom?

MRS. CAGLE — No, Emmy cain't help who her paw wuz. She's a good gal,
and so wuz her maw.

RUFE — I've done ask Emmy to live here with ye, Mom, so's ye won't be
all by yo'self.

MRS. CAGLE — *Well*, the gal will be company, and she's welcome, but I
calculate we'll have the old man and Bud most of the time.

RUFE — No, I done told Bud to eat at home, and let his Pap do the cookin'.
I told him plain I wuz a-payin' him fer his work without eats. Bud ain't no
fool, if he is a little queer.

The thought of Rufe's getting married is also a little disturbing. The Widow Cagle can't just understand how it is he has growed up so quick, seein' it was only yesterday that he was a-playin' around with mud pies. But she is philosophical about it. " I reckon if ye air old enough to fight ye air old enough to git married," she tells him. But she can't quite understand how a man just getting married can want to leave home. He ought to stay with his wife.

RUFE — Mom, I hate to go off and leave ye feelin' like that 'bout my goin'. I wish ye could see it like I do. If ye cain't now, maybe ye will some day.
MRS. CAGLE — Yo' pap wuz a brave man.
RUFE — Mom, it's because I'm pap's son that I want to go. He died for whut he thought wuz right. Why, Mom, way back fifty years ago even ole Pap Todd had a chance to fight the Yankees. Now, Mom, it's fer ye, and the ole women like ye, that I want to go. They say they air goin' to make us slaves this time. We air almost slaves now, bein' so poor, but it could be worse, Mom. Ye know I kin shoot like hell. Nobody kin handle an old gun any better than I kin. Ain't ye willin' to trust me, Mom? Ain't ye willin' fer me to go?
MRS. CAGLE — Ye air yo' own man, Son, I ain't one to hold ye back if ye air sot on goin'. But don't ye let 'em make ye go, or scare ye into goin'!
RUFE — I'm goin' of my own free will.
MRS. CAGLE — Then it ain't fer me to say no more.

Soon Bud's over to announce the coming of Pap and Emmy with the preacher. And to bring Rufe a pistol. The neighbors have always looked upon Bud as a little weak minded, but he has his moments of sane reasoning. Something might go wrong with Rufe's rifle — it might kick or something — and then, he figures, the pistol would come in mighty handy. But Rufe knows his rifle. And he wants Bud to keep the revolver to take care of Mom and Emmy.

The preacher is a typical mountaineer, tall and rangy, and he brings to the Cagle home such gossip as he has picked up on the way. He chaws his tobacco in place of smoking, seeing he's forgot his pipe, and he and the Widow Cagle visit and ruminate on the sinfulness of war and the probabilities of Rufe's getting shot. But there isn't much time to visit. Rufe is going to camp at sundown and he feels like it will be just as well if they get the wedding over with.

" All right," agrees the preacher, " Rufus, you and the
bride stand here." He places them at the top of the table.
Mrs. Cagle and Pap Todd calmly continue their smoking
at the other side of the room. Bud looks on with great
interest. " I reckon you both air willin'."

RUFE — I reckon.
PREACHER — You, Miss Emmy?
EMMY —I reckon. (*Sheriff appears at door.*)
PREACHER — Reckon none of the rest of you's got any objections? (*Mrs.
Cagle shakes her head, no.*)
TODD — Reckon me and Bud ain't got nothin' agin it.
SHERIFF — I've got a lot agin it, but I reckon it ain't no use.
MRS. CAGLE — Too late, Jim Weeks.
PREACHER — 'Lo, Jim.
SHERIFF — Go on, preacher, I'm agin it, but I'll hold my peace.
PREACHER — Now join hands. (*They do so awkwardly.*) Rufe Cagle, before
God and the law, do you take this woman, Emmy Todd, to be your wedded wife?
RUFE — Yes sir.
PREACHER — Emmy Todd, do you take this man, Rufe Cagle, before God and
the law to be your wedded husband?
EMMY — Yes sir.
PREACHER — Do you both promise to love and help each other until death
parts you?
RUFE — Yes, sir.
EMMY — Yes, sir.
PREACHER — Then, in the name of God and the law, I now call you man
and wife.
TODD — Amen!
MRS. CAGLE — Sorry Preacher that cain't marry two folks without pullin' in
the law.
SHERIFF — Law's law, Miss Cagle.

Pap Todd misses something. In his day they always
celebrated when the " young uns got hitched." But the
best he can stir up is an invitation to supper with the
Widow Cagle, who was " calculatin' to feed 'em " all the
time — providing they stay sober.

Rufe can't stay. He must be in camp by sundown.

Their good-byes to him are typical. The preacher
offers to pray for him. Pap Todd undertakes to instruct
him in the art of dodging Yankee bullets. Let him
always be sure to stand sideways so they'll have to hit
him the narrow way. Bud agrees to come to his aid
if he sends word back the Yanks are getting too much
for him.

Now they are all gone — all but Emmy.

Rufe — Come here, little un, and give me a kiss while we air by ourselves.

Emmy — (*quickly throwing her arms about him. He holds her in a close embrace*). O, Rufe, cain't yer stay? Why do ye have to go? Why do ye have to leave me?

Rufe — Don't, little woman, ye most break my heart, I don't want ter leave ye.

Emmy — Then why do ye go?

Rufe — I have to go, Emmy. That is, I'd be ashamed not to go.

Emmy — Cain't ye wait a week, Rufe? Maybe the war will be over then.

Rufe — No, Emmy, I cain't. Don't tell Mom, but I'm whut they call drafted. They have called my name and I've got to be there tomorrow, some time.

Emmy — In France?

Rufe — I reckon.

Emmy — Then they air a-forcin ye to go.

Rufe — No, I don't have to go. I could stay and hide right here on my place, and they never would find me, but I'd be ashamed to face ye and Mom if I stayed, Emmy.

Emmy — But why, Rufe?

Rufe — I cain't explain it, I don't exactly know, I ain't got no education, yet, and I couldn't understand all the soldiers I talked to told me. But hit's somethin' like this, honey. This here country is ourn, cause God let us be born here. (*Mrs. Cagle stands in doorway. Rufe and Emmy do not see her.*) It's fed us, and kinder brung us up. We love it, don't we, Emmy?

Emmy — Yes, Rufe, but ——

Rufe — Yes we do, I do, Emmy, I love every rock, and every tree, and every hill 'round here. (*Points.*) Out thar on that hill my Pap died fer whut he thought was right. He's at rest down thar in the valley near to your maw. Some day Mom will lie there, and you, and maybe — me. Hit's ourn, Emmy. We don't own all the land, but hit's ours jest the same, to love and enjoy 'cause God A'mighty give it to us. There's lot o' folks, Emmy, that's got a home somew'ers else that wants ours too. I got to go help defend my hills, and my home, and my wimen folks, ain't I, honey? (*Mrs. Cagle goes back into the other room.*)

Emmy — I didn't know all that. Yes, Rufe, ye air a man, and ye got to fight fer what's right. Ye go, and I'll be a-waitin' fer you, and a-lovin' ye. And if ye don't come back ——

Rufe — I reckon I will, honey.

Emmy — I reckon ye will, but if ye don't, I'll know ye died like yo' Pap. I'll be proud of ye. Jest seems like I cain't stand it, but I kin, 'cause other women have stood it, and I reckon ye ain't no more to me than other women's husbands air to them.

Mother and son are still inarticulate when it comes time for the last word. For long, silent moments Mrs. Cagle sits moodily at the table smoking her pipe while Rufe busies himself with the collection of his pack. Occasionally a short observation, made poignant by its very irrelevancy, breaks the silence.

Now Rufe stands, his pack over his arm, his gun in his hand, ready to go.

Rufe — Bud will be over and milk for ye, Mom.

Mrs. Cagle — All right, son.

Rufe — (*after a painful pause*). Well, reckon I'll have to be goin'.

MRS. CAGLE — (*smoking calmly on*). Take keer o' yeself.
RUFE — Ye do the same, Mom.
MRS. CAGLE — Ye kin write. Emmy kin read the letters.
RUFE — I'll write. (*There is another pause.*) Well — goodbye, Mom.
MRS. CAGLE — (*putting out her hand*). Goodbye, son.
EMMY — Ain't ye goin' to kiss him, Mom?
MRS. CAGLE — (*without emotion*). What's the use o' sech foolishness?
RUFE — All right, Mom, God bless ye. (*Tears himself away.*)
MRS. CAGLE — If ye fight, son, shoot to KILL.
RUFE — (*going off followed by Emmy*). I will, Mom. Goodbye.
MRS. CAGLE — Take keer o' yo'self.

Rufe and Emmy go off together. For a moment or two Mrs. Cagle calmly smokes on. Then she rises and follows to where she can watch Rufe as he goes down the path. The shadows deepen. She appears to strain her eyes as if to catch a last look at him. Then, she goes slowly back to the doorway. The hoe Rufe left leaning against the house attracts her attention. She lifts the hoe up tenderly, as if it were a living thing, and moves her hand over the handle as if to caress it. She puts the hoe inside the cabin door. She sits down in the doorway and goes on with her smoking. Darkness comes as the curtain falls.

ACT III

It is February and there is a blinding snowstorm howling past the Widow Cagle's cabin. It is midnight and the room is but dimly lighted by the lantern on the table and fitful flashes from the fire on the hearth.

Mrs. Cagle sits by the fire smoking her pipe. In her hand she holds a yellow envelope and her restlessness is apparent. Frequently she glances anxiously toward the door. Now she walks to the table and studies intently the address on the envelope. Then she hangs the lantern on the nail by the side of the window and opens the wooden shutter that its beams may shine across the trackless snow outside.

She is back at the fire, smoking, when suddenly above the whistling of the storm a man's voice is heard halloo-

ing. Thinking it is Bud Todd, the Widow Cagle unbars the door and opens it. She is about to close it again when she sees the man outside is a stranger. With a hoarse plea to be let in he stumbles past her. He is "a young man from civilization. He is bare-headed and without an overcoat. His coat and trousers are much too large for him. His shoes are tan and well fitted."

The Stranger, it appears, has lost his way in the storm and is half starved. He has come a long way, he says, and Mrs. Cagle thinks perhaps he may have come from France. But he hasn't. He is from down Asheville way and he is going—— Well, he is going too far for him to make it that night and he would like to buy board and lodging if she will take him in.

The Widow Cagle "don't keep no boarders," but she reckons the Stranger is welcome to as good as she has to offer — if he is honest, which she thinks he is. He can have Rufe's room, she tells him, and half of Emmy's supper — Emmy being expected any minute. Which gives her the idea that perhaps the Stranger can read her letter for her.

He is willing to try — until she hands the letter to him and he has a hasty glance at its contents. Then he is quick to admit that he can't read — not that particular letter. Which does not surprise the Widow Cagle. Lots of people can't read letters. But Emmy can — and Emmy's Rufe's wife.

STRANGER — How long has your son been gone?
MRS. CAGLE — Since last September. Hit's kinder lonesome since he left. I'm glad ye come.
STRANGER — Thank you. Was your son drafted?
MRS. CAGLE — He registered — that whut ye mean?
STRANGER — Well, yes, and then afterwards they called him — made him go.
MRS. CAGLE — No, he went of his own free will.
STRANGER— (*with something like bitterness*). I suppose you're very proud of him?
MRS. CAGLE — He's a good boy, Rufe is.
STRANGER — Yes, of course, but I suppose you're very proud of him because he joined the army of his own free will.
MRS. CAGLE — No, I think he'd a showed more sense if he had a stayed home and gathered his crop.
STRANGER — Then you were opposed to his going? I mean you weren't willing for him to go?

MRS. CAGLE — Well, he wuz sot on goin'. Seemed to think he oughter I
didn't say nothin' to keep him from doin' whut he thought wus right. In
spite of whut the Guv'ment done to his pap, Rufe figured he oughter help 'em
out agin' the Yankees.
STRANGER — (with surprise). The Yankees —— ?
MRS. CAGLE — Yes. Who he's a-fightin'.
STRANGER — (laughing good naturedly). Oh, I see.
MRS. CAGLE — Did ye register?
STRANGER — Yes.
MRS. CAGLE — Air ye figurin' on goin'?
STRANGER — There's no way out of it.
MRS. CAGLE — If ye air a man thar is. If ye stay at home they cain't do
no more than shoot ye. That's whut they'll do to ye out thar. I'd ruther die
at home than somew'eres out thar in the mud.
STRANGER — You mustn't talk that way. If you were heard saying that, they
might — shoot you.
MRS. CAGLE — Let 'em shoot. The law killed my man. Hit's got my boy
out thar somew'eres. Shootin' me wouldn't matter. (There is a pause.) Have
ye got a maw livin'?
STRANGER — Yes, and she's getting old too. I'm her only son. I'm on my
way to see her now — if nothing happens ——

But something does happen. Jim Weeks, the sheriff,
and another man named Bob happen. They come suddenly up to the cabin and, after a short discussion, request entrance. The Stranger is immediately excited.
Hoarsely he begs Mrs. Cagle not to let the men in.
They're after him. He knows that. And he has got to
get home ——

She holds the Sheriff off until she hears the Stranger's
plea that he has done nothing wrong — nothing really
wrong — and that he wants to get home to see his mother.
Which is enough to fix her decision. Sending him into
the other room to hide in Emmy's bed, she calmly takes
up the gun that has been standing by the side of her own
bed and opens the door.

The Sheriff and Bob are looking for a deserter from
one of the army camps, they tell her, and they have
tracked him as far as the cabin. Which doesn't surprise
her. The tracks they've seen were probably made by
Bud's big feet — and if there ain't none showin' that he
also went the other way it's probably because Bud went
the back way.

" If ye had a little more common sense and less law I'd
respect ye more, Sheriff," she says. " Tain't nobody in

the house but me and Emmy. Emmy is in bed asleep.
Ye kin search all ye want to so's ye don't wake Emmy.
She's bin a-settin' up with old Pap Todd. He's bin
mighty low."
They search the bedroom and find nothing. And they
search the loft. They are just about to go when suddenly
the door opens and Emmy bursts innocently into the
room. The Sheriff, who has been amiably fixing the fire,
starts up with an exclamation of pleasant surprise. Mrs.
Cagle, noticeably confused but still equal to the situation,
merely grips her gun a little tighter.

SHERIFF — Well, I'll be doggone! Howdy, Miss Emmy.
EMMY — Howdy, Sheriff. Mis' Cagle, Bud said ——
MRS. CAGLE — I don't keer whut Bud said. Whut ye mean by foolin' me
like that? Trottin' off in the storm when I thought ye wuz in thar a-sleepin'.
EMMY — Why, Mis' Cagle ——
MRS. CAGLE — Up to some o' yo' tricks again. Puttin' things in yo' bed to
make me believe it's ye.
SHERIFF — (striding toward the back door). Yes, Miss Emmy, whut did you
put in your bed? Let's pull it out and see.
EMMY — Why, Mis' Cagle ——

Mrs. Cagle shakes her head at Emmy, who seems to
realize that something is expected of her. With her gun
in her hand, Mrs. Cagle follows the Sheriff to the door.

MRS. CAGLE — 'Pears to me like ye air mighty much at home, Jim Weeks.
SHERIFF — (from inside of back room). Let's see who else makes himself
at home. (Mrs. Cagle steps to one side of the door, and is about to lift her
gun when the Sheriff appears in the doorway holding up a big feather bolster.
He laughs.) Well, Miss Emmy, that's one on me, unless ——
BOB — (Coming down ladder). Nothin' alive up thar but rats.
SHERIFF — Well, look whut was in bed, Bob. Better come and look under
the bed again.
BOB — All right. (Pause. The Sheriff goes to the fire.)
SHERIFF — How's your paw, Miss Emmy?
EMMY — He's gettin' better tonight.
BOB — (entering). Nothin' under thar except these here pertaters. (He
slips the potatoes he holds into his pocket.)
SHERIFF — All right. Well, that bolster, Miss Emmy, is a pretty good joke
on me and Mis' Cagle both.
EMMY — Yes ——
SHERIFF — I'm powerful sorry, Mis' Cagle, that I had to 'pear to doubt
your word. It wus one of them things that has to be done now and then.
MRS. CAGLE — Well, I hope ye air satisfied. And now if ye be through
searchin', I reckon ye kin go. I ain't got nothin' agin ye, Jim Weeks, but
I ain't powerful fond of yo' job. When ye come and ain't representin' the law,
ye're welcome. When ye air, ye ain't.
SHERIFF — (going to door, followed by Bob). All right, Mis' Cagle. If I
didn't know you so well, I'd shore think you wuz a moonshinin'.

Mrs. Cagle — I would be if it warn't so cold that the mash would freeze.
Sheriff — (laughs as he goes out door). Good night, Mis' Cagle. Good
night, Miss Emmy.

Mrs. Cagle doesn't feel altogether secure even after the
Sheriff has left, and she can't quite understand what
has become of the " furriner." He must have crawled
through the " winder hole," she decides, for all he did
not look that small.

Emmy is finishing her supper and getting ready to
read Rufe's letter when the Stranger reappears. He had
been hiding, he tells them, back of the potato pile, and
he is mighty grateful for their protection. He has begun
to feel that he has been wrong from the first about the
army. He should have offered his services, as Rufe did,
and not waited to be drafted. But he was afraid —
afraid of being shot. That is some better than being just
plain afraid, Mrs. Cagle insists.

The Stranger doubts that. If he had been a man, and
done less whining around when he was called, both his
mother and the girl who threw him over would have had
more respect for him. And now that he is being hunted
as a deserter as well, his loss of respect for himself is
even lower than it was. Yet he had only wanted to get
home long enough to reassure his mother that he would
be all right.

Mrs. Cagle is glad Rufe wa'n't afraid to go, and wa'n't
fo'ced to go. But she still resents the gov'ment's action
in calling him. Wars are foolish things, caused by men
" always seein' some terrible thing ahead." " My maw
told me about that other war," she reports; " but I kin
remember it. Always they wuz a-skeerin' 'em, and
a-teilin' 'em about the Yankees a-comin'. They did come
to some places, but she never seed one. She wuzn't
afeered then, and I ain't askeered of no Yankee now."

The Stranger tries to explain to her that it is not the
Yankees they are fighting now, but she insists they will
always be Yankees to her. And as for the Yank and the

Rebel fighting on the same side — that's quite too much
for anyone to believe.

MRS. CAGLE — Ye mean they air fightin' on the same side, Stranger?

STRANGER — Yes, side by side.

MRS. CAGLE — Who air they fightin', Stranger?

STRANGER — The Germans.

MRS. CAGLE — I reckon they've come 'long since my time. I never heard
of 'em. Whut's it over, Stranger?

STRANGER — Well, for one thing, to protect our country.

EMMY — That's what Rufe said, Mis' Cagle. He knowed.

MRS. CAGLE — Yes, I heared him, but I didn't think the boy knowed so
much. I heared him say this country belonged to us case God A'mighty let us
be born here. He said this land had brung us up, and nursed us — kinder
pretty speech for a boy like mine, ain't it, Stranger?

STRANGER — Yes. He is right.

MRS. CAGLE — (taking envelope from bosom and handing it to Emmy). Read
his letter, Emmy. Rufe could always write nice letters. I reckon ye won't
mind hearing it, Stranger?

STRANGER — (with some uneasiness). No.

EMMY — (looking at the letter). Why, Mis' Cagle, your name is printed.
(Emmy goes to the lantern and looks at the envelope closely. Mrs. Cagle
follows and looks over her shoulder.)

MRS. CAGLE — Read the inside, Emmy.

EMMY — (cries out). 'Tain't from Rufe, Mom. 'Tain't from him.

MRS. CAGLE — (fiercely). Who's it from?

EMMY — I cain't read it. I cain't read it.

MRS. CAGLE — (takes the letter from the girl and stares at it). Great God,
why didn't I larn to read? (Hands letter back to Emmy.) Spell it out,
Emmy. Maybe the Stranger kin help ye. He kin read a little.

EMMY — (sobs as she takes the letter. The Stranger starts forward as if
to take the letter, but stops). I so afeered ——

STRANGER — I'll help you.

EMMY — (spells out a letter or two and then speaks the name). M — R — S.
L — That's yo' name. Mis' Liza Cagle. We r-e-g-r-e-t ——

STRANGER — That means — are sorry.

MRS. CAGLE — (repeats). We air sorry ——

EMMY — To i-n-f-o-r-m ——

STRANGER — That means — to tell ——

MRS. CAGLE — We air sorry to tell ——

EMMY — You — that — your — son, Rufe Cagle, died ——

MRS. CAGLE — (speaks before the Stranger. She stands erect, and rigid,
but does not evidence any great emotion otherwise). DIED ——

EMMY — (sobbing). O, Mom, Mom ——

STRANGER — (taking the telegram from her hand and reading). February
fifth, in action. That means he died — fighting.

MRS. CAGLE — (very calmly, but with deep emotion). It means my boy is
dead. It means the law's got my boy same as his pap.

The curtain falls to denote a lapse of time.

It is early morning, the next day. Mrs. Cagle is
already astir. Breakfast is cooking on the hearth.
Through the window the first streaks of dawn can be
seen. Emmy is still asleep on the bed in the corner.
Mrs. Cagle wakens her — wakens her from a peaceful

dream about Rufe living and at home, to the realization
that he is dead and is never to come back again. Dreams,
admits Mrs. Cagle, are mighty comfortin', sometimes —
but the wakin' up ——

Rufe's mother has not done much sleeping the night
through. Or much dreaming, either. But she has been
doing a lot of thinking — thinking of Rufe when he was
little, when he used to be " a-sleepin' thar in the bed and
me a-settin' up with him sick. I jest kept a-waitin' fer
him to cry out so's I could take him up in my lap. I kin
remember when he used to stump his toe, or hurt hisself,
I'd feel the pain as much as him. And jest like he wuz
little agin, somew'eres in here (*clutches her breast*) I kin
feel the hurt of a bullet. Jest like when he wuz little,
and had hurt hisself."

They call the Stranger. It's getting near sun-up and
time for him to be on his way. He has made up his
mind during the night that he is going back to camp and
face them before they can catch him and bring him back.
They put him up a snack that he may have something to
eat on the way, and he is just about to leave them when
there is a heavy knocking at the door and he is obliged to
hide again.

Sheriff Weeks is back. And he is not to be fooled
again. He knows now his man is there and he sees by the
table things that he has had his breakfast.

Mrs. Cagle makes no pretense at subterfuge now. She
is frank to tell the Sheriff that the Stranger was there the
night before and that he is there now.

SHERIFF — I kinder thought so. Well, I'm mighty sorry to disobleege you,
or your company, Mis' Cagle, but law is law.

MRS. CAGLE — Don't ye know no other word but law, Jim Weeks? Why
don't ye put yo' law to some use? If ye want to fight why don't ye go fight
like Rufe? Ain't you fitten to use yo' law again nothin' but wimen, and
men folks whut's without guns?

SHERIFF — Now, Mis' Cagle, all this talk ain't going to soften my heart to
let this here deserter go ——

MRS. CAGLE — I ain't tryin' to soften yo' heart. Ye air goin' to let the
stranger go anyway. He ain't no deserter. He ain't nothin' more than a boy.
He wuz homesick, and he is a-goin' back to war this mornin'.

SHERIFF — But Mis' Cagle, I'm obleeged to ——

Mrs. Cagle — Ye ain't a-goin' to tech him, Jim Weeks.

Sheriff — Well, now, Mis' Cagle, me and your son had some differences, of course, but after all I ain't got nothin' agin Rufe.

Mrs. Cagle — Whut's Rufe got to do with it?

Sheriff — Well, there ain't no use of you denyin' that Rufe's run away, and come home.

Mrs. Cagle — (looks at him in amazement; Emmy bursts into tears. Mrs. Cagle speaks very quietly). Rufe? No, Sheriff, Rufe ain't come home.

Mrs. Cagle throws a shawl over her head and goes into the yard, and the Sheriff does not find it easy to comfort Emily after she tells him of Rufe's death. And it is still more embarrassing for him to explain why it is he is there, ready to arrest a man he thought was Rufe, when he has been protesting his friendship for the family.

Mrs. Cagle is back with Bud Todd. The boy is hard hit by the news of Rufe's death. He can't believe it, seeing that he had brought the letter from Rufe the day before. But if it's true then he (Bud) must go to war to avenge his friend.

Bud — Rufe's kilt, Mis' Cagle. I got to go. Sheriff, will ye take keer my wimen folks?

Mrs. Cagle — Ye don't know whut ye talkin' 'bout, Bud. This ain't no feud whar ye have a chance. Hit air murder, and the law air back of hit.

Sheriff — Mis' Cagle's got it wrong, Bud, but thar ain't no use o' yo' goin' tell they call ye.

Mrs. Cagle — They won't call Bud.

Sheriff — I'm mighty sorry 'bout Rufe, Mis' Cagle, and I'm powerful sorry to force the law at a time like this, but I'm obleeged to take this here deserter to headquarters.

Mrs. Cagle — Sheriff, the law ain't never took nobody outen my house.

Sheriff — Then ye admit that this deserter is hid here?

Mrs. Cagle — Yes, he's hid in the back room.

Sheriff — (starts toward the back room door and then stops. After a moment's pause, he turns back). All right, Mis' Cagle. Outen respect to you in yo' trouble I'll jest wait outside for him. My deputies wuz to be here at sun-up. We'll surround the house. Thar ain't no use of him tryin' to git away. If he's a man he'll come out and give hisself up.

Mrs. Cagle — A man ain't givin' hisself up to the law.

Sheriff — (becoming irritated). Now, Mis' Cagle. I'm a-hatin' to say these things to you, when you're in trouble, but last night you harbored a deserter. That's the same as givin' aid to the enemy. Fer that thing I kin throw ye into jail today. I ain't a-wantin' to do hit, but I'll have to if you interfere any further with the law.

Mrs. Cagle — I've been a-breakin' the law fer nigh on to sixty years, and I ain't afeered to break it agin.

Sheriff — Well, I warn ye. If you make another move to help this deserter git away I'll arrest ye, Mis' Cagle, and take ye to prison. (He goes toward the door, and then stops.) I'll wait outside, Mis' Cagle.

They call the Stranger. He has overheard what has

been said and he is determined to give himself up. **He will not hide behind Mrs. Cagle any longer.**

But he gets no support from the old lady in this resolve. The deputies are coming. Very well, let them come. There are three of them and Jim Weeks is putting them around the house. So are there four inside the cabin, if the Stranger can shoot, argues Mrs. Cagle.

"What chance have we against the law?" parries the Stranger. "If we open fire on these officers it will mean that all of us will be tried on a more serious charge. I alone am guilty. Let me take the consequences."

It is his idea that he had better run for it. He'll take a chance of their getting him in the back, and thinks he can make the woods ——

Jim Weeks is again at the door, asking for a parley. Mrs. Cagle stands, gun in hand, daring him to enter. If he has any talkin' to do he can do it through the door. But when he convinces her that he has news that is of interest to her, and that he is not up to any tricks, she sends the Stranger back into the bedroom and tells Emmy to open the door. Sheriff Weeks glances a little nervously at Mrs. Cagle's gun as he enters.

SHERIFF — No use for gun play, Mis' Cagle. I ain't after touchin' ye. (*He comes close to her and speaks in a low voice.*) My deputies have jest come, and they brung me the name of this here deserter. (*He takes out a paper.*) Hit mought be interestin' for ye to know who it is ye air riskin' yo' own liberty to hide.

MRS. CAGLE — In my house, Jim Weeks, we ask no man his name.

SHERIFF — In this case, it mought have been better if yer had. (*He reads from paper.*) This is a warrant for the arrest of Zeb Turner, Jr.

MRS. CAGLE — Zeb Turner? (*Pause. She shakes her head.*) No, ye air wrong, Sheriff. Zeb Turner air old. The stranger ain't more than a boy.

SHERIFF — Yes, Mis' Cagle, but this is Zeb Turner, Junior. That means — son of — Zeb Turner.

MRS. CAGLE — (*rigid with emotion*). Ye mean this boy air — the son — of my man's murderer?

SHERIFF — Yes — this deserter — the same.

MRS. CAGLE — The son of Zeb Turner ——

SHERIFF — Now, I'll leave it to yo' judgment, Mis' Cagle, if ye hadn't better jest turn him out to me.

MRS. CAGLE — (*looking at back door, and then studying the Sheriff closely*). Air ye — lyin' to me, Jim Weeks?

SHERIFF — No, and if ye don't believe me, let Miss Emmy read this ——

MRS. CAGLE — Read it, Emmy.

SHERIFF — (*pointing*). Right here, Miss Emmy.

EMMY — (*spelling out words*). Z-e-b, Zeb — T-u-r-n-e-r ——

SHERIFF — That spells Turner. (*Taking the warrant from her.*) Ain't that right, Miss Emmy?

EMMY — Yes, sir.

SHERIFF — Now, Mis' Cagle, if ye air satisfied, I reckon I can take my prisoner.

MRS. CAGLE — (*after a moment's hesitation*). No, Sheriff, ye kin wait outside.

SHERIFF — All right, as ye say. If ye need me, jest call. (*Satisfied with his triumph he goes out smiling.*)

Mrs. Cagle stands staring at the bedroom door. Gradually over her hard old face there is spread a look of unalterable hatred lined with sneering triumph. When Emmy, frightened, would interfere she pushes her roughly aside. " I fed him ——" she mumbles to herself. " And I hid him. I wuz about to shoot to save him. The son of the man who killed Rufe's pap!"

" Rufe's dead!" wails Bud Todd from a corner.

"Rufe's dead — and one of his murderers air in thar," Mrs. Cagle answers. " Come out, Stranger!"

He comes, somewhat relieved to know the Sheriff's gone, but feeling the tenseness of the scene into which he has stepped.

MRS. CAGLE — Yo' name, Stranger?

STRANGER — My name is Zeb Turner.

MRS. CAGLE — And yo' pap's name? Wuz hit Zeb Turner, too?

STRANGER — Yes, Zeb Turner.

MRS. CAGLE — Wuz he a revenuer?

STRANGER — Yes, one of the bravest that ever crossed the mountains. You don't know him, do you?

MRS. CAGLE — Know him? Well, Stranger, Zeb Turner killed my son's pap.

STRANGER — Great God!

MRS. CAGLE — Shot him in the back while he wuz protectin' his own property.

STRANGER — God Almighty!

MRS. CAGLE — And I've protected ye ——

STRANGER — I didn't know, Mrs. Cagle, I ——

MRS. CAGLE — Hid ye in my own house — ye, the son of my man's murderer.

STRANGER — I didn't know. Besides, you've got to remember, it was law.

MRS. CAGLE — Law! Law! Allus that word, law. Well, Stranger, the feud has a law, and it air a life fer a life.

STRANGER — I would not have come here and accepted your hospitality for the world if I had known. I understand how you feel. Call the Sheriff and give me up.

MRS. CAGLE — Give ye up? No, Stranger, ye air mine to deal with.

EMMY — Mom!

STRANGER — Mrs. Cagle, for your own sake, turn me over to the Sheriff. I'll get what's coming to me.

MRS. CAGLE — If ye've got a gun, Stranger, use hit. The feud will give ye a chance the law won't.

STRANGER — I have no gun.

MRS. CAGLE — Thar's Bud's. I'll give ye time to reach hit.

STRANGER — Why I can't fight you, Mrs. Cagle.

Mrs. Cagle — I'm givin' ye a chance.

Stranger — I can't take it.

Mrs. Cagle — Then ye better run ——

Stranger — Mrs. Cagle, think what you are about to do. They will take your life for this. (*The Stranger shows his fear of her.*)

Mrs. Cagle — My life! What does that matter? They've took every life that belonged to me. My pap's — my man's — my son's — my little son's life, they took hit, them that hide behind a thing called law ——

Stranger — But Mrs. Cagle, you don't understand ——

Mrs. Cagle — I understand that ye air a son of the law, and that ye air in the power of the feud.

Stranger — (*pleadingly*). Have mercy, Mrs. Cagle ——

Mrs. Cagle — I'm offerin' ye a chance fer yo' life, but if ye air too much of a coward to take hit, I'll ——

Emmy — (*throwing herself between Mrs. Cagle and the Stranger*). Mom, ye shan't kill him, ye shan't.

Mrs. Cagle — Git away, Emmy.

Emmy — Mom, he's goin' out thar to shoot the dogs that killed Rufe ——

Mrs. Cagle — I ain't a-believin' him.

Emmy — Him and Rufe was a-fightin' on the same side ——

Mrs. Cagle — Out of the way, Emmy.

Emmy — Mom, he can't help whut his pap done.

Mrs. Cagle — He's a son of the law. Air ye fergettin' whut the law done to yo' pap?

Emmy — My pap was a-breakin' the law.

Mrs. Cagle — Air ye fergettin' that the law killed Rufe?

Emmy —No, Mom, I ain't a-fergittin' ever. But hit warn't the law, Mom, hit wuz hate — hate like this thing in yo' heart toward him — (*pointing toward the Stranger*) fer somethin' he's got nothing to do with. It's hate, Mom, Rufe told me the day he went off — (*She breaks into hysterical sobs.*) Rufe told me ——

Stranger — (*stepping from behind Emmy*). Wait a moment, Mrs. Cagle, and then you can shoot. I'm all that you say. I'm a coward, a deserter, a son of the law, and afraid. I'm not fit to live, but I want to tell you that she is right. Hate is the thing that makes feuds and wars. I had nothing to do with the killing of your husband — I had no say about this war, but it has got me, trapped me. (*He speaks hysterically.*) I'm through, Mrs. Cagle, — shoot.

"Rufe's dead!" again wails Bud. Suddenly Mrs. Cagle lowers her gun. The expression of bitter hatred gradually fades from her eyes, and something resembling a smile takes its place. She stares into space, and listens, listens ——

"Hit's music," she mumbles.

"It's the wind on the snow," ventures Emmy.

"Hush! It's him —— Can't ye hear him?"

From afar off there is the sound of a quick, martial air. But only Mrs. Cagle can hear.

"Yes, son —— " she mutters, bending her old head closer to her vision. "Whut is it, son? Yes — yes —— (*To the others.*) Cain't ye hear him speakin'?"

They cannot hear.

"Say hit again, son, so's I kin tell 'em. As long as
thar air hate — thar will be — feuds. As long as thar
air women — thar will be — sons. I ain't no more — to
you — than other sons' mothers — air to them —— Yes,
son — whut else? Take keer of — yo'self — yes, son
— and Emmy. Whut else, son ——?"

She strains to hear more, but there is no more. The
music fades away, and as she turns to the others her gun
slips to the floor. The spirit of her exaltation is still
upon her. She takes their denials calmly. Maybe the
dead can't come back, as Emmy says. If so she reckons
her love went on — out yonder — and reached him.

Anyway, now she knows what to do. "I reckon ye
better go, boy," she says to young Turner, and Emmy is
posted at the window to watch the deputies and see
when the way is clear.

Turner is reluctant to leave them, but Mrs. Cagle's new
faith reassures him. "I ain't afeered," she says, "and
thar ain't no danger unless ye air afeered."

Now there's a chance and he makes a run for it. From
the window Emmy watches him eagerly. She sees Jim
Weeks turn, as if he saw him, and then turn back. Now
the boy has reached a clump of trees and is safe from
capture, and there is great rejoicing in Emmy's heart.
Presently Jim Weeks comes again to the door and knocks.

MRS. CAGLE — Bud, see who that is that can't open the door fer hisself.
The Stranger's gone, Sheriff.
SHERIFF — You let *him* go?
MRS. CAGLE — He air a mother's son, Sheriff.
SHERIFF — Well, I warned ye, Mis' Cagle.
MRS. CAGLE — I'm ready to go to jail.
SHERIFF — All right, come along.
EMMY — No, no, Sheriff, please ——
MRS. CAGLE — Ye kin stay at yo' pap's, Emmy. Ye kin sell the place. Jim
Weeks will buy hit.
EMMY — Sell the place? But, Mom, whut would ye do when ye come
back?
MRS. CAGLE — I reckon these here hills that borned me, and nursed me
kin take keer of me fer a little while.
EMMY — Sheriff, ain't ye rememberin' yo' own ma? Ain't thar no love is
yo' heart that can make ye see why Mom done this?

SHERIFF — Duty, Miss Emmy, is a hard thing, but thar must be some of us to carry hit out.

MRS. CAGLE — (*wrapping herself in a large shawl*). Emmy, ye kin move my things down to yo' pap's — (*She goes to the door where Rufe's hoe stands and caresses the handle.*) And — don't ye fergit — Rufe's hoe — Emmy. I'm ready, Sheriff.

SHERIFF — (*looking at her, he shakes his head, and lowers it as if ashamed. As he goes out, he says somewhat brokenly*) Well, not now — Mis' Cagle, not — now.

EMMY — O Mom!

MRS. CAGLE — Ye go ahead, Emmy, and get yo' pap's breakfast, and I'll lig the snow outen the yard.

EMMY — (*almost in tears*). He ain't a-comin' back, Mom.

MRS. CAGLE — Maybe not, Emmy. I ain't afeered, nohow, and there ain't no danger if yer ain't afeered.

EMMY — Air ye all right, Mom?

MRS. CAGLE — Yes, Emmy.

EMMY — I'll be back soon. And I reckon you better do the wash today.

MRS. CAGLE — Yes, hit's blowed up so fair hit won't take the clothes no time to dry.

EMMY — I won't be long. Come, Bud.

Mrs. Cagle, finished brushing the hearth, draws her shawl over her head again, and stopping at the door, fingers Rufe's hoe. The music comes again — soft, and seemingly from far away. She listens, and hearing no voice, speaks.

" I heered ye, Rufe. I never knowed nothin' about lovin' anybody but you till you showed me hit was lovin' them all that counts. It was sundown when yer left me but hit's sun-up now and I know God Almighty is a-takin' care of you, son."

THE END

"CHICKEN FEED"

("WAGES FOR WIVES")

A Comedy in Three Acts

By GUY BOLTON

THERE was no outstanding success among the lighter domestic comedies produced last season. None, at least, comparable with the hit scored by "The First Year" three years ago, or with that of "Six Cylinder Love" the year following.

In late September, 1923, John Golden produced a comedy written on a "wages for wives" theme by Guy Bolton called "Chicken Feed" which gave considerable promise, and did, in fact, continue for five months to exceptionally good business. It was then withdrawn temporarily because Lawrence Weber, a partner with Mr. Golden in the lease of the Little Theater, needed a home for "Little Jessie James," a musical comedy which was potentially the greater money maker of the two.

"Chicken Feed" was not sent on tour in mid-season, but held for a fresh start in Chicago in August, 1924, where it is to be recast. I have included it in this volume because I believe it best represents its particular type of play, inspiring as much laughter as a farce without losing too completely its hold upon its theme, which is fundamentally both sound and serious.

"Chicken Feed" is concerned with the experience of a group of husbands, wives and sweethearts the year neighbor Nell Bailey organized a strike to determine the rights of wives to a proper share in the net income of the family.

Nell is "an honest-minded, practical, attractive girl of 22." She is engaged to marry Danny Kester, "a good-

looking boy — very romantic and sentimental, about
28," and we meet them first the morning of the day set
for the wedding.

Danny, having inherited a few thousand dollars from
his mother's estate, has invested it in a portable cottage
business. These are known to the trade as the "Kester
Cottage." He has brought one on from the western
manufactory and set it up both as a sample and a home.
It is all furnished and ready for the wedding. The
neighbors and friends helping with the final decorations
of the house include the Logans, Hughie and Luella.
Hughie, a young business man of the village, "is a
tight wad, but not a bad sort," and Luella, his wife, is a
pleasant, sober-faced, dry-humored but observing and
determined little woman, easily led but not easily held.

Luella has had her troubles with Hughie. She has
soon discovered that his pockets are lined with fishhooks,
and she declares frankly "if the moths had to live on
the dresses my husband buys me they'd starve to death."

Asking a husband for money, it has been Luella's
observation, is like dropping a nickel in a slot to hear:
"What do you want it for?" or "What did you do with
the five dollars I gave you Monday?" And they're all
alike.

Jim Bailey, Nell's father, is certainly true to type. A
"small town sport" of fifty, he has always missed being
a success by the narrowest of margins. The cards, he
feels, have been stacked against him up till now, but he
is still hopeful. Some day he is going to show 'em ——

Danny runs in hoping there will be a chance to re-
hearse the wedding march. Luella is to play it and
Hughie is to act as best man. Getting married is mighty
serious to Danny. But so is everything else. And he
is terribly sensitive.

Nell Bailey also dashes over. She had promised
Danny she wouldn't come until everything was ready —
but she just couldn't wait, and here she is. It is all

much prettier than she expected and she is quite thrilled. But she is keen-eyed and a little critical, too. And Danny, accepting everything she says as a criticism of his taste, is alternately crushed and buoyed by her remarks. Nor do Luella's side comments help much.

LUELLA — When are you going to put on your wedding dress, Nell?

NELL — There's lots of time. I don't want to be sitting around in it. Who knows — I may need it again some day.

DANNY — Nell!

NELL — (affectionately). There — there — it's a shame to tease him!

LUELLA — (rising). Well, I guess you two'd like to be alone.

NELL — Yes, in the movies the girl always takes this time just before the wedding to ask the man about his past.

LUELLA — You'll not get anything out of him now. The time to start askin' questions is when a man's just dozin' off an' his mind don' work fast. I'll see if your mother wants anything in the village, Nell.

DANNY — You're not going near the depot?

LUELLA — Right by it.

DANNY — I wonder — I wonder if you'd ask old Tevis ——

LUELLA — Ask him what?

DANNY — He's getting us a drawing room on the night train to Maine. Well, I want it on the side that gets the moonlight.

LUELLA — For pity's sake!

DANNY — If I ask him that he'll laugh — or — say something — you know.

LUELLA — I can just imagine that old crab being asked to furnish moonlight for married couples!

DANNY — I hate to have anyone laugh! You see, it — it seems kind of sacred to me.

NELL — (patting his cheek). Dear old Danny. (To Luella.) He is sweet, you know.

LUELLA — So you're really going off camping on your wedding trip?

NELL — Yes. We're going to sleep right out on the ground. Danny swears it isn't cold once you're inside your sleeping bag!

LUELLA — Sleeping with spiders and caterpillars crawlin' over you all night don't sound like much of a honeymoon to me. (She goes to the kitchen.)

NELL — Oh, poor Danny! Don't look hurt. I think it's a wonderful idea for a honeymoon. Yes, and I think the Kester Kottage is a tremendous success!

DANNY — You're a darling! (Going to sofa.) Look, here's the sofa I've always talked about, where I can sit with your head against my shoulder and look in the fire and kiss your hair and ——

NELL — How about the fireplace — does it draw well? I'd hate that nice inglenook to get all spoiled with smoke.

DANNY — (damped). I think it's all right.

NELL — Sweet old snicklefritz! I do believe his feelings are hurt again. Come right here to mother! (She puts her arms about him; he kisses her.)

DANNY — And you're really going to marry me?

NELL — You try and stop me.

Danny has but little time to expand under this new vote of confidence before Chester Logan interrupts him. Chester is " the small town wit and ' wise cracker,' but he jests with a sad face and mournful air." He has been pretty much in love with Nell for a long time, and he can't quite understand yet how she happened to pick Danny Kester instead of him. Being a fairly good loser, however, Chester covers his disappointment by making sport of the institution of marriage. Not for him, this voluntary martyrdom. " I believe in looking at the wrecks along the seashore before I order myself a sailor suit. After all, freedom is rather nice. You can just come and go as you please. And a wife is so expensive — a terrible handicap for a young chap just starting out in life. Sure, I know: two can starve as cheap as one ——"

His banter worries Danny but it never touches Nell. She thinks it funny. And she had a lot rather take her chances with a serious little fellow with the keenness to recognize the chances of success in a portable house business, and the courage to put all his money into it, than she would with any joker on earth. She has faith in Danny — with herself to help him and to share all his troubles and worries ——

" Oh," exclaims the delighted bridegroom, " oh, what a wonderful thing marriage is!"

At which moment there is a crash of dishes in the kitchen, followed by the sound of the Father and Mother Bailey voices raised in anger.

Chester, it appears, being the local agent of the insurance company in which Jim Bailey carries a policy, has come to collect the last premium. And Jim is furious when he discovers that, although he had given Mrs. Bailey the money, she had spent it on Nell's wedding. How dare she do such a thing? It's just plain stealing, that's what it is!

Mrs. Bailey is crushed and Nell is excited. And more excited a moment later when she learns that not only the last installment but the last four installments had not been paid. In addition to which Mr. Bailey has borrowed $1,500 cash on the policy.

NELL — (*to her father*). Is that true? You've used up fifteen hundred dollars of your endowment policy?

JIM — Well, what if I have?

NELL — Why, Popper, that's the only money you've ever saved for a rainy day. What in the world did you do with it?

JIM — Never mind what I did with it.

NELL — (*indignantly*). You think you had a perfect right to take all that money and yet you call Mother a thief for taking the little bit she did.

JIM — The difference is — it was *my* money.

NELL — No more than it was Mother's.

JIM — I'm the one who earned it!

NELL — No more than Mother did! Hasn't she worked for you and kept house for you? What do you think you'd have to pay for all she's done for you for twenty-five years? Why, even at servant's wages you owe Mother thousands of dollars!

JIM — Your mother isn't a servant.

NELL — No, if she had been she would have been paid for all her hard work — that's the difference.

MRS. BAILEY — Don't say any more, Nell. Not here before everybody. I was never more ashamed in my life! (*She goes into the kitchen.*)

NELL — Poor Mother — she's just worked and worked all these years — and what has she had? Nothing.

JIM — She's had me.

CHESTER — That's what Nell said!

NELL — Chester, can't you fix it so Popper won't lose what's left of that policy? You're the insurance company's lawyer.

CHESTER — (*doubtfully*). I know, but ——

NELL — Do try — for my sake.

CHESTER — All right, Nell. (*Hughie enters.*)

NELL — Thanks, Chester.

HUGHIE — You'd better go in to your mother, Nell. She seems pretty well upset.

NELL — I should think she would be. I just hate to go away and leave her when she's in trouble.

Danny comes to the rescue. If Mr. Bailey can't pay the $1,500, he will pay it, he tells Chester. But he is curious to know what has become of the money. It is Hughie Logan's opinion that the old sport has gambled it away playing stud poker, but Jim resents the suggestion. He has, if they must know, invested it. And he stands a chance of being a rich man as a result — if he can only find a way to take advantage of his great opportunity.

Finally Danny worms the admission out of him that he has bought $80,000 worth of the old trolley company's bonds for ten cents on the dollar. True, the company's busted. But its old power house still stands and Jim has a tip the new electric light company is thinking of buying it. If it does buy it Jim will have a fortune — providing, of course, he can hold on to his bonds.

The investment is a great joke to Hughie. But it isn't to Danny, and he is willing to help his future father-in-law out. He has $7,000, and he needs it to finance his own business — but he's willing to take a chance. He will let Jim have the needed $6,500. And Jim is delighted.

"Do you mean it?" he shouts. "Give me your hand! Danny, I'm proud of you! Listen, I want to tell you the truth. I didn't approve of you at first — thought Nell was making a mistake — but I was wrong! I apologize! (*Embracing him.*) Welcome — welcome into the Bailey family. Could you let me have the money now?"

But there is more trouble brewing in the next room. And now it is brought out. Nell and her mother, their faces long and sober, return to announce that they have had a serious talk about the lost money and father's handling of it. And Nell has decided that her father and mother must come to an understanding concerning the disposition of the family income before she will feel content to get married.

"Before I leave home today," she says to her surprised father, "we want you to promise that every Saturday after you've paid your weekly expenses whatever's left you'll divide equally with Mother."

"Do you think I'm crazy?" demands her father, angrily.

NELL — (*going to him*). You've never been fair with Mother about money. You've had everything; your poker games — your cigars — your holiday fishing trips! Twice in the past five years you've gone to Atlantic City for the Redmen's Convention — but you didn't take Mother!

JIM — I'm the Redman — not your mother!

NELL — Yes, you've been everything. You were always out at some lodge meeting, or snake dance, or something, while Mother sat around home, watching the stove in case you wanted some supper when you came in.

JIM — Do you hear that, Hughie? Really, what's the use of a fellow trying to be unselfish?

MRS. BAILEY — But your father's always been called the livest wire in Johnsburg.

NELL — Well, I think it's your turn to be a live wire. (*Hughie laughs.*) And that's why I'm asking you to pay her a definite salary instead of making her come to you like a beggar for every penny she gets.

HUGHIE — Most wives have to ask their husbands for money, and I've noticed they don't stutter much.

NELL — (*going to Hughie*). There isn't a wife in the world who wouldn't sooner have less money to spend if only she knew it was her own and she could do what she liked with it without answering those everlasting questions: "What do you want it for?" and "What did you do with the last I gave you?"

JIM — I tell you women aren't to be trusted with the handling of money.

NELL — (*fighting back — Luella enters*). And if we aren't, *why* aren't we? It's because you men never let us have a share in the responsibility of saving. You dare us to try and get money out of you. You make us *dig* for it — and then you have the nerve to call us "gold diggers."

LUELLA — What *is* all this?

HUGHIE — (*rises quickly, grabs Luella by the hand and rushes her to the door*). Say, come on out of here — this is private.

NELL — No, Luella, you stay. (*Hughie and Luella pause.*) I'm just saying that I think every wife has a right to part of what her husband makes.

LUELLA — Sure she has.

JIM — Just for taking care of a home?

NELL — Yes, and for keeping her husband amused and seeing that things are smooth and pleasant. For watching over his health and his children's health, and nursing him and for trying to get him the things he likes to eat for — over — a thousand meals a year!

JIM — (*laughing*). Housework! Women make a lot of fuss about it but it isn't anything really.

MRS. BAILEY — It isn't anything?

LUELLA — It's the old story — a husband's a relative and it don't pay to work for relatives.

NELL — (*coming to Jim*). Won't you — won't you admit that Mother is entitled to part of what you get?

JIM — I will not.

NELL — And you won't agree to divide with her?

JIM — No. (*He turns his back on her.*)

NELL — Well then, we'll have to do it, Mother. Let him shift for himself for awhile!

MRS. BAILEY — Oh, Nell, no — I can't do it.

NELL — This is your last chance, Mother. If you're ever going to take a stand, it's got to be now.

JIM — (*pulling Nell around by the shoulders*). Look here, Nell — what do you think you're doing?

MRS. BAILEY — Don't you start scolding Nell!

JIM — What?

MRS. BAILEY — She's right in everything she says. She knows how I've worked and worked for you, and you don't appreciate it. You say it's nothing!

JIM — And I meant what I said!

MRS. BAILEY — Well, if it's nothing, I might just as well stop doing it.

JIM — (*shocked for a minute — Nell pats her mother on the back*). Do you really mean to say that after twenty-five years of peaceful married life you'd let Nell come along and upset everything with her crazy ideas?

NELL — They're not crazy. If you want to make silly investments and waste half the money you ought to save, that's your business. But the other half belongs to mother, and I'm going to help her stand up for her rights.

HUGHIE — Well, I'm surprised at you! Making trouble like this between your parents.

LUELLA — She isn't making trouble — the trouble's *there*. She's trying to cure it.

HUGHIE — Luella, don't *you* dare to mix up in this.

LUELLA — Don't you dare to dare me!

HUGHIE — Oh, maybe *you're* going to walk out and leave *me*!

LUELLA — Maybe I am! Lord knows, Jim Bailey can't be any closer with his wife than you are with me.

JIM — (*going to Nell*). This is a fine thing you've started.

NELL — Well, now that I have started it, I mean to see it through.

HUGHIE — I don't know what Danny will do, but if you were *my* wife ——

LUELLA — What would you do? I'm your wife, so I'd like to know.

HUGHIE — Why, I wouldn't give you any money at all as long as you didn't appreciate it.

LUELLA — (*indignantly*). Yes, I know you. You think that's the way to keep a woman pleasant — waiting around hoping you'll throw her some of your chicken feed!

HUGHIE — If you ain't satisfied with what you get and want to start actin' up, just go ahead.

JIM — What's the use of arguin'? Come into the kitchen, Hughie, we'll have a little drink of apricot brandy to celebrate my return to bachelor life.

NELL — (*breaking in*). Then that's the understanding, Popper — everything is over between you and Mother until you come to your senses.

JIM — All right. Let her go. There's nothing she does I can't learn to do in a day. Who are all the best cooks? Men!

HUGHIE — Gosh, think of the card parties you can have! Stay out as late as you like!

JIM — You bet! And I never knew a strike yet when you couldn't find a few strike breakers!

Mrs. Bailey is dissolved in tears and of a mind to weaken, but Nell is firm. Rather than give in, rather than see her mother unfairly treated, she and Danny will give up their honeymoon and stay right there.

But Danny is not so enthusiastic. He has counted a good deal on his honeymoon. The first thing he says to Luella now, as he comes bursting into the room, is to inquire about the moonlit drawing room she was to engage for him. It's all right, she tells him, looking questioningly at Nell, it's all right—if he still wants it.

Want it? Danny's crazy about it. "Why, it's just things like that which lift marriage up and keep it from being commonplace and matter-of-fact. That's the trouble with most marriages, Mrs. Logan. Folks don't start right. But Nell and I — we aren't going to be like that; right from the start we're going to make our marriage a romance — a beautiful adventure!"

"Anybody that can think like that about marriage seems a shame they can't stay single," laconically observes Luella.

And then Nell breaks the news to him. They are not going on their honeymoon. They are going to stay right there — and help mother, and explains why. Mother wanted Popper to give her half of what he earned like wages, and he refused.

Danny — Where did she ever get such a horrible idea?

Nell — Why, she got it from me!

Danny — From you?

Nell — I certainly never thought that you wouldn't agree with me about that.

Danny — I know exactly how your father feels — The greatest fun in the world for a man is giving his wife money!

Nell — It is? Well, you just tell that to Popper.

Danny — Listen — in the olden days a man used to go out to kill something that he could bring home to his mate, — he can't do that nowadays but he can bring a present to surprise her with — and instead of that you want everything cut and dried. He can't bring anything home to lay at her feet because it isn't his — it's hers already. She earned it by being his wife!

Nell — Danny, how would you like it if you had a boss and he said — "Look here, Danny, I won't pay you a regular salary. I'll just give you presents when I feel like it. It makes me feel so nice and generous and I like to hear you thank me. And in case you need something just tell me and I'll see if I think you ought to have it." What man would ever stand that?

Danny — It isn't the same thing.

Nell — It's exactly the same thing.

Danny — Well, dear, what is it you want me to do?

Nell — I want you to help me about this trouble with Papa and Mother.

Danny — How?

Nell — You see, Danny, we can't go to Maine.

Danny — (repeating). We can't go to ——

Nell — (breaking in). Don't you understand I've got to stay here with Mother? You and Mother and I can all move in here today — won't everybody in town be surprised?

Danny — You and Mother and I — do you really mean to say that you'd let a silly little quarrel of your mother's interfere ——

Nell — It isn't silly or little! It's a lot bigger than where we spend our honeymoon. Oh, I know how you've set your heart on this trip, but won't you do this for me?

Danny — It isn't for you! It's just this idea of money that your father and mother ought to settle between them. It's for that that you want to take all the romance and beauty out of our wedding.

Nell — Oh! So romance and beauty depend on the place we go to! Very well, then, if you've got your heart so set on this romantic honeymoon of yours, we'll just have to postpone the wedding until we can go!

Danny — (going to her). What? You're only saying that to try and force me to give in!

Nell — (half-crying). No, I'm not. I mean it!

Danny — If you really love me you'll prove it by going to Maine with me this afternoon.

Nell — I can't, Danny — I've given Mother my word.

Danny — (turning away). I see! (He turns back to her sharply.) Your mother ought to be ashamed of herself to suggest such a thing!

Nell — Don't you dare say a word against my mother. She didn't suggest it. I suggested it and if you don't like it you don't need to marry me.

Danny — You don't love me.

Nell — Yes, I do.

Danny — Then I won't let you make our marriage into the kind of thing you're trying to.

Nell — You won't let me! You talk as if this trip meant more to you than I do! Very well then, since we can't go we'd better break off our engagement until you come to your senses!

Danny — You wouldn't dare!

Nell — (getting her hat). Oh, wouldn't I?

Danny — Where are you going?

Nell — To the church to tell Dr. Harper.

Danny — (catching her roughly). Nell, you don't know what you're doing.

NELL — Yes, I do. (*She is about to leave when Luella enters.*)

LUELLA — Nell! I've just made up my mind. You don't need to stay with your mother — I will. I'm going to quit Hughie!

NELL — You are? But you're too late to help me, Luella. I'm on my way up to see Dr. Harper. I'm going to postpone the wedding.

LUELLA — You don't mean it, Nell!

NELL — There's nothing else to do. (*She hurries out of the door, crying.*)

LUELLA — Danny! I can't believe it!

DANNY — She doesn't love me!

LUELLA — Yes, she does.

DANNY — No — she doesn't — and I love her so much!

(*Mr. Tevis enters. He wears the shabby make-up of a station-agent — spectacled — a man nearing sixty.*)

TEVIS — It's all right, Mrs. Logan. I done what you asked me. I've got 'em a drawing room with moonlight as far as Albany! After that they'll either have to go to sleep or else move over to the other side of the train!

The curtain falls

ACT II

Two weeks later Hughie Logan enters the living room of his own cottage late in the afternoon. The morning paper and the morning milk are still at the door, and the room suggests a late party the night before.

The center table is strewn with cards and poker chips. There are empty beer bottles scattered about, and the place has a stale and dejected look.

Hughie, however, has become somewhat accustomed to the new routine. He pours a saucer of milk for the cat and sits down comfortably with a bottle of beer and a cigar to glance through the paper before he takes up the serious work of getting his own dinner. He can throw his cigar ashes wherever he likes and the thought is pleasing.

A knock at the door disturbs him, however, and he is at some pains to straighten up the room before admitting guests. The caller is only Mr. Tevis, the station agent. Naturally curious, Tevis is eager to know just what is happening. He knows Hughie has been lying about Luella's having been called away to take care of her sick sister. He knows Jim Bailey's wife disappeared the same

day, and he knows Nell Bailey has broken her engagement to Danny Kester. Furthermore, he is reliably informed that all three women are boardin' at Gene
Powell's farm not five miles away.

"Everybody's wonderin' just why Luella left you,"
reports Mr. Tevis. "There was some pretty lively bettin'
about it up at prayer meetin' last night. Some favored
another woman — and some favored poker and drink.
Gene Powell says it's because you wouldn't give her half
your wages."

HUGHIE — Well, s'pose it were — would you give your wife half *your* wages?
TEVIS — Should say I would!
HUGHIE — You *would?*
TEVIS — Sure! My wife takes *all* mine.

The real Tevis errand, it appears, was to bring Hughie
a telegram from Judge MacLean. The Judge is the
moneyed man of the village and for some time he and
Hughie have been working together on real estate deals.
Now there is some suggestion of a partnership and the
Judge has wired that he would like to come over, stay to
dinner and talk over details.

The plan suits Hughie, and he is eager to please the
Judge. But who is to get the dinner? Dinner means a
lot to a man talking business. He is much more
approachable full of food. But Hughie's only chance
of having anything cooked for the Judge is to get Jim
Bailey to cook it. He is away in search of Bailey when
Luella appears, followed a moment later by Nell Bailey.

They were to have met at the drugstore and ride back
to the Powell farm together. But, missing Luella, and
suspecting she might be weakening, Nell has followed
her to the Logan cottage and finds her sneaking stealthily
and a little unhappily through the disordered rooms.

She is aching to clean the place up, and homesick clear
through, but she won't admit it. "I only came in to get
a warm nightgown and a hot water bottle!" she insists.

Nell seriously doubts that these husband substitutes

are all that interest Luella. Both girls, if the truth were
told, are pretty well discouraged.

They have both been looking for jobs in the village,
and neither has found one.

LUELLA — Trouble is we haven't tried for the only job we're any good at.
NELL — Housekeeping! (*Luella nods.*) I don't know anyone who needs a
housekeeper — do you?
LUELLA — Hughie does. Go and look at that kitchen.
NELL — (*amused*). Well, there's an idea! I might come here and work for
Hughie. He wouldn't pay you but he'd *have* to pay me!
LUELLA — But he'd never want me back if you came here and did every-
thing for him!
NELL — I shouldn't do everything. You used to rub his back every night
with Omega Oil. I certainly shouldn't do that.
LUELLA — Well, we've got to do something. I've only got two dollars.
NELL — You're rich! Mother and I have hardly got car fare.
LUELLA — (*resignedly*). Well, if we have to give in ——
NELL — Give in! I wouldn't dream of giving in. Just think how they'd
crow over us. I wish I had something I could pawn — I couldn't pawn my
engagement ring ——
LUELLA — (*looking at her ring*). I know I couldn't pawn *mine*. Hughie
didn't believe in spendin' money on jewelry! So you didn't send back your
engagement ring?
NELL — I wouldn't know where to send it.
LUELLA — Isn't Danny at the bungalow?
NELL — How do I know? I haven't heard a word from him since — since
that day.
LUELLA — Where do you think he is?
NELL — Maybe he went off on his old wedding trip by himself!
LUELLA — I've heard of men going on wedding trips without their wives, but
I've never heard of them going by themselves.
NELL — Oh, you can trust Danny. He's different from other men.
LUELLA — If you can trust him he's different. I know of two kinds of
husbands. One that's true while you're watching him and one that isn't even
that.
NELL — (*protesting*). Luella!
LUELLA — You'd like to have Danny back, wouldn't you?
NELL — (*walking away*). No. (*Turns.*) What?
LUELLA — I said you'd like to have him back! You don't have to be
ashamed to admit it. I know I'd like to have Hughie back.
NELL — Why, surely you don't think ——
LUELLA — I'll tell you what I do think. I think we ought to have thought
a whole lot more about this before we went into it! (*Sniffs.*) Do you get
that smell of stale tobacco?
NELL — Yes. It's terrible.
LUELLA — It makes me so homesick!
NELL — It's only natural that we'd miss them. We train our minds to think
of the things they're interested in — we train our memories so we can find
their books and papers and collar buttons ——
LUELLA — I feel like a piece of toast after the poached egg's been lifted
off of it.
NELL — Well, maybe they're every bit as lonely and dissatisfied as we are!
LUELLA — Lonely? Don't make me laugh. Look at those poker chips — and
those bottles — that's some of Joe Snyder's home-brew. Oh, they've been havin'
a wild time, all right — kicked the boards right out of their stalls. (*She walks
about, scuffing the carpet and searching intently for something.*)

NELL — What in the world are you looking for?
LUELLA — Hairpins — I don't see any. Now that the girls are taking to wearing their hair bobbed, a wife's lost one more protection!
NELL — Never mind, Luella, it'll be all right if we can only — Good Lord, there's Hughie's car! He must have forgotten something.

They manage to sneak out without Hughie's seeing them. Jim Bailey, having arrived with his arms filled with canned goods, goes busily about getting the expected Judge MacLean a meal. Jim has had a drink or two, which serves to make him a bit garrulous and to stimulate his natural sense of independence. He is, he insists, having a fine time enjoying his freedom. Does what he darned pleases when he pleases. In addition to which blessing he is still certain that he is about to become one of the town's richest men. The idea fills Hughie with mirth, and Hughie's mirth so disgusts Jim that he is about to quit his job as cook when there is another knock at the door. It may be the Judge. But it isn't. It's Luella. And Hughie's joy at seeing her is most pronounced.

She has not come to stay, however, as he had hoped. She has come, she says, in response to his note asking her to sign a check. He wants to be ready to make a payment on the partnership he hopes Judge MacLean is going to offer him. But Hughie is ever so hopeful she may stay. He dismisses Jim Bailey a little curtly on the strength of these hopes. But Luella is already moving slowly toward the door.

HUGHIE — Oh, Lou, you're not going?
LUELLA — As soon as I get some of my music.
HUGHIE — Now that you're here, won't you stay?
LUELLA — Do you want me to?
HUGHIE — Want you to? I should say I do! Why, Lou, I was almost on the point of going after you when you rang the doorbell!
LUELLA — You wanted me back as much as that?
HUGHIE — More than that, dear — I needed you! Needed you somethin' awful!
LUELLA — (softly). Hughie! (Goes into his arms.)
HUGHIE — Guess who's coming to dinner tonight?
LUELLA — Company?
HUGHIE — Judge MacLean.
LUELLA — Is he back?
HUGHIE — Yes, and I want you to cook him a good dinner. You'll have to hurry, dear, because I've got ——

LUELLA — (*drawing back from him*). So that's what you needed me for — a dinner!
HUGHIE — But, Lou ——
LUELLA — I'm nothing but a cook to you! (*She opens the door and calls.*) Nell — oh, Nell! (*Pause — Nell enters — stops — then goes to Hughie.*) Now go ahead and have your business talk with Hughie.
NELL — Business?
LUELLA — About that idea of yours. Judge MacLean is coming here to dinner and I'm going back to Powell's Farm.
HUGHIE — But, Luella, you came to stay — you know you did!
LUELLA — I came to get my "Ave Maria" and "Love Lies Dying" — and if I want anything more I'll send for it.
HUGHIE — (*angrily*). Now, you listen to me ——
LUELLA — I did! Good-night!

Nell offers her services as housekeeper. Hughie is a little surprised but grateful — until she names $30 a week as the salary she expects. He balks at that — but what can he do — with Judge MacLean on the way? Nothing! So the bargain is made and Nell starts the dinner.

The Judge's visit proves more important than anticipated. Not only is he ready to take the Logan $20,000 savings and declare Hughie a partner in the business, but he seems particularly anxious to buy into Danny Kester's portable cottage enterprise. So anxious, in fact, that when he inadvertently admits that Danny has a good thing, and Nell overhears him, Hughie has to think quick for an excuse to get Nell out of the house, so she will hear no more.

It is agreed between the new partners that now is the time to approach Kester. Danny appears to have lost interest in his cottage business, they agree, and he has all his working capital tied up in the power plant scheme, which, the Judge insists, is not going through.

Jim Bailey, a little more tight than he was before, comes back to finish up the dinner he had started for the Judge. When Nell walks in on him he is much inclined to suspect the quality of the home brew he has been sampling, and his demands of Hughie for an explanation naturally arouse Judge MacLean's suspicions.

JUDGE — (*rising*). Has your wife left you, Hughie?

HUGHIE — Oh, it's nothing. Just a little domestic argument — his wife is in it — and his daughter ——

JIM — It wasn't Hughie's fault, Judge. It was just a matter of money. And I've got a scheme to end it. If Nell thought Danny was in trouble she'd go back to him like a shot. And then our wives would come back to us.

HUGHIE — (*disgusted*). Oh, shut up.

JIM — (*moving his chair close to the Judge*). I'll tell it to you, Judge. I wanted Danny to tell Nell he's flat broke — that the power house investment had gone wrong — but he won't do it — said he couldn't found his happiness on a lie.

JUDGE — But it happens that it isn't a lie!

JIM — What do you mean?

JUDGE — I mean it's true. I happen to know that the committee decided not to buy the old power house!

JIM — You mean — they're going to build a new power house?

JUDGE — That's it exactly.

JIM — (*hopelessly*). That's the way it's been all my life — whenever I bet on 'em, they start runnin' backwards. (*Nell enters.*)

NELL — What time do you want dinner, Mr. Logan?

HUGHIE — (*to Nell*). Just a minute.

JUDGE — (*to Hughie*). Is his money in this investment?

HUGHIE — Yes.

JUDGE — I thought you said it was young Kester's.

NELL — What does he mean? Has anything happened to Danny?

HUGHIE — It looks as if he'd lost all his money.

NELL — Lost it? How?

HUGHIE — Your father got him into a speculation and it went wrong.

NELL — (*to Jim.*) Oh, Popper!

JIM — I'm broke — busted! Haven't got so much as a thin dime! (*Nell turns and goes to desk, pulling off her apron.*)

HUGHIE — Nell, where are you going?

NELL — To Danny!

JUDGE — Let me get this straight — (*To Jim.*) This young woman is your daughter ——

NELL — Yes, and I'm going to be Danny Kester's wife. (*Exits.*)

HUGHIE — There goes the cook!

JIM — She's gone to him! I said she would! And that's what I'm going to do. I'm going to my wife and tell her she can have half of all I've got!

The curtain falls

The scene changes to the living room of Danny Kester's cottage. "The place looks even more forlorn than Hughie's living room. The decorations of rambler roses and laurel are still up. They are quite dead. Garlands have parted and are hanging in strips; there are some blueprints scattered about and a collar with a tie threaded through it, socks and pair of trousers are thrown over the back of the lounge which is now facing the room, made up with blankets, sheet and pillow."

Danny is home, having supper. At least Danny is eating canned beans, drinking cold coffee and patiently munching what appears to be dry bread. Life is not meaning much to Danny these days. Even when Oscar, his office boy, rushes in full of enthusiasm and a report that the manager of a near-by hotel has been inquiring about the Kester Cottage with the idea of ordering twelve of them, Danny is not greatly stirred. With all his cash tied up he could not finance the deal now, even if it were to go through. But Oscar manages to get him to agree to at least talk with the prospective purchaser.

They are gone when Nell arrives. She knocks timidly first, and then tries the living room windows. Finding one open she promptly sneaks in. Her arms are filled with groceries. Slowly and a little tearfully she surveys the wreck of her hopes, and there is a catch in her throat as she comes upon the pathetic remains of Danny's supper. Then she starts in to clean up.

When Chester Logan calls she lets him in through the window and promptly utilizes him as a furniture mover. Chester would, if Nell would let him, take advantage of the situation to further his own suit. He does get as far as a definite proposition. " Fifty per cent of the surplus income and no questions asked." That's Chester's idea. " Pictures three times a week — semiannual trip to New York — man of the house to help with the dishes on the cook's night out."

But Nell has other plans. She expects to marry Danny the next day. " Danny's in trouble," she explains. " He's lost all his money and he's going to have a hard fight to keep his head above water. I'm going to keep this bunga- low looking so attractive that everyone will want one. And I'm going to try to cheer Danny up so he'll have the courage to go on fighting!"

Chester can't quite understand why she wants to take such an awful chance with Danny and poverty, and he is sure she is all wrong in thinking Judge MacLean is trying in any way to cheat Danny, but he has to make the best of the situation. Nell is not without some little regret that she is forced to so completely disappoint him. "There'll always be a chair here for you, Chester," she promises, sympathetically. But he is not to be cheered. "I can imagine how comfortable it will be if Danny picks it out," he grumbles as he leaves.

Now there is a noise at the door, followed by the sound of a key in the lock. Nell hurriedly disappears into the kitchen. Danny has come back. The sight of the place, the aroma of fresh coffee in the air, the sight of the fire in the fireplace completely dumfound him. A second later he hears Nell blithely singing in the kitchen. He is staring a bit wildly at the door as she comes cheerily in with a plate of celery.

NELL — I didn't hear you come in. Just sit down here and put on your dressing gown, dear. There's your pipe and evening paper. I've got something you like, I think. I found it in one of mother's preserving jars. (*Starts back to kitchen.*) That stove is just the quickest thing I ever saw. (*Exits.*)

Danny goes to the sofa in a kind of daze. He takes off his coat, picks up the dressing gown. Nell enters with soup tureen and takes it to the table.

DANNY — And you said once that life wasn't a fairy story!
NELL — Come over here and eat this while it's hot. Where have you been — out seeing somebody — hmmm? (*She serves him — spreads napkin for him.*)
DANNY — I went to see a man — but he wasn't home. Oh, Nell, it's too wonderful to be true!
NELL — Does the place seem different?
DANNY — As different as misery and happiness. (*She is in his arms.*) I've been so lonely!
NELL — I'll let you into a secret — I've been lonely, too.
DANNY — And we aren't going to quarrel any more?
NELL — (*freeing herself gaily*). Oh, I won't promise that! But I'll marry you — if you don't mind taking a chance.
DANNY — When?
NELL — I thought maybe tomorrow if you haven't any previous date.
DANNY — Nell!
NELL — Sit down — eat that!
DANNY — You know that little bag you brought over here all packed for the train. (*She nods.*) I can't tell you how often I've opened it and taken out the soft, fluffy pink robe and the two little slippers ——
NELL — Have you, dear? (*Starts to cry.*)
DANNY — Oh, darling, what's the matter? Please don't cry, dear.
NELL — Can't you let me enjoy myself my own way?
DANNY — (*taking his handkerchief out and dabbing her eyes*). And when

I wasn't lonely I was jealous. I knew Chester would have looked you up wherever you were. I'd think of him seeing you — (*Uses handkerchief vigorously.*)

NELL — Please, dear, don't punch *me* in the eye — I'm not Chester.

DANNY — And now suddenly everything's changed — (*Pause.*)

NELL — Danny ——

DANNY — Yes, dear?

NELL — There's something I've got to tell you. It's rather bad news. That investment Father made you put all your money in — it's no good.

DANNY — The power house deal?

NELL — It's awful to realize that you lost all your money through my father — but don't be discouraged, Danny.

DANNY — Did you hear this from your father or Hughie?

NELL — From both of them. You may have a struggle at first ——

DANNY — Nell, I can't pretend with you. I haven't lost my money. This was your father's idea. He thought it would make you come back and then your mother would have to come back to him.

NELL — (*rising slowly*). Thank you for telling me. (*Pauses irresolutely.*) What time is it?

DANNY — Quarter to eight.

NELL — I mustn't miss the car. (*Goes for her hat.*)

DANNY — There's another one at nine.

NELL — But I've got to see Mother before Papa does.

DANNY — Nell, why did you come here tonight? Was it just because you heard this story?

NELL — Why did you suppose it was? Did you think I couldn't stay away any longer and came to beg you to take me back?

DANNY — And you said you'd marry me tomorrow just out of pity?

NELL — When I said that I didn't know they lied to me — and I thought you needed me.

DANNY — So you're going to break your word to me again!

NELL — But things are just as they were. I can't desert Mother and Luella.

Danny breaks into wild laughter that is near to sobbing and buries his face in his arms. Nor does knocking at the door, followed by the entrance of Judge MacLean and his new partner, Hughie Logan, stop him. He manages to control himself, however, long enough to hear the judge's proposition. The judge has come to confirm the report that the power house deal is off and that the investors in the bonds have lost their money. Danny at first accepts it as a part of the same story Jim Bailey told Nell to get her to come back, and sneers at it. Later he is convinced it is true. When the judge intimates that he and Hughie are willing to help him meet the strain his losses will put upon the Kester Cottage business by buying a half interest in it, Danny offers to sell the whole thing to them. Nor will he listen to Nell, pleading with him not to let them trick him.

NELL — Danny — Danny, listen to me. They want to get your business away because they know it's worth a fortune. (*Danny turns abruptly away from her.*)

JUDGE — Really, young lady ——

NELL — (*turning on the Judge*). Yes, you do. I heard what you said about the Kester patents to Hughie tonight. You can talk of friendship all you like, but you've come here to get the best of Danny because you think he's helpless.

DANNY — I don't care why you've come — and I don't care whether you get the best of me or not. All I want is to sell out this business right now and forget it.

NELL — Oh, Danny, please ——

DANNY — And I want to get away and forget this place, too. (*He removes his dressing gown and puts on his coat.*)

NELL — Won't you listen to me — you always said I was going to be your partner!

DANNY — No — we don't think alike. Marriage means one thing to you — to me it means something quite different. You're a practical girl with practical ideas about partnership and family incomes, and all that. And I'm just a romantic fool. We'd never be happy together because we don't agree. (*He crosses to Hughie who gives him a check.*) I suppose you want a receipt.

HUGHIE — It's all on the back of the check.

DANNY — " In full for all ownership rights and patents to the Kester Portable Kottage."

NELL — Don't take it, Danny ——

DANNY — I'll send an order to Oscar to give you all the plans and papers and what to do with my things. I'm going to the depot.

HUGHIE — You're not going tonight?

DANNY — (*going for his hat*). I don't want to hang round just to hear people saying what a poor dub I am.

NELL — They don't!

DANNY — Oh, yes, they do. And I don't blame them. I *am* a dub. Other men's wives leave them after a year or two and it's a tragedy. Mine left me on my wedding day and it's a joke. Oh, yes, I'm a dub all right. But I'm going somewhere where everybody I meet on the street doesn't know it.

NELL — Danny!

DANNY — Good-bye.

He is out the door before she can try further to stop him and she sinks wearily into a chair. Even Hughie is unhappy at seeing Danny quit like that, but the judge is greatly pleased. Luella tries to comfort Nell. Whatever it is, Danny'll get over it, she predicts.

NELL — No, he won't. I've hurt him too much. (*She is sobbing.*) This was to have been our home, Luella. All the thought Danny put in it was for me — and now it all belongs to that — (*suddenly she breaks off*). Luella! Luella! I've got an idea! You can save it for him!

LUELLA — I can!

NELL — His whole business, if you would ——

LUELLA — I'll do anything I can.

NELL — You've often told me you didn't like the judge and you wished Hughie weren't with him.

LUELLA — Yes, I know, but ——

NELL — He'd probably get the best of Hughie before he was through. Oh, Lou, here's our chance!

LUELLA — I'll do anything I can, but Hughie'll never listen to me.

NELL — You will?

LUELLA — Yes, anything. But Hughie'll never listen to me.

Nell — Oh, if we ——

Huchie — (*entering, followed by the judge*). We didn't ask him what he wanted done with his furniture.

Judge — We must move it out of here right away and turn this place into an office.

Nell — Judge MacLean, you'll let Mr. Kester's furniture alone!

Judge — I don't want his furniture — you can have it if you like — only it can't stay here.

Nell — It won't be taken out of here if I can help it.

Judge — Well, you can't help it.

Nell — I'm going to try. And you're not going to cheat Danny Kester out of his business. I won't let you, Judge MacLean.

Judge — What do you think you're going to do?

Nell — I'm going to help Luella run this business. She owns it — not you! It was bought with her check and the receipt on the back will be hers, too.

Huchie — But, Nell, every penny in that account is my money!

Nell — I know. You think Luella ought to be satisfied all her life with your little handfuls of chicken feed — and you claim all this money belongs to you! Well, you're wrong. It isn't yours! It's her back pay for working and cooking and slaving for you for eight years! That's what it is!

The curtain falls

ACT III

It is two months later. The living room of Danny's cottage has again been transformed. It is now the main office of the "Kester Kosy Kottage Kompany," of which Nell Bailey and Luella Logan are the directing heads. There is a gate and a wooden rail at the entrance, the bookshelves are filled with samples of materials and collections of blueprints. A table supports a model cottage in miniature, and there are desk and typewriter for the office secretary.

Around the wall there are advertising posters and window cards. "The Kester Kottage Takes Half the Care — Gives Twice the Joy," reads one. "Buy a Kester Kottage and You'll Have Enough Left Over to Buy an Automobile" is another.

It is a bustling place. Oscar, the boy, is as active as office boys always are (in plays), and Miss Johnson, the secretary, is apparently much more interested in the mail than she is in her side curls. As for Luella Logan, she is so busy she has completely lost a day. What has become of Wednesday?

Still, there is trouble brewing. At Towanda, where the company is building ten cottages, the workmen are threatening to strike. Not a gentlemanly thing to do, Miss Johnson insists, but there it is.

Chester Logan, who has been retained as the company's attorney, gives Luella a moment's cheer by insisting that even should there be a strike she and Nell would not have to pay a forfeit, inasmuch as he had inserted in the contract the usual strike clause relieving them of responsibility in such a contingency. Luella is really worried. She does not want to lose Hughie's twenty thousand dollars, even if she does feel that she has a right to use it. She is, she admits to Chester, afraid of money. " I should say I am," says she; " why, I never had over twenty dollars at any one time before — but Hughie was always sittin' there harder to get a nickel out of than a weighing machine. I didn't worry about his losing our money — I never realized what a nice, safe feeling it gave you to have a tight wad for a husband."

Now Hughie himself appears. He has been standing outside all the time, it appears, waiting for Chester. He was a little timid about coming in without an invitation. But Luella wants to talk with him on business.

HUGHIE — Well, here I am.

LUELLA — Will you sit down?

HUGHIE — No! thanks.

LUELLA — Are you sore at me?

HUGHIE — Why shouldn't I be? First you desert me and then you rob me!

LUELLA — That money was in the bank in my name, and your own brother says you can't get it back unless I choose to give it to you!

HUGHIE — (after a long pause). Well — I didn't say I could!

LUELLA — Well, then perhaps we can make an agreement about it.

HUGHIE — Agreement?

LUELLA — There was over twenty thousand dollars in that account — twenty thousand! It's all I can do to say it!

HUGHIE — Do you realize how much that money would make if invested with Judge MacLean?

LUELLA — Oh, Nell and I are going to pay you interest.

HUGHIE — What rate?

LUELLA — Oh, we'll do the right thing by you — just leave it to us.

HUGHIE — You don't intend to pay back the money?

LUELLA — We can't.
HUGHIE — Not even the balance in the bank?
LUELLA — There isn't much of anything left.
HUGHIE — But Chester says the business is showing a wonderful profit.
LUELLA — It is not. We're making a profit, but the Lord knows it don't show! The more business we do the more money it costs to do it; if the business keeps on improving we'll be taking a taxi to the poor house.
HUGHIE — And so you propose keeping my money?
LUELLA — For the present. If business gets bad enough we'll begin paying you back!
HUGHIE — Why — why don't you come home? (Luella looks at him astonished.) You struck to get half my money, didn't you?
LUELLA — Yes.
HUGHIE — Well, you've got it all. What's keeping you away now?
LUELLA — I didn't know you wanted me to come back!
HUGHIE — (suddenly giving in). Well, I do! Gosh, it's awful there without you, Lou.
LUELLA — (going to him). Poor old Hughie! (She stops — almost in his arms.) Wait a minute! Are you trying to get hold of me for my money?

The Logan reconciliation is interrupted by the arrival of Jim Bailey — a crushed and humbled Jim Bailey. Things have not been going well for Jim. He has given up housekeeping and is going to boarding, and he has come now to leave some of his wife's personal things he didn't know what else to do with. He had some thought of asking his wife to come back to him, but after his bond deal went wrong he lost his job and all his courage and independence went with it. He admits as much to Hughie.

HUGHIE — Say, what's come over you?
JIM — I just got wise to myself, and found out I'm a great, big, wonderful, zero! But as long as Annie was there I never knew it. Hughie, that's the one thing about this wife business we didn't reckon on. Pay 'em? Gee, you couldn't give 'em too much for bein' the one person in the world who really believes in you!
HUGHIE — (uncomfortably). Gosh, I never thought I'd hear Jim Bailey spoutin' mush like that.
JIM — "Mush," is it? Huh! Listen — I guess p'rhaps big, successful men don't need their wives — I don't know — but, God, how we poor dubs need 'em! You're a nobody at the office — an' you're afraid to ask for a raise for fear the boss will notice your name on the pay roll and fire you — but once you get home it's different. There you're the boss — and wifie's there to take care everyone knows it. Maybe the kid asks some question about her school work — a question you couldn't answer on a bet — but your wife says, "Don't bother father, he's had a hard day at the office and he's got a lot on his mind." Probably you're only sitting there wonderin' what chance the Yanks have got to win the pennant, but you look wise and you know that to the little gang around the reading lamp you're somebody — and somehow or other, you begin to feel like a somebody!

All the men are more or less depressed. Jim is beaten. Hughie admits that he is suffering from housemaid's knee and even Oscar is irritated excessively by the demands the sex can make on even a lowly errand boy. They are always wanting to know about something. "Gee," explodes Oscar, "but these dames make you sick! Automatic clothes washers, vacuum sweepers, sewin' and darnin' machines — all they need now is a machine to give the baby its bath and they're fixed fine. Ask me, I think the world'd be a whole lot better off if there weren't any women at all."

"If there weren't any women," Miss Johnson counters, "who'd look after you and mend your clothes and —— "

"If there weren't any women I wouldn't wear any clothes," declares Oscar.

There is a report that Danny Kester is in town, but Nell doesn't know it. She is no sooner in the office than she is head over heels in the strike complication. Luella tells her of Chester's strike clause assurance, but she can't remember it and a moment later her worst fears are confirmed. Chester has found the contract and there is no strike clause in it. Yet he is willing to swear it was there when he drew up the paper. If there should be a strike, and the Kottage Kompany did have to pay a forfeit, it would mean ruin.

"I'd just die if I lost your money, Luella," Nell admits to her partner.

"It'd be just my luck to live!" predicts Luella.

But Nell is still for making a fight. She has started out to save the business for Danny and she is not going to give up until she is completely beaten. And she will not, even with Chester's urging, agree to call in Judge MacLean and sell to him until she absolutely has to. She is more than a little convinced, anyway, that the Judge has had a hand in stirring up the workmen to strike.

Nell is the only one who has any spirit left. Luella is cheerless and Mrs. Bailey, looking for her husband and learning that he has been there and gone, is unhappy

and blames her daughter for that. Nell is a headstrong
girl, her mother charges. If it had not been for her they
might all be happy now, and Danny wouldn't be running
around with painted-up women, drinking and everything,
as it is reported he has been doing.

Nell is pretty miserable and about ready to consider
any proposition that will get them all out of their difficulties when Judge MacLean calls. Chester has telephoned him and, of course, the Judge is only too eager
to do anything he can. Nell sends him into the inner
office that he may talk matters over with Chester and
agree upon what shall be done. As she turns back into
the room she sees Danny standing in the doorway, watching her intently.

NELL — Danny Kester! Why have you come?

DANNY — (hiding his emotion — speaking calmly). For my trunk. (Pause.)
I had to come over from Binghamton on business today — I didn't know a thing
about you and Luella getting hold of this place until I saw your father.

NELL — Were — were you surprised?

DANNY — More than surprised — cleverest trick I ever heard of. Beat the
Judge at his own game — you've proved more than you started out to, Nell.

NELL — I — I don't know what you mean.

DANNY — Not only that men can't get along without women, but that
women can easily get along without men. Just see what success you've made
in almost no time at all.

NELL — I'm not so sure about the success.

DANNY — You're too modest. I've heard all about it. Fifteen cottages
sold already. It is really wonderful! And this room — why, it's a monument
to your business ability.

NELL — (uncertainly). Thank you. Do you know why I got Luella to hold
on to this business?

DANNY — Why, it gave you a chance to show how clever you are!

NELL — But I had to stop Judge MacLean from getting it.

DANNY — Did you? Why?

NELL — Would you rather the Judge had it?

DANNY — I don't care a rap who has it. (Goes to door.)

NELL — But, Danny, suppose you could have it.

DANNY — Have it back? I wouldn't take it as a gift!

NELL — (stunned). Oh!

DANNY — It's all wrapped up in my mind with things I want to forget!

NELL — (after a short pause). Me, you mean. (She crosses to the door —
turns slowly and comes back to him.) I'll tell you one thing, Danny Kester.
You've talked about being a fool, but you've never begun to be the fool
that I am. I don't want to show I'm clever at business — I — I don't care
anything about that kind of success — but I loved you — and I saw you being
cheated — and I thought it was because I'd hurt you — and I just couldn't
stand it — so I got Luella to hold on to it — and I've been working as I
never worked before to save it for you. But I'm through now! Through
forever! Judge MacLean can have it and welcome — and no matter how much
you hate it, I hate it a hundred million times more.

Danny is lost in astonishment as Nell sweeps by him and into the inner office to complete her part of the deal with Judge MacLean. But he recovers in time to extract considerable information from Luella. Among other things he learns of the threatened strike and the contract clause that has been left out. "And in spite of all this Judge MacLean is willing to buy this business and assume your liabilities?" he demands.

He is, Luella reports. Which sets Danny working on a new thought and in no time at all he has discovered that the contract with the strike clause left out was not copied on the same typewriter as that in which the clause was included. A minute later he is dashing across to the bank, leaving instructions with Luella not to do anything about selling the business until he gets back.

She tells Chester the news when he comes to report cheerily that the deal is all fixed up — Nell is ready to sell for $22,000 if Luella is, and the Judge is prepared to sign on the dotted line as soon as they bring him a blank check. But there isn't going to be any blank check for any sale, Luella informs him. Not, at least, until Hughie approves. Hughie has been sent for.

Chester is a little peeved at this. "First you say you'd like to sell," he explodes; "then you walk in and say you won't — then Nell walks in and says you will — then I come out and you say you won't. No wonder women get run over by automobiles."

They are still waiting for Hughie when Tevis, the station agent, rushes in excitedly, calling for Mrs. Bailey. He wants her to come and look at her husband. A moment later Jim Bailey himself appears, resembling nothing half so much as a circus horse ready for parade. He is wearing a new shepherd's plaid suit, a new straw hat with the gayest of bands and he carries, and twirls, a nifty cane. He has called to inquire, he would have them know, for Mrs. James Bailey, who stares at him wild eyed and a little tearful. The truth comes out when

Judge MacLean walks into the room and Jim catches
sight of him.

JIM — (crossing to Judge). Hello! You're the wise one that said my trolley
bonds was no good, aren't you?
JUDGE — They weren't then — the committee changed their plans at the meet-
ing last evening.
JIM — Changed, eh? And none of you smart Alecks could figure it out!
Ha! I never had a doubt in the world about it.
MRS. BAILEY — Jim, you're — you're rich?
JIM — Rich! Ask the Judge! (Mrs. Bailey bursts out crying.) Hello —
the dam's busted! What is there to bawl at?
MRS BAILEY — If you're rich, Jim, you won't want me back.
JIM — Oh, I see. Well, just because I got to the top of the heap I'm not
the kind to throw the old girl overboard and take up with a doll-faced cutie!
And you're goin' to get your share of the money — save it or blow it in, as you
like.
MRS. BAILEY — Oh, I don't care about that — I only want you. (Luella
enters.)
JIM — 'Atta baby! That's the way to have 'em trained! You know, Annie,
that for Jim Bailey's wife — you look — seedy! Come along with me and you
can get yourself a new dress.
MRS. BAILEY — Jim, do you mean it?
JIM — Come on and see.
MRS. BAILEY — I'll get my hat.
JIM — You don't need a hat. I'll buy you one. And you can walk down
the street with me while I give the laugh to all these poor simps that have
been calling me a failure! Imagine the nerve of them —— Me — a failure
—— (He takes Mrs. Bailey's arm.) Come on, old girl, let's go.

The Judge has brought the bill of sale with him for
Luella's signature. Nell has already signed and everything is agreed upon. Luella is still intent on waiting
for Hughie, but the Judge assures her that Hughie knows
all about it and, being a partner, is naturally in favor of
the deal. She is about to sign when she looks up and
catches sight of Danny coming through the door.

Danny is loaded with information and money. He has
also sold his bonds. He knows, for one thing, that the
contract has been altered at some one's suggestion, and
he suspects the Judge. He knows the Judge owns most
of the hotel company's stock and he discovers, when
Hughie arrives, that the contractor putting up the Kester
cottages was to be paid to call the strike. That is a little
too much even for Hughie to stomach and he very
frankly tells the Judge so.

Before they are through with him the Judge is ready
to cry quits and do what he can to call off the strike.

He has no desire to face in court a charge of conspiracy. But he has one parting shot. He will have nothing further to do with Hughie as a partner. Which tickles Luella a lot. Now Hughie can take over her share of the business and go in partnership with Danny. " The only place I want to be boss is around home," she confesses.

When Nell comes from the inner office she is wearing her hat and carrying her pocketbook. She is ready to leave and tries to pass Danny without comment. But he stops her.

DANNY — Nell! Before we part again I feel that I'd like to straighten the record a little. I thought you'd made rather a mess of things interfering between your father and mother ——

NELL — Don't worry. As long as I live I'm never going to interfere or give one word of suggestion or advice to anybody.

DANNY — Wait! Everything you've done has turned out to be the gosh-darndest success!

NELL — Is that some more of your sarcasm?

DANNY — Good Lord, don't you see it yourself? Look at Luella and Hughie — they were just a humdrum married couple. Now they've suddenly blossomed out like a pair of honeymooners, and you taught your father some-thing he hadn't learned in his whole married life. You've taught him how much your mother means to him and made him *want* to share everything with her and do his best to make her happy! (*Nell looks astounded.*) You should have seen their faces when I met them, arm-in-arm, parading down the street just now.

NELL — (*smiling with pleasure*). Mother and Dad. (*Realizes she is smiling — changes expression and turns away.*)

DANNY — (*fingering torn pocket*). Yes — oh, they've made up fine. There are two pretty good bits of work, I should say. I've got a meeting of the bondholders at the Village Hall, and I don't want to look ragged.

NELL — (*going up to bookcase for sewing basket*). Then for heaven's sake let me sew up that pocket.

DANNY — Oh, don't bother.

NELL — Stand around here to the light. (*She begins to sew pocket.*)

DANNY — And look at the business. I couldn't have come within a mile of making this the success that you have. Ouch!

NELL — Did I stick you?

DANNY — It's all right.

NELL — I'm sorry.

DANNY — And then — there's me. When I leave today I'm going to take something away with me I'll never forget. You've made me see at last what a damned fool I've been with all my romantic slush. From now on I'm going to be a sensible, practical — ouch! (*He winces once more*). You're sewing, not tattooing! (*Nell laughs hysterically — Danny listens as if not believing his ears.*) Nell, have I really made you laugh?

NELL — Of course you have. (*Breaks off thread.*) Oh, what is the matter with me? I've sewn the coat right through to the trousers!

DANNY — That's all right. It'll keep me from getting my suits mixed. As long as you haven't sewn them to the other things. (*Pulls pocket.*) No — you haven't — why, you're laughing again! (*Nell's shoulders are shaking — her head buried in her arm on back of chair.*) No, you're not — you're crying. Please don't do that. You make me feel exactly the way I don't want to feel — if I'm to be sensible and practical ——

NELL — Oh, you and your " practical " — make me sick.

DANNY — (*surprised*). Why, don't you want me to be practical?

NELL — You know I don't. You're only talking that way to be contrary!

DANNY — I am not.

NELL — You are so. Whatever I am you're bound you're going to be the opposite.

DANNY — You! Don't tell me you've turned ——

NELL — Romance! Real romance — is worth all the practical ideas in the world.

DANNY — Good Lord, it's hopeless!

NELL — Oh, you're just the most impossible man! Danny — I want to ask you something.

DANNY — All right — ask away.

NELL — You want me to shout it, I suppose. (*He crosses to her.*) I want to whisper!

(*Danny bends down — her arm goes round his neck. Danny looks at her, surprised, and goes to the desk and picks up the telephone.*)

DANNY — Main two-seven — That's right!

NELL — Danny!

DANNY — Yes?

NELL — Tell him it must be on the side that gets the moonlight!

THE END

" TARNISH "

A Drama in Three Acts

By Gilbert Emery

THE season was practically two months old when Gilbert Emery's " Tarnish " was produced at the Belmont Theater, October 1, 1923. But there had been no striking success scored with the dramas presented ahead of it. It was therefore the more gratefully received by the professional and semi-professional section of the playgoing public that hungers for a hit to talk about through the early season.

" Tarnish " is another of those serious dramas of American family life and problems that serve well to distinguish the American theater. It achieves theatrical effectiveness without sacrifice of those fundamental truths of character lacking which the best of drama is but extravagant fiction told in dialogue.

It begins in the living room of the Tevis flat in West One Hundred and Eighty-Ninth Street, New York. It is New Year's Eve. The Tevises include Josephine Lee Tevis, the mother, born a Lee and eager her world should know it; Adolph Tevis, the father, a somewhat spineless gadabout, and Letitia Lee Tevis, the daughter, at once the strength and the hope of the family.

" The room itself is typical of its kind, cheaply made and cheaply decorated," writes Mr. Emery. "The paper on the walls is quiet in tone, but the electric light fixtures — a central chandelier and side brackets — are of a common and vulgar pattern. This commonplace room gives evidence of being inhabited by people of good taste — for such, indeed, are the Tevises. The pieces of furni-

263

ture, shabby and worn, still bear the stamp of refinement and former prosperity."

At the moment Mrs. Tevis is having tea. She is " a lady of some fifty-five years, very worn and thin and faded, yet with evidences still which suggest rather tragically — or perhaps humorously — what she was: ' The beautiful Josephine Lee.' Her expression is fretful, dissatisfied, complaining, rather haughty; her face has deep lines of disappointment, disillusion, illness, combined with a kind of long-suffering triumphant virtue. For long ago she made up her mind, whatever happened, to be the impeccable wife and mother. Mrs. Tevis is at all events a lady, born and bred to the conventions of a good old New York society, and still clinging tenaciously to them. She is simply dressed in black."

Later Mrs. Tevis is joined, to her apparent but politely guarded disgust, by her upstairs neighbor, Mrs. Stutts. " Mrs. Stutts's attitude is that of the lesser to the greater, try as she will to maintain an equality and to remember that she ' is just as good as anybody else.' She is, alas! past forty, inclined to plumpness; considerably ' made up '; showily dressed in the extravagance of the latest mode; and with painfully ' elegant ' manners. A common, vulgar, good-natured creature."

It is Mrs. Stutts's first call, and she has quite obviously accepted the New Year holiday as a fitting excuse to satisfy her neighborly curiosity. She is observing and full of gossip. She has had the " Lee family story " from the society columns, she has met Mr. Tevis in the elevator and the halls and knows him for the sort who would, as her husband says, appreciate a nice bottle of port wine for New Year's, and she has set Letitia down as being rather reserved and retiring.

Being a " bootlegger's bride," as the charge goes, Mrs. Stutts may be classed with the social liberals. She sees what she sees and knows what she knows, and from these observations evolves her own philosophy of life. Just

now she is considerably exercised over the things she has
seen that afternoon.

MRS. STUTTS — . . . Well, I lunched with some lady friends at the Palace
Hotel, and afterwards they would sit around in Peacock Alley ——
MRS. TEVIS — In what?
MRS. STUTTS — Peacock Alley! Did you ever? Of course I think it's just
too common for words, but you do see some of the — Well! I think it's
awful, the way those women carry on. Girls that one day haven't got more
than one pair of — well, you know — to their names and the next you see 'em
in sables. As I tell Ed — there's two ways to get a fur coat, and one of 'em is
to buy it. But Ed says some women are just like fruit cake; the more you keep
'em, the better they are.
MRS. TEVIS — (shuddering). Mrs. Stutts — Really!
MRS. STUTTS — (in full swing). Why, if you'll believe me, there's that
manicure of mine who — well, how that girl manages to ——
MRS. TEVIS — (passing the gingerbread in an attempt to divert her). Did
you have a pleasant Christmas, Mrs. Stutts?
MRS. STUTTS — (taking more gingerbread). Lovely — just lovely! As I
was saying, that manicure of mine — would you believe me if I told you she
calls herself Ant'n'ette LeeNawr? French it is — for dark. Ay-ugh! And
her name is Nettie Dark. Can you beat it ——?
MRS. TEVIS — (still trying to stem the tide). I don't know what the world
is coming to! Let me give you some tea, Mrs. Stutts.
MRS. STUTTS — No, thank you! That cup was lovely. Kinda saving up for
my cocktail when Ed comes. Well, she's a fast one, that Dark girl is ——

Mrs. Healey, " a kindly, shrewd old Irish woman who
rather reluctantly consents to give a few hours of her
time daily to the heavier tasks of the Tevis household," is
in to take the tea things. Also to save some of the gingerbread she has served for her favorite of the family,
" Tishy," the daughter, and to observe that inasmuch as
she is to be home for the New Year's holidays she would
like her pay before she goes.

The request greatly embarrasses Mrs. Tevis. She has
no money. Letitia runs the family budget, and Letitia is
not at home. So Mrs. Healey is forced to depart with a
promise that is not altogether satisfying to her.

A few moments later Letitia appears. " She is a very
pretty girl, quietly and simply dressed, of some twenty-
two or twenty-three years of age. Notwithstanding her
great good looks she has an air of self-reliance, cap-
ability, youthful dignity — for she bears a heavy burden
of responsibility. She is the moving force of the family,
the one on whom the others rely. Since childhood she

has had to face unpleasant facts, deal with unpleasant situations, adjust unpleasant conditions. Her natural buoyancy and keen sense of humor have kept her from any settled bitterness and pessimism; and a fastidious taste has kept her so far from absorbing any of the commonness of the workers' life she is a part of. She presents the figure of a charming, straightforward, clean-minded, cultured girl, yet one who is neither ignorant of, nor afraid of, nor a falsifier of the phases of human nature she comes in contact with."

Tishy, as she is called, is accompanied by a young man. His name is Emmet Carr. "He is a young man with plenty of charm and physical attractiveness; and he is intelligent, ambitious, proud — the pride which often results from a feeling of being inferior socially to those about one and the assurance that one is worth as much as the next person. He has two pretty distinct sides — a common one and a fine, delicate one, the latter evoked by Tishy. His lack of sureness in the Tevis *milieu* gives him a rather taking shyness at times. He is some twenty-seven or twenty-eight years old — quietly dressed in a business suit."

They have evidently been romping a bit on their way home from the office in which they are both employed. And though it is plain to Carr that he is not particularly popular with Mrs. Tevis, his happiness at being with Tishy is of so much greater importance he is barely conscious of that fact.

Now Mrs. Stutts has taken her delayed departure, after adding further to the Tevis family unrest by reporting having seen Mr. Tevis "with a certain little lady" she could name but won't. Mrs. Tevis has retired to her room, after vainly signalling to Tishy to get rid of Carr. And Carr and Tishy are hanging up a couple of New Year wreaths they have brought home with them.

CARR — (*facing Tishy with a droll little smile*). You know, sometimes I almost think your mother doesn't quite like me.

Tishy — (*with affected solemnity*). Sometimes I almost think she doesn't.
Carr — (*sincerely*). I'm sorry — awfully sorry. (*They smile ruefully.*) She thinks I'm not your sort. Well, I guess I'm not.
Tishy — (*seriously*). Emmet, you mustn't mind Mamma. Please don't. She's had a lot to lose — besides money. And she's not well, not at all well. Me, I don't like being poor a bit more than she does — I'm no early Christian. Only I —— You see, I was only ten when the bottom fell out of our high estate, and we fled to Europe and cheap *pensions*, and then fled back again because the war made even that impossible. So now I —— Oh, don't let's talk of it! (*Taking the wreaths from him.*) Where'll we hang the rich, round wreaths?
Carr — By George, you're a plucky girl!
Tishy — I'm not. But what you've got to do, you've got to do. That's my little motto.
Carr — (*smiling*). And if it hurts ——?
Tishy — Then it hurts. What would be your feeling about one on each of these doors? Or would it be too Christmas-cardy? (*She stands with a wreath at arm's length before her, looking particularly charming.*)
Carr — (*his eyes on her adoringly*). Beautiful! I think it's beautiful! Do you know something? I've never hung up a holiday wreath before in my life. Our family — we weren't the holiday kind. These — with you — they're my first. Funny, isn't it?
Tishy — No, it isn't funny. It's rather — heartbreaking.
Carr — And I've never had a present from any one in my family — six of us there are. My mother — she prays a good deal, but she never remembers.
Tishy — Oh!
Carr — So, when you gave me this — (*touching a blue silk handkerchief in his breast pocket*) — the other day — made it yourself — well!
Tishy — (*lightly*). It's a shower and a blower both — that handkerchief. I couldn't let you go on — could I, leaving little bunches of flowers on my desk, day after day, without making a ladylike return for the delicate attention?
Carr — (*with growing fervor*). The first time I left a bunch of posies on your desk — do you remember? It was the day after I brought you those deeds to copy. And we talked — (*a pause — their eyes meet*). I talked and you answered.
Tishy — (*smiling reminiscently*). Yes. We — we talked.
Carr — I was afraid of you, a little. I am yet. I always will be.
Tishy — (*pretending dismay*). Emmet, you must be psycho-analyzed at once!
Carr — The nicest thing about you is that you're so nice, Tishy! When I saw you that first day in the office, I thought, "O Lord! If only I can get to know that girl! If she'll only condescend to look at me, once a week even! And if she'll say 'good morning,' well ——!"
Tishy — (*smiling*). How absurd you are, Emmet.
Carr — You'd be absurd too if a lady-angel suddenly up and said, "Hello" to you. It's a funny thing. You think you're set; that you'll just go on, plugging along in your that's-good-enough way; and then you break your shoe string, or lose a filling out of your tooth, or — a girl says, "good morning," and everything is changed — forever.
Tishy — Maybe it just seems changed.
Carr — No — changed — beautifully.
Tishy — I don't know. I don't think I have much faith — my life has been too quicksandy. Sometimes I feel a hundred years old.
Carr — (*warmly*). I tell you I know! About myself I know. Things are changed for me.
Tishy — I don't believe you can know. You think you're singing grand opera, sublimely, at the top of your lungs; and the next thing you know you're bawling some horrible hand organ tune. It's like that. It's all in the way you're made.
Carr — I don't believe that. I won't believe it. Once a man realizes the thing that's best inside him, he isn't going back to the worst of himself again. Not — not unless his heart breaks.

TISHY — I'm not sure.

CARR — Some day you will be. I'll make you. Yes! Tishy, I can't tell you what you are to me. But I know — inside me I know. I knew the first day! I've always known there was you in the world. I knew — sort of blindly — dumbly. Something was always wrong at home. I felt it as a kid. Wrong with us. Only I didn't know what it was — how to get anything better. There's my kid brother — I'll tell you about him — only not tonight. I came down to Columbia — worked through the University — like a dog. It was like a dog. And I've dogged it through the Law School. And dogged it into Layton & Gray's. And all the time I'd do things that didn't seem so — so bad at the time. But afterwards I'd — be ashamed. Things ——

TISHY — I know. Things. Yes, I know all about that.

CARR — You understand? Things — Oh, God, I don't know! Most men have them, I suppose.

TISHY — It's — it's a kind of — tarnish, isn't it?

CARR — Tarnish? You can clean tarnish, can't you? Perhaps, if I hadn't got to know you, I'd have gone on getting tarnished, and finally, at last, not minding, not knowing — only now — there's you. And that's the other side — the shiny side — that's in me somehow. And so — you see — well, there's you. Don't laugh.

TISHY — (deeply touched). Laugh? I'd sooner cry. Has it been all that? So much? Me, I mean?

CARR — All that?

TISHY — Now I'm a little afraid. But I'm — glad, Emmet.

He tells her then, his enthusiasm mounting, of his chances for investing his $1,000 savings on the advice of the member of the firm most interested in him, and of his better chances of being taken into the firm itself later as a junior partner. She is happy for him, and quotes him a motto for his guidance: " Good luck have thou with thine honor; ride on because of the word of truth; and thy right hand shall teach thee terrible things."

But she cannot rise to his enthusiasm over the firm member who has helped him. She has, as it happens, that day quit her job — for reasons she refuses to tell him. Tonight she would like to think she is " sort of happy." Another moment and they are laughing and singing again, " very youthfully and gayly."

CARR — (radiant). Tishy — let's have a Happy New Year — together.

TISHY — (defensively). The drawback to that is, you must go — this minute. Table not even set. Allez! (Carr takes her in his arms and kisses her.) No, Emmet, no! (For an instant she lets herself go, her lips on his. Then she draws quietly away.) That much — that little much — I take for my New Year. To keep. To remember.

CARR — Tishy Tevis — I'm in love with you — head over heels — I can't see straight — I can't think. You're just like God to me — I want to worship you — I feel small and mean and big and tall all at the same time — I — I — I —— Are you in love with me? Are you?

TISHY — (with a smile). Oh — for a nickel — I could be.

Carr — You are! Oh, praise God, you are!

Tishy — I'm not going to be! No, wait! I could have stopped your saying — what you've just said. I ——

Carr — You couldn't!

Tishy — (*trying to conceal her emotion*). Well, anyhow, I didn't. It just suddenly seemed to me that I — I — I couldn't go on unless someone ——

Carr — Who?

Tishy — Well, you, then — said I was a nice girl. Tomorrow I'm going to be brave and bold again. Only tonight — (*wiping away a little tear*). Oh, Emmet, say I'm a nice girl again!

Carr — You're — you're — you're ——

Tishy — (*quickly — smilingly*). It's all right. You needn't go on. I just wanted to be sure. And tomorrow it's going to stop.

Carr — Tomorrow it *begins!*

Tishy — (*firmly*). *Stops.* The posies — the wreaths — you — everything.

Carr — Why do you say that?

Tishy — Because there isn't any chance in the world for you and me. Because ——

Carr — Go on.

Tishy — My mother and — and my father — I've got them. And they've got me — that's all they have got. No, I can't leave here.

Carr — (*quietly*). I'm not asking that.

Tishy — What *are* you asking?

Carr — I'm asking you to let me love you. I'm asking you to love me. All the rest is simple — after that.

Tishy — Simple? Simple? I tell you it's impossible. Us — us on your shoulders? That's where we'd be. Oh, you don't know what you're talking about!

Carr — I know I want you — and I — Oh, Tishy, you *do* want me! Don't you?

Tishy — (*trying to be resolute*). An engagement between us — it would be absurd! Something to drag out and grow soiled and faded and — and hopeless — as time goes on. It would kill me to see you get bored and tired and mechanical — to see you giving up your chances, your beautiful chances, because you are tied. Oh, there are relations in this world between men and women that don't tarnish — I'm big enough to see that — splendid, true relations — when a man really gives himself —and a woman gives herself— (*As he attempts to speak.*) No, no! Please! It's just hopeless for us, you and me.

Mrs. Tevis — (*from her room*). Tishy — hasn't your father come in yet?

Tishy — No, not yet, dear.

Carr — And isn't it anything to you that I love you? (*She is silent.*) Isn't it?

Tishy — (*feebly*). The wreaths *are* pretty aren't they?

Carr — Answer me! Isn't it — isn't it?

Tishy — (*in a scarcely audible voice*). Ye-e-s —— (*Carr puts his hands on her temples and turning her face up to his looks adoringly, reverently, into her eyes.*)

Carr — You've got me — and I — oh, I've got you! (*Tishy releases herself; then drops with a sigh into his arms. After a pause.*) I feel like the day I went to war. Tishy, all my life I'm going to love you and fight for you.

Again the querulous voice of Mrs. Tevis interrupts them, and with a half promise to meet him later Tishy hurries Emmet away.

Mrs. Tevis doesn't like Carr, and is emphatic in stating her objections. She has heard something from Mrs. Stutts of his rather common family. And the less they have to do with people of that sort the better will she be pleased. Tishy's own father should serve as a warning to her when it comes to that type of man.

The paternal Tevis, it appears, is at the moment under suspicion. The major portion of the family income is $1,000 a year which comes from the estate of a deceased aunt. The half-yearly check for $500 came that morning, and in a thoughtless moment Mrs. Tevis gave it to Mr. Tevis to have it cashed, that the accumulated bills might be paid. Mr. Tevis, departing gayly with the check, has not been heard from since.

Tishy is frankly upset by this news, and greatly disappointed in her mother. Mrs. Tevis should have known better, after experiences they have gone through with her father and knowing, as she does, what he does with whatever money he is able to get hold of. And the bills! They are heavier than ever this time. Mrs. Tevis's last operation hasn't been paid for yet, nor the rent ——

A moment later the discussed Tevis appears. "He is secretly much agitated but makes a very debonair effort to appear at his ease. Tevis is sixty-five years old, or thereabouts — unhealthily fat, white-haired, with signs of long self-indulgences; puffy eyes, flabby skin, etc. He still betrays the evidences of the dandyism of his younger days — the too bright tie, the flower in the buttonhole, the clothes carefully brushed, clothes much worn and of a somewhat antiquated fashion. His manners are florid, his gestures courtly. His indulgences have undermined him physically, leaving him weak, nervous and fatuous. He presents the painfully undignified figure of an old man who has squandered almost everything of value in his character and is still ridiculously at the mercy of his ungovernable, senile, sexual desires."

TEVIS — My Lambkin! (*He enters with an affectation of sprightliness.*) Give your venerable parent a kiss! (*He kisses Tishy. Mrs. Tevis follows.*) Ah, ha! Wreaths! Wreaths! Makes our little love nest as cosy and bright as — as a little love nest. Eh, Mother?
MRS. TEVIS — (*inflexibly*). Adolph! Where have you been?
(*Tishy takes his hat, stick, muffler and coat.*)

TEVIS — (*sitting*). Been? I? Oh, flâné-ing. Here! There! Everywhere! Like a bird! Yes, like a bird! Like a bird!

TISHY — Did you have a nice walk, Daddy?

TEVIS — Delightful — delightful! Alluring shops — festive scenes — bright faces — " eyes looked love to eyes that spake again " — *Espièglerie!* The New Year — always the New Year! Eh, mother?

(*Mrs. Tevis sniffs.*)

TISHY — (*disregarding the pantomime of Mrs. Tevis indicative of her conviction that Tevis's gayety bodes no good.*) Well, you seem to have caught the spirit of the occasion beautifully. Did you go far? Did you meet anyone you knew?

TEVIS — Far? to the utmost ends of the earth! Meet anyone I knew? I met them all, knew them all, loved them all — the world, my brothers, my sisters.

MRS. TEVIS — Don't be a fool, Adolph! Did you go to the bank?

TEVIS — The bank? Stately pile — floors of silver, doors of gold — what joys, what sorrows there! The Bank, ah!

MRS. TEVIS — Oh, *mon Dieu!* May I infer from your ridiculous conversation, that you did go to the bank?

TEVIS — (*blandly*). Josephine — you may.

MRS. TEVIS — And you've got the money?

TEVIS — Got it? (*Slapping his pockets elaborately.*) Oceans — barrels — oodles of it!

MRS. Tevis — Thank God for that! Now give it to Tishy.

TISHY — (*good-naturedly going over to him*). Come along, Daddy. Produce the guilty gold. And I'll put it in the trusty dispatch box.

TEVIS — Miseress!

TISHY — " Hands up! The money or —— "

The fact is, Tevis has not got the money. He puts them off as long as he can, and then makes a bold show of searching his pockets for it. But it is not to be found. He has been robbed! He must have been robbed! There is no other explanation.

That explanation pleases him so well he begins to dramatize it. He remembers how it might have occurred. There was an accident — a taxi — a crushed child — a weeping mother. And while he was weeping over " that bruised little body " some miscreant had taken his money. What, oh, what, is he to do? Let him die! Let him go that he may throw himself into the river.

But Tishy is not to be fooled by this performance. After a little burst of tearful impatience with both her parents, during which she tries to make them realize the position they are in — with her own job gone — she takes her father in hand and, though she regards him " contemptuously, despairingly, struggling with her impulse to rush away forever from such scenes as these," she speaks to him gently, which she knows is the only way to win him.

Step by step she goes over with him his reported experiences of the day, and soon she has him so tangled in his own misstatements that she knows he is lying. Then she reminds him that he was seen that afternoon by Mrs. Stutts when he was walking with another woman, and she wants to know about that other woman.

TISHY — (*quietly*). Father — you're lying! You've been lying all the time.

TEVIS — (*in the last attempt*). Tishy, if it were my dying word, I'd swear ——

TISHY — Stop! Don't go on! It — it isn't any use. This isn't the first time. (*Wearily, without much hope.*) What have you done with it? Answer me! What have you done with it?

TEVIS — I — Tishy, have pity on me. You don't know. You don't understand. You're — you're a young girl — you —

TISHY — (*trying to master her repulsion*). Father — you've given it to somebody. Is that it? Is it?

TEVIS — I — I — had to —— (*Tishy gives a little cry.*) I — Oh, I can't talk to you about it! A man would understand, but you ——

TISHY — You've given the money to — some woman — haven't you?

TEVIS — Oh, Tevis — Tevis — why does God let you live?

TISHY — *Who was it?*

TEVIS — Oh! What does it matter who it was now?

TISHY — It matters just this: you or I have got to try to get the money back — from her — the woman you were with today.

TEVIS — (*sincerely*). You — my daughter ——! Go to her? No! Not if we starve, all of us — in the gutter!

TISHY — Then will you go?

TEVIS — (*whimpering*). I don't know how she got it from me — Tishy, as God sees his poor little children, I didn't mean to give it all to her — only a few dollars to help a poor young girl. But, but ——

TISHY — (*in the last appeal*). Father, will you go to her?

TEVIS — Me? I — I — No! (*His voice drops to a whisper.*) I'm afraid of her — afraid ——

TISHY — You must!

TEVIS — I can't — I can't ——

TISHY — Then I've got to go! Who is she? Where is she?

TEVIS — (*moaning*). Tishy! Don't tell your mother — don't tell her ——

TISHY — Who is she?

TEVIS — I won't tell! I won't tell!

TISHY — (*in desperation*). I've got to get it — I've got to get it! Can't you understand? Oh, why don't you help me — help me? Tell me — tell me! Daddy! Why don't you help me?

TEVIS — Too late — too late ——

(*One hears Mrs. Stutts again at "The Love Nest."*)

TISHY — I've got to find out. I've got to find out — somehow —— (*Looking up.*) Oh! That! (*In anguish at the thought of further humiliation at Mrs. Stutt's hands.*)

TEVIS — (*agonizedly; comprehending*). My Baby! My Lamb! No! No!

MRS. TEVIS — (*running from her room*). What is it? Oh, God, what is it now? Tishy! Where are you going?

TISHY — (*at the door, with a hard little laugh*) I? I'm going to call on the "bootlegger's bride."

The curtain falls

ACT II

A few hours later that evening Nettie Dark bustles
into her dowdy apartment somewhere "in the Forties,
near Sixth Avenue." As an apartment it consists of "a
small sitting room opening out of what is a bed room,
or, one might say, an alcove, since the larger part of the
back wall has been cut to form an arch, thus making the
rear room almost entirely visible. This arch is curtained
with cretonne of a very vivid new art pattern. The walls
of the sitting room and bed room are covered with a
rather muddy-colored, brown-yellow-green paper, usually
referred to as 'tapestry.' The furniture is meretricious,
vulgar, cheap and of different varieties — in short, anything that has happened to take Miss Dark's lively fancy.
Near the fireplace is a *chaise longue* on which is a red
velvet cover. A plate of frosted cup cakes, two other
plates, cigarettes in a holder, matches and ash tray, two
large highball glasses, etc. The view one has of the
bed room gives a sight of the bed set in the middle of the
room, its head against the rear wall."

As Nettie enters " one perceives that, while not pretty,
nor beautiful, she has the 'certain something' which
attracts — that is to say, attracts men. She is small,
lithe, dark-haired, rather sallow of skin, but her eyes are
brilliant and bold and expressive; and her face, a little
dull and sullen in repose, lights up when she is in a good
humor, with a curious youthful charm, heightened by a
warm, sensuous smile. She looks what she is to men:
companionable and dangerous. As she comes into the
room, she is wearing a gray fur coat and a small bright
turban. As soon as the packages are disposed of, she
pulls off her hat and throws it into a chair. As she
removes her coat she regards the much worn lining and
whistles a single rueful note at its sorry state. Her dress
is of plain black with a little white collar, and she has
discarded all ornaments except one or two of the
simplest, and a wrist watch. She goes to the tahle near

the fireplace, finds and lights a cigarette, then regards herself critically in the mirror, nodding disapproval at the effect.

Being New Year's Eve, Nettie would like to have a party. And it has occurred to her that if she can get hold of a certain old friend of hers she could organize one without much trouble. But she suspects if she were to call him herself he would not come. So she rings up her friend, Aggie, who lives in the apartment above her, and asks her to do the calling for her.

NETTIE — Say, Ag — you want to do something for me?
AGGIE — What — *me?*
NETTIE — Ay-ugh.
AGGIE — What do you want me to do?
NETTIE — (*abruptly*). Ag — telephone to Emmet Carr for me, will you?
AGGIE — What — *me?*
NETTIE — Ay-ugh! Listen! I want to see him. I gotta. I want to see him tonight.
AGGIE — But ——
NETTIE — I know. But he won't come for me. He won't. I phoned to him twice before I came in tonight, and he threw me down — cold. You phone him for me.
AGGIE — But if he — Lord, what'll I say?
NETTIE — Tell him — Oh, tell him I'm in trouble — awful — that I need help or something — and that I don't know you're telephoning, see? And that you knew he was my best friend — you know the kind of song-and-dance. Will you? I've helped you out before now. Will you?

Aggie's technique is a little crude and she stammers considerably over the phone, but she manages finally to convince Emmet that his old friend's condition is precarious and that the least he can do is to drop around and see her, if only for a minute.

"He'll come," she reports to Nettie; "he'll come — for a minute. He's going somewhere afterwards. God, I hate to lie like that."

Nor does Nettie's happy gratitude cheer her perceptibly. Fact is, Aggie is the one who is in serious trouble. Her man is sick upstairs — with pneumonia, she thinks — and the landlady has given them until Monday to raise the rent. She's just gotta make a touch somewhere. There ain't nothing else for her to do. She's gotta stick to her man.

"It's hell when you fall for 'em, isn't it?" Nettie sympathizes. "Especially when they don't fall back."

The problem of the loan is easily met, and when Aggie returns to her sick friend she carries with her one of Nettie's hundred dollar bills. The sight of so much money has nearly floored her, and she fears the worst. But Nettie reassures her.

"Oh, no, dearie! Don't think it! I didn't have to pay the 'awful price.' He's just a poor old boob that falls for the 'young-girl-in-trouble' stuff if you cry a little and let him hold your hand under the table. He's mush now, but I guess he was some little Bluebeard in his day. Ain't it awful, though, to see these old birds lick their chops? Well, I borrowed some from him 'on account.'"

Nettie is happy fixing the room for Carr's reception, adding a final touch when she extracts a half bottle of gin from back of the fire screen to go with the glasses on the table. She also lights the incense that the atmosphere may be properly seductive.

But when Emmet comes, mystified by the cheerfulness of her greeting and her feigned surprise at seeing him, he does not even notice the preparations in his honor and he hates the incense. Also, he would like to know exactly what help it is Nettie needs, as his time is somewhat pressing.

But Nettie is not for having this happy reunion so quickly spoiled. Her invitation to him to make himself comfortable is not only earnest but insistent, and before he knows it she has taken his coat and hat and tossed them on her bed and has him seated in the best of the rockers, smoking his favorite brand of cigarettes and still wondering why she has sent for him.

She is much more interested in learning what has happened to him the last several months, and what progress he is making at the office. She has heard from his boss — rather a "rapid baby" with the girls, this boss — that he (Carr) is doing beautifully. This is not unpleasing news to Emmet, but he is still insistent on finding out what it is she wants of him, and she continues dissembling.

NETTIE — . . . Well, old Sunshine, don't bite my head off! Gosh, it's nice to see you sitting there in Nettie's little old rocker! I — I've missed you, Metty.
CARR — (hastily). Ay-ugh? Aggie said over the phone you were up against it, Nettie. What's the difficulty?
NETTIE — I'll tell you — in a minute. Oh, I've had an awful time! Honest, I never thought I'd ——
CARR — (not unkindly). Better spit it right out. I've got to be on my way, you know.
NETTIE — (wistfully). Where you going? To celebrate?
CARR — (casually). No. I've got an engagement.
NETTIE — With the iceman, I suppose.
CARR — (smiling). Ay-ugh.
NETTIE — (Ingratiatingly). 'Member last New Year's, Metty? (Carr nods embarrassedly. Nettie puts her hand on his knee.)
CARR — (moving away). Say, Nettie — shoot out anything you want to tell me, and if I can be of any help, why ——
NETTIE — Wasn't it fun? Out with the bunch raising Cain — and then coming home, by ourselves, just you and me, and — oh, we did have good times together, didn't we? Playing around? (Jumping to her feet.) Oh, my good Lord! What will you think of me? What? And me "the grand little homemaker," as you used to say. I've never offered you a drink! Watch Little Sister while she —— (She runs to the table and begins to prepare the drink.)
CARR — (emphatically). I don't want a drink, Nettie. I ——
NETTIE — Oh, my Lord! I never heard such a dog! Don't want a ——
CARR — I don't! Don't fix it, not for me.
NETTIE — Why, Emmet Carr! Do you stand there and say you won't have a drink with me, Nettie, on New Year's Eve? Pig!
CARR — (yielding). Honestly, I — oh, well, if ——
NETTIE — Oh, well, I guess so! Just as if I didn't know how a certain rising young lawyer didn't like his "Tom Collins." (As she works.) 'Member last year at this time when you looked at me with those old brown eyes of yours and said, "Net, by God, I'm going to make 'em sit up in that office!" Do you? (As she pours the gin, making a stiff drink, Carr interjects, "Easy there!")
CARR — (smiling). Did I? Damn cheek, eh?
NETTIE — No! Gosh! I'm so proud of you — (Going to the bathroom.) I got a cold siphon in the bathroom. (Carr rises and consults his watch, moving uneasily to the fireplace.) Is she pretty?
CARR — Who?
NETTIE — The iceman!
CARR — (laughing in spite of himself). That iceman sort of worries you, doesn't he?
NETTIE — (making a face at him and adding the siphon-water to the glasses). Here you are, old dear! (As she gives the glasses.) You! Me! Us! To old times, Metty, God bless 'em! And a Happy New Year — to us both! (She clinks her glass on his.)
CARR — A Happy New Year! (His mind on Tishy.) A new year — a new year! (They drink.)

The drink revives a little of their old intimacy, but not much. Emmet is still on his guard. He sympathizes with Nettie and her loneliness, and is sorry to hear that she has been so discouragingly up against it the last few months. If a loan will help —— But it is not money that Nettie wants, seeing that she has just been lucky. " It's never been a question of money between us," she reminds him, " and it's never going to be — *no, sir!"* Nettie's lonesome, that's all. She wants company.

Aggie calls again. She is distressed because her friend upstairs is seriously ill with the flu, or something, and she wants help. Nettie is reluctant to go back with her for fear she will lose Emmet while she is gone. Anyway, there's no hurry.

NETTIE — (*her arm on his shoulder*). —Metty? Do you know I was soppy in love with you once? A year ago tonight? Right here in this little old room? Do you know that?

CARR — (*in an attempt to laugh it off*). See here, Nettie, no bunk. What's the use of ——

NETTIE — I was.

CARR — (*as kindly as possible*). What happened between us, happened. That's all. I guess there wasn't much falling in love done — not on my part or on yours. You and I — well, I was a man and you were a girl — and — well, you know. There wasn't any special reason why we — I guess we were both a little lonely and — you were a good pal, Nettie. I don't want you to think I don't appreciate — but — oh, hang it! Things change. They've got to. It's nobody's fault — it's — well — they change.

NETTIE — They change all right. Only — oh, I'm a poor mutt, I am! But honest and true, Metty, there never was a fellow I ever met — and that's going some — that — that ——

CARR — (*more brusquely*). Oh, get down to brass tacks, Nettie! What is it you want to talk to me about tonight? Anything?

NETTIE — (*abruptly*). Met? Who's your new girl?

CARR — (*irritatedly*). Look here! Do you think I came here to be asked fool questions like that?

NETTIE — O don't be so darned up-stage! You used to be able to take a joke, but now — Oh, gosh, look at the coffee-pot doing the Gilda Gray! Gimme your handkerchief! — To lift it off with! Quick! It'll be hard-boiled! Gimme it! (*She snatches the blue silk handkerchief Tishy has given him, from his pocket.*)

CARR — (*jumping to recover it*). No — here — hold on — let go of that! If you burn ——

NETTIE — (*seeing that he is really angry, throws the handkerchief back*). Aw, take your old wipe! (*Carr replaces it solicitously.*) I never did like blue anyway. I can do it with my little old skirt. (*She lifts away the coffee-pot.*) Pull out the plug, will you? Gosh, I see I gotta learn to make handkerchiefs if I want to get a beau.

CARR — (*significantly*). There's more you've got to learn to forget, Nettie. You'd better begin right now.

NETTIE — Oh! — (*Starting to retort but thinking better of it.*) You don't

say! — Gee, doesn't it smell grand? Still the same old coffee-hound you use
to be, are you?
    CARR — Uhn — hmn.
    NETTIE — (at his arm). Say, Met, wasn't the coffee good last New Year's
Eve? O Boy! And wasn't it good the next morning? I'll tell the world!
Come on, let's have a cup now, Met. (She thrusts her arm in his affectionately.
She sees their two reflections in the glass.) O Gee, don't we look cute in there
together? Old Darling!

Emmet gently, but positively, disengages himself from
her tightening embrace, and is again ready to leave her.
But she begs so hard that he stay and have at least a cup
of coffee — for the sake of old times and that other New
Year's — that he again weakens. He makes another
effort to get away when she discovers there is no cream.
He will go to the store and — " And send it back by the
boy " she finishes for him. He will not!

Aggie is in again, terrified at the goings on of her
delirious friend and begging that some one come. Finally
it is decided that Emmet will go upstairs and see if he
can quiet the sick man while Nettie goes for the cream.
But once Emmet is gone she changes her mind. Instead
of wasting time buying cream she will use it to reset the
stage.

Out goes the ceiling light, and on goes the phonograph.
The next minute she has dashed into the bed room,
thrown off her street clothes and put on an elaborate
negligée, " calculated to display her charms to the
utmost." She is barely dressed when the bell rings, and,
hoping to startle Emmet with her adjusted loveliness, she
throws open the door.

Letitia Tevis stands waiting on the other side.

" Well," demands Nettie, as soon as she can recover
from her surprise and disappointment; " what is it?
Income tax or birth control?"

Tishy is deadly serious and a little frightened. She has
come in search of a Miss Le Noire, and she has not come
as a client or as an agent. She has come because she
knows her father was with Miss Le Noire at the Palace
Hotel that afternoon.

NETTIE — (*insolently*). Well, what if I was at the Palace today? What of it? Maybe I do know your father. I know Grant's Tomb and the Woolworth Building and Jack Dempsey — but what of it? What of it?

TISHY — (*coldly*). It is just that — that's the reason for my coming here.

NETTIE — (*rising and looking at her watch*). Well, you'll have to excuse me, I'm afraid ——

TISHY — I am afraid you will have to listen. (*Nettie sits.*) Miss Le Noire, I have to earn my living — I am, or was till recently, in Layton & Gray's law office ——

NETTIE — (*with a swift look*). O-o-oh! Were you?

TISHY — My people lost their money — some time ago — when I was a child. I have a father and a mother who are dependent on me, who are old, in ill health, unable to keep themselves; our circumstances are straitened, very; we have only what I can earn — and just now I am out of employment — only what I earn and a very small amount of money yearly, left us by an aunt — I'm sorry to bore you with all this, but I have to tell it in order to make things quite clear to you why ——

NETTIE — Layton & Gray's, you say? Do you know a fellow down there named Carr?

TISHY — Yes. In order to make it quite clear to you ——

NETTIE — He's a great friend of mine — a great friend.

TISHY — Please! I have to count every penny — every penny — I want you to believe this. Today we received a part of our little money, the half of it — five hundred dollars. My father cashed the check at the bank — and he ——

NETTIE — (*rising*). Excuse me, Miss Tevis, but I gotta tell you my friend will be here any minute — and if you're getting round to borrow money of me, as you seem to be, I might as well tell you now that I am not in a position to ——

TISHY — (*flushing*). Oh! How can you speak like that?

NETTIE — I'm sorry you're up against it, as you say you are — but I don't see why you should come down here to my flat and spill it all over me. It's not my notion of a pleasant New Year's Eve.

TISHY — No, nor mine.

NETTIE — Well?

TISHY — Miss Le Noire — the money my father cashed today he gave to you. I know that.

NETTIE — What do you mean — gave it to me?

TISHY — He gave it you. I don't know why — I don't want to know why. He is an old man, a very broken, unfortunate, old man — and — and not — not quite responsible very often — for what he does — not quite — O you must have *seen* that! Miss Le Noire, I am going to ask you — for my mother's sake, for my father's sake — not for mine — to keep them from actual want, I ask you to — to give me back the money my — my father gave you this afternoon.

NETTIE — I don't care if you're asking it for the Lord on High! You can't come here and insult me right in my own house. I want you to get out of here. I want you to get out of this room!

TISHY — I'm not going to leave here, until I have that money ——

NETTIE — We'll see abou ——

TISHY — I'm not insulting you — I'm not accusing you of — of anything. All I am doing is to try to show you, to make you feel how — how — Miss Le Noire, you *must* give that money back. You *must!*

NETTIE — (*lashing herself to a rage*). I don't know how you dare say such things! I don't know how you dare! You! Who are you, anyway? What do I know about you, or your sob-story? Just because you pretend to be a lady — I suppose that's what you do! — with a ga-ga old father, " not quite responsible " — he's *rotten!* (*Tishy interrupts with: " Stop, Miss Le Noire!"*) I'll say he's rotten! — and because a nasty, bleach-haired, gossiping old bootlegger's *kept woman* comes to you and tells you she happened to see me say " Hello " to your lovely father, you come crashing down here to me — *me* — a girl who works a darned sight harder than you do to get along — to me, who's just as good as you are, yes, just as good — and accuse me of stealing — sure, that's what it amounts to! *Me!* Because you think I'm not in your class.

That's why you try it on! Well, Miss Tevis, let me tell you one thing, and let
me tell you straight, I can sue you — sue you for defamation of character. You
better be sure next time you and your father get into trouble that you know
who it is you're trying to hang your dirty work on to! — *You get out of here!*
    TISHY — (*angrily*). Oh! How dare you speak to me like that? How dare
you? I won't leave this room I tell you — not till you give me that money!

The outer door swings open and Emmet bursts cheerfully through, calling to Nettie. "Hello, darling," she
calls back, without taking her eyes off Tishy, who stands
as if she were turned to stone.

"There's nothing the matter with that fellow," reports
Emmet from the hall. "He only wanted a drink. Did
you get your old cream?"

He comes gayly into the room but stops stock still,
the words faltering on his lips, as he sees Tishy. She
is motionless, expressionless. Nettie looks from one to
the other, uncertain of what will happen. The pause is
long and tense. At last, as he suddenly realizes the
position in which he appears.

"Oh, my God!" he mutters. The keys he holds
fall unheeded from his hand. "Tishy — what — what
are you doing here?"

She is like ice. "I — I need hardly ask that of you,"
she answers.

"Is there any reason why he shouldn't be here, I'd
like to know?" demands Nettie. "He's a very old
and very dear friend of mine, Emmet is. Aren't you,
Emmet? He's having a little supper here with me —
that's what he's doing here."

Excitedly Emmet denies the statement. Let Tishy believe nothing she hears, and let him explain what she
has seen.

But Tishy is of no mind to listen to anything as common as an explanation. What she has seen and heard
is enough.

    TISHY — (*in cold scorn*). What does it matter to me where you go? You
have a perfect right, haven't you, to — choose your — your diversions? I don't
know why you feel that what you call explanations are necessary. I don't ask
— I don't want them.
    CARR — But you — my being here ——
    TISHY — Isn't it enough that you *are* here ——

Nettie — Ay-ugh — tell her! Tell her you're a good boy. She'll believe you — I don't think!

Carr — (*to Nettie*). For God's sake, keep quiet! (*Going to Tishy and putting his hand on her arm. With all his heart.*) Come away, Tishy — come away with me ——

Tishy — Don't touch me! Don't dare to touch me!

Carr — (*very humbly*). I won't — I won't, Tishy — but, oh, if you've got any pity, — any — Why it's only common justice to hear me — you wouldn't treat me like that — you mustn't — Tishy — it isn't like you — it isn't *like* you! Tishy, won't you come away from here? (*He takes a step toward the door, his eyes on her pleadingly.*)

Nettie — (*running up to the door and intercepting him*). She ain't going — not yet she ain't going — not till I tell her, she ain't! (*To Tishy.*) Listen — listen to me! — I'm going to tell you! He and I used to be lovers ——

Carr — Tishy — for God's sake — come away!

Nettie — Lovers — and he came here tonight again — and he got caught — by his girl — and now he's trying to short-skate out of it — that's the kind of fellow he is! Judas! *Judas!* That's what he is!

Carr — Tishy — you won't believe that — you can't believe that — you ——

Nettie — (*sobbing*). Judas — Judas Carr!

Carr — Tishy, listen to me — listen to me! She's lying — she's lying, I tell you she's lying! — O won't you come away from here?

Tishy — Oh, stop — stop!

Carr — It's horrible — horrible — everything I say — everything I do — *here!* It's all against me — but if you'll only come away with me — somewhere — anywhere ——

Nettie — Four-flusher!

Carr — (*barring Tishy's way — wildly, at the door*). No — you're not going — not yet. (*To Nettie.*) You've done this! You've done this! By God, you're going to pay for it, too! You planned all this. That's why you got me here, you and your Aggie! That's why you — (*To Tishy.*) That's it, isn't it? Why *you're* here? What *you're* doing here? (*To Nettie.*) How'd you get her here? She wouldn't come here herself — she wouldn't come here to *you!* You planned it somehow — God knows how! You lied to *her*, too — you ——

Nettie — I didn't — I didn't — I didn't — I ——

Carr — You did! Do you think *she* 'd be here otherwise? *She* — in *your* filthy, slimy ——

Tishy — Oh, stop! Oh, stop! Oh, please stop!

Nettie — (*terrified*). Metty — my God — listen! I *never* got her here — I *never* got her here — I *never* got her here — I've never seen her before ——

Carr — That's a lie!

Nettie — I didn't — I didn't — (*To Tishy.*) You! You're his girl! You — *you!* Tell him! Tell him!

Tishy — She — she's right.

Nettie — There!

Tishy — I — I came here of my own free will.

Carr — Came — here? What *for*, then — what *for*? (*Tishy looks straight at Nettie in silence.*) What *for*?

Tishy — It — it doesn't matter now what for.

Carr — (*taking her arm*). Tell me what you're here for?

Tishy — Let me go! How dare you question me — *you?* How dare you? Ask her! Ask your friend! Ask that woman why I'm here. She'll tell you. Then you'll know. That's the only part of the whole beautiful story you've missed. Ask her! (*She pushes past him hysterically and goes out.*)

"The outer door slams. Carr turns to Nettie, who stands with her hands on her hips, looking at him insolently, trying to hide her apprehension." Nettie — "Well, she's gone — your girl's gone. Ain't she?"

" With an affectation of indifference she goes to the victrola and starts, ' Yes! We Have No Bananas '."

NETTIE — Well — she's gone. What are you going to do now?
CARR — (*in a low voice — approaching her slowly, his fists clenched*). I — I — don't — know — but — but I think — I'm going to kill you — (*Nettie backs away in terror as he advances.*) I think — I'm going to kill you ——
NETTIE — (*in a little fearful voice*). No, Metty — No, Metty — I — I didn't mean to — I ——

" Carr makes a sudden movement forward and seizes her. With her head in both hands he pushes her slowly against the wall."

CARR — (*about to choke her*). You beast — you little beast— you dirty little beast — (*For a long moment he holds her there. Nettie is hypnotized by her fear. Suddenly he lets her go — pushes her away — and begins to laugh.*) O my God! O my God! O my God! — " Good luck — have thou — with thine honor!" — O Christ! Stop that music!

" All at once he breaks down and drops by the table; buries his head among the remains of the supper and sobs his heart out. Nettie stares at him in distress, amazement, pity." Nettie — (*weakly*). " This is a hell of a New Year's party, this is."

The curtain falls.

ACT III

It is nearing midnight. The scene is again the Tevis living room, in darkness. Through the windows intermittent sounds of the street celebrations are heard.

Tishy is just back from her visit to Nettie Dark's apartment. She " is in a state of moral, mental and physical collapse. The hopelessness of extricating the family from the desperate situation they find themselves in, coupled with her discovery of Carr at Nettie's gives a grim face to the New Year just breaking."

Mrs. Tevis has awakened, her senses still a little numbed by the sleeping powder Tishy has given her. There is a moaning in the kitchen. It is Mr. Tevis threatening to cut his unworthy throat with a dull bread knife. These new problems divert Tishy's mind from her own troubles for the moment.

Finally she gets her mother back to bed, with another sleeping powder, and listens patiently to the whining defense of her unhappy father, and his slushy but measurably sincere regrets that she, his baby, was forced to do what she did for him, and to learn what she has learned of his life.

Tevis — (*groaning*). Oh, oh! (*Clinging to her dress.*) Tishy — My Baby — I didn't mean to do it — I didn't mean to ——

Tishy — (*in a revulsion of disgust*). Father — Don't — don't ——

Tevis — Don't tell *her* — don't tell your mother — You haven't told her, have you? You won't tell her, will you?

Tishy — No — No — I won't tell her.

Tevis — You've been good to me — always — but she — I've always been afraid of her — I wasn't her sort — Oh, I loved her once — she was so beautiful and beyond me — like a star — and afterwards, beyond, always beyond! God, how they treated me, her lot! What's a man to do, married to the Social Register? When I — I made up my little mistakes, my little peccadillos, what *was* she? She was a glacier — she was the *Mer de Glace*, that woman! Oh, why didn't she let me *go* — let me go?

Tishy — (*goaded to retort*). Why didn't you go? Why didn't you go? You stayed, didn't you? Even after you stopped loving her, you stayed. You were a coward, weren't you? You've always been a coward. Tonight with your talk of suicide — Oh! — Yes, I went to her — I went there — and while I was there — I — I found out that the man who had told me only today he loved me — that he and the woman you were with this afternoon, had been — Oh! — Ever since I was a child I've had the shame of something dreadful around me. Scandals with — women, talked of and whispered about, before me, by the servants. Then, the money gone, the house gone, friends gone — gone. And those ghastly, ghastly years — wandering penniless about Europe — with terrible *déclassés*, men and women — Oh, you know what our life was there — yours was! Perhaps I don't understand. Perhaps there's something wrong with *me*. Everything I touch seems pitch. Oh, isn't there *anything* clean, *anywhere?* Girls, girls like me, who try to live decently, to — to —— Aren't there men who try to live that way, too? Perhaps it's the way you're born — perhaps you can't help it, being decent or being rotten. I don't know. All I know is that I'm sick — sick — sick — of this horrible life I'm living! (*Tevis bursts into tears again.*) Oh, don't cry — It's too late for that.

Tevis — Tishy — don't hate me — don't hate me — don't hate me ——

Tishy — (*miserably*). Hate you? Oh, Daddy, would that help any? I've borne things and borne things and borne things, but (*falteringly*) but I can't bear much more — I don't — know — what — I'm going — to do!

Tishy goes to her own room and Tevis, still a little maudlin but genuinely affected by Tishy's reproaches, prays that the Lord look down and pity him; that he may be washed and made whiter than snow. The tolling of the bells announcing the New Year gave him quick hope that his prayer may be answered.

There is a ring at the doorbell. Then another. Hesitantly Tevis goes to the door to be confronted by Emmet Carr holding Nettie Dark firmly by the arm. Now he half drags her into the room. Nettie is thoroughly angry, but she realizes that Carr is in no mood to be trifled with and has defiantly submitted to his demand that she shall come with him and explain to Tishy the real reason for his having been in her rooms that afternoon.

Tevis is anxious to get them out before either his wife or Tishy hears them, but Emmet will not budge. He must see Tishy. Mrs. Stutts, arriving with a bottle of port wine, tied with a large bow of red ribbon, as her intended contribution to Mr. Tevis's New Year's, complicates matters and adds to the confusion. Nettie recognizes Mrs. Stutts as an enemy with a loose tongue who has talked too much. Which brings a countering charge from " the bootlegger's female mate," and the exchange of compliments reveals to Emmet the details of how Tishy knew about Nettie and her father, and how she happened to be in Nettie's rooms. It also forces an admission from Nettie that she had taken her aging admirer's money.

> NETTIE — (*blazing*). O God, I'm sick of this! What right have you got, all of you, sticking your noses in my business? I'll tell you — yes, I'll tell you! This old baboon — he's been hanging 'round me every chance he got — the dirty old thing! And I was hard up — I been hard up — just because I was trying to keep straight ——
> MRS. STUTTS — Ha!
> NETTIE — O I *was!* Do you think I'd let that Old Cream-Puff touch me? And he came 'round today — with his pockets full of it — and I hadn't a cent and it was New Year's (*choking back a sob*) and — Why shouldn't I take it? Why shouldn't any girl take what she can get from rotten old things like him? 'Tisn't *us.* It's him and *his* kind that makes all the trouble!

Tishy finds them thus when she comes, trembling with anger, to demand a last explanation of Carr. He has come, he tells her, and brought the unwilling Nettie, that

she (Tishy) may hear the truth of all that has happened,
insofar as he has been concerned with it. Nor will he
listen to her orders that he leave.

TISHY — (*her eyes flashing*). Will you leave this room?

CARR — (*earnestly*). Whatever you may feel about it afterwards, Tishy, there's
one thing you've got to hear — not maybe for you, but for *me*. I know how
you feel about that business down there tonight — and I know how *I* feel about
it. I've brought her here — I made her come ——

NETTIE — You near killed me, you big brute!

CARR — And she's going to tell you she lied to you — about why I was there
— that I wasn't having supper with her, that I haven't seen her in months, that
it was all a put-up job. That's why I brought her. (*To Nettie.*) You lied about
me, didn't you? Tell her!

TISHY — What does it matter — whether she lied or not — what difference
does it make?

CARR — It matters the whole world to me. Doesn't it matter anything to you?

NETTIE — (*feeling somehow that she is mistress of the situation*). You poor
fool! You poor fool! She knows I lied. She knew it all the while. Do
you think that's what's the matter with her? Not it! She's sore — sore because
you ain't a virgin, or whatever you call it. She's sore because you traveled
around with me — *me!* Oh, if it had been one of her kind — that you'd had an
" affair " with, it would have been different. But I'm spotty — and you're
spotty — because you liked me once. That's the kind she is. And you want
to know what else she is? Well, she's jealous. Ay-ugh! That's what it is —
just plain jealous! Sure, I lied! Why shouldn't I? I was in love with you. I
wanted you. And who wins? Me? No! You? No! 'Cause she won't take you
back. Her? No — 'cause she don't know enough to keep you. And so everybody has a happy New Year's. I didn't come up here to cry and tell her I
lied — not if you did about twist my arm off. I come up to see what she'd do
when she saw us and heard your spiel — Well, I've seen. (*Turning to Tishy.*)
And let me tell *you* a thing: you don't know much. No, you don't! Not as
much as I do. And I got to tell you this, too: if I was in your shoes tonight,
and he wanted me, I wouldn't care what he'd done or what he was, I'd — (*With
a laugh to hide her emotion.*) I'd count my lucky stars, all of 'em! And
that's all you'll ever get out of me! Good night!

Now Nettie has gone, the slamming door a last evidence of her anger and disgust. Carr and Tishy have
stood in silence during the girl's outburst. Now he
turns toward her. His thoughts are all for her. " His
heart is full of pity and love and distress for what has
happened. What he wants now is forgiveness, to begin
again, to take her in his arms, unworthy as they are."

Tishy drops into a chair and he moves over beside
her. " Tishy, I love you," he says, pleadingly. She
does not answer. " Nobody'll ever love you like me,
Tishy." Still she does not answer. He hurries on.
" Won't you take me back, Tishy? You can't go back
on me, Tishy — you can't! It's been, why, it's been

heaven. You wouldn't shut me out now. Today after
I left you, I didn't know what I was doing or saying —
I just knew I'd gone to Heaven. I talked to myself in
the streets and gave away all my money and it was
summer and everything was singing: ' Tishy — Tishy!
Tishy!' But now, if I lose you — if I lose you ——
(No answer.) Tishy — every man — when he meets his
girl — he wants to come to her — white — only he
can't — it breaks his heart, maybe, but he can't ——
(No answer.) A man doesn't live very straight, I guess,
unless he's got some one to live straight for — Tishy —
ever since that first day — when you said, ' good morning ' — I've been trying to scrub and polish and wipe
out — and then tonight — happened. Tishy — won't
you take me back? (No answer.) You've got to let
me help you, Tishy. You've got to. This money I
was going to give to Leighton — you've got to take it,
dear. Tishy — you must — you must!"

There is a gesture of refusal from Tishy, but she does
not answer. " Tishy," he pleads, " do you love me?"

Her answer, after a long pause, is almost inaudible.
But it is " Yes."

" Do you doubt my love? Do you? Tishy, if you
doubt love you'll doubt everything."

" I doubt everything now."

" Do you know what a man is, Tishy? He's just what
his love is. Just that."

" Just what his love is?" The words are forced out
of her. " Just what his love is? Yes, just that. And
what do I know, how can I know, what yours will be
ten — five — two years, even, from now? What did
my mother know of my father's? What does any woman
know? All she can do is to throw herself blindly, pitifully, into love — and take her chance, her little terrible
chance — of keeping love somehow."

She is afraid. Afraid to trust her love to him. The
men she has known — her father, the man she worked

for, and then Emmet — have offered little as examples.
The tones of her voice convey to Emmet the sense of
his defeat. He is leaving. Not without a final plea,
and not until he has insisted that she shall take the
money he has saved to help her over the loss of the
other. With a last despairing promise — " I — I'd make
you so happy, dear — I'd try so hard to make you happy
——" He is at the door.

The New Year breaks " with all its gay, wild noises
outside." Emmet pauses. " It's the New Year," he
ventures, a little lamely. Still she does not answer.
" Well — I'll — I'll — I don't blame you, dear — I —
I —— Good bye."

Tishy lets him go, stifling her sobs as she turns
toward the door. The wreaths they had hung earlier in
the day catch her eye. She tears them down and hurls
them through the window, crashing the window closed
again to shut out the New Year celebration.

She is on the floor, her head buried in a chair, sobbing
bitterly when old Mrs. Healey lets herself in. Mrs.
Healey had seen the lights as she was passing and she
had come to wish Miss Tishy a happy New Year and to
ask her if she had found her gingerbread that morning.
Gingerbread! At such a time! The incongruity throws
Tishy into something like hysteria. She is laughing and
crying, and reaching out for Mrs. Healey's sympathy.

MRS. HEALEY — (*going to her and taking her in motherly arms*). Miss
Tishy, love — don't darlin' — don't ——
TISHY — (*the tears come at last and she sobs her misery out on Lizzie
Healey's breast*). Lizzie — Lizzie Healey — I'm all alone — all alone ——
MRS. HEALEY — (*half carrying her to a chair, where she sits and holds her*).
There — Miss Tishy, love, there — there, now ——
TISHY — (*as the clamor outside continues*). O Lizzie — why don't they stop
— why don't they stop? What are they glad for? What is anyone glad for?
MRS. HEALEY — (*patiently*). 'Y God, Miss Tishy, love, they're glad because
they're beginning again — and that there's something to begin. And they're glad
because they can forget all the divilishness they've got into, and start all
over. They don't know what's going to happen, and God help 'em, they don't
want to. They're — *hoping* — that's all. (*Tishy's sobbing becomes less violent
now. The crisis is over, the storm has begun to cease.*) Miss Tishy, love,
there's a lad on the stairs out there — 'Y God, I think his poor little heart
is breaking — (*Tishy murmurs.*) Darlin', I don't know what you said to him nor
he to you, but if you love him, keep him, for there's nothing worth keeping

in this world, but love — (*With a large embrace, Mrs. Healey rises, leaving Tishy kneeling by the chair.*) 'Y God, they're a poor lot, the men, all of 'em, and dirty, too — but the thing is, darlin', to get one that cleans easy.

" Mrs. Healey moves softly out of the room, leaving Tishy, whose tears now come healingly and gently. Carr appears presently at the door, all his love and his honesty of soul in his pleading eyes. Tishy smiles through her tears. Her decision is made. She and Carr will set out together on their journey of life — not because he ' cleans easy ' but because of the love for him in her heart that will not let him go; because she knows that the man of her choosing is clean. And so the play ends; the confusing, bewildering, torturing day is over; and this young man, this young woman, begin another, a truer experience."

THE END

THE PLAYS AND THEIR AUTHORS

"The Swan. By Ferenc Molnar. Translation by Melville Baker. Copyright, 1923, by Charles Frohman, Inc. Earlier version translated by Benjamin Glazer. Copyright, 1923, and published by Boni and Liveright, New York.

Ferenc Molnar, long prominent as a dramatist in Hungary and in all continental theatrical centers, has appeared once before in these volumes. His " Liliom " was included in the year book of 1920–1921. Born January 12, 1878, of wealthy Jewish parents, he was a journalist in 1896 and has been a playwright since 1902. Several translations of " The Swan " were made before Gilbert Miller of the Charles Frohman company accepted that of Melville Baker, a Harvard man, who is a play reader in the Frohman office.

"The Show-Off." By George Kelly. Copyright, 1923, 1924, by George Kelly. Published by Little, Brown & Co., Boston.

George Kelly is a Philadelphian — a young Philadelphian, seeing he is still in his early thirties. Deciding to become an actor when he was twenty-one he played juvenile rôles in and around New York, drifted into vaudeville five years later and for the next five years wrote and played in a series of original vaudeville sketches. His first long play, " The Torchbearers," was produced in New York the season of 1922–1923 and was an immediate though not an altogether consistent success. Having amused the special public of Little Theater enthusiasts, about whom it was written, it failed to stir the bigger general public.

"The Goose Hangs High." By Lewis Beach. Copyright, 1923, by Lewis Beach. Published and copyrighted, 1924, by Little, Brown & Co., Boston, Mass.

Lewis Beach, born in Saginaw, Michigan, took his A.B. and A.M. at Harvard. The first plays he wrote were in one act. Four of these: " The Clod," " A Guest for Dinner," " Love Among the Lions," and " Brothers,"

289

have been published by Brentano's. His first long play, "A Square Peg," was produced in New York and was enthusiastically hailed by the reviewers but not by the public. "Ann Vroome" is another full length effort.

"Outward Bound." By Sutton Vane. Copyright, 1923, by Sutton Vane. Published by Boni and Liveright, New York.

Vane Sutton Vane is the complete name. The young author of the most unusual of the season's dramas (he is only thirty-three) was born in England. Thirty years and more ago his father wrote melodramas of the wilder type in London. Sutton Jr. did no writing of consequence until after two years of hard fighting in the war. He went in in 1914 and came out of hospital, full of malaria and shell shock, in 1916. The story of "Outward Bound" came to him while he lay in the hospital contemplating what might happen to his soul if he were suddenly to pass out. While he was writing the play he played a part in the London production of "The Thirteenth Chair." No manager would buy "Outward Bound," so Vane, by saving and borrowing six hundred dollars, managed a production of the play himself at the Everyman's Theater, one of London's centers of experimental drama. Success followed.

"Hell-Bent fer Heaven." By Hatcher Hughes. Copyright, 1923, by Hatcher Hughes. Published and copyrighted, 1924, by Harper Brothers, New York.

Hatcher Hughes was born on a farm in the foothills of North Carolina forty years ago. He was graduated from the University of North Carolina in 1907, and became an instructor in English at the same university two years later. In 1911 he took graduate work in the drama at Columbia University under Brander Matthews and became Professor Matthews's assistant in 1912. He was a captain in the war, serving with the 18th Division at the front. His first play was "Wake Up, Jonathan," written in collaboration with Elmer Rice. Mrs. Fiske produced and starred in "Jonathan" in 1922.

" Beggar on Horseback." By George Kaufman and Marc Connelly. Suggested by " Hans Sonnenstoesser's Hohlenfahrt," by Paul Apel. Copyright, 1923, by Kaufman and Connelly. Published and copyrighted, 1924, by Boni and Liveright, New York.

During the four years they have been collaborating playwrights the Messrs. Kaufman and Connelly have produced " Dulcy " (see " Best Plays of 1921–1922 "), " To the Ladies," " Merton of the Movies " (" Best Plays of 1922–1923 "), " Deep Tangled Wildwood " and " Beggar on Horseback." They are newspaper men and both come from Pennsylvania, Kaufman from Pittsburgh and Connelly from McKeesport.

" Sun-Up." By Lula Vollmer. Copyright, 1923, by Lula Vollmer. Published and copyrighted, 1923, by Brentano, New York.

Lula Vollmer, born in Aberdeen, North Carolina, did considerable amateur playwriting when she was going to boarding school, but her first real acquaintance with the professional theater, even as a spectator, was made in New Orleans when she was twenty years old. She lived in Atlanta ten years after that and reached New York in 1918, just as America was going to war. Inspired by the stories her friends brought her of the attitude of the Carolina mountain folk toward the draft, she wrote " Sun-Up " in two weeks — and peddled it for five years before she found a purchaser. During that time she accepted a position as a box-office executive with the Theater Guild. Last year she wrote her second folk play, " The Shame Woman," which also ran the season through in New York.

" The Changelings." By Lee Wilson Dodd. Copyright, 1923, by Lee Wilson Dodd. Published and copyrighted, 1923, by E. P. Dutton & Co., New York.

Lee Wilson Dodd is a Pennsylvanian, born in Franklin in 1879. He graduated from Yale in the class of '99 and from the New York Law School two years later. He was admitted to the bar in 1902. Five years after that he gave up law and took up matrimony and litera-

ture. Since then he has written novels, poems and a
few plays. Two of the plays were " Speed " and " The
Return of Eve."   He also dramatized " His Majesty
Bunker Bean " and " Pals First," returning to literature
to write " The Book of Susan " and " Lilia Chenoworth."
" The Changelings " followed these.

" Chicken Feed," renamed, 1924, " Wages for Wives." By Guy Bolton. Copyright, 1923-1924, by Guy Bolton. Published by Samuel French, New York and London.

Guy Reginald Bolton was born in England, which
accounts for the Reginald. It was his family's idea that
he would make a good architect, but he preferred another
kind of creative building and in 1911 went in for playwriting. That season he and Douglas J. Wood col-
laborated on a piece called " The Drone." Since then
he has written many plays and numerous books for
musical plays. His plays include " Adam and Eva "
(with George Middleton; see " Best Plays of 1919–
1920 ").

" Tarnish." By Gilbert Emery. Copyright, 1923, by Gilbert Emery. Published and copyrighted, 1924, by Brentano's, New York.

This is also Gilbert Emery's second appearance in
these volumes, his fine after-the-war drama, " The Hero,"
having been included in the 1921–1922 issue of " Best
Plays." Mr. Emery is a young literary man and actor
who has written considerable fiction under his family
name of Emery Pottle. He was born in Naples, New
York, and educated at the Oneonta Normal School and
Amherst University. He lived ten years abroad and
was active in the war.

PLAYS PRODUCED IN NEW YORK

June 15, 1923 — June 15, 1924

" GEORGE WHITE'S SCANDALS "

A revue in two acts, lyrics by B. G. DeSylva, Ray Goetz and Ballard McDonald; music by George Gershwin; book by George White and W. K. Wells. Produced by George White at the Globe Theater, New York, June 18, 1923.

Principals engaged —

Johnny Dooley
Lester Allen
Tom Patricola
Richard Bold
Newton Alexander
Harry Lang
Tip Top Four
    Staged by George White.

Winnie Lightner
Beulah Berson
Marga Waldron
Helen Hudson
Margaret Breen
London Palace Girls
The Breens

" HELEN OF TROY, NEW YORK "

A musical comedy in a prologue and two acts by George Kaufman and Marc Connelly; music and lyrics by Bert Kalmar and Harry Ruby. Produced by Rufus Lemaire and George Jessel at the Selwyn Theater, New York, June 19, 1923.

Cast of characters —

Elias Yarrow..Tom Lewis
C. Warren Jennings..Roy Atwell
Baron de Cartier....................................Joseph Lertora
Theodore Mince..................................Charles Lawrence
Harper Williams..................................Clyde Hunnewell
David Williams..Paul Frawley
Helen McGuffey..Helen Ford
Maribel...Queenie Smith

Grace Yarrow...Stella Hoban
Mme. Pasanova.......................................Joan Clement
    Prologue—Corridor in the Yarrow Collar Factory, Troy, N. Y.
Act I.—The Directors' Room.   Act II.—Baron de Cartier's Studio,
New York City.   Staged by Bertram Harrison and Bert French.

Helen McGuffey, stenographer to the president in a
Troy, N. Y., collar factory, loses her job because the
boss's son takes a fancy to her and the boss objects.
She later invents the semisoft style of collar, causing
a rival factory to boom, a merger to be effected, and
Helen to win the manufacturer's son after all.

"VANITIES OF 1923"

A musical revue in two acts; lyrics and music by
Earl Carroll.   Produced by Earl Carroll at the Earl
Carroll Theater, New York, July 5, 1923.

Principals engaged —

Joe Cook	Peggy Hopkins Joyce
Bernard Granville	Roy Giusti
Harry Burns	Irene Ricardo
Jimmy Duffy	Amy Frank
J. Frank Leslie	Dorothy Neville
Loretta Marks	Al Thomas
Dorothy Knapp	Renoff and Renova
	Charles Alexander

Staged by Earl Carroll.

"FASHIONS OF 1924"

A musical revue; music by Ted Snyder; lyrics by
Harry B. Smith.   Produced by Alexander Leftwich at
the Lyceum Theater, New York, July 18, 1923.

Principals engaged —

Arnold Daly	Edith Taliaferro
Jimmy Hussey	Florence Morrison
Ina Hayward	Marie Nordstrom
Dinazarde	Carlotta Monterey
Helen LaVonne	De Jari
John V. Lowe	Alden Gay
Gene Delmont	Masters and Kraft

Staged by Alexander Leftwich.

"TWO FELLOWS AND A GIRL"

A comedy in three acts by Vincent Lawrence. Produced by George M. Cohan at the Vanderbilt Theater, New York, July 19, 1923.

Cast of characters —

Lea Ellery..Ruth Shepley
Thomas Ellery..Jack Bennett
Jack Moorland...John Halliday
Jim Dale...Allan Dinehart
Johnson..George Smithfield
Doris Wadsworth....................................Claiborne Foster
Act I.—Lea's Home. Act II. and III.—The New Home.

Lea Ellery, courted by two attractive young men, Jack Moorland and Jim Dale, can't decide which one to accept until she flips a coin. She cheats a little, continuing the flipping until it comes Moorland's way. They are married and Dale, depressed but game, goes away. Five years later he returns still single and a millionaire. Lea finds herself still a little in love with him, and a little tired of Moorland's contented air of proprietorship. She begins what might have resulted in a serious flirtation if Dale had not decided suddenly to marry Doris Wadsworth and put an end to Moorland's jealousy.

"IN LOVE WITH LOVE"

A comedy in three acts by Vincent Lawrence. Produced by William Harris, Jr., at the Ritz Theater, New York, August 6, 1923.

Cast of characters —

Julia...Maryland Morne
William Jordan..Berton Churchill
Ann Jordan..Lynn Fontanne
Robert Metcalf...Henry Hull

Frank Oakes...Robert Strange
Jack Gardner..Ralph Morgan
Marion Sears..Wanda Lyon
    Act I., II. and III.—William Jordan's Home. Staged by Robert
Milton.

Ann Jordan, fond of attention, lets both Bob Metcalf
and Frank Oakes make desperate love to her. Oakes,
being the older and more aggressive, finally gets her to
accept a ring from him and permit him to announce their
engagement. But Metcalf, spurred on by his friend,
Jack Gardner, refuses to be beaten. He continues his
campaign for Ann more strenuously than ever. Ann,
both amused and worried by the two excited suitors,
gradually comes to realize that she loves neither seriously, but has been completely bowled over by young
Mr. Gardner, the little fixer. She never has been really
in love with anyone before, she admits. Just in love with
love.

" THUMBS DOWN "

A melodrama in a prologue and three acts by Myron
C. Fagan. Produced by C. C. Wanamaker at the Forty-
ninth Street Theater, New York, August 6, 1923.
Cast of characters —

Officer O'Neill......................................John Wylie
Officer McGraw.......................................Earl Mitchell
Emmett Sheridan......................................Howard Lang
James Cantwell......................................Purnell Pratt
Virginia Sheridan....................................Thais Lawton
Florence Sheridan....................................Sue MacManamy
Dopey Brown..William Ives
Billy Camp..H. Dudley Hawley
Charlie...Harvey Hays
Larry Fowler..John Marston
Samuel Hart...J. Hammond Dailey
Judge Richard Fowler................................William Ingersoll
Coroner Reynolds....................................W. J. Townsend
Officer Moulton.....................................Thos. H. McKnight
Harding...Herbert Bruce
    Prologue—Two Years Ago. At the Sheridan Home in an American
City. Act I.—Larry Fowler's Studio Apartment in Same City.
Act II.—Office of District Attorney. Act III.—Same as Act I.
Staged by Priestly Morrison.

For years Emmett Sheridan has been leading, so far
as his family is concerned, a double life, getting his

income from questionable sources, and specializing in
plain and fancy bootlegging. Cornered at last, he confesses to his wife and daughter, and demands that they
help him escape the law. In place of which they dis-
own him. He goes to prison, serves two years and
comes out looking for revenge. Trying the patience of
his daughter too far she fires a revolver at him and
is about to be tried for the murder when it is discovered
that the murder was really done by a man higher up who
was the real leader of the bootleg gang.

"THE MAD HONEYMOON"

A comedy in three acts by Barry Conners. Produced
by William A. Brady in association with Wilmer and
Vincent at the Playhouse, New York, August 7, 1923.

Cast of characters —

Mrs. Shannon	Louise Sydmeth
Rufus Colgate	George Pauncefort
Marie Wilson	Mayo Methot
Duke Wilson	Edward Arnold
Bill Cripps	George Probert
Kennedy	A. Francis Lenz
Peggy Colgate	Boots Wooster
Wally Spencer	Kenneth MacKenna
Cousin Jimmie Rawlinson	Benedict MacQuarrie
Mrs. Eads	Blanche Latell
Parson Crandall	William Gerald
Obediah Eads	Herbert Heywood
Captain Hines	Lawrence Williams

Act I.—Rufus Colgate's Home—La Chevral, Ind. Act II.—Parlor of
Eads Hotel—Pee Wee, Michigan. Act III.—Same as Act I. Play
staged by Hal Briggs.

Peggy Colgate is ready and willing to elope with
Wally Spencer, and her father secretly hopes she will
make it. He pretends to be greatly angered, however,
and the housekeeper steals Peggy's clothes while she
is in the bath, to prevent her meeting Spencer. Peggy,
out of the bath, grabs her lace pajamas and a fur coat
and elopes anyway. Which would have been all right

if certain crooks had not secreted a bundle of stolen government bonds in the coat. A comic pursuit follows and there are complications delaying the consummation of the elopement until 10.45 p.m.

" THE NEWCOMERS "

A musical revue in two acts by Joe Burrows and Will Morrissey. Produced by Will Morrissey at the Ambassador Theater, New York, August 8, 1923.

Principals engaged —

William Morrissey
Al Fields
Paisley Noon
Larry Beck
Frank Gaby
Joe Burrows
Henry Streml
Mason and Shaw
   Staged by Will Morrissey.

Frankie James
Sophie Romm
Florence Stone
Grace Masters
Gail Beverley
Elsie Lamonte
Constance Evans
Cecil and Kaye

" TWEEDLES "

A comedy in three acts by Booth Tarkington and Harry Leon Wilson. Produced by Robert McLaughlin at the Frazee Theater, New York, August 13, 1923.

Cast of characters —

Mrs. Ricketts..................................Cornelia Otis Skinner
Mrs. Albergone..Patti Cortez
Winsora..Ruth Gordon
Julian...Gregory Kelly
Mrs. Castlebury..................................Florence Pendleton
Mr. Castlebury...Wallis Clark
Adam Tweedle..George Farren
Ambrose..Irving Mitchell
Philemon..Donald Meek
   Act I., II. and III.—Mrs. Albergone's Antiquity Shop and " Tea Terrace," Old Tweedle Mansion.

Winsora Tweedles is a waitress in her aunt's antiquity shop and tea terrace. Julian Castlebury is one of the summer folk living nearby. Julian, buying tea, falls in love with Winsora and starts a collection of Bristol glass to cover his visits to the shop. Still a scandal threatens and both the Castleburys, proud of their long line of family somebodies, and the Tweedles, equally proud of their family's beginnings in revolutionary days, seek to prevent it. Julian, much upset, exposes both his own and Winsora's folks as family-proud snobs, and likewise discovers rotten branches on both family trees. After which he and Winsora decide to stage their own wedding in their own way.

"THE GOOD OLD DAYS"

A comedy in three acts by Aaron Hoffman. Produced by A. H. Woods at the Broadhurst Theater, New York, August 14, 1923.

Cast of characters —

John Miller	Harry Lester Mason
Gus Rausch	Charles Havican
The Bum	John G. Fee
Fritzie Zimmer	Mathilde Cottrelly
Tim	Ralph Wiedhaas
Ted Schloss	Stewart Wilson
Nick Schloss	George Bickel
Jim Knowles	Charles Mather
Rudolph Zimmer	Charles Winninger
Mrs. Mahoney	Nan Karew
Officer Kelly	Joseph Slaytor
Katie Zimmer	Beatrice Allen
William J. Parker	John Junior
Sweeney	Harry Linkey
Jack	Harry Curtin
Doyle	John Kuhns

Act I.—Scene 1—Nick and Rudolph's Cafe, New York City, 1916. Scene 2—The Same, Four Years Later. Act II. and III.—Living Room in Rudolph's Home. Staged by Howard Lindsey and the Author.

Before the days of prohibition Rudolph Zimmer and Nick Schloss ran a German beer saloon. After the Volstead law was put in force Zimmer, getting religion, became an enforcement officer and Schloss took up bootlegging. As a result they had many comic adventures, resulting finally in Zimmer's decision that he believed prohibition to be all right but he knew it to be all wrong. Which makes it possible for the Zimmer daughter to marry the Schloss nephew.

"THE WOMAN ON THE JURY"

A drama in a prologue and three acts by Bernard K.
Burns. Produced by A. H. Woods at the Eltinge Theater,
New York, August 15, 1923.

Cast of characters —

Betty Brown	Mary Newcomb
George Wayne	Fleming Ward
Miss Matilda Slade	Adelaide Fitz Allan
Marion Masters	Frieda Inescort
Fred Masters	Henry Daniell
Judge Davis	Stanley Jessup
Emmet	Elwood F. Bostwick
Nellis	John Craig
Mrs. Pierce	Mabel Colcord
Grace Pierce	Florence Flinn
James McGuire	John Sharkey
Baliff	Jules Ferrar
Garrity	Wilson Reynolds
Tom Lewis	Bennett Southard
Mr. Simons	Royal Tracy
Otto Schmidt	Harry Vokes
Clerk of Court	Thomas Hood

Prologue—A Cottage in the Mountains in Vermont. Act I.—Living
Room in the Masters's Home. Act II.—A Court Room in New Jersey.
Act III.—The Jury Room. Staged by Lester Lonergan.

Betty Brown, trusting George Wayne, lives with him
through one summer in a mountain cottage. It is to be
a "daring adventure in sincerity." But at the end of the
summer George is through, and as he coldly leaves her
Betty sends a bullet through the door after him. Three
years later she is happily married to another man and is
called, with her husband, to jury duty on a murder case.
Midway in the trial she discovers that the man killed
was George Wayne, and that he had also deceived the
woman who had shot him after her child was born.
Eleven men on the jury are for making an example of
the woman accused. Betty holds out for two days and
nights for acquittal. Finally, being able to convince
them in no other way, she confesses her experience with
Wayne, risking the loss of her reputation and her husband rather than vote to convict the woman accused.
The jury agrees on acquittal and Betty's husband for-
gives her.

"LITTLE JESSIE JAMES"

A musical farce in three acts by Harlan Thompson; music by Harry Archer. Produced by L. Lawrence Weber at the Longacre Theater, New York, August 15, 1923.

Cast of characters —

```
Tommy Tinker...........................................Allen Kearns
Juliet..............................................Miriam  Hopkins
Mrs. Flower........................................Winifred  Harris
Geraldine Flower........................................Ann  Sands
Paul  Revere.............................................Jay  Velie
S.  Block........................................James  B.  Carson
Mrs. Jamieson.......................................Clara  Thropp
Jessie Jamieson.......................................Nan  Halperin
William J. Pierce.......................................Roger  Gray
Clarence..............................................Carl  Anderson
Harold..............................................Herbert  Bostwick
Lucila...............................................Lucila  Mendez
Loretta..............................................Loretta  Flushing
Bobbie..............................................Bobbie  Breslau
Blanche..............................................Blanche  O'Brien
Frances..............................................Frances  Upton
Edna..................................................Edna  Howard
Emily..................................................Emily  Stead
Agnes................................................Agnes  Morrisey
Bonnie................................................Bonnie  Shaw
     Act I. and II.—Living Room of Paul's Apartment, Central Park
West, New York City.
     "The James Boys," a Paul Whiteman Band, Ernest Cutting,
Director.
```

Jessie Jamieson, from Kansas, has a reputation for getting whatever she goes after. Hence they call her Jessie James. Coming to New York she takes a fancy to Paul Revere. And is still for Paul even after he is forced to hide in a trick bed with another man's wife to escape an enraged bill collector.

"THE BREAKING POINT"

A drama in three acts by Mary Roberts Rinehart. Produced by Wagenhals and Kemper at the Klaw Theater, New York, August 16, 1923.

Cast of characters —

Bill	Stephen Maley
Clare	Lucille Sears
Lucy	Zeffie Tilbury
David	John Doyle
Dr. Miller	Reginald Barlow
Dick	McKay Morris
Elizabeth	Regina Wallace
Beverly	Gail Kane
Bassett	Robert Barrat
Curley	Robert Vaughn
Joe	Maurice Darcy
Sheriff	John Morrissey
Indian Woman	Marie Valray
Riley	Robert Vaughn

Act I.—Home of Dr. David Livingston. Act II.—The Clark Ranch, Norada, Wyoming. Act III.—Home of Dr. Livingston. Play Staged by Collin Kemper.

Once, when he was young and wild and in love with a married vamp, Dick killed the vamp's husband in a fight. Escaping, he was found by a friend, his memory of the affair completely obliterated by the shock. The friend, Dr. David Livingston, took Dick east and tried the experiment of reclaiming his soul while he was a victim of amnesia. Ten years later Dick is a fine fellow and a successful physician. He knows, however, that his past is clouded, and before he can honestly ask Elizabeth to marry him he feels he must clear his memory. He goes back to the scene of his youthful adventures, suffers a second shock, remembers all connected with the murder but forgets all that happened in the ten years he has lived since. A third shock completes his recovery and makes a happy ending possible.

" CHILDREN OF THE MOON "

A drama in three acts by Martin Flavin. Produced by Jacob A. Weiser in association with A. L. Jones and Morris Green at the Comedy Theater, New York, August 17, 1923.

Cast of characters —

Thomas	Whitford Kane
Walter Higgs	Harold Winston
Madame Atherton	Henrietta Crosman
Jane Atherton	Florence Johns
Dr. Wetherell	Grant Stewart
Major John Bannister	Paul Gordon
Judge Atherton	Albert Perry
Laura Atherton	Beatrice Terry

Act I., II. and III.—The Sitting Room of the Atherton Home

In an out-of-the-way place, on a bluff above the sea, the Athertons have for years remained partly in hiding because of a curious moon madness that is a family affliction. Crashing into their garden an attractive aviator is badly jarred and compelled to rest up at the Atherton cottage. Falling in love with the Atherton daughter, who is unaware of the strain of insanity in her family, he proposes and is accepted — by everybody except the girl's mother, a neurotic and morbid soul who insists, in the name of mother love, that she shall dictate every action of her children. Defied by her daughter, the mother tells her of the insanity taint, just as she had told her son in an effort to keep him from going to war. But the boy had gone and had flown his airplane into the path of the moon and had been killed. And the girl now rides away with her lover into the fog in search of the moon and is heard from no more.

" HOME FIRES "

A comedy in three acts by Owen Davis. Produced by
the Messrs. Shubert at the Thirty-ninth Street Theater,
New York, August 20, 1923.

Cast of characters —

Betty...Lillian Ross
Abner...Eugene Powers
Aunt Martha...Marion Ballou
Tommy..Morgan Farley
Mary..Frances Underwood
Henry Bedford...Charles Richman
Flora...Marian Warring-Manley
Julia..Juliette Crosby
Jack Harvey...Alan Bunce
Walter Harvey..Howard Gould
Dana Roberts..Dodson Mitchell
Bill Maxwell...John Bingham
Lucy..Marion Benda
Quinn..Lester Scharff
Doctor Norton...Jay Strong
Act I.—Henry Bedford's Suburban Home. Act II.—Scene 1—The
Same. Scene 2—Paradise Inn. Scene 3—Same as Scene 1. Act
III.—Same as Act I. Staged by Hugh Ford.

The Bedfords live on Long Island. He is a bond
salesman, weak, vain, conceited, but able to make
$10,000 a year. She is a practical, sane, thrifty wife
who has managed to keep the family together and happy.
There are two restless daughters, one fourteen, the other
eighteen. Suddenly everything goes wrong. The oldest
girl, thinking herself jilted by a rich man's son, goes
with him to a dance place to hear his explanation. Her
father, taking a neighbor's wife for a ride, stops there,
sees daughter, and is horrified. Daughter, trying to
run, falls off a balcony and breaks an arm. The husband of the woman who came with father threatens
divorce. But, despite all the black clouds, Mrs. Bedford sticks to the home fires and finally gets everything
straightened out again. The rich man's son proves to
be an upright young man; the neighborly husband gives
up his divorce ideas and father finds a golf chum who
is willing to back him in business.

" WE'VE GOT TO HAVE MONEY "

A comedy in three acts by Edward Laska. Produced by A. L. Jones and Morris Green at the Playhouse, New York, August 20, 1923.

Cast of characters —

David Farnum..Robert Ames
Thomas Campbell..Stewart Kemp
Toney Platt...Jerome Cowan
Robert Brady..Leo Donnelly
Richard Walcott...Robert McWade
Prof. Bigley..Louis Mount Joy
Lucas...James Robb
James Doolin..Alex Derman
M. Levante..Joseph Granby
Kennison..Milton Nobles, Jr.
Otto Shultz...Manuel A. Alexander
Henry Mack..J. D. Walsh
Dunn..Richard Warren
A Barber..R. M. D'Angelo
Olga Walcott..Vivian Tobin
Evelyn Russell..Doris Marquette
Betty Clark...Marie Louise Walker
Miss Doolittle..Eden Gray
Miss Davis..Louise Segal
Miss Finney...Flora Finch

Act I.—At Farnum and Campbell's Apartment Near Columbia University, Commencement Day. Act II. and III.—In the Woolworth Building. Staged by Bertram Harrison.

Dave Farnum, being rich and wild, did not want to go to college. Thomas Campbell, poor and studious, did. So they put up a job on Farnum's guardian — Dave to do as he pleased, Thomas to graduate and get his degree and give it to Dave to take home. On Commencement Day at Columbia Dave's guardian arrives with his daughter, Olga, Dave's sweetheart, and discovers the deception. He stops Dave's allowance and forbids his pursuit of Olga. Dave goes on his own, organizes a Brains Promoting concern, tumbles on to a leather patent, bluffs a rich man into backing him and emerges triumphantly as a smart business man and Olga's affianced husband in the last act.

" BROOK "

A play in three acts by Thomas P. Robinson. Produced by McKee and Stevens at the Greenwich Village Theater, New York, August 20, 1923.

Cast of characters —

Mooney Blackburn................................George Thompson
Dan Peltry..Benjamin Kauser
Brook Blackburn....................................Mary Carroll
Bryce Hammond..................................Donald Cameron
Norman Tracey............................Theodore Westman, Jr.
Joe Cochran...George Barbier
Adah Cochran..Ellis Baker
    Act I., II. and III.—Mooney Blackburn's Cabin in the Alleghany Mountains.   Staged by John McKee.

Brook Blackburn is a mountain girl crudely reared and lacking all suggestion of sophistication. Loving a summer visitor, Bryce Hammond, she does not hesitate to give herself to him. Nor to frankly confess that she has done so when accused. She loves Bryce and he loves her. If God put so great a love in their hearts He must naturally have expected them to acknowledge it. Even the girl who was going to marry Bryce, Adah Cochran, is beaten by such logic. And Bryce, who had entered upon the adventure lightly and in the mood of an investigator, refuses to accept the freedom Brook offers him. He will stay on in the mountains and marry her for love, rather than return to town and marry Adah for convenience, and to avert town talk.

" ARTISTS AND MODELS "

A musical revue in two acts. Produced by Messrs. Shubert at the Shubert Theater, New York, August 20, 1923.

Principals engaged —·

Frank Fay   Adele Klaer
Harry Kelly   Charlotte Woodruff
George Rosener   John Adair

Bob Nelson	Nikola Cunningham
Rose Boylan	Lee Morse
Veronica	Annie Pritchard
Bob O'Connor	Buddy Doyle
Harriet Gimbel	Marie Pettes
Beth Elliott	Clare Thompson
Arthur Boylan	Rollo Wayne
Kyra	Fatelle Levelle
Etta Pillard	Grace Hamilton
James R. Liddy	

Staged by Harry Wagstaff Gribble and Francis Weldon, under the supervision of J. J. Shubert.

"RED LIGHT ANNIE"

A drama in three acts by Norman Houston and Sam Forrest. Produced by A. H. Woods in association with Sam H. Harris at the Morosco Theater, New York, August 21, 1923.

Cast of characters —

Fanny Campbell	Mary Ryan
Tom Campbell	Frank M. Thomas
Mr. Clark	Edward Walton
Nick Martin	Edward Ellis
Dorothy Martin	Warda Howard
Mr. Wilson	W. H. Prendergast
A Man	Albert Carberry
Another Man	Fred McLean
A Judge	Harry Hammill
Ned	Al Britton
Chester	Henry Vincent
Flo	Monita Gay
Marie	Ann Martin
Al	John Waller
An Office Boy	Billy Gillen
Mr. Fulton	Francis Dunn
Robert Dugan	Paul Nicholson

The First Act is in Ten Thumbnail Sketches: 1—A Railroad Station, upstate. 2—At the Martins in Brooklyn. 3—An Office in a Bank in New York. 4—Outside of an Office Building. 5—A Corner in a Court Room. 6—At the Martins. 7—Fanny's Bedroom. 8—A Private Parlor. 9—Fanny's Bedroom. 10—An Office. Act II. and III.—An Apartment on the West Side. Staged by Sam Forrest.

The Campbells, Fanny and Tom, just married in an upstate town, go to New York, where Tom is to become a bank clerk. In New York they fall under the influence of Fanny's step-sister and her husband, Nick and Dorothy Martin, keepers of a resort and dealers in dope. Tom is framed for the theft of $50,000 in Liberty Bonds from his bank, and after he is sent to prison Fanny is taught to use dope and becomes a regular visitor to the Martin resort, where she is known as Red Light Annie. After a year she reforms, and is waiting for Tom when he gets out of Sing Sing. For a few months they are happy. Then Martin tries to blackmail Annie back into the old life. She shoots him dead and a friendly detective refuses to arrest her.

" ZENO "

A drama in three acts by Joseph F. Rinn. Produced by the Hampton Play Corporation at the Forty-eighth Street Theater, New York, August 25, 1923.

Cast of characters —
```
Officer Burke.........................................Charles J. Sims
James O'Brien........................................James T. Ford
William Donegan.......................................Thomas Gunn
Chief Inspector Parker..............................Walter Wilson
Sniffy Gordan.......................................Martha McGraw
William King........................................William Shelley
James Cartier.......................................Hugh O'Connell
Marie...................................................Helen Gill
Mrs. Hampton.......................................Mina C. Gleason
Grace Hampton..............................Margaret Shackelford
Harry Williams ....................................Frederick Bickel
Charles Baker..........................................Paul Byron
Mr. Hampton..........................................Albert Sackett
Professor Dodge.......................................Leigh Lovell
Dr. Moore...........................................William B. Mack
Officer Dillon..........................................J. A. Curtis
```
Act I.—Scene 1—Office of Chief Inspector Parker. Scene 2—Library in the Hampton Home. Act II.—Same. Act III.—Scene 1—Garret in the House Next Door. Scene 2—Same as Act II. Staged by Edward Elsner.

Zeno is a notorious crook who has been defying the police for months. No one has ever seen him. He issues orders to his gang by wireless, and divides the swag by leaving it in the center of a hayfield and notifying them to go get it. Police Inspector Parker combs the town unsuccessfully, and is finally induced to accept the coöperation of Dr. Moore, a psychic, who has been engaged to hold a séance at the home of the Hamptons in the hope of getting in touch with the spirit of the Hampton son, cruelly murdered weeks before. At the séance Dr. Moore performs wonderfully until Inspector Parker breaks in, reveals the house to have been wired and uncovers Zeno's headquarters in the house next door. Dr. Moore, however, is only one of the gang, and the capture of Zeno himself exposes the least suspected member of the cast.

" MAGNOLIA "

A comedy in three acts by Booth Tarkington. Produced by Alfred E. Aarons, Inc., at the Liberty Theater, New York, August 27, 1923.

Cast of characters —

General Rumford..J. K. Hutchinson
Madame Rumford..................................Elizabeth Patterson
Elvira...Phyllis Schuyler
Lucy..Martha Bryan-Allen
Tom..Leo Carrillo
Major Patterson.......................................John Rutherford
Joe Patterson....................................James Bradbury, Jr.
General Orlando Jackson..........................Malcolm Williams
Blackie...John Harrington
Mexico..Ethel Wilson
Rumbo...Barrington Carter
    Act I.—General Rumford's Estate, Magnolia Landing, Mississippi, 1841. Act II.—General Jackson's Gaming Resort, Natchez. Act III.— Drawing Room of the Mansion. Staged by Ira Hards.

In the 1830's the Rumfords live at Magnolia Landing, Mississippi. Young Tom Rumford, taken north when a boy, was brought up by relatives of Quaker tendencies living near Philadelphia. Returning to Magnolia Landing a young man, he refuses to accept the duel as the only means of settling a dispute between gentlemen. He does not believe in fighting. Insulted by a bully, he refuses to fight. Which so angers his fire-eating father that Tom is sent to the woodshed to live. Running away from home he drifts into a gambling house in Natchez just in time to see the proprietor shoot down a couple of faro cheaters. From the gambler Tom learns that courage is merely a question of preparedness. "The brave man is the man who feels he is safe." Under which spur Tom fights another bad man who has insulted him, acquires an acquaintance with the use of firearms and seven years later returns to Magnolia Landing as " the notorious Cunnel Blake," terror of the lower Mississippi. Here he is romantically revenged upon his male enemies and wins the love of his most adorable cousin.

" LITTLE MISS BLUEBEARD "

A comedy in three acts by Avery Hopwood. Produced by Charles Frohman in association with E. Ray Goetz at the Lyceum Theater, New York, August 28, 1923.

Cast of characters —

Larry Charters	Bruce McRae
Eva Winthrop	Margaret Linden
Smithers	William Eville
Sir John Barstow	Arthur Barry
The Hon. Bertie Bird	Eric Blore
Bob Talmadge	Stanley Logan
Colette	Irene Bordoni
Gloria Talmadge	Jeannette Sherwin
Lulu	Eva Leonard-Boyne
Paul Rondel	Burton Brown

Act I. and II.—Larry Charters' Flat in London. Act III.—Reception Hall of the Talmadges' Villa in Deauville. Staged by W. H. Gilmore.

Colette is an attractive French girl, with a secret love for Larry Charters, composer. Introduced to him as the wife of Charters's friend, Bob Talmadge, who has inadvertently committed bigamy, using Charters's name, she asks the privilege of remaining in his apartment, his wife in name only, until she can get a divorce. Char-

ters agrees to help his friend and within the hour is
deeply in love with Colette. For an act and a half she
keeps him at half-arm's length, pretending jealousy of
his other inspirations. But eventually she capitulates.

"THE WHOLE TOWN'S TALKING"

A comedy by John Emerson and Anita Loos. Produced by A. H. Woods at the Bijou Theater, New York,
August 29, 1923.

Cast of characters —

Henry Simmons	James Bradbury
Mrs. Simmons	Lucia Moore
Chester Binney	Grant Mitchell
Ethel Simmons	June Bradley
Roger Shields	Gerald Oliver Smith
Lela Wilson	Violet Dunn
Sally Wilson	Alice Dunn
Donald Swift	Harold Salter
Letty Lythe	Catherine Owen
Sadie	Jeanne Greene
Annie	Eleanor Kennedy
Taxi-Driver	Ellsworth Jones

The Action Takes Place in the Living Room of the Simmons
Family in Toledo, Ohio. Staged by Mr. Emerson.

Chester Binney, a kind but crude merchant in Toledo,
Ohio, is eager to marry Ethel Simmons, the daughter
of his business partner. Ethel, however, although she
admires Chester, is romantic and demands a lover who
has lived. Hoping to please her Chester invents a past
for himself, inscribing the back of a movie queen's
photograph with subtle references to the " happy, hectic,
Hollywood hours " he had spent with her. Ethel is duly
impressed until the movie queen, Letty Lythe, appears
on the scene, accompanied by her director and fiancé,
a large, pugnacious gentleman named Swift. Chester,
exposed, is forced to " fight in the dark," just like a
movie hero, to defend his honor. At the end of which
comic contest he emerges victorious and Ethel is proud to
marry him.

" THE JOLLY ROGER "

A comedy in four acts by A. E. Thomas. Produced at
the National Theater, New York, August 30, 1923.

Cast of characters —

```
Barney  Blum.............................................Le Roi Operti
Long  Tom.....................................C. Norman Hammond
Flint....................................................Reynolds Evans
Zeno......................................................J. R. Lee
Toohy.................................................P. J. Kelly
Red  Dominique...........................................Ernst Rowan
Teach...............................................Murray Darcy
Sam........................................William H. Stephens
Van  Kirk................................................Allen Thomas
Martin..................................................William  Sauter
Sebastian...............................................Paul Gilfoyle
Hilda  Borner.......................................Carroll McComas
Adam  Trent.....................................Pedro De Cordoba
Helmsman.............................................Marcel Dill
Nat....................................................Joseph Latham
Purrington..........................................H. E. Humphrey
Mistress Purrington..............................Ruth  Chorpenning
        Act  I.—The  Deck  of  a  Pirate  Brig.  Act  II.—Captain's  Cabin.
Acts  III.  and  IV.—The  Beach  of  a  Desert  Island.
```

Off the coast of Somewhere, some time or other, Adam
Trent mysteriously boards a pirate ship which has
stopped to take on prisoners and loot from a captured
brig. He finds the pirate captain dead and the crew in
mutiny, but, preying upon the superstitions of the men
through certain devil's symbols tattooed on his chest,
Adam takes command. Among the prisoners from the
brig is Hilda Borner, proud and pretty, disguised as a
cabin boy to protect her from the bad men. Adam,
penetrating the disguise, falls in love with Hilda, who
defies him until after they have been marooned on a
desert island for a month. After that she discovers
she loves him and a mysterious way of delivery is found
for them.

"POPPY"

A musical comedy in three acts; book and lyrics by Dorothy Donnelly; music by Stephen Jones and Arthur Samuels. Produced by Philip Goodman, at the Apollo Theater, New York, September 3, 1923.

Cast of characters —

Sarah Tucker	Maude Ream Stover
Amos Sniffen	Jimmy Barry
Mary Delafield	Luella Gear
William Van Wyck	Alan Edwards
Princess Vronski Mameluke Pasha Tubbs	Emma Janvier
Mortimer Pottle	Robert Woolsey
Prof. Eustace McGargle	W. C. Fields
Poppy McGargle	Madge Kennedy
Judge Delafield	Hugh Chivers
Premier Dancer	Marion Chambers

Act I.—Outside of the Fair Grounds, Greenmeadow, Connecticut. 1874. Act II.—The House on the Hill. Act III.—At Mrs. Tucker's. Staged by the Author and Julian Alfred.

Poppy's mother ran away with a circus, serving as a wardrobe woman, and died soon after Poppy was born. The baby was adopted by Professor McGargle, one of the smoothest of the show's " grifters," who brought her up to be a fortune teller and his assistant. When she was twenty the show played the home town of Poppy's deceased parent. She discovered she was an heiress and she left the show to marry a rich but decent city fellow she had met on the grounds.

" CONNIE GOES HOME "

A comedy in three acts by Edward Childs Carpenter, from a story by Fannie Kilbourn. Produced by Kilbourn Gordon, Inc., at the Forty-ninth Street Theater, New York, September 6, 1923.

Cast of characters —

Edna St. Cloud	Valerie Vallaire
Josephine Pierce	Audrey Hart
Connie	Sylvia Field

Hilda..Martha Madison
Chester Barclay..................................Fred Irving Lewis
Albert...Harry E. McKee
Isobel Wayne.....................................Ethel Remey
Mrs. Merrick.....................................Lorna Elliott
George M. Barclay................................Berton Churchill
Jim ....Donald Foster
Mrs. Gibbs.......................................Florence Earle
Molly Latimer....................................Arlina McMahon
    Prologue—A Room in the Forties, West of Broadway, New York.
Act I.—The Library of George M. Barclay's House, Chicago. Act
II.—III.—The Library. Staged by Frederick Stanhope.

Connie, coming to New York from a home for destitute girls in Illinois, tries to get on as an actress. Her
specialty is playing " kid " parts. Out of work for
months she faces a choice of three ways out: She can
kill herself, she can go back to the home, or she can
accept the favors of rich men. She decides to go back
to the home. Not having enough money to pay her full
fare she makes up as a kid and tries to travel for half
fare. One conductor catches her and is about to throw
her off the train when a nice but slightly eccentric youth
rescues her. Thinking her a child he takes her to his
uncle's house in Chicago, where uncle keeps her on as
a sort of junior secretary, and finally she helps straighten
out a domestic problem which lands her in the young
man's arms.

" THE CROOKED SQUARE "

A comedy drama by Samuel Shipman and Alfred C.
Kennedy. Produced by Mrs. Henry B. Harris at the
Hudson Theater, New York, September 10, 1923.

Cast of characters —
Pete Darnell's Assistant..............................Edward Power
James Darnell...John Park
Barbara Kirkwood......................................Edna Hibbard
Thomas Harvey...Claude King
Robert Colby..Kenneth McKenna
Tessie..Agnes Mare
Peggy...Patricia Calvert
Pinkie..Rita Romilly

```
Matron.................................................Lida  Kane
Annie  Jordan.........................................Ruth  Donnelly
Laura.................................................Dorothy  West
Tony..................................................Jack  Larue
Laura's Father........................................John  Hall
Mrs.  Emily  Burnham..................................Leonore  Harris
Mr.  Edgemore.........................................C.  Henry  Gordon
Miss  Darby...........................................Grace  Burgess
Mr.  Dodson...........................................Franklyn  Hanna
Toyo..................................................T.  Tamamoto
Lissette..............................................Patricia  Calvert
Prince Stefano Solenski...............................Georges  Renavant
Alice  Harvey.........................................Gladys  Hanson
Smith.................................................Walter  Howe
```
    Act I.—Scene 1—Private Office of James Darnell's Detective
Agency. Scene 2—Discharge Room of the Woman's State Reform-
atory. Act II.—Private Room at Edgemore's Information Bureau.
Act III.—Drawing Room at the Harvey Residence. Staged by Fred
G. Stanhope.

Barbara Kirkwood, from the South, comes to New York seeking self-expression and a job. Down to her last cent she asks help of men on the street and is arrested as a street walker. Sent to the woman's reformatory she is released through the influence of a fake detective agency and smuggled into the home of the Thomas Harveys to spy out a scandal. Being in love with the son of the house she double-crosses her employers and saves everybody, including a fiancé for herself.

" MARY, MARY, QUITE CONTRARY "

A comedy in three acts by St. John Ervine. Produced by David Belasco at the Belasco Theater, New York, September 11, 1923.

Cast of characters —
```
Mrs.  Considine......................................Winifred  Fraser
Sheila...............................................Nora  Swinburne
Geoffrey.............................................Francis  Lister
Sir Henry Considine, K. C. M. G.....................C.  Aubrey  Smith
Rev.  Canon  Peter  Considine,  M.  A...............Orlando  Daly
Mary  Westlake  (Mrs.  James  Westlake)..............Mrs.  Fiske
Tori.................................................Naoe  Kondo
Mr.  Hobbs...........................................A.  P.  Kaye
Jenny................................................Audrey  Cameron
Ellen................................................Gladys  Burgess
```

Miss Mimms..Florence Edney
Mr. Beeby..Lennox Pawle
Act I.—The Garden of Hinton St. Henry Vicarage. Act II.—The
Drawing Room of the Vicarage. Act III.—The Garden. Time, the
Present. Staged by David Belasco.

Mary Westlake, a popular actress in London, journeys
to the vicarage of a country town in England to hear
a young poet read a play about Joan d' Arc. While
there she manages to stir the family up considerably by
fascinating the boy, Geoffrey Considine, who is engaged
to his cousin Sheila, and by making something of a
fool of Sir Henry Considine, previously a confirmed
bachelor. After which she exits laughingly and returns
to London.

" THE LULLABY "

A drama in a prologue, four acts and an epilogue
by Edward Knoblock. Produced by Charles Dillingham
at the Knickerbocker Theater, New York, September 17,
1923.

Cast of characters —

The Old Woman.......................................Florence Reed
The Young Girl.......................................Rose Hobart
Mariette...Alice Fleming
Claudet...Leonard Mudie
Elise...Mary Robson
Madelon...Florence Reed
Jacques...Harold Elliott
Bouillard...David Glassford
Rosalie...Grace Perkins
" La Poule "...Marianne Walter
Salignac...Henry Plimmer
Freddie Maynard...................................Charles Trowbridge
Victor Lebeau...Rupert Lumley
Count Carlo Boretti..................................Frank Morgan
Baroness Dax...Alice Fleming
Felix de Parme.......................................Peter Carpenter
A Young Sailor.......................................Leonard Mudie
An Older Sailor.......................................Bernard Thornton
Prologue—A Paris Street. Act I.—In Normandy. Act II.—Rosalie's
Attic, Paris; Maynard's Garden, Barbizon; Salignac's Rooms, Paris.
Act III.—Madelon's Boudoir, Paris; Restaurant Pompadour. Act IV.—
Old Wall, Tunis; A Prison Cell. Epilogue—A Paris Street. Staged
by Fred G. Latham.

Old Madelon, walking the streets of Paris, pauses to
advise a young girl not to keep the assignation with her

lover upon which she is bent. As she relates her own
life the action slips back to the days of Madelon's youth
in Normandy. There she found herself in trouble at
eighteen. The parents of the boy who was the father
of her child refuse to let him marry her. To Paris she
goes, and there, to support her baby, she becomes the
mistress, first of an American painter who leaves her,
and later, of an international jewel thief, who is dragged
from her by the police. Down she drifts until she is a
painted harlot on the streets of Tunis with but one fixed
idea of honor. She will have nothing to do with the
sailors because she knows her son has entered the navy.
When one who is drunk tries to force his attentions
upon her he is shot and Madelon serves twenty years
in prison for his murder. Out of prison she drifts back
to Paris, where the epilogue leaves her finishing her
story to the young woman.

" THE CHANGELINGS "

A comedy in three acts by Lee Wilson Dodd. Produced by Henry Miller's Theater Co., at the Henry Miller
Theater, New York, September 17, 1923.

Cast of characters —

Dora Faber.....................................Laura Hope Crews
Karen Aldcroft..Blanche Bates
Fenwick Faber......................................Reginald Mason
Wallace Aldcroft.......................................Henry Miller
Fisher...Elmer Brown
Wicky Faber...Geoffrey Kerr
Kay Faber...Ruth Chatterton
Clyde Halstead...Felix Krembs
Degan...Walter Baldwin

Act I.—A Room in the Apartment of Wallace Aldcroft. Act II.—
Clyde Halstead's Bachelor Quarters. Act III. and Epilogue—Same as
Act I.

(See page 188.)

"PETER WESTON"

A drama in four acts by Frank Dazey and Leighton Osmun. Produced by Sam H. Harris at the Sam H. Harris Theater, New York, September 18, 1923.

Cast of characters —

Isabelle Weston.....................................Millicent Hanley
James Weston...Jay Hanna
Jessie Weston.......................................Judith Anderson
The Maid..Hope Drown
Peter Weston..Frank Keenan
John Weston...Clyde North
Henry Vannard...Fred Mosley
Paul Vannard.......................................Wilfred Lytell
The Butler..Geo. W. Barnum
William Harris.......................................Paul Everton
The Police Officer...................................A. O. Huhn
    Act I., II., III. and IV.—The Home of Peter Weston, in the Town of Weston, New York. Staged by Frank Keenan.

Peter Weston is an old and successful man, iron willed and selfish. His wife dead, worn out by his domination, he tries to direct the lives of his three children and fails. The artist son he had forced into his pump works accidentally kills the man who has discovered a shortage in his accounts. His daughter confesses that she had been the sweetheart of the man slain and that she expects to bear him a child. His youngest son, made miserable by the family scandals, goes into a consumption brought on by drinking. Unable, with all his boasted influence, to obtain a reprieve for his convicted son, Peter Weston is left mumbling into the telephone at dawn of the day set for the boy's electrocution.

" CHAINS "

A drama in three acts by Jules Eckert Goodman.
Produced by William A. Brady at the Playhouse, New
York, September 19, 1923.

Cast of characters —
John Maury..William Morris
Maud...Maud Turner Gordon
Harry..Paul Kelly
Grace...Katherine Alexander
Richard...Gilbert Emery
Jean Trowbridge.....................................Helen Gahagan
    Act I., II. and III.—The Home of John Maury. Staged by William A. Brady, Jr.

Jean Trowbridge and Harry Maury had been more
than sweethearts while both were at college, expecting
at the time to be married later. They quarrel, however,
and separate, to meet again in New York after five years
have passed. The sight of Jean, flashily independent
and rather " jazzy," convinces Harry that she has come
to reproach him for his desertion of her. He seeks to
be rid of an unhappy conscience by going away, which
exposes the story of his trouble to his somewhat horrified parents. They seek a settlement with Jean. But
she refuses money, and will not think of marriage. She
is content to bear her share of the blame for anything
that has happened. Believing there has been a child
born to her the Maurys insist that it shall be made
respectable by the marriage of its parents. But again
Jean refuses. Respectability, so called, may be gained
that way, but not self-respect. She is still holding
her ground at the end, but she has agreed to consider
the proposal of Harry's Uncle Richard, who is older
and more understanding than any of the others.

"GREENWICH VILLAGE FOLLIES"

A revue in two acts, lyrics by Irving Cæsar and John M. Anderson; music by Louis A Hirsh and Con Conrad. Produced by The Bohemians, Inc., at the Winter Garden Theater, New York, September 20, 1923.

Principals engaged —

Marion Green
George Rasely
Al Sexton
Tom Howard
Denman Maley
Joe Lyons
Sammy White
Johannes Jossefson
The Mandels

Daphne Pollard
Eva Puck
Ruth Urban
Irene Delroy
Josephine Adair
Ula Sharon
Martha Graham
The Cansinos

Staged by John Murray Anderson.

"MUSIC BOX REVUE"

A musical revue in two acts; lyrics and music by Irving Berlin. Produced by Sam H. Harris at the Music Box Theater, New York, September 22, 1923.

Frank Tinney
Joseph Santley
John Steel
Robert Benchley
Hugh Cameron
Solly Ward
Phil Baker
Charles Columbus
Nelson Snow

Florence Moore
Grace Moore
Ivy Sawyer
Lora Sanderson
Florence O'Denishawn
Mme. Dora Stroeva
Brox Sisters
Frances Mahan
Dorothy Dilley
Nellie King

Staged by Hassard Short.

"A LESSON IN LOVE"

A comedy in three acts by Rudolph Besier and May Eddington. Produced by Lee Shubert at the Thirty-ninth Street Theater, New York, September 24, 1923.

Cast of characters —

Captain Andre Briquette..........................William Faversham
Beatrice Audley.......................................Emily Stevens
Dean Carey...Edward Emery

Sir Nevil Moreton..Hugh Buckler
Mrs. Carey..Grace Henderson
Laura Westerly..Gilda Leary
Masters...Marian Hutchins
Waiter..F. S. Merlin
    Act I.—II.—Living Room in Mrs. Audley's House at Norman Arches.
Act III.—Private Rooms in Savoy Hotel, London. Staged by William
Faversham.

Captain Andre Briquette, following Beatrice Audley
home from the seaside resort at which he had first been
impressed by her beauty, finds her not only engaged to
Sir Nevil Moreton, but a good deal of a stickler for the
conventions and something of a prude. He sees her,
for instance, turn from her door Laura Westerly, a
friend of her girlhood, because Laura has so far forgotten her responsibility to society as to run from an
unloved husband to live with an ideal lover in the
Transvaal. Thereupon the Captain, being French and
a defender of love for its own sake, determines to teach
Miss Beatrice something of passion's power. Within a
fortnight he has so completely charmed her that she
throws over her fiance and is willing to fly with Briquette,
either as his wife or his mistress, whenever he says the
word. Extracting this confession from her the Captain
proves himself a better man than even Beatrice suspected
and all is as it should be.

" CHICKEN FEED "

(" WAGES, FOR WIVES ")

A comedy in three acts by **Guy Bolton**. Produced by
John Golden at the Little Theater, New York, September
24, 1923.

Cast of characters —

Jim Bailey..Frank McCormack
Annie Bailey...Marie Day
Luella Logan..Leila Bennett
Hughie Logan.......................................Arthur Aylsworth
Danny Kester..Stuart Fox
Nell Bailey..Roberta Arnold
Chester Logan...Frank Allworth

```
Mr. Tevis..........................................Mart Fuller Golden
Judge MacLean...........................................Sam Reed
Oscar.....................................................Bert West
Miss Johnson......................................Katherine Wilson
Harry Taylor..........................................George Spelvin
```
    Act I.—Danny's Living Room. Act II.—Scene 1—The Logan Home.
Scene 2—Same as Act I.   Act III.—Office of the Kester Kosy Kottage
Kompany. Staged by Mitchell Smith.

(See page 235.)

" NIFTIES OF 1923 "

A musical revue in two acts by Sam Bernard and
William Collier. Produced by Charles Dillingham at
the Fulton Theater, New York, September 25, 1923.

Principals engaged —

William Collier	Hazel Dawn
Sam Bernard	Ray Dooley
Frank Crumit	Helen Broderick
Gus Van	Helyn Eby Rock
Joe Schenk	Jane Greene
Florenz Ames	Twelve Tiller Girls
William Holbrook	Cortez and Peggy

" CASANOVA "

A drama in a prologue and three acts by Lorenzo de
Azertis, translated by Sidney Howard. Produced by A.
H. Woods and Gilbert Miller at the Empire Theater, New
York, September 26, 1923.

Cast of characters —

```
Columbine...........................................Beatrice Belreva
A Guitar Player...............................................Doris
Pulcinella.............................................George Royle
Battista, His Page.....................................Herbert James
A Fat Man..........................................Harry Fielding
A Gentleman in Black..............................Horace Healy
A Roman Soldier..................................George Blackmore
Alfani-Celli..............................................Philip Wood
Manzoni..................................................B. N. Lewin
A Waiter............................................Walter Soderling
A Gambler...............................................William Marr
Giulietta ............................................... Dinarzade
Captain Michael Echedy...........................Mario Majeroni
Henriette.......................................Katherine Cornell
Giacomo Casanova, Chevalier de Seingalt...........Lowell Sherman
```

A Lieutenant...Ralph Belmont
An Innkeeper..Edward Le Hay
First Archer...J. C. Wallace
Second Archer.......................................Edward F. Snow
Leduc...Ernest Cossart
A Banker in Cesena.................................Harold Hartsell
A Gambler...Harry Redding
Monsieur Dubois......................................Victor Benoit
The Abbe Bernis....................................Horace Braham
The Innkeeper.......................................A. G. Andrews
Monsieur Antoine...................................David Glassford
First Postillion......................................James Powers
Second Postillion................................Jacob Kingsberry
Third Postillion...................................Frank Newcomb
Fourth Postillion.................................Charles Vincent
The Beautiful Governess.............................Gypsy O'Brien
The Dancer from Milan.................................Mary Ellis
The Courtesan......................................Judith Vosselli
Rose..Shelia Hayes
Manon...Nellie Burt

   Act I.—" The Hours." The Principal Room of an Inn at Cesena,
Italy; in the year 1755. Act II.—" The Days." A Private Room
in the Hotel des Balances, on the Shores of the Lake of Geneva.
Act III.—" The Century." The Same Room, Twenty-two Years
Later. Incidental Music by Deems Taylor.

Giacomo Casanova, the self-styled Chevalier de Sein-
galt, having had many mistresses in his youth, meets and
is supremely impressed by the beauty and charm of
Henriette, who has fled the home of a husband she loathes.
Ardent is the wooing of Casanova and he elopes with
Henriette at dawn the next day, taking with him much
gold that he has won at cards. For ninety days they live
gloriously on the shores of Lake Geneva. Then Casanova, having fallen deeply in love with Henriette, permits
her friends to come for her, rather than that she should
know the poverty his adventurous life has again forced
upon him. She is no sooner gone than Casanova finds
himself again in funds, and learns, too, that she has been
sewing baby caps. Sending wildly over all the known
roads leaving Geneva he seeks to bring his love back,
but though his postillions find many Henriettes for him,
they cannot overtake the right one, and the great lover
is distressed. Twenty years later, returned to Geneva to
renew his memories of his greatest romance, he meets his
and Henriette's daughter and expires in an ecstasy of regret that he cannot make himself known to her.

" TARNISH "

A play in three acts by Gilbert Emery. Produced by
John Cromwell, Inc., at the Belmont Theater, New York,
October 1, 1923.

Cast of characters —

Josephine Lee Tevis..............................Mrs. Russ Whytall
Mrs. Healy......................................Mrs. Jacques Martin
Apolline Stutts...Marion Lord
Letitia Tevis...Ann Harding
Emmett Carr..Tom Powers
Adolph Tevis...Albert Gran
Nettie Dark...Fania Marinoff
Aggie..Mildred MacLeod
    Act I.—Sitting Room of the Tevis Flat at 189th Street. Act II.—
An Apartment West of Broadway. Act III.—Same as Act I. Staged
by John Cromwell.

(See page 263.)

" FLORIANI'S WIFE "

A drama in three acts by Luigi Pirandello, adapted by
Ann Sprague MacDonald. Produced by Cornelia Pen-
field Lathrop at the Greenwich Village Theater, New
York, October 13, 1923.

Cast of characters —

The Widow Naccheri..............................Marion Beckwith
Roghi...Hamilton MacFadden
Don Camillo Zonchi..................................Harold Webster
Vanna Floriani...................................Margaret Wycherly
Marco Mauri.......................................Jacques Lebaudy
Dr. Roberto Floriani.........................George Bergen George
Betta..Eleanor Hutchison
Livia Floriani..Mary Hone
Signorina Ernestina Galiffi.......................Jennie A. Eustace
Don Cesarino.......................................Francis Sadtler
Barberina..Gladys Clarke
A Nurse..Gladys Clarke
    Act I.—The Sitting Room of the Pension Zonchi, Northern Italy.
Act II. and III.—A Room in Dr. Floriani's Villa. Staged by Margaret
Wycherly and Henry Stillman.

Dr. Robert Floriani, marrying young, divorces his
wife, Vanni, when their daughter is three years old, retaining custody of the child. Thirteen years later Flori-

ani, called as a surgeon to attend Vanni, saves her life. When she is well he, remorseful because he believes he may have been partly to blame for the wife's weakness as a young woman, proposes a remarriage, with the understanding that the daughter, who believes her mother dead, shall look upon her now as her stepmother. Because of her eagerness to be near her daughter Vanni agrees. The girl, resenting another woman in her sainted mother's place, hates her supposed stepmother and, because there is no record of a ceremony, believes Vanni to be her father's mistress. When a second child is born to Vanni the daughter announces her belief that it is illegitimate, at which accusation Vanni rises in rebellion and announces herself the mother of her accuser. Then she takes her baby and again leaves her husband's house.

"THE MAGIC RING"

A musical comedy in a prologue and three acts by Zelda Sears; music by Harold Levey. Produced by Henry W. Savage, Inc., at the Liberty Theater, New York, October 1, 1923.

Cast of characters —

```
Zobeide..................................................Madge North
Vizier..................................................Joseph Macaulay
Abdullah..............................................Worthe Faulkner
Henry Brockway.....................................Sydney Greenstreet
Phoebe Brockway......................................Janet Murdock
Mrs. Bellamy...........................................Phoebe Crosby
Iris Bellamy.......................................Jeanette MacDonald
Tom Hammond..........................................Boyd Marshall
Policeman................................................Ed Wakefield
Policeman...................................................John Lyons
Polly Church.....................................................Mitzi
Minnie.........................................Wait Until You See Her
Moe Bernheimer......................................James B. Carson
Stella..................................................Estelle Birney
Specialty Dancers..................................Carlos and Inez
    Prologue—A Room in the Seraglio of a Grand Vizier. Act I.—
Henry Brockway's Antique Shop. Act II.—Studio of Mrs. Bellamy's
Home. Act III.—Same as Act I.
```

Polly Church, poor but gifted, is making a living with a monkey and a hand organ when she bumps into a magic ring at an antique store and finds herself next act the center of a romance which turns out to be positively the grandest adventure she ever had.

" WHAT'S YOUR WIFE DOING?"

A farce comedy in three acts by Herbert Hall Winslow and Emil Nyitray. Produced by Arthur Klein at the Forty-ninth Street Theater, New York, October 1, 1923.

Cast of characters —

Gerald Warner, known as " Jerry "	Glenn Anders
Hawkins	Harry Lilliford
Officer Corrigan	J. Edward O'Malley
Edith Somers	Isabelle Leighton
Burr Shrewsbury	Joseph Bell
Judge Somers	Norman Hackett
Christopher Skinner	Louis Simon
Beatrice Skinner	Dorothy Mackaye
Lyman Webster	Hal Munnis
Bellamy Warner	Shep Camp
Samuel Peabody Skinner	George Pauncefort
Detective Magee	George Spelvin
Detective Moriarty	Frank Emmett

Act I.—Scene 1—On the Front Steps of Judge Somers's Home. Scene 2—Drawing Room of the Somers's Home. Act II.—Jerry's Rooms. Act III.—Scene 1—The Front Steps. Same as Act I. Scene 2—The Drawing Room.

Christopher Skinner is in bad with a rich uncle because he married Beatrice. Uncle is coming to town and the Skinners decide to frame a divorce, using uncle as a witness so he can see for himself. Then, after Christopher is again in uncle's will, the Skinners will meet in Paris, remarry and spend the money. Jerry Warner agrees, for a price, to act as the necessary co-respondent. The scene is set for Jerry's apartments, but everything goes wrong except Beatrice. She gets squiffy on champagne, which leads her husband to believe the worst. An adjustment of sorts is effected at 10.45 p. m.

" VIRGINIA RUNS AWAY "

(" FORBIDDEN ")

A comedy in three acts by Sydney Rosenfeld. Produced by John Cort at Daly's Theater, New York, October 1, 1923.

Cast of characters —

```
Roger Carlyle.........................................Cyril Keightley
Ormsby................................................Roy Cochrane
Rachel................................................Nellie Callahan
Miss Alice Carson.....................................Mary Young
The Mother Superior...................................Lillian Kingsbury
Frederick Titus, M. D.................................Harry Minturn
Virginia..............................................Josephine Stevens
Hastings Westover.....................................John Daly Murphy
Mrs. Westover.........................................Rose Winter
Peter.................................................William Leonard
    Synopsis: Act I.—Roger Carlyle's Apartment. Act II.—At Miss
Carson's. Act III.—Same as Act I.
```

Virginia, at seventeen, is curious as to the meaning and significance of life, and rebellious. She runs away from the convent where she is studying and elopes with a young man who is no more knowing than she and considerably less courageous. She takes him to a lecture on birth control and then insists on going home with him rather than back to the convent. A sane aunt understands Virginia well enough not to oppose her, treats her and her young man as though they were adventuring children and soon straightens out Virginia's complexes.

" CYMBELINE "

A romance by William Shakespeare. Produced by Lee Shubert at the Jolson Theater, New York, October 2, 1923.

Cast of characters —

```
                        BRITONS:
Cymbeline, King of Britain..........................V. L. Granville
Cloten..............................................France Bendtsen
Posthumous Leonatus.................................E. H. Sothern
Belarius............................................Albert Howson
```

```
Guiderius...............................................Murray Kinnell
Arviragus...............................................H. Fisher White
Pisanio................................................Vincent Sternroyd
Cornelius....................................................Frank Peters
First British Lord...................................John MacFarlane
Second British Lord...................................Forbes Dawson
Queen............................................Lenore Chippendale
Helen.......................................................Florence Fair
A Lady to the Queen................................Eugenie Webb
Imogen..................................................Julia Marlowe
```

ROMANS:

```
Iachimo...............................................Frederick Lewis
Philario...................................................T. G. Bailey
Caius Lucius.........................................Wallis Roberts
A Roman Captain.....................................Denis Auburn
A Roman Captain......................................Verne Collins
A French Gentleman.................................Milano Tilden
```

An acting version originally arranged by Mr. Sothern in two acts and twenty scenes. During this engagement Mr. Sothern and Miss Marlowe also played " The Taming of the Shrew," " Twelfth Night," " Hamlet," " Merchant of Venice " and " Romeo and Juliet."

" HAMMERSTEIN'S 9 O'CLOCK REVUE "

A musical revue by Harold Simpson and Morris Harvey. Presented by Arthur Hammerstein at the Century Roof, New York, October 4, 1923.

Principals engaged —

Morris Harvey	Cicely Debenham
William Valentine	Phyllis Joyce
Wynn Richmond	Irene Olsen
Frank Hector	Ann Rogers
Colin Campbell	Eva Brick

A favorite late evening entertainment of English sketches and specialties brought over from the Little Theater, London.

" WINDOWS "

A comedy in three acts by John Galsworthy. Produced by the Theater Guild at the Garrick Theater, New York, October 8, 1923.

Cast of characters —

Geoffrey March	Moffat Johnston
Joan March	Helen Westley
Mary March	Frieda Inescort
Johnny March	Kenneth MacKenna
Cook	Alice Belmore Cliffe
Mrs. Bly	Henry Travers
Faith Bly	Phyllis Povah
Blunter	George Baxter
Mr. Barnabas	Francis Tweed

Act I., II. and III.—The Dining Room after breakfast, lunch, dinner.

Three of the Marches, Geoffrey, the father; Johnny, the son, and Mary, the daughter, are idealists of a sort. Mrs. March is as definitely practical. To the Marches comes the chance to take on Faith Bly as a maid, Faith being the daughter of a philosopher who washes the windows. She is just out of jail after serving a commuted sentence for infanticide. She had smothered her illegitimate child to save it from the curse of living. The idealist Marches are in favor of helping Faith; Mrs. March is against it, but gives way. Faith goes to work and two weeks later is caught kissing Johnny. Mrs. March insists she shall leave. Johnny insists she shall stay. A kiss is nothing, and the girl still needs their help. But Faith has other plans. She wants to be loved. So she leaves. " Things are not what they seem, and ideals six-a-penny unless founded on realities," is the Galsworthy text.

"BATTLING BUTTLER"

A musical comedy in three acts, adapted by Ballard MacDonald from the original of Brightman, Melford and Furber; music by Walter L. Rosemont. Produced by George Choos at the Selwyn Theater, New York, October 8, 1923.

Cast of characters —

Deacon Grafton...................................Eugene McGregor
Mrs. Alfred Buttler.....................................Helen Eley
Nancy...Helen La Vonne
Marigold...Mildred Keats
Edith...Marie Saxon
A Chauffeur..George Sands
Alfred Buttler......................................Charles Ruggles
Frank Bryant..Jack Squire
Ernest Hozier......................................William Kent
Sweeney...Guy Voyer
Spink..Teddy McNamara
Battling Buttler.......................................Frank Sinclair
Bertha Buttler.....................................Francis Halliday
Feature Dancers................................Grant and Wing
Eccentric Dancers...................George Sands and Mack Davis
Exceptional Dancer................................George Dobbs
Act I.—The Home of Alfred Buttler, Silver Lake, N. H.   Act
II.—" Sweeney's " at Malba, L. I.   Act III.—The Four Hundred
Athletic Club, New York City.   Staged by Guy Bragdon.

Alfred Buttler, somewhat resembling in appearance the welter-weight champion boxer, whispers to his trusting wife that he is, indeed, the champion himself. Which gives him a chance to leave home for weeks at a time to attend to his training. In the second act, however, his wife and all the chorus follow him and the real Buttler, liking the joke, insists that the fake Buttler shall take his place in the ring.

"THE NERVOUS WRECK"

A comedy in three acts by Owen Davis, founded on a story by E. J. Rath. Produced by Lewis and Gordon at the Sam H. Harris Theater, New York, October 9, 1923.

Cast of characters —

Sally Morgan..June Walker
Henry Williams..Otto Kruger
Tim...Jay Wilson
Chester Underwood....................................Albert Hackett
Jerome Underwood.....................................William Holden
Harriet Underwood............................Winifred Wellington
Andy Nabb...Riley Hatch
Mort...Hobart Cavanaugh
Dan..J. Elmer Thompson
Bob Wells..Edward Arnold
Jud Morgan...Joseph Brennan

Act I.—Scene 1—Black Top Canyon, Arizona. Scene 2—Living Room of Bar M Ranch. Act II.—The Exterior of the Ranch House. Act III.—Living Room of the Ranch House. Staged by Addison Pitt.

Henry Williams, a clerk from Pittsburgh, worries himself into the last stages of nervous exhaustion. On the advice of his physicians he goes to an Arizona ranch for a long and quiet rest. He is there but a few weeks when the rancher's daughter, to escape marrying a bulky sheriff to whom she has been promised, tricks Henry into eloping with her. They run out of gasoline, are forced to hide on a strange ranch, where they accept jobs as cook and waiter, and finally are pursued by both the girl's father and her sheriff fiance. All of which is hard on the nervous wreck, though he suddenly finds himself quite able to stand it.

" LAUNZI "

A drama in three acts by Ferenc Molnar, adapted by
Edna St. Vincent Millay. Produced by Arthur Hopkins
at the Plymouth Theater, New York, October 10, 1923.

Cast of characters —

Claire	Adrienne Morrison
Frederick	Charles Millward
Anna	Xenia Polinoff
Launzi	Pauline Lord
Imre	Saxon Kling
Redempta	Mary Hubbard
Honorata	Irene Shirley
Firmina	Edith Yeager
Dativa	Mildred Whitney
Louis	Edward Robinson
Dr. Jeki	Edgar Stehli
Dr. Anton	William J. McClure
Policeman	Benedict MacQuarrie
Ivan	Albert Bruning
Dr. Barody	Lark Taylor
Madame Ivan	Christine Compton

Act I.—Scene 1—Living Room in Villa on the Adriatic. Scene
2—Bedroom in Same Villa. Act II.—Scene 1—Lower Quay of
Embankment, Budapest. Scene 2—Room in Ivan's Apartments. Act
III.—Tower Room in the Country House of Ivan's Mother. Staged
by Arthur Hopkins.

Launzi, innocent and impulsive at eighteen, is desperately in love with Imre, a youth of twenty. But Imre
has achieved an even more desperate passion for Launzi's
mother, a worldly fascinator of thirty-nine, who will have
nothing to do with him. Realizing the hopelessness of
her love Launzi throws herself into the Danube, hoping
to die. She is rescued, but insists upon believing that
so far as Imre is concerned she is dead. She asks that
a beautiful bier be prepared for her and Imre invited
to see her in her shroud. Alienists advise that Launzi
be humored in this and the bier is prepared. Imre is
inspired with pity but not with love. Thereafter Launzi
lives with the conviction that she is dead. Strapped to
her back constantly are a pair of angel's wings, and her
family and nurses treat her as they assume angels should
be treated. One night Launzi puts her angel's wings
to the test and tries to fly from her tower window with,
it is assumed, disastrous results.

" THE GRAND GUIGNOL PLAYERS "

From the Grand Guignol Theater, Paris. Presented by the Selwyns at the Frolic Theater, New York, October 15, 1923.

UNE NUIT AU BOUGE
(" A Night in a Den ")
Drama in One Act by M. Charles Mere

Lucienne de Martiny...........................Mlle. Marcelle Gylda
Le Prince Attalonga..............................M. Leo. Brizard
Le Garcon..M. Robert Seller
Le Rouge...M. Louis Defresne
Petit Louis......................................M. Jules Sylvere
Bebert...M. Ernest Machard

LE COURT CIRCUIT
(" The Short Circuit ")
Comedy in One Act by MM. Benjamin Rabier et Eugene Joullot

Anatole Loupy....................................M. Robert Seller
Robert...M. Marcel Des Mazes
Nina de Cansac...............................Mlle. Simone Hermann
Felicie......................................Mlle. Andree Duchesne

SUR LE BANC
(" On The Bench ")
Comedy in One Act by M. Henry Hirsch

Une Midinette (a Shop Girl)...............Mlle. Simone Hermann
Un Vieux Monsieur (an Old Man)............M. Maurice Henriet
Un Etudiant (a Student).....................M. Marcel des Mazes

AU RAT MORT, CABINET NO. 6
(" At Dead Rat, Room No. 6 ")
Drama in One Act by MM. Andre de Lorde et Pierre Chaine

Le General Gregoroff.............................M. Paul Bernier
Comte de Lutzi...............................M. Jacques Derives
Lea...Mlle. Jane Meryem
Alice.......................................Mlle. Estelle Duclos
Victor...M. Louis Defresne
Un Garcon, I er Agent, et 2 eme Agent, 1st Gendarme, 2d Gendarme.

During a ten-weeks season, of which the above was the opening bill, the Grand Guignol Players presented the following short plays:

Nounouche, Au Coin Joli, L'Horrible Experience, Sur La Dalle, Alcide Pepie, Les Crucifies, Un Peu de Musique, Catherine Goulden, Les Trois Masques, Seul, Gardiens De Phare, Le System du Docteur Goudron et du Professeur Plume, Le Kama Sontra, Le Bonheur, Le Laboratoire des Hallucinations, La Fiole, Prenez Ma Dame, Sol Hyam's Brocanteur, La Griffe, Petite Bonnie Serieuse.

During one week Alla Nazimova, having been barred from the Keith Vaudeville Circuit because of the boldness of her sketch, " The Unknown," joined the Guignol Players.

"FOR ALL OF US"

A play in three acts by William Hodge. Produced by Lee Shubert at the Forty-ninth Street Theater, New York, October 15, 1923.

Cast of characters —

Frederic Warren	Frank Losee
Walter Fisher	Echlin Gayer
Joey	Florence Mason
Mrs. Warren	Marion Abbott
Dr. Shipman	Frank Burbeck
Ethel Warren	Belle Murry
Tom Griswald	William Hodge
Eugene Merrick	Robert Middlemass
Frederic Warren, Jr.	Frederick Howard
Mr. Dysart	Philip Dunning
A Maid	Rita Sherman

Act I.—Sleeping Room in the Home of Mr. Warren. Act II.—Library in the Home of Mr. Warren. Act III.—Same as Act II. Staged by William Hodge.

Tom Griswald is foreman of a gang of ditch diggers. He whistles as he works. Outside the house of Frederick Warren, banker, his whistling attracts the attention of Warren, confined to his room by the paralysis of his lower limbs. Warren, out of curiosity, sends for Griswald, finds him a happy Irishman who had found a satisfying philosophy of life in the Bible while he was spending thirty days in jail for drunkenness. Basicly the Griswald philosophy is founded in the belief that the body can be no healthier or cleaner than the mind that directs its functioning. Right thinking makes right living. Gladly he passes on his good thoughts to the banker and in time is able to clear the old gentleman's mind of a beautiful stenographer who had gotten him into trouble. Then the paralysis disappears. Griswald, too, is rewarded by finding the beautiful stenographer in the banker's thoughts to be his own lost daughter, taken from him in his days of sin.

" THE SHAME WOMAN "

A drama in nine scenes by Lula Vollmer. Produced by the Independent Theater, Inc., at the Greenwich Village Theater, New York, October 16, 1923.

Cast of characters —

Lize Burns....................................Florence Rittenhouse
Lily...Thelma Paige
John Crombie...................................John J. Ward
Mrs. Burns.....................................Minnie Dupree
Martha Case....................................Florence Gerald
Craig Anson....................................Edward Pawley
Ezra Case......................................Claude Cooper
Matron...Jessie Graham
Jailer...Allen W. Nagle
Minister.......................................G. O. Taylor
   Scene 1, 2 and 3—Lize Burns's Cabin. Scene 4—Outside Big Jim's Store. Scene 5, 6, 7 and 8—The Cabin. Scene 9—A Room in a Prison.

Lize Burns has for twenty years lived in a lonely cabin in the North Carolina mountains, shunned by her neighbors as one of the " hill women " who had sinned, Craig Anson, the mayor's son, being the author of her shame. With her is living Lily, an adopted daughter, an orphan she adopted following a fever epidemic. The girl is the idol of her heart, though she feels herself unworthy. Hearing Lily has been meeting a man at night Lize tells her the story of her own shame in the hope of protecting her from a similar fate. At the story's conclusion it is evident she is too late. The girl kills herself, and when Craig Anson calls at the cabin and Lize realizes he again is the man responsible, she stabs him to prevent his " laughin' and tellin'." She refuses to permit her little girl's name to be brought into the case, and calmly goes to the gallows for the murder of Anson.

" THE PLAYER QUEEN "

A " poetic farce " by William Butler Yeats. Produced
by the Neighborhood Players at the Neighborhood Playhouse, New York, October 16, 1923.

Cast of characters —

First Old Man	Albert Carroll
Second Old Man	John Scott
Third Old Man	Leonard Carey
Old Woman	Reba Garden
Septimus	Dennis Cleugh
First Poet	Perry Ivins
Second Poet	John F. Roche
First Citizen	Philip Mann
Second Citizen	Polaire Weissmann
First Countryman	John Taylor
Second Countryman	Marian Morehouse
Big Countryman	Charner Batson
His Wife	Joanna Roos
Old Beggar	Perry Ivins
Prime Minister	Douglas Garden
Nona	Pamela Gaythorne
Fourth Player	Dan Walker
Sixth Player	Lily Lubell
Two Musicians	Martin Wolfson, Ira Uhr
The Queen	Esther Mitchell
Decima	Aline MacMahon
The Bishop	John Campbell
Four Pages	Joanna Roos, Ruth Lee, Ann Schmidt, Frances Cowlei
Two Hangmen	Philip Mann, Alfred Hagnauei
Other Citizens	Adeline Ruby, Charles Wagner, Blanche Talmud, Arthur Reed

Scene 1—An Open Space at the Meeting of Two Streets. Scene 2
—The Throne Room.

During this, its tenth subscription season, the Neighborhood Players also presented Bernard Shaw's " The
Showing-up of Blanco Posnet " (given in conjunction with
" The Player Queen ") ; " This Fine-Pretty World," a folk
play of the Kentucky mountains by Percy Mackaye; the
Festival Dancers in " An Arab Fantasia " and " Buffoon,"
and " The Grand Street Follies." Nine special performances of H. R. Lenormand's " Time Is a Dream "
were also given.

"GINGER"

A musical comedy in two acts by Harold Orlob and H. I. Phillips. Produced by Harold Orlob at Daly's Theater, New York, October 16, 1923.

Cast of characters —
```
Ruth Warewell...........................................Nellie Breen
Mrs. Warewell...........................................Olive May
Willie Fall.............................................Joe Mack
Marjorie Frayne.........................................Sibylla Bowhan
A Buyer.................................................Virginia Andersen
Dick Warewell...........................................Walter Douglas
Clix Young..............................................Norman Sweatser
Virginia Warewell — "GINGER".............................Leeta Corder
Joe Bagley..............................................Thos. F. Swift
Joe Bagley, Sr..........................................Chas. J. Stine
```
Act I.—Porch Bazaar at Mrs. Warewell's Country House, Bronxville, N. Y. Act II.—Scene 1—Joe Bagley's Camp, Catskill Mountains. Scene 2—A Forest in the Catskills. Scene 3—Bagley's Camp.

"THE DANCERS"

A play in four acts by Gerald du Maurier. Produced by the Messrs. Shubert at the Broadhurst Theater, New York, October 17, 1923.

Cast of characters —
ACT I
```
Nat.....................................................Kevitt Manton
Tony....................................................Richard Bennett
Mack....................................................Fuller Mellish, Jr.
Maxine..................................................Jean Oliver
Settler.................................................Monroe Childs
"Little Willie".........................................Alfred Holborn
Nellie..................................................Barbara Bennett
Wal.....................................................Edwin Hensley
Billie..................................................Almerin Gowing
John Carruthers.........................................Templer Powell
Charlie Paxton..........................................William J. Donovan
Silas...................................................Edmund Gurney
Buke....................................................James Velton
Pete....................................................Henry Skelton
Mike....................................................Alex Huban
Charley.................................................Barton Hepburn
Indian..................................................John Whiffen
```
ACT II
```
Mrs. Gabrielle Mayne....................................Daisy Belmore
Miss Phoebe Pringle.....................................Vera Mellish
```

```
George  Fothering.................................H.  Langdon  Bruce
Una  Lowery...........................................Flora  Sheffield
Evan  Carruthers......................................Pat  Somerset
```

ACT III

```
Una  Lowery...........................................Flora  Sheffield
Dar...............................................Affie  Chippendale
Mrs.  Mayne...........................................Daisy  Belmore
George  Fothering.................................H.  Langdon  Bruce
Lord  Anthony  Chieveley............................Richard  Bennett
Billy.................................................Almerin  Gowing
Gustave.................................................Jean  Delval
Pierre.............................................Francois  Godchaux
Another  Waiter........................................Anton  Cucci
```

ACT IV

```
Stage  Manager..........................................Jean  Delval
Evan  Carruthers......................................Pat  Somerset
Jeanne,  Maxine's  Maid............................Georgette  Passedoit
Maxine................................................Jean  Oliver
John  Carruthers....................................Templer  Powell
The  Duke  of  Winfield..............................Wilfred  Noy
Lord  Anthony  Chieveley............................Richard  Bennett
```
Act. I.—Western Canada. Act II.—London. Act III.—Hotel Savoy, London. Act IV.—Back Stage in a French Hotel.

As plain Tony, Anthony Chieveley is running a saloon and a cabaret in Western Canada, when he is notified that he has succeeded to a title and a fortune in England. He is eager to return because he has left Una Lowery, the sweetheart of his youth, waiting for him over there. But also he hates to leave Maxine, a dancer, of whom he has grown fond in his own café. In England Una has been less faithful. She, too, is a dancer, though in society, and has succumbed to the insidious influences of the supper club, American jazz and the importunings of a handsome dancing partner. When Tony comes for her she finds it impossible to marry him and put upon him the burden of her shame, so she kills herself. Six years later, Tony, still heavy hearted, finds Maxine dancing in Paris and they decide to patch up their old romance.

" WHITE DESERT "

A drama in four acts by Maxwell Anderson. Produced by Brock Pemberton at the Princess Theater, New York, October 18, 1923.

Cast of characters —
```
Michael Kane.........................................Frank Shannon
Mary Kane.............................................Beth Merrill
Sverre Peterson.......................................George Abbott
Annie Peterson........................................Ethel Wright
Dugan.................................................John Friend
     Prologue—A Snow-Covered North Dakota Prairie.  Act I., II., III.
and IV.—Inside and outside Michael Kane's Claim Shack.  Staged by
Mr. Pemberton.
```

Michael and Mary Kane have moved on to a North Dakota homestead in the middle of winter. Their nearest neighbors are the Petersons, Sverre and Annie. Peterson, a bantering, romantic type, welcomes the coming of Mary, younger and more attractive than his wife, with such a show of pleasure that the moody Michael grows jealous. Knowing Mary had come to him when they were engaged he has long harbored ugly suspicions of her self-control and finally openly accuses her of frailty, calling her scarlet names. Angered and resentful Mary determines to be even with Michael. When a blizzard ties up the countryside while Michael is away, she invites young Peterson to keep her company. When Michael returns she confesses. Feeling his share of blame, Michael tries to forgive her and cry quits. But at sight of Peterson he knows he cannot. Mary starts away and Michael, taunted beyond his endurance, grabs a shotgun and shoots her dead.

" ZIEGFELD FOLLIES "

A musical revue in two acts; lyrics by Gene Buck;
music by Victor Herbert, Rudolph Friml, and Dave
Stamper. Produced by Florenz Ziegfeld at the New
Amsterdam Theater, New York, October 20, 1923.

Principals engaged —

Brooke Johns	Fanny Brice
William Roselle	Olga Steck
Bert Wheeler	Paulette Duval
Hap Ward	Marie Callahan
Lew Hern	Betty Wheeler
Arthur West	Edna Leedom
Harland Dixon	Hilda Ferguson
Faul Whiteman	Linda
Alexander Yarkovleff	Dave Stemper
The Empire Girls	Harry Short
Paul Whiteman's Orchestra	
Staged by Ned Wayburn.	

" NOBODY'S BUSINESS "

A comedy in a prologue and two acts by Frank Mandel
and Guy Bolton. Produced by Robert McLaughlin at
the Klaw Theater, New York, October 22, 1923.

Cast of characters —

Brakeman..Alfred West
Vera Smith...Josephine Drake
Marjorie Benton...............................Francine Larrimore
Jerry Moore..Louis Bennison
Train Conductor......................................Arthur Sparks
Pullman Conductor.....................................Paul Yaple
" Uncle " Willie Travers.............................Burke Clarke
Arthur Moore.......................................Charles Webster
Dick Abbott....................................Fred Irving Lewis
Hines..Caryl Gillin
Vincent..Frank Dae
Paul Gregory...Frank Conroy
Oliver Pratt..Wallace Ford
Savannah...Elaine Davies
Prologue—Rear of an Observation Car. Act I.—Scene 1—Jerry
Moore's Apartment, New York. Scene 2—Vera Smith's Apartment,
New York. Act II.—Scene 1—Vera's Apartment. Scene 2—Jerry
Moore's Apartment. Staged by Frank Conroy.

Marjorie Benton believes it possible for a girl to go
to New York and work out her destiny just as a man

does. So she starts from Chicago with her sketchbook in her hand. On the train she meets Jerry Moore, one of the rich, helpful young men of Broadway always willing to assist pretty girls out of difficulties. He offers to buy an option on Marjorie's future, but she refuses to sell. Later, in New York, after she has discovered a poor pianist to be a rotter, and a young banker to be her true love, she is forced to confess that on one occasion Jerry Moore had spent the night in her rooms. But that was all. The banker believes her, though his friends do not, and they are married.

" THE SWAN "

A comedy in three acts by Ferenc Molnar, translated from the Hungarian by Melville Baker. Produced by Charles Frohman at the Cort Theater, New York, October 23, 1923.

Cast of characters —

Dr. Nicholas Agi	Basil Rathbone
George	George Walcott
Arsene	Alan Willey
Princess Beatrice	Hilda Spong
Alexandra	Eva LeGallienne
Father Hyacinth	Halliwell Hobbes
Symphorosa	Alice John
Prince Albert	Philip Merivale
Colonel Wunderlich	Henry Warwick
Count Lutzen	Carl Hartberg
Alfred	Stanley Kalkhurst
Caesar	Richie Ling
Maid	Nancie B. Marsland
Princess Maria Dominica	Alison Skipworth
Countess Erdley	Geraldine Beckwith
Ladies in Waiting	Jane Shaw and Margaret Farr
Lackeys	Boswell Davenport and Tom Collins
Hussars	Jack Cobb and Stanley Grand

Act I.—A Pavilion in the Garden of Beatrice's Castle. Act II.—A Reception Room in the Castle. Act III.—The Drawing Room of a Suite in the Castle. Staged by Gilbert Miller.

(See page 77.)

" SCARAMOUCHE "

A romantic play in four acts by Rafael Sabatini.   Produced by Charles L. Wagner at the Morosco Theater, New York, October 24, 1923.

Cast of characters —

Lesarches	William Crimans
Le Chapelier	Stanley Howlett
Florimond Binet	H. Cooper-Cliffe
Pierrot	Knox Herrold
Polichinelle	J. M. Kerrigan
Harlequin	Allyn Joslyn
Rhodomont	Walter Timmis
Pasquariel	Herbert Belmore
Leander	Arthur De Langis
Scaramouche	Sheldon Stanwood
Climene	Vivienne Osborne
Columbine	Dorothy Tierney
The Duena	Mary Cecil
Phillippe de Vilmorin	E. J. Ballentine
Andre Louis Moreau	Sidney Blackmer
Jacques	Orlo Sheldon
Quentin De Kercadiou	John L. Shine
Comtesse De Plougastel	Percy Haswell
Aline De Kercadiou	Margalo Gillmore
Gervais De La Tour	Frederic Worlock
Chevalier De Chabrillane	Louis Le Seuer
Sergeant of Gendarmerie	Tim Walters
Fencing Master	John Turner
Duroc	William Crimans

Act I.—The Garden of the Breton Inn at Gavrillac.   Act II.—A Barn Near Guichen.   Act III.—Green Room of the Feyday Theater at Nantes.   Act IV.—Mme. De Plougastel's Salon in Paris.

Andre Louis Moreau, an orphaned aristocrat, sees his friend, the Abbe Phillippe de Vilmorin, killed before his eyes by the Marquis of Azyr, who resents his (Phillippe's) revolutionary utterances. Andre thereupon turns revolutionist and swears revenge upon Azyr. Escaping the home of his godfather, where he is sought by the government agents, he joins a band of strolling players as Scaramouche and continues to foment interest in the revolution from the stage. Finally he comes upon Azyr and is about to impale him upon his sword when he learns that he is his own father.

" ŒDIPUS REX "

Adapted by W. L. Courtney. Produced at the Century Theater, New York, October 25, 1923.

Cast of characters —

Œdipus Rex..Martin Harvey
Jocasta...Miriam Lewes
Creon..Gordon McLeod
Tiresias...Fred Grove
Messenger from Corinth..............................Walter Pearce
An Old Servant of Laius.............................Harvey Braban
Messenger from the Palace.........................Eugene Wellesley
A Priest..G. Fredericks
Leader of the Chorus................................Hubert Carter
1st Attendant on Jocasta...............................Mary Gray
2d Attendant on Jocasta...............................Ann Furrell
    Incidental Music by W. H. Hudson

The Sir Gilbert Murray translation of the Sophoclean text. During this engagement Sir Martin Harvey also played " Via Crucis," " Burgomaster of Stilemonde," and " Hamlet."

" STEADFAST "

A drama in three acts by Albert Koblitz and S. J. Warshawsky. Produced by George H. Brennan, Inc., at the Ambassador Theater, New York, October 29, 1923.

Cast of characters —

Rabbi Nathan Judah................................Frank McGlynn
Mamma..Marie Reichardt
Dr. Philip Judah...................................Henry Mortimer
Morris...Rexford Kendrick
Sarah...Leona Hogarth
Bennie..Billy Pearce
Solomon Marcuson..................................Robert Conness
Florence Marcuson.............................Lulu Mae Hubbard
Marian Burton................................Marie Louise Walker
Cantor Maravitz...........................George Henry Trader
Butler...Charles H. Cline
    Act I. and III.—Living Room in the Rabbi's Home. Act II.—Study
in the Marcuson Home.

Rabbi Nathan Judah, content, serene and steadfast in his allegiance to the orthodox Jewish faith, is sorely tried when he learns that his daughter, Sarah, has been betrayed by the son of his best friend, and that his son, Morris, is determined to take unto himself a Gentile wife. He manages to bear up under these calamities, though his heart is threatened at the end.

" RUNNIN' WILD "

A musical comedy in two acts by F. E. Miller and A. L. Lyles; music and lyrics by James Johnson and Cecil Mack. Produced by George White at the Colonial Theater, New York, October 29, 1923.

Cast of characters —

Uncle Mose	C. Wesley Hill
Uncle Amos	Arthur D. Porter
Tom Sharper	Lionel Montagas
Ethel Hill	Revella Hughes
Jack Penn	George Stephens
Detective Wise	Paul C. Floyd
Mrs. Silas Green	Mattie Wilkes
Mandy Little	Ina Duncan
Adalade	Adalade Hall
Steve Jenkins	F. E. Miller
Sam Peck	A. L. Lyles
Willie Live	Eddie Gray
Chief Red Cap	Tommy Woods
Head Waiter	Charles Olden
Ruth Little	Elizabeth Welsh
Silas Green	J. Wesley Jeffrey
Boat Captain	James H. Woodson
Sam Slocum	George Stamper
Lucy Lanky	Katherine Yarborough
Ginger	Bob Lee
Lightning	Ralph Bryson
Angelina Brown	Georgette Harvey

Act I.—Scene 1—Market Place, Jimtown. Scene 2—Railroad Station. Scene 3—Four Corners, St. Paul, Minn. Scene 4—Rondo Street, St. Paul, Minn. Scene 5—Cabaret, St. Paul, Minn. Act II.—Scene 1—Levee, Jimtown. Scene 2—Street, Jimtown. Scene 3—A Deserted Barn, Jimtown. Scene 4—Street, Jomtown. Scene 5 —Country Club, Jimtown.

A colored vaudeville loosely strung with the adventures of Sam Peck and Steve Jenkins, the familiar team of sharper and boob.

"CYRANO DE BERGERAC"

A poetic comedy in five acts by Edmond Rostand.
Produced by Claude Bragdon at the National Theater,
New York, November 1, 1923.

Cast of characters —

Cyrano de Bergerac	Walter Hampden
Christian de Neuvillette	Charles Francis
Comte de Guiche	Paul Leyssac
Ragueneau	Cecil Yapp
Le Bret	Ernest Rowan
Carbon de Castel-Jaloux	H. E. Humphrey
Ligniere	William Sauter
Vicomte de Valvert	Reynolds Evans
A Marquis	Thomas F. Tracey
Second Marquis	Joseph Latham
Montfleury	C. Norman Hammond
Bellerose	Antonio Salerno
Jodelet	Le Roi Operti
Cuigy	William H. Stevens
Brissaille	Albert G. West
A Busybody	P. J. Kelly
A Musketeer	John Alexander
D'Artagnan	Louis Polan
A Spanish Officer	William Sauter
A Light Horseman	Jay Fassett
A Porter	Allen Thomas
A Man	Marcel Dill
Another Man	John E. Trevor
A Guardsman	Bernard Savage
A Citizen	H. E. Humphrey
His Son	Anthony Jochim
A Pickpocket	Cedric Weller
Betrandou the Fifer	Allen Thomas
A Capuchin	C. Norman Hammond
Roxane	Carroll McComas
Her Duenna	Ruth Chorpenning
Lise	Mary Hall
An Orange Girl	Mabel Moore
A Soubrette	Margaret Barnstead
A Flower Girl	Elsie Herndon Kearns
A Comedienne	Isabelle Garland
Another Comedienne	Anne Tonetti
Mother Marguerite de Jesus	Mary Hall
Sister Marthe	Mabel Moore
Sister Claire	Elsie Herndon Kearns
A Little Girl	Ethel Fisher

Act I.—A Performance at the Hotel de Bourgoyne. Act II.—
The Bakery of the Poets. Act III.—Roxane's Kiss. Act IV.—The
Cadets of Gascoyne. Act V.—Cyrano's Gazette. Staged by Walter
Hampden. Incidental Music from Walter Damrosch's Opera,
"Cyrano."

This new English version of the Rostand classic done
in verse by Brian Hooker follows the familiar adventures

of the valiant longnose from the Hotel de Burgoyne to
the Bakery of the Poets, and later through the poetic
episode of his pleading with the fair Roxane beneath her
balcony as her handsome lover's substitute, followed
by the battle of the Cadets of Gascoyne and Cyrano's
death in the yard of the convent to which Roxane retired after the passing of Christian.

"THE DEEP TANGLED WILDWOOD"

A comedy in three acts by George S. Kaufman and
Marc Connelly. Produced by George Tyler and Hugh
Ford at the Frazee Theater, New York, November 5,
1923.

Cast of characters —

James Parks Leland	James Gleason
Harvey Wallick	Robert McWade
J. Warren Patterson	T. M. Cahill
Amy Meade	Devah Morel
Aunt Sarah Parks	Blanche Chapman
Edwin Palmer Corliss	George Alison
Francine La Forge	Angela Warde
Pearl Corliss	Mary Daniel
Tom Wilson	McKay George
Joe Inglis	Ralph Sipperly
Bates	Fred J. Nicholls
Mary Ellen	Mildred Booth
Deacon Flood	James K. Appleebee
Mayor Gombel	Harry Cowley
Phyllis Westley	Gertrude Hitz
The Photographer	Harry Irving
The Electrician	Sam Janney
Schwartz	George Spelvin
Willetts	Denman Maley

Prologue—Apartment of James Parks Leland, New York City.
Act I.—Aunt Sarah Parks's Home in Millersville. Act II.—Scene 1
—Aunt Sarah's Home. Scene 2—W O Z, Millersville. Act III.—
Aunt Sarah's Home. Staged by Hugh Ford.

James Parks Leland is a Broadway playwright. Home
from the failure of his newest drama he decides there
must be something wrong with him. He has become, he
believes, too hard and sophisticated, too cynical and
blase. What he needs is a touch of the old home atmosphere. He must get back to where people are real and

life is earnest. So he goes home to Millersville — and finds the " hicks " smoking, jazzing, drinking and wearing nifty clothes. The only real, old-fashioned human among them is another visitor, Mary Ellen, also an adopted New Yorker. They stir up a romance and go back to Broadway for their honeymoon.

" WHITE CARGO "

A drama in three acts by Leon Gordon. Produced by Earl Carroll at the Greenwich Village Theater, New York, November 5, 1923.

Cast of characters —

The Doctor	Conway Wingfield
Witzel	A. E. Anson
Ashley	Frederick Roland
The Missionary	J. Malcolm Dunn
The Skipper	Curtis Karpe
The Engineer	Tracy Barrow
Longford	Richard Stevenson
Tondeleyo	Annette Margules
Worthing	Harris Gilmore

Act I., II., and III.—A Bungalow on the West Coast of Africa. Staged by Leon Gordon.

On the West Coast of Africa, doing their four-year stretches on the rubber plantations, are certain young Englishmen trying to escape the attacks of the dry rot that eats into men's souls as well as their vitals in this lonesome country. Among them is Longford, newly arrived and defiant, swearing he will not succumb as the others have, giving up to whisky or the native women or both, until he is pathetically beaten. For a year he sticks it out, but finally Tondeleyo, a half-caste native girl with a beautiful body but a warped and shallow soul, undermines his resistance. With a last stand for respectability he marries the girl. A year of this and he, too, is beaten — ready to be shipped home by his cynical friends, so much additional " white cargo " for the river boats.

" A LOVE SCANDAL "

A comedy in three acts by Carlos de Navarro and Sydney Stone. Produced by Calvert, Inc., at the Ambassador Theater, New York, November 17, 1923.

Cast of characters —

Aunt Jeanne..Charlotte Granville
Constance Adair.......................................Mona Kingsley
Winthrop Field..Percy Waram
Dr. Besson (afterwards Arthur Presby)..............Norman Trevor
Lady Armsford..Marjorie Chard
Bettina Tilton..Edith Taliaferro
  Act I.—A Cottage in the North of Scotland. Act II. and III.—
Presby Hall.

Bettina Tilton, American and flapperish, is visiting in Scotland and falling in love with Winthrop Field. Her success in this direction excites the jealousy of Constance Adair, who might have married Winthrop but didn't, because he was poor. So Constance, to keep Winthrop single, intimates to Bettina that he is now her (Constance's) lover in fact rather than in fancy. But Betty is too smart for her and, with the help of Constance's husband, explodes the plot, and captures Winthrop.

" STEPPING STONES "

A musical comedy in two acts by Anne Caldwell and R. H. Burnside; music by Jerome Kern; lyrics by Anne Caldwell. Produced by Charles Dillingham, at the Globe Theater, New York, November 6, 1923.

Cast of characters —

Peter Plug...Fred Stone
Prince Silvio...Roy Hoyer
Otto DeWolfe..Oscar Ragland
Remus..John Lambert
Richard..Harold West
Captain Paul...Jack Whiting
Antoine..Gerald Gilbert

Gypsy Jan...Bert Jordan
Eddie...Willie Torpey
The Landlord...George Herman
Roughette Hood......................................Dorothy Stone
Widow Hood..Allene Stone
Lupina..Evelyn Herbert
Radiola..Primrose Caryll
Mary...Lucille Elmore
Nurse Marjorie...Lydia Scott
Charlotte..Lilyan White
Eclaire..Ruth White
Rose..Hazel Glen
    Act I.—Scene 1—The Nursery. Scene 2—The Puppet Play. (With Tony Sarg's Marionettes.) Scene 3—The Corridor. Scene 4—The Sweet Shop. Scene 5—Cherryville Square. Scene 6—The Road to Broughton Woods. Scene 7—The Garden of Roses. Act II.—Scene 1—The Haunted Inn. Scene 2—The Mystic Hussars. Scene 3—The Ghost of the Inn. Scene 4—The Dolls' Village. Scene 5—Outside the Inn. Scene 6—The Palace of Prince Silvio. Staged by R. H. Burnside.

A musical comedy version of Little Red Riding Hood's adventures with a villain named DeWolfe, from whom she is rescued in song, dance and acrobatic comedy by one Peter Plug, errand boy and wild plumber from the Pampas.

"SPRING CLEANING"

A comedy in three acts by Frederick Lonsdale. Produced by the Selwyns at the Eltinge Theater, New York, November 9, 1923.

Cast of characters —

Walters...Lewis Broughton
Margaret Sones......................................Violet Heming
Ernest Steele...A. E. Mathews
Fay Collen...Blythe Daly
Lady Jane Walton................................Pauline Whitson
Archie Wells..Gordon Ash
Bobbie Williams......................................Robert Noble
Billy Sommers............................C. Haviland Chappelle
Connie Gillies......................................Maxine McDonald
Richard Sones.......................................Arthur Byron
Mona..Estelle Winwood
    Act I. and III.—Living Room at Richard Sones's, London. Act II.—Dining Room.

Richard Sones is distressed because his beautiful young wife, Margaret, insists on running with a terrible set of social degenerates. For the sake of their two children

he determines upon a heroic course to save her. Going
into the streets one evening when Mrs. Sones is giving
a dinner party to her particular pets he invites a painted
lady to go home to dinner with him. At the party he
introduces her as his friend, and when the guests resent
the insult he pretends great surprise that amateurs should
feel so toward sitting at the table with a professional.
The shock drives Mrs. Sones to the arms of the man with
whom she has been flirting and she threatens to marry
him. But it isn't marriage of which the friend has been
thinking. Discovering her philanderer's true character
Margaret is thankful to be taken back by her husband
and promises to be good.

"A ROYAL FANDANGO"

A comedy in three acts by Zoë Akins. Produced by
Arthur Hopkins at the Plymouth Theater, New York,
November 12, 1923.

Cast of characters —

H. R. H. Prince Peter	Cyril Keightley
H. R. H. Princess Amelia	Ethel Barrymore
Prince Michael	Teddy Jones
Prince Alexander	Charles Eaton
Princess Titania	Lorna Volare
Lady Lucy Rabid	Virginia Chauvenet
Mr. Wright	Harold Webster
Henriette	Denise Corday
Parrish	Walter Howe
Arthur	Drake deKay
Chucho Panez	Jose Alessandro
Ampero	Beverly Sitgreaves
Pascual	Edward G. Robinson
Pilar	Aileen Poe
Skelly	Frank Antiseri
Holt	Spencer Tracy

Act I.—A Drawing Room in Prince Peter's Villa at Biarritz.
Act II.—The Private Sitting Room of the Princess Amelia. Act
III.—The Courtyard of Chucho's Little Castle in Spain. Staged by
Arthur Hopkins.

Being a little overbred, the Princess Amelia, married
to Prince Peter in Plotzvitch and the mother of his three

children, is given to occasional attacks of love madness. During one she summons Chucho Panez, a handsome matador she has seen in Biarritz, to her apartment. Chucho is brave with the bulls but timid in the presence of feminine beauty and when the Princess makes frank love to him he swoons at her feet. Later, visiting her matador in his mountain home where he lies ill of a fever, the Princess discovers the natives preparing to blow up the Prince, her husband, with a bomb. This discovery serves to normalize her mind and she flies home in the airplane the Prince has brought to fetch her.

"THE CUP"

A play in three acts by William Hurlbut. Produced by Joseph E. Shea at the Fulton Theater, New York, November 12, 1923.

Cast of characters —

Paula...Rosita Mantilla
Slick...Alfred Rigali
Harry...John Irwin
Tony...Carlos Calde
Eddie...Tom Moore
Mary...Josephine Victor
The Priest...O. P. Heggie
    Act I. and II.—Eddie's Flat on the Lower East Side in New York.
    Act III.—Scene 1—The Same. Scene 2—The Rectory.

On the lower side of New York Eddie, a gangster, and his girl, Mary, are living in a cheap apartment supported by Eddie's success as a thief and a thug. Nearby lives Slick, previously a rival of Eddie's for Mary's favors, and still under suspicion. Hearing that Slick has just made a swell haul, having stolen " the most valuable thing in the whole woild," Eddie determines to be even with him by grabbing the loot for himself. While he is doing this the parish priest, called to urge Mary and Eddie to marry, tells the girl of a report that the " Chalice of Antioch," the sacred cup of the Last Supper, dug up years ago in Syria, has been stolen and is in New York. Being of a religious bent the story impresses Mary so deeply that when Eddie returns home with what proves to be the cup and threatens to destroy it before it gets him into trouble she protects it with her life, taking a beating but retaining enough strength to stagger with the sacred relic to the priest's home. There Eddie follows her, and some measure of reform and forgiveness is promised both.

" GO WEST, YOUNG MAN "

A comedy in three acts by Fay Pulsifer and Cara Carelli. Produced by the Westminster Productions at the Punch and Judy Theater, New York, November 12, 1923.

Cast of characters —

Mrs. Hector Brumble	Aline McDermott
Mrs. William Merrill	Enid Gray
William Merrill	Reginald Barlow
Claude Merrill	Percy Helton
John Sterling	Everett Butterfield
Laura Harper	Kay Johnson
Mr. Comstock	Benedict MacQuarrie
Hortense DeWolf	Minna Phillips
Lucille Winterbottom	Marion Trabue
Dottie Dulcye	Ann Anderson
Miss Carbury	Blanche Latell
Joe Harper	Leslie Stowe
Hernandez	Benedict MacQuarrie

Act I.—Merrill Home, Arrowhead, Connecticut. Act II.—Miss De-Wolf's Studio, New York City. Act III.—Living Room, Harper's Ranch, Texas.

Claude Merrill's mother, denied artistic expression in her youth, determines to express herself through him. She makes a Greek dancer of him. But Claude, under the influence of Laura Harper, rebels, goes West, and becomes enough of a he-man to give the villain a beating.

" THE CAMEL'S BACK "

A comedy in three acts by Somerset Maugham.   Produced by the Selwyns at the Vanderbilt Theater, New York, November 13, 1923.

Cast of characters —

```
Hermione.......................................Violet Kemble Cooper
Enid Lefevre..........................................Joan Maclean
Mrs. Lefevre....................................Louise Closser Hale
Sarah ...................................................Margaret Moffat
Annie................................................Dorothy Stokes
Valentine Lefevre........................................Charles Cherry
Denis Armstrong.........................................Gavin Muir
Dr. Dickinson..........................................Arthur  Lewis
      The Action Takes Place in the Drawing Room at Valentine's Home
at Hampstead, England.
```

Valentine Lefevre is a dull and stubborn **English** gentleman who hopes to stand for Parliament.   Seeking to impress his rightful importance upon his family he forbids his ward, Enid, to marry, objects to the color of his wife's hair and insists his mother shall live in his home or lose her allowance.   To make him more tractable Hermione, his wife, lies and tricks him into believing all sorts of things — that she has been unfaithful to him among other things — until he is half crazed with doubts and glad to patch up a truce when he discovers the truth.

" QUEEN VICTORIA "

A drama in seven episodes by David Carb and Walter Prichard Eaton.   Produced by the Equity Players, Inc., at the Forty-eighth Street Theater, New York, November 15, 1923.

Cast of characters —

```
Alexandrina Victoria...........................   .........Beryl  Mercer
Duchess of  Kent............................... .....Winifred  Hanley
Baroness Lehzen.............................. ..........Anita  Rothe
Lady Gay Hawthorne..............................Frances Goodrich
```

Prince Albert of Coburg................................Ulrich Haupt
Edward, Prince of Wales.............................Arthur Maude
Viscount Melbourne...............................Donald Cameron
Duke of Wellington................................Edward Fielding
Archbishop of Canterbury...........................Albert Tavernier
Lord Palmerston....................................William Ingersoll
Lord Conyngham.............................Herbert Standing, Jr.
Baron Stockmar..Hubert Wilke
Sir James Clark....................................Herbert Farjeon
Benjamin Disraeli.................................Clarence Derwent
William Ewart Gladstone............................George Farren
A Footman..Borden Harriman
    First Episode—Kensington Palace, June 20, 1837. Second Episode
—Buckingham Palace, October 10, 1839. Third Episode—Buckingham
Palace, October 11, 1839. Fourth Episode—Buckingham Palace, Jan-
uary, 1854. Fifth Episode—Windsor, December 14, 1861. Sixth
Episode—Buckingham Palace, May 24, 1870. Seventh Episode—
Buckingham Palace, June 20, 1897. Staged by Priestly Morrison.

An historical drama told in seven episodes carrying
Victoria through from the morning of her ascension in
1837 to the celebration of her diamond jubilee in 1897.
Three episodes are devoted to the courtship of Alfred
and Victoria's happy life with him, one to his death, one
to the mourning queen's reluctant return to public life,
and one each to the ascension and jubilee.

" OUT OF THE SEVEN SEAS "

A drama in three acts by Kilbourn Gordon and Arthur
Cæsar. Produced by Kilbourn Gordon at the Frazee
Theater, New York, November 19, 1923.

Cast of characters —

Phyllis Stanton..Audrey Hart
Hanson...William A. Norton
Anne Stanton..Lotus Robb
Ted Mason...Norval Keedwell
Leonard Mason......................................Stapleton Kent
An Englishman...Wallis Clark
Papa Dubois..George Marion
Chang...Joseph Selman
A Woman...Olga Lee
A Sailor...John Q. Dunn
Another Sailor...Ray Hart
Li Sing..Walter Plunkett
    Act I.—Living Room of the Stanton Apartment in New York.
Act II. and III.—Café de Petit Paris, Hongkong.

Phyllis Stanton, being just naturally weak and wilful,
buys herself pretty things on money she gets from help-

ing men smuggle opium. Also she teaches her good sister's fiancé, Ted Mason, to smoke the stuff. Ted, remorseful, runs away to China, and Anne Stanton, his fiancée, follows after. They get mixed up in Papa Dubois's Cabaret in Hongkong, are set upon by thugs, smugglers and such like, and suffer considerable inconvenience from nine-thirty till eleven-fifteen o'clock, when Ted turns out to be a secret service agent.

"THE FAILURES"

A drama in fourteen scenes by H. R. Lenormand, translated from the French by Winifred Katzin. Produced by the Theater Guild at the Garrick Theater, New York, November 19, 1923.

Cast of characters —

Montredon	Dudley Digges
He	Jacob Ben Ami
She	Winifred Lenihan
Second Phantom	Sterling Halloway
The Musician	Erskine Sanford
The Bell Boy	Philip Loeb
Larnaudy	Henry Crosby
A Dresser	Helen Westley
The Ingenue	Helen Tilden
The Duenna	Alice Belmore Cliffe
An Actor	Ernest A. Daniels
Saint-Gallet	Henry Travers
The Magistrate	Morris Carnovsky
The Private	Ernest A. Daniels
The Corporal	Jo Mielziner
The Librarian	Philip Loeb
His Wife	Ida Zeitlin
The Rake	Herbert Ashton
The Chemist	Henry Clement
The Barmaid	Nell Barnes
An East Indian	Jo Mielziner
A Commissioner of Police	Morris Carnovsky
Waiter	Sterling Halloway
Magistrate's Daughter	Hildegarde Halliday
A Hunchbacked Girl	Polly Craig

Fourteen episodes from the lives of He and She — He a struggling playwright trying to preserve his ideals, She a struggling actress of similar ambition. They marry, She gets a job with a touring company to keep them from starving, He goes along and when She can support him no other way she sells herself to the small-town lovers who pursue her. Learning which He kills her and himself.

MOSCOW ART THEATER

Second repertoire season under the direction of F. Ray Comstock and Morris Gest. Played at Jolson's Fifty-ninth Street Theater (November, 1923; January, 1924) and the Imperial Theater (May, 1924), New York.

Cast of characters —
" BROTHERS KARAMAZOFF "

Fyodor Pavlovitch Karamazoff	Vassily Luzhsky
Alyosha Karamazoff	Boris Dobronravoff
Ivan Karamazoff	Vassily Katchaloff
Dmitry Karamazoff	Leonid M. Leonidoff
Smerdyakoff	Lyoff Bulgakoff
Grigory	Vladimir Gribunin
Katerina Ivanovna	Lydia Korenieva
Grushneka	Alla Tarasova

During this and two later return engagements the Moscow company presented in addition to Dostoievsky's "Brothers Karamazoff," Goldoni's "Mistress of the Inn," Tchekhoff's "Ivanoff" and "The Cherry Orchard," Knut Hamsun's "In the Claws of Life," Ibsen's "An Enemy of the People," Ostrovsky's "Enough Stupidity in Every Wise Man," Tchekhoff's "Uncle Vanya," Saltnikoff-Schedrin's "The Death of Pazukhin," Tolstoy's "Tsar Fyodor," and Gorky's "The Lower Depths." They gave ninety-seven performances in New York.

"ROBERT E. LEE"

A play in nine episodes by John Drinkwater. Produced by William Harris, Jr., at the Ritz Theater, New York, November 20, 1923.

Cast of characters —

Of the U. S. Army:

Major Perrin..Earl Gray
An Orderly...Nelan H. Jaap
General Scott.......................................Burr McIntosh
Robert E. Lee....................................Berton Churchill
Tom Buchanan..John Marston
Ray Warrenton....................................Richard Barbee
David Peel...Alfred Lunt
Duff Penner.....................................James Spottswood
John Stean...William Corbett
Marianne...Jean May
Elizabeth...Ann Cuyle
Mrs. Stean...Martha Mayo
A Servant at Lee's Home...............................Fred Miller

Of the Army of the Confederate States:

General J. E. B. Stuart............................James Durkin
His Aide..Frank Russell
An Aide to General Lee.............................Gerald Cornell
A Sentry...Ralph Macbane
General " Stonewall " Jackson.......................David Landau
Captain Mason......................................George Willis
Captain Udall....................................James Henderson
Colonel Hewitt...............................William R. Randall
Jefferson Davis.....................................Eugene Powers
His Secretary.....................................Stewart Robbins
Mrs. Meadows...Millie James

The life of the famous Southern leader told in nine episodes, beginning with the secession of Virginia, and continuing through Lee's resignation from the union army, the conferences preceding and the attack upon Malvern Hill, a meeting with President Jefferson Davis at the peak of the South's successes, the defeat at Spottsylvania Courthouse and the retreat from Richmond. Woven through these is the story of four young southerners who were close to the great general throughout the war.

" TOPICS OF 1923 "

A musical revue in two acts by Harold Atteridge and Harry Wagstaff Gribble; music by Jean Schwartz and Alfred Goodman; lyrics by Harold Atteridge.   Produced by the Messrs. Shubert at the Broadhurst Theater, New York, November 20, 1923.

Principals engaged —

Alice Delysia	Herbert Corthell
Lora Hoffman	Jay Gould
Fay Marbe	Barnett Parker
Billie Shaw	Jack Pearl
Marie Stoddard	Ben Bard
Frank Green	Roy Cummings
Paisley Noon	Dorothy Vance
Delano Dell	Harry McNaughton
Allan Prior	Nat Nazarro, Jr.

Staged by J. C. Huffman, supervised by J. J. Shubert.

" SHARLEE "

A musical comedy in two acts by Harry L. Cort and George E. Stoddard; lyrics by Alex. Rogers; music by C. Luckyeth Roberts.   Produced by John Cort at Daly's Theater, New York, November 22, 1923.

Cast of characters —

Mr. Watson Holmes	Winn Shaw
Oscar Riley	Eddie Nelson
I. Kahn	Joe Morris
Tom Mason	Sydney Grant
Dolly Dare	Frances Arms
Jack Vandeveer	Joseph R. Dorney
Sharlee Saunders	Juliette Day
Annabelle	Mitti Manley
Jane Caldwell	Ottilie Corday
Masenia	Masenia
May, June	Field Sisters
Mrs. Vandeveer	Mrs. Mary Leroy

Act I.—Scene 1—Interior of Cabaret. Scene 2—Living Room of Sharlee's Apartment. Scene 3—Same as Scene 1. Act II.—Porch and Lawn of Jack Vandeveer's Summer Home.

" SANCHO PANZA "

A comedy in a prologue and four acts based on certain episodes in Cervantes's story, " Don Quixote De La Mancha," by Melchoir Lengyel; music and songs by Hugo Felix. Produced by Russell Janney at the Hudson Theater, New York, November 26, 1923.

Cast of characters —

Sancho Panza	Otis Skinner
Don Quixote	Robert Robson
Dapple	Robert Rosaire
A Scrivener	Charles Halton
Chamberlain	Frederick Tiden
Duke of Barataria	Russ Whytal
Father Hyacinth	H. H. McCollum
Donna Rodriguez	Marion Barney
Arvino	Stewart Baird
Hernando	Richard Cramer
Mayor of Barataria	Harry Lewellyn
Gralva	Anthony Andre
The Young Duchess	Marguerite Forrest
Gregory	Herbert Delmore
Altisidora	Grace Elliott
Dolorida	Kathleen George
Isabella	Marguerite Ingram
The Page with the Mirror	Olga Treskoff
The Page with the Cape	Roberta Renys
The Page with the Crown	Merle Stevens
The Page with the Pin	Elizabeth Page
The Page with the Staff of Office	Helen Grenelle
The Page with the Insignia	Aileen Grace
The Court Physician	Stewart Baird
A Tailor	Charles Halton
A Fruit Woman	Olga Treskoff
A Farmer	Robert Robson
A Dancer	Helen Grenelle
A Citizen	William H. Browne
An Old Man	Royal Cutter
A Young Thief	Kirk Allen
A Drab	Ruby Trelease
A Drover	Meyer Berenson
A Street Singer	Malcolm Hicks
Another Singer	Harold Brown
Another Singer	Walker Moore
The First Guard	Michel Barroy
The Second Guard	William Venus
The Third Guard	Arthur C. Tennyson
The Fourth Guard	Richard Trott
A Citizen	Smiley W. Irwin
Another Citizen	Jack Cronin
Another Citizen	Fred Kotek

Prologue—A Roadside in the Province of Andalusia. Act I.—The Pavilion of the Duke of Barataria. Act II.—The Governor's Throne Room in Barataria. Act III.—The Square Before the Cathedral. Act IV.—The Throne Room Again.

The incident taken from the story of "Don Quixote" in which Sancho Panza is made the ruler of the island Barataria. Being a good and democratic ruler he manages the wedding of the young duchess and her knight, rights the wrongs of the suffering people, deals justly with the poor and ruthlessly with the sharpers. When the wicked councillors turn upon him he calls upon the people to rise against them and is triumphant. After which he takes Dapple, his wise and comic ass, and goes back to his farm.

"MEET THE WIFE"

A comedy in three acts by Lynn Starling. Produced by Stewart and French at the Klaw Theater, New York, November 26, 1923.

Cast of characters —

```
Gertrude Lennox.........................................Mary Boland
Harvey Lennox..........................................Charles Dalton
Doris Bellamy........................................Eleanor Griffith
Victor Staunton........................................Clifton Webb
Gregory Brown........................................Humphrey Bogart
Philip Lord............................................Ernest Lawford
Alice.................................................Patricia Calvert
William..............................................Charles Bloomer
    Act I., II. and III.—The Living Room of the Home of Gertrude
Lennox.
```

Gertrude Lennox is a celebrity-worshipping tuft hunter living in the suburbs. Twice married, she thanks goodness she still is "the captain of her soul." Her latest crush is Philip Lord, London novelist, whom she has invited to a luncheon. Mr. Lord, on arrival, turns out to be Mrs. Lennox's first husband whom she has mourned as dead ever since he disappeared in the San Francisco fire and earthquake. She is considerably taken aback, not to say disturbed, by the discovery that she is, in effect, a bigamist, but Mr. Lord is quite content to disappear a second time. Mr. Lennox, the second husband, is busily inquiring the way to other earthquake centers at the play's close.

" TIME "

A comedy in three acts by Arthur Henry. Produced by Stuart Walker in association with Lee Shubert, at the Thirty-ninth Street Theater, New York, November 26, 1923.

Cast of characters —

Mabel Prescott..Lucile Nikolas
John Barrett..William Kirkland
Ruth Prescott...Dorothy Francis
Georgette Barrett.....................................Margaret Mower
Jim Prescott..A. H. Van Buren
Patsy Prescott..Marie Curtis
Joshua Prescott.......................................William Evarts
　　　Act I. and II.—Jim Prescott's Camp in the Maine Woods. Act III.—Living Room in Joshua Prescott's Home in Mayville.

Jim Prescott, at forty, believes himself indifferent to the attractions of Ruth, his wife, and turns to Georgette Barrett, a widow and a camp neighbor, for sympathy and understanding. They agree to go honorably to Ruth, assure her of their mutual esteem and ask her please to divorce Jim. Before the arrangement can be completed young John Barrett elopes with the equally young Mabel Prescott, and Grandma Prescott, hearing of the domestic flareup, chaperones the youngsters on their honeymoon. A year later Mabel is to have a baby, and the thought of being a proud grandfather proves more attractive to Jim than that of being Georgette's second husband.

" HAMLET "

A tragedy by William Shakespeare. Revived by Arthur Hopkins at the Manhattan Opera House, New York, November 26, 1923.

Cast of characters —

Francisco...John Boyd
Bernardo..Lark Taylor
Horatio...J. Colville Dunn

```
Marcellus...........................................John Connery
Ghost of Hamlet's Father............................Reginald Pole
Hamlet, Prince of Denmark...........................John Barrymore
Claudius............................................Kenneth Hunter
Gertrude............................................Blanche Yurka
Polonius............................................Moffat Johnston
Laertes.............................................Sidney Mather
Ophelia.............................................Rosalind Fuller
Rosencrantz.........................................Boyd Clark
Guildenstern........................................Larence Cecil
First Player........................................Lark Taylor
Player King.........................................Burnel Lundee
Second Player.......................................Jose Ruiz
Lucianus............................................Vadini Uraneff
A Gentlewoman.......................................Winifred Salisbury
King's Messenger....................................H. C. Smith
First Grave Digger..................................Whitford Kane
Second Grave Digger.................................Russell Morrison
A Priest............................................Reginald Pole
Osric...............................................Edgar Stehli
Fortinbras..........................................Richard Morton
```
The Play Presented in Three Parts, with Intervals Following the First Players' Scene and the Queen's Closet Scene.

" DUMB-BELL "

A comedy in three acts by J. C. Nugent and Elliott Nugent. Produced by Richard Herndon at the Belmont Theater, New York, November 26, 1923.

Cast of characters —
```
Ma Hutchenson......................................Jessie Crommette
Romeo..............................................J. C. Nugent
Aggie..............................................Ruth Nugent
Ted Stone..........................................Kenneth McKenna
Mrs. Stone.........................................Ethel Winthrop
Ann Worthing.......................................Gladys Wilson
Jones..............................................John Daly Murphy
```
Act I., II. and III.—Mrs. Stone's Country Residence in Kentucky.

The village grocer calls Romeo " Dumb-bell " and the name sticks, because the boy is something of a nit-wit. Romeo likens all the people about him to characters in the fairy stories that were read to him in his childhood, and that helps the plot. This is concerned with the love of Ted for the poor but honest Aggie, when his stylish mother is trying to marry him off to the proud and haughty Ann. Romeo also invents a mouse trap which Ted turns into a novelty toy and makes everybody rich and happy.

"ONE KISS"

A comedy with music in two acts by Clare Kummer, from the French "Ta Bouche," by Y. Mirande and A. Willemetz; music by Maurice Yvain. Produced by Charles Dillingham at the Fulton Theater, New York, November 27, 1923.

Cast of characters —

Marguerite	Jane Carroll
Margot	Alden Gay
Meg	Dagmar Oakland
Meregrette	Pauline Hall
Madame Doremi	Ada Lewis
Eva	Louise Groody
General Pas-De-Vis	John E. Hazzard
Bastien	Oscar Shaw
Jean	John Price Jones
Mme. De Peyster	Josephine Whittel
Georges	Fred Lennox
Riquette	Patrice Clark
Bebe	Janet Stone
Babette	Elaine Palmer
Berte	Irma Irving
Beatrix	Gertrude McDonald

Synopsis: Act I. and II.—Terrace of the Hotel at Morny-sur-Mer.

Bastien and Eva, never being able to forget the thrill of one stolen kiss, are determined to marry. But Mme. Doremi, Eva's mother, and Gen. Pas-de-Vis, Bastien's father, are equally determined they shall not. Bastien and Eva pretend to have spent a night at an inn, expecting their parents will then insist that they marry at once to save their honor. But the parents are modern and practical. Still they only succeed in keeping the lovers apart for another act.

" IN THE NEXT ROOM "

A melodrama in three acts by Eleanor Robson and Harriet Ford.   Produced by Winthrop Ames and Guthrie McClintic at the Vanderbilt Theater, New York, November 27, 1923.

Cast of characters —

Philip Vantine	Wright Kramer
Lorna Webster	Mary Kennedy
James Godfrey	Arthur Albertson
Rogers	Morris W. Ankrum
Parks	George Riddell
Felix Armand	Claude King
Inspector Grady	Leighton Stark
Simmonds	Edward Butler
Tim Morel	William J. Kline
Madame De Charriere	Merle Maddern
Julia	Olive Valerie

Act I.—The Sitting Room, Vantine's House, Washington Square, New York.   Act II. and III.—The Vantine Drawing Room.   Staged by Guthrie McClintic.

Philip Vantine has bought a rare copy of an original Boule cabinet and ordered it shipped to his New York home from Paris.   When it arrives it is found to be the original itself, the possession of which is desired by many strange people.   Before the mystery concerned with the cabinet's shipment can be cleared up two persons meet mysterious deaths fooling with it and the happiness of many otherwise happy actors is threatened.

" LAUGH, CLOWN, LAUGH! "

A drama in three acts by David Belasco and Tom Cushing, from the Italian of Faurto Martini's " Ridi, Pagliaccio."   Produced by David Belasco at the Belasco Theater, New York, November 28, 1923.

Cast of characters —

Tito Beppi	Lionel Barrymore
Luigi Ravelli	Ian Keith
Prof. Gambella	Henry Herbert

Federico..Guy Nichols
Signora Calvaro....................................Vaughn De Leath
Signora Del Papa..................................Thomas Reynolds
Flik..Lionel Barrymore
Flok..Sidney Toler
Simonetta...Irene Fenwick
Lilly Blanchette.......................................Myra Florian
The Rienzi Sisters.....................Susanna Rossi, Leah LeRoux
Bibi...Nick Long
Usher...Jose Yovin
Giacinta...Rose Morison
Father Saverio....................................Giorgio Majeroni
Signora Del Monte...............................Kathleen Kerrigan
Margherita...Lucille Kahn
Conte Castiglione.................................Giorgio Majeroni
Signora Capelli....................................Agnes McCarthy
Signora Felice......................................Jenny Dickerson
Signorina Crispi...................................Micheline Keating
Signora Torre...Alice Horine
First Ragamuffin............................Charles Firmbach, Jr.
Second Ragamuffin.....................................Harry Craven
    Act I.—The Waiting Room in Professor Gambella's Sanatorium.
Act II.—Simonetta's Dressing Room in the "Paradiso" Theater.
Act III.—Tito Beppi's Lodgings, Rome, in 1923. Staged by David
Belasco.

Tito Beppi, famed as a clown in Italy, consults a
psychologist to discover why he, Beppi, cannot control
his nerves. He is forever breaking into tears at the
most inconvenient times. The specialist diagnoses the
case and discovers that the clown is in love with his own
ward, the young and beautiful Simonetta. He orders
them to be much together without telling the girl of the
clown's passion. In the same specialist's office Simonetta meets a young nobleman who is afflicted at times with
uncontrollable laughter, and the specialist suggests that
he, too, follow the players into the country in search of
new thoughts and scenes. Simonetta then falls in love
with the young nobleman, but tries to remain true to
Beppi. The clown, realizing that her loyalty to him
stands in the way of her happiness, kills himself.

ELEONORA DUSE

Farewell engagement under the direction of Morris Gest and F. Ray Comstock, starting at the Metropolitan Opera House, New York, Monday evening, November 29, 1923.

Cast of characters —

" THE LADY FROM THE SEA "

Ellida Wangel	Eleonora Duse
Stranger	Memo Benassi
Dr. Wangel	Alfredo Robert
Boletta	Enif Robert
Hilda	Ione Morino
Lyngstrand	Gino Fantoni
Arnholm	Ciro Galvani
Ballested	Leo Orlandini

Following this gala performance Mme. Duse appeared in repertory at the Century Theater, New York, giving two performances each of Ibsen's " Ghosts," Gallarati-Scotti's " Cosi Sia," Marco Praga's " La Porta Chiusa," and D'Annunzio's " La Citta Morta."

" THE TALKING PARROT "

A comedy in three acts. Produced at the Frazee Theater, New York, December 3, 1923.

Cast of characters —

Aunt Truefitt	Ruby Hallier
Millie Scudder	Kathleen Arthur
Albert Scudder	Jack Cherry
Roger	Walter Connolly
Felix Barlow	Oswald Yorke

A husband's ghost reappears in Greenwich Village and has fun with the bachelor friends who are trying to marry his widow.

" PELLEAS AND MELISANDE "

A drama in five acts by Maurice Maeterlinck. Produced by the Selwyns in association with Adolph Klauber, at the Times Square Theater, New York, December 4, 1923.

Cast of characters —

The Doorkeeper..Gordon Burby
Melisande...Jane Cowl
Golaud...Louis Hector
Arkel..J. Sayre Crawley
Genevieve...Grace Hampton
Pelleas...Rollo Peters
Little Yniold..William Pearce
The Old Servant.......................................Jessie Ralph
A Doctor...Vernon Kelso
Maid Servants........Alma Reeves Smith, Marion Evanson, Mildred Wall, Lucile Wall, Edith Van Cleve, Mary Holton, Katherine Wray.
Three Beggars......Harry Taylor, Laurence Adams, Richard Bowler.
    Act I.—Scene 1—The Castle Door. Scene 2—The Forest. Scene 3—A Hall in the Castle. Scene 4—Before the Castle. Act II.—Scene 1—A Spring in the Park. Scene 2—A Room in the Castle. Scene 3—Before a Cave. Scene 4—A Room in the Castle. Scene 5—A Room in the Castle. Act III.—Scene 1—One of the Castle Towers. Scene 2—The Castle Vaults. Scene 3—A Terrace at the Entrance of the Vaults. Scene 4—Before the Castle. Act IV.—Scene 1—A Passage in the Castle. Scene 2—A Room in the Castle. Scene 3—A Spring in the Park. Act V.—Scene 1—A Low Hall in the Castle. Scene 2—A Room in the Castle.

The story of Melisande, the beautiful princess, found wandering in the wood by Golaud, the mighty hunter, and taken to his gloomy castle, where she falls in love with Pelleas, his younger and handsomer, though no more cheerful, brother. Golaud, suspecting the worst, slays Pelleas. Melisande dies shortly after with a wound over the heart no bigger than a scratch.

" THE LADY "

A melodrama in a prologue, four acts and an epilogue by Martin Brown. Produced by A. H. Woods at the Empire Theater, New York, December 4, 1923.

Cast of characters —

A Sailor..Marcel Le Mans
A Navvy..Marcel Morelli

Lizette...Stephane de Leger
Julie...Adelaide Wilson
The Loafer...Edward La Roche
Polly Pearl...Mary Nash
The Traveler...Leonard Willey
Blackie..Herbert Heywood
A Young Man..Brandon Peters
Fanny Le Clare.......................................Elisabeth Risdon
Call Boy...Hugh Brooke
Florine..Betty Williams
Phyllis..Teddy King
Leonard St. Aubyns...................................Austin Fairman
Tom Robinson...Victor Morley
Mr. St. Aubyns.......................................Ethelbert Hales
Lady " Dido " Huntington.............................Irby Marshal
A Girl...Nera Badeloni
Madame Blanche.......................................Ludmilla Toretzka
Josef..Edward La Roche
First Sailor...Edward Fetbroth
Second Sailor..Hugh Brooke
Mrs. Cairns..Cecelia Radcliffe
A Lawyer...Herbert Heywood
A Nurse..Sylvia Little
A Gentleman..Clement O'Loghlen
A Bobby..Frank Horton
A Lady...Virginia Langdon
A Little Boy...Junior Durkin
A Doctor...Rudolpho Badaloni
A Police Agent.......................................John Fulco
Prologue—The Brixton Bar at Havre. Act I.—Polly's Dressing
Room. Act II.—The Terrace of a Hotel at Monte Carlo. Act III.
—The Café of the " Maison Blanche " at Marseilles. Act IV.—
The Corner of a London Square. Epilogue — The Brixton Bar.
1921.

Polly Pearl was a serio-comic travelling the English
provinces. Leonard St. Aubyns, although a gentleman,
loved her true and married her legally. After which,
on the Riviera, he grew conscious of her grammar, or
lack of it, and sympathized not at all with her ambition
to be a lady. So he ran away and when her son was
born Polly was destitute. She went to work in cabarets
to support her boy and kept herself pure so he need never
be ashamed of her, and when his grandfather tried to
snatch him from her she sent him to England and never
saw him again. Not, at least, until the last act, when
she discovers him in her own cabaret, and in something
of a mess, seeing he has just shot a man. But she is
happy, knowing that at least he has courage and is a
gentleman, and there is a promise the shooting was only
accidental anyway.

" THE POTTERS "

A comedy by J. P. McEvoy. Produced by Richard Herndon at the Plymouth Theater, New York, December 8, 1923.

Cast of characters —

Ma Potter..................................Catharine Calhoun Doucet
Bill Potter..Raymond Guion
Mamie Potter...Mary Carroll
Pa Potter..Donald Meek
Red Miller..Douglas Hunter
Gladys Rankin...Mary Stills
Friend...Tom Burton
Mr. Rankin..Edwin Walter
Mr. Eagle..Dean Raymond
Conductor..R. Henry Handon
Motorman...William Fairchild
Medium...Josephine Deffry
Iceman...Russ Carter
Her Daughter....................................Josephine Mostler
Waiter..Daniel Kelly
Check Room Girl................................Adelaide Lawrence
Mrs. Rankin..Maud Cooling
Pullman Porter.......................................James Hagen
Bill...Daniel Kelly
Mike...Tom Burton
Girl's Voice...Dorothy Deuel
Boy's Voice.......................................Arthur Christian
Mrs. Peterson..Isabel Hill
Mr. Peterson.......................................Raphael Byrnes
Mechanic...Russ Carter
Jack...Raphael Byrnes
Anabelle..Helen Chandler

A series of connected episodes from the family life of the Potters, showing Ma, Pa, Bill and Mamie at home and later following them through Pa's investment in oil stock and Mamie's elopement with her red-headed steady.

" THE BUSINESS WIDOW "

A comedy in three acts by Gladys Unger. Produced by Lee Shubert at the Ritz Theater, New York, December 10, 1923.

Cast of characters —

Pennington...Albert Morrison
Billy Windsor.......................................James Dyneforth

```
Rex Ramsdell......................................Elwood  Bostwick
Natalie Frisson.........................................Baby  Fleury
John...................................................Palmer  Young
Paul Bucklaw......................................Leo Ditrichstein
Helen Lesley...........................................Marjorie  Wood
Ruby Bucklaw...........................................Lola  Fisher
Standish...............................................Robert  Lowing
Muey Fah...............................................Alice  Hung
Phidias Caravopulo...................................John Davidson
```
Act I.—Paul Bucklaw's Office in New York. Act II. and III.—
The Living Room in Paul Bucklaw's Home in Larchmont.

Paul Bucklaw, older than his wife, Ruby, is hard
pressed by her determination to have a good time at
any cost.   She runs him ragged socially and keeps him
broke financially.   Finally he gives up, makes her flirtation with her latest glostora possible and has the satisfaction finally of hearing her beg to be taken back to his
aging arms, and dependable pocketbook.

" THE SHADOW "

A play in three acts by Dario Nicodemi. Produced
by A. H. Woods and Lee Shubert at the Thirty-ninth
Street Theater, New York, December 18, 1923.

Cast of characters —
```
Berta Tragni...........................................Tilla  Durieux
Gianettina, a Nurse......................................Polly  Craig
Michael Delatti...........................................Paul Dietz
Helene Previlla.......................................Grete Sandheim
Gerhard Tragni (Berta's Husband).....................Carl Schmidt
Doctor Magre..........................................John Feistel
Louise.................................................M. Lange
```
Act I.—Living Room in an old Italian Palazzo in Milan. Act II.—
Studio of Gerhard Tragni. Act III.—The same room as Act I.

Berta Tragni, twelve years married to Gerhard, has
for six years been confined to an invalid's chair by paralysis. Suddenly she is cured. Thinking to thrill her
husband with the great happiness that has come to them
she waits until she can walk and then she goes to visit
him in his studio. Here she discovers that for three

years her husband has been living with her best friend, that a child has been born to them and that Gerhard was about to ask his invalid wife to divorce him. For the sake of the child she sorrowfully agrees to this arrangement.

" THE OTHER ROSE "

A play in three acts by George Middleton, from the French of Edouard Bourdet. Produced by David Belasco in association with William Harris, Jr., at the Morosco Theater, New York, December 20, 1923.

Cast of characters —

```
Rose  Coe...............................................Fay  Bainter
Prof. Andrew Coe.....................................Ernest Stallard
Johnny Coe...................................Andrew J. Lawlor, Jr.
Mrs. Mason...........................................Effie Shannon
Tony Mason.............................................Henry  Hull
Rose Helen Trot...................................Carlotta Monterey
Etty  Doolittle.........................................Maud Sinclair
Gideon...........................................Harry MacFayden
     Act I., II. and III.—Whale Harbor, Maine, in a cottage rented to
the Coes by Mrs. Mason.  Staged by David Belasco.
```

Rose Coe, taking care of her aging scientific father and her twelve-year-old brother, rents a cottage for the summer at Whale Harbor, Me. Arrived there she finds the son of the owner, Tony Mason, in rebellion against his mother for having let the cottage go. It is to him a shrine, because there he devotedly loved a widow, another Rose, the year before. Miss Coe, however, refuses to give way to so silly and preposterous a youth and keeps the cottage — with the result that Tony falls more deeply in love with the new Rose than he ever had been with the other.

" HURRICANE "

A drama in four acts by Olga Petrova.   Produced by Richard Herndon at the Frolic Theater, New York, December 25, 1923.

Cast of characters —

```
Martha Olczewski (Deeney)........................Camilla Dalberg
Masha..............................................Katharine Roberts
John Arkwright.....................................Lewis Willoughby
Richard Peterson...............................Manuel A. Alexander
Rose Peterson.........................................Dorothy Ellin
Ilka...................................................Olga Petrova
Joe Jennings.........................................Joseph Granby
Michael Deeney.......................................Patrick S. Barrett
Walter Welch, M.D.......................................Percy Carr
Butler.................................................Dan O'Brien
        Act I.—Kitchen of a Texas Farmhouse. Act II.—A Room in a
Lodging House in Kansas City. Act III.—The Balcony of the New
Miramar Hotel at Miami, Florida. Act IV.—Living Room in Ilka's
House, Long Island.
```

Ilka, born in Russia, transferred to a Texas ranch, hates her brutal stepfather with a consuming hatred.   To escape him she accepts the money of a white slaver, stabs father in the back and starts for Kansas City.   Two years as a bad woman net her much misery but handsome profits, with which she does much good and finally establishes herself as an interior decorator in New York. Here her past follows her, but she eludes it finally and recovers her soul before she dies.

" THE WILD WESTCOTTS "

A comedy in three acts by Anne Morrison.   Produced by Lewis and Gordon at the Frazee Theater, New York, December 24, 1923.

Cast of characters —

```
Helen Steele................................................Norma Lee
Sybil Blake.........................................Claudette Colbert
Robert Cummings.......................................Leslie Adams
John Westcott.........................................Douglas Wood
```

Agatha Westcott...Vivian Martin
Eddie Hudson...Elliott Nugent
Capt. Hippesley Trenchard...........................W. Boyd Davis
Geraldine Fairmont.............................Cornelia Otis Skinner
Anthony Westcott.....................................Morgan Farley
Muriel Westcott.......................................Isabel Withers
Henry Hewlett...Charles Laite
Mrs. Westcott...............................Edith Campbell Walker
Philip Morgan.....................................Fred Irving Lewis
Mrs. Taylor...Helen Broderick
    Act I. and III.—The Westcott Library, Greenwich, Conn. Act II.
—The Hewlett Apartment, New York.

Muriel Westcott marries Henry Hewlett against her
family's wishes and advice. Agatha Westcott falls desperately in love with Captain Trenchard, who is twice
her age. Anthony Westcott thinks his sister a poor fish
and the world in general hopelessly a mess. The parent
Westcotts are well meaning, but excitable. The explosion occurs the day Muriel leaves Henry and takes their
week-old baby home with her, which happens to be
Agatha's wedding day, she having finally decided to take
Eddie Hudson (seeing her captain has married another.)
Nothing goes right and everything goes wrong and the
wild Westcotts rage until finally Muriel goes back to
Henry and Agatha starts for the altar.

" THE ALARM CLOCK "

A comedy in three acts by Avery Hopwood from " La
Sonnette d'Alarme " of Maurice Hennequin and Romain
Coolus. Produced by A. H. Woods at the Thirty-ninth
Street Theater, New York, December 24, 1923.

Cast of characters —
Wills..John Troughton
Lulu Deane..Helen Flint
Charlie Morton.....................................Ernest Lambart
Mrs. Dunmore..Gail Kane
Dr. Wallace..George Alison
Bobby Brandon.......................................Bruce McRae
Mrs. Susie Kent......................................Blanche Ring
Mary Kent...Marion Coakley
Homer Wickham...................................Harold Vermilye

Theodore Boom...Charles Abbe
Reggie Wynne...Vincent Serrano
    Act I., II. and III.—A Room in Bobby Brandon's House, New York City.

Bobby Brandon, forty and tired, entertains his nephew, Homer Wickham, and Homer's fiancée, Mary Kent, in his New York apartment as the result of a suggestion made in his interests by his friend, Mrs. Dunmore. They should serve to brighten Bobby's life. And they do. Homer acquires himself a " Follies " girl and Mary Kent turns from her country boy to her city host. The rearrangement serves every purpose.

" MARY JANE McKANE "

A musical comedy in three acts by William Cary Duncan and Oscar Hammerstein, 2d; music by Herbert Stothart and Vincent Youmans. Produced by Arthur Hammerstein at the Imperial Theater, New York, December 25, 1923.

Cast of characters —

Joe McGillicudy...Hal Skelley
Maggie Murphy...Kitty Kelly
Mary Jane McKane...Mary Hay
Cash and Carrie...Keene Twins
Martin Frost...Dallas Welford
Andrew Dunn, Jr...Stanley Ridges
Doris Dunn...Laura De Cardi
Louise Dryer...Eva Clark
George Sherwin...Louis Morrell
Andrew Dunn, Sr...James Heenan
    1. Mary Jane Leaves Slab City, Massachusetts. 2. Her First Sight of New York City. 3. View from Her Bedroom Window. Act.—I.—Scene 1—In the Subway. Scene 2—Private Office of Andrew Dunn, Jr. Scene 3—Mary Jane's Room—On the East Side. Scene 4—Same as Scene 2. Act II.—Office of the " Dandy Dobbin Novelty Company." Act III.—Scene 1—Garden of Andrew Dunn's Home. Scene 2—Mary Jane's Room. Scene 3—Central Park.

Mary Jane, cute and from the country, applies for a job in the offices of the Dunns. She is a good stenographer-secretary, but too pretty, they think, for young

Mr. Dunn. So she slicks down her bobbed hair, puts on goggles and comes back. She gets the job and later goes into business with young Dunn when his Daddy fires him. They embrace matrimony and each other in the last act.

"THE RISE OF ROSIE O'REILLY"

A musical comedy in two acts by George M. Cohan. Produced by George M. Cohan at the Liberty Theater, New York, December 25, 1923.

Cast of characters —

Jimmy Whitney	Bobby Watson
Bob Morgan	Jack McGowan
Lillian Smith	Marjorie Lane
Kitty Jones	Dorothy Whitmore
Casparoni	Albert Gloria
Mrs. Casparoni	Adelaide Gloria
Buddie O'Reilly	Bobby O'Neill
Johnson	George Bancroft
Rosie O'Reilly	Virginia O'Brien
Polly	Mary Lawlor
Cutie Magee	Emma Haig
Pete	Georgie Hale
Mrs. Montague Bradley	Margaret Dumont
Steve	Johnny Muldoon
Molly	Pearl Franklin
Hop Toy	Eddie Russell
Fannie	Betty Hale
Annie	Bernice Speer
Ethelbert	Tom Dingle
Gertrude	Patsy Delany
Roscoe Morgan	Walter Edwin
Flower Girls	Woods Sisters

Act I.—Scene 1—Under the Brooklyn Bridge (Brooklyn Side). Scene 2—A Few Blocks Beyond. Scene 3—Reception Room in Mrs. Bradley's Brooklyn Home. Act II.—Scene 1—Madame Regay's Florist Shop. Scene 2—In Front of the Draperies. Scene 3—Exterior of Morgan's Brooklyn Home. Staged by Julian Mitchell and John Meehan. Supervised by George M. Cohan.

Rosie runs a flower stand under the Brooklyn bridge. Bob Morgan, son of wealth, meets and loves her. Papa Morgan cuts Bob off at the pockets, thus forcing him to go to work singing and dancing in an uptown flower shop. And in the last act they (Rosie and Bob) get married.

" THE BLUE BIRD "

A fairy tale in two acts by Maurice Maeterlinck.   Produced by Lee Shubert at the Jolson Theater, New York, December 24, 1923.

Cast of characters —

```
Mummy Tyl...........................................Ethel Jackson
Daddy Tyl...........................................Stapleton Kent
Tyltyl................................................Ben  Grauer
Mytyl.................................................Mary  Corday
The  Fairy  Berylune..................................Thais  Lawton
            (By Arrangement with George Broadhurst)
Bread..............................................J. K. Hutchinson
Fire...............................................Cleveland Bronner
Tylo, the Dog......................................Reginald Barlow
Tylette, the Cat...................................Harold de Becker
Water...............................................Ingrid  Solfeng
Milk..............................................Catherine  Collins
Sugar..............................................George  Sylvester
Light..............................................Virginia  Hammond
Granny Tyl.........................................Jennie A. Eustace
Gaffer Tyl...........................................Walker  Walker
          The Tyl Brothers and Sisters—Blue Children
The  Boy  Lover....................................Patricia  Barclay
The  Girl  Lover...................................Suzanne  Powers
The  Unborn  Tyl....................................Alfred  Little
Time................................................Walter  Walker
The  Hero  Child......................................Teddy  Jones
Happiness of Being Well..............................Nina  Oliver
Night...............................................Gladys  Hanson
Cold-in-the-Head......................................Billy  Quinn
Neighbor Berlingot...................................Thais  Lawton
Neighbor Berlingot's Daughter....................Francene  Wouters
     Act I.—Scene 1—The Woodcutter's Cottage.  Scene 2—Outside the
Window.  Scene 3—At the Palace of the Fairy Berylune.  Scene 4—
On  the  Way  to  the  Land  of  Memory.  Scene 5—The  Land  of
Memory.  Scene 6—Outside the Graveyard.  Scene 7—The Kingdom
of the Past.  Act II.—Scene 1—The Palace of Night.  Scene 2—
The Corridor.  Scene 3—The Kingdom of the Future.  Scene 4—
Before the Curtain.  Scene 5—The Palace of Happiness.  Scene 6—The
Leave Taking.  Scene 7—The Awakening.
```

Revival of the familiar Maeterlinck fantasy, detailing Tyltyl and Mytyl's search for the bluebird of happiness.

" NEIGHBORS "

A comedy in three acts by Leon Cunningham. Produced by the Equity Players, Inc., at the Forty-eighth Street Theater, New York, December 26, 1923.

Cast of characters —

Mr. Hicks...Frederick Burton
Mrs. Hicks...Josephine Hull
Phoebe Hicks...Ruth Nugent
Johnnie Hicks..Tom Brown
Mr. Stone..Sydney Macy
Mrs. Stone...Helen Strickland
Crawford Stone.......................................Warren Lyons
Lillian Stone..Helen Macks
Mrs. Blackmore.......................................Georgie Drew Mendum
Nettie Blackmore.....................................Alton Goodrich
Mr. Tulliver, LL.D...................................Bruce Elmore
Aunt Carrie..Jessie Crommette
Act I., II. and III.—Outside the Suburban Homes of the Messrs. Hicks and Stone.

In a suburb of Detroit the Hicks and Stones live in adjoining houses. Professor Hicks is experimenting with odorless onion plants. Mrs. Stone is the proud owner of a prize-winning rooster. The day young Crawford Stone is to marry Phoebe Hicks a jealous neighbor leaves the rooster's gate open and the rooster proceeds to demolish the odorless onion plants. War follows. The Stones shut off the Hicks's gas and the Hicks retaliate by shutting off the Stones's water. An armistice is agreed upon at eleven p.m.

" THIS FINE-PRETTY WORLD "

A drama in three acts by Percy MacKaye. Produced at the Neighborhood Playhouse, New York, December 26, 1923.

Cast of characters —

Beem Spaulding......................................E. J. Ballantine
Lark Fiddler..John F. Roche
Goldie Shoop..Joanna Roos

```
Granny Shoop (Rhody Melindy)........................Reba Garden
Roosh Maggot............................................Albert Carroll
Gilly Maggot.............................................Perry Ivans
Mag Maggot.........................................Aline MacMahon
Arminty Sprattling................................….Esther Mitchell
Polly Ann Clem...............................Pamela Gaythorne
Witty Shepheard..............................T. Lewis McMichael
Reason Day................................................Dan Walker
Dug Cheek.............................................William Stahl
Squire Green Cornet...............................Robert Le Sueur
Andy Caudle..........................................…George Brett
Judy Dishman................................Polaire Weissmann
Ruthie Madders.........................................Lily Lubell
Delphy Boggs......................................Marion Morehouse
Sarah Jane..............................................Grace Hooper
Sie.....................................................A. T. Wenning
Bige Boker............................................Charles Wagner
Gid....................................................Remon La Joie
Jasper................................................John Crawford
Asa...................................Reginald Carrington
    Act I.—Outside the Palings of Gilly Maggot's Cabin Yard.  Act
II.—Inside the Palings of Beem Spaulding's Cabin Yard.  Act III.—
Interior of a Log Schoolhouse.
```

Represents the author's attempt to preserve in play form something of the character and quaint speech of the hill people living far from the railroads in Kentucky. The story is of Gilly Maggot who is eager to be rid of his wife, Mag, that he may take up with the younger and buxomer Goldy Shoop. Gilly hires Beem Spaulding, a " defamin' attorney," to do a lot of " lie-swearing " which will prove Mrs. Maggot a bad woman. Judge and jury, however, accept the lady's defense as true, and Goldy elopes with Gilly's nephew.

" SAINT JOAN "

A chronicle play by Bernard Shaw. Produced by the Theater Guild at the Garrick Theater, New York, December 28, 1923.

Cast of characters —

```
Bertrand de Pulengy....................................Frank Tweed
Steward...........................................William M. Griffith
Joan...............................................Winifred Lenihan
Robert de Baudricourt..............................Ernest Cossart
The Archbishop of Rheims............................Albert Bruning
La Tremouille.....................................Herbert Ashton
```

Court Page.....................................Jo Mielziner
Cilles de Rais..................................Walton Butterfield
Captain La Hire................................Morris Carnovsky
The Dauphin....................................Philip Leigh
Duchess de la Tremouille.......................Elizabeth Pearre
Dunois, Bastard of Orleans.....................Maurice Colbourne
Dunois's Page..................................James Norris
Earl of Warwick................................A. H. Van Buren
Chaplain de Stogumber..........................Henry Travers
Bishop of Beauvais.............................Ian Maclaren
Warwick's Page.................................Seth Baldwin
The Inquisitor.................................Joseph Macaulay
Canon D'Estivet................................Albert Perry
Le Courcelles..................................Walton Butterfield
Brother Martin Ladvenu.........................Morris Carnovsky
The Executioner................................Herbert Ashton
An English Soldier.............................Frank Tweed
A Gentleman of 1920............................Ernest Cossart

The story of the Maid of Orleans told in seven
episodes. Joan seeks support at Vaucouleurs. She is
sent to Chinon, where she picks the Dauphin from the
crowd and wins the support of Dunois and the army.
She carries the armies through a successful campaign,
helped by God's answer to her prayer that the direction
of the wind be changed. She sees Charles crowned at
Rheims, breaks with Dunois, is captured by the Burgun-
dians, tried at Rouen and sent to the stake. In an
epilogue all those having to do with her life reappear in
the spirit on the anniversary of her canonization and beg
her to remain dead, and a saint. If she were to return
to life she probably would again be flouted by a stupid
world.

" ROSEANNE "

A drama about colored people by Nan Bagby Stephens.
Produced by Mary H. Kirkpatrick at the Greenwich
Village Theater, New York, December 29, 1923.

Cast of characters —

Roseanne.......................................Chrystal Herne
Son..Blaine Cordner
Leola..Kathleen Comegys
Rodney...Murray Bennett
Cicero Brown...................................John Harrington
Sis Tempy Snow.................................Marie Taylor

```
Sis Lindy Gray.........................................Tracy L'Engle
Winnie Caldwell.......................................Irma Caldwell
Alec Gray...............................................Robert Strauss
Dacas Snow............................................Leslie M. Hunt
Morninglory Trimble................................Conway Sawyer
    Acts I., II. and III.—A Small Town in Georgia.  Staged by John
A. Kirkpatrick.
```

Roseanne, a colored laundress, is a devout church-
woman, a worker in the Ladies' Aid and a worshipful
admirer of her pastor. All her faith in God is reflected
in her faith in the Rev. Brown. To him she entrusts
the eighteen-year-old orphaned girl she has raised from
infancy that she may be properly set upon the spiritual
paths that lead to glory. Then she discovers that Brown
is wrong, a sinner covering his sins with a cloak of
religion. When her girl dies she drags the unworthy
Brown from his pulpit to meet the "sperrit" of the
dead girl, and urges the congregation to hang him.
Later she relents and leaves his punishment to God.

"THE SONG AND DANCE MAN"

A comedy drama in four scenes by George M. Cohan.
Produced by George M. Cohan at the Hudson Theater,
New York, December 31, 1923.

Cast of characters —

```
Curtis...................................................William Walcott
Chas. B. Nelson......................................Frederick Perry
Joseph Murdoch......................................Louis Calhern
John Farrell...........................................George M. Cohan
Crowley...............................................Wm. J. Phinney
Jim Craig..............................................Robert Cummings
Jane Rosemond.....................................Eleanor Woodruff
Mrs. Lane..............................................Laura Bennett
Leola Lane.............................................Mayo Methot
Freddie..................................................Al. Bushee
Miss Davis...........................................Mary Agnes Martin
Tom Crosby...........................................John Meehan
Anna....................................................Alice Beam
    Scenes 1 and 2—Nelson's Apartment.  Scenes 3 and 4—Nelson's
Business Office.
```

"Hap" Farrell of the team of "Farrell and Carroll,
songs, dances and funny sayings," makes Broadway after

having been seventeen years a "hick trouper." At the theatrical boarding house where he stops he finds Leola Lane, who had been kind to his partner when the latter was ill, in arrears for board. He pays the bill, which straps him, and three days later, hungry and desperate, he tries to hold up a pedestrian with a prop revolver. He is bested in the fight that follows and started for jail, but on the way tells his story and is given a chance to prove it. When he does prove it he finds friends and success follows. Then he goes back to being a song and dance man.

"KID BOOTS"

A musical comedy in two acts by William Anthony McGuire and Otto Harbach; music by Harry Tierney; lyrics by Joseph McCarthy. Produced by F. Ziegfeld at the Earl Carroll Theater, New York, December 31, 1923.

Cast of characters —

```
Peter Pillsbury......................................Harry Short
Herbert Pendleton....................................Paul Everton
Harold Regan.......................................John Rutherford
Menlo Manville.....................................Harland Dixon
Tom Sterling.........................................Harry Fender
Polly Pendleton......................................Mary Eaton
First Golfer....................................Morton McConnachie
Second Golfer.......................................Jack Andrews
First Caddie.........................................Dick Ware
Second Caddie.....................................William Blett
Third Caddie.........................................Frank Zolt
Fourth Caddie....................................Waldo Roberts
Fifth Caddie........................................Lloyd Keyes
Kid Boots..........................................Eddie Cantor
Beth..................................................Beth Beri
Carmen Mendoza..................................Ethelind Terry
Jane Martin.......................................Marie Callahan
Dr. Josephine Fitch............................Jobyna Howland
Randolph Valentine...............................Robert Barrat
Federal Officer...................................Victor Munroe
                 George Olsen and His Orchestra
   Act I.—Scene 1—The Exterior of Everglades Golf Club, Palm Beach,
Florida. Scene 2—The Ladies' Locker Room. Scene 3—The Caddie
Shop. Scene 4—Patio of the Everglades Club. Act II.—Scene 1—
The Trophy Room. Scene 2—The Eighteenth Hole. Scene 3—The
Exterior of Caddie House—"The Nineteenth Hole." Scene 4—The
Cocoanut Ball.
```

Boots is the caddie master and official bootlegger of a Palm Beach golf club. He also deals in crooked golf balls and is tricked at his own game when his best friend, the club champion, gets hold of one of the loaded balls by mistake and loses the season's biggest match.

"HELL-BENT FER HEAVEN"

A melodrama in three acts by Hatcher Hughes. Produced by Marc Klaw, Inc., at the Klaw Theater, New York, January 4, 1924.

Cast of characters —

David Hunt	Augustin Duncan
Meg Hunt	Clara Blandick
Sid Hunt	George Abbott
Rufe Pryor	John F. Hamilton
Matt Hunt	Burke Clarke
Andy Lowry	Glenn Anders
Jude Lowry	Margaret Borough

The three acts of the play occur in the Hunt home in the Blue Ridge Mountains between four o'clock in the afternoon and nine o'clock at night of a midsummer day.

(See page 49.)

"THE SPOOK SONATA"

A fantasy in three movements by August Strindberg. Produced by Kenneth McGowan, Eugene O'Neill and Robert Edmund Jones.

Cast of characters —

The Milk Girl	Mary Blair
The Student	Walter Abel
Old Hummel	Stanley Howlett
The Dark Lady	Mary Morris
The Janitress	Ruza Wenclawska
The Fiancée	Marion Berry
The Young Lady	Helen Freeman
Ghost of the Consul	Allen Nagle
Johansson, Hummel's Servant	Charles Ellis
Baron Skansenkorge	James Light

Beggars..............Murray Bennet, Bernard Simon, Samuel Selden
Bengtsson..Allen Nagle
The Mummy..Clare Eames
The Colonel..................................Romeyn Park Benjamin
The Cook...Rita Matthias
    First Movement—Outside the House. Second Movement—Inside the
House: The Round Room. Third Movement—The Hyacinth Room.

A weird tragedy of ugly and distorted souls, human and superhuman.

" OUTWARD BOUND "

A play in three acts by Sutton Vane. Produced by William Harris, Jr., at the Ritz Theater, New York, January 7, 1924.

Cast of characters —
Scrubby...J. M. Kerrigan
Ann..Margalo Gillmore
Henry..Leslie Howard
Mr. Prior..Alfred Lunt
Mrs. Cliveden-Banks...........................Charlotte Granville
Rev. William Duke...................................Lyonel Watts
Mrs. Midget...Beryl Mercer
Mr. Lingley...Eugene Powers
Rev. Frank Thompson.............................Dudley Digges
    Act I.—In Harbor. Act II. and III.—At Sea.

(See page 105.)

" THE NEW POOR "

A comedy in three acts by Cosmo Hamilton. Produced by Alex. A. Aarons and Vinton Freedley at the Playhouse, New York, January 7, 1924.

Cast of characters —
Mrs. Curtis Wellby...................................Beth Franklyn
Constance Wellby.....................................Irene Purcell
Betty Wellby..Myra Hampton
Mary Maxwell Maudsley............................Norma Mitchell
Amos Wellby...Herbert Yost
Alice Wellby...Anita Booth
Miller C. Guttbridge............................Morton L. Stevens

Princess Irina..................................Lillian Kemble Cooper
The Grand Duke Boris...............................Lyn Harding
Count Ivan..William Wiliams
Prince Vladimir.....................................George Thorpe
Kirk O'Farrell.....................................Ralph Sipperley
    The three acts take place in the Living Room of the Wellbys's
Country House in Connecticut.

The Wellbys's servants have deserted them. Alice, the oldest daughter, engages a quartet of impoverished representatives of the Russian nobility to take their places. The Russians are so wonderful all the young Wellbys fall in love with them, and social standards are amusingly distorted. Finally the new servants are suspected of being English picture thieves, but prove, in freeing themselves of the charge, that they are only four good actors.

"ANDRE CHARLOT'S REVUE OF 1924"

A musical revue in two parts by Andre Charlot. Produced by the Selwyns at the Times Square Theater, New York, January 9, 1924.

Principals engaged —

Jack Buchanan
Fred Leslie
Robert Hobbs
Herbert Mundin
Ronald Ward
Douglas Furber
    Staged by Andre Charlot.

Beatrice Lillie
Gertrude Lawrence
Dorothy Dolman
Marjorie Brooks
Barbara Roberts
Jill Williams

"GYPSY JIM"

A drama in three acts by Oscar Hammerstein, 2d, and Milton Herbert Cropper. Produced by Arthur Hammerstein at the Forty-ninth Street Theater, New York, January 14, 1924.

Cast of characters —

Harry Blake...George Farren
Mary Blake...Elizabeth Patterson

```
Craig.............................................George Anderson
Lucy Blake.......................................Martha-Bryan Allen
Tom Blake............................................Wallace Ford
Gypsy Jim...........................................Leo Carrillo
Worthing...........................................Harry Mestayer
Dan.................................................Fleming Ward
Estelle................................................Ethel Wilson
Kent................................................Averell Harris
Grace..............................................Virginia Wilson
Butler...............................................Joseph Spence
```

Act I. and II.—Home of the Blakes. A Small Town in the Middle West. Act III.—Home of Mr. Prentiss.

The Blake family is about to crash. Harry, the father, is a broken attorney, ready to run; Mary, the mother, is a hopeless hypochondriac; Lucy, the daughter, unhappy at home, plans to elope; Tom, the son, a discouraged inventor, is thinking of suicide. Then Gypsy Jim knocks at the door, convinces them he is possessed of something resembling supernatural powers, restores their faith in themselves and leaves them happy. Later he is discovered to be an eccentric millionaire who takes this means of applying practical charity where it is the most needed.

" THE MIRACLE "

A legend in eight scenes by Max Reinhardt; book by Karl Vollmoeller. Produced by Ray Comstock and Morris Gest at the Century Theater, New York, January 16, 1924.

Cast of characters —

```
Madonna.......................................Lady Diana Manners
Sexton................................................Charles Peyton
Assistant Sexton...................................David Hennessey
Old Sacristan.........................................Elsie Lorenz
Old Nun Attendant..............................Mrs. John Major
Mother of the Nun.......................Claudia Carlstadt Wheeler
Grandmother of the Nun..............................Laura Alberta
The Nun........................................Rosamond Pinchot
The Abbess.........................................Mariska Aldrich
A Peasant.............................................Louis Sturez
The Burgomaster...................................Lionel Braham
The Knight.........................................Orville Caldwell
A Blind Peasant..............................Rudolph Schildkraut
His Son..............................................Schuyler Ladd
```

```
A Crippled Piper.....................................Werner Krauss
The Archbishop...........................................Luis Rainer
The Shadow of Death...................................Luis Rainer
A Czardas Dancer..............................Maria Cherer-Bekefi
A Guest of the Count............................Mariska Aldrich
The Prince...........................................Schuyler Ladd
Majordomos...............................Fritz Field, Carl Linke
The Emperor.....................................Rudolph Schildkraut
The Spirit of Revolution.......................Maria Cherer-Bekefi
Chief Officers.....................Nicholas Glowatski, Louis Sturetz
Judges.......................Messrs. Balieff, Auburn, Linke, Burns
Revolutionist................................................Fritz Feld
Executioner.............................................Lionel Braham
Priest..............................................Monsieur Friedli
```

The Max Reinhardt staging of the old legend in which
Megildis, a young nun, dreams that she is lured into
the world, where she learns much through suffering, and
returns to the great cathedral from which she fled to
discover that the compassionate and understanding
Madonna has descended from her niche and performed
her duties during the years she was away.

" MERRY WIVES OF GOTHAM "

(" FANSHASTICS ")

A comedy in three acts by Laurence Eyre. Produced
by Henry Miller at the Henry Miller Theater, New York,
January 16, 1924.

Cast of characters —

```
                    PROLOGUE
Jimminy................................................Eddie Quinn
Patsy...............................................William Quinn
Phelim Hennessy.......................................Tom Maguire
Sister Mercedes..........................................Avis Hughes
Brigid Shannahan.........................................Mary Ellis
Mother Agnes...........................................Judith Vosselli
Miss Mortimer.......................................Ann Winston
Cathy Donovan..................................Mignon O'Doherty
                    THE PLAY
Denbeigh...........................................Bertha Ballenger
Dirk DeRhonde......................................William Hanley
Anne DeRhonde........................................Grace George
Lambart DeRhonde...............................Berton Churchill
Annie O'Tandy...................................Laura Hope Crews
Seumas O'Tandy...................................Arthur Sinclair
Andy Gorman............................................Arthur Cole
Ophelia O'Tandy...........................................Mary Ellis
```

Paperhanger...George Wilson
Pomeroy..Lewis A. Sealy
Major Fowler...John Miltern
Widow Gorman......................................Mignon O'Doherty
A Small Gorman.....................................William Quinn
Angelo...Herbert Farjeon
Hudson Bess.......................................Judith Vosselli
    Prologue—St. Ann's Orphanage, Ireland, 1830. Act I.—Scene 1—A
Room in the DeRhonde Mansion, New York. 1873. Scene 2—A Room
in the O'Tandy Dwelling, Upper Fifth Avenue. Scene 3—Major Fow-
ler's Law Offices. Act II.—Outside the O'Tandy Dwelling. Act
III.—Scene 1—The Olympic Halls. Scene 2—Outside Bellevue
Hospital.

Forty-three years before the action of the play begins,
twin girl babies were taken from St. Ann's orphanage
in Ireland, one adopted by a farmer's wife and the other
taken by an actress on her way to America. In the
play they meet but never discover their relationship.
One is the wife of a wealthy and influential New Yorker,
Lambart DeRhonde, and the other the wife of Seumas
O'Tandy, a " squatter " on the DeRhonde " goat hills "
at 69th Street and Fifth Avenue in 1873. The wives feel
a curious bond of sympathy and share a sense of humor
that permits them to understand and manage their respective prigs of husbands, who mean well, for all they
are " fanshastic," as Annie O'Tandy puts it.

" THE ROAD TOGETHER "

A play in four acts by George Middleton. Produced
by A. H. Woods at the Frazee Theater, New York,
January 17, 1924.

Cast of characters —

Warren..John Dwyer
Tom Porter...H. Reeves-Smith
Dora Kent.......................................Marjorie Rambeau
Wallace Kent...A. E. Anson
Julia Deering...Ivy Troutman
Fred Safford...Harry Minturn
George Gilmore..................................Charles W. Guthrie
Fred Taintor.......................................William Balfour
Armour Deering......................................Robert Adams
Mary..Ethel Tucker
    Act I. and II.—At the Kents's. Act III.—At Julia Deering's. Act
IV.—At the Kents's again. In a Large Eastern City.

Dora Kent feels that the career of her successful husband, District Attorney Kent, is like a child she has watched over and protected. When she discovers that he has failed her, and is about to sell his honor to the corporations to save the family home, she demands that he remain true to her faith in him in payment for the sacrifices she has made — notably when she refused to go away with a man she loved more. Her confession goads Kent to an admission that he, too, has loved another woman and he proposes that now they know neither really loves the other they separate. They find, however, that having come along the road together for ten years it is not easy to bear the thought of separation. The past is past. A new love has come to them.

"THE LIVING MASK"

A satirical comedy in three acts by Luigi Pirandello. Produced by Brock Pemberton at the Forty-fourth Street Theater, New York, January 21, 1924.

Cast of characters —

Landolfo..Thomas Chalmers
Arialdo...Rex K. Benware
Ordulfo...Ralph Macbane
Bertoldo..Gerald Hamer
Giovanni..Arthur Bowyer
Marquis Carlo Di Nolli................................Stuart Bailey
Baron Tito Belcredi...................................Warburton Gamble
Dr. Dionisio Genoni...................................Thomas Louden
Donna Mathilde..Ernita Lascelles
The Marchesina Frida..................................Kay Strozzi
"Henry IV."...Arnold Korff

Act I.—The Drawing Room of a Lonely Villa in Umbria. Act II.—An Adjoining Room in the Villa. Act III.—Same as Act I.

A young Italian, preparing to appear as Henry IV of the Holy Roman Empire at a masquerade ball, suffers a fall from his horse, bumps his head on a stone and thereafter imagines he is the monarch himself. To humor him and keep him quiet his friends and relatives surround him with the trappings and attendants of Henry's supposed court. This has been going on for twenty years when the play opens. A new alienist is about to try a new cure based on the reënactment of certain scenes connected with the original accident. In the midst of these preparations the insane man suddenly makes it known that he had recovered his mind years before, but preferred the freedom from contact with a hypocritical world that insanity gave him. Also, finding among his regathered friendships the woman who had jilted him and the man who had taken her from him, he kills the man, upbraids the woman and goes back to madness with every indication of making a thorough job of it this time.

" LOLLIPOP "

A musical comedy in three acts by Zelda Sears; music by Vincent Youmans. Produced by Henry W. Savage, Incorporated, at the Knickerbocker Theater, New York, January 21, 1924.

Cast of characters —

Mrs. Mason	Adora Andrews
Virginia	Gloria Dawn
Tessie	Aline McGill
Don Carlos	Leonard Ceiley
Omar K. Garrity	Nick Long, Jr.
Petunia	Virginia Smith
Laura Lamb	Ada May
Rufus	A Dark Secret
George Jones	Gus Shy
Bill Geohagen	Harry Puck
Mrs. Garrity	Zelda Sears
Helene	Florence Webber
Specialty Dancers	Addison Fowler, Florenz Tamara
Parkinson	Mark Smith
Lindsay	Karl Stall
Adrian	Leonard St. Leo

Act I.—Adoption Day at the Franco-American Orphanage. Act II.—Mrs. Garrity's Summer Home. Act III.—Laura's Home.

Laura Lamb is called " Lollipop " at the orphanage, and the name sticks to her, naturally, after she is adopted by Mrs. Garrity, a rich but catty lady. At the Garritys's Laura meets an attractive plumber, frees herself from the accusation of having stolen Mrs. Garrity's purse, and attends the masked ball in costume in the last act.

"SWEET LITTLE DEVIL"

A musical comedy in three acts by Frank Mandel and Laurence Schwab; music by George Gershwin. Produced by Laurence Schwab at the Astor Theater, New York, January 21, 1924.

Cast of characters —

Rena...Rae Bowdin
Joyce West...Marjorie Gateson
May Rourke..Ruth Warren
Sam Wilson..Franklyn Ardell
Virginia Araminta Culpepper........................Constance Binney
Tom Nesbitt...Irving Beebe
Fred Carrington.....................................William Wayne
Jim Henry...Charles Kennedy
Susette...Mildred Brown
Joan Edwards..Bobbie Breslaw
Richard Brook.......................................William Holbrook
Marian Townes.......................................Olivette

Act I. and II.—Joyce West's Apartment on the Roof of a New York Apartment Building. Act III.—Sierra Notre, Peru.

Virginia Culpepper is visiting Joyce West in New York, Virginia being a simple child and Joyce a "Follies" girl. Tom Nesbitt, a South American engineer, strikes up a correspondence, as he supposes, with the "Follies" girl, but Virginia writes all the letters. Tom comes to New York to collect $40,000 and his girl, discovers that she is interested only in the money and turns finally to Virginia, the "sweet little devil" who tricks the show girl into revealing her true character.

" MR. PITT "

A play in three acts by Zona Gale. Produced **by** Brock Pemberton at the Thirty-ninth Street Thea**ter,** New York, January 22, 1924.

Cast of characters —
```
Rachel Arrowsmith.................................Antoinette Perry
The Reverend Barden............................Frederick Webber
Mrs. Barden..........................................Laura Sherry
Mrs. Arrowsmith..............................Adelaide Fitz-Allen
Milly..................................................Marion Allen
Marshall Pitt.......................................Walter Huston
Barbara Ellsworth...............................Minna Gombell
Mis' Hellie Cooper....................................Ethel Wright
Buck Carbury.....................................Parker Fennelly
Mayme Carbury.....................................Helen Sheridan
Winnie................................................Florence Barrie
Elsie................................................Catherine Sayre
Carrie.................................................Mildred Miller
Mis' Matt Barber...................................Emily Lorraine
Mis' Henry Bates....................................Marie Haynes
Mis' Nick True.......................................Minnie Milne
Max Bayard.......................................C. Henry Gordon
Jeffrey Pitt......................................Borden Harriman
Bonny...............................................Florence Peterson
```
Act I.—1902. Scene 1—Mrs. Arrowsmith's Drawing Room. Interlude—Town Talk. Scene 2—Arbor at Barbara Ellsworth's. Interlude—Upstreet. Scene 3—Mrs. Arrowsmith's Drawing Room. Interlude—Downstreet. Scene 4—Alcove of Hotel Lobby. Act II.—Scene 1 and 2—Living Room at Pitt's House. Scene 3—Bedroom at Eltovar Hotel. Scene 4—Living Room at Pitt's House. Act III.—1922. Mrs. Arrowsmith's Drawing Room.

Marshall Pitt, selling canned goods in a small mid-West town, meets Barbara Ellsworth, whose father has just died. His sympathy appeals to Barbara. Also she needs a man around the house. So they are married. But Barbara begins to find Marshall an awful boob almost immediately. A year later she can stand him no longer and runs away with the trombonist of a jazz band. Marshall, still pathetically in love with Barbara, goes to the Klondike and comes back with $125,000, only to discover that his son, become a college boy in his absence, is almost as much ashamed of him as his wife used to be. Barbara never comes back.

" THE GIFT "

A drama in three acts by Julia Chandler and Alethea
Luce. Produced by Anna Lambert Stewart at the Greenwich Village Theater, New York, January 22, 1924.

Cast of characters —

Madame Lambert...Ida Mulle
Lucia Cavelli.................................Leonore McDonough
Richard Bain..................................Pedro de Cordoba
Paul Bain..G. Davison Clark
Daphne.......................................Elizabeth Bellairs
Suchecki...Effingham Pinto
Yvonne Dubois.......................................Doris Kenyon
John Armstrong.............................Frederick R. Macklyn
Harriet Bain...Alice Parks
Margaret Marshall...............................Madeline Davidson
    Act I., II. and III.—Richard Bain's Studio, in the Latin Quarter,
Paris. Staged by Clifford Brooke.

Richard Bain, painting in Paris, is given to late
parties and gay ladies. Yvonne Dubois, applying for
a job as his model, falls desperately in love with him
and seeks to save both his talent and his health by
inspiring him to a cleaner life and better work. She
succeeds, eventually, but, being physically frail, she
dies just as her painter triumphs.

" THE WAY THINGS HAPPEN "

A drama in three acts by Clemence Dane. Produced
by Guthrie McClintic at the Lyceum Theater, New York,
January 28, 1924.

Cast of characters —

Mrs. Farren..Zeffie Tilbury
Shirley Pride.....................................Katharine Cornell
Martin Farren..Tom Nesbitt
Harness..Augusta Haviland
Muriel Hanbury......................................Helen Robbins
Chussie Hare.......................................Reginald Sheffield
Bennett Lomax.. Ivan Simpson
Mrs. Hanbury.......................................Lillian Brennard

Dr. Rodson......................................T. Wygney Percival
A Porter...Orlando Smith
    Act I., II. and III.—Sitting Room at Mrs. Farren's in a suburb of London. Staged by Guthrie McClintic.

Shirley Pride has been brought up in the family of the Farrens in a London suburb and has always been in love with Martin Farren, her foster brother. Learning on the eve of his marriage to another girl that he is in danger of exposure as a thief at his office, because he temporarily has borrowed certain securities, and being offered the incriminating evidence in exchange for her virtue by the villain who holds it, Shirley completes the bargain. But when Martin learns what she has done he angrily denounces her and insists upon confessing his guilt and going to jail rather than accept such a sacrifice from her. Two years later Martin, broken and cynical, returns home to find his mother dead and Shirley still waiting. Circumstances finally open his eyes to the girl's great love of him, and his love of her.

"THE GOOSE HANGS HIGH"

A play in three acts by Lewis Beach. Produced by the Dramatists' Theater, Incorporated, at the Bijou Theater, New York, January 29, 1924.

Cast of characters —
Bernard Ingals......................................Norman Trevor
Eunice Ingals.......................................Katherine Grey
Noel Derby..William Seymour
Leo Day...Purnel Pratt
Rhoda...Florence Pendleton
Julia Murdoch.......................................Lorna Elliott
Mrs. Bradley..Mrs. Thomas Whiffen
Hugh Ingals...John Marston
Ronald Murdoch......................................Geoffrey Wardwell
Lois Ingals...Miriam Doyle
Bradley Ingals......................................Eric Dressler
Dagmar Carroll......................................Shirley Warde
Elliott Kimberley...................................Harry Cowley
    Act I., II. and III.—The Living Room of the Ingals's House in a Small City of the Middle West.

(See page 132.)

" MOONLIGHT "

A musical comedy in two acts by William Le Baron;
music by Con Conrad; lyrics by William B. Friedlander.
Produced by L. Lawrence Weber, at the Longacre Theater,
New York, January 30, 1924.

Cast of characters —

Jimmie Farnsworth	Louis Simon
George Van Horne	Glen Dale
Betty Duncan	Maxine Brown
Louise Endicott	Allyn King
Suzanne Frank	Elsa Erst
Brooks	Robinson Newbold
Peter Darby	Ernest Glendinning
Marie	Helen O'Shea
Special Dancers	The Lorraine Sisters

Act I. and II.—Jimmie Farnsworth's Home on Long Island.

The plot of this one is from a farce called " I Love
You," written by Mr. Le Baron some years back. One
society man wagers another dress suit fellow that he
can cause any two young people to fall in love by
maneuvering them into a comfortable seat under a rose-
colored lamp while a violinist plays soulful music in
the next room. The scheme works perfectly, but always
on the wrong people.

" RUST "

A drama in three acts by Robert Presnell. Produced
by Devsilck, Incorporated, at the Greenwich Village
Theater, New York, January 31, 1924.

Cast of characters —

El Viejo	Ralf Belmont
Paula	Selena Royle
Miguel	Richard La Salle
Jose	Clarke Silvernail
Martin	Leslie King
Carlos Ortega	William Bowman
Pio	John Maroni
Lola	Lisle Leigh
Matto	Jack McElroy

```
1st Sailor..............................................Bradford Hunt
2d Sailor..............................................Carlin Crandall
Rosa....................................................Abbe Corbeau
Juan....................................................A. M. Bush
Gypsy Dancer..........................................Lola Florisca
Gypsy Guitarist.......................................Solly Maldona
```
    Act I.—Interior of House of El Viejo, Ancantes, Barcelona. Act
II.—Café Villa Martin, Valencia. Act III.—Same as Act I.

Jose is a writer of songs but also a junkman. Born
in the Ancantes, " a stinking morass of junk," a " thieves'
market," near Barcelona, Spain, he is bound to spend
his life " in the bondage of tradition." Jose loves Paula
and, thinking he has killed a rival, Miguel, runs away to
Valencia. There he takes up with smugglers and cabaret
singers, and writes a popular song that makes him rich.
But when he gets back to Barcelona Paula has married
Miguel. Which complicates matters until Jose's father
stabs Miguel and leaves the way clear for love and song
writing.

" FASHION "

A revival of the comedy of 1845 by Anna Cora Mowatt.
Arranged by Brian Hooker and Deems Taylor. Pro-
duced by the Provincetown Players at the Provincetown
Playhouse, February 3, 1924.

Cast of characters —

```
Zeke...................................................George Brown
Millinette.............................................Mary Blair
Mr. Tiffany............................................Romeyn Benjamin
Mrs. Tiffany...........................................Clare Eames
Snobson................................................Allen W. Nagle
Seraphina..............................................Helen Freeman
T. Tennyson Twinkle....................................Charles Ellis
Augustus Fogg..........................................Harold McGee
Count Jolimaitre.......................................Stanley Howlett
Adam Trueman...........................................Perry Ivins
Gertrude...............................................Mary Morris
Colonel Howard.........................................Walter Abel
Prudence...............................................Ruza Wenclawska
Mrs. Tiffany's Harpist.................................Marietta Bitter
Mrs. Tiffany's Violinist...............................Macklin Marrow
```

Mrs. Tiffany's Guests............................Eloise Pendleton
Cynthia Barry, Lucy Ellen Shreve
Act I.—Scene 1—A Splendid Drawing Room in the House of Mrs.
Tiffany. Scene 2—The Interior of a Beautiful Conservatory. Act
II.—Scene 1—Mrs. Tiffany's Ball Room. Scene 2—Housekeeper's
Room. Act III.—Mrs. Tiffany's Drawing Room.

The first native comedy to achieve a "run" in an American theater. Written by Anne Cora Mowatt, and produced at the Park Theater, New York, in 1845, it achieved a record of eighteen consecutive performances. In the current revival a half dozen songs of the period, including, "Come, Birdie, Come," "Call Me Pet Names, Dearest" and "The Gypsy's Warning" are included.

"THE SHOW OFF"

A comedy drama in three acts by George Kelly. Produced by Stewart & French, Incorporated, at the Playhouse, February 5, 1924.

Cast of characters —
Clara...Juliette Crosby
Mrs. Fisher..Helen Lowell
Amy...Regina Wallace
Frank Hyland...Guy D'Ennery
Mr. Fisher...C. W. Goodrich
Joe...Lee Tracy
Aubrey Piper...................................Louis John Bartels
Mr. Gill...Francis Pierlot
Mr. Rogers...Joseph Clayton
Act I., II. and III.—The Big Room at Fisher's.

(See page 26.)

"SIX CHARACTERS IN SEARCH OF AN AUTHOR"

A revival of the play by Luigi Pirandello. Produced by Brock Pemberton at the Forty-fourth Street Theater, New York, February 6, 1924.

Cast of characters —
The Father...Moffat Johnson
The Mother...Margaret Wycherly

```
The Step-Daughter...............................Florence  Eldridge
The Son..............................................Dwight  Frye
The Boy...............................................Knox  Kincaid
The Little Girl......................................Mildred  Lusby
Madame Pace  (Evoked)..............................Ida  Fitzhugh
The Manager........................................Ernest  Cossart
The Leading Man.......................................Fred  House
The Leading Lady.....................................Ethel  Jones
The Juvenile......................................Borden  Harriman
The Ingénue.......................................Kathleen  Graham
The Character Woman...............................Maud  Sinclair
The Third Actor........................................Jack  Amory
The Fourth Actor.................................William  T.  Hays
The Third Actress...................................Leona  Keefer
The Fourth Actress...............................Blanche  Gervais
The Fifth Actress...............................Katherine  Atkinson
The Stage Manager................................Russell  Morrison
The Property Man...................................John  Saunders
      Scene—The  Stage  of  a  Theater.   Staged  by  Mr.  Pemberton.
```

" THE NEW ENGLANDER "

A drama in four acts by Abby Merchant. Produced by the Equity Players, Incorporated, at the Forty-eighth Street Theater, New York, February 7, 1924.

Cast of characters —
```
Mrs. Ellery........................................Katherine  Emmet
Helen Estabrook.......................................Louise  Huff
Robert Keene.........................................Gilbert  Emery
Annie Bennett.....................................Helen  Strickland
Seth Ellery.......................................Alan  Birmingham
James McCall.........................................Arthur  Shaw
      Act I., II., III. and IV.—The  West  Parlor  of  the  Ellery  Home  in
a  Suburb  of  Boston.
```

Mrs. Ellery, a Spartan mother representative of the New England aristocracy, discovers that her son, Seth, has misappropriated funds belonging to his fiancée, Helen Estabrook. The girl has given him a power of attorney, and urged him to use the money, but the mother cannot accept this as an excuse. Having been similarly lenient with Seth's father she is convinced she materially weakened his character. She insists upon Helen's prosecuting Seth and sending him to jail, determined that the boy shall acquire a sense of responsibility. Seth runs away and threatens to jump his bond. Before he can carry the threat into execution his mother kills herself and leaves him her fortune, seeking thus to complete his lesson and also to prove the quality of her devotion.

"BEGGAR ON HORSEBACK"

A play in two parts by George S. Kaufman and Marc Connelly. Produced by Winthrop Ames at the Broadhurst Theater, New York, February 12, 1924.

Cast of characters —

Dr. Albert Rice	Richard Barbee
Cynthia Mason	Kay Johnson
Neil McRae	Roland Young
Mr. Cady	George W. Barbier
Mrs. Cady	Marion Ballou
Gladys Cady	Anne Carpenter
Homer Cady	Osgood Perkins
A Butler	Pascal Cowan
Jerry	Edwin Argus
A Business Man	Maxwell Selzer
Miss Hey	Spring Byington
Miss You	Fay Walker
A Waiter	Charles A. House
A Reporter	James Sumner
A Juror	Paul Wilson
A Guide	Walker M. Ellis
A Sightseer	Norman Sweetser
A Novelist	Bertrand O. Dolson
A Song-Writer	Chappell Cory, Jr.
An Artist	Henry Meglup
A Poet	Hamilton MacFadden

The Play Begins in the Apartment of Neil McRae
The Pantomime—During Part II
A KISS IN XANADU

H. R. H. The Crown Prince of Xanadu	George Mitchell
H. R. H. The Crown Princess of Xanadu	Grethe Ruzt-Nissen
First Lady in Waiting	Spring Byington
First Lord of the Bedchamber	Drake DeKay
A Lamplighter	Tom Raynor
A Policeman	Edwin Argus
Cæsar and Pompey	Joseph Hamilton and Herbert James

Scene 1—The Royal Bedchamber. Scene 2—A Public Park. Scene 3—The Bedchamber Again. Otto Ore, Solo Pianist.

(See page 160.)

"THE WONDERFUL VISIT"

A drama in five acts by H. G. Wells and St. John Ervine. Produced by the Players Company, Incorporated, at the Lenox Hill Theater, New York, February 12, 1924.

Cast of characters —

```
Grummett...........................................Edmond Norris
Peter Jekyll...........................................Tom Fadden
Delia...........................................Virginia MacFadyen
Mrs. Hinijer...........................................Kate Mayhew
Rev. Richard Benham, M. A..........................Robert LeSueur
Mrs. Mendham...................................Marion Beckwith
Nicky...........................................Theodore Hecht
The Angel...........................................Margaret Mower
Rev. George Mendham, M. A...........................Albert Reed
Henry Crump, L.R.C.P., L.R.G.S...................Mortimer White
Lady Hammergallow...........................Nellie Graham-Dent
Sir John Gotch, K.B.E............................Warren William
```

Act I.—The Garden of Siddermorton Vicarage. Act II.—The Vicar's Study. Act III.—The War Memorial. Act IV.—Same as Act II. Act V.—Same as Act I. The Spring of 1919. Staged by Eugene Lockhart.

The Rev. Richard Benham, M.A., dozing in the garden of the vicarage, imagines an angel, wounded in the belief that it was a particularly brilliant flamingo, falls to earth at his feet. He takes it in, and thereafter has a vast amount of explaining to do to the neighbors. The angel is properly disgusted with the meannesses of the people living in a world that hatches war and such like crimes. Defending the mother of an illegitimate war baby the celestial visitor brings scandal about the ears of the vicar, and finally is burned up in a vicarage fire, together with the baby and its mother. It returns later to reassure the vicar that the world is improving gradually, which he is pleased to believe when he awakes.

"THE ASSUMPTION OF HANNELE"

A dream play in two acts by Gerhardt Hauptman. Produced by John D. Williams at the Cort Theater, New York, February 15, 1924.

Cast of characters —

Hannele	Eva Le Gallienne
Gottwald, a Schoolmaster	Basil Rathbone
Sister Martha	Alice John

Inmates of the Almhouse

Tulpe	Mrs. Edmund Gurney
Hete	Olive Valerie
Pleschke	Edward Forbes
Hanke	Charles Ellis

Seidel, a Woodcutter	Henry Warwick
Berger, a Magistrate	Paul Leyssac
Schmidt, a Police Official	Stanley Kalkhurst
Dr. Wachler	Morris Ankrum

Apparitions in Hannele's Delirium

Mattern	Charles Francis
The Form of Hannele's Dead Mother	Merle Maddern
The Deaconess	Alice John
The Village Tailor	Owen Meech
The Stranger	Basil Rathbone
First Woman	Florence Walcott
Second Woman	Agnes McCarthy
Third Woman	Georgia Backus
Pleschke	Edward Forbes
Hanke	Charles Ellis
Seidel	Henry Warwick
A Child	Teddy Jones

The dream play of Gerhardt Hauptman in which a bruised and beaten child, dying, visualizes her entrance into heaven. She sees the Saviour in the person of her most sympathetic friend, the schoolmaster. Her enemies are punished, including the stepfather who has beaten her, and the playmates who had made fun of her quaint imagination and tattered clothes are properly impressed. The play was in Mrs. Fiske's repertoire some fourteen years ago.

" NEW TOYS "

A comic tragedy in three acts by Milton Herbert Gropper and Oscar Hammerstein, 2d. Produced by Sam H. Harris at the Fulton Theater, New York, February 18, 1924.

Cast of characters —

Ruth Webb	Vivienne Osborne
Will Webb	Ernest Truex
George Clark	Robert McWade
Mrs. Warner	Louise Closser Hale
Kate Wilks	Frances Nelson
Sam Wilks	Robert E. O'Connor
Natalie Wood	Mary Duncan
Tom Lawrence	James Spottswood

Act I., II. and III.—The Living Room of the Webbs.

The Webbs, Ruth and Will, have entered the second year of matrimony. Their months-old baby is at once a joy and a responsibility. Ruth, growing restless, wants a career and accepts an offer to go on the stage. Will, to be even, resumes an old flirtation with a lipstick and rouge beauty. Both forget the baby — until Ruth's show is a failure and Will's flirtation goes wrong. Then they realize their foolishness and are happily reconciled.

" ANTONY AND CLEOPATRA "

A revival of the Shakespearean drama, in four acts. Produced by the Selwyns in association with Adolph Klauber, at the Lyceum Theater, New York, February 19, 1924.

Cast of characters —

Antony	Rollo Peters
Octavius Caesar	Vernon Kelso
Lepidus	Gordon Burby
Sextus Pompeius	George Carter
Domitius Enobarbus	Louis Hector
Ventidius	Richard Bowler
Eros	J. Sayre Crawley
Scarus	James Diffey

Dercetas...James Meighan
Maecenas...Charles Brokaw
Agrippa...C. Bailey Hick
Proculeius...Grandon Rhodes
Thyreus...Charles Brokaw
Menas...James Meighan
Menecrates...Cyrus Staehle
Varrius...Edward Brooks
Euphronius...Walter Knapp
Alexas...Robert Ayrton
Mardian...Harold Webster
Seleucus...Lionel Hammond
Diomedes...Willard Joray
A Soothsayer...Lionel Hogarth
A Clown...Milton Pope
A Messenger...Dennis King
Other Messengers..........James Difley, Albert Bliss, John Gerard,
                                   Harold Webster, Edward Brooks
Cleopatra, Queen of Egypt...............................Jane Cowl
Octavia...Edith Van Cleve
Charmian...Marion Evensen
Iras...Grace Hampton
    Action of the play occurs in several parts of the Roman Empire.
The music arranged by Alfred Dalby.

The Shakespearean tragedy in a playing version of four acts and fourteen scenes. Directed by Frank Reicher.

" THE CHIFFON GIRL "

A musical comedy in three acts by George Murray; music and lyrics by Carlo and Sanders. Produced by Charles Capehart at the Lyric Theater, New York, February 19, 1924.

Cast of characters —

The Spider...Leah May
Tough Boy...William Green
Mario Navarro...Joseph Lertora
Edward Lewis...John Park
Betty Lewis...Gladys Miller
Tonita Rovelli...Eleanor Painter
Tim Delancy...Shaun O'Farrell
Woolsey...Frank Doane
Specialty Dancers...........................Si Layman, Helen Kling
Lieutenant Dickie Stevens...........................James Marshall
Mortimer Stevens...............................James E. Sullivan

Premier Danseuse...Mlle. Pam
Jeffrey...Arthur E. Viall
    Act I.—" Little Italy " in Lower New York. Act II.—Edward
Lewis's Home on Long Island. Act III.—Café Bohème, New York
City.

The story of an Italian girl with a big voice and an
interest in a banana shop. A wealthy patron sends her to
Italy to have her voice cultivated. Four years and one
act later she returns a great prima donna. And still
true to her Mario, who gave up selling statuary to
become a successful bootlegger.

" THE MOON-FLOWER "

A play in three acts by Zoë Akins, adapted from the
Hungarian of Lajos Biro. Produced by Charles L.
Wagner at the Astor Theater, New York, February 25,
1924.

Cast of characters —

Peter...Sidney Blackmer
Diane...Elsie Ferguson
Waiter..Edward Broadley
The Baron...Edwin Nicander
The Duke...Frederic Worlock
Another Waiter.....................................Hubbard Kirkpatrick
Le Maître d'Hôtel......................................Gustav Roland
    Act I.—The Terrace. Act II. and III.—A Salon in the Suite
Imperial. Time and Place—A Hotel at Monte Carlo.

Peter, a lawyer's clerk in Budapest, inherits a few
thousand crowns from his father. Being a dreamy sort
he is determined to spend it all on one glorious spree
and then throw himself into the sea. In Monte Carlo
he organizes the spree — falls in love with Diane, a
duke's mistress, and includes her in it. But next morning
he forgets the sea and wants to live on — always with
Diane. Being a practical person, Diane, though also
in love with Peter, cannot see her way clear to desert
the duke and his fatter income, and sails, as scheduled,
on his yacht.

" THE STRONG "

A drama in three acts by Karen Bramson. Produced by Henry Baron at the Forty-ninth Street Theater, New York, February 26, 1924.

Cast of characters —
```
Guerhard Klenow..................................Henry Herbert
                                 (Courtesy of David Belasco)
Marie.....................................................Angela Jacobs
Aneta......................................................Helen Weir
Theodore Forsberg.........................................A. P. Kaye
Eric Wedel..........................................Brandon Peters
A Hotel Servant..................................Maurice McCrae
     Act I. and III.—Professor Klenows Study, Copenhagen, Den-
mark.  Act II.—The Sitting Room of a Hotel in the South of
France.
```

Guerhard Klenow, an old and crook-backed professor, rescues Aneta from a cruel father who was using her as a decoy in his winery. Later he seeks to win the love of the girl by pitting his helplessness and need against the youth and strength of her lover, Eric. Aneta, torn between a sense of gratitude to the professor and love for Eric, kills herself.

" FATA MORGANA "

A drama in three acts by Ernest Vajda, translated by James L. A. Burrell. Produced by the Theater Guild, at the Garrick Theater, New York, March 3, 1924.

Cast of characters —
```
George................................................Morgan Farley
His Mother............................................Josephine Hull
Annie, His Sister..................................Patricia Barclay
His Father.........................................William Ingersoll
Peter.................................................James Jolley
Rosalie..............................................Helen Westley
Blazy...........................................Charles Cheltenham
Mrs. Blazy..........................................Armina Marshall
Therese.................................................Aline Berry
Katharine..............................................Edith Meiser
Henry..............................................Sterling Holloway
Franciska...........................................Helen Sheridan
```

Charley Blazy..Paul E. Martin
Mathilde Fay..Emily Stevens
Gabriel Fay..Orlando Daly
    Act I., II. and III.—At the Home of George's Parents, St. Peter,
on the Great Hungarian Plain Known as the Puszta. Staged by
Philp Moeller.

George, eighteen, having been rebellious, is left at home
when his family goes to a village celebration and all-
night dance. Mathilde Fay, an attractive and flirtatious
second cousin living in Budapest, comes unexpectedly
to visit and finds George alone. The boy, immediately
stricken by her charms, is a willing victim of her rather
deliberate seduction. Next morning, when Mathilde's
husband arrives and offers her a trip to Ostend, she
forgets all about George. But to the boy she is still the
romance of his life and he would have her divorce her
husband and marry him. She takes him for a walk on
the Puszta and points out to him that his love is like a
mirage, which she cannot afford to indulge. Her tastes
and extravagances demand the realities of life.

" THE OUTSIDER "

A drama in three acts by Dorothy Brandon. Produced by William Harris, Jr., at the Forty-ninth Street
Theater, New York, March 3, 1924.

Cast of characters —

Mr. Frederick Ladd, F.R.C.S........................Whitford Kane
Sir Montagu Tollemache, F.R.C.S................T. Wigney Percyval
Mr. Vincent Helmore, F.R.C.S......................Kenneth Hunter
Sir Nathan Israel, F.R.C.S.............. ....John Blair
Mr. Jasper Sturdee, M.S........................ ..Lester Lonergan
Lalage Sturdee....................................Katharine Cornell
Madame Klost.....................................Fernanda Eliscu
Anton Ragatzy..Lionel Atwill
Pritchard...Florence Edney
Basil Owen...Pat Somerset
    Act I.—The Honorary Staff's Room at St. Martha's Hospital, S. E.
Act II.—Lalage's Sitting Room, Harley Street. Act III.—Lalage's
Flat, Regent Park.

Anton Ragatzy, apprenticed as a boy to a maker of
bandages and splints for surgeons, patents a rack on

which he is later able to stretch patients afflicted with
malformed joints and cure them, often after recognized
surgeons have failed.   Lacking a technical education,
however, the Royal College of Surgeons is vigorous in
its denouncement of him as a quack.   Ragatzy, embittered
by this opposition, conspires to get Lalage Sturdee,
daughter of the most famous of the Royal surgeons and
lame from birth, to try his rack.   A year later she is
cured.   And during the year she has forgotten one lover
and found another in Ragatzy.

M. MAURICE DE FERAUDY

First American engagement of the French star, presented by Wendell Phillips Dodge at the Fulton Theater,
New York, March 10, 1924.

Cast of characters —

" AFFAIRES SONT AFFAIRES "

Comédie en Trois Actes, en Prose, d'Octave Mirbeau

Mlle. Bianchini..Madame Lechat
    Henriette Lorèze..Germaine
MM. Hector..Jean
    Pierre Caillabet..................................Lucien Garraud
    De Feraudy...Isidore Lechat
    Guy ....Phinck
    Couderc ....Grucch
    Ronet..M. de La Fontenelle
    Henry Vermeil.......................................Xavier Lechat
    Pierre de Rigoult............................Marquis de Porcellet

During a two weeks' engagement, of which the above
was the first performance, Maurice de Feraudy appeared
in the following plays: " L'Avare," " Monsieur Broton-
neau," " La Nuit de Mai d'Alfred de Musset," " Il ne
Faut Jurer de Rien," " La Nouvelle Idole," " Blanchette "
and " Le Legataire Universel."

" WE MODERNS "

A comedy in three acts by Israel Zangwill. Produced by Harrison Grey Fiske, at the Gaiety Theater, New York, March 11, 1924.

Cast of characters —

```
Robert Sundale, K.C..................................O. P. Heggie
Katherine Sundale....................................Isabel  Irving
Richard...........................................Kenneth Mackenna
Mary..................................................Helen  Hayes
Beamish.............................................Galwey Herbert
Feodosia Moskovski.....................................Olin  Field
John Ashlar, C.E....................................Harris Gilmore
Sir William Wimple..............................St.  Clair Bayfield
Dorothy................................................Gilda  Leary
Oscar Pleat............................................James  Dale
Joanna Herzberg........................................Mary  Shaw
     Act I.—Mrs. Sundale's Drawing Room in a Quiet London Square.
   Act II.—Richard Sundale's Studio in Chelsea.   Act III.—Mrs. Sun-
dale's Drawing Room.  Staged by Harrison Grey Fiske.
```

Richard and Mary, children of the Sundales, have taken up with the rapidly advancing younger set of London, including Oscar Pleat, a free-loving poet, and Dorothy Wimple, daughter of the king's surgeon, who is frankly living with Pleat as his soul's mate. Richard and Mary consistently defy their old-fashioned and misunderstanding parents until they are brought up with a turn — Richard by his discovery that he loves Dorothy enough to marry her and father Oscar Pleat's expected heir, and Mary when she learns that her mother's life is endangered by a necessary operation.

"THE LADY KILLER"

A farce in three acts by Alice and Frank Mandel. Produced by the Morosco Holding Company, Incorporated, at the Morosco Theater, New York, March 12, 1924.

Cast of characters —

```
Gordon Kennedy.....................................George Alison
Peters..........................................William A. Norton
Mrs. Kennedy.......................................Ethel Jackson
```

```
Rena Blake.................................................Doris Kelly
Henry Meecham.......................................Harold Vermilye
Joan Smith.............................................Claiborne Foster
Lucy........................................................Lucile Webster
Jack Kennedy.............................................Paul Kelly
Frank Burnham.......................................Charles Hammond
Gregory..................................................James Gleason
Hogan.......................................................James Donlan
Malcolm Smith.........................................Lyle Clement
        Act I., II. and III.—The Home of Gordon Kennedy.
```

Joan Smith, working as secretary to a Hollywood picture scenarist, acquires the cinema point of view. When the boy she loves is charged with murder she takes the crime on her own shoulders, because she knows no jury will ever convict a pretty girl. The crime being a comic attempt on the part of one lawyer to convince another of the plausibility attaching to circumstantial evidence, Joan escapes trial, but not matrimony.

" MACBETH "

Produced by the Equity Players at the Forty-eighth Street Theater, New York, March 15, 1924.

Cast of characters —

```
Macbeth...........................................James K. Hackett
Macduff............................................Moffat Johnston
Duncan...............................................Henry Mortimer
Banquo............................................Douglass Dumbrille
Malcolm.............................................Lawrence Cecil
Ross.................................................William P. Adams
Lennox...............................................Harvey D. Hayes
Seyton ...............................................John Connery
Porter...............................................Louis Wolheim
Doctor...............................................Charles Warburton
Witch, Messenger, Armor-Bearer.....................Barry Macollum
Murderer..............................................Robert Lawler
2nd Messenger......................................Russell Morrison
Donaldbain...........................................Howard Claney
Seward, Apparition...................................Joseph Singer
Fleance, Apparition...................................Teddy Jones
2nd Apparition........................................Evelyn Ware
Lady Macbeth.........................................Clare Eames
Gentlewoman......................................Catherine Proctor
1st Witch..........................................Helen Strickland
2nd Witch.........................................Helen Van Hoose
```

The Shakespeare tragedy in a playing version of five acts and nineteen scenes.

" WELDED "

A drama in three acts by Eugene O'Neill. Produced by Kenneth Macgowan, Robert Edmund Jones and Eugene O'Neill in association with the Selwyns, at the Thirty-ninth Street Theater, New York, March 17, 1924.

Cast of characters —

Eleanor Owen..Doris Keane
Michael Cape..Jacob Ben-Ami
John Darnton..Curtis Cooksey
A Woman..Catherine Collins
    Act I.—The Capes's Apartment.   Act II.—Scene 1—Darnton's Library.   Scene 2—A Room.   Act III.—The Capes's Apartment.

Eleanor Owen is an actress, Michael Cape, her husband, a playwright. So intense is their love for each other that both resent its absorption of their respective individualities. There are frequent quarrels and many disturbing jealousies, followed by feverish scenes of forgiveness. At the height of one quarrel they break, each swearing the other is trying to degrade their love. Both rush from the apartment to be avenged. Eleanor goes openly to the apartment of one who would be her lover, but finds she can go no farther. The memory of her love for her husband stands as a barrier before her. Michael, picking up the first girl of the streets he meets, suffers a similar revelation in her rooms. The concluding act finds them returned home, admitting that, like it or not, each must protect the inspired affection born of their meeting.

" SWEET SEVENTEEN "

A comedy in three acts by L. Westervelt, John Clements, Harvey O'Higgins and Harriet Ford. Produced by John Henry Mears at the Lyceum Theater, New York, March 17, 1924.

Cast of characters —

Ida Farnum..Grace Filkins
Grace Farnum..Isabel Leighton

```
Peeks Farnum.........................................Marian Mears
Bozo...................................................By Himself
Rannie...............................................Jennie Eustace
Russell  Farnum.......................................Douglas  Wood
Bill Boyd............................................Stanford Jolley
Diana Edgerton...................................Josephine Drake
Ted Rutherford...................................Edward H. Wever
Donald  Brown..........................Charles  Trowbridge
       Act I., II. and III.—The Farnum Home in a Suburb of New York.
```

Peeks Farnum is seventeen and active. Eager to help her daddy meet the problems of a house mismanaged by her extravagant mother, who never learned to add, and to save her petting-party sister from marrying the wrong petter, she gets herself tangled in a lot of amusing situations and a suit of boy's clothes. Finally, when she is locked in her room and her clothes taken away from her, she manages a sort of elopement for herself with her big sister's beau, and extracts a promise or two of domestic reform from her parents.

MME. SIMONE

A special engagement, directed by George C. Tyler, in which the famous French actress played a series of matinée performances at the Gaiety Theater, New York, beginning March 21, 1924.

Cast of characters —
" LA VIERGE FOLLE "
```
Marcel Armaury.........................................Jose Ruben
Duc de Charence........................................de Rigoult
Gaston  de  Charence....................................Delaquerere
L'Abbe Roux.............................................Villemain
Le Secretaire d'Armaury....................................Morrell
Fabian  ................................................Dupius
Fanny Armaury....................................Mme. Simone
Diane de Charence (Courtesy of Gilbert Miller)——Eva Le Gallienne
Duchess  de  Charence.....................................Burani
Ketty  ...............................................Tilden
Secretaire de Charence.....................................Soutzo
       Act I.—Drawing Room of the de Charence Home.  Act II.—Li-
    brary, Office of Marcel Armaury.  Act III.—Parlor in a Hotel,
    Greenwich, England.  Act ᵀV.—Drawing Room, Private Suite of a
    Hotel, London.
```

Mme. Simone also revived Alfred Savoir's "La Couturierre de Lunéville," and De Porto Riche's "Le Passe " during this engagement.

" ACROSS THE STREET "

A comedy in three acts by Richard A. Purdy. Produced by Oliver Morosco at the Hudson Theater, New York, March 24, 1924.

Cast of characters —

Mildred Martin..Ruth Thomas
Oberly Musgrave.......................................Elmer Grandin
Harry Stapleton....................................Hooper Atcheley
Joe Bagley...Fred Raymond
Cyrus Perkins....................................James K. Applebee
Calvin Abbott......................................George Neville
Agnes Ellery...Lucile Nikolas
Kenneth Dodge...............................Robert Emmett Keane
Col. Wentworth Dodge..............................Peter Raymond
    Act I.—The Bagley Dry Goods Store. Act II.—Editorial Room of the Glendale Observer. Act III.—The Town Hall. Staged by Oliver Morosco.

Kenneth Dodge, son of an old-time editor, is sent by his father to Glendale, Vermont, to take over and make something of the *Glendale Observer*. Joe Bagley, son of a Glendale dry goods merchant, is left his father's store as his inheritance. Kenneth wants to be a business man and Joe wants to write. They secretly change jobs, Joe dictating the editorial policy of the *Observer*, and Kenneth putting on gingham sales at the emporium. Both are tremendously successful. After a rousing town meeting they are elected selectmen and marry two of the village girls.

" THE MAN WHO ATE THE POPOMACK "

A tragi-comedy in four acts by W. J. Turner. Produced by the Cherry Lane Players, Incorporated, at the Cherry Lane Theater, New York, March 24, 1924.

Cast of characters —

Hon. Rupert Clavelly.....................................Bert Young
Mr. Anthony....................................Charles Welsh-Homer
A Woman...Esther Belford

```
A Man............................................Thurston Macauley
First Young Man....................................Walter Plunkett
Second Young Man..................................Neal Caldwell
Muriel Raub.........................................Vera Tompkins
Lord Belvoir......................................William S. Rainey
Parlourmaid........................................Esther Belford
Lady Olivia.............................................Sarah Truax
Lady Phaoron........................................Ethel Martin
Sir Philo Phaoron................................Reginald Travers
Sir Solomon Raub..................................Dennis Cleugh
A Mandarin.....................................Charles Welsh-Homer
First Chinaman...............................Arthur William Row
Second Chinaman....................................Walter Plunkett
Harringham..........................................Lionel Ferrend
Nosegay..........................................Arthur William Row
    Act I.—A Picture Gallery off Regent Street.  Act II.—Drawing
Room at Sir Solomon Raub's.  Act III.—Lord Belvoir's Flat.  Act
IV.—The Same.  Staged by Reginald Travers.
```

Putting the hypocrisy of the world to test, Lord Belvoir
eats heartily of the popomack, the most delicious of
eastern fruits but of an odor most offensive to western
nostrils. Within a short space he is deserted by all those
friends who previously had found him vastly entertaining
and worth while. Disgusted that so trivial a thing as a
smell could so affect intelligent humans he blows out his
brains.

" THE MAIN LINE "

A comedy in three acts by Grace Griswold and Thomas
McKean. Produced by the Comedy Productions Com-
pany, Incorporated, at the Klaw Theater, New York,
March 25, 1924.

Cast of characters —

```
Izzy Goldstein............................................Sam Jaffe
Mrs. Fogarty.........................................Emily Francis
Betty Beverley..........................................Jo Wallace
Simmons.............................................Kevitt Manton
Lucy...............................................Hazel Harroun
Parks..............................................George Tawde
Bob Rittenhouse....................................Murray Bennett
Trevor Burton......................................Courtney White
Katy...................................................Mary Ricard
Alice Miller...........................................Elsie Esmond
Mrs. Daisy Rittenhouse............................Grace Griswold
```

Mrs. Du Billy..Millie Butterfield
Marjory..Mattie Edwards
Edith...Eleanor Seybolt
    Scene—The Servants' Hall. At the Home of Mrs. Rittenhouse, Bryn Mawr, Pa. Staged by Horace Sinclair.

Betty Beverley, from the south, goes into service in the home of Mrs. Daisy Rittenhouse, who lives along the aristocratic " main line " of the Pennsylvania Railroad running through Philadelphia's most exclusive suburbs. Being a social reformer and keen to reëstablish the old understandings between " the help and the helpless," Betty puts a parlor in the servants' quarters which becomes the most comfortable and most generally frequented room in the house. Also she inspires Bob Rittenhouse with ambition, frustrates a diamond robbery and finally manages to draft the Rittenhouse estate as a model intelligence office, where mistresses and maids will both be handed questionnaires before it is decided they will be permitted to live and work together.

" VOGUES OF 1924 "

A musical revue in two acts by Fred Thompson and Clifford Grey; music by Herbert Stothart. Produced by the Messrs. Shubert at the Shubert Theater, New York, March 27, 1924.

Principals engaged —

Odette Myrtil
May Boley
Irene Delroy
Anette Bade
Beatrice Swanson
Marcella Swanson

J. Harold Murray
Fred Allen
Jimmie Savo
George Anderson
Hal Van Rensalear
James Alderman

" NANCY ANN "

A comedy in three acts by Dorothy Heyward. **Pro**duced by Richard Herndon at the Forty-ninth **Street** Theater, New York, March 31, 1924.

Cast of characters —

Nancy Angeline Van Cuyler Farr	Francine Larrimore
Binner	Harry Blakemore
Miss Dexter	Pauline Armitage
Aunt Angeline (Mrs. Chiverick—née Farr)	Edith Shayne
Aunt Kate (Mrs. Flemming—née Van Cuyler)	Marie R. Burke
Aunt Emily (Miss Van Cuyler)	Louise Randolph
Aunt Nancy (Mrs. Webster—née Farr)	Ada C. Neville
Mr. Llewylln	Charles Angelo
Marcia Haddon	Mary Rose McGlynn
Mr. Brandon	Ralph Carter
Lulu Treman	May Hopkins
Billie Claridge	Clare Weldon
Beth Worthington	Mary Tarry
Mr. Capper	Frank Knight
James Lane Harvey	Tom Nesbitt
Dan Dennis	Wallace Ford
Waiter	Walter T. Jones
Jerry O'Connell	William W. Crimans

Act I.—Aunt Kate's Living Room. Act II. and III.—James Lane Harvey's Offices.

Nancy Farr, strictly reared and closely guarded by four Boston aunts, acquires a dislike for society and a passion for a leading stock actor. She bolts her coming out party, pawns her party gown for a working dress, beards the actor in his den, is properly repulsed and threatened with punishment, only to cry herself into a job and a romance before the evening is finished.

" PARADISE ALLEY "

A musical comedy in two acts by Charles W. Bell and Edward Clark; lyrics by Howard Johnson; music by Carle Carlton, Harry Archer and A. Otvos. Produced by Carle Carlton at the Casino Theater, New York, March 31, 1924.

Cast of characters —

Little Annie Rooney	Hallie Manning
Sweet Marie	Evelyn Martin

```
Mother O'Grady.....................................Dorothy Walters
Casey the Cop......................................William Renaud
Quinnie La Salle...............................Ida May Chadwick
Bonnie Brown.......................................Helen Shipman
Spike Muldoon.........................................Arthur West
Jack Harriman....................................Chas. Derickson
Rudolf Zotz........................................George Bickel
Sylvia Van de Veer...................................Gloria Dawn
Edward Harriman.....................................Edward Wonn
Dusty.................................................Ben Benny
Benny..............................................Burke Western
Four of the Finest and Reporters—Four Entertainers....Lloyd Balliot,
          William Renaud, Frank Stanhope, Garfield Brown
Alex Huxley...........................................Leslie Barrie
Stage Door Keeper...............................Arthur Atkinson
    Act I.—Paradise Alley, New York.  Act II.—Piccadilly Theater,
London.
```

Bonnie Brown, the pet of Paradise Alley, has stage ambitions. Quinnie La Salle, having gone from the Alley to the stage, eggs her on. Bonnie, in London, is a hit in "The Gaiety Girl," which subjects her for two acts to the proposals of the English bounders and delays her marriage to Jack Harriman, the American lightweight champ.

"THE ANCIENT MARINER"

Produced by the Provincetown Players at the Provincetown Playhouse, New York, April 6, 1924.

Cast of characters —

```
The Ancient Mariner................................E. J. Ballantine
First Wedding Guest.....................................James Shute
Second Wedding Guest............................H. L. Rothschild
Third Wedding Guest..................................Charles Ellis
Chorus..........Clement Wilenchick, William Stahl, Harold McGee,
          Benjamin Keiley, Robert Forsyth, John Taylor
Helmsman...........................................James Meighan
Bride..............................................Rosalind Fuller
Bridegroom............................................Gerald Stopp
Life-in-Death...........................................Rita Matthias
First Spirit..........................................Henry O'Neill
Second Spirit.........................................Gerald Stopp
Pilot.................................................Rupert Caplan
Pilot's Boy..........................................John Brewster
Hermit............................... .........................Henry O'Neill
```

"GEORGE DANDIN"
By Molière

George Dandin..Charles Ellis
Angèlique..Rosalind Fuller
M. de Sotenville.......................................Henry O'Neill
Madame de Sotenville..............................Kirah Markham
Clitandre..Gerald Stopp
Claudine..Rita Matthias
Lubin...Rupert Caplan
Colin..John Brewster
The scene is before the house of George Dandin.

A dramatic setting of the Coleridge poem, slightly rearranged. "George Dandin" is a Molière revival in which the great Frenchman has been credited with including many personal domestic experiences.

"HELENA'S BOYS"

A comedy in three acts by Ida Lublenski, dramatized from a story by Mary Brecht Pulver. Produced by Charles L. Wagner, at the Henry Miller Theater, New York, April 7, 1924.

Cast of characters —

Helen Tilden...Mrs. Fiske
Harold "Beansy"...................................Gay Pendleton
Henry...Reggie Sheffield
Moresby Girard.......................................Ralph Shirley
James Truesdell.....................................William Courtleigh
Tot Raymond...Irene Purcell
Ann Kimball...Elaine Temple
Tibby McNair..Louie Emery
Mr. Parr..Carlton Rivers
Lucy...Eunice Osborne
Richard..John A. Willard
Act I., II. and III.—The Living Room in the Home of Mrs. Tilden in a Small Town near New York.

Helena Tilden is the widowed mother of two sons, Henry and "Beansy." "Beansy," having shouted, "Bunk!" in the midst of his college professor's oration on patriotism and the late war, is sent home. He runs to brother Henry, and Henry, being a young radical, supports him. When mother mentions her son's rudeness and intimates that he will have to apologize, they counter with windy defenses of the new freedom and the rights of the individual. Forced to do something drastic to convince them of their lack of judgment, Helena pretends to embrace their most extreme views, gets squiffy on what they think is Scotch and threatens to live openly with a village manufacturer. They beg her finally to desist, and are tamed radicals when their visit is finished.

"TWO STRANGERS FROM NOWHERE"

A drama in three acts by Myron C. Fagan. Produced by Myron C. Fagan at the Punch and Judy Theater, New York, April 7, 1924.

Cast of characters —

```
Dr. Allan Gordon.....................................Richard Gordon
John Gordon.........................................James Bradbury
Florence Gordon...................................Frances McGrath
Angelo Desdichado......................................Fritz Leiber
Bob Grant............................................Norval Keedwell
Helen Hessler............................................Gail Kane
Jerome Hessler...................................Theodore Babcock
Aunt Martha..........................................Thais Lawton
Bryerly...............................................Frank Allworth
Louise Huldane.......................................Peggy Allenby
     Act I. and III.—Living Room in the Home of the Gordons. Act
II.—The Home of the Hesslers.  Eleven o'Clock the Same Evening.
```

Angelo Desdichado, posing as a philanthropic scientist, is really Satan incarnate. Doomed to tempt all those with whom he comes in contact to the degradation of their souls, for every one that repulses him he is given a good mark in heaven. In the play he works with two families, destroying one (the Hesslers) by selling Helen to the wicked Jerome for a mess of diamonds, and saving the other (the Gordons) when Florence overcomes the temptation to desert Allan for her girlhood sweetheart, Bob Grant, and eludes also the tentacular clutch of Jerome Hessler.

" SITTING PRETTY "

A musical comedy in two acts by Bolton, Wodehouse and Kern. Produced by F. Ray Comstock and Morris Gest at the Fulton Theater, New York, April 8, 1924.

Cast of characters —

Mrs. Wagstaff	Marjorie Eggleston
James	Albert Wyart
Roper	Harry Lilford
" Bill " Pennington	Rudolph Cameron
Judson Waters	Eugene Revere
Babe LaMarr	Myra Hampton
May Tolliver	Gertrude Bryan
Dixie	Queenie Smith
Jasper	Edward Finley
Wilhelmina	Jayne Chesney
Otis	George Sylvester
Wilhelmina	Marian Dickson
Mr. Pennington	George E. Mack
Horace	Dwight Frye
Joe	Frank McIntyre
Professor Appleby	George Spelvin
Bolt	George O'Donnell
Jane	Terry Blaine

CHARACTERS AT THE BALL

Jenny Lind	Wynthrope Wayne
Edgar Allan Poe	George Sylvester
Barbara Frietchie	Mariettea O'Brien
Stonewall Jackson	Edward Finley
Rachel	Marjorie Eggleston
Harriet Beecher Stowe	Frieda Fitzgerald
Louisa M. Alcott	May Clark
George Sand	Charlotte Wakefield
Florence Nightingale	Jayne Chesney
Empress Eugénie	Dorothy Janice

Act I.—Garden of Mr. Pennington's Summer Home at Far Hills, N. J. Act II.—Patio of Mr. Pennington's Winter Home at Belle Air, Florida.

Joe's a fat old thief who plays a system. With the help of the authors he gets Horace, his youthful accomplice, adopted into the homes of rich men where he locates the wall safes and the jewels. At the Penningtons's, however, Horace meets May Tolliver and loves her, and Dixie, her sister, helps him go straight. After which Dixie mates with Bill Pennington, the real Pennington heir.

" MAN AND THE MASSES "

A tragedy in seven scenes by Ernest Toller, translated by Louis H. Untermeyer. Produced by the Theater Guild at the Garrick Theater, New York, April 14, 1924.

Cast of characters —

The Woman	Blanche Yurka
The Man—Her Husband	Ullrich Haupt
The Nameless One (The Spirit of the Masses)	Jacob Ben Ami
The Companion (A Dream Figure)	Arthur Hughes
First Banker	A. P. Kaye
Second Banker	William Franklin
Third Banker	Erskine Sanford
Fourth Banker	Leonard Lean
Fifth Banker	Barry Jones
Sixth Banker	Charles Tazewell
The Condemned One	John McGovern
First Working Man	Maurice McRae
Second Working Man	Allyn Joslyn
Third Working Man	Marling Chilton
Fourth Working Man	Samuel Rosen
A Working Woman	Pauline Moore
An Officer	Barry Jones
A Priest	Erskine Sanford
First Woman Prisoner	Zita Johann
Second Woman Prisoner	Mariette Hyde
Messenger Boy	Sidney Dexter

In this tragedy of the social revolution in Germany, The Woman, a pacifist, assumes the leadership of the Communistic party, despite the protests of her husband, representing patriotism and the state. Thereafter her adventures are tragic. Her followers revolt against her insistence on a bloodless revolution, she suffers a series of distorted dreams and she finally is executed as a traitor by her own party.

" CHEAPER TO MARRY "

A play in three acts by Samuel Shipman. Produced by Richard Herndon at the Forty-ninth Street Theater, New York, April 15, 1924.

Cast of characters —

Florence Lowery	Ruth Donnelly
Filomena	Olga Lee

Evelyn Gardner.......................................Florence Eldridge
Melville Masters.......................................Horace Braham
Jim Knight...Robert Warwick
Charles Tyler...Allan Dinehart
Beulah Parker.......................................Claiborne Foster
Everett Riddle....................................Berton Churchill
    Act I.—Miss Gardner's Apartment. Act II.—The Tyler Apartment. Act III.—Same as Act I. Place, New York.

Jim Knight and Charlie Tyler are partners in a glove business and personally devoted to each other. Jim, being a free lover, does not believe in marriage and takes a mistress. Charlie, more old-fashioned, is keen for the sanctity of the home and wants to marry. They nearly split on the issue, but when they discover that Beulah, the wife, and Evelyn, the mistress, are quite content to accept each other as social intimates and business partners, they let it go at that. Six months later it is discovered that Jim has stolen the firm's money to keep Evelyn in luxury, and Evelyn has stolen Jim's money to provide against the day he will quit her. Charlie and Beulah are poorer but happier, though they, too, have their problems.

"EXPRESSING WILLIE"

A comedy in three acts by Rachel Crothers. Produced by the Equity Players, Incorporated, at the Forty-eighth Street Theater, New York, April 16, 1924.

Cast of characters —

Minnie Whitcomb....................................Chrystal Herne
Mrs. Smith..Louise Closser Hale
Simpson...Douglas Garden
Reynolds...John Gerard
Willie Smith...Richard Sterling
Taliaferro...Alan Brooks
Dolly Cadwalader....................................Molly McIntyre
George Cadwalader..................................Warren William
Frances Sylvester....................................Merle Maddern
Jean..Laura Richards
    Act I., II. and III.—The House of Willie Smith on Long Island. Staged by Rachel Crothers.

Willie Smith is the son of a toothpaste king and worth millions. His shrewd Yankee mother sees him falling under the influence of a group of cheating self-expressionists and seeks to save him by inviting his old small-town sweetheart, Minnie Whitcomb, to visit him in his Italian villa on Long Island. Minnie and the self-expressionists are there over the same week-end. She is awkward and unhappy, but she knows music and is the only real soul among them. Which Willie discovers in time to save himself and his money.

" LEAH KLESCHNA "

A revival of the play by C. M. S. McLellan. Produced by William A. Brady at the Lyric Theater, New York, April 21, 1924.

Cast of characters —

Kleschna	Arnold Daly
Schram	Jose Ruben
Leah Kleschna	Helen Gahagan
Valentine Favre	Hal Crane
Sophie Chaponniere	Katherine Alexander
Raoul Berton	Lowell Sherman
Paul Sylvaine	William Faversham
General Berton	Arnold Korff
Madame Berton	Edith Barker
Claire Berton	Mary Hone
Baptiste	Henry Davies
Sergeant de Valle	Ulric Collins

Act I.—Kleschna's Lodgings in Paris. Act II.—Paul Sylvaine's Home at St. Cloud. Act III.—Same as Act II. Act IV.—Same as Act I.

Leah, the daughter of Kleschna of Vienna, the most skillful of Continental thieves many years ago, suffers a change of heart in the midst of robbing Paul Sylvaine, a deputy of France and an amateur criminologist, who had helped to save her life in a railroad wreck. Determining to go straight, she quits Father and the gang with some difficulty, but strongly backed by the Sylvaine interest. In this revival an epilogue in which Leah was reunited with Sylvaine was dispensed with.

" FLAME OF LOVE "

A romantic drama by Maurice V. Samuels and Malcolm
La Prade.   Produced by G. W. McGregor at the Morosco
Theater, New York, April 21, 1924.

Cast of characters —

Wu-chen	Brandon Peters
Chang-chin	Bernard A. Reinold
Toy-ting	Gilda Kreegar
Sin-yang	J. Hammond Daly
First Weaver	Romney Brent
Second Weaver	Samuel Baron
Third Weaver	Hall Higley
Hai-lung	C. Porter Hall
Men-sin	Kay Strozzi
Fong-lee	Lynn Pratt
Yuen-kai	James Malaidy
Shi-king	Leon Barons
Guest at Fong-lee's House	Guido Orlando
Premier Danseuse	Aysa Kass
First Dancer	Ange
Second Dancer	Bertha Stemmerman
Third Dancer	Eve Jounger
Fourth Dancer	Lydia Langdon
Lo-song-oi	Isidore Marcil
Kuzar	Reginald Carrington
Fong-lee's Maid Servant	Venus Scularekes
Zara	Lenita Lane
First Workman	Roger Phipps
Second Workman	Fred McNally
Third Workman	Olof Laven
Yen-chee	Charles LaTour
Chow-king	Robert Resley
Li-nin	Kenneth Diven
Court Dignitary	William Dean
First Soldier	Randolph Beckwith
Second Soldier	Robert Randolph
Mandarin	Reginald Carrington
First Silk Girl	Mary Cecilia Hilton
Second Silk Girl	Florence Quinn
Third Silk Girl	Gloria Glayde
Fourth Silk Girl	Nancy Lee
Fifth Silk Girl	Mary Taylor
Sixth Silk Girl	LaBelle Cairone
Seventh Silk Girl	Carmen Sanchez

Scenes in Old China, Centuries Ago.

Wu-chen, entering a competition of weavers, seeks to
reproduce the flaming pattern favored by Si-Ling, the
weavers' goddess, because in such a weave her soul
was wafted to heaven the night her lover deserted her
somewhere near the altar.   According to a popular

legend he must remain pure in spirit and body to win the prize, and he falls before the temptations offered by Zara, a gorgeous Circassian. The goddess Si-Ling, however, takes pity on him and sends the flaming silk to help him win the contest and the Circassian as well.

" COBRA "

A drama in four acts by Martin Brown. Produced by L. Lawrence Weber at the Hudson Theater, New York, April 22, 1924.

Cast of characters —

Sophie Binner....................................Dorothy Peterson
Jack Race..Louise Calhern
Tony Dorning..Ralph Morgan
Elise Van Zile.....................................Judith Anderson
Judith Drake...Clara Moores
Rosner..William B. Mack
    Act I.—Tony Dorning's Rooms at New Haven. Act II., III. and IV.—Jack Race's Office at " Dorning's," New York.

Jack Race and Tony Dorning are chums in College. Jack is a crew man and ever so popular with the ladies. Tony is rich and generous, but none too successful as a lady's man. Elise Van Zile, brought up to marry money, loves big Jack but marries little Tony. Four years later, still determined to break down Jack's resistance to her charms, she lures him to a shady hotel for dinner. But he will not stay. That night the hotel burns and Elise with it. Jack has a hard time deciding whether or not he should tell Tony the truth about Elise and destroy his idolatrous memory of her or let him go on mourning an unworthy wife and believing in his would-be disloyal friend. Tony learns the truth about Elise in another way and Jack marries a pure stenographer and settles down.

" WHITEWASHED "

A comedy in three acts by John Goldsworthy and Charles McNaughton. Produced by John Goldsworthy at the Fifty-second Street Theater, New York, April 23, 1924.

Cast of characters —

The Duke	John Goldsworthy
Holly	Victor Tandy
Mrs. Claridge De Casie (nee Casey)	Lorena Atwood
Vivian	Marion B. Hall
Roberta Langdon	Paula Shay
Dick Harmon	Donald Stuart
Count de Rochefort	Olaf Hytten
Alice	Mona Glynne
Mr. Jones	Louis Haines
The Constable	Edward Jephson
Deputy Constable	George Slivers

Act I., II. and III.—The Hall at Catskill Lodge.

" THE DUST HEAP "

A melodrama in three acts by Bernard J. McOwen and Paul Dickey. Produced by Lyle D. Andrews in association with James Shesgreen, at the Vanderbilt Theater, New York, April 24, 1924.

Cast of characters —

Father Paul	Albert Tavernier
Robert Hawthorne	William Hanley
Abraham Levy	George Farren
Alf Jennings	E. J. Blunkall
No Shoes	Miriam Lipps Crawford
Jules Toussaint	Louis Bennison
Nina Moosha	Inez Plummer
Pat O'Day	Robert Strange
Sam Yen	George W. Barnum
Harry Mims	Harry R. Allen
Charlotte	Adda Gleason
Pietro Sorrato	Herbert Farjeon
" Stony " Phil	John Sharkey
" Limpy " Ross	Phillip Bosner

Act I.—Father Paul's Cabin in the Canadian Yukon. Act II. and III.—" The Dust Heap."

Abraham Levy, a wandering Jew in the Yukon, is searching for his lost daughter. He finds her in the last act, but not before as Nina Moosha, the supposed half-breed foundling brought up by a priest, she is pursued by Jules Touissant, a lecherous and blasphemous French Canadian, and rescued by Pat O'Day of the Royal Mounted, assisted by God, who strikes Touissant down with a shaft of lightning just as he is about to overpower the girl.

" THE ADMIRAL "

A play in five acts by Charles Rann Kennedy. Produced by the Equity Players at the Forty-eighth Street Theater, New York, April 17, 1924.

Cast of characters —

```
A Queen.....................................Edyth Wynne Matthison
A Girl.............................................Margaret Gage
A Sailor......................................Charles Rann Kennedy
     Scene—The Pavilion of a King and Queen at War.
```

A three-cornered discussion of an Italian sailor's vision of a new world to be won — the talkers being Christopher Columbus, Queen Isabella and a girl who was Columbus's friend and a stanch partisan.

" GARDEN OF WEEDS "

A drama in three acts by Leon Gordon. Produced by Leon Gordon in association with W. Herbert Adams at the Gaiety Theater, New York, April 28, 1924.

Cast of characters —

```
Delphine...............................................Lola Maye
Hazel Harbury......................................Lilyan Tashman
Vera Carlton........................................Maxine Flood
Nick................................................Harry Morvil
Marion..............................................Ruby Gordon
Phyliss...............................................Jean Bell
Betty............................................Florence Huntley
Patsy.............................................Bobbie Storey
Madge............................................Shiela Desmond
Jack Lane.........................................Norman Hackett
Archie Duffing...................................Clarence Derwent
```

Henry Poulson..Robert T. Haines
Douglas Crawford...............................Warburton Gamble
Phillip Flagg...Lee Baker
Daisy Field...Elizabeth North
Dorothy Deldridge....................................Phoebe Foster
Anna...Carrington North
    Act I.—Reception Hall in the House of Phillip Flagg, Asbury Park,
N. J. Act II.—The Crawford Apartment, New York. Act III.—The
Crawfords's Dining Room. Staged by Leon Gordon.

Phillip Flagg is a rich man of degenerate tastes.
Holding a theory that the most beautiful flowers are
weeds at the root, he proves it by conducting a sort of
forcing ground for human weeds in his Asbury Park
home. Taking the most attractive of Broadway chorus girl
types home as his guests, he mixes the coarser of them with
the finer and observes with pleasure the gradual weedy
deterioration of the crowd of them. His failure completely to conquer Dorothy Deldridge gives him pause.
When Dorothy marries and does not tell her husband
of her past, Flagg plans to renew his pursuit of her.
But husband learns the truth and throws Flagg down-
stairs so hard the weed gardener breaks his neck.

" THE BRIDE "

A mysterious comedy in three acts by Stuart Olivier.
Produced by Jewett & Brennan, Inc., at the Thirty-ninth
Street Theater, New York, May 5, 1924.

Cast of characters —
Henrietta Travers......................................Isabel Irving
James...George Pauncefort
Mortimer Travers...............................Ferdinand Gottschalk
Wilson Travers....................................Donald Cameron
Marie Duquesne..Peggy Wood
Officer O'Brien.......................................Jefferson Lloyd
Isaac Walton Pelham..........................George Henry Trader
Inspector Gillson...............................Henry W. Pemberton
Dr. Sandross....... ....Robert Harrison
    Act I., II. and III.—Library of the Travers Home.

Marie Duquesne, running away from a distasteful marriage, crosses a few roofs and bolts into the first area-
way she finds open. It leads to the apartment of bachelor

brothers. One is young, handsome and timid, the other
freakish and fussy. One collects rare jewels, the other
rare bugs. Against their better judgment they agree
to help hide the bride. Follow adventures in which the
rare jewels are stolen and the bride suspected. But
she isn't that kind of bride at all.

" PEG-O'-MY-DREAMS "

A musical comedy in two acts by J. Hartley Manners;
lyrics by Anne Caldwell; music by Hugo Felix. Produced by Richard Herndon at the Jolson Theater, New
York, May 5, 1924.

Cast of characters —

Peg	Suzanne Keener
Jerry	Roy Royston
Alaric	G. P. Huntley
Ethel	Roberta Beatty
Monica	Gilberta Faust
Arkady	Paul Kleeman
Alexis	Chester Hale
Jarvis	Oscar Figman
Una	Albertina Vitak
Blanche	Lovey Lee
Banbury	Joseph McCallion
Chris	William Ladd
Rita	Henrietta Brewster
Blossom	Gladys Baxter
Fay	Jean Ferguson
Muriel	Helen Haines
Joan	Katherine Spencer
Diana	Julia Lane
Bill	Richard Ford
Guy	John R. Walsh
Fred	Charles Baum
Michael	Michael
Pet	Pet

Act I.—Mrs. Chichester's House, Scarborough, England. Act II.—
The Garden.

In this musicalized version of " Peg-O'-My-Heart " there
is no change in the story of Margaret O'Connell, who
inherits English money and is taken in by her rich
and snobby English relatives because of it. She still
wins Sir Gerald with her wit, but she gets a singer and
dancer, as well as a lord, when she marries him.

LITTLE THEATER TOURNAMENT

Conducted by Walter Hartwig, in coöperation with the New York Drama League for three $100 prizes and a David Belasco trophy, at the Belasco Theater, New York, the week of May 5, 1924.

MONDAY EVENING, MAY 5

The Montclair Repertoire Players of Montclair, N. J., in "On Vengeance Height," by Allan Davis and Cornelia C. Vencill.

The cast —

    Cheridah Gormley...Anna Dolloff
    Hope...Althea Brodsky
    Lem Carmalt..Elton Swenson
    Clay...Hugh Burtis
        Scene: A Cabin in the Tennessee Mountains, Thirty Years Ago.
    Scenic effect designed and executed by Frank Stout.

The Manor Club Players of Pelham Manor, N. Y., in "The Man in the Bowler Hat," by A. A. Milne.

The cast —

    John...Roland Wood
    Mary..Nancy Greene
    Hero..Andrew Fox
    Heroine..Ann Hollister
    Chief Villain.......................................William Bradley
    Bad Man..Stacey Wood
    Man in the Bowler Hat...........................Northrup Dawson
        Scene: In Mary's Sitting Room. The Play Directed by Vernon
    Radcliffe.

The Bensonhurst Theater Guild of Brooklyn, in "Beauty and the Jacobin," by Booth Tarkington.

The cast —

    Anne de Laseyne....................................Olga Biederman
    Louis Valny-Cherault..............................Frederick Kraut
    Eloise d'Anville....................................Emily T. Oppa
    Valsin..Stuart Seymour
    Dossonville...Harold Shapiro
    Officer...Herman J. Cohn
    Soldiers.........................Sidney Fischer and Benjamin Flax
        Scene: The Attic of a Rusty Lodging House of the Lower Town,
    Boulogne-sur-Mer. November, 1793. The Play Directed by Stuart
    Seymour and Bernard Katz.

TUESDAY EVENING, MAY 6

The Lighthouse Players from the New York Association for the Blind of Manhattan, in " My Lady Dreams," by Eugene Pillott.

The cast —
```
The Lady.................................................Mary Bierman
Marie, her maid..........................................Anna Beach
Little Old Lady.........................................Lillian Hillman
The Other Woman.......................................Hazel Crossley
The Two Adorable Children.........Rose Resnick and Ruth Askenas
    Scene: My Lady's Boudoir. The Play Directed by Rosalie Mathieu.
```

The Brooklyn Players of Brooklyn, in " The Wrists on the Door," by Horace Fish.

The cast —
```
Henry Montague.......................................Henry Schacht
George Steele.....................................William L. Felter
The Visitor........................................Bennett Kilpack
The Waiter.............................................Archie Gellis
The Cigarette Girl....................................Judy Fairfield
Guests.......Norma Watson, William H. Ryalls, Florence Herbert,
        William A. Clark, Jr., Louise Schacht, James Watson,
        Ruth Rebhann
    The Scene is Laid at the Source of Ideas. The play Directed
by Evelyn Kingsland.
```

The Alliance Players of Jersey City, in " Caleb Stone's Death Watch," by Martin Flavin.

The cast —
```
Caleb Stone.............................................John Bruns
His Nurse..............................................Mabel Hisor
Carrie, his sister.......................................Viola Bley
Antoinette, his daughter............................Edith Finkeldey
Henry, his daughter's husband.......................John Ehrhardt
Tony, his granddaughter.............................Helen Choffy
Tom, his son...........................................Alan Stark
His Doctor............................................Harry Dippel
Fred..................................................Walter Dippel
Jim..................................................Charles Wessling
    Scene: A Mortuary Chamber.
```

The Fairfield Players of Greenwich, Connecticut, in "The Warrior's Husband," by Julian F. Thompson.

The cast —

Hippolyte	Marjorie Brush
Homo	Kenneth K. Wheeler
Buria	Edna M. Chamberlain
Antiope	Miriam Macauley
Herald	Nat W. Morrow
Theseus	Wilton A. Pierce
Hercules	Lee W. Gibbons
Sentinel	Gladys Bang
Amazon Warriors	J. Mildred Schwarz, Mary Heaton, Carroll Ferguson, Clarissa MacRae, Jane Ely, Grace Rhoads, Grace Cutler, Elizabeth Kellogg, Becky Lanier and Virginia Storm

Scene: Frontier Camp of the Amazon Army. Play Directed by Belford Forrest.

WEDNESDAY EVENING, MAY 7

The Stockbridge Stocks of Manhattan, in "The Poor," by John Merrick Yorke.

The cast —

The Undertaker's Young Man	George B. Jenkins, Jr.
Granny, the rag picker	Edith Coombs
Annie	Dorothy Stockbridge
Tina Maroni	Jane Gaeta
Marta, a neighbor	Emma Miazza
Maggie, her daughter	Sally Walton
Tracy, a neighbor	Robert Irwin
Tracy's Girl Friend	Helen Lieder
Pat, the Man with the Black Eye	Philip Welch
Mamie, his wife	Eleanor Coates
The Street Corner Lounge Lizard	Ross Anderson
The Fruit Peddler	Raymond Seymour
Kid Lewis, Annie's " steady "	Kemp Wyatt McCall
Pop Stacey, Annie's stepfather	Robert Lance
Girl from the Delicatessen Shop	Alice Harrison
Janitress from down the street	Hulda Kloenne
Officer O'Clarty	Godfrey Irwin

Scene: A Street Corner in a Slum. The Setting Designed by Willard Van Ornum.

Adelphi College Dramatic Association of Brooklyn, in "'Op-o'-Me-Thumb," by Frederick Fenn and Richard Pryce.

The cast —

Madame Jeanne Marie Napoleon de Gallifed Didier	Ruth Merritt
Clem (Mrs.) Galloway	Wilma Libman

Rose Jordan..Edith Campbell
Celeste...Edith Hurd
Amanda Afflick.......................................Frances Patton
Horace Greensmith...................................John A. David
    Scene: Working Room at Madame Didier's Laundry. The Play
Directed by J. Harry Irvine.

The Little Theater Company of Dallas, Texas, in " Judge Lynch," by William R. Rogers, Jr.

The cast —
    Mrs. Joplin..Julia Hogan
    Ella, her daughter-in-law..............................Louise Bond
    Stranger...Joe Peel
    Ed. Joplin, Ella's husband...........................Louis Quince
    Scene: Somewhere in the South. The Play Directed by Oliver
Hinsdell. The Scenery Designed by Olin Travis.

THURSDAY EVENING, MAY 8

The Kittredge Players of Manhattan, in " In the Darkness," by Dan Totheroh.

The cast —
    Lissie, a homesteader's wife.........................Jennie Baumel
    Nathan, the homesteader...........................Joseph Greenidge
    Bess, Nathan's sister...............................Madelon Porod
    Arth, a sheep herder................................William Sewert
    Scene: The Lean-to of Nathan's Cabin in the Mid-Western Plains.
The Play Directed by Pearl Byrd.

The Playshop of Pelham Manor, N. Y., in " When the Whirlwind Blows," by Essex Dane.

The cast —
Madame Elizabeth Andreya, wife of General Andreya of the
    Army of the regular Government............Elizabeth Hubbard
Josepha, mother of Oswald, a blacksmith and a member of
    the Workman's Council set up in the District...Eleanor Randall
Anna, lately lady's maid to Madame Andreya........Violet Townsend
    Scene: Josepha's House, Situated Near a Town in Europe in the
Throes of Labor Struggles and Political Upheavals. The Play Directed by Vernon Radcliffe.

The Gardens Players of Forest Hills, L. I., in " **Crabbed** Youth and Age," by Lennox Robinson.

The cast —

Mrs. Swan, a widow.................................Agnes Kiendl
Her Daughters:
   Minnie Swan.....................................Catherine Jones
   Eileen Swan..Elsa Youngs
   Dolly Swan...................................Geraldine Claypoole
Gerald Booth.......................................Melville Greig
Charlie Duncan.......................................Ordway Tead
Tommy Mims......................................Edward H. Moir
   Scene: The Sitting Room at the Swans.

The Community Players of Mount Vernon, N. Y., **in** " **The** Nursery Maid of Heaven," by Thomas **Wood Stevens.**

The cast —

Sister Benvenuta...........................Dorothy Stiles Wellington
Sister Grimana...................................Madge Taylor Tubbs
Sister Rosalba..Eva B. Hull
The Abbess......................................Genevieve H. Cheney
The Sister Sacristan................................Vera M. Weaver
Atalanta Badoer, a novice.........................Florence Tompkins
The Puppet Man....................................Donald Willson
Beelzebubb Satanasso.....................................Grayte Hull
Nuns..................Eleanor Berry, Ruth Bush, E. Dorothy Fogg,
               Helen Kavanaugh, Katherine Mazziotta, Bertha
               Hand,, Marjorie Smith and Elizabeth Temple
   Scene 1—The Chapter Room of the Convent of Our Lady of **the** Rosebush, Cividale. Scene 2—Benvenuta's Cell. Scene 3—The Chapter Room. Early in the Eighteenth Century. The Play Directed **by** Ina Hammer Hards. Costumes Designed and Executed by Ruth **W.** Spears. Miss Ethel Stevens at the Organ.

FRIDAY EVENING, MAY 9

The Huguenot Players of New Rochelle, N. **Y., in** " **Lamplight,**" by Claire Carvalho.

The cast —

Bateese, a Canuck Guide.............................Engene Beaupre
Roger, a gossip...Mark **Harris**
Adrienne Vaugh, the Silver Lady.....................Blanche Greene
John Brenton, an artist........................H. Cleveland Harris
   Scene: A Cabin in the Maine Woods. The Play Produced **under the** Supervision of the Author and Herbert A. Weiller.

The MacDowell Club Repertory Theater of Manhattan, in " Tired," by Juliet Wilbor Tompkins.

The cast —
```
Carrie Sullivan, clerk in a store...............Edith Chapman Goold
Susie Sullivan, a school teacher...............Harriet Stuart Colter
Clarence Sullivan.....................................Paul P. Goold
Agnes, the baby's nurse.............................Isabel Garland
The Baby..................................................
```
Scene: The Main Room of a Two-room-and-bath Suite, the Home of Carrie and Susie Sullivan. The Play Directed by Harriet Stuart Colter. The Stage Setting Designed by William Howard Hart.

The Fireside Players of White Plains, N. Y., in " **The** Game of Chess," by Kenneth Sawyer Goodman.

The cast —
```
An Aristocrat..............................................Warren Ives
An Officer........................................Gustav Michelbacher
A Servant..............................................Adriel Harris
A Peasant..........................................Thomas Scofield
```
Scene: A Room in the House of an Aristocrat. During the Reign of the Czar. The Play Directed by James Wallace and R. C. Turner. The Setting Designed by Donald Earle.

" CATSKILL DUTCH "

A drama in three acts by Roscoe W. Brink. Produced by Richard Herndon at the Belmont Theater, New York, May 6, 1924.

Cast of characters —
```
Case Steenkoop......................................Frank McGlynn
Cobby..................................................Louis Wolheim
Sait Wolleben.........................................Minnie Dupree
Brammy Wolleben.....................................Frederic Burt
Peetcha.........................................Kenneth MacKenna
Irey's-Anne...........................................Helen Reimer
Neelia-Anne..............................................Ann Davis
Elder Shauny Fronce...................................David Landau
Deacon Irey Valter....................................Thomas Irwin
Deacon Mauny Tenneych............................William Hasson
Deacon Ikey Meyers.............................William R. Randall
Nautcha Tenneych...................................Dorothy Sands
Viney Fronce......................................Evelyn Carrington
Mait Meyers............................................Ada Barbour
Charity Logendyke...................................Adele Schuyler
Naomi Van Kill.........................................Helen Tower
```

Leah Van Hovenburgh...................................Kate Kerin
Jacob Onderdonk..............................Willard Mac Hargue
    Act I., II. and III.—The " Stoop," or Summer Living Room, of
Case Steenkoop's Farmhouse in a Small Dutch Hamlet on the Eastern
Side of the Catskill Mountains.

Fifty years ago, in a Dutch settlement at the foot of
the Catskills, Neelia-Anne was a handmaiden in the home
of Brammy Wolleben. Also she was being sparked by a
young fellow named Peetcha. While Peetcha was away
Wolleben, although an elder in the church, tempted the
girl into sin and then denied her before the church.
As there had to be a father for her baby the elders
decided Peetcha must be guilty and forced him to make
her, as the saying is, an honest woman. Peetcha rebelled,
but submitted with the understanding that Neelia-Anne
should never again refer to the matter and never, under
any circumstances, name the father of her firstborn.
Everything was lovely until the girl, moved to hysteria
at a " persuasion " meeting of the church folk, confessed
her sin, accused Elder Wolleben and broke her word
to Peetcha. After which she was pretty miserable until
Peetcha, because of their other children, agreed to forgive her.

" THE MELODY MAN "

A comedy in three acts by Herbert Richard Lorenz.
Staged by Lawrence Marston and Alexander Leftwich,
at the Ritz Theater, New York, May 13, 1924.

Cast of characters —

Jessie Sands...Eleanor Rowe
Sidney...Jerry Devine
The Saxophone...Fred Starwer
The Cornet...Joe Lindwurm
The Trombone...Dave Stryker
The Piano..Al Schenck
The Drums...Bill Tucker
Ruth Davis...Louise Kelley
Stella Mallory..Eva Puck
Al. Tyler...Donald Gallaher
Bert Hackett...Sam White

```
Rita La Marr.............................................Renee Noel
Elsa Henkel.............................................Betty Weston
Donald Clemens.......................................Fredric March
Franz Henkel..............................................Lew Fields
Dave Loeb.................................................Jules Jordan
A Chauffeur..........................................Joseph Torpey
A Maid....................................................Sara Chapelle
A Piano Player with the Company....................Jimmy Kapper
    Act I.—Office of the Al. Tyler Music Publishing Company.  Act
II.—Henkel's Flat.  Act III.—Al. Tyler's Apartment on Riverside
Drive.
```

Franz Henkel, an Austrian composer, finds himself, after years of struggle in America, an arranger of music for Al Tyler, a seller of jazz in Tin Pan Alley. He suffers many indignities, but rebels openly when Tyler rearranges his (Henkel's) " Dresden Sonata " as " Moonlight Mama " and sells it for a popular hit. Later, his daughter Elsa marries Tyler and he is privileged to go back to writing real music.

" PLAIN JANE "

A musical comedy by Phil Cook and McElbert Moore; lyrics by Cook; music by Tom Johnstone. Presented by Louis I. Isquith and Waller Moore at the New Amsterdam Theater, New York, May 12, 1924.

Cast of characters —

```
Jane Lee.........................................Lorraine Manville
Mrs. McGuire.......................................Alma Chester
Kid McGuire......................................Joe Laurie, Jr.
Rollins.........................................John M. Troughton
Julian Kingsley.....................................Ralph Locke
Countess Suzanne D'Arcy..........................Helen Carrington
Pierre...............................................Lew Christy
Lord Gordon Hemmingsworth...................Charles McNaughton
Ruth Kingsley.........................................Marion Saki
Buddy Smith......................................Lester O'Keefe
Dick Kingsley...........................................Jay Gould
Happy Williams.........................................Dan Healy
Little Miss Ritz.................................May Cory Kitchen
Champ Kelly...........................................Allie Nack
Kelly's Second.........................................Jay Gerrard
Referee...............................................Jack Stanley
Stenographer..........................................Pearl Howell
Japanese Doll.........................................Edna Coigne
Spanish Doll.........................................Liane Mamet
```

Russian Doll...Pearl Howell
Hawaiian Doll...Pauline Williams
    Act I.—Scene 1—Jane Lee's Room in the Garret of the McGuire Home, Lower East Side, New York City. Scene 2—Corridor in the Kingsley Studio. Scene 3—The Kingsley Studio, Downtown, New York City. Act II.—Scene 1—Outside the Doll House. Scene 2—The Prize Ring in Madison Square Garden. Scene 3—Same as Scene 1. Scene 4—Up in the Skies. Scene 5—In the Doll House.

Jane Lee is a poor but talented tenement girl who enters her rag doll creation in a doll contest and wins nothing but a duet with the doll manufacturer's son. Later, the son quits his barking father's home, stays five rounds with the lightweight champion at $1,000 a round, sets the poor little doll girl up in business and tells his father to run and jump into the Hudson River. Or the East River, if he prefers.

" THE KREUTZER SONATA "

A drama in four acts by Jacob Gordin. Adapted by Langdon Mitchell. Revived by Lee Shubert at the Frazee Theater, New York, May 14, 1924.

Cast of characters —

Raphael Friedlander...................................Edwin Maxwell
Rebecca Friedlander...................................Engel Sumner
Miriam Friedlander....................................Bertha Kalich
Celia Friedlander.....................................Clelia Benjamin
Samuel Friedlander....................................Burt Chapman
David...Graham Lucas
Ephroym Randar..Jacob Katzman
Beila Randar..Feriake Boross
Gregor Randar...Manart Kippen
Natasha...Myra Brooks
Katia...Jeane Wardley
John..Francis Sadtler
Mary Hopewell...Haidee Javne
Foster..Jacob Kingsberry
Flint ....Martel
Mrs. Hill...Daisy Lucas
    Act I.—Raphael Friedlander's House, Kremenschug, Russia. Act II.—Gregor Randar's Flat, New York City. Act III.—Friedlander's Farm House in Connecticut. Act IV.—Ephroym's Conservatory of Music, East Houston Street, New York City.

Miriam Friedlander, deserted by her Christian lover in Russia when she stands most in need of him, is pro-

vided with a young husband by her rich father and **sent**
away to America to avoid the results of a scandal **at**
home.   In America the young husband beats Miriam**'s**
child and loves her younger and more cheerful **sister.**
Catching the lovers in their sin when they claim to **have**
attended an operatic performance that was not **given,**
Miriam flies into a rage and shoots them both dead.

" HEDDA GABBLER "

A drama by Henrik Ibsen.   Revived at a series **of**
special matinees by the Equity Players, Incorpora**ted,**
at the Forty-eighth Street Theater, New York, May **16,**
1924.

Cast of characters —

George Tesman	Dudley Digges
Hedda Tesman	Clare Eames
Miss Juliana Tesman	Augusta Haviland
Mrs. Elvsted	Margalo Gillmore
Judge Brack	Roland Young
Eilert Lovborg	Fritz Leiber
Berta	Helen Van Hoose

Staged by Robert Edmond Jones.

" I'LL SAY SHE IS "

A revue in two acts; book and lyrics by Will **B.**
Johnstone; music by Tom Johnstone.   Produced **by**
James P. Beury at the Casino Theater, New York, **May**
19, 1924.

Cast of characters —

Theatrical Agent	Edward Metcalfe
Office Girl	Bunny Parker
Doctor	Herbert Marx
Poorman	Leonard Marx
Lawyer	Julius H. Marx
Beggarman	Arthur Marx
Chief	Frank J. Corbett
Merchant	Phillip Darby
Thief	Edgar Gardiner

Chorus Girl..Hazel Gaudreau
Nanette...Alice Webb
Social Secretary.....................................Florence Hedges
Beauty...Lotta Miles
Pages..Melvin Sisters
White Girl and Hop Merchant..Cecile D'Andrea and Harry Walters
Street Gamins..Bower Sisters
Chinese Boy..Florence Hedges
Bull and Bear.................Hazel Gaudreau and Edgar Gardiner
Gold Man..Ledru Stiffler
Pierrots...........................Jane Hurd and Evelyn Shea
Hazel..Hazel Gaudreau
Marcella..Marcella Hardie
Martha...Martha Pryor
    Two acts and twenty scenes. Staged by Eugene Sanger and Vaughan
Godfrey. Supervised by James Beury.

A riotous vaudeville into which the Four Marx
Brothers, popular entertainers for many years in vaudeville, have injected the best of their specialties.

" BLOSSOM TIME "

A revival of the musical play in three acts by Dorothy
Donnelly with a Schubert score. Produced by the Messrs.
Shubert at the Jolson Theater, New York, May 19, 1924.

Cast of characters —

Mitzi...Margaret Merle
Bellabruna..Fenita de Soria
Fritzi...Alma Keller
Kitzi..Bee Brady
Mrs. Kranz...Isabell Vernon
Greta..Verna Shaff
Baron Franz Schober.................................Arthur Geary
Franz Schubert...Greek Evans
Kranz...Robert Lee Allen
Vogl...Cliff Whitcomb
Kupelweiser...Edward Orchard
Von Schwind..William Lilling
Binder...Lee Bright
Erkmann......................................Oliver T. McCormick
Count Sharntoff.....................................Gregory Ratoff
A Violinist..Ulysses Morell
Novotny..Otis Sheridan
Rose..Ryth Randall
Mrs. Coberg......................................Elizabeth Hunt
Waiter...Harry F. Scott
Dancer...Ruth Remington
    Act I.—The Prater in Vienna, 1826. Act II.—Drawing Room in
the House of Kranz. Act III.—Schubert's Lodgings.

" INNOCENT EYES "

A musical revue presented by Lee and J. J. Shubert. Book by Harold Atteridge; lyrics by Harold Atteridge and Tot Seymour; music by Sigmund Romberg and Jean Schwartz. Produced at the Winter Garden, New York, May 20, 1924.

Principals engaged —

Mistinguett
Cleo Mayfield
Edythe Baker
Vanessi
Frances Williams
Marjorie Leach

Cecil Lean
Lew Hearn
Ted Doner
Earl Leslie
Frank Dobson
Charles Howard

Supervised by J. J. Shubert.

" GRAND STREET FOLLIES "

A burlesque presented at the Neighborhood Playhouse. Music by Lily Hyland; book and lyrics by Agnes Morgan. Presented May 20, 1924.

Principals engaged —

Helen Arthur
Aline MacMahon
Esther Mitchell
Agnes Morgan
Lily Lubell
Betty Prescott
Joanna Roos
Florence Levine

Albert Carroll
John F. Roche
Dan Walker
John Scott
George Bratt
Edmond Rickett
Edmund Kent
Junius Matthews
Evan Mosher

Staged by Helen Arthur.

" ROUND THE TOWN "

A musical revue assembled by Herman Mankiewiez and S. Jay Kaufman. Produced at the Century Roof, New York, May 21, 1924.

Principals engaged —

Julius Tannen
Heywood Broun
Harry Fox
Jay Velie
Jack Haley
Charles Crafts
Tom Nip

Janet Velie
Elise Bonwit
Irene Delroy
Gloria Foy
Mabel Stanford
Rose Rolanda
Roberta Medrano

"KEEP KOOL"

A musical revue. Book and lyrics by Paul **Gerard** **Smith;** music by Jack Frost. Produced by E. K. **Nadel** **at the** Morosco Theater, New York, May 22, 1924.

Principals engaged —

Johnny Dooley	Hazel Dawn
Charles King	Jessie Maker
Dick Keene	Dorothy Van **Alst**
Hal Parker	Ina Williams
Edward Tierney	Helen Fables
Lon Hascall	Ann Butler
	Rita Howard

Staged by Earl Lindsay. Supervised **by** Edgar MacGregor.

"THE RIGHT TO DREAM"

A drama in three acts by Irving Kaye Davis. Produced by S. K. and B. S. Knauer, Incorporated, at the **Punch** and Judy Theater, New York, May 26, 1924.

Cast of characters —

Mrs. Anna Hermuller	Augusta Burmester
Sylvia Emerson-Dean	Bertha Broad
David Dean	Ralph Shirley
Typewriter Clerk	Edward Colebrook
Mrs. Ethel Emerson	Marion Barney
Dr. Emil Meyer	Sardos Lawrence
Edward R. Steele	James Hughes
Milkman	George **Jones**

Act I. and II.—Sylvia and David's Room in Mrs. Hermuller's Furnished-Room House. Act III.—Living Room of Sylvia and David's Apartment on the Upper West Side, New York City.

Sylvia Emerson-Dean, married to David Dean **against** her rich family's wishes, lives happily with him in a tenement and starves cheerfully to give him a chance to write the things he wants to write, even if he can't sell them. When their affairs reach a crisis and Sylvia's mother interferes, David takes a horrid job as editor of a mystery story magazine. In two years he is rich but unhappy and kills himself.

"THE FATAL WEDDING"

A comedy in three acts by Theodore Kremer. Revived by Mary H. Kirkpatrick at the Ritz Theater, New York, June 2, 1924.

Cast of characters —
Howard Williams......................................Milano Tilden
Robert Curtis......................................Courtney White
Toto..Harry Hougenot
Swartz...William Ker
O'Reilly..Arthur Dober
Rev. Lanceford.......................................Frank Knight
Mabel Wilson.....................................Mildred Southwick
Cora Williams..Ann Crawford
Jessie...Little Georginna
Frankie Wilson.......................................Master Harry
    Prologue—Scene 1—Home of the Wilsons. Scene 2—Corridor of Divorce Court. Scene 3—Home of the Wilsons. Act I.—Scene— An Attic Room in a New York Tenement. Act II.—Scene 1—The Wilson Mansion. Scene 2—Corridor in Wilson Home. Scene 3—The Hut on the Palisades. Act III.—Scene—Interior of Grace Church. Staged by Harry McRae Webster.

Cora Williams, the jealous cat, seeks to break up the marriage of her best blonde friend, Mabel Wilson, to Howard Williams. With the aid of Howard's best friend, Robert Curtis, she succeeds in doing this. But the day she and Howard are to be married Mabel faces them at the altar and busts up the party.

"FLOSSIE"

A musical comedy in two acts. Book and score by Armand Robi; lyrics by Ralph Murphey. Produced by Charles Mulligan at the Lyric Theater, New York, June 3, 1924.

Cast of characters —
Marie...Jeanne Danjou
Mr. Van Cortland................................Harry McNaughton
Nellie...Mildred Kent
Mildred...Viola Boles
Ki Ki...Trix Taylor
Sally..Jane McCurdy
Irene...Paula Lee

```
Adrienne..............................................Betty Garson
Poppy................................................Mildred Brown
Mary.................................................Helen Warren
Liza.................................................Mary O'Rourke
Elsie................................................Nellie Roberts
Jane.................................................Carol Seidler
Bessie...............................................Alice Cavanaugh
Flossie..............................................Doris Duncan
Archie...............................................Sydney Grant
Senor Don Ribeiro....................................Robert Mameluch
Tommy................................................Jack Waldron
Mrs. Van Cortland....................................Rose Kessner
Peggy................................................Jane Van Rein
Flick and Flock......................................Handers and Millis
Uncle Ezra...........................................Shep Camp
Chummy...............................................Edward Fetherston
    Paul Specht's Lido Venice Orchestra, Mr. Harold Lewis, Conductor.
    Synopsis—Act I. and II.—A Studio Apartment adjoining a Fifth
Avenue Millinery Establishment.
```

In order to fool Uncle Ezra, Flossie pretends she is
married to Archie, who is timid and engaged to Bessie.
And Uncle Ezra, pretending to be fooled, makes Archie
kiss Flossie in front of Bessie, and even walk right into
her bedroom with nothing but his undies and his garters
to protect him. After which all is explained and Flossie
marries Chummy, who comes from her home town and
sings second tenor.

" ONE HELLUVA NIGHT "

A revue by members of the Cheese Club. Produced at
the Sam. H. Harris Theater, New York, June 4, 1924.

Cast of characters —

```
The Cop..............................................Sam Fischer
The Stale Bun Kid....................................Ruth Harding
The Stick-Up.........................................Fay Roope
The Scrub Woman......................................Ruby Blackburn
The Girl.............................................Gwen Burroughs
The Detective........................................Ben H. Roberts
The Burglar..........................................Arthur Villairs
The Mysterious Stranger..............................Frank Ortway
    Prologue—An Alley Off Washington Square, New York City. Act
I.—Sitting Room in the Vandervent Home, New York. Act II.—
Same as Act I. Act III.—Boyle's Thirty Acres, Jersey City. N. J.
```

A special production of " the world's worst drama " by
an organization known as the Cheese Club. It cheated
the storehouse for one night only.

" SHE STOOPS TO CONQUER "

By Oliver Goldsmith, Esq.   Revived by the Players'
Club, June 9, 1924, at the Empire Theater, New York.

Cast of characters —

Sir Charles Marlow	Frazier Coulter
Young Marlow	Basil Sydney
Squire Hardcastle	Dudley Digges
George Hastings	Paul McAllister
Tony Lumpkin	Ernest Glendinning
Diggory	Henry E. Dixey
Roger	A. G. Andrews
Dick	John Daly Murphy
Thomas	Theodore Babcock
Jeremy	Francis Wilson
Stingo	Maclyn Arbuckle
Slang	J. M. Kerrigan
Mat Muggins	Milton Nobles
Tom Twist	Robert McWade
Aminadab	Harry Beresford
A Farmer	Augustin Duncan
A Postillion	John Davenport Seymour
Mrs. Hardcastle	Effie Shannon
Kate Hardcastle	Elsie Ferguson
Constance Neville	Helen Hayes
A Maid	Pauline Lord
A Bar Maid	Selina Royle

Act I.—Scene 1—A Room in Mr. Hardcastle's House. Scene 2—A
Room in an Alehouse.   Act II.—A Room in Mr. Hardcastle's House.
Act III.—The Same. Act IV.—The Same.   Act V.—Scene 1—The
Back of the Garden at Mr. Hardcastle's.   Scene 2—A Room in
Mr. Hardcastle's House.

The third in the series of Players' Club revivals of
classic comedies, the others having been " The Rivals,"
1922, and " The School for Scandal," 1923.

STATISTICAL SUMMARY

(June 15, 1923–June 15, 1924.)

Plays	Performances
Across the Street	32
Admiral, The	4
Alarm Clock, The	32
Ancient Mariner, The and George Dandin	33
Antony and Cleopatra	31
Artists and Models	312
*Battling Buttler	288
*Beggar on Horseback	144
Blossom Time	24
Blue Bird, The	33
Breaking Point, The	68
*Bride, The	30
Brook	16
Bros. Karamazoff, The	40
Burgomaster of Stilemonde	4
Business Widow, The	32
Camel's Back, The	15
Casanova	77
Catskill Dutch	7
Chains	125
Changelings, The	128
*Charlot's Revue	173
Chauve-Souris (return)	36
*Cheaper to Marry	71
Chicken Feed	144
Chiffon Girl, The	103
Children of the Moon	117

Plays	Performances
*Cobra	63
Connie Goes Home	20
Crooked Square, The	88
Cup, The	16
Cymbeline	15
*Cyrano de Bergerac	232
Dance of Death, The	1
Dancers, The	133
Deep Tangled Wildwood	16
Dumb-bell	2
Dust Heap, The	20
Eleonora Duse	10
*Expressing Willie	69
Failures, The	40
Fanshastics	93
*Fashion	152
Fashions of 1924	13
Fatal Wedding, The	8
*Fata Morgana	120
Flame of Love	32
Floriani's Wife	16
*Flossie	16
For All of Us	216
Forbidden	8
Garden of Weeds, The	16
George Dandin and The Ancient Mariner	33

444

Plays	Performances	Plays	Performances
Two Fellows and a Girl	132	What a Wife! (What's Your Wife Doing?)	72
Two Strangers from Nowhere	56	*White Cargo	257
Tyrants	16	White Desert	12
Vagabond, The	3	Whitewashed	13
Vanities of 1923	204	Whole Town's Talking, The	173
Via Crucis	4	Wild Westcotts, The	24
*Vogues of 1924	92	Windows	48
Way Things Happen, The	24	Woman on the Jury, The	77
Welded	24	*Wonderful Visit, The	56
We Moderns	22	Zeno	89
We've Got to Have Money	56	Ziegfeld Follies	333

* Still playing, June 15, 1924.

PLAYS THAT HAVE RUN OVER FIVE HUNDRED PERFORMANCES ON BROADWAY

(To June 15, 1924)

Lightnin'	1291	Rain	632
The Bat	867	Adonis	603
Abie's Irish Rose	839	Kiki	600
The First Year	760	Blossom Time	576
Seventh Heaven	704	Sally	570
Peg o' My Heart	692	The Music Master	540
East Is West	680	The Boomerang	522
A Trip to Chinatown	657	Shuffle Along	504
Irene	670		

WHERE AND WHEN THEY WERE BORN

Abarbanell, Lina........Berlin 1880
Adams, Maude..........Salt Lake City, Utah...1872
Adelaide, La Petite......Cohoes, N. Y..........1890
Allen, Viola............Huntsville, Ala.........1869
Ames, Robert...........Hartford, Conn.........1893
Anglin, Margaret........Ottawa, Canada........1876
Arbuckle, Maclyn.......San Antonio, Texas....1866
Arliss, George..........London, England.......1868
Arthur, Julia...........Hamilton, Ont.........1869
Atwell, Roy............Syracuse, N. Y.........1880
Atwill, Lionel..........London, England......1885
Bacon, Frank..........California 1864
Bainter, Fay...........Los Angeles, Cal.......1892
Barbee, Richard........Lafayette, Ind..........1887
Barrymore, Ethel.......Philadelphia, Pa.......1879
Barrymore, John........Philadelphia, Pa.......1882
Barrymore, Lionel......London, England.......1878
Bates, Blanche.........Portland, Ore..........1873
Bayes, Nora...........Milwaukee, Wis........1880
Beban, George..........San Francisco, Cal......1873
Beckley, Beatrice.......Roedean, England......1885
Beecher, Janet..........Chicago, Ill...........1884
Belasco, David.........San Francisco, Cal.....1862
Ben-Ami, Jacob.........Minsk, Russia.........1890
Bennett, Richard........Cass County, Ind.......1873
Bennett, Wilda.........Asbury Park, N. J......1894
Benrimo, J. Harry.......San Francisco, Cal.....1874
Bernard, Barney........Rochester, N. Y........1877
Bernard, Sam..........Birmingham, England...1863
Bernhardt, Sarah.......Paris, France..........1844
Bingham, Amelia.......Hickville, Ohio........1869
Binney, Constance.......Philadelphia, Pa.......1900

Conroy, Frank.........London, England.......1885
Cooper, Violet Kemble...London, England.......1890
Corrigan, Emmett........Amsterdam, Holland....1871
Corthell, Herbert........Boston, Mass...........1875
Courtenay, William......Worcester, Mass........1875
Courtleigh, William......Guelph, Ont...........1869
Cowl, Jane.............Boston, Mass...........1887
Crane, William H.......Leicester, Mass.........1845
Craven, Frank..........Boston, Mass..........1875
Crews, Laura Hope......San Francisco, Cal.....1880
Crosman, Henrietta......Wheeling, W. Va.......1865
Crothers, Rachel........Bloomington, Ill........1878
Cumberland, John.......St. John, N. B..........1880
Dale, Margaret..........Philadelphia, Pa.......1880
Dalton, Charles..........England 1864
Daly, Arnold...........New York.............1875
Daniels, Frank..........Dayton, Ohio..........1860
Dawn, Hazel............Ogden, Utah...........1891
Day, Edith.............Minneapolis, Minn......1896
De Angelis, Jefferson.....San Francisco, Cal.....1859
Dean, Julia.............St. Paul, Minn.........1880
De Belleville, Frederic...Belgium 1857
De Cordoba, Pedro......New York.............1881
Dickson, Dorothy.......Kansas City...........1898
Dillingham, Charles B....Hartford, Conn.........1868
Dinehart, Allan.........Missoula, Mont.........1889
Ditrichstein, Leo........Temesbar, Hungary....1865
Dixey, Henry E.........Boston, Mass...........1859
Dodson, John E.........London, England......1857
Dolly, Rosie...........Hungary 1892
Dolly, Jennie..........Hungary 1892
Donnelly, Dorothy Agnes.New York.............1880
Doro, Marie...........Duncannon, Pa.........1882
D'Orsay, Lawrence.......England 1860
Dressler, Marie.........Cobourg, Canada......1869
Drew, John.............Philadelphia, Pa.......1853
Drew, Louise...........New York.............1884

Frohman, Daniel........Sandusky, Ohio........1850
Fulton, Maude..........St. Louis, Mo..........1883
Garden, Mary...........Scotland 1876
Gaythorne, Pamela.......England 1882
George, Grace...........New York..............1879
Gillette, William.........Hartford, Conn.........1856
Gillmore, Frank.........New York..............1884
Gillmore, Margalo.......England 1901
Glaser, Lulu............Alleghany, Pa..........1874
Glendinning, Ernest......Ulverston, England.....1884
Gottschalk, Ferdinand....London, England......1869
Grey, Jane..............Middlebury, Vt.........1883
Grey, Katherine.........San Francisco, Cal.....1873
Hackett, James K........Wolf Island, Ont......1869
Haines, Robert T.........Muncie, Ind...........1870
Hale, Louise Closser.....Chicago, Ill...........1872
Hall, Laura Nelson......Philadelphia, Pa.......1876
Hamilton, Hale..........Topeka, Kansas........1880
Hampden, Walter........Brooklyn, N. Y........1879
Harding, Lyn...........Newport 1867
Hawtrey, Charles........Eton, England.........1858
Hayes, Helen...........Washington, D. C......1900
Hazzard, John E.........New York..............1881
Hedman, Martha........Sweden 1888
Heggie, O. P............Australia 1879
Heming, Violet..........Leeds, England........1893
Herbert, Victor..........Dublin, Ireland........1859
Herne, Chrystal.........Dorchester, Mass.......1883
Hilliard, Robert S........New York..............1857
Hitchcock, Raymond.....Auburn, N. Y..........1870
Hodge, William.........Albion, N. Y..........1874
Hopper, DeWolf.........New York..............1858
Hopper, Edna Wallace...San Francisco, Cal.....1874
Holmes, Taylor..........Newark, N. J..........1872
Howard, Leslie..........London, England......1890
Huban, Eileen...........Loughrea, Ireland......1895
Hull, Henry.............Louisville, Ky..........1893

Illington, Margaret....... Bloomington, Ill·.......1881
Irving, Isabel........... Bridgeport, Conn.......1871
Irwin, May............. Whitby, Ont...........1862
Janis, Elsie............. Delaware, Ohio........1889
Joel, Clara............. Jersey City, N. J.......1890
Jolson, Al............. Washington, D. C......1883
Keane, Doris........... Michigan 1885
Keenan, Frank.......... Dubuque, Ia...........1858
Keightley, Cyril........ New South Wales, Aus..1875
Kennedy, Madge......... Chicago, Ill............1890
Kerrigan, J. M.......... Dublin, Ireland........1885
Kerr, Geoffrey.......... London, England.......1895
Kershaw, Willette........ Clifton Heights, Mo.....1890
Kosta, Tessa............ Chicago, Ill............1893
Kruger, Otto........... Toledo, O.............1895
Lackaye, Wilton......... Virginia 1862
Larrimore, Francine...... Russia 1888
La Rue, Grace.......... Kansas City, Mo........1882
Lauder, Harry.......... Portobello, Eng........1870
Lawton, Thais........... Louisville, Ky..........1881
Lawrence, Margaret...... Trenton, N. J·.........1890
Lean, Cecil............. Illinois 1878
LeGallienne, Eva........ London, England......1900
Levey, Ethel............ San Francisco, Cal.....1881
Lewis, Ada............. New York.............1871
Lewis, Mabel Terry...... London, England......1872
Loraine, Robert......... England 1876
Lorraine, Lillian........ San Francisco, Cal.....1892
Lou-Tellegen .... Holland 1881
Mack, Andrew........... Boston, Mass..........1863
Mack, Willard.......... Ontario, Canada.......1873
Mackay, Elsie.......... London, England......1894
MacKellar, Helen........ Canada 1896
Mann, Louis............ New York.............1865
Mantell, Robert B........ Ayrshire, Scotland.....1854
Marinoff, Fania......... Russia 1892
Marivale, Philip......... India 1886

Thomas, Augustus.......St. Louis, Mo..........1859
Thomas, John Charles....Baltimore, Md..........1887
Tinney, Frank...........Philadelphia, Pa.......1878
Tobin, Genevieve........New York.............1901
Tobin, Vivian...........New York.............1903
Toler, Sidney...........Warrensburg, Mo.......1874
Trevor, Norman.........Calcutta 1877
Truex, Ernest...........Denver, Col............1890
Tynan, Brandon.........Dublin, Ireland........1879
Ulric, Lenore...........New Ulm, Minn........1897
Valentine, Grace.........Indianapolis, Ind......1892
Varesi, Gilda............Milan, Italy...........1887
Victor, Josephine........Hungary 1891
Wainwright, Marie.......Philadelphia, Pa........1853
Walker, Charlotte........Galveston, Texas.......1878
Warfield, David.........San Francisco, Cal......1866
Warwick, Robert.........Sacramento, Cal........1878
Ware, Helen.............San Francisco, Cal.....1877
Weber, Jos..............New York.............1867
Welford, Dallas.........Liverpool, England.....1874
Westley, Helen..........Brooklyn, N. Y.........1879
Whiffen, Mrs. Thomas....London, England.......1845
Whiteside, Walker.......Logansport, Ind.........1869
Wilson, Francis.........Philadelphia, Pa........1854
Winant, Forrest.........New York.............1888
Winwood, Estelle........England 1883
Wise, Tom A............England 1865
Wood, Peggy............Philadelphia, Pa........1893
Wycherly, Margaret......England 1883
Wyndham, Olive........Chicago, Ill...........1886
Wynn, Ed...............Philadelphia, Pa........1886
Zabelle, Flora...........Constantinople 1885
Ziegfeld, Florenz, Jr......Chicago, Ill...........1867

NECROLOGY

June 15, 1923–June 15, 1924

Bert Savoy, comedian, 35. Born Boston. Of the vaudeville team of Savoy and Brennan. Traveled over this country and in Alaska as female impersonator. Was in Ziegfeld " Follies " and " Greenwich Village Follies." Killed by lightning at Long Beach, L. I., June 26, 1923.

Gustave Adolph Kerker, composer, 66. Born Westphalia, Germany. Moved to Louisville at age of 12, New York in 1884. Some of his compositions were: " The Belle of New York," " Winsome Winnie," " The Whirl of the Town," etc. Vice-president and a director of the Society of Composers, Authors and Publishers, and a member of the Lambs and the Green Room Clubs. Died June 29, 1923, New York.

J. J. (" Jake ") Rosenthal, theatrical manager and agent, 60. Born in Ohio. Manager of Bronx Opera House for Cohan and Harris, and the Woods Theater in Chicago. Father of Jack Osterman. Died July, 1923.

Percy G. Williams, vaudeville manager, 66. Born Baltimore. After building up an independent vaudeville circuit, he sold to the Keith interests for $5,000,000, in 1912. Died East Islip, L. I., July 21, 1923.

Louis Calvert, Shakespearean actor, 64. Born England, 1859. Made his début in 1886. Came to America in 1887 with Mrs. Langtry. Later played with Sir Herbert Tree and Sir Charles Wyndham. In 1889 was made classical director of the New Theater, New York. Last important work was done with the Theater Guild. Died July 9, 1923.

Albert Chevalier, English comedian, 62. Born 1861 in England. A famous entertainer in vaudeville, both in England and America. Died in a London nursing home, July 11, 1923.

Sir Charles Hawtrey, British actor and manager, 65. Made stage début in 1881 in " The Colonel." Made three trips to United States. Played in several American plays in London. Last appearance in " Ambrose Applejohn's Adventure," produced in America as " Captain Applejack." Died London, July 30, 1923.

Dorothy Follis, actress, 31. Born Newark, N. J., 1892. Wife of Karl K. Kitchen, special writer of the " World." First stage appearance in " Mary's Lamb." Later one of " Follies " beauties. Died New York, August 15, 1923.

Marie Wainwright, actress, 70. Born in Philadelphia. Began stage career as member of Boston Museum Company. Played Shakespearean rôles. Appeared with Edwin Booth, Tomaso Salvini and Lawrence Barrett. With William Gillette in " Dear Brutus." Died Scranton, Pa., August 17, 1923.

Franklyn H. Sargent, head of Sargent School of Dramatic Art in New York. Died Plattsburg, N. Y., August 29, 1923.

Frank H. Westerton, actor. Born in London. Came to this country in 1902. Played in " Everyman." Last year in " It is the Law." Died New York City, August 25, 1923.

Ernest C. Warde, actor, stage manager, and motion picture director, 49. Son of Frederick Warde. Died Los Angeles, Sept. 9, 1923.

Harry Braham, actor, 73. Born in London and came to this country in 1874. On stage here 46 years. Died Staten Island Hospital Sept. 21, 1923.

Jerome Patrick, actor, 40. Born in New Zealand. First stage appearance in Australia. Came to this country 12 years ago and played in "Ben Hur." Leading man with Frances Starr and Emily Stevens. Last appearance with Alice Brady in "Zander the Great." Appeared in films. With Agnes Ayres in "The Furnace." Died New York, Sept. 26, 1923.

Mrs. Tony Pastor (Josephine Pastor), widow of Tony Pastor, 68. Organizer of the State Children's Christmas Festivities. Died Elmhurst, L. I., Oct. 6, 1923.

Mrs. Beatrice M. DeMille, widow of Henry C. DeMille, the dramatist. Mother of Cecil B. and William C. DeMille. Some years ago was head of DeMille play agency in New York. Died Hollywood, Cal., Oct. 8, 1923.

Adelaide Winthrop, vaudeville star, 32. Of the team Ames and Winthrop. Wife of Florenz Ames. Died New York, Oct. 13, 1923.

Victor Maurel, actor and singer, 75. Member of Metropolitan Opera Company. Moved to New York in 1909. Survived by his wife, Mme. De Grissac, a playwright. Died New York, Oct. 22, 1923.

Kenneth Douglas, English comedian, 52. At time of death was appearing in "Spring Cleaning" in Chicago. Played in "A Pair of Silk Stockings," "Too Many Husbands," "Mr. Pim Passes By," and "The Demi-Virgin."

James O'Neill, Jr., actor 43. Son of late James O'Neill and brother of Eugene O'Neill, playwright. Died Trenton, N. J., Nov. 8, 1923.

Ralph Delmore, actor, 70. Prominent character actor many years. Played Johnson in "Too Much Johnson," with William Gillette. Died Nov. 21, 1923.

Tom McNaughton, English comedian, 57. Born England. Played mostly in America after 1909, notably in "The Spring Maid." Brother of Charles and Harry McNaughton. Died London, Nov. 28, 1923.

Percival Knight, English comedian and playwright, 50.

Appeared in this country in " The Dollar Princess,"
" The Arcadians," " The Marriage Market " and
" Thin Ice." Was author of " Thin Ice." Went to
Switzerland last spring, where he died Nov. 27,
1923.

Herbert Standing, actor, 77. Father of Wyndham, Herbert, Sir Guy, Percy and Aubrey Standing. Died
Los Angeles, Dec. 5, 1923.

H. B. Marinelli, international vaudeville agent, 59. Born
in Thuringe, Germany, in 1864. Came to America
in 1885. Organized Marinelli vaudeville agency.
Died Paterson, N. J., Jan. 7, 1924.

Forrest Robinson, actor, 65. Played in " Quo Vadis."
Prominent in " The Fortune Hunter." Twice married. First to Eugenie Blair, and then to Mabel
Burt, who survives him. Died Los Angeles, Jan.,
1924.

Tarkington Baker, publicity man and film executive, 45.
Cousin of Booth Tarkington. One time dramatic
critic of the Indianapolis " News." President of
Visugraphic Picture Corporation. Died New York,
Jan. 1, 1924.

Kate Terry (Mrs. Arthur Lewis), actress, 80. Sister of
Ellen Terry. Made London début as Robin in
" Merry Wives of Windsor." Died London, Jan.
5, 1924.

Herbert C. French, dancer and stage director, 33. Produced " The Torchbearers," " Meet the Wife " and
" The Show Off." Died New London, Conn., Jan.
27, 1924.

Charles A. Gardner, actor and composer, 76. Began
career in Brooklyn with Hooley Minstrels. Author
of song hits: " Apple Blossoms," and " Little Bunch
of Lilies." Played in " Fatherland " and " Karl, the
Peddler." Died February 15, 1924.

John J. Murray. Member of old theatrical team of
Murray and Mack. Started as circus clown. Was

manager of two theaters in Warren, Ohio. Died
St. Petersburg, Fla., Feb. 18, 1924.

Arthur C. Aiston, 58. Producer of popular priced road
shows: " At the Old Cross Roads," "After Office
Hours " and " Tennessee's Pardner." Recently revived " Ten Nights in a Bar Room." Died Feb. 26,
1924.

May Tully, actress and authoress, 40. Born in Victoria,
British Columbia. First played in stock companies.
Made New York début in cast of " The Christian."
Wrote and produced " Mary's Ankle." Died New
York, March 9, 1924.

Leonard P. Phelps, theatrical manager, 72. Born in
Baltimore. Appeared in minstrels. Long time asso-
ciate of Charles Hoyt and Frank McKee. Died
New York, March 15, 1924.

Barney Barnard, comedian, 46. Born in Rochester,
N. Y. Made début as monologist. Played in many
Weber and Fields successes and in musical comedies.
With Alex. Carr he created the " Potash and Perl-
mutter " series. Died New York City, March 21,
1924.

Glen MacDonough, musical comedy librettist, 57. With
Victor Herbert wrote " Babes in Toyland." Started
as reporter on New York " World." Did many of
May Irwin pieces. Died Stamford, Conn., March
30, 1924.

Macey Harlam, character actor. Prominent in the casts
of " The Yellow Jacket," " Eyes of Youth " and
" The Wanderer." Last few years played in many
picture dramas. Died April 9, 1924.

Eleonora Duse, actress, 65. Shared with Sarah Bernhardt
honor of being the greatest actress of her day.
First appearance at age of 14 in " Les Miserables."
She was nearing the completion of a farewell American tour when she died at Pittsburg, Pa., April 23,
1924.

John Russell Vokes, vaudeville actor, 52. Born in Australia. Appeared in vaudeville act " Officer Vokes
and Don," Don being a famous trick dog. Died
Minneapolis, Minn., April 21, 1924.

Alma Belwin, actress, 29. Was leading woman in a
number of Broadway productions. Died Boston,
May 3, 1924.

Kate Claxton, actress, 74. Born in Somerville, N. J.
Celebrated particularly for her portrayal of the
blind girl in " The Two Orphans." Died New York,
May 5, 1924.

Louis A. Hirsch, composer, 42. Born in New York. One
of foremost light opera composers. Wrote music
for six Ziegfeld " Follies." Composer of " The
O'Brien Girl," " Going Up " and " The Kiss Waltz."
Died New York, May 13, 1924.

Victor Herbert, composer, 64. Born in Ireland. Came
to America at an early age. First post as conductor was at Koster and Bial Music Hall, New
York. Wrote the scores for many musical comedies,
incidental music for several " Follies," a cantata,
oratorio, and a grand opera, " Natoma." Among
his better known light operas are " Babes in Toyland," " Mlle. Modiste," " It Happened in Nord-
land," and " Orange Blossoms." Died New York,
May 26, 1924.

Aaron Hoffman, playwright, 43. Author of many popular plays, including " Friendly Enemies," " Nothing
But Lies," " Welcome Stranger," " Give and Take,"
etc. Died New York, May 27, 1924.

Henrietta Byron (Mrs. Barney Fagan). Long a vaudeville favorite with her husband. Died National
Stomach Hospital, Philadelphia, June 1, 1924·

INDEX OF PLAYS AND CASTS

INDEX OF AUTHORS